EXPLORATION OF THE SOUTH SEAS IN THE EIGHTEENTH CENTURY

EXPLORATION OF THE SOUTH SEAS IN THE EIGHTEENTH CENTURY

Rediscovered Accounts

Edited and Translated by Sandhya Patel

Consultant Editor
Odile Gannier

Volume II

Voyage Round the World Performed
under the Direction of Captain Etienne Marchand
in the *Solide* of Marseilles 1790–1792

LONDON AND NEW YORK

First published 2017
by Routledge
2 Park Square, Milton Park, Abingdon, Oxon OX14 4RN

and by Routledge
711 Third Avenue, New York, NY 10017

Routledge is an imprint of the Taylor & Francis Group, an informa business

British Library Cataloguing in Publication Data
A catalogue record for this book is available from the British Library

Library of Congress Cataloging-in-Publication Data
A catalog record for this book has been requested

ISBN: 978-1-8489-3070-4 (Set)
ISBN: 978-1-138-68986-2 (Volume II)
eISBN: 978-1-315-53735-1 (Volume II)

Typeset in Times New Roman
by Apex CoVantage, LLC

Publisher's Note

References within each chapter are as they appear in the original complete work

CONTENTS

VOLUME II

ILLUSTRATIONS

INTRODUCTION*

1. The Narrative

In 2005, more than two hundred years after the fact, Odile Gannier and Cécile Piquoin published the first critical edition of Etienne Marchand's manuscript journal of his voyage round the world in the *Solide* during the years 1790–1792.[1] The *Solide*, a three-master of 310 tons, was 72 feet in length and specially built for the purpose. Marchand describes her thus: *Mr Maistre and his nephew had built a vessel with no faults. This vessel was to be sheathed in copper. I had all the bolts of the keel, the stern and the stern post made in this metal, as all the nails of the bottom. From here to the wales, they were half copper and half iron. She was named the Solide and launched in May 1790.* She was privately owned by the Bauxs, and the principal object was trade. She was the first French ship to venture to the Northwest coast of America to trade for skins, which were then to be sold in China for supposedly great profit. Her route took her round the Cape Horn to the Marquesas, and then onto the Northwest coast. From there, after a stop at the Sandwich Islands (Hawai'i), she sailed to China. After weaving her way across the China Sea, she sailed across the Indian Ocean to Ile de France (Mauritius). After a two and a half month stay there (of which there is no account in the manuscript journal), Marchand took the ship to Ile Bourbon and immediately afterwards made the final run home, round the Cape of Good Hope to Toulon, via St Helena, arriving in August 1792, after a twenty-month voyage round the world.

French maritime initiatives, contrary to British enterprise had, until then, often ended in disaster and death, though Louis-Antoine de Bougainville in the *Boudeuse*

---

* In order to adopt coherent editorial policy in Volumes 1 and 2 of this Rediscovered Accounts series, full bibliographical references to primary material (for the large part) are given in the footnotes (rather than in a final list). As in Volume 1, an index is not included.

1 Odile Gannier and Cécile Picquoin, *Le Voyage du Solide autour du monde (1790–1792)*, 2 vols., Paris, CTHS, 2005 (referred to as *Journal* and *Annexes* in this *Introduction*). This transcription contains detailed accompanying text and must be read in conjunction with this critical translation which does not reproduce Gannier *et al.*'s footnotes. Marchand's manuscript journal is held at the Bibliothèque Alcazar in Marseilles, France (Ms 1120 and 1121).

had survived his circumnavigation from 1766 to 1769, "discovering" Tahiti just a few months after Samuel Wallis in the *Dolphin* (1766–1768). Other contemporaneous voyages however included that of Surville who was in New Zealand in 1769 in the privately owned *St. Jean Baptiste*, at the same time as Cook in the *Endeavour* (1768–1771), the latter in the midst of mapping the two islands and claiming them for Britain. Surville drowned in 1770 at Callao. Marion Du-Fresne left for Tahiti in 1771 in the *Mascarin* with the Tahitian *Aoutourou*, brought to France by Bougainville. Aoutouru died on the voyage and Du-Fresne was killed by Maoris in New Zealand in 1772, having charted parts of the North Island, as he thought, for the first time. La Pérouse in the *Boussole* (sailing with the *Astrolabe* in 1785–1788), an expedition mandated by the King, after crossing the Pacific, arrived in Botany Bay in January, 1788, as the First Fleet was taking material possession of New South Wales. His journal and other papers were sent on to France from Botany Bay, but La Pérouse continued his voyage and was wrecked on Vanikoro. D'Entrecasteaux (*Recherche* and *Espérance*) was sent out by the government in search of La Pérouse in 1791, but to no avail; this Commander died of cholic in 1793 off New Guinea. In this overview of a rather laboured maritime context, set against the fraught political backdrop, the twenty-month voyage round the world of the French merchant ship *Solide* (1790–1792) was not to prove as useful, or textually profitable, as perhaps it may have done in other, more favourable circumstances. It did not have wide-reaching commercial repercussions, neither did it provoke debate or discussion, as Bougainville's voyage had after the quasi-immediate publication and translation of the shipboard journals in 1771[2] and 1772,[3] respectively. It was however one of the two successful circumnavigations in eighteenth-century French maritime history, if one measure of success is considered as the return home of the Commander and most of the crew in relatively good health. Gannier and Picquoin's exhaustive introduction, annotations and annexes (which will not be reproduced *in extenso* here) to the long overdue transcription of the journal, provide detailed, contextual insights into this voyage.[4] In the editors' view, the voyage could be considered as exemplary in spite of the commercial failure of the venture as Marchand was unable to sell his skins in China.[5] The voyage was remarkably rapid with only seven stop-offs, there was very little damage to the ship and the crew came back in good health,

---

2 *Voyage autour du monde par la frégate du roi la Boudeuse et la flûte l'Étoile; en 1766, 1767, 1768 & 1769*, Louis Antoine de Bougainville, à Paris, chez Saillant & Nyon, Libraires, rue S. Jean-de-Beauvais, 1771.

3 *A voyage round the world: Performed by order of His Most Christian Majesty, in the years 1766, 1767, 1768, and 1769 by Lewis de Bougainville, Colonel of Foot, and Commodore of the Expedition, in the Frigate La Boudeuse, and the Store-Ship L'Etoile; translated from the French by John Reinhold Forster*, J. Nourse and T. Davies, 1772.

4 See Gannier (*Journal, op. cit.*, pp. 3–119) for the historical background and the rationale, the planning and the fitting-out of the expedition.

5 Ibid., p. 5.

there being only one death from apoplexy. Captain Etienne Marchand, according to his papers, also made a major discovery in June 1791, namely the Iles de la Révolution (present day Northwest Marquises).[6] Unfortunately, like Bougainville following in the immediate footsteps of Englishman Samuel Wallis, like Surville in the wake of Cook, Marchand's mapping of the Northwestern Marquises, and his encounter with these islander peoples, came two months *after* American Joseph Ingraham's[7] first contact with them in April 1791. The French authorities, informed of the discovery by letter from Marchand in Macao, sent at the end of November 1791, were not made aware of this claim, despite Marchand's prior knowledge of Ingraham's appropriation of the islands in question. Marchand, as suggested in this *Introduction*, very probably knowingly withheld the information in order to add lustre to what he perhaps understood as an otherwise unsuccessful venture. Thus, Marchand himself published *Découverte des Iles de la Révolution dans l'océan Pacifique meridional* in 1793, two years after his return home to France. This short *Brochure* gives an account of the most important aspect of the voyage, namely the discovery of the Northwest Marquises, and takes up whole sections of the manuscript journal from the 13th to the 24th June, 1791. Marchand does not discuss the legitimacy of his discovery of the Iles de la Révolution in the *Brochure*. If his deliberate refusal to acknowledge Ingraham as first discoverer had by now become common knowledge, thanks to the other *Solide* journals,[8] the long-lasting lack of interest in the publication of the whole of Marchand's personal story of the voyage may seem more reasonable.

An account of the circumnavigation did however appear in print in 1797, but in the form of a critical compilation by Fleurieu.[9] Gannier discusses this publication[10] and suggests that Fleurieu, having been involved in organising La Perouse's ill-fated voyage, but not having played an instrumental part in editing the narrative, became interested in writing up a report of the *Solide's* voyage.[11] Gannier

---

6 Gannier *et al.* consider this discovery as one of Marchand's greatest achievements.

7 The manuscript of Joseph Ingraham's journal is held at the Library of Congress, Manuscript Division, Washington, D.C.

8 Namely those of Second Captain Prosper Chanal (*Second Capitaine*) and Surgeon Claude Roblet (*Chirurgien-Major*). *Second Capitaine* is translated as "Second Captain" in the English version of Fleurieu, but "Mate" by William Falconer in his *Dictionary*.

9 *Voyage autour du monde, pendant les années 1790, 1791 et 1792, par Étienne Marchand, précédé d'une introduction historique, auquel on a joint des recherches sur les terres australes de Drake et un examen critique du voyage de Roggeween par C.-P. Claret Fleurieu*, Paris, An VI, Imprimerie de la République.

10 See Gannier, *Journal, op. cit.*, pp. 96–101.

11 *Voyage de La Pérouse autour du monde. Texte établi par Louis-Antoine Milet-Mureau, Imprimerie de la République, 1797. Voyage de La Pérouse autour du monde. Publié conformément au décret du 22 avril 1791, et rédigé par M. L. A. Milet-Mureau*, Paris, Imprimerie de la République, An V. (1797). Milet-Mureau provides the following rather vague explanations for Fleurieu's lack of involvement in the La Pérouse publication: *"Le public regrettera sans doute avec moi, que l'ex-ministre de la marine Fleurieu, aujourd'hui membre de l'institut national et du bureau des*

provides a detailed description of Fleurieu's principal sources[12] and they were the journals of Captain Prosper Chanal (*Second Capitaine*) and Surgeon Claude Roblet (*Chirurgien-Major*). Fleurieu was, in his own words, unable to gain access to Marchand's journal itself. The compilation, in addition to the actual relation of the voyage, includes an extensive historical introduction, notes on Drake's search for the Southern Land, a critical examination of Roggeveen's voyage, an assessment of the calculations of longitude and latitude, an evaluation of the effects of the currents on the course taken, a section on the natural history of the birds, fish and sea creatures encountered on the voyage, observations and new propositions on the

---

longitudes, savant d'un mérite rare et distingué, qui avait bien voulu se charger d'abord de la rédaction de cet ouvrage, ait été forcé par les circonstances de l'abandonner. Le même intérêt qui m'avait fait manifester, à la tribune de l'Assemblée constituante, le plus grand zèle pour la publication de ce voyage au profit de l'estimable veuve de la Pérouse, me fit chercher à diriger le choix du gouvernement sur un marin capable de remplacer celui qui avait été d'abord nommé pour le rédiger : mais la France avait déjà perdu, en grande partie, les officiers de la marine les plus distingués; et les autres étaient employés, ou s'étaient éloignés volontairement. Le ministre ne put que jeter les yeux sur quelqu'un qui eût du moins fait une étude des sciences exactes et naturelles, base essentielle d'un tel ouvrage. Le choix d'un homme qui possédât préférablement ces connaissances, était d'ailleurs conforme à l'intention de la Pérouse; car il écrivait à un de ses amis à peu près en ces termes : « Si l'on imprime mon journal avant mon retour, que l'on se garde bien d'en confier la rédaction à un homme de lettres; ou il voudra sacrifier à une tournure de phrase agréable, le mot propre qui lui paraîtra dur et barbare, celui que le marin et le savant préféreraient et chercheront en vain; ou bien, mettant de côté tous les détails nautiques et astronomiques, et cherchant à faire un roman intéressant, il commettra, par le défaut de connaissances que son éducation ne lui aura pas permis d'acquérir, des erreurs qui deviendront funestes à mes successeurs : mais choisissez un rédacteur versé dans les sciences exactes, qui soit capable de calculer, de combiner mes données avec celles des autres navigateurs, de rectifier les erreurs qui ont pu m'échapper, de n'en point commettre d'autres. Ce rédacteur s'attachera au fond; il ne supprimera rien d'essentiel; il présentera les détails techniques avec le style âpre et rude, mais concis, d'un marin; et il aura bien rempli sa tâche en me suppléant, et en publiant l'ouvrage tel que j'aurais voulu le faire moi-même.

Ce vœu m'ayant servi constamment de règle, je déclare à ceux qui, dans leurs lectures, n'ont d'autre objet que leur amusement, qu'ils ne doivent pas aller plus loin; je n'ai point travaillé pour eux, mais seulement pour les marins et les savans. J'ai cherché dans un ouvrage où le fond doit l'emporter sur la forme, et où la fidélité dans les faits et l'exactitude dans l'expression sont les qualités les plus importantes, à être clair et précis; je n'ai rien sacrifié à la grâce aux dépens de la justesse : cet aveu est mon excuse, en même temps qu'il sollicite l'indulgence des lecteurs.

C'est dans cette vue, que j'ai respecté religieusement le caractère du style de chaque auteur, en soumettant simplement ses formes aux règles reçues du langage : mais quand il m'est venu quelque idée qui pouvait servir de liaison aux autres, une expression qui pouvait compléter une image, la rendre plus saillante, ou donner à la phrase plus d'harmonie sans altérer le fond, j'ai cru pouvoir l'employer.

L'ouvrage qu'on va lire eût sans doute été plus précieux, s'il fût sorti de la plume de l'ex-ministre Fleurieu, qui l'eût enrichi de ses profondes connaissances : je dois cependant annoncer que je l'ai consulté toutes les fois que j'ai eu quelques doutes; et j'ai toujours trouvé en lui cette complaisance et cette modestie, compagnes inséparables du vrai talent et de la science."

12 Gannier, *Journaux, op. cit.*, pp. 94–96.

hydrographical divisions of the world, maps and finally, a series of plates.[13] What is interesting in this compilation is that even at this later date, Fleurieu seems unwilling to clarify who actually discovered the Iles de la Révolution. Gannier cites Fleurieu's reference to Chanal's theory that Ingraham had met with the same islands as Marchand. On close reading, however, it is surprising that Fleurieu does not choose to immediately identify the Captain in the body of the text, leaving him in continued anonymity until the *Third Addition to the Narrative For the Group of Islands to the North-west of the Marquesas de Mendoça*, at the end of the volume. In this *Addition*, Fleurieu makes it clear that the American Captain's name was unknown to all until the publication of *Voyage dans les Etats Unis par La Rochefoucauld Liancourt* in 1797, the same year as his own compilation, in which La Rochefoucauld refers to a Captain Josiah Roberts who mentions Ingraham (by name) and his discovery of the Northwest Marquesas. Fleurieu is here forced to recognise that Marchand was not the first discoverer of the Northwest group, but he does so with rather convoluted reasoning.[14] He argues it was well known (by whom?) that Ingraham had had only a "glimpse," whereas Marchand had managed to acquire more detailed knowledge of the islands and the peoples living there, and was able to provide the necessary longitudes and latitudes. He ends with quite a vibrant homage to Captains Marchand and Chanal (both well

13 The actual account of the voyage was published in two forms, six volumes in-octavo (2763 pages), and four volumes in-quarto (2091 pages) (Gannier, *Journal, op. cit.*, p. 96). The actual account of the voyage makes up approximately one and a half volumes of the six in-octavo edition, and the first volume of the four in the in-quarto edition. The *Introduction* is extremely long (pp. i to cci in the first, and pp. i to cxxxvii in the second) and the account of the voyage is 823 (out of 2763) and 591 (out of 2091) pages long, respectively. It is clear then that Fleurieu's publication is a very personal approach to relaying the account of the voyage of the *Solide*.

14 "*These islands had been seen the preceding year (1791) by Captain Ingraham of the ship Hope of Boston but he had done no more than perceive them and point out their situation. Captain Roberts says [. . .] that, while the Solide lay in Macao Road, Captain Chanal was sent on board an American ship, the captain of which was ill, and that he learnt from him that, in the beginning of the month of May 1791, in standing from the Mendoça Islands to the north-west coast of America, he had discovered to the northwest of that group, another group as extensive as the former that he had given names to the islands of which it is composed, but had not stopped there. It could not be doubted, from the latitude and the bearing which he indicated, that these were the same islands which Captain Marchand had discovered a month later; but we were ignorant of the name of this Captain who had seen them first without examining them: the extract of Captain Roberts's Voyage informs us that the former Captain is named Ingraham, and that he commanded the Ship Hope of Boston.*" From the English translation of Fleurieu (*Voyage Round The World, Performed During The Years 1790, 1791, And 1792, By Etienne Marchand. Preceded By A Historical Introduction, And Illustrated by Charts. Translated From The French of C. P. Claret Fleurieu, Of The National Institute Of Arts And Sciences And Of The Board Of Longitude of France*, Longman and Rees and Cadell, 1801, p. 282).

aware of Ingraham's discoveries having compared notes and coordinates with him, as will be discussed later) and considers that:

> Captain Marchand, undoubtedly, cannot aspire to the honour of priority but he has not, on that account, like the American captain who anticipated him, the less pretension to the honour of the discovery; for he could not know, in the month of June 1791, while he was navigating in the Great Ocean, that a month before, another navigator, standing the same course with himself, had made the same discovery.[15] We must, however, grant to the French Captain an additional merit, that of having made known to us the natives of the new islands, and of having fixed the geographical positions of this group with an exactness sufficient for the safety of navigation.

This implies then that Fleurieu had never read the 1793 publication by the Massachusetts Historical Society on Ingraham's discovery. Neither was he familiar with the same Society's 1795 *Collections* in which Josiah Robert's article (referenced in La Rochefoucauld) on *The Discovery And Description Of The Islands Called The Marquesas, In The South Pacific Ocean. With A Farther Account Of The Seven Adjacent Islands, Discovered First By Capt. Joseph Ingraham, And Since By Capt. Josiah Roberts. Compiled From Dalrymple's Collection Of Discoveries; Cooke's Second Voyage, And The Journals And Log-Book Of The Ship Jefferson, Of Boston was published.*[16]

Nevertheless, Marchand was not to go down in history as a great explorer and navigator thanks to Fleurieu's compilation, considering first the fact that his (Marchand's) journal was not used in the account. Fleurieu though suggests that Marchand's influence is perceptible for the close collaboration between Marchand and Chanal, who every day (according to Fleurieu) compared their astronomical observations, implied an exchange of information which then was recorded or copied into the respective journals. Second, the discovery, the triumph of the voyage, is not one as such, even if, as noted above, this is not put forward in such

---

15 Ingraham comes across the Northwest Marquises two months before Marchand.

16 *"In 1791, Capt. Joseph Ingraham, in the brigantine Hope, of and from Boston, bound to the N. W. coast of America, touched at Resolution-bay; and in his passage from thence to the N. N. W. made a new discovery of seven other islands, belonging to this cluster; an account of which was published in the Collections of the Historical Society for the year 1793, page 20, &c. to which the reader is referred. Before Ingraham's discovery was known, Capt. Josiah Roberts sailed from Boston on a voyage to the N. W. coast, in the ship Jefferson. This ship carried the frame and rigging of a schooner, which was set up and launched at Resolution-bay, in the island of Christina; where Capt. Roberts lay from Nov. 11, 1792, to Feb. 21, 1793; a much longer time than any European or American vessel had lain in that or any other port of the Marquesas, since the first discovery of those islands."* Kaplanoff (Mark, D. Kaplanoff, Joseph Ingraham's journal of the Brigantine Hope. *Voyage to the Northeast Coast of North America 1790–1792*, Imprint Society, Barre, Massachusetts, 1971.) also indicates that excerpts from a letter from Macao written by Ingraham were printed in the Boston Gazette on the 27th August, 1792.

forthright terms by Fleurieu. Finally, that the description of the circumnavigation itself counts for less than a third of the whole work contributes to what may be termed its diminishing returns. Fleurieu's emendations, comments and additions dominate the story of the voyage as Gannier makes clear.[17] Etienne Marchand's personal account of the voyage was as a result lost to history until 2005 when Gannier and Picquoin finally transcribed and annotated the manuscript journal.

The English translation of Fleurieu's *Voyage* appeared in 1801 but, according to a *nota bene … was printed in Paris in the year 1797 though from various causes not published till the present*, that is the French and English editions were apparently to have been published simultaneously. But even this international recognition had little impact on the voyaging cultures of the time. In the opening pages (see *Advertisement*),[18] the translator (unknown) explains his editorial choices and his scrupulous respect of Fleurieu's text, even if the volumes not directly relating the voyage are omitted:

> The two volumes of natural history, descriptive of the birds, fishes, &c. &c. seen in the course of the voyage, being intended more as a vehicle of instruction to navigators in general, than a fresh source of information to persons already versed in that interesting science, we have thought that those who might be desirous of reaping in so extensive a field would prefer consulting the original to having recourse to a translation; and, for that reason, we have declined rendering them into English. Impressed with the same idea, we have omitted the "*Recherches sur les Terres Australes de Drake, et un examen critique du Voyage de Roggeween*", which, together with the "*Système métrique decimal appliqué à l'Hydrographie aux calculs de la Navigation*" may be considered rather in the light of an Appendix than forming an integral part of the original work.

The *Observations and New Propositions on the Hydrographical Divisions of the World* section is not translated either and the justification is:

> This part of our Author's labour, which he now offers to the world at large, was first submitted to the National Institute of Arts and Sciences and to the Board of Longitude of France, and the judgment of his peers has proclaimed the correctness of his views and the clearness of his conceptions. Persons who, may wish for further information on this head, or may be desirous of analyzing the Author's motives, for this innovation, will find them detailed in the *Observations sur la division hydrographique du Globe, et changements*

---

17 See Odile Gannier, "Consigner l'événement : Les journaux du voyage de Marchand (1790–1792) et les Iles de la Révolution," *Annales historiques de la Révolution française*, 320, 2000, pp. 101–120.
18 See *Voyage Round The World, op. cit.*

*proposés dans la nomenclature générale et particulière de l'Hydrograp*hie given in the fourth volume of the 4to edition of the original.

The maps and charts are also abridged in the work in English, but perhaps for other, more partisan reasons: ... *we have suppressed such as were either copies, the originals of which are to be found in the narratives of our English voyages, or as, from subsequent information, have, in some measure, become superfluous. These different suppressions have enabled us to make a proportionate reduction in the price of the English work, without having in the smallest degree lessend its value to the general reader.* The translation contains nine charts and figures whereas the French contains fifteen. The translator chooses not to include John Meare's chart of North America, J.N. de l'Isle's 1752 chart of Admiral Fuente's discoveries, the chart of Norfolk Bay by Prosper Chanal, a chart of the Magellan Straits and a chart of the Great Equinoctial Ocean.[19] This removal of the bulk of Fleurieu's textual presence was to do little towards elevating Marchand to the ranks of intrepid and successful explorer.

In *The Naval Chronicle*[20] for example, which was a periodical and a recognised reference in naval matters, no mention was made of Fleurieu's account of 1797 in Volumes 1 to 5, covering January 1799 to July–December 1801. It was only in Volume 6 of the *Chronicle*, three years after *Voyage* appeared in print (presumably when the translation appeared in 1801), that the *Naval Chronicle* of 1801 took note of the publication. The entry in the category "Naval Literature" provides a very brief summary of the book and does not mention the discovery of the Northwest Marquises at all. Marchand's voyage itself is considered as having scarcely deviated from the *usual track of English navigators*. The authors are also cautious of some of the positions which Fleurieu takes up, but predictably complimentary of founding British maritime ventures which have been the source of "essential benefits" for "mankind." The *Chronicle* considers that the publication was used by Fleurieu to *promulgate his [own] ideas* but because he is a respected man of science having a respectable publishing record he may be excused for a

---

19 The Great Equinoctial Ocean is described in the *Naval Chronicle* (Volume VI, 1801) as being the part of the Great Ocean between the Tropics and Fleurieu is cited as preferring "the appellation of Equinoctial, and gives his reasons, deduced from the term, passing the line, being more used by Mariners than passing the Equator, and also that geologists and naturalists, in their descriptions of regions and animals use the word Equinoctial." The authors are here quoting from Fleurieu's *Voyage Round the World* and the volume on the new hydrographical division and nomenclature (which was not translated into English).

20 The first version of the *Chronicle* was published by J. Fuller (3 volumes) in 1760 and entitled *The Naval Chronicle, or, Voyages, travels, expeditions, remarkable exploits, and atchievements of the most celebrated English navigators, travellers, and sea-commanders, from the earliest accounts to the end of the year 1759.* Then, from 1799 to 1818 the periodical was published as (the title given in Volume 6) *The Naval Chronicle: Containing a General and Biographical History of the Royal Navy of the United Kingdom with a Variety of Original Papers on Nautical Subjects* (J.S. Clarke, A.J. McArthur, S. Jones and J. Jones).

few excursions into the *region of fancy*. The flight of fancy in question is Fleurieu's indignation concerning British domination of St Helena and Gibraltar, which worked towards forestalling other European attempts at establishing trade routes. The *Chronicle* judges Fleurieu's "invective" and "phillipick" as being the war-mongering of a disappointed foe. The work is otherwise praised as being informative in nautical, topographical and natural philosophical terms, even if a footnote sardonically questions the coincidence between the theories expounded by Fleurieu and Bligh's conclusions in his chart of the track from England to St Helena in the *Director*.[21]

In another entry, also in Volume 6, the author focuses on the section on the hydrographical division of the globe and the nomenclature which the official translation into English omits (as noted above) acknowledging that *even allowing it to be only a reverie, it is the reverie of a man of genius, and therefore to be respected*. As recognition of the "genius" of the previously-descried Fleurieu, the *Chronicle* translates certain sections of this particular volume into English arguing that they *were further induced to the following translation on being informed, that the Nomenclature is not included in a very able translation of Marchand's voyage by a man of science, which will shortly be given to the public by Messrs. Longman and Rees.* The *Chronicle* warns though that *our space will not permit the appearance of the whole of his nomenclature; we therefore hope to be excused in deferring it to the next number.* The *Chronicle* also promises to reproduce translated passages from the actual account of the voyage in the future, for their readers' amusement, in almost serial fashion. In a search through the indexes of Volume 7 (January to June 1802) however, there seems to be no further mention of neither Marchand nor Fleurieu. In Volume 8, there is only one citation of the translated edition of *Voyage* in a newly-created section reserved for "Naval Works Newly Published." Marchand makes a very brief appearance in 1806 (January to June) in Volume 15 (in the "Naval Anecdotes" section): The *Chronicle* specifies that *the following letter (unsigned), dated from the port of St. Peter and St. Paul, in Kamtschatka, the 24th of August, 1804, has been received from an officer in the Russian expedition under M. de Kreusenstern*:

> On the 6th of May we perceived Hood's Island, and about noon of the same day Riou's Island, which form a part of the group called Marquesas, which the French navigator, M. Marchand, has denominated the islands of the Revolution. That which is considered the largest of them received from him the appellation of Baux, but in the language of the country it is called Nukahiwah. On the 7th, one of our ships, the Nedeshda made that island: the natives immediately came on board in crowds, and appeared

---

21 *A Chart for the purpose of exhibiting the track of His Majesty's Ship Director in a voyage to St. Helena and return to England. By Capt. W. Bligh. By A. Arrowsmith with "Remarks,"* London, 1800.

highly delighted at our visit: we observed among them an Englishman and a Frenchman, who have been naturalized in the country. About noon our vessel came to an anchor in the gulf of Anna Maria, and the next day went on shore. After viewing the country we thought fit to pay a visit to the chief of these savages. The women of this island are all excessively ugly; but this proceeds rather from the disproportion of their limbs, than the coarseness of their features: they generally go naked, their whole dress consisting of a few leaves rudely sewed together, with which they cover the parts of generation, Nature, who has been niggardly of her favours to the women, seems, by a singular caprice, to have lavished them all on the men: these savages are of a noble stature, and perfect proportions, and we met with none diminutive or deformed: their dress is very extraordinary; they make use of none excepting for the head, the arms, and the legs, the other parts of the body being entirely naked. Their food is the bread-fruit, cocoa-nuts, fish, pork, and even human flesh: these islanders devour not only their prisoners of war and the enemies whom they have killed, but even their wives and children in times of scarcity. Their arms are slings, lances, and clubs made of the wood of the casuarina. The Englishman, whom we had on board, and who appears to have resided a considerable time among these cannibals, warned us not to place too much confidence in their apparent joy. As nature seems to have made ample provision for their ordinary wants, they spend their time in feasting and drinking; they however manifested great solicitude to serve us. They use the skin of a whale for making a kind of drum, which is their national music. Their chief or king, whose name is Topeka Ketenue, exercises no authority over them; but he and his family are considered as inviolable: they pay him a heathen tribute on the fishery, because they look on him as the master of the ocean. They worship a certain god called Atua, who is nothing more than the corpse of their high priest; for as soon as he dies his body undergoes various operations: after he has been cleansed and washed with cocoa-nut oil, it is exposed in the air to dry, and then embalmed: it is then wrapped in skins sewed together, and deposited in the place consecrated to this purpose: they sacrifice to him their prisoners of war, whose flesh they devour with great avidity. The 8th of June the Nedeshda arrived at the island of Owhyhee, the inhabitants of which are much more industrious than those of the Marquesas, but they are less handsome. On the 15th of this month we arrived at the port of St. Peter and St. Paul. The number of the Kamtschadales has diminished exceedingly, in consequence of epidemic diseases, which have made dreadful ravages among them. During our residence in these parts, our crews opened a subscription for the erection of an hospital, which soon amounted to the sum of four thousand rubles.

In this letter then, Marchand as discoverer of the Islands of the Revolution gains very fleeting prominence, and no corrective remarks on the part of the *Chronicle* seem to indicate otherwise in spite of the fact that in 1793, news of Joseph Ingra-ham's mapping of the islands, preceding Marchand's, was published by the Massa-chusetts Historical Society. Further, no "serialisation" of the voyage was offered to the public, as promised in Volume 6 of the *Chronicle*, in the five years following the publication of the translation. Very briefly then, at the beginning of the nineteenth century, in the *Chronicle* at least, the hero (or anti-hero) was not Marchand but Fleurieu, whose judicious addition of notes and calculations is understood as mak-ing the published account a vitally useful addition to any necessarily meagre ship-board library. Thus, despite Etienne Marchand's successful circumnavigation, and putative discoveries, reviewers in England, at least in the *Chronicle*, overlooked the voyage and Marchand's primary role in the undertaking as a whole. Perhaps knowl-edge of the tenuousness of the claim to first discovery may explain why Marchand, in spite of being only the second French Captain, since Bougainville, to have come back alive from a voyage round the world, remained so firmly in the background.

2. The Navigator

Etienne Marchand the man, like his account, remained elusive, supplanted then to a certain extent by Fleurieu. The latter provides very little information about him, describing him as "a French Captain." He is reduced in *Voyage* to a discussion with a certain Captain Portlock in 1788 at St Helena. Marchand, on his way home from Bengal, stops off at St Helena. Portlock, returning home from the Northwest coast in the *King George*, supposedly furnishes him with all necessary detail con-cerning the economic potential of the fur trade. Fleurieu relates that these insights were to serve as incentives for the Bauxs, on the advice of Marchand, to fit out a trading expedition to the Northwest. Marchand himself makes no mention of such a meeting in his own journal. Portlock in his published account[22] does not refer to any such encounter either. Neither are there any entries to that effect in the *King George's* logbook.[23] Fleurieu ends his account of the voyage with a description of Marchand as an admirable navigator (*estimable navigateur*) who brings his ship home safely and then takes up another commission on a vessel bound for Ile de France (present-day Mauritius), where he apparently decides to stay.

Subsequent nineteenth century biographies (Gannier lists a comprehensive selec-tion in her bibliography)[24] provide scant, supplementary information about Etienne Marchand, though the fact that he appears in them at all may be considered as a form of public recognition of his worth. Many of these refer to the leitmotiv return voyage from Bengal and the chance encounter with Portlock at St Helena. In the

---

22 *A voyage round the world but more particularly to the north-west coast of America: performed in 1785, 1786, 1787, and 1788, in the King George and Queen Charlotte, Captains Portlock and Dixon*, London: J. Stockdale and G. Goulding, 1789.
23 National Archives, London, ADM 55/84.
24 Gannier, *Annexes, op. cit.*, pp. 204–207.

1820 *Biographie Universelle Ancienne et Moderne* (Tome 26) for example, the entry specifies that Marchand was an eighteenth-century navigator, born in Grenada on the 13th July, 1755. The biography mentions several voyages in the Caribbean on merchant ships, before an expedition to Bengal, as Mate, in a ship from Livourne sailing under Tuscan colours. Fleurieu's remarks on the background to the voyage are taken up in this biographical dictionary in a condensed version, sometimes almost word for word. The biographer though does add some additional detail. Marchand apparently is unanimously elected to the office of Commander of the battalion of the Marseilles seamen in the National Guard. In 1793, appointed Captain of a ship bound for Ile de France, as Fleurieu notes, he sails from France for good. This reference to a "unanimous" vote of confidence may be understood as peer acknowledgement of Marchand's standing as a successful navigator, even if celebrated posthumously in the biography, but at this late date, the explorer myth could not take hold. In comparison, in the entry for Louis-Antoine de Bougainville (volume published in 1812, a year after Bougainville's death), the tone is decidedly more complimentary and Bougainville's academic, military and professional background is presented in minute, hagiographical detail.

Some years later, in Léon Guérin's *Histoire Maritime de la France* published in 1842, Marchand, is recognised as having been a good man, modest, courageous, enterprising and able, whose voyaging endeavour would have gone unnoticed if Fleurieu had not patriotically decided to write up the voyage according to Chanal's journal. Guérin attributes the general lack of interest in the voyage as being due to the upheaval of the French Revolution. In the 1848 edition of the *Histoire*, more information about Marchand's background comes to light. His education is described as being above the average expected in the merchant navy thanks to his distinguished relations in the East India Company. Guérin this time also describes the *Solide* voyage as being one of the two most illustrious in French maritime history (the second being Entrecasteaux's expedition in search of La Pérouse). Marchand is considered by Guérin as having been potentially prime material for the Republican Navy, but his death, soon after having sailed the brig *Sans-Souci* to Ile de France, put an end to a possibly memorable career.

Efforts at giving Marchand his due were then made, but they did not necessarily have any significant impact on prospects of publication of his personal account. This was in spite of concerted attempts on the part of the surviving members of his family, notably in a very enthusiastic article (unsigned) which appeared in the 10th January, 1843 edition of the *Semaphore*,[25] written most probably by a member or a friend of the family considering that Marchand's "honorable" relations are mentioned as having inherited nothing but this manuscript *in memoriam*. The article suggests that Marchand actually gave his notes to Fleurieu in person (which is contradicted by Fleurieu himself). The article fustigates the latter's polished style which removes all spontaneity from Marchand's day-to-day record of his intrepid voyage. The critical stance which the piece partially takes up is particularly pertinent today

---

25 Printed in Gannier, *Journal, op. cit.*, p. 116.

as it addresses (in obviously more emotional than academic terms) past and present concerns related to the re-writing of travel accounts. It argues, for example, that first impressions (*pensées premières*) are lost in elaborate second hand, erudite compilations like Fleurieu's. As in Cook's preface to the published account of his second voyage, the writer of the article insists on the fact that Marchand the navigator had no authorial objectives in mind, which perhaps we know to be untrue considering that Marchand wrote a fair copy from a proleptic perspective which included earnest apostrophes and calls for more trade, more exploration, more measure (morally speaking). The article finishes on an almost lyrical, and perhaps contradictory, note with the manuscript being described as progressively moving away from the cataloguing of dry nautical detail, to an artless, textual idyll, with a rare degree of attraction compared to other, like relations of voyages.

Gannier also prints a transcript of a memorandum[26] from this period which is in the same vein, and which, in addition, also fills some of the gaps (however unreliably) in the published sources as to the life of Marchand. Thus, in a "note" on the Captain and his family, by Maria Marchand and her daughter Louise (the Captain's sister-in-law and niece), which is not dated but which was written before the purchase of Marchand's manuscript journal by Marseilles' *Conseil Municipal* from Maria herself[27] in 1843, Captain Marchand, born in Grenada, or having arrived in La Ciotat at an early age, is presented as being of distinguished stock (his parents were André Marchand who married Miss Therese Persillé). The document specifies that both Etienne and Louis, his brother[28] studied there and in approximately 1782–1783, Etienne Marchand undertook his first voyage to Calcutta for the Amalrics. On his return, he married Mlle Julien of Marseilles and soon after took command of the *Solide* in 1790 – the note points to the fact that the voyage was financed in equal proportion by the Bauxs and by the government (but there is no evidence of this joint funding of the expedition in Gannier's appraisal of all the available sources). After Marchand's return, alive and well, with the discovery of the Iles de la Révolution as proof of the geographical and strategic success of the voyage, the note specifies that the government acknowledged Marchand's achievements by appointing him Commander of the Fleet at Toulon, a position which Marchand

---

26 "Notice sur le capne Marchand et sa famille," Gannier, *Annexes, op. cit.*, p. 135.

27 Maria was Louis Marchand's (Etienne Marchand's brother) widow and inherited the manuscript from her husband. The latter had inherited it from his sister Louise on her death in 1806. Louis attempted to have the manuscript published by petitioning Napoleon, Louis XVIII and then Louis Philippe but with no apparent success. Gannier (*Journal, op. cit.*, p. 92) also mentions a *Précis historique du journal du Capitaine Marchand commandant le navire Solide, destiné pour la côte Nord-Ouest d'Amérique passant par le Cap Horn, depuis son départ de Marseille jusqu'à son arrivée en Chine*. This document was sent to France by David Charpentier-Cosigny (to an unknown correspondent), Governor of Isle de France from 1790 to 1792, on the 21st April, 1792. The accompanying letter (printed in Gannier) describes the *Précis* as Captain Marchand's journal. Gannier points out that it is an unknown hand. This then may be another fair copy, an abridged version, of the voyage of the *Solide*.

28 Louis Marchand, 21 at the time, was First Lieutenant on the *Solide*.

refused. He was then given command of a battalion of the *Garde Nationale* but he again declined the offer, as the Marchand brothers, wishing to avoid the disruption of revolutionary France, decided to take to the seas once more. This interesting detail is perhaps at odds with the sentiments which Marchand expresses in his journal (see *Journal* and translation), particularly concerning the homage paid to the newly acquired liberty of the French people. Etienne Marchand dies in Mauritius in a hunting accident, according to Maria. His brother Louis Marchand, who died in 1837,[29] was in England at this time, acting as tutor to George Augustus Frederick, Prince of Wales. Maria and Louise are also quite vehement as far as Fleurieu's *Voyage* is concerned, and the note is overtly critical of his (Fleurieu's) use of Chanal's journal (which, in their view, is nothing more than an abridged version of the Captain's manuscript) for his compilation without the authorisation of the Marchands. Chanal is accused of having dishonestly reaped the rewards from the *Solide* voyage. The "letter" ends on rather a pecuniary note as the hope is that the sale of the manuscript to Marseilles's *Conseil Municipal* (by Maria), will finally benefit the family thanks to publication.

Maria Marchand in another very similar note, which also appeared in the *Semaphore*,[30] again insists on official governmental implication in the voyage of the *Solide*. At one point in this particular letter, she thus indicates that Marchand refuses the honour of being addressed as King by the Marquesan islanders because he was acting on behalf of the French government, and not in any personal capacity. Gannier points out that this may have been a means of lending more weight to the prominence of the expedition. Both of Mrs Marchand's notes seem then to be the outpourings of a wronged member of the Marchand family, there being financial motives behind the panegyrics, the objective being to force the *Mairie*'s hand as far as publication was concerned.

Unfortunately, as Gannier shows, this type of initiative did little to bring the Captain and his first-hand account of the voyage into the public eye. In 1843, the *Conseil Municipal* decided against publishing the manuscript, in spite of Marchand's "well-deserved" reputation, presumably as navigator-explorer.[31] The justification was that Fleurieu's *Voyage* provided sufficient detail, and even if Marchand's manuscript were to be acquired (at a moderate price), it would be held in a library collection.

In biographies then, until the middle of the nineteenth century, Marchand had become an estimable character, but Fleurieu, as publisher, remained the more privileged object of attention. Little progress had been made in bringing the manuscript journal into the limelight. In ensuing biographies, in *Nouvelle Biographie générale depuis les temps les plus reculés jusqu'à nos jours* (1860) for example, cited in Gannier's bibliography, Maria Marchand's recurrent references

---

29 Gannier, *Annexes, op. cit.*, p. 137.
30 *Ibid.*, p. 138.
31 Gannier, *Journal, op. cit.*, p. 94.

to governmental commitment to the voyage, are omitted. Marchand's personal qualities are however highlighted. His courage, loyalty and authoritative but compassionate personality, allied with an innate gentleness, are recognised as having made him the ideal commanding officer. The publication of Fleurieu's account, based, according to the author Levot, on Marchand and his companions' journals, is nonetheless considered in the concluding paragraphs as being compensation for revolutionary French neglect of the discoveries made on this voyage, implying thus that Marchand's account had been worked into the compilation (which was not the case). In the 1866 publication *Gloires Maritimes de la France*, by the same author, the entry is much shorter and the complimentary tone has disappeared. Marchand the man, after a slight peak in the cataloguing of his personal qualities, fades yet again into the background.

In 1879, Jules Verne in his *Histoire Générale des grands voyages et des grands voyageurs* (cited in Gannier's bibliography) provides an account of the voyage taking up the leitmotivs developed over the century, the meeting with Portlock and the promise of riches in China, the discovery of the Iles de la Révolution (with descriptions of the peoples encountered), the purchase of furs on the Northwest coast, the impossibility of trade in China, and finally the run home. Verne ends with a question as to the scientific success of the voyage. His conclusion is the following: geographically speaking, the voyage was only moderately successful thanks to the discovery of a chain of islands in the Marquesan archipelago (which Cook had not sighted) and to a more thorough understanding of the people living there, and on the Northwest of America. These achievements may be considered minor if, as Verne suggests, the voyage had been an "official" expedition of which expectations were necessarily higher than of those commissioned by *simples particuliers*, or ordinary individuals. The Marchand voyage, of the latter category, may, on the contrary, be considered a fruitful *amateur* attempt. Verne thus congratulates the Captain and his men (Chanal and Masse) on their remarkable navigational skills and their attentiveness to the mechanics of their predecessors' successes and failures. Verne's entry in the *History* only mentions Fleurieu's publication in passing, he does though extensively borrow from it and does not specifically mention that it was a compilation of personal comment and journals other than Marchand's.

Marchand and his manuscript remained out of sight and mind until 1897 when an official publication of a part of the personal manuscript was undertaken by the *Société géographique*. The *Bulletin*, or the academic journal of the *Société*, in an article by Georges Saint-Yves in the 1895 edition, focused specifically on Marchand's manuscript, which was now held in local library collections in Marseilles. The biographical detail, as presented in Mrs Marchand's note and in the various biographies, resurfaces. Marchand's dislike of revolutionary change as the reason behind his departure from France, leaving his manuscript behind in his sister's care, is made clear. According to this article, Marchand is given command of a war ship but he refuses and leaves France for Ile de France. Fleurieu thinking that the manuscript is lost, publishes Chanal's account. The Marchand family makes fruitless attempts at publication during the first few decades of the nineteenth century. The author (George Saint-Yves) then goes on to suggest that Captain Marchand's journal would be difficult to publish in its entirety, but that it is his intention to publish a detailed account of the voyage, based exclusively on the manuscript, in order to pay homage to this intrepid but luckless navigator. This abridged version of the journal would bring to the fore all that Fleurieu had not thought to include in his edition of what was in fact Chanal's journal.

In sum, only two published documents (though only partially) were to relate the voyage of the *Solide* according to her Captain. The first was written by Marchand himself (discussed earlier)[32] and published in 1793. George Saint-Yves's account in the above *Bulletin* was to be the only other publication, just over a hundred years after the fact, based on Marchand's own record. Saint-Yves in his then very limited reproduction of the Marchand manuscript, focuses inevitably on the discovery of the Northwest Marquises, transcribing passages from the entries in the journal between 12th June to the 25th of June 1791, which specify the locations of the islands and provide details as to the people living there. As in the *Brochure*, the description of sexual mores is omitted.[33] Saint-Yves lauds the rapidity of the circumnavigation and above all the "discovery" of the Iles de la Révolution. In a footnote he makes it clear that some, not all, of the said islands had been sighted before Marchand came across them, by Ingraham in the *Hope*, but that the latter had only very superficially reconnoitred them (thus taking up Fleurieu's dubious justifications and errors).

Marchand was almost entirely forgotten in the twentieth century as Gannier's bibliography shows, and in 2005, the journal finally appeared in print. Gannier brings together the disparate data available in her remarkable *Introduction* and *Annexes*, confirming some of the biographical elements, and raising some questions.[34] Marchand marries in La Ciotat in December 1789 and has a son in 1790. He does become Commanding Officer of a Navy's battalion on his return from his voyage around the world in November 1792, but resigns a month later in order to take command of the *Suzette* whose destination, according to Gannier, was deliberately kept secret (why this was so is not specified). Marchand in Port Louis leaves behind documentary evidence which Gannier presents in her biography. An order for indebted Marchand's arrest is issued in October 1795, he is described as having betrayed Payan and Jouve's (the owners of the *Suzette*) trust by gambling away the proceeds of the cargo, and the monies from the sale of the *Suzette*. In an exchange of correspondence between the Governor of Ile de France and the Admiralty (*Ministère de la Marine*), it appears that Marchand kills himself

---

32 Gannier, *Annexes, op. cit.*, p. 57.

33 In the *Brochure*, Marchand is not as forthcoming as in his manuscript when discussing the contacts with the Marquesan women. Marchand writes: "No sooner did we find ourselves in the cove that they hurried to offer us very pretty women. In the journal, Marchand is just a little bit more forthright about the episode: I remarked that the women were not as comely as had been described to me, though they were enough so to bring into subjection even a difficult man."

34 Gannier, *Annexes, op. cit.*, pp. 106–119.

well before the order is received, supposedly wracked by his conscience, and in order to avoid arrest. Gannier underlines the fact however that no death certificate is available to corroborate the date of his inglorious demise, or one or the other account (hunting accident or suicide) of how he died.

Another question, more directly related to the voyage, which Gannier's biography raises, concerns the meeting with Portlock. She argues that it most probably did take place even if there is no trace of a return voyage from Bengal in Marchand's career history. Gannier proposes that Marchand may either have been a clerk on a French ship (which according to Gannier may explain why there is no mention of his voyage on his record (*état de service*) or he may have been on a foreign ship (two Tuscan ships were in St Helena in June 1788). But as mentioned earlier, Portlock makes no mention of a French or Tuscan ship at St Helena in his journal and Marchand does not specifically refer to a meeting in his journal as mentioned earlier. That Fleurieu and the biographies all cite this meeting as providing the basis for Marchand's apparent fervent arguments in favour of a voyage to the Northwest coast, and then to China to sell the skins for significant profits, is perhaps not sufficient confirmation of whether the two actually met.

Gannier concludes her analysis of the *Solide's* papers[35] by pointing to the fact that like many shipboard journals, Marchand's account was written in spates, when circumstances allowed for it. The fact that the Captain and officers borrowed from each other is a recognised and documented feature of shipboard writing. Gannier provides examples of acknowledged or unacknowledged textual appropriation amongst the officers and concludes that Marchand and Roblet's journals are close in content as compared to Chanal's more "personal" texts.[36] Who copied from whom, or who borrowed whose notes, is unclear. Gannier also suggests that Marchand used the published, translated versions of the Cook journals to write up his own. The extent of Marchand's plagiarising procedures though has become clearer in this translation (see footnotes in the body of the translation). For example, right from the very beginning, in the introductory remarks, Marchand makes extensive unacknowledged use of *A Voyage Around the World; but more particularly to the North-West coast of America Performed in the Years 1785, 1786, 1787, 1788 in the King George and the Queen Charlotte. Captains Portlock and Dixon*, published in 1789. This account (Dixon's) unusually in the form of letters, was written by William Beresford (supercargo on the *Queen Charlotte*) and translated into French the same year by M. Lebas (*Voyage autour du monde, et principalement à la côte Nord Ouest de l'Amérique fait en 1785, 1786, 1787 et 1788 A bord du King George et de la Queen Charlotte par les Capitaines Portlock et Dixon*).

---

35 Gannier, *Journal, op. cit.*, pp.101–116.

36 In *Le voyage du capitaine Marchand [1791] : les Marquises et les îles de la Révolution* (Odile Gannier et Cécile Picquoin, Papeete, Au Vent des îles, 2003) the Marchand, Chanal and Roblet accounts of the Marquesan discoveries are transcribed. The Chanal and Roblet journals have never though been transcribed or translated in full.

Marchand makes fewer references to Portlock's narrative, in spite of the purported meeting with him in 1788, as compared to Dixon's. There is some doubt as to whether a translation of Portlock had appeared at that time, so the more limited recourse to Portlock may have been because the text Marchand had with him was in English. Further in the journal, it becomes clear that Marchand has read Bougainville, Cook, King and many others who all argue for accrued fur trade initiatives to the Northwest coast. Marchand's journal is also extremely descriptive in terms of the flora and the fauna and his interest in natural philosophy is obvious. He frequently refers for example to Buffon's *Histoire Naturelle, générale et particulière, avec la description du cabinet du Roi* sometimes even going as far as challenging Buffon's theories (see footnote for 7th–8th January 1791). Gannier provides a list of the sources used by Marchand which shows that his library was very well stocked.[37] He compiles vocabularies and writes descriptive sections, again in keeping with the formatting of journals kept on the exploratory expeditions he had so obviously read of in such great detail. Marchand hence adopts not only the form of eighteenth century journals of exploration, but also the content, in his attempt to produce a putatively authentic "exploration" narrative, though his was first and foremost, a trading expedition. From this perspective, for Etienne Marchand, the discovery of the Iles de la Révolution may very well have taken precedence over the other mediocre results of the voyage as his only publication focuses specifically on this aspect. As evoked above, questions remain, notably relating to Marchand's account of the discovery and the extent of his knowledge of Joseph Ingraham's prior claim to the islands, preceding his by only two months.

3. The Northwest Marquises

Joseph Ingraham, Mate on the *Columbia* (1788–1790), amongst the first American ships to attempt to integrate the fur trade route (Northwest coast of America to China), was appointed Captain of the *Hope* immediately after his return to Boston in 1790. Like the French expedition, the voyage of the *Hope* was a commercial venture with the fur trade in mind. Like Marchand, Ingraham writes descriptions of the peoples and places encountered, and in addition to the text, not as thorough as Marchand's, Ingraham also constituted an iconographical archive which Kaplanoff[38] considers, rightly so, as comprising "beautifully drawn" charts and figures.

---

37 See Gannier, *Journal, op. cit.*, p. 198.
38 Mark D. Kaplanoff, *Joseph Ingraham's Journal of the Brigantine Hope. Voyage to the Northwest coast of North America 1790–1792 illustrated with charts and drawings by the author. Edited with notes and an introduction*, Imprint Society, Barre, Massachusetts, 1971. The manuscript journal is in the Library of Congress (USA) and there are microfilm and paper copies in the Yale Library (Beinecke Library) and in the Archives of British Columbia. The version which Gannier refers to in her transcription is the translation into French of the 1793 excerpts from the journal published by the *Massachusetts Historical Society* entitled *An Account of a recent discovery of seven Islands in the South Pacific Ocean, by Joseph Ingraham, Citizen of Boston, and Commander of*

The *Hope* left Boston on September 16th, 1790, sailing round Cape Horn; after a halt at the Falklands, the ship reached the Marquesas (those that had been mapped by Cook) on the 15th April, 1791: *We plainly saw five islands – Magdalena, St. Pedro, La Dominica, St. Christina, and Hood's Island.* Marchand is in sight of La Magdalena on the 12th June, 1791, barely two months later. Both men have very similar encounters with the islanders. For example, in Port Madre de Dios, they both raise white flags of peace, they both attach the symbols of peace in "a conspicuous place," they are both surrounded by between fifty (Marchand) and sixty (Ingraham) canoes and six hundred islanders (in the water and in the canoes around the *Hope*, the same number in the water swimming around the *Solide*). Both men are rather overwhelmed by the Marquesans. Ingraham, with just fifteen men, decides to weigh anchor in order to avoid rising to the bait and firing at them, noting that *they continued to be troublesome and mischievous, I determined to weigh my anchor and leave them as I found them, lest they should provoke me to fire among them, by which, no doubt, many must have been killed. This above all things I wished to avoid. The old men all behaved well and endeavoured to check the young ones in their idle, noisy career. Perhaps they all remembered the fate of their unfortunate countryman who was shot by the British fifteen years before for a trifling circumstance* (18th April). Marchand also has to deal with unruly islanders and their *disturbance and riot* (see the entries for 13th–14th June). Like Marchand, Ingraham is involved directly in a skirmish with a Marquesan. He is struck on the head *by a small stick of wood* which is thrown over the netting. Ingraham fires his musket loaded with small shot over him. Marchand is threatened by a man with a spear, he takes aim *but fortunately for him, the gun miscarried. I immediately gave orders to two of the officers to fire their pieces over his head. When he heard the balls whistle past him, he retreated forthwith and the others followed his example and left us in peace.* Ingraham does not go ashore and cannot give a *copious description* as his passage through the islands was so brief. Marchand on the contrary, stays longer, he goes ashore and is able to provide a long, detailed description of these islands, already known to the world. Nevertheless, he does, like Ingraham, perhaps out of false modesty, express the same sentiment. Both men were to go on and discover the "New Marquesas."

On the 18th of April, the *Hope* leaves Port Madre de Dios and that same day Ingraham discovers two new islands. He writes the following account of the discovery:[39]

April 19. [a day ever memorable to Americans.] We steered N. N. W. from the island of Dominica, and at 4. P.M. saw two islands under our

---

the brigantine Hope, of seventy Tons burthen; of and from this Port, bound to the N. W. Coast of America. By permission of the Owners, copied from the Journal of said Ingraham and communicated to the Publick, by the Historical Society.

39 Kaplanoff specifies two publications of this portion of Ingraham's journal, one in 1793 in the *Collections of the Massachusetts Historical Society* and the other – a translation of the 1793

lee; one bore N. W. by N. from us, and N. N. W. distant 35 leagues from the N. W. end of Dominica; the other bore W. of us. This sight was unexpected, as I knew we had seen and passed all the group called the Marquesas. On this I examined Capt. Cook's chart of the world, his voyages, Quiros's voyage, who was with the Spanish Admiral, that discovered the Marquesas in 1595, M. Bougainville's account of circumnavigators and lands discovered by them, all my charts and globes of modern date; but could find no account of but five islands in the group, called Marquesas de Mendoca, or any land laid down where these islands we then saw were. Of course I had reason to conclude ourselves the first discoverers. On which I named the first Washington's island, in honour to the illustrious President of the United States of America. The other I called Adams's island after the Vice-President. At 5 o'clock two more islands were seen, one of which was between Washington's and Adams's island; this I called Federal island. The other was a small island which bore about S. from Adams's, this I named Lincoln's island, in honour to General Lincoln. The situation of these four islands is as follows:

Latitude S.	Longitude W. of London.	
Washington's	8° 52'	140° 19'
Adams's	9'° 20'	140° 54'
Lincoln's	9° 24'	140° 54'
Federal	8° 55'	140° 60'

All four may be seen at once when sailing towards them from the East. I stood for Washington's all night. At six the next morning, April 20. We were abreast of the E. end of it; and by 10 we were under its N. W. side. A canoe in which were three men came towards us; when they were within about 300 yards of us, they laid still a while as it were to view us; frequently calling out hootah, which is, land, or, on shore, in the language of the Sandwich islands, and I judged theirs was the same. After many gestures and signs of friendship, we prevailed on them to come near enough to receive a few cents and nails. They talked to us a great deal but to little purpose, as all we understood was an invitation to go ashore; but as I saw no place proper to anchor in, I bore away more to the W. and they paddled in shore again, giving us a song, as at the Marquesas. These people resembled those we had left, except one young man, who had his hair stained white at the ends, as is common at the Sandwich

---

publication – *Le Voyage d'Ingraham aux Iles Marquises (Oslo, 1937)* which Gannier uses for reference purposes in her transcription. This excerpt is taken from the former (as Kaplanoff seems to have made minor changes and additions).

islands. The canoe was curved at each extremity, both being alike and resembling the stern of those at the Marquesas.* It was my intention to have anchored at this island and taken possession; but I could find no place on its lee side proper for a vessel to anchor, unless in case of great necessity. I therefore called my officers and seamen together, and acquainted them, that I had every reason to believe the island we were then under, and the three seen the night before, were never seen by any civilized nation except ourselves; thereto witness, that I claimed them as a new discovery, and belonging to the United States of America. On which we all gave three cheers and confirmed the name of Washington's island. After this we bore away for another island, which we saw bearing, W. by N. distant 10 leagues. Washington's island is about ten leagues in circuit; of a moderate height, diversified with hills and vallies, and well wooded; the whole having a vastly pleasant appearance. It is accessible for boats in many places; but, as I before observed, there appeared no good anchorage. As to the number of inhabitants, I cannot say, as we saw only two canoes; the one beforementioned, and one, which by the help of a glass I saw two men launch; but they concealed themselves again and did not venture off to us. Houses we saw none; though no doubt these were concealed below the trees, as at Port Madre de Dios. Federal island and Adams's island appeared about the same extent and height as Washington's, from what I could judge by the distance we passed them.

At six in the evening we were within two leagues of the island which we discovered and bore away for at noon. It was much higher than Washington's; but appeared about the same extent. The N.E. part is much broken and divided; its summits terminating in ridges and peaks, of a pyramidical form; the whole bearing a volcanick appearance. Night approaching, I could not examine this island particularly, although I much wished to have done it. To have remained for no other purpose might perhaps be deemed inconsistent by the gentleman of the concern; hence I hawled my wind to the northward. This island I named Franklin's island, in memory of Doctor Benjamin Franklin. I cannot pretend to describe this island very particularly, for the reasons beforementioned. It appeared however well wooded, and was inhabited; for as soon as we had hawled off, the natives made fires, as it were to entice us to remain. The latitude of Franklin's island is 8° 45' S. its longitude 140° 49' W. Its centre bears W. by N. 10 leagues from Washington's.

From this island we steered N. till six o'clock the next morning. April 21, when we saw two more islands bearing W.N.W. distant 8 leagues. We bore down for them. One I named Hancock's island in honour to the governor of Massachusetts; the other Knox's island, after General Knox. I hawled towards Hancock's island; but finding no anchorage, bore away under Knox's. We passed several fine bays, in which was good shelter from the trade wind; but the bottom I judged was bad, from the surrounding rocky shores. One of the bays seemed, as to shelter, convenience of landing, &c. equal to Port Madre de Dios; but its shores indicated a bad bottom. Hence every ship or vessel on such voyages, that sails in unknown seas, and that necessity obliges to anchor among rocks, would do well to be provided with a chain of 25 or 30 fathom; which would enable them to anchor any where, without the risque of losing their anchor or endangering the ship.

In the best bay abovementioned, which I named Brattle's bay, we saw one house, on the brow of a hill, above a fine grove of coconut trees; but we saw no .person stirring. One house we had passed before and gazed in vain for inhabitants. Opye+ said they were afraid, as at Atooi, when they first saw a vessel. He said they hawled all their canoes up and kept close till a few seeing the near approach of the vessel, had courage to venture off, and returned with beads, trinkets, &c. when many, allured by their good fortune, launched to visit the strangers, biassed by curiosity and the hope of gain.

From the houses we saw, I am led not to doubt that Knox's island is inhabited. The approach of night prevented any further examination, and I bore away to the westward. The wind came off the land in frequent heavy gusts and squalls, which rendered it dangerous plying under it all night; besides, under land in tropical climates the wind generally shifts in the night, from the natural trade wind, and blows from the W. which was, as we were situated, directly on shore. To remain under such a risque would therefore have been imprudent.

Knox's island is about 6 or 7 leagues in circuit; it appears fertile and pleasant to the eye, on all sides; but more particularly on the W. and N.W. sides, which are well wooded, and have many fine groves of coco-nut trees. Hancock's island is about 5 leagues in circuit. It appears to have no harbour or place of shelter for ships; but is accessible in many places for boats. It has a good verdure, with both trees and bushes Hancock's island lies in Lat. 8° 3' S. Long. 141° 14' W. Knox's island in 8° 5' S. Long. 141° 18'.

As to the positions of these seven islands which we have discovered and given names to, I presume they cannot be far from the truth. Federal island, which we saw late in the afternoon, is most liable to a small mistake, as I had no opportunity to work its distance by angle; yet being pretty sure of the situation of Washington's and Adams's, Federal island cannot be missed, as it lies between them; and as I before observed, all may be seen at once, coming from the E.From what M. Bougainville says,++ it is pretty evident these islands were not seen by the Spaniards in 1595, when they discovered the Marquesas. They pretend only to four islands in this group, nor ever saw any more. Capt. Cook, who visited the Marquesas in 1774, discovered a small round island, which bears about N.N.E. from the E. end of Dominica, and which he named Hood's island. This may be plainly seen in running from the E. and steering to sail between San Pedro and Dominica. Indeed we saw the four, discovered by the Spaniards, all at one view.

As I could not, from the most diligent search find the least account of these Islands, I conceive there could be no impropriety or presumption in naming them, and claiming the discovery as my own. Should it be hereafter proved that islands in the same situation have been seen before, I renounce my claim with as little ceremony as I assumed it.

It seems from M. Bougainville's account of the several voyages performed round the globe and the discoveries made, that none ever sailed nearer these islands than the Spaniards, who discovered the Marquesas; their next discovery on the same voyage was the island San Bernardo which is 24° W. from which I judge they steered S. W. or W. S. W. from Port Madre de Dios. Capt. Cook, in 1774, steered S. W. and the group which I discovered, at least the first four lies N. W. from that port. I shall now take my leave of these islands, leaving it to be determined by future investigation, who first discovered them.

April. 22. Course N. Knox's island in sight distant 14 leagues. The variation, by amplitude was 4° 30' E. Latitude observed at noon 7° 34' S.

The foregoing account is faithfully extracted from the journal of Capt. Joseph Ingraham, in his own hand writing, by JEREMY BELKNAP, Corresponding Secretary of the Historical Society.

Since the above extract was made, the College Librarian, Mr. Harris, has consulted all the books of maps and voyages in the library, particularly Dalrymple's and Cook's, and cannot find any islands laid down between the Marquesas and the Equator. Several other maps and voyages have been searched; among which is Harrison's New Atlas, printed in 1791; but nothing appears from any of them to militate with the claim of our citizen, to the first discovery of these seven islands; to which the publick voice will in justice to him, in future give the denomination of Ingraham's Islands.

* These are thus described in another part of the journal "The bottom of their canoes is dug out of a single log, and the sides are sewed on with line made of coco nut fibres. At the head and stern they have a small piece of board fixed perpendicularly, which repels the water and prevents it entering the canoe as she goes ahead. The stern is considerably higher than the head, being a curve terminating in a point. The prow is flat and horizontal, so that the water continually washes over it. The single canoes have outriggers, the double ones are lashed together. Their sails are made of mats in a triangular form: but neither canoes nor sails possess that neatness which marks the superior genius of the Sandwich Islanders."

+ A native of one of the Sandwich islands, who had been at New-York and Boston, and was returning home in the Hope, after an absence of twenty months. "I was much surprised (says Capt Ingraham) to find that Opye could not understand the natives of the Marquesas; but still more to find he could converse but very indifferently with the people of his own country. Nay, on our first arrival, I could apparently talk better with them than Opye; for he, by blending the American language with his own, formed a kind of jargon unintelligible to every one but himself; but it soon wore off, and his mother tongue became natural."

++ Introduction to the English edition by Dr. Forster, page 21

Ingraham is in sight of Washington Island on the 19th April and sails away from the chain on the 21st. Marchand's discovery of the North Marquises on the 21st of June, 1791 is recounted in detail in the journal – Marchand leaves the islands on the 24th June. Marchand's lyrical description of these islands, as compared to Ingraham's rather more matter of fact approach (summarised by the "vastly pleasant appearance" of the island), is unsurprisingly reminiscent of Bougainville's description of Tahiti. The account of the first encounter with the Marquesans of Ile Marchand/ Washington's Island/Ua Pou is, on the contrary, very similar to Ingraham's, where three extremely cautious men approach in a canoe, the Captains convince them to come on board after giving them trinkets. Marchand is certain that they had never before seen a ship (like Dorr on board the *Hope*).[40] The Frenchmen have more face to face contact with the New Marquesans, they take possession of the islands in the name of the King, whereas Ingraham does not go ashore to do so but performs the ceremony nonetheless. After coming in sight of Ile Baux/Nuka Hiva, Marchand, like Ingraham, decides against further exploration.

Later, Marchand, in citing Roblet's report, considers that the warm welcome which the party receives on shore is most certainly evidence of their unfamiliarity with the violence of preceding European encounters. Throughout the account, he insists on this "newness" of the place, even the presence of women is considered as being a sacred mark of hospitality. He affirms that they have no knowledge of iron, but Ingraham makes presents of nails to the three islanders who approach the ship.

The insistence in Marchand's journal, and in his *Brochure*, on *his* discovery of the Iles de la Révolution is surprising, as both ships are in China, in Macao Road, according to both journals, at the end of November 1791 and they discuss the discovery of the islands in question. The accounts of the contact between the two ships differ however. In Ingraham's journal, this meeting is recounted in detail:

29 November. We weighed at four next morning and at one o'clock we anchored in Macao Roads . . . At this time from anxiety and fatigue in the late gales I was taken extremely ill with a fever. There was a French ship at anchor about two leagues to windward of us; on board her I sent

40 See Kaplanoff, *op. cit.*, pp. 58–59.

Mr Cruft, my chief officer, for their doctor. He came on board and obligingly rendered me every assistance in his power. The ship, he informed
me, was named La Solide belonging to Marseilles and was performing a
voyage round the globe. They had been at the Marquesas about twenty
days after us[41] and were last from the N.W. Coast of America, where they
had been collecting furs – but had not been very successful. The doctor
returned on board his own ship in the evening.

30 November. He visited me next morning accompanied by a gentleman who I understood to be their second officer and draughtsman. I told
the doctor the day before that we had discovered seven islands in the
South Seas and I was soon convinced that the business of this officer
was to learn the situation of these isles. I frankly told him their situation,
showing him my journal with the particulars. He immediately acknowledged that they had seen four of the same islands some days after us and
claimed them as a new discovery. As I before observed, they were at the
Marquesas about twenty days after us. Steering the same course from
the Marquesas, they fell in with part of the same islands. Our latitudes
and longitudes exactly agreed as to the position of the isles. He brought
a chart of them which he showed me by which I found they had seen
Washington's Island, Federal Island, and run between Knox's and Franklin's Islands but that these four were all they saw.

[. . .] 2 December. Next morning the captain of the French ship beforementioned came on board and with a politeness characteristic of his
nation enquired after my health, apologizing that he was not able to call
on me before. He was a very agreeable, good looking man and usually
an officer in the navy. He wore a uniform and informed me he was once
before in Macao as a lieutenant on a French frigate. I am vexed with
myself for being so remiss as not to enquire the name of so obliging
and good a man as he appeared to be. He informed me he was going to
sail for the Ile de France without selling his furs but I was afterwards
informed that he had smuggled them onshore through the interest of the
padres,[42] which I believe was the case, as the ship sailed shortly after and
it did not seem probable they would take their skins with them.

---

41 There seems to be some confusion in Ingraham's journal about when the *Solide* was in the
Marquesas.
42 Marchand did not necessarily "smuggle" all the furs into Macao as Gannier reproduces the record
of the goods landed at Marseilles in 1792, which lists 7 bales of skins for the Bauxs (an estimate
of a thousand skins on the part of Ingraham). But he may have managed to sell some of them.
Marchand did stay with a French priest whilst ashore in Macao. On the other hand, he also admits
to going on shore on the 30th November to attempt to sell skins illicitly but apparently to no avail
according to the journal. Ingraham may have heard about this attempt and jumped to obvious,
perhaps erroneous conclusions.

[. . .] 3 December Next morning I went to Larks Bay, where I found the Hope safe at anchor. Riding there besides her were the Grace, Captain Coolidge, the Hancock, Captain Crowell, and the Gustavus, Captain Barnett – all from the N.W. and all having furs on board.

At a moderate estimation there were not less than 7,000 sea otter skins on board them all – besides those landed by the French ship before mentioned – and it was reported that 3,000 were in the custom house of Macao, which were consigned to the Spanish company from Manila. Allowing the Frenchman to have a 1,000, there were for sale at that time 11,000 in all, which may readily account for the decrease of the former price.[43]

Thus, if Ingraham's account is considered as reliable, Roblet treats Ingraham for fever and fatigue. Chanal shows his chart of the Iles de la Révolution to Ingraham and Captain Marchand visits Ingraham the next day. Ingraham seems perfectly aware of the French officers' probing and writes that he shows them his journal in all frankness, which may explain the close correspondence between the accounts outlined above. It seems then clear that Marchand was perfectly aware of Ingraham's prior discovery, and that Roblet had had access to the journal. However, Marchand omits any mention of such a discovery in his journal (see *Journal* and translation). He also adroitly avoids specifying the name of the ship, the name of the Captain and his own visit. His studied unawareness of these essential details seems improbable as Marchand provides other information (the "natives" attack on a boat from an American ship, two deserters joining the *Hope* at Hawaii, the fact that the ship stopped off at the known Marquesas with two young Hawaiians on board), but curiously enough, he cannot identify the ship or the Captain. Marchand, perhaps quite cleverly, suggests that the American Captain was out of his senses as a result of a terribly debilitating fever which lasted a few days. Whether this was to discredit any rival claims (figments of Ingraham's feverish imagination?) which Ingraham so obviously made to Roblet and Chanal, and to Marchand himself, is unclear. According to the journal, during his stay in Macao (see the entry for the 27th–28th November 1791), he sends news back to France on board ships sailing back to Europe. Gannier cites Fleurieu who explains that this was how Messrs Baux were informed of the discovery. Chanal's map of the Iles de la Révolution was included in the packet.[44] The meeting with Ingraham took place at exactly the same moment, which may account perhaps for the precipitate despatching of the correspondence at this time. Marchand chooses then to relay "his" discovery, knowing full well that Ingraham had preceded him, had claimed possession and named the islands. Ingraham's magnificent drawing of three islanders in a canoe was probably not of the three New Marquesans he met with at sea, but it carries symbolic weight here (see Figure 1).

---

43 Kaplanoff, *op. cit.*, pp. 175–178.
44 Gannier, *Journal, op. cit.* p. 470.

Figure 1 Untitled drawing in Book 1 of Joseph Ingraham's journal
Courtesy of the Library of Congress

Marchand seems then to have been particularly concerned with safeguarding and consolidating his reputation as explorer/navigator of repute, even perhaps resorting to the above subterfuge. This is otherwise noticeable in his journal as he has a marked tendency to compare his actions to those of his predecessors. He finds faults with the latter, principally British navigators who, though masters of the seas, act in his view irresponsibly, while his own conduct is portrayed in a favourable light. This was however a feature of travel narratives in general. If we compare this aspect of Marchand's reporting strategy to George Vancouver's, who was travelling at this same period, the latter is conversely critical of the body of anonymous traders (of whom Marchand was one). Vancouver was of course largely aware of the violent encounters between for example the Polynesians and Wallis, Cook, Bligh, and Christian between 1766 and 1790, obviously because of his direct implication in some of the events.

In the context of the Marquesan encounters, Greg Dening writes[45] of "unthinking violence" from the very first contact with the Europeans onwards, namely the Spanish in 1593: 200 shot dead. James Cook came next, almost 200 years later, in 1774, one shot dead for stealing a stanchion. Next came Joseph Ingraham in 1791, he reports no casualties, though at one point, as mentioned above, he fires

45 *Islands and Beaches Discourse on a Silent Land Marquesas 1774–1780*, University of Hawaii Press, 1980, p. 9.

his musket at one of the islanders who gets away and thus avoids being killed. Marchand, near La Magdalena on the 13th June, sees Marquesan canoes paddling along the coast, and from a cross referencing perspective, his first remark is the following:

> Though we directed our course towards the canoes, making signs of friendship and showing to them nails, mirrors, etc., they never came near us. In all appearance, they remembered still Captain Cook who ordered musquet balls to be fired at them in 1774. What followed convinced me of this for they repeated often Toute, Pouhi, Matté. The first signifies Cook which they cannot pronounce better, the second is some allusion to the sound of our firearms for they name them in no other way than this, and the third means killed, dead or hurt.

Here Marchand relates the violence of previous encounters with the British navigators. He implicitly invites favourable comparison with his own subsequent initiative, which, like Ingraham, was to hoist a white flag of peace on approaching the Marquesans. He goes further in this virtuous vein and suggests that Cook's use of violence was unjustified, the Marquesans cowering at the display of English colours: *They remembered yet the colours of Mr Cook for it is true to say that it is most difficult to forget any harm done us above all when we are convinced that it is not deserved.* Nevertheless, the next day Marchand is himself, like those who came before him, faced with pressing crowds of Marquesans. This encounter becomes violent and very near fatal. Marchand is, according to his own account, forced to resort to armed riposte, but unlike Cook, even takes up his own musket and fires at a Marquesan. The gun miscarries. The people are then ordered to fire over the Marquesan's head. It is clear then that if his gun had not miscarried, another dead Marquesan would have been added to the list of casualties. The comparative/contrastive objective, which seems to be characteristic of Marchand, is nevertheless pursued as he concludes with: *I did not see, as did Mr Cook, the canoes laden with stones and the men with slings. It is likely that the honest manner in which we had received the natives on board the preceding day had removed their fears.* Marchand contextualises his actions within limits set by the excess of others. Even when on another occasion, Marchand takes up arms after the theft of his handkerchief and musket, the unequivocal gesture is mediated by textual posture which puts forward the reasonableness of French conduct, as implicitly opposed to English behaviour, thus: *I desired much to live peaceably with them in order not to be obliged to have recourse to some extreme measure of which they would undoubtedly be the victims* (almost word for word Ingraham's sentiment). This cross-referencing is understandable in that Marchand is navigating in known waters, but when he does finally come across islands which he thinks he is the first to discover, his reporting of the encounter cannot be, at least overtly, directed by previous practice. As a consequence, the islands are described as being the most beautiful and welcoming of all the known Marquesas, the islanders are:

> like those who we are told lived on this earth during the golden age, they enjoy the fruits of nature with no other desires, no fear and no troubles. Not knowing neither who we were, nor our intentions, they came however to meet our people with confidence, which is near sure proof that they had never before seen neither Europeans nor their terrible arms, and understood the troubles they have caused in this sea.

Marchand claims possession but only with a view to protecting these innocents. Not only does the French Captain discover particularly beautiful islands, but he also encounters the most amiable of peoples:

> It is a most particular circumstance that all the peoples observed by Mr Cook were possessed of pride – or even a fierceness of which he at last proved to be the most unfortunate victim. Those we have just met with form a perfect contrast, owing to the many marks they shewed us of their sweetness of temper and of their obliging disposition.

Here the implication is pride and fierceness breeds pride and fierceness, violence breeds violence. This "compare and contrast" strategy of "texting"[46] the violent history of encounter is then one means of transliteration of unequal engagement which may have as its aim the legitimation of personal, and perhaps national, litigious conduct. Marchand's *records* his condemnation of British exploratory and exchange practice, but in so doing, he attempts perhaps to cover the like nature of his own engagement with the islander peoples.

In conclusion, these voyages took place after intense exploration of the Pacific from 1764 onwards. There was little left to discover in the 1790s, when Marchand set out, in theory, to reap commercial rather than personal rewards. But by now, in Igler's[47] terms ... *the early modern Pacific had developed an imaginary past, one in which intrepid explorers encountered exotic natives on distant beaches and together they enacted harmonious ceremonies.*[48] A close reading of Marchand's

---

46 Greg Dening in *The Death of William Gooch. A History's Anthropology* (Melbourne, Melbourne University Press, 1995, p. 14–21) argues that the writing-down of experiences creates an "artifact," an object of displayed memory, which serves historical and cultural purpose. Here, Marchand, like many others before him, engages in that complex process of texting history.
47 David Igler, "Hardly Pacific: Violence and Death in the Great Ocean," *Pacific Historical Review*, Vol. 84, No. 1 (February 2015), pp. 1–18.
48 *Ibid.*, p. 16.

journal makes it clear that he was deeply interested in contributing to those illusory annals. He was eager to become one of the historical actors who had written about expeditions and exploration, contact and conflict, but the lack of new territories to discover pushed him into making spurious claims and inventing a coded textual artefact. These processes are "embedded" in the European historical record and Gannier's transcription, and this translation of Marchand's manuscript journal into English for the first time extends that existing, complex and contradictory archive.

VOYAGE ROUND THE WORLD PERFORMED UNDER THE DIRECTION OF CAPTAIN ETIENNE MARCHAND IN THE *SOLIDE* OF MARSEILLES 1790–1792

First volume

INTRODUCTION

Though Captain Cook, during his last voyage to the Pacific Ocean, opened up for privateers and navigators a new branch of commerce in the most precious of furs on the North West Coast of America, and though all of Europe was thus convinced of it, this most useful discovery did not immediately give birth to, nor widely encourage, the desire to make profitable use of it. Only in 1785 did some persons look this way. I will except nevertheless M. William Bolts who, so early as 1781, freighted and fitted out the *Cobenzell* of 700 tuns at Trieste, under imperial colours, and set out for the North West Coast of America. She was to be accompanied by a small vessel of 45 or 50 tuns named the *Trieste*. It seems that these ships were to be engaged in other than commerce, and were to undertake discoveries as several natural philosophers and artistes were to be taken on board. This undertaking was very well purposed and could not but have brought great benefits to the shareholders, and this at a time when Mr Bolts would have met with no concurrence neither on the coast of America nor in China. But the design was not to be carried out on account of the intrigues, most likely at the Court of Vienna, by persons who had it in their interest to abort the plan.[1]

---

1 Marchand seems here to be quoting almost directly from the French translation of *A Voyage Around the World; but more particularly to the North-West coast of America Performed in the Years 1785, 1786, 1787, 1788 in the King George and the Queen Charotte. Captains Portlock and Dixon*, published in 1789. This account, in the form of letters, was written by William Beresford (supercargo on the *Queen Charlotte*) and translated into French the same year by M. Lebas (*Voyage autour du monde, et principalement à la côte Nord Ouest de l'Amérique fait en 1785, 1786, 1787 et 1788 A bord du King George et de la Queen Charlotte par les Capitaines Portlock et Dixon*). Marchand seems to have relied heavily on this account throughout his own narrative, and here he reproduces the French text almost word for word. Lebas writes: *Sans entrer ici dans une énumération de voyages, qui deviendroit inutile, il nous suffira de dire que pendant le dernier voyage du capitaine Cook à l'océan pacifique, outre les avantages qui en sont résultés pour les sciences, on a ouvert aux navigateurs à venir un champ nouveau et inépuisable pour le commerce des fourrures les plus précieuses, sur la cote au nord-ouest de l'Amérique. Cette découverte, quoiqu'étant une source d'où l'on pouvoit tirer des richesses immenses, et quoique plusieurs personnes en fussent convaincues, dès l'année 1780, ne fit pas naître sur-le-champ l'envie de tenter d'en profiter* (op. cit., p. 4). Marchand then discusses William Bolts and gives a condensed, again mirror account, of how William Bolts'

3

Notwithstanding, I believe, and it is to be supposed, that immediately after the publication of the third Voyage of Mr Cook,[2] the Russians of Kamtchatka, who are infinitely better placed than we, would have benefited from the discoveries of this most well-known navigator, above all in the region near the river which carries his name, but this is not known to us for this power has forever kept a profound silence on what their subjects undertake in this part of the globe.

We know only that the first vessel sent to this coast in order to do commerce in furs was a small vessel[3] fitted out and armed for the voyage in China, commanded by Captain Hanna and which sailed from Macao in 1785 and returned at the end of that year. The Captain was sent out again the following year, that is to say in 1786, in the 100 tun *Sea Otter*, he returned in 1787. *The Lark*, a snow captained by Mr Peters, 220 tuns, was also sent out in 1786. But it is said that she was lost on one of isles between Asia and America (it is believed on Copper Island), and only two of the people are thought to have been saved.[4]

At the beginning of this very same year of 1786, a 300 tun snow, the *Captain Cook*, Captain Lowrie,[5] and the 100 tun snow the *Experiment* captained by Captain Guise, commanded by Mr James Strange, were sent from Bombay and

---

expedition in the *Cobenzell* was truncated (see pp. 15–16 in Lebas). Odile Gannier (op. cit., p. 123) in her annotated transcription of Marchand's journal (*Journal de bord d'Etienne Marchand. Le Voyage du Solide autour du monde (1790–1792)*, Paris, CTHS, 2005) underlines this frequent occurrence of introductory evaluative analyses eighteenth-century travel books. Marchand not only adopts the usual format, but also here has recourse to a heightened degree of borrowing.

2 *A Voyage to the Pacific Ocean. Undertaken, by the Command of His Majesty, for Making Discoveries in the Northern Hemisphere, to Determine the Position and Extent of the West Side of North America; Its Distance from Asia; and the Practicability of a Northern Passage to Europe. Performed under the Direction of Captains Cook, Clerke, and Gore, in His Majesty's Ships the Resolution and Discovery, in the Years 1776, 1777, 1778, 1779, and 1780* was first published in London in 1784. The translation of this official account appeared in 1785: *Troisième Voyage de Cook, ou voyage à l'Océan Pacifique, ordonné par le Roi d'Angleterre, pour faire des Découvertes dans l'Hémisphère Nord, pour déterminer la position & l'étendue de la Côte Ouest de l'Amérique Septentrionale, sa distance de l'Asie, & resoudre la question du passage au Nord. Éxécuté sous la direction des capitaines Cook, Clerke & Gore, sur vaisseaux la "Résolution" & la "Découverte," en 1776, 1777, 1778, 1779 & 1780*. Unofficial accounts had appeared beforehand and had also been translated into French, for example John Rickman's *Journal of Captain Cook's Last Voyage to the Pacific Ocean* was published in 1781 and translated in 1782: *Troisième voyage de Cook ou Journal d'une expédition faite dans la mer Pacifique du sud et du nord en 1776, 1777, 1778, 1779 et 1780. Traduit de l'anglois*. See A. Charon, T. Claerr and F. Moureau (*Le livre maritime au siècle des Lumières: Edition et diffusion des connaissances maritimes (1750–1850)*, Paris, PU Sorbonne, 2004, pp. 203–205) for details of editions in French of the official and unofficial publications. Marchand must have been familiar with these French editions as his own narrative draws heavily on them.

3 According to William Falconer's *An Universal Dictionary of the Marine* (1780), *brigantin* in French (the term used by Marchand) is . . . a small light vessel, navigated by oars and sails; but differing extremely from the vessel known in England by the name of brig or brigantine. Dixon though uses the term "brig" to describe Hanna's ship and Lebas translates as *brigantine*.

4 Here again Marchand's narrative is an abridged version of Lebas' translation of Dixon (pp. 12–14).

5 Capitaine Lorié in the Marchand manuscrit.

4

fortunately returned to Macao. From Bengal were sent two vessels, the 200 tun *Nootka* captained by Meares, and the 100 tun *Sea Otter*, Captain Tipping. This latter vessel is believed to have been lost for no more was heard of her.[6] The *Nootka* returned to Macao.

However, of all these numerous expeditions, the first vessels to depart from Europe to do this commerce were the *King George*, Captain Portlock, and the *Queen Charlotte*, Captain Dixon. They were sent from England in 1785 by individuals who called themselves *The King George's Sound Company* after having procured a charter from the *South Sea Company*, which enjoys exclusive rights to all the trade in the North Pacific Ocean, and which gave to them the unique right to carry on this commerce of furs on the North West Coast of America.[7]

These two vessels returned to England in 1788. This same Company equipped two further ships in the year 1786, the *Prince of Wales*, Captain Collnet, and the *Princess Royal* whose Captain was Mr Duncan. The two Captains were charged with establishing a colony at Staten's Land in order to protect the fishing of whales, sea lions and sea bass which the English do with much success. The vessel *Imperial Eagle* captained by Mr Berkley, was also sent to sea in this same year. From Boston, several expeditions were made to this coast.

All these expeditions which in general, it is said, had produced profits, gave me the idea of proposing to Mr Jn and Dd Baux, merchants of Marseilles, to fit out two vessels in order to engage in this commerce. After serious consideration and having obtained information relative to this proposal, they were fully decided and

---

6 See *Lebas*, op. cit., p. 15.

7 See Lebas, pp. 20–21. Nathaniel Portlock in his *Voyage round the World; but most particularly to the North-West Coast of America: Performed in 1785, 1786, 1787, and 1788, in the King George and the Queen Charlotte, Captains Portlock and Dixon*, published in 1789, provides more details: *While those adventures were thus performed from the Eastern extremities of Africa to the Western shores of America, private persons undertook a more arduous voyage of a like kind from England. It was in May 1785, that Richard Cadman Etches and other traders entered into a commercial partnership, under the title of The King George's Sound Company for carrying on a fur trade from the Western Coast of America to China. For this purpose they obtained a license from the South Sea Company, who, without carrying on any traffic themselves, stand in the mercantile way of more adventurous merchants. They procured also a similar license from the East India Company, who at the same time engaged to give them a freight of teas from Canton. This enterprise of The King George's Sound Company alone evinces what English copartnerships and English capitals could undertake and execute, were they less opposed by prejudice and restrained by monopolies* (pp. 4–5). Marchand makes scant reference to Portlock, as compared to Dixon, though he does refer to Mr Portlock's journal several times, for example on 17th February, 1791. Théophile Mandar in *Voyage en retour de l'Inde, par terre, et par une route en partie inconnue jusqu'ici* (published in An V, *after* Marchand's voyage round the world) alludes though to its forthcoming translation: *J'ai donné la traduction du voyage de Nathanial Portlock autour du monde, et particulièrement à la côte nord-ouest de l'Amérique. Cet ouvrage dont les circonstances actuelles avaient retardé la publication, paraîtra incessamment chez Maradan, libraire à Paris.* Marchand may then have had only Portlock's journal in English with him, which may explain why he does not refer to it as much as he does to Dixon. Whether this translation appeared is unclear.

asked me if I cared to command and direct the two vessels. I said I would with much pleasure as I had always desired to make a voyage of this sort. This was in 1789. But as the period of the year was much advanced, we decided to plan the execution of the proposal for the following year. At the end of the said year, I received the order to select two ships in the port which would suit my purpose so that they could be purchased. Not finding any suitable ships, the gentlemen decided to have one constructed following my needs, and they were very certain to have sufficient time to procure the second.

I only desired of them a low vessel from afore to abaft, of 320 tuns with only two decks and flat floor timbers strong enough to be run aground, for I think the vessels of this burthen and of this kind of construction are the best suited for all sorts of navigation in the most secure conditions. Everything was carried out to my satisfaction and it must be said that Mr Maistre and his nephew had built a vessel with no faults. This vessel was to be sheathed in copper. I had all the bolts of the keel, the stern and the stern post made in this metal, as all the nails of the bottom. From here to the wales, they were half copper and half iron. She was named the *Solide* and launched in May 1790. The ship that was to accompany me was purchased at this time and had left the ship wright's yard.

We were fitting out both ships to make ready for sail in August when the disputes which arose between Spain and England as regards this commerce, obliged us to make delay. This was all the more troublesome that the cargoes and the provisions had been purchased and were in the storehouse. However in the middle of the month of November, having learned that Spain and England had settled the matter, the owners of the ship decided to make me depart all at once. I made them understand that it was now a little late to pass beyond the Cape Horn and to undertake this voyage, for I could not reasonably purpose to repair to the North West coast of America before the beginning of the month of August of the following year, consequently I would not be able to prolong my stay enough to profitably trade there. My reasons did not convince them and I decided to depart. I informed them however that my intention being to do all that was possible to hurry my arrival on the coast of America, I desired to depart alone for two ships which keep company lose time as most know. This was granted me.[8]

---

8   In *Voyage autour du monde pendant les années 1790, 1791 et 1792, par Etienne Marchand précédé par une introduction historique* . . . published in An VI (1797), Fleurieu attributes the House of Baux's eagerness to continue with the project to patriotic rather than simply pecuniary motives. Marchand is rather less enthusiastic. Fleurieu's account was translated and printed in Paris in 1797 but published in London only in 1801 as is made clear by the translator: *N. B. The original of the following work was printed in Paris in the year 1797 though from various causes not published.* In the *Introduction* to the account, Fleurieu notes that he did not have access to Marchand's journal (using as his principal source that of Chanal's, a second Captain): *It has not been in my power to procure the identical journal of Captain Marchand: that estimable navigator, after having happily brought back the Solide into one of our ports of the Mediterranean, took the command of another ship bound for the Isle of France, where he ended his days and I am ignorant into whose hands his papers may have fallen.* This may account for the difference in tone referred to above.

We set to work without delay and with such vigour that the ship was careened, sheathed with the copper bottom, loaded and ready for sail in 25 days. I must here give my owners credit for nothing was refused me regarding neither the safety of the ship nor that which could contribute to the good health of the crew and ensure the success of the voyage. I took on 22 months of provisions, these were of the best quality having been minutely inspected by myself. Moreover I had taken on board all the antiscorbutics I could get, like cabbage and other vegetables pickled in vinegar, coffee, sugar, malt wort, malt, purl beer, spruce beer, balsam fir, tobacco, etc. I had also provided myself with portable soup and clothes for the crew in case of need. The owners had given me a ventilator to convey fresh air between decks in case we were unable to keep the hatchways open. I owe to all this caution, and to the utmost cleaness on board throughout, the very few men sick with the scurvy during this voyage of near 20 months. I lost only one man out of fifty in the Strait of Sunda. He died from an apoplecktik fit to which he might have fallen on land.[9]

To render this voyage as useful as I am able to those seamen who might do the same, I had supplied myself with the best of instruments and with all the books and maps I thought necessary. I had only one regret, I was not able to procure a chronometer or a time-piece for I had waited too long. I hoped to remedy this matter by recourse to the lunar method[10] in order to calculate the longitudes.

1790 December

On the 12th December,[11] I was sent for by the Admiralty from whom I received my commission, from the Bureau des classes I received a copy of the new Penal code for maritime affairs which had been decided by the National Assembly. The owners gave me my last instructions which said in substance that I was to go as soon as possible to the North West coast of America and trade as many furs as I could, and from there to make sail for China where I would receive further orders. The

---

9 Dixon (op. cit.) makes almost identical remarks in his journals: *But pecuniary emolument did not altogether engross the attention of the owners on this occasion; for in addition to the provisions usually allowed in Merchants service (and of which the greatest care was taken to procure the very best of every kind) a plentiful stock of all the antiscorbutics was laid in which could be thought of as preservatives to health. These, and an unremitting attention to the rules observed by Captain Cook, have, under Providence, been the means of preserving the health of the people, in every variety of climate; for during the present Voyage, which has been of more than three years continuance, the Queen Charlotte, out of thirty-three hands, lost only one person.*

10 Gannier (*journal*, op. cit., pp. 82–84) examines in detail the methods which Marchand had recourse to on board the *Solide*. Fleurieu in his account of the voyage explains that the observations resulting from the lunar method . . .*may at least be considered as approximations, which cannot be very wide of the truth and in their state of imperfection, they will still be of great utility to ships that shall traverse the tracts of sea which the Solide crossed in her circumnavigation of the globe* (p. 316).

11 All the pages of the journal are numbered and Marchand inserts the date in the margin (omitted here) until Wednesday 29th.

crew was composed in total of fifty one men, but this was reduced to fifty,[12] of which circumstance I shall soon give an account.

On the 14th, we made sail from the port of Marseilles with the help of a gentle breeze at East and towed by three boats. I was honoured by the owners and several of my friends who came on board and breakfasted with us. We plyed off and on while waiting for several of the people who had not yet come on board.

At 10 o'clock, the wind veered to the North West and desiring to make the most of such favourable conditions to our route, upon receiving the ship's company and finding that only five men were not yet on board, among them the gunner and the hospital prentice, I decided on replacing them immediately with four willing sailors who were on board and who expressed a great wish to make the voyage with me. As soon as this new arrangement was put in place, the gunner came to tell me that he found the allowance of £72 a month I had given to be insufficient, and that when he had accepted it he thought me bound for Canton by the Cape of Good Hope. But he had learned since, whatever I had given him to understand, that I was to double the Cape Horn and he did not care to make the voyage at this price. I could very well have kept him, but I saw in him a want of good will, and in other respects, during the fitting out of the ship, I had discovered him to be careless of his duties, I let him know that I could very well do without him and he could leave the ship as soon he please. He then proceeded to make his excuses which I did no longer want to hear and I sent him away very willingly as he had not yet brought his things on board. It was known to me that the replacements that I had only just done were expressly forbidden by the statute, but I could not bring myself to depart for so long a long with four less men and to lose such favourable weather for as I think I have previously said I could not conceal from myself that the proper time for for doubling the Cape Horn was very much advanced. The ship's company was thus reduced to fifty men for five had not come on board and I had augmented the ship's company by four only. The crew was composed of the following:

Etienne Marchand Cap.n	11 shown here	27 shown here
Pr Masse	3 Petty officers	15 Sailors
V. Prosper Chanal Second Cap.n	1 Boatswain	3 Young sailors
Ls Etne Marchand 1st Lieutenant	2 Carpenters	5 cabin Boys
Ls Antoine Infernet 2nd *ditto*	2 Coopers	*50 in all*
Hiacinthe Murat 3rd *ditto*	1 Steward	
Claude Roblet 1st Surgeon	1 Cook	
Pre Regnier 2nd Surgeon	1 Baker	
Pre Etne Caihe	1 Armourer	
Amédée Chanal Volunteers	2 Furriers	
Augstin de Cani	*27*	
11 officers		

12 See Gannier (*journal*, op. cit., pp. 57–59) for a list of the members of the crew.

At ½ past ten o'clock, we received on board the powder. After dinner, we drank to the voyage, the owners and our friends left us. We bid them goodbye with cries of joy and very gaily as if we had but just returned from our voyage. I must here honour the ship's company who carried off everything with much cheerfulness.

At eleven o'clock, the pilot left us and we put to sea with a gentle gale at North West. I found the ship did not carry sail at all, but I consoled myself for firstly the ship was extraordinarily obstructed and extremely heavy, for the between decks and the great cabin were much crowded and did not allow anything more to be there stocked there, not even a hawse bag. In the second place, the masting and the yards of the ship were too heavy. As for the first reason, I was sure to lighten the ship soon due to the expenditure of the provisions. The second was wholly in my power to remedy as I could reduce some of the weight of the masting and the yards of the vessel, and this is what I resolved to do as soon I was able.

At noon, the North West wind blew a hard gale with a heavy swell from SSW. We brought under the mizen and close-reefed top-sails. We were employed in the afternoon in stowing our anchors in order to ease the ship and putting the cables and various other cordage down below. We stood SW¼S to in order to reconnoitre Minorca. At sun-set, from 9 leagues, Mayre lay NE¼NW, and Cape Sicié bore E 6° S. In indicating these bearings, and our route, I will make use of the points of the compass and make no account of the variation, which I supposed to be 20° NW in the Mediterranean sea, unless I find it expedient to proceed otherwise.

From Wednesday 15th[13]

During the night, we had a gale at NW which continued to blow fresh. At 5 o'clock AM, the wind abating, we set all sails out, and at 7 o'clock, set the studding sails. At noon, we had run 36 leagues SW¼S by reckoning, and the latitude by observation was 41° 17' N, the difference being 16 North arising no doubt from the heavy sea from the SSW which had retarded our progress.

During the remainder of this day and night, a gentle gale blew from WNW, it being a little hazy[14] we shortened sail to the four main courses.

From Thursday 16th

In the morning, we had sight of Minorca, Mount Toro bearing W¼SW, distant 7 leagues. We can most easily know this mountain for it is the highest of the island, and even at a distance, the white edifice which is on the summit, is visible enough.

---

13 All the dates are in bold and *in italics* in this translation for clarity. Marchand uses larger lettering for dates. I have attempted to respect Marchand's punctuation habits (use of commas and lack of semi-colons).

14 This is the spelling which is indicated in Samuel Johnson's dictionary though Cook in his journal uses *hazey*.

The wind veered to WSW at 8 o'clock and obliged us to haul close upon a wind on the starboard tack.

We perceived a brig in the SSE, plying Northward.

At noon, for the second time, Mount Toro bore W¼NW, distant 7 leagues, which exactly agrees with the latitude by observation, which was N 39° 56'.

We had fine weather during the whole of the afternoon, with a light wind varying from W to WSW. At 10 o'clock PM, the wind began to blow a hard gale from the same direction, I took two reefs in the top-sails keeping on the starboard tack as before. We had the same weather during the remainder of the night.

From Friday 17th

At 9 o'clock AM, we got the topgallant yards down in order to reduce their length and their thickness, and in consequence we unbent the sail.

At 12 o'clock, the latitude by observation was N 39° 8', which did not differ from that by reckoning. In this situation, the North point of Port Mahon bore North, distant 20 leagues.

I served slops to the three men who had come on board on the day of our departure, P^re Simon, Louis and Ch^es Candi, to whom I each gave 3 wool shirts, 2 wool caps, 2 pairs of wool stockings and one pair of shoes, which I allowed them in reckoning.

At 8 o'clock PM, we tacked and stood to the North. At 2 o'clock AM, the wind blew once again a hard gale at WSW attended with squalls, and as before mentioned, the ship not carrying sail very well, we were brought under the mizen and the main top-sail, close-reefed.

From Saturday 18th

At 7 o'clock AM, we perceived a brig at WSW, plying North to windward, as we were. At 8 o'clock, we tacked and stood again to the South. At noon, it being very cloudy we were not able to observe the latitude. At 2 o'clock PM, it began to blow so hard and the sea was so very great from WSW, with heavy gusts of wind one after the other, that I was obliged to bring to and lay under the stay-sails and get down the top-gallant masts along-side the main top masts.

We were taking in so much water from all sides that I feared we would spoil all the bread we had between decks and in the great cabin. The officers' cabins were wetted through from the water which came in from the portholes[15] which I had

---

15 Gannier (*journal*, op. cit., p. 133) points to the usage of the word *hublot* or *houblot* in 1773, though in which source is not specified. William Falconer's dictionary (1780) does not list either. The *Dictionnaire de la marine françoise avec figures* (Charles Romme, 1792) makes no mention of *hublot* or *houblot*. I have chosen to use the term portholes (transated into French as *sabords*), defined in Falconer as *embrasures or openings in the side of a ship of war, wherein the artillery is ranged in battery upon the decks above and below*. Samuel Johnson in the 6th edition (1785) of

caused to be made in order to air the between decks, but everything was so full that I could not come to any resolution.

At 4 o'clock PM, in a squall, the wind veered to the NE, but the sea being very heavy from WSW, the ship laboured much and we made very little progress W¼NW. The fear caused by the dirty weather made Girard, who had come aboard as furrier in order to make ready the furs we proposed to trade for on the NW coast of America, a victim of a form of madness. He came to me trembling and in a great fright, asking why I had resolved to forsake him alone in the ship and to make our escape in the boats. Having understood the matter, I did what I could to remove his fears, but I only fully succeeded the next morning. He told me afterwards that a common sailor, who most certainly wished to make a fool of him, and seeing that he was greatly frighted, had seized a chicken coop and told him that those who could save themselves should. This could have caused a fright to any man but more to he who had never seen the sea, and to whom had been told around fifty tales of this sort. I must say he was very quiet for the remainder of the voyage.

At 10 o'clock PM, it fell calm with a great Westerly swell. At midnight, we suffered heavy squalls from NNW. We shortened sail and were reduced to the mizen and the stay-sails.

From Sunday 19th

At 7 o'clock AM, the wind moderating, we loosed all the reefs out of the top-sails and set the mainsail. At 9 o'clock, we saw a vessel at SW¼S, standing ESE. At 10 o'clock, the wind, now very light, shifted to NNE. We stood to the WSW.

At noon, the latitude by observation was 38° 56' North, Port Mahon bearing North, distance 20 leagues.

At 3 o'clock PM, we saw a vessel to the windward, leading on the larboard tack. At 7 o'clock, the wind having shifted to the W and blowing a hard gale, we put about and stood to the North under close-reefed top-sails. At midnight it blew an excessive gale and the wind caused such a terrible great sea, that we were once again obliged to bring to and lie under the stay-sails. We had thunder, lightning and hail for the best part of the night. Though the ship did not carry sail well, she had other good qualities and sailed swiftly, with little rolling or pitching, which spared her masts.

Monday 20th

At 8 o'clock AM, the wind abated and shifted to the North, we steered WSW under the four main courses and close-reefed the top-sails. During these two squalls, we

---

his Dictionary (first published in 1755) lists porthole for the first time (defined as *holes cut like windows in a ship's sides where the guns are placed*).

lost 60 of our fowls and three hogs. Why these hogs died is a matter of surprise as I had never seen such animals die at sea as they are hardly liable to dirty weather.

The remainder of the day was at intervals calm and squally, with the wind at NNE and rain.

From Tuesday 21st

At 4 o'clock AM, we got the NNE trade wind which blew a hard gale, we steer'd West under the foresail and close-reefed main top-sail. We had the same weather all day, however, the wind moderating a little, brought us under the top-sails with two reefs in. At noon, we were unable to observe the latitude on account of a thick haze.

From Wednesday 22nd

At daybreak, we had sight of the land which I knew to be a high mountain in the adjacent parts of the East of Alicante, called by sailors the Sabre de Rolland due to a sort of opening at the summit which is said to have been cut with Rolland's sabre. At 8 o'clock AM, it bore N 27° W, distant 20 leagues. We steered West in order to make Cape Palos.

At noon, our latitude by observation was 37° 33' N. Cap Palos lay W¼SW distant 21 Leagues. We made sail with clear weather and a light breeze at North, all sails set.

At 7 o'clock PM, the wind blowing from the NW we worked to windward upon the starboard tack.

From Thursday 23rd

At 8 o'clock AM, we perceived Cape Palos to the NW, distant 9 leagues, the most Westerly land bore WNW. During the night, the wind had shifted to NNW.

In the morning, we examined the bread in the great cabin. We found 150 pounds to be spoilt by seawater which we had taken in by the false windows[16] and which we caulked without delay. The bread was not all lost for it served our animals.

We saw several ships, some sailing to the West and the others East. I would have much liked that some of those sailing East pass by us, I would have spoken to them with my signals and by this way, in case the vessels were bound for Marseilles, I would have sent news of the voyage to the owners. But they passed very much in the offing.

During the afternoon, a gentle gale at N, made sail, all sails set, directing our course W¼NW. We made observations to determine the variation of the magnetic needle. By means of the azimuth, we found the variation to be 21° 40' and by means of the amplitude, 21° NW.

---

16 Marchand uses *fausses fenêtres* here instead of *houblots*. See note 15.

At ½ past 5 o'clock PM, Cape de Gata bore W¼NW, distant 15 leagues. The mountains adjacent to Cape Palos bore NNE½E, and the entrance of Carthagena NNE½N.

After one hour of calm, at ½ past 7 o'clock PM, the wind settling at WSW and blowing a light gale, we worked to windward upon the larboard side. The wind was constant all night with a great Easterly swell.

From Friday 24th

At 3 o'clock AM, we put the ship about into the offing, being quite close to the land. At 6 o'clock, the wind shifted to NNW and we directed our course towards Cape de Gata, which at 8 o'clock bore W¼SW, distant 4 leagues. During the morning, we got up the top-gallant mast, having got it down to reduce the thickness and to cut the top two feet above the shrouds and rigging. I have before said that the masts were too heavy for the ship and that by consequence, it was of the greatest necessity to lighten them. This has been my utmost endeavour.

At noon, our latitude by observation was 36° 57' N. At 2 o'clock PM, we got the NNE trade wind blowing a gentle gale, stood W¼SW, all sails set, with very clear weather. At 7 o'clock, we were abreast of Cape de Gata which bore North, distant 1 and a half leagues. We steered West in order to avoid the sandbanks of Almeria.

From Saturday 25th

At 4 o'clock AM, having doubled them, we steered WSW, having fresh gales at ENE which fell at 8 o'clock. At noon, it fell dead calm. Windmill Hill bore NW¼W, distant 9 leagues and the latitude by observation was 36° 27' N.

Though we were in view of the mountains of Grenada, whose tops were covered in snow, and which are thus nearly the whole of the year, it was very hot.

A very light breeze at SW sprung up after the calm which had lasted until 4 o'clock. We stood in for the shore. We were in sight of 19 vessels.

At sun-set, the variation of the magnetic needle, by means of the amplitude observed with an azimuth-compass of 10 inches diameter, made by J. Roux & Son of Marseilles, was found to be 22° 8' NW.

At 5 o'clock PM, Windmill Hill bore WNW½W, distant 7 leagues. The most Westerly land bore W¼NW. The very light wind air at W continued all night, we kept on the starboard tack or on the larboard tack, according to our distance from the shore.

From Sunday 26th

At sunrise, I was in my cabin when I was much surprised to hear the firing of a great gun, I demanded the reason for this. My officers then all embraced me and wished me my name day. I was much pleased at the honour they did me. They hoisted the ship's ensign also and displayed one at each mast until evening. We were very near to three ships steering the same way and which displayed flags of truce. I gave to each mess one of our fowls in addition to the usual allowance, and they had a double allowance of wine.

At day-light, I had noticed by our bearings that we had driven Eastwards 5 to 6 leagues owing to the currents.

At 8 o'clock AM, we got sight of the Malaga Velez Mountain which bore NNW, distant 7 leagues; we were 4 leagues from the nearest land. At noon, our latitude by observation was N 36° 20'. It was calm during the afternoon and the whole of the night on account of which we were not able to steer.

Monday 27th

At 8 o'clock AM, having not the least puff of wind, I gave orders to shorten the excessive length of the main top-gallant mast and of the mizen top mast, as we had done for the top-gallant mast, that is to cut off the tops above the shrouds and rigging. This was done by 11 o'clock. I intended to have the main and fore top yards lightened also. At noon, our latitude by observation was 36° 9' N.

At 2 o'clock PM, I sent the boat to examine the outside of the ship. We found that the canvas coat of the rudder had been carried away owing to the heavy seas. I gave orders to have it removed intirely as the rudderhead was within a block which did render the coat unnecessary. While the boat was out, we saw a turtle on the surface of the water which we took, it weighed 30 pounds. At 5 o'clock, Velez Malaga bore NNW and the Westermost land in sight bore NW¼N. At 8 o'clock, we tacked on the larboard side, having a very light wind at West. At midnight, we found a very strong current running ESE. The sea was white and luminous, most especially in the stream of the current.

From Tuesday 28th

At 2 o'clock AM, having a gentle gale from the same quarter and being close to the land, we tacked on the starboard side. A quarter of an hour after having tacked, we saw a very large ship sailing before the wind, we hailed her but she did not reply. I presumed she was a Spanish frigate bound for Carthagena.

The wind continued at West during the whole of this day and we continued to make boards.

I was informed by the Surgeon that four of our people had got the venereal distemper. I recommended that he take the utmost precaution. Some seamen had been hurt at work but this was of small significance.

Knowing, after the several experiments of the most famous Captain Cook, that the cleaning of a ship was of the greatest consequence for the health of the seamen, and above all on a voyage such as the one I was to undertake, I gave orders that the slops and hammocks be aired and the between decks washed with vinegar each time the weather and such a cumbered ship would allow. At noon, our latitude by observation was 36° 32' N. The Castel de Fero bore at this time N 27° E, distant 3 leagues. The gentle gale at WSW was still with us.

At 1 o'clock PM, we got sight of a ship which was sailing before the wind which I knew to be *Provençal*, I worked the ship in order that we speak to her after having hoisted the colours and the ensigns. She put herself abreast of us. It was Captain Vigne in command of the *Jeune Camille* bound for Genoa. I requested that he would on his arrival at Genoa write to Messers J and D Baux of Marseilles and give them news of us, which he accordingly promised to do.

At ½ past 5 o'clock, the town of Motril which is to found deep within a great bay, bore N 12° E, Cape Sacratif N 18° E and Castel di Ferro N 40° E.

Near 7 o'clock, the ship lay almost becalmed with overcast weather all round the horizon. At 10 o'clock, the wind at SSE after a squall, we steered W¼SW.

The wind shifted, little by little, to East with continuous squalls and very dark and dense in the horizon. We thus directed our course to the WNW in order to reconnoitre Windmill Hill and from there, proceed to the Straits.

From Wednesday 29th

At 8 o'clock AM, we perceived Windmill Hill at N½W, distant 3 leagues. We crowded sail WSW in order to pass in sight of Mount Gibraltar. The weather was still very dark with squalls one after another. At noon, the weather clearing, we observed Mount Gibraltar bearing W½N, distant 5 leagues. At 3 o'clock PM, though the wind was blowing very hard, we set the studding sails in order to reach the open sea as soon as possible.

At 5 o'clock, Cape Spartel bore W 18° S, Point Europa N 56° E and the tower of Tarifa N 57° W, Ceuta Point bore E 22° 30 S. We had sight of 17 ships.

At 8 o'clock, Cape Spartel bore SSW, distant 2 leagues. We took our departure in the latitude of 35° 52' N and longitude 8° 12', West of Paris, after the chart of Verdun, Borda and Pingré.[17] Fresh gales at East, squalls and lightning continued, we steered West.

---

17 Marchand is here most probably referring to *Carte Réduite d'une partie de l'Ocean Atlantique ou Occidental Comprise entre le 13me et le 49me Dégré de Latitude Septle. et entre le 2me et le 78me Dégré de Longitude a l'Occident du Merider. de Paris. Dressée sur plusiers Observations Astronomiques et d'apres des Déterminations de Longitude faites a la Mer avec les Horloges Marines dans le Campagne de l'Isis en 1768 et 1769 sous le Commandement de Mr. de Fleurieu et dans celle de la Flore en 1771 et 1772 sous le Commandement de monsieur du Verdun de la Crenne*, published in 1775. The account of the voyage of the *Flore* was published in 1778: *(Voyage fait par ordre du roi n 1771 et 1772 en diverses parties de l'Afrique et de l'Amérique pour vérifier l'utilité de plusieurs methodes et instruments servant à déterminer la latitude et la longitude tant du vaisseau que des côtes, isles et écueils qu'on reconnaît, suivi des recherches pour vérifier les cartes hydrographiques)*. This narrative does not seem to have been translated into English as the *Royal Society* collections only list the French publication. James King in the introduction to Cook's

I had taken care while we were in the straits to have the lanterns lighted abaft in order to prevent boarding.

During the remainder of the night, we had clear weather and light breezes at ENE, all sails set. At day-light, we had sight of a ship astern of us keeping the same course, we lost sight of her in two hours.

Until this day, I have reckoned the day according to the civil account but in the remainder of this journal I will reckon the day from noon to noon in the astronomical fashion as being the most convenient.[18]

From Wednesday 29th at 9 o'clock PM to Thursday 30th December at noon[19]

101 Miles[20]

Very clear weather, winds varying from the NE to East.

The variation of the magnetic needle by reckoning was 21° NO.

During the morning, I had the hold of the ship opened to bring up water for we had finished that which was on the deck. We got up three barrels of 18 gallons each which we put on deck. These were then replaced by heavy articles which we were carrying for trade, and which had hitherto been stored between decks. This left us with a little room for the people to sleep therein, as they had until now been sleeping on the decks.

Latitude by observation at noon 35° 23'.[21]
Longitude by reckoning 10° 7'.

---

third Voyager op. cit., refers to the Atlantic ocean chart in the following terms: *First then, I have followed closely the very excellent and correct charts of the North Atlantic Ocean, published by Messers. De Verdun de la Crenne, de Borda, et Pingré in 1775 and 1776* . . . Cook met with Borda in August 1776 : *The Chevalier de Borda, Commander of the French frigate* (which was the *La Boussole*) *now lying in Santa Cruz road, was employed in conjunction with Mr Varila, a Spanish gentleman, in making astronomical observations for ascertaining the going of the two time-keepers which they had on board their ship. For this purpose, they had a tent pitched on the pier head, where they made their observations, and compared their watches every day at noon, with the clock on shore, by signals. These signals the Chevalier very obligingly communicated to us; so that we could compare our watch at the same time. But our stay was too short, to profit by his kindness.*

18 Gannier (*journal*, op. cit., pp. 139–140) points to the change in the format of the journal at this point. The contents of the column labelled *Observations métérologiques, astronomiques et autres* provides the material (as transcribed by Gannier) for this translation.

19 From the 29th onwards, each page of the journal contains a table (as in a log) of the time, the direction of the wind, the course and the distance sailed. Gannier has published these tables in the substantial Annexes to her transcription and thus they are not reproduced here.

20 The distance sailed is included in Gannier's transcription and I have retained this formatting (though in the manuscript itself, this figure appears in the table and not in the *Observations* column).

21 I have indented all the latitudes and longitudes for clarity.

We had 10' of difference to the Northward from the reckoning of the latitude, which seemed to me extraordinary in this space of sea, where the currents set very certainly to the SSW following the Barbary coast.

After the observations computed on the King's Frigate *La Flore*,[22] which found that the measure of a mile by the loglines was excessive at 47½ feet, I had them marked at 45 feet which was the length chosen by the observers who were employed on this frigate, amongst whom was the Chevalier de Borda.

From Thursday 30th to Friday 31st December[23]

89½ miles

Fine weather, cloudy, light breezes at NE with a great swell from the North, all sails set. I gave J[h] Pecou 2 woollen shirts, and woollen breeches to Ch[es] Candi.

At 10 o'clock the wind at NE began to abate and shifted to NNW and gradually varied at W, SW and SSW, I determined to tack on the larboard side in order not to approach the Barbary coast too near.

At 10 o'clock AM, the wind blowing a hard gale at SSW with rain, we took the lower reefs in the top-sails.

At noon, we could not take the sun's altitude on account of the weather which was very overcast, the latitude by reckoning was N 34° 45', and longitude by reckoning was W 11° 39'. The variation of the magnetic needle by reckoning was 21° NW.

Saw many seagulls, large and small.

From Friday 31st December to 1st January 1791

118½

At 3 o'clock PM, the wind having shifted to SSE, though with continuous rain, we loosed a reef out of the main top-sail and the fore top-sail. Soon afterwards, the wind veered to the SE with a great swell from the SW and one from the North, which excessively worked the ship and slowed her progress.

At 3 o'clock AM, the trade wind settling at NE and ENE, we set all our sails.

The variation of the compass by reckoning was 20° NW after the observations I had made in this same sea space during my previous voyage to India.

At noon, the latitude by observation was 33° 51' N, and the longitude by reckoning was W 13° 41'. We had only one and a half minutes of difference between the latitude by observation and that given by dead reckoning.

We were losing 5 to 6 fowls every day.

---

22 See note 16.
23 The months are sometimes abrreviated in Marchand's journal. They are written in full throughout this translation.

From Saturday 1ˢᵗ to Sunday 2ⁿᵈ January 1791

136

The winds were variable this day from N to ENE, blowing fresh gales with a great swell from the NNW.

At 8 o'clock PM, we steered WSW.

At sunrise, the variation determined from several observations of the amplitude, made with different compasses, was NW 19° 16'.

We had heavy showers of rain at intervals in the morning

Latitude by observation N 32° 17'.
Longitude by reckoning W 15° 17'.

I had remarked with great pleasure that since our departure, the ship was sailing better, more especially in light winds, which was most advantageous for a voyage as long as the one which we had undertaken for generally winds are most often light than strong, though with these latter much progress is made.

The carpenter was constantly employed in lightening the spare yards, and then hauling them up accordingly. The second carpenter being sickly, the work did not go forward as quickly as I would have wished.

From Sunday 2ⁿᵈ to Monday 3ʳᵈ January 1791

113

The winds were variable from North to NE, blowing gentle gales with at intervals lighter winds. The weather was otherwise fine though overcast.

The variation of the compass was by reckoning NW 19°.

During the morning, we suffered violent squalls of wind.

Latitude by observation 31° 8'
Longitude by reckoning W 17° 28'.

7' more to the North than by reckoning.

Salvage Island bore S 54° 45' W, distant 25 leagues.

At 8 o'clock AM, I gave the order to lash up all the hammocks in the hind part of the between decks which was somewhat cleared as we had got up all the seamen's chests upon deck. After having washed the place with vinegar, at 11 o'clock the rain obliged me to put all in order again.

From Monday 3ʳᵈ to Tuesday 4ᵗʰ January 1791

46½ miles

Gentle breezes varying from NW to NNW, attended with a thick haze and some rain from time to time.

As we were in the vicinity of the Salvages, and choosing not to pass their latitude during the night, and above all, in such hazy weather, we close hauled on the starboard tack and at 8 o'clock PM, we shortened sail to the four main courses. By means of several azimuths and an observation of the Westerly amplitude, the variation of the compass was found to be NW 19° 23', mean result. These observations were made with different compasses.

We saw many common sterns or large sea swallows which proves M. Ray's assertion, as reported by Mr de Buffon, that this species of bird is generally found to nest in the Salvages.[24]

Having made little progress during the night, at 8 o'clock AM we steered SW to examine this island. Indeed we saw it directly a-head at 10 o'clock, about 4 leagues distant, and as the wind was very light and variable from N to NNW, attended with a strong swell from the NNW, we directed our course to W and W¼NW in order that we not come too near because I had learnt several times by experience that the currents set in the direction of the island, when coming from the North.

At noon, I found the latitude by observation with Dolland's[25] well-tried sextant, to be 30° 29'. At this moment, the Salvages bore true South, at no more than 4 leagues distant. On Messers Verdun, Borda and Pingre's chart, this island is situated in latitude 30° 8' and we should have observed but 30° 20'. However we found the latitude to be 30° 29' and several of my officers, amongst whom was M. Chanal who possessed an exceedingly good sextant, manufactured by Gilbert and Wright, found it to be 30° 30', from which it is clear that the island is laid down 9 or 10' more to the South than it really is. Some may make the objection that I was mistaken as to the real distance at the time of the observation, but I may assert that we were certainly no more distant than 4 leagues for I could readily discern the shore. My longitude here by reckoning was 18° 15', which is that laid down in the chart of which I have spoken, in consequence of which I continued my reckoning without taking a new departure. I found the currents had driven us 14' to the Southward, which is usual in this sea, and seamen who find themselves obliged to spend the night near to this island must take the utmost care.

Salvage Island is a low island and in fine weather it is hardly visible and can be seen from the mast-heads, only when 7 leagues distant. The highest land is in the SW, and in the SE there are some breakers which extend, I have been told, 1 mile in the offing. It is uninhabited.

---

24 Marchand obviously had copies of Buffon's *Histoire Naturelle, générale et particulière, avec la déscription du cabinet du Roi* on board ship. Here he refers to Mr Ray as cited by Buffon in Volume 23: *Ray observes, that they are usually found fifty leagues from the most western part of England, and are even met with the whole way to Madeira; and that a vast multitude resort to breed on the Salvages, desert islets at a small distance from the Canaries* (from the 1793 English translation *The Natural History of Birds from the French of the Count de Buffon, Illustrated with Engravings and a Preface, Notes and Additions by the Translator. In Nine Volumes*, Volume VIII, p. 297).

25 See Gannier, *journal*, op. cit., p. 143.

From Tuesday 4ᵗʰ to Wednesday 5ᵗʰ January 1791

58

During the afternoon, it was exceedingly hazy with intervals of calm and sudden, violent gusts of wind from N to NNW, attended with a great swell from the NW.

At 5 o'clock PM, Salvage Island bore S¼SE, distant 3 leagues.

The winds during this night were very light and variable from N to NE with a great rolling swell from the North.

At day-light, we saw our first flying fish. During other voyages I had got sight of them two degrees more to the North, which made me think that these fish retire to the South during the winter. At 9 o'clock, the variation of the compass, by the means of several azimuths by different compasses, was NW 17° 53'.

A gentle breeze at NE succeeded the haze and we had in consequence clear weather. I took all advantage possible of this moment and had all the hammocks taken down and gave orders to wash the between decks with vinegar.

Latitude by observation N 30° 8'.
Longitude by reckoning W 19° 16'.

1' more to the North than by reckoning.
We saw many sheerwaters and stormy petrels.

From Wednesday 5ᵗʰ to Thursday 6ᵗʰ January 1791

126¾

We stood our course with a gentle breeze varying from NE to E and all sails set. At ¾ past 2 o'clock, we got sight of the high mountains which form the base of the Peak of Teneriffe, bearing S¼SW, the Peak could not be seen on account of the haze, and following the latitude we had just observed, we were distant 35 leagues.

Several gulls were fluttering about the ship.

At 8 o'clock, we directed our course to WSW in order to pass West of the the Isle of Palma. During the night, we had very fine weather.

At 4 o'clock AM, I gave orders to steer SW¼ but at ¾ past 5 o'clock having seen land at SSW, we again directed our course to WSW in order to pass it at a distance, we then doubled it at a distance of 5 or 6 leagues.

At 11 o'clock, we rigged the fore top yard, its length had been shortened to 6 feet and it had been reduced to 1½ inches in diameter.

Latitude by observation N 28° 36'.
Longitude by reckoning W 21° 1'.

14' more to the North than by reckoning.
At this instant, the SW point of Palma bore E 33° 45' S, our longitude was 20° 40', that is to say that we were 6 leagues more to the East than by reckoning.

We took our departure from this point. Our latitude as known by observation agreed by a minute to the bearings.

We saw very few flying fish.

We were losing daily many of our fowls, a hundred of which were already dead since leaving Marseilles.

From Thursday 6th to Friday 7th January 1791

116¾

At half past noon, we had sight of the Isle of Ferro through the haze, of which a point bore S¼SW and which we were hardly able to distinguish. At 2 o'clock PM, we rigged the main top yard which I had lessened in much the same way as the fore top yard, and the yards were thus equal in all.

At 3 o'clock PM, the Southermost point of the Isle of Ferro bore South.

During the afternoon, the winds were very variable with a very heavy sea from the North.

At 10 o'clock, the wind blowing a fresh gale at SE, we took a reef in each top-sail, which we loosed at 3 o'clock AM, and at day-light we set the studding sails.

As I had been sickly these several days, during the morning an emetic and some physick very soon afterward, did me the greatest good.

Latitude by observation N 26° 50'.
Longitude by reckoning W 21° 30'.

5' more to the South than by reckoning.
The variation of the compass by reckoning was NW 16°.

From Friday 7th to Saturday 8th January 1791

151¼

The wind blew constantly this day from E to ESE with clear weather though with some little haze.

At sun-set, by means of several observations of the amplitudes, we found the variation of the compass to be NW 14° 30'.

At 8 o'clock AM, we steered SSW, a route by which we passed West of Cape Blancs, distant 45 leagues.

We saw but few flying fish in this sea though there are many such fish here in general. As for the birds, we saw only stormy petrels which do not always herald the coming of bad weather as the ancient navigators believed it to be.[26]

---

26 Here Marchand may be challenging Buffon's description of the *oiseau de tempête*: *By force of instinct, it perceives those indications which escape our senses; and its motions and its approach warn the sailors to be prepared for the tempest. When, in calm weather, these little petrels are*

Since our departure, and not including dolphins, we had not got sight of a single fish along-side the ship and I would have believed the copper bottom to be the cause of their staying away if this were not a prejudice much belied by experience.

Latitude by observation N 24° 19'
Longitude by reckoning W 22° 16'.

From Saturday 8th to Sunday 9th January 1791

We had hard gales which continued to blow at East.

Réaumur's thermometer of which I have not yet spoken, was at +17° in my cabin and on the deck of the ship, at 16°. During all the time that we had been in the Mediterranean sea, it had been between +13 and 14½°. On leaving the Straits, it had risen to 15° and had remained thus until the Canaries. It surprised me not a little to see it so low in the sea in which we were. Indeed, the winds were fresh and the declination of the sun was very South.

At 3h, 20' 14" o'clock PM, by means of four observations of the distance of the ☉-☾, we found the longitude to be 21° while the longitude by reckoning was at this moment 22° 18', which was 1° 18' more to the East.

The variation of the compass by the Westerly amplitude was NW 14° 16'. At 7 o'clock PM, we crossed the Tropick of Cancer in longitude 22° 20' W by reckoning.

The ship's company wished to practice the ordinary ceremony but I would not suffer them to do so for I had constantly seen this diversion end in quarrels.

At day-light, we saw a ship to the windward of us, steering SSW. At 7 o'clock AM, having steered S½SW, we came near to her. We hoisted the ship's ensign at which she displayed a flag of truce. We each continued our route, not having spoken to each other.

The sea appeared to be of a green colour, paler than general, and I would have sounded if the wind had not been as fresh.

Latitude by observation N 21° 24'.
Longitude by reckoning W 22° 36'.

5° more to the North than by reckoning.
Thermometer +15°[27]

---

seen to flock behind a vessel, flying on the wake, and sheltering themselves under the stern, the mariners hasten to furl the fails, and prepare for the storm, which infallibly comes on a few hours after. Thus, the appearance of these birds at sea is at once dismal and salutary; and nature would seem to have dispersed them over the wide ocean to convey the friendly intelligence (The Natural History of Birds, op. cit., Volume IX, p. 280).

27 Marchand systemmatically notes the temperature and sometimes notes the ° symbol and sometimes he omits it. All the temperatures in this translation include the degree symbol.

From Sunday 9th to Monday 10th January 1791

149¼

We had a fresh breeze of wind, more or less, and constant at E. In the horizon there was some little haze.

At 3h 27' 41" o'clock PM, the longitude by observation of five distances of the ☉-☾ was 21° 45' W, which was 51' to the Eastward of the reckoning.

The variation of the magnetic needle by the Westerly amplitude was found to be NW 13° 10'.

I had observed since our departure that the articles between decks had been very ill stowed and that our officers were much cumbered. The quantity of heavy goods, which would have better been accommodated in the hold, made the ship drive slowly and roll. These reasons, added to the prodigious use of our stock of water, and due to the number of animals we had on board, determined me to put in at Praya, Isle of St Jago. There we would effect the changes that had become necessary in the stowage, which would thus allow us to make ready to navigate with a degree of safety in the hard seas which we were to find after rounding Cape Horn. We would also there make water and examine the barrels of our bread in the between decks, which I much feared was spoilt by the two hard squalls we had suffered in the Mediterranean after our departure.

A 4 o'clock AM, we steered South.

At 8 o'clock AM, we saw our first tropic bird. I saw a land bird at this moment which had come to the bow of the ship and which, in an instant, I lost sight of. It was of the heron kind. The sea was still of a green whitish colour.

Longitude by observation N 18° 45'.
Longitude by reckoning W 22° 22'.

5° more to the South than by reckoning.
Réaumur's thermometer +15°.

From Monday 10th to Tuesday 11th January 1791

92½

This day, the breeze varied from NE to ESE, attended with a haze and rain at intervals. During the night, the sea was white and illuminated.

The variation of the magnetic needle by reckoning was found to be 13° NW.

At ½ past 4 o'clock, I saw the traces of many fish, but at day-light we saw them no more. The appearance of a great shark was no doubt the reason of their retreat. The sea was covered with a sort of *Mollusca* commonly called by the seamen a Portuguese Man of War.

We saw several small stormy petrels.

The carpenters were still employed in lightening the yards. They finished their work on one main yard in the morning which had been shortened one foot in length and which was now four and a half inches in diameter.

Several of the people had made known to Mr Roblet, the Surgeon, their wish to be purged in order that they might enjoy a better state of health on the voyage. He gave them the medicine in order to purge them and he was of the opinion that all the people should proceed thus. We saw some sheerwaters[28] and flying fish in great number.

Latitude by observation N 17° 20'
Longitude by reckoning W 22°

5° more to the North than by reckoning.
Thermometer +15½°.

From Tuesday 11ᵗʰ to Wednesday 12ᵗʰ January 1791

129¼

The weather continued hazy though we had gentle breezes at North which varied at ESE. This haze is common and is often met with in this sea surrounding the Cape de Verde islands which makes that extreme care must be taken in meeting with them, most particularly at night.

The variation of the magnetic needle by reckoning was 13° NW.

The sea continued to be illuminated during the night.

At 5 o'clock AM, we steered SSW. At 6 'clock, our latitude was 15° 50' N by reckoning and 21° 39' Longitude W, I shaped the course to Westward, in order to pass near St Jago, by keeping to the wind which was at this time blowing a fresh gale at North. We were sailing under the four main courses.

During the morning, all the seamen's chests and boxes were moved forward to get the cables clear of them.

Latitude by observation N 15° 43'.
Longitude by reckoning 22° 18W.

Thermometer +15°.

From Wednesday 12ᵗʰ to Thursday 13ᵗʰ January 1791

128¼

A gentle gale at North continued to blow with the horizon very hazy and a great swell owing to the wind.

---

28 Cook in his *Endeavour* journal writes "sheer water" with an irregular use of the hypen. Banks (*Endeavour* journal) and Forster (in his 1777 *A voyage round the world, in His Britannic Majesty's sloop, Resolution, commanded by Capt. James Cook, during the years 1772, 3, 4, and 5. By George Forster, F. R. S. Member of the Royal Academy of Madrid, and of the Society for promoting Natural Knowledge at Berlin. In two volumes*) both use "shear-water" (Banks does not use the hyphen).

At 3 o'clock PM, we steered W½S,W, directing our course North for the Northern point of the the the Isle of Mayo.

At ½ past 5 o'clock, we saw a prodigious number of dolphins.

We attempted with little success to strike them with a harpoon.

I also got sight of a grey white bird of the sea swallow sort, flying to the Southward.

At 7 o'clock, a flying fish threw itself on board the ship. It was approximately five inches in length from head to tail.

At 1 o'clock AM, the wind began to blow hard with violent gusts one after the other, we were unable to see a cable's length before us and I did not think it safe to stand in for the shore in such weather and gave orders to work to windward upon the larboard tack under the top-sails.

When day-light came, we crowded sail W¼NW in order to examine the coast. The wind abated at this moment and we now had clearer weather.

All through the night, the sea was exceedingly illuminated of which the reflection on the sails was most beautiful.

At noon we had not been able to make our observations of the latitude due to the haze, it was 15° 10' by reckoning and longitude 24° 3' W.

In this position, the middle of the isle of Mayo bore North 13° W, I mean W 13° N, distant 21 leagues.[29]

Thermomter +15½°

From Thursday 13th to Friday 14th January 1791

98¼

Gentle gales at N and at NNE, with the horizon very hazy most particularly from North to South round by West. All sails set, stood in for the land.

At 4 o'clock, we took a porpoise which was served to the ship's company. We dined only on the liver which we found to be as sweet as that of the hog.

At 8 o'clock PM, the wind began to blow a hard gale, with showers of rain at intervals. I stood in for the shore notwithstanding. At 11 o'clock, the weather was so dirty that we tacked and stood to the East under the foresail and the top-sails with two reefs in.

At ½ past 3 o'clock, we tacked again on the larboard side and worked to windward NNW, the wind was at this moment at NE. At day-light, we steered WNW.

During the night, the sea was once again very illuminated.

At ½ past 9 o'clock, we saw the land through the haze, which was very thick, it stretched from N 15° E to N 17° W. I reckoned its distance to be 5 leagues. It seemed to be very high, the mountains ending in peaks. Not seeing any land

---

29 Gannier points out (*journal*, op. cit., p. 150) that the entries in the official logs and journals could not be crossed out and especially if any nautical data was concerned. Cook's *Endeavour* journal contains many crossings out but his journal of the second voyage is impeccable.

a-head of us, and our position being most incertain, as we had not been able to observe the latitude the previous day, I resolved to steer NNW directly for the land, for if it were indeed the Isle of St Jago, it was to my advantage to approach it. If on the contrary it was found to be the Isle of Mayo, I was by this method still to the windward.

At noon, the latitude by observation was 14° 59', and the land thus proved to be the Isle of Mayo. We steered WSW to make the East point of the Isle St Jago before night came on. The SW point of the Isle of May bore N 45° W, and the East point, N 56° 30' E. The longitude by reckoning was found to be 25° 36', and that resulting from two observations that we had made was 24° 55'. Our true position according to the maps of Mr Verdun, Borda and Pingré, was longitude 25° 27' West. We saw many frigate birds, boobies and a kind of sea swallow with a split tail and named by the seamen *tailleurs*[30] for this reason, we saw gulls and stormy petrels. The South part of the Isle of Mayo is edged by sea beach of which the sand is white.

Thermometer + 15½°

From Friday 14th to Saturday 15th January 1791

57½

I have before mentioned that we had steered WSW to make the Isle of Yago before the night came on, with a light breeze at ENE, attended with a thick haze. At 4 o'clock PM, we saw land directly a-head. It bore W to W¼ SW with the most Easterly low point bearing NW½W, distant 1 league. There was not light enough to come to anchor in Praya, we tacked on the larboard side in order to stand on and off during the night. Each hour during the night we sounded and never found any bottom with 80 fathoms of line.

At 7 o'clock AM, we got sight of the island through the haze, of which the most Northerly point bore N 62° W, with the most Southerly, which in truth was the most Easterly point of the Island, bearing S 40° W. We stood for this point. At ½ past 8 o'clock, we were abreast of it and steered for the Easterly point of the Bay of Praya bearing SW 2° W. At ¼ past 9 o'clock, we rounded this point and came to anchor at ½ past 9 o'clock in 8 fathom water, ooze and sand bottom. The fort bore NW¼N, the middle of the Green Island bore W, and all round the West point, which bore SW¼W, were breakers. Much care is required when entering this bay for the squalls of wind are very violent.

We saw a Portuguese vessel from Lisbon bound for the Coast of Guinea, an American schooner bound for St Eustache, and a French ship for Gorée, to which I gave letters for my owners and for my family, for there is at La Praya almost never any occasion to send directly to Europe. As the French ship was leaky, she

---

30 May be translated as cutters or perhaps tailors. Marchand describes the bird as having a tail in the form of shears (scissors).

had put into the port for repairs and she would never have succeeded in such an undertaking but for the assistance of an English frigate and sloop of war which were in her wake and which procured her all the help that she was in need of.

We immediately came to anchor and veered away two thirds of the cable

Remainder of Friday 14ᵗʰ to Saturday 15ᵗʰ January 1791

... then I gave orders to unrig the main top-gallant yards and to immediately hoist out all the boats.

At 10 o'clock, I sent the longboat to the watering place and I and an officer went in a boat to visit the Governor and the Commander. The first I was not able to see for he was engaged in what the Spanish call a siesta. I was able to speak only to his Secretary and asked leave to procure water and other provisions, which I obtained. As for the second, he asked questions in a very laconic way as to from whence I came, where I was bound, what was my business, and made me understand by way of an interpreter (not apparently desiring to say the thing himself for he had seen that I spoke the language) that it was usual for all the captains who put in at this place to make him a present. He hoped I would accept to do likewise. I made use of shifts for my answer and withdrew most determined to do nothing and filled with indignation at so base a proceeding.[31]

From Saturday 15ᵗʰ to Sunday 16ᵗʰ

No sooner had I made my visits than I went to the watering place which is upon a beach of black sand to the Westward of the town. I found there the officer and the longboat crew employed in getting on board the water. There are two wells to this purpose though Mr Forster in the second voyage of Cook[32] says there is but one.[33] It is true to say that perhaps there was only a single one at that date, and it is certainly the one at 200 paces in from the shore of which he was speaking. But

---

31 Captain Dixon (op. cit., p. 22) does indeed give the Commander of the Fort a small gift: *The Commander of the Fort treated them at first in rather a haughty manner, but on having a trifling present made him, he grew civil and gave them leave to water the ships; this being it seems all that is in his power.* ... Captain Portlock op. cit., tells a slightly different story having accompanied Captain Dixon to see the Commander: *After waiting on the commander of the fort, who is styled the "Captain Moor" and paying a port charge of four dollars for each vessel, I went to inspect the wells* (op. cit., p. 17).

32 Marchand is probably quoting from a translation into French of the narrative of the second voyage of Cook *Voyage dans l'hémisphère austral et autour du monde* (Hotel de Thou, 1778). The translator makes it clear that his text is a collation of the Cook and Forster (in quotation marks) texts.

33 *The water is tolerable but scarce; and bad getting off, on account of the surf on the beach.* Forster underlines that *At Porto Praya there was only a single well set round with loose stones, and containing muddy, brackish water in such small quantities, that we drew it quite dry twice a day* (op. cit., p. 37). Cook also refers to the well: *You water at a well that is behind the beach at the head of the bay* (*A Voyage towards the South Pole, and round the World. Performed in His Majesty's ships the Resolution and Adventure, in the years 1772, 1773, 1774, and 1775. Written by James Cook,*

the water is worth nothing and muddy. The second place of which we made use, was at 500 paces from the shore and the water was of a much better sort. We are there able to roll the casks or bring the barrels to the longboat and within fill the casks. We employed both ways and at 5 o'clock PM in the evening, we came on board loaded with 9 full casks.

Before going ashore, we had got down the top-gallant masts, and carried out a kedge anchor at SW. The Quartermaster made ready to make the alterations I considered necessary in the stowing of the between decks and in a part of the hold.

In the morning of the 16ᵗʰ, I did not wish to go ashore but rather to accompany and hurry the men employed in making all the arrangements for sailing. I must say in honour of the crew that I had never seen them work so heartily.

At 9 o'clock AM, the French ship got under sail bound for Gorée.

The remainder of Saturday 15ᵗʰ to Sunday 16ᵗʰ January 1791

At 11 o'clock AM, I sent Mr Chanal with the steward to purchase some provisions and I gave leave to several other officers to go ashore and visit the place.

Brief description of Port Praya

Port Praya is situated on a steep elevation and a path though winding, leads up to it. The fortifications are very old and now almost in ruins.[34] Facing the land, there is a very low and imperfect dry stone parapet. The inside of the fort is guarded by soldiers, three quarters are black and almost naked and they have some few huts and inside of which shelter from the rain is hardly be had. A rather fine building is to be found in the plain which I was told belonged to a Lisbon company of merchants whose agent is engaged in the commerce of livestock. The inhabitants suffer the weight of a despotick power and what is the most surprising is that the people may not take leave of the island as they wish. There are but a very few white men in Port Praya and I saw no more than six or seven, amongst which I include the Governor and the Commander and I am sure that I have seen all the inhabitants. These are lazy for I desired to employ some in the watering place and

---

commander of the Resolution, 1777, Volume 1, p. 8). Both references to the well in question appear in the translated version.

34 Gannier (journal, op. cit., p. 155) points to the similarities between Marchand's description and Cook's. In fact, Forster, not Cook, gives this description in his journal: *Porto-Praya stands on a steep rock, to which we climbed by a serpentine path. Its fortifications are old decayed walls on the sea side, and fences scarce breast-high, made of loose stones, towards the land [. . .] A tolerable building, at a little distance from the fort, belongs to a company of merchants at Lisbon, who have the exclusive right to trade to all the Cape-Verd Islands, and keep an agent here for the purpose* . . . (Volume 1, op. cit., p. 34).

I found hardly more than four or five who had to be paid near to 45 sous of our money. The purchase of provisions has to made with great care as they ask three times the price of the thing but I had fortunately had warning of the case from the Captain of the French ship.

As for the productions of this island, they are much the same as those which are to be found in the West Indies, but from I what I have been able to observe the people do not cultivate the land and prefer to tend livestock which costs them less labour.

In order to anchor in Port Praya when coming in from the East, following the coast is of the greatest importance and the chart of M. D'Après[35] is very true.

At the East point of the island, which is very low and around which there are breakers, there is a bay of a kind and in the bottom of it, a sandy beach and a wood of coconut trees behind, this is the false bay which some navigators have taken for Port Praya. But unless it is night, I cannot conceive of this for both the town and the port may be distinctly recognised, and added to this there is no house to be seen in the false bay. The direction of the coast must prevent this mistake. From the East, or rather North point of this false bay, to the West point (which is Eastward of Port Praya) the coast trends SW½ S on the one side and NE ½ N on the other, whereas the East and West points of Port Praya bear E¼NE and W¼SW.

It is of use I think to relate what Mr d'Après says:

> *Three leagues before coming to anchor at La Praya, there is a cove edged with trees and some few houses (of which I saw only one). It is very much like the cove of Praya: (I found it bore no sort of resemblance to it). Several ships have by the appearance mistaken it for Port Praya and have found themselves at risk of being destroyed on the submerged rocks within the cove. Fort Praya, situated on an elevation, though is a sure sign of the distinction between the two. The most certain means is that around the East or North point of this false bay there are breakers, whereas Port Praya, which follows, is high ground with no submerged rocks. It is necessary always to coast along this bay to come to anchor. The ensign of the fort must bear NW 3 to 4° N by compass and the West*

---

35 Most of Marchand's entry here is a transcription of the description in *Neptune Oriental* (Jean-Baptiste d'Après de Mannevillette, 1745), see Gannier, *journal*, op. cit., p. 155. This book was adapted and published in English under the title *The Oriental Navigator; or, new directions for sailing to and from the East Indies. Also for the use of the country ships, trading in the Indian and China Seas; to New Holland, &c. &c. Collected from the manuscripts, journals, memoirs, and observations, of the most experienced officers . . . Being a companion to the East India pilot, by the late Mr. Robert* Sayer; *which have been greatly augmented with many corrections and improvements* (Joseph Huddart, 1794).

point of the bay at the extremity of which we may see the sea break upon a reef, must so be at WSW.[36]

This is what Mr Cook says during his voyage to the South Pole.

Port Praya is a small bay, situated about he middle of the South side of the island of St. Jago in the latitude of 14° 53' 30" North, longitude 23° 36' [37] *West of Greenwich. It may be known especially in coming from the East, by the Southermost hill on the island; which is round, and peaked at top; and lies a little way inland, in the direction of West from the port. This mark is the more necessary, which strangers may mistake for Port Praya, as we ourselves did, a small cove about a league to the East-ward, with a sandy beach in the bottom of it, a valley and cocoa-nut trees behind. The two points which form the entrance of Port Praya bay, are rather low and in the direction of WSW and ENE, half a league from each other. Close to the West point, are sunken rocks on which the sea continually breaks. The bay lies in NW, near half a league and the depth of the water is from 14 to four fathoms. Large ships ought not anchor in less than eight.* [38]

The principal seamark in this bay which Mr Cook gives is a hill which is peaked at the top, which cannot be seen if a ship comes to the anchoring place from the East, for it is necessary to coast

The remainder of Saturday 15th to Sunday 16th January 1791

Very closely along the shore, and besides this, the haze very often covers it.

---

36 My translation. In Huddart's adaptation in English (op. cit., 1794), the false bay is described as follows: *The South East part of the Island of St Jago appears a long low point when you are to the Northward or Southward of it; and from this point S. W. by S. about 6 or 7 miles lies the East point of Port Praya Bay. Between the two, and near the former, lies a Bay which so much resembles that of Port Praya, that many vessels, deceived by this likeness, have ran the hazard of being lost in this dangerous place-, at the bottom of it are several cocoa nut trees, and a few houses; the land between this and the aforesaid point of Port Praya is mostly perpendicular, in some places appearing like the Berry Head in Torbay; and though the Fort of Port Praya, which stands on a small cliff, is a mark by which the true bay may be distinguished from the false one, yet the most certain mark is that the North or East point of the false bay is surrounded with breakers, whereas the point of Port Praya is high and steep, and free from shoals; you must haul close round this point, and keep within a cable's length of the shore to go to the anchoring place.*

37 In the Cook account (as well as in the translation) the coordinates are 23° 30'.

38 This is a slightly truncated version of Cook's entry in the published account and in the 1778 translated version. Both these latter though do not include "of Greenwich" and the longitude is noted as 23° 30'. Gannier (*journal*, op. cit., p. 156) points out that Port Praya is in 23° 31' longitude.

These two most famous navigators each laid down Port Praya in a chart. Following our very exact observations, I found the bay to be of too great an extent after Mr d'Après but well drawn. The chart of Mr Cook, in respect to the extent, I found to be exact but the form was not wholly correct.[39]

From Sunday 16th to Monday 17th

In the afternoon, I resolved not to send the longboat to the watering place as I had at first thought to do, and this in order that more of the people be employed about the ship. At 7 o'clock PM, the boat I had sent a shore came back and the officer had procured only 13–1400 oranges, six small hogs, some few eggs, some small bananas[40] and very few greens. Fresh meat for the people was impossible to be had, the promise however of some for the next day was made but they did not keep their word. Having hoisted in the boat, I served oranges to the ships company. At 8 o'clock, we had completed our stowage. We disposed the main top masts, and the spare yards, save a foreyard (and the pieces of oak timber which cumbered the deck), in the between decks.

At 8 o'clock in the morning I sent the longboat ashore to complete our water for I was intent to get under sail in the evening, or during the night if I was able. Immediately afterwards, I sent some officers in the boat to procure all the refreshments they could find.

At sunrise, after the observations of the sun made by different compasses, the variation of the magnetic needle was determined to be 14° 17' NW, and by the mean of 10 azimuths, it was found to be 13° 59'.

At noon, the latitude by observation was 14° 53' 2", with only 38' of difference from that which is given by Messers Verdun, Borda and Pingré on their chart, and who lay down this bay in 14° 53' 40". Mr Cook observed it to be 14° 53' 30". The haze prevented us from verifying by observation its longitude.

From Monday 17th to Tuesday 18th 1791

At ½ past 2 o'clock PM, the longboat returned with water, and the yawl with refreshments such as oranges, greens, cabbages, cocoa-nuts, a goat and a kid. They made us hope that the next day we should get everything we were in need of for there was to be a market. I was very little concerned by this news and did not desire to delay getting under sail, though it be only for a quarter of an hour, as I could very well make shift without. We had some difficulty this day in making our water on account of the surf and a great swell at ESE at ten paces from the beach. The sea became so heavy in time that the officer who had the charge of the

---

39 There is no chart of Port Praya in Marchand's journal.
40 Marchand uses the term *figues bananes*.

watering was obliged to throw himself in the water and swim to get on board the longboat. He thus left behind a part of the cable which had parted.

Five of our people had remained ashore, the Surgeon, the cooper, the two furriers and the armourer. I discovered from the officers who had been ashore that the three latter were in an ale-house, very likely drinking. For the two remaining, they had not dared embark in the longboat on account of the swell, and the officer seeing that she was ready to break in two, did not care to wait for them.

When there is a heavy sea in this bay, the best landing place is situated on the most Northern point of the East of the Bay. In this situation, one is able to disembark on the rocks in dry places. There is a path to be found there which leads up to the fort. This point is easy to find out for to the North it forms a cove with a border of coconut trees which is situated below the South of the town.

At Praya, the price for anchorage is four Spanish pieces of eight.

In the afternoon, we caulked the portholes as it is impossible for us to open them even in the least heavy of seas. A new canvas coat for the rudder was put on. As soon as the water casks had been taken out from the longboat, I gave orders to atrip the small anchor at SW.

At 5 o'clock PM, the people ashore had still not come on board, I sent a boat with two officers to bring them back. I strongly censored the furriers and the armourer as to their ill conduct.

At 9 o'clock, we hoisted in the long boat and the two boats and I kept only the yawl in the water.

Remainder of Monday 17ᵗʰ to Tuesday 18ᵗʰ January 1791

As the people had continually been at work this day and were prodigiously tired, I resolved to get under sail the next morning in spite of my desire to leave this place at once. I had forgot to mention that the bread we had in the barrels in the between decks, which I had very much feared was spoilt, was in the best of condition.

Remainder of Monday 17ᵗʰ to Tuesday 18ᵗʰ January 1791

At 5 o'clock AM, we made ready to weigh and at 8 o'clock we got under sail accompanied by a fresh breeze at NNE. We shortened sail until 9 o'clock in order to see the anchors clear, hoist in the yawl and clear the cables. At this moment we set all the sails and made much progress to the South, with the very fresh breeze at NE. At ½ past 8 o'clock

the East point of the bay bore N 33° 45' E
the West point N 40° W
the Westermost low point of the island in sight bore N 57° W
& the Eastermost low point, or rather Northermost of the false bay, bore N 50° E.

From thence we took our departure in latitude 14° 50' North and 25° 49' W longitude.

During the whole of our stay in La Praya, we constantly had steady winds at ENE in the day, and at NE during the night, they blew always very fresh accompanied by more or less haze. The thermometer on board at noon was at +17½°, and onshore, close to the well, it was at 20°.

At noon, we reckoned we had run 23½ miles Southward. Our latitude by observation was 14° 27' N, which agreed exactly with that found by reckoning. Our longitude by reckoning was 25° 44' W.

I was much pleased to notice that the working of the ship had much improved on account of the new alterations we had made and she rolled much less. I hoped she would work better when no longer sunk as low in the water.

From Tuesday 18th to Wednesday 19th 1791

159½

At noon, we steered S¼SE with a fresh breeze at ENE which stayed with us throughout the day attended by a light haze. We saw boobies, tropic birds, porpoises and flying fish.

At 7 o'clock AM, we unrigged the cross jack yard of the mizzen top-sail in order to reduce the length as well as the thickness.

We took down all the hammocks to air the between decks.

The variation of the compass by reckoning was 13° NW.

Latitude by reckoning N 12° 8'.
Longitude by reckoning 24° 39'.

5' more to the North than by reckoning.
* Réaumurs's thermometer +21° and Fahrenheit's *ditto* 79°.
* The thermometers are always exposed at noon, in the sun and in the shade

From Wednesday 19th to Thursday 20th January 1791

136

The wind blew a gentle gale and continued at NE to ENE. At noon, we examined the bread and the other stores in the great cabin, and smoked the ship by fires. Two hundred weight of bread was spoilt but could be fed to the poultry and livestock.

I desired to manage with economy our fresh water as long as it was possible, without recourse to an allowance, and so I gave orders that the water jars be locked with a padlock and the officer of the watch was charged with giving water to those who asked for it. I also regulated the amount of water to be given to the cook room.

By means of the Westerly amplitude of the ☉, and of several azimuths, the variation of the magnetic needle was found to be 11° 10' NW.

Latitude by observation N 10° 4'
Longitude by reckoning W 23° 45'.

Réaumur's thermometer +21°, Fahrenheit's thermometer 79°.

From Thursday 20th to Friday 21st 1791

85½
A light breeze now succeeded that which had been blowing. The weather, which had been clear though a little hazy, now became cloudy. The variation of the compass was found to be 12° 19' NW by the mean of the Easterly and Westerly amplitudes of the ☉ with different compasses, and several azimuths.

At 4 o'clock PM, we had rigged the cross jack yard which had been altered. During the morning, we saw many flying fish, tunny fish, dolphins and porpoises.

We struck the main yard and in its place we got across the yard which had been reduced and shortened. No sooner had this been done than the carpenters were employed in doing the same to the yard we had just unrigged.

Latitude by observation N 8° 41'
Longitude by reckoning W 23° 13'

We now started to feel a strong heat.
Réaumur's thermometer +21° 30', Fahrenheit's thermometer 80°.

From Friday the 21st to Saturday 22nd January 1791

76¼
The whole of this day, we had a light variable breeze at NNE to ENE or a perfect calm. There was a large hollow sea from the North and a small swell from the South East.

The variation of the compass, determined by the amplitudes and azimuths was 12° 21' NW.

The air was very hot and hazy.

Latitude by observation N 7° 31'
Longitude by reckoning W 22° 31'.

Réaumur's thermometer 22°, Fahrenheit's thermometer 81°.

From Saturday 22ⁿᵈ to Sunday 23ʳᵈ January 1791

67½

We had successively quite hard squalls from ENE to N, with intervals of light airs next to a calm.

We were nearing a region where we would soon lose the Northeasterly trade winds.

We saw some tunny fish but could not catch any.

The variation of the needle by the mean of six sets of azimuths and the Easterly amplitude, was found to be 11° 44' NW.

Latitude by observation N 6° 31'
Longitude by reckoning W 21° 53'
4 minutes more to the South than by reckoning.

The water got at Praya had now begun to smell disagreeable and I gave orders to the Surgeon to prepare three bottles of Seltzer Water, by the method of fixed air,[41] and this was poured into the water casks, which gave the water an acid taste which was very agreeable. Several chemists have recommended this method to be a wholesome device and an antiscorbutic medecine.

Réaumur's thermometer +22°, Fahrenheit's *ditto* 81°.

From Sunday 23ʳᵈ to Monday 24ᵗʰ January 1791

23½

Much fog and very hot weather with intervals of perfect calm and light variable airs at E round by the North to NNW.

We saw a shark and some bundles of sea grape,[42] a booby, a stormy petrel and many bonito but which did not come near the ship as most certainly we were making but little progress.

---

41 *The method of impregnating water with fixed air, of which a description is given in this pamphlet [. . .] was lately communicated to the Royal Society [. . .] Judging that water thus impregnated with fixed air must be particularly serviceable in long voyages, preventing or curing the sea-scurvy, according to the theory of Dr Macbride . . .* (see *Directions for Impregnating Water with Fixed Air,* Joseph Preistly, 1772). Portlock op. cit., makes a specific reference to Seltzer water (though Dixon does not) when Dixon is sick with scurvy: *This unwholesome weather had likewise affected the health of several seamen on board the Queen Charlotte; and Captain Dixon in particular being very bad, I went on board the Queen Charlotte, and found his disorder to be the scurvy. At my return, I sent him a cask of fine mould, with sallad growing in it, together with some krout, garden seeds, and a few bottles of artificial mineral water, which was prepared by Dr. Melville, in imitation of Seltzer water, and supposed to be a most excellent antiscobutic* (pp. 55–56). Marchand may here have had no personal knowledge of these chemists

42 Most probably cuttle-fish eggs, as Portlock op. cit., in the same area, recounts passing . . . *through a prodigious quantity spawn, some of which was taken up, and on examination it was found to be the spawn of shrimps; each seperate particle was about the size of a small bean, of a substance like*

A 5 o'clock PM, the variation of the compass by the mean of 4 azimuths, observed with several compasses, was 12° 20' NW.

I am pretty well convinced that the exercise of the body will best prevent the scurvy for this distemper has as its principle cause, the thickening of the blood, I gave the people drums with which they amused themselves in dancing and in games.

Latitude by observation N 6° 12'
Longitude by reckoning W 21° 40'

Réaumur's thermometer +22° and Fahrenheit's *ditto* 81°.

From Monday 24ᵗʰ to Tuesday 25ᵗʰ January 1791

28½

We had during the whole of this day, very light variable winds next to a calm, perfect calm, rain and thunder and lightning.

At noon, we steered S¼S to gain more South.

We had very rainy weather this night.

In the morning, we took two small tunny fish.

At 10 o'clock AM, we were near becalmed with rain which poured down upon us with thunder and lightning. We got up the awnings to collect fresh water for the livestock. I recommended to the people that they wash their clothing in the fresh water which is without measure more healthful than seawater, for that which is washed with this latter will never dry. No sooner had I myself set the good example before them, than this they did,

Being unable to observe the latitude, it was found to be 5° 46' N by reckoning and longitude 21° 28' W.

After the observations we had made the preceding days, the variation of the compass was by reckoning 11° 15' NW.

Réaumur's thermometer +22° and Fahrenheit's *ditto* 81°.

---

blubber or jelly, quite transparent, and contained a small shrimp alive but not matured (op. cit., p. 25). Gannier (*journal*, op. cit., p. 166) also refers to Fleurieu and his reference to Pernety's description of *raisin de mer*. Pernety himself writes: *On the evening of the 25ᵗʰ, we again met with some seagrass, which the seamen call Goemon de grappes de raisin, I have already observed, that the seeds with which it abounds are small bladders, of the size of the largest swan-shot. They are not collected into separate clusters, but dispersed over the stems and branches. When the seeds grow dry, they dwindle to the size of a middling pin's head. The leaves which are very small, almost like those of parsley piert, become brittle. Some of the stems, and a great number of the seeds, are incrusted with a very small kind of shell, or spawn of fish, which is white and hard, and when rubbed against wood acts as a file, or the herb called shave-grass* (The History of a Voyage to the Malouine (or Falkland) Islands, made in 1763–1764, under the command of M. de Bougainville, Translated from Dom Pernety's Historical Journal written in French, *1771, p. 255).*

From Tuesday 25ᵗʰ to Wednesday 26ᵗʰ January 1791

33½

We continued to have light, variable winds, attended with thunder, lightning and rain. Dark clouds were all round the horizon.

At 3 o'clock PM, we took a fish of near three pounds. It had a very small mouth with teeth like those of a rat. It was of a dark blue colour on its back which lightened towards the belly, and spotted with a light blue very near to white. The scales with which it was covered were rather large and very hard for we were obliged to skin it in order to be able to eat it. It was tolerably good.

When the fish was in the water, I remarked that, to swim, only two fins were employed of which one was on its back and the other below, those which it possessed on its sides were no more than half an inch in length.

We had much rain in the night and we continued to collect the water.

At 7 o'clock AM, the wind veering to South we stretched WSW, all sails set.

At ½ past 11 o'clock, the wind varied to the North and we once again steered S¼SE.

We saw many fish but could not take any.

Latitude by reckoning N 5° 22'.
Longitude *ditto* W 21° 23'.

Réaumur's thermometer +20°, Fahrenheit's thermometer 77°.

From Wednesday 26ᵗʰ to Thursday 27ᵗʰ 1791

46

The winds continued variable from NNE to East and very light, attended with continuing rain, thunder and lightning. We caught two tunny and a bonito. I took all necessary precautions that the seamen not leave wet clothes in between decks on account of the fetid smell which was caused by them if shut in there.[43]

At 5 o'clock PM, we saw the sun and we made good use of it and made observations of several azimuths in order to determine the variation of the compass, which was found to be 11° 50' NW.

At 7 o'clock in the morning, I served an allowance of spirits[44] to the people as it is an excellent antiscorbutick.

---

43 Cook, on leaving Port Praya, makes the same observation on 27ᵗʰ August 1772 (2ⁿᵈ voyage): *I took every necessary precaution by airing and drying the ship with fires made betwixt decks, smoking, etc. and by obliging the people to air their bedding, wash and dry their cloaths, whenever there was an opportunity. A neglect of these things causeth a disagreeable smell below, affects the air, and seldom fails to bring on sickness; but more especially in hot and wet weather* (*Voyage to the South Pole*, op. cit., Volume 1, p. 10).

44 Recipes for the *elixir de longue vie* or the *sirop de longue vie* are given in Diderot's *Encyclopedia*, but there seems to be no mention of a *baume de longue vie*.

We saw many sea swallows of a small size with white bellies and the rest of a dark grey colour with the wings, the tails and the head, brown.

Latitude by reckoning N 4° 40'.
Longitude by reckoning W 21° 5'.

We found currents which I judged to be carrying us to the NW
Réaumur's thermometer +20°, Fahrenheit's *ditto* 77°.

From Thursday 27th to Friday 28th January 1791

72½

Until 4 o'clock PM, we had drizzling rain, the wind was at ENE and at ESE, light, all sails set. The weather cleared a little and continued thus through the night. On account of two great swells from the NE and from the South, the ship made very slow progress.

I discovered that the ship was making but a quarter of her usual progress. This we attributed to the rain which had been continuous for three days, and to the shrouds which had stiffened by degrees in the most extraordinary manner. At 5 o'clock PM, we rigged the sprit-sail yard which had been struck three days earlier in order to reduce the size. We caught tunny fish, of which there were many about the ship, along with flying fish.

At 8 o'clock AM, the weather being tolerably clear, I ordered the hammocks to be lashed up and the seamen's clothes to be dried. During the morning, I served punch to the people.

Latitude by observation N 3° 35'.
Longitude by reckoning W 20° 39'.

The latitude not being observed these four last days, I was much surprised to find no difference between the reckoning and the observation, especially as we had perceived the currents.

Réaumur's thermometer +20°, Fahrenheit's *ditto* 77°.

From Friday 28th to Saturday 29th January 1791

38½

The winds continued very variable from S to ESE, with intervals of calm the whole of this day. We heard thunder at times, attended with lightning.

By six azimuths, we found the variation of the compass to be 13° 10' NW. In the afternoon we caught two tunny fish and a bonito. We saw sea swallows and stormy petrels.

At sunrise, we saw a ship at SE. Seeing her bearing up to us, we hoisted our ensign and brought to in order to wait for her. As there was little wind, she came within call only at noon. Wishing to dispatch letters to my owners, we hoisted out the yawl and I sent an officer to her with my packets and those of several other people. I had also given the officer a dozen oranges to make a present to the Captain. She was the *Bonhomme Richard*[45] of La Rochelle, whose Captain was Papin le Jeune, bound for Port au Prince from Porto Novo on the Guinea coast. On board, he had 542 captives, among which he had lost 2 on the Guinea Coast and 2 since his departure. He gave us his longitude which was 23°, which was 2° 18' more to the Westward than ours. At half past noon, the yawl returned accompanied by that of the *Bonhomme Richard*. There was an officer aboard the boat who, on the part of his Captain, requested if I might part with some onions, cheeses and sugar. Despite our own need to preserve these provisions, I gave him what I could and M. Papin expressed his gratitude to me. We hoisted up the yawl and made our goodbyes and each continued his way.

Latitude by reckoning at noon N 2° 57'
Longitude by reckoning W 20° 42'.

Réaumur's thermometer +21°, Fahrenheit's *ditto* 77°.

From Saturday 29th to Sunday 30th January 1791

48½

In the afternoon, we saw large flocks of birds but I could not tell the species for they were far and took flight to the Southward in the evening.

At sun-set, the *Bonhomme Richard*, standing WNW, bore NW, distant about 2 leagues.

The weather continued very variable the whole of this day with squalls all round the horizon and intervals of calm, lightning and rain.

Latitude by reckoning N 2° 28'.
Longitude by reckoning W 21° 2'.

I served a dish of coffee to each of the sailors.
Réaumur's thermometer +21°, Fahrenheit's *ditto* 79°.

From Sunday 30th to Monday 31st January 1791

63

At 5 o'clock PM, we had fresh gales with squalls from the NE with the help of which we steered South. From 9 o'clock to 2 o'clock AM, we had a calm which

---

45 The *Bonhomme Richard* was a slaver and Captain Papin was in the Atlantic during this particular period (from October 1786 to May 1788 and then from July 1790 to October 1791 (see *Dictionnaire des chefs de brigade, colonels et capitaines de vaisseau de Bonaparte, Premier Consul*, Danielle and Bernard Quintin, Editions Paris, L'Harmattan, 2012, p. 415).

was followed by gentle gales at SE and very clear weather. I was much pleased that we had got the general winds for we were in the region where they are usually to be had.

We made several observations and found the variation of the compass to be NW 12° 36' by the amplitude, and 12° 18' by the azimuth.

We saw several boobies and caught 16 tunny fish and bonitos. As far as we could see, we perceived this sort of fish giving chase to the flying fish.

At 8 o'clock AM, I ordered the hammocks to be taken down which we had not been able to do on account of the continuous rain.

At noon, the latitude by observation was found to be N 2° 26' with 50' of difference more to the North than by the reckoning, which gave 1° 36'. The longitude by reckoning was 21° 19'.

We can account for this great difference in three days only by the currents.

Réaumur's thermometer +21°, Fahrenheit's *ditto* 79°.

From Monday 31ˢᵗ to Tuesday 1ˢᵗ February 1791

89¾

The breeze continued variable from SE to SSE. Fine weather though cloudy. At 4 o'clock AM, we had some rain which gave us a little wind.

During the morning, we hauled up a fore-yard which we had had thinned and shortened. This was the last, as all the others had suffered the same. This diminution of all the yards had afforded the ship the best of qualities for she now carried sail very well indeed. We took near fifty tunny fish or bonitos and the people had as much as they could eat. There were so many about the ship that it was sufficient to throw a hook and line to catch them.

Latitude by observation N 1° 26'.
Longitude by reckoning W 22° 11'.

12' of difference more to the North than by reckoning.
We saw boobies and stormy petrels.
Réaumur's thermometer +21°, Fahrenheit's *ditto* 79°.

From Tuesday 1ˢᵗ to Wednesday 2ⁿᵈ February

102½

We had a gentle breeze the whole of this day at SSE and SE, very clear weather and a smooth sea which is not often to be seen between the Tropics.

The variation of the compass determined from the mean of 10 azimuths and the Westerly amplitude, was found to be NW 10° 13' with very little difference between the observations themselves.

We took as many fish as we desired until evening. A company of porpoises along-side the ship at night made them go out of sight in such a manner that we could not see a single one of them at day-light. This caused me much disappointment as I preferred to see the company dine on fish than salt meat.

By the Easterly amplitude, the variation of the magnetic needle was found to be 10° NW.

Latitude by observation N 0° 12'.
Longitude by reckoning W 23° 15'.

7' of difference more to the North than by reckoning.
We saw boobies and stormy petrels.
Réaumur's thermometer +22°, Fahrenheit's thermometer 81½°.

From Wednesday 2nd to Thursday 3rd February

98½

The breeze kept from SE to SSE the whole of this day, attended with serene weather.

At about 4 o'clock PM, we crossed the Equator in longitude W 23° 27' by reckoning.

At sun-set, the variation of the compass was found to be NW 9° by the amplitude.

At half past midnight, being very near to the latitude and longitude of the Ile de Sable and the sandbank to the Westward of it, marked on the chart of Messrs Verdun, Borda and Pingré, I judged it prudent to bring to and not to cross the line during the night. We lay to until day-light. I had determined on such a course for we had seen a great number of birds during the afternoon and the way we had been making had taken us between the isle and the bank, and finally, since our departure from La Praya, we had not been able to make an observation even once, during the day or at night, consequently our longitude was very uncertain.

The Ile de Sable lies in 30' latitude South and in 21° 27' longitude W on this chart.

The bank or shallow water in 30° latitude South and 24° 10' longitude West.

Latitude by observation at noon 0° 26' South.
Longitude by reckoning W 24° 13'.

Réaumur's thermometer +23°, Fahrenheit's thermometer 83°.

From Thursday 3rd to Friday 4th 1791

122¾

The breeze continued to blow a gentle gale at SE and SSE the whole of the day, attended with a swell from the South and clear weather.

We saw sheerwaters and many birds of a small size and of the species of the swallow. They are quite black all round except their bellies which are white and the tail is split, half white and half black. By the mean of eight azimuths and the Easterly amplitude, the variation of the compass was 7° 27' NW.

Latitude by observation S 2° 29'.
Longitude by reckoning W 25° 22'.

Réaumur's thermometer +22°, Fahrenheit's thermometer 81°.

From Friday 4th to Saturday 5th February 1791

115

A gentle gale at SE and ESE, clear weather, smooth water.

During the afternoon, we saw infinite numbers of porpoises. We took one by curiosity and opened its belly. Its stomach was full of small worms of a white colour from 2 to 2½ inches in length, there being nothing else in the stomach or in the entrails.

I had always been told, and seen, that if one of these species of the whale was caught, the others would flee from the spot. But these were not so timid for they remained along-side the ship in spite of their fellow being taken, though it is true to say that they did not come so near as to be struck with a harpoon.

There may often be found in this journal, remarks which may appear (with reason perhaps) to be of a trifling nature to those who have never been to sea. But it should be allowed that a navigator who is condemned, if I may say in this manner, for a great part of his life, to be at sea, to amuse himself with all the things that he sees and with the writing of an account of these, for there is no other amusement to be had.

By the mean of eight observations of the azimuth and the Easterly amplitude, the variation was found to be at 6° 50' NW.

We saw a considerable number of sheerwaters in the South, flying Eastwards.

Latitude by observation S 4° 11'.
Longitude by reckoning W 26° 13'.

Réaumur's thermometer +23°, Fahrenheit's thermometer 83°.

There was no longer any difference North, which we had had these few days, for the latitude by observation and that by account exactly agreed.

From Saturday 5th to 6th February 1791

86

A fresh breeze of wind at SE¼E, fine weather though cloudy.

By several azimuths, the variation of the magnetic needle was found to be 5° 30' NW.

I served coffee to the people this morning.
We saw sheerwaters and many flying fish.

Latitude by observation S 5° 38'.
Longitude by reckoning W 26° 48'.

Réaumur's thermometer +21½°, Fahrenheit's thermometer 80°.

From Sunday 6ᵗʰ to Monday 7ᵗʰ February 1791

93

The breeze blowing a gentle gale, varying from SSE to ESE. Smooth sea and clear weather.

In the afternoon, we observed four sets of five distances each of the distance of the sun and the moon, in order to determine the longitude. These observations made with a good watch and reduced to 4h 17 and a half minutes, apparent time, gave longitude W 28° 4' 22". The longitude by reckoning from La Praya was found to be 26° 53' at this time. A difference of W 1° 11' 22". It is worthy of note that the four observations differed but 8' from each other.

The variation of the compass by the amplitudes was found to be NW 5° 30',

Latitude by observation South 7°.
Longitude by observation W 28° 44'.
Longitude by reckoning *ditto* 27° 33'.

4' of difference more to the South than by reckoning.

Réaumur's thermometer +22°, Fahrenheit's thermometer 81°.

During the night, we took two sea swallows on the riggings which were of a sort which is not described by Mr de Buffon. They were quite dark brown excepting the top of their heads which was of a dirty white colour becoming dark towards the neck. Their bills were pointed and somewhat curved and one and a half inches in length, and on the top of which was a groove at whose extremity there were the nostrils, which quite pierced holes from one side to the other. Their eyes (which were black and lively) were bordered on the lower edge with white and on the upper with black. Their feet had three toes which were joined together with a very thin membrane. Each toe had a weak nail and two, three and four joints, that is to say that the interior one had two, the middle one three and the exterior four. They had at the heel a small spur with only one joint. The lower parts of their legs were naked of feathers. The extension of its wings was 2 feet and 4 inches, and 14 inches from the extremity of the bill to that of the tail, which was formed of eight large beam feathers separated in the middle by a tuft of white feathers which made it forked. They make a noise which can be taken for that of the crow, though not as loud. We attached to their necks a small piece of parchment on which we had written the name of the ship, my name, the latitude and the longitude and the date, we gave them their liberty of which they could hardly take advantage for they were so very benumbed.

From Monday 7*th* to Tuesday 8*th* February 1791

126½

We had a fresh breeze of wind from SSE to E the whole of this day. We had clouds at intervals which were attended with hard squalls. We carried as much sail as we could during the day and at night, in order to advance our progress to Cape Horn for the season for the doubling of it was well advanced.

In the afternoon, we observed five sets of six distances each of the distance of the moon and the sun, the mean of which gave the longitude W 29° 8' 22" at 3h 54' 58", apparent time. Yesterday, the longitude computed from 4 observations was, at that time, 28° 56' 11". Sum 58° 2' 11". The mean of the nine observations was 29° 2' 11", which must be near to the truth as the observations were made with the greatest care and with the assistance of very good sextants. The computations were made as well as could be.

> Latitude by observation at noon 8° 55' South.
> Longitude by observation 29° 48' 31" West.
> Longitude by reckoning W 28° 33' W.

The variation of the compass by observation was NW 4° 39'.

Réaumur's thermometer +22°, Fahrenheit's thermometer 82°.

Note. I shall in this journal employ *longitude by observation* to speak of those longitudes which are observed, and of those which are computed from the observations most lately made. *Longitude by reckoning* shall refer to longitudes computed from from the last point of departure.

From Tuesday 8*th* to Wednesday 9*th* February 1791

121

Blowing gentles gales varying from SSE to ESE, cloudy weather and quite a large swell from the SE.

At 2 o'clock PM, we saw a sail 3 leagues to the Eastward, steering SW, and at 4 o'clock, we saw yet another. She was a brig steering NE. At 3ʰ 38' 52" apparent time, the second mate M. Chanal, observed two sets of six distances each, of the moon and the sun, the longitude was found to be at W 29° 55'. At 3ʰ, 56' 46" by means of two sets, I found it to be 30° 4'.

The mean result 29° 59' 30'.

The observations we had made on previous days, reduced to this moment, gave 29° 58' 30". A difference of 0° 1' between the two.

At sun-set, we could no longer see the ships.

The variation of the compass, by several azimuths and the Easterly amplitude, was found to be 3° 13' NW.

Latitude by observation S 10° 43'.
Longitude by observation W 30° 49' 30".
Longitude by reckoning W 29° 33'.

3' of difference more to the South than by reckoning.
Réaumur's thermometer +22°, Fahrenheit's thermometer 81°.

From Wednesday 9th to Thursday 10th February 1791

123½

We had a gentle gale at SE and ESE the whole of this day. At ¾ past 3 o'clock PM, we had a shower of rain attended with a wind at South, but which was with us but a very short time, after which the breeze returned.

At 5ʰ 6' 29" apparent time, I observed two sets of distances of the moon and the sun and found the longitude to be W 31° 32' 153. At 4h 57' 29", M. Chanel found it to be 31° 5'.

The mean result 31° 18' 37½".

The variation of the compass determined by means of several azimuths and the Westerly amplitude was found to be 2° 7' NW.

We saw a sheerwater.

Latitude by observation S 12° 35'.
Longitude by observation W 31° 56' 30".
Longitude by reckoning W 30° 20'.

2' of difference more to the North than by reckoning.

The crew was served coffee and I began now to give a small measure of sour krout in their soup every day.

Réaumur's thermometer +22°, Fahrenheit's thermometer 81°.

From Thursday 10th to Friday 11th February 1791

113¾

Blowing gentles gales at ESE, grey weather with a swell at SSE.

At ½ past 5 o'clock PM, the variation of the compass was 1° 14' NW by the mean of four sets of azimuths.

We saw no birds and very few flying fish.

Latitude by observation S 14° 26'.
Longitude by observation W 32° 40' 7".
Longitude by reckoning W 31° 3'.

6' of difference more to the South than by reckoning.
Réaumur's thermometer +22°, Fahrenheit's thermometer 81°.

From Friday 11ᵗʰ to Saturday 12ᵗʰ February 1791

95¼

A fresh breeze of wind at ESE and E, clear weather, a smooth sea.

The variation of the needle was found to be 44' NW by the mean result of five azimuths.

In the morning, we were employed in painting the upper works.

Latitude by observation S 16° 10'.
Longitude by observation W 33° 20' 7".
Longitude by reckoning W 31° 43'.

18' of difference more to the South than by reckoning.
Réaumur's thermometer +21½°, Fahrenheit's thermometer 80°.

From Saturday 12ᵗʰ to Sunday 13ᵗʰ February 1791

74¾

The breeze was variable from ESE to NE this day. Sea very smooth and clear weather, all sails set and steering SW¼ S.

We saw no birds.

The variation of the needle was 0° 28' NW determined by ten azimuths and by the amplitudes.

In the afternoon, we observed four sets of six distances each of the moon and the sun in order to determine the longitude. They were all taken at 4ʰ 19' 28" apparent time and the results of them were as follows

The 1ˢᵗ by Mr Chanal   33° 44' 15".
The 2ⁿᵈ by the same   33° 38' 45"
The 3ʳᵈ by myself   33° 38' 45"
The 4ᵗʰ *ditto*   33° 47' 45"

At 8ʰ 53' 41" apparent time, we took six distances of Pollux and the moon, which gave the longitude 34° 00' 15" and which at 4ʰ 19' 28" was reduced to 33° 51' 15".

Sum 169° 7'. The mean result 33° 49' 24" and a difference of 21° 17' more to the Westward than by that computed from the observations made most recently.

Latitude by observation S 17° 17'.
Longitude by observation W 34° 23'.
Longitude by reckoning W 32° 27'.

46

6' more to the South than by reckoning.

I have remarked that since we have been taking observations of longitude in a regular manner, these put us always more to the West. This West difference added to the South difference that we had daily, was certainly on account of currents here setting between the South and West.

I gave orders to serve coffee to the people twice a week.

Réaumur's thermometer +22½°, Fahrenheit's thermometer 82°.

From Sunday 13ᵗʰ to Monday 14ᵗʰ February 1791

46½

This day, we had at intervals light variable winds attended with rain and calms, which I accounted for by the sun being so near to the zenith.

We saw a bird of black colour of the gull kind and a tropic bird.

At 8h 46' 56" apparent time, we observed two sets of five distances each of Regulus and the moon, which gave the longitude of 33° 52', which was 31' more to the East than by that determined from five observations we had made yesterday. Reducing them all to the above, our longitude was found to be 34° 25' 50" W by the mean result of the six observations.

The variation of the compass determined from several sets of azimuths and amplitudes, was 0° 38' NE.

We had crossed the line where the magnetic needle perfectly indicated the meridian.

Latitude by observation S 18° 3'.
Longitude by observation W 34° 46' 50".
Longitude by reckoning W 32° 56'.

10' more to the South than by reckoning.
Réaumur's thermometer +23°, Fahrenheit's thermometer 83°.

From Monday 14ᵗʰ to Tuesday 15ᵗʰ February 1791

45½

In the course of the last twenty four hours, we had had light variable airs with heavy and cloudy weather attended with rain from time to time. We saw dolphins and took one. When this fish is taken out of the water, nothing may be compared to the beauty of its colours which are lost by degrees as it expires.

We saw a booby[46] with a white belly, the head and the tail were black and the wings of a fallow colour.

---

46 Marchand uses here *fol* instead of the common *fou*. Buffon himself says *On a donné le nom de fols à ces oiseaux, à cause de leur grande stupidité, de leur air niais, et de l'habitude de secouer continuellement la tête, et de trembler lorsqu'ils sont posés sur les vergues d'un navire ou ailleurs, où ils se laissent aisément prendre avec les mains.* In the English translation of Buffon (op. cit.,),

We felt a suffocating heat.

During the morning, there arose a hollow swell from the South and the wind seemed to settle at NE, light.

By the mean of eight observations of azimuths and by the amplitudes, the variation of the compass was 1° 16' NE.

Latitude by observation S 18° 54'.
Longitude by observation W 35° 13'.
Longitude by reckoning W 33° 23'.

14' more to the South than by reckoning.
Réaumur's thermometer +22½°, Fahrenheit's thermometer 82°.

From Tuesday 15ᵗʰ to Wednesday 16ᵗʰ February 1791

78¼

This day we had a light variable breeze from NNW, round by the North to ENE, attended with a great swell from the South and clear weather.

During the afternoon, we saw a fish which very much resembled the shark but the fins were of a greater length and width.

By several sets of azimuths and by the amplitudes, the variation of the compass was 1° 59' NE.

At 30' past 8h, apparent time, we observed two sets of five distances each of the moon and the Star Aldebaran, which was to the West of the moon, and of Regulus which was to the East, the mean result of which gave the longitude 36° 10' 15", which put us 44' more to the West than the last observations.

Latitude by observation S 20° 1'.
Longitude by observation W 36° 40' 35".
Longitude by reckoning W 34° 6'.

9' more to the South than by reckoning.
Réaumur's thermometer +22°, Fahrenheit's thermometer 81°.

From Wednesday 16ᵗʰ to Thursday 17ᵗʰ February 1791

83

After having observed 20° 1' latitude, I shaped our course to the South in order to cross the line during the day and to make the island of Ascension. This isle is

---

no distinction is made between the usual *fou* and the more unusual *fol* which Marchand uses (*These birds are called boobies (*fous) because of their great stupidity, their silly aspect, and their habit of continually shaking the head . . .*, Volume XVIII, p. 327.

laid down very ill on all the charts and the true position has never been exactly determined to my knowledge, by any navigator.

Mr D'Après, in *Neptune Oriental*, says with relation to these two isles of Trinity and Ascension, that the first is situated in the latitude of 20° 25' South and in the longitude of 32° 45' West from the Meridian of Paris, the second is 15' more to the South and 100 leagues to the Westward of the first, in this manner Ascension is to be found in the latitude of 20° 40' and in the longitude of 37° 51' West. However, in the journal of Mr Duponcel de la Haye, upon which Mr D'Après depends for the position of these islands, it is unfortunate that it is but a reckoning.[47]

M. Bellin[48] in his chart of the Southern Atlantic Ocean lays down these two islands about 100 leagues more to the East than the position in which they are to be found, following what has been above mentioned. It is a matter of much surprise that, in a century in which the art of navigation has been brought to such perfection, no Captain in his Majesty's command, bound for India, has been ordered to make these islands and fix their latitude and longitude. I would have greatly wished to make Ascension and assign the island its true position by means of the good observations we had got of the longitude on previous days, and those we would have made when in sight of this island. But the object of the expedition made it impossible for me to undertake such an enquiry, for the time I had at my disposal was rendered all the more precious as the success of the voyage depended upon it. On the English chart of Mr John Hamilton Moore, this island lies in the longitude of 37° 45' West of Paris and in the latitude of 19° 45' S. This difference in the latitude appears to be most singular. I did not

Remainder of Wednesday 16th to Thursday 17th February 1791

possess this chart but I had at my disposal the journal of Mr Portlock, *Voyage autour du monde*.

We had not gained sight of any land, nor was there any sign of it being near, and so once more I directed the course to SW¼S, attended with a light breeze at NNE, keeping a good watch a-head. In the evening, by the observation of two sets of five distances each of the moon and Aldebran, reduced to 9h PM, the longitude was 37° 29' 56", and by two sets of distances of the moon and Regulus, got at the same hour, 36° 44' 30". The mean result 37° 7' 13".

---

47 … *the existence of Portuguese Ascension has been confirmed in 1760, by M. Duponcel de la Haye, Capatain of the French frigate La Renommée, who having sailed by the rocks of Martin Vaz the 4th of June, passed afterwards to the Northward of Trinidad, from which he kept a West course, and on the 8th of June made the Isle of Ascension [. . .] According to the above course of La Renomée, Ascension should be about 100 leagues distant Westward of Trinidad, and its latitude 15 minutes more Southerly* (Oriental Neptune, op. cit., p. 34).

48 On his *Carte réduite de l'océan meridional* (1753), Bellin notes that some navigators are very much convinced that these two islands are the one and the same (*Quelques navigateurs assurent que la Trinité et L'Ascension ne sont que la même isle*).

The longitude determined the previous day from two observations was at this time 36° 41', mean result 36° 54' 6".

The differences West and South that we have suffered daily in our observations, have assured me in my opinion that the currents set nearly SW in this space.

At 3 o'clock AM, the Island of Ascension bore West, distant 14½ leagues following the position assigned to it by Mr d'Après.

This day, we had a gentle breeze from NNE to NE attended with clear weather and a swell from the South.

We saw a petrel with the whole of the top of the body a smoke black colour, and the belly white.

The variation of the compass determined from the azimuths was 3° 7' NE.

Latitude by observation S 21° 21'.
Longitude by observation W 37° 29'.
Longitude by reckoning W 34° 46'.

11' more to the South than by reckoning.
Réaumur's thermometer +23°, Fahrenheit's thermometer 83°.

I gave orders to rig two top-sails and two courses and to make ready in case of necessity, and at the same time to examine all the remaining spare sails. In one of the main sails we found some small holes made by the rats.

From Thursday 17ᵗʰ to Friday 18ᵗʰ February 1791

128½

At 3 o'clock PM, we saw in the sea, a-head of the ship, wide streaks of a yellowish colour. Some of the water thus coloured was taken up and with the assistance of a microscope found to be full of innumerable atoms pointed at the end and of a dark yellowish colour. They were no more than half a line in length. It is generally thought that this is the spawn of fish. I myself could not distinguish whether they were animal or vegetable substances.

This day we had a fresh breeze, varying from NE¼N to North, attended with clear weather and a swell from the South.

By several azimuths and by the observation of the passage of the sun upon the prime vertical, the variation of the compass was found to be 4° 13 NE'.

Latitude by observation S 23° 22'.
Longitude by observation W 38° 52'.
Longitude by reckoning *ditto* 36° 9'.

19' more to the South than by reckoning.
Réaumur's thermometer +22°, Fahrenheit's thermometer 81°.
We saw sea swallows.

From Friday 18th to Saturday 19th February 1791

71½

The breeze at North continued more or less fresh until 9 o'clock PM, when it shifted to SE during a squall. During the night, and the morning, we had light variable winds from NW to SSW with very cloudy weather and rain all round the horizon.

We saw sea swallows and a great number of flying fish.

We were not able to observe the variation of the compass which by reckoning was found to be NE 5° 30'.

Latitude by reckoning S 24° 21'.
Longitude by observation W 39° 14'.
Longitude by reckoning W 36° 31'.

11' more to the South than by reckoning.
Réaumur's thermometer +20°, Fahrenheit's thermometer 77°.

From Saturday 19th to Sunday 20th February 1791

63½

The winds continued variable from SSW to South until 4 o'clock PM attended with continual rain. At this time, they veered to the SE, still very variable, with overcast weather attended at intervals with squalls and a hollow swell from the South. We were now near to the region where we were to lose the trades, a sure sign of which were these variations.

The variation of the compass was by observation NE 6°.

We saw a sheerwater.

Latitude by observation S 24° 58'.
Longitude by observation W 39° 45'.
Longitude by reckoning W 37° 2'.

7' more to the North than by reckoning of these two days.
Réaumur's thermometer +20°, Fahrenheit's thermometer 77°.

From Sunday 20th to Monday 21st February 1791

93

This day, the light breeze continued at E, cloudy weather. The sea from the South which had been prodigiously heavy until midnight, abated by degrees and I was in hopes that the winds at East would continue a few days more.

We saw several sea swallows, which fluttered about the ship during the night.

By the mean result of the observation of six sets of azimuths, the variation of the compass was found to be 7° 22' NE.

Latitude by observation S 26° 10'.
Longitude by observation W 40° 51'.
Longitude by reckoning W 38° 8'.

4' more to the South than by reckoning.
Réaumur's thermometer +21½°, Fahrenheit's thermometer 80°.

Mr Portlock in the journal of his voyage to the North West Coast of America and round the world in 1785, 1786, 1787 and 1788,[49] writes that in latitude 26° 24' South and in longitude 41° 46' West of Paris, he altered his course during the night, for in this position there is to be found a rock marked on the chart of John Hamilton Moore; these are his own words.[50] In speaking of this, it is very unfortunate that he chooses however not to indicate the true position of this rock on the chart for you may have at your disposal the journal of M. Portlock, but not the chart of which it is question. But as this rock was not marked on either the French nor the English charts I had on the ship, I was much in doubt of its existence. I was provided with a large chart of the world entitled *A Chart of the World*,[51] the publication of which was by Arrowsmith in 1790, and which accounts for the new discoveries.

49 Here Marchand refers explicitly to the journal of Captain Portlock (see above as to the feasibility of Portlock's journal having been translated into French). In the English original, Portlock points out that: *John Hamilton Moore, in his chart of the Atlantic Ocean, lays down an island called Ascencas, about 19° 45' South latitude, and 35° 25' West longitude; and judging myself at this time nearly in the same latitude, and not being certain of its situation as to longitude, I brought-to and lay by during the night; at day-light next morning we bore away and stood South West till ten o'clock, and afterwards West South West until noon, when our observation giving 20° South latitude, which is more than five leagues to the Southward of Ascencas, and it being only a needless waste of time to search for that island, I altered our course to South West by South, in order to make Port Egmont as speedily as possible* (op. cit., p. 23).

50 *In the evening of the 6ᵗʰ, being in 26° 24' South latitude, and 39° 26' West longitude, we steered South West during the night, as there is a rock laid down in Moore's chart nearly in that situation. Fortunately, however, we saw nothing of it; and next morning we again steered our proper course with a fresh Easterly breeze* (Ibid., op. cit., p. 25).

51 *Chart of the world on Mercator's projection*, Aaron Arrowsmith, April 1790. Arrowsmith's indicates the tracks of Cook, Furneaux and Surville. In the English version of Fleurieu's narrative (op. cit.,), the translator adds a note at this point concerning Arrowsmith: *On consulting Mr. Arrowsmith, we find that he copied this group of islands into his maps of 1790 and 1794, from the general Chart of Cook's Third Voyage; but that he never had an opportunity of informing himself from Captain Roberts, who is now dead, from what authority it had there found a place. It does not appear that such a group has yet been seen by any navigator. Translator.*

From Monday 21st to Tuesday 22nd February 1791

114¼

At half past noon, I saw pass by the ship a piece of the fungus which grows on the trunk of trees and which serves to make tinder, I was much surprised to see such a production so distant from any land for we were more than a 100 leagues from the coast of Brazil.

During the afternoon, we had squalls at ENE and NE which brought much rain and little wind.

The variation of the compass determined from azimuths, amplitudes and the observation of the sun upon the prime vertical, was found to be 8° 26' NE, mean result.

Latitude by observation S 27° 10'.
Longitude by observation W 42° 17'.
Longitude by reckoning W 39° 34'.

9' more to the South than by reckoning.
Réaumur's thermometer +21½°, Fahrenheit's thermometer 80°.

From Tuesday 22nd to Wednesday 23rd February 1791

109½

We had a gentle breeze at NE the whole of this day, attended with a smooth sea and grey and hazy weather. This state of sky gave the sea a very dull colour much more so than was usual.

We saw a great number of sheerwaters and two Colliers called *Charbonnier* by M. De Bougainville.[52] This navigator gives a description of such birds in the account of his voyage around the world. As we were now approaching regions in which the winds are generally more violent than between the Tropics, we set up all the shrouds and hauled taught the stays.

---

52 From Buffon (English version, Volume IX, pp. 369–370): *XXXII. The* Collier (charbonnier) *so called by Bougainville, and which, from the first characters, we might take for a sea swallow, but in the last ones, if they be exact, it seems to differ. The* Collier *says Bougainville is of the size of a pigeon; its plumage is of a deep gray, and the upper side of the head white encircled with a gray cord more inclined to black than the rest of the body, if the bill is slender, two inches long, and a little curved at the end, the eyes are bright, the toes yellow, resembling those of ducks; the tail is abundantly furnished with feathers, rounded at the end; the wings are much cut out and each of about eight or nine inches extent. The following days we saw many of these birds (it was in the month of January and before his arrival at the river del Plata. Voyage autour du Monde, tom. 1, pp. 22 & 33.*

The variation of the compass was by reckoning NE 9°.

Latitude by observation S 29° 20'.
Longitude by observation W 43° 42'.
Longitude by reckoning W 40° 59'.

14' more to the South than by reckoning.
Réaumur's thermometer +22°, Fahrenheit's thermometer 81°.
The weather was hot and sultry notwithstanding the breeze.

From Thursday 24ᵗʰ to Friday 25ᵗʰ February 1791

80¼

At 1 o'clock PM, the wind shifted to the NW after a sudden squall and blew a fresh gale, and although it filled most of the top-sails, I observed with much pleasure that the ship did not much roll.

The reduction of the yards and all the alterations we had made in regard to the stowage at La Praya had occasioned the improvement. I had also put five of the large water casks in frame and removed them from the hold. This place served to stow other effects which had previously been between decks, which conduced not a little to the ship being a better sailor. In the afternoon, the weather cleared and I gave orders to clear and air in the between decks for I was convinced that the smallest neglect in this part of the direction would prove most fatal to the crew.

By the result of the mean of ten azimuths, the variation was determined to be 10° 44' NE. The wind varied from NNW to N and then round by NE¼N, returning at North, attended by grey weather. At 7 o'clock AM, the weather cleared which enabled us to make the observations as follows.

Mr Chanal observed three sets of five distances each of the moon and the sun and obtained the results as follows:

The first   47° 24' 22".
The second   47° 58'.
The third   47° 43' 15".

I also made the observations which gave

The first   47° 44'.
The second   48'.

The third 47° 35' 45". Sum 286° 25' 22'. Mean result 47° 44' 13".

These observations were all reduced to 7h 4' 15", at which moment the longitude was found to be 45° 52' determined from the last observations, which gave 1° 52' 13' of difference more to the East than by our observations. The longitude by reckoning was likewise 4° 35' 13" more Easterly.

Remainder of Thursday 24ᵗʰ to Friday 25ᵗʰ February

28½

I did not wonder at these differences to the Westward which we constantly found by our observations for we had suffered differences to the South for some little time, and it was plain to me that this was occasioned by the currents setting to SW or SSW, off the coast of Brazil.

Latitude by observation S 31° 45'.
Longitude by observation W 47° 56'.
Longitude by reckoning W 43° 16'.

20' more to the South than by reckoning during two days.
Réaumur's thermometer +21½°, Fahrenheit's thermometer 80°.

From Friday 25ᵗʰ to Saturday 26ᵗʰ February 1791

32

At noon, the wind which was at N, shifted to the NW, attended by squalls. Afterwards, we had calms and heavy rain. I made use of the rain to procure water for the livestock and likewise had the casks filled, from which the people most happily drank.

We saw whales, sheerwaters and colliers. At 5 o'clock PM, the wind shifted to NNE, blowing a very light air and continued thus until 7 o'clock in the morning, during which we had a calm.

At ¾ past 3 o'clock AM, we had heard birds passing over the ship whose cry was like the whistle of an owl. At day-light, I saw I believe, very high in the sky, one of these birds flying to the West. It appeared to be a land bird. At 8 o'clock AM, we hoisted out the yawl to try the currents but the swell proved to be a little too heavy, which put an end to the experiment. We found only a current setting to the SE but could not determine the rate. This gave us the opportunity to make use of the yawl in order to scrub the sides of the ship clean of seaweed at the water line. During the morning, we observed six sets of five distances of the moon and the sun in order to compute the longitude. Mr Chanal observed three, the results of which are as follows:

The first gave   48° 18'.
Second   48° 1' 45".
Third   48° 7' 30".

The remaining three were observed by myself:

The first gave   48° 50' 30".
Second   48° 36' 45".
Third   48° 26' 30". Sum 290° 21'. Mean result 48° 23' 30".

The longitude, determined from the observations carried out the preceding evening, was found to be 48° 23', the observations we had made above being reduced to 8 o'clock AM. The difference between them was only 30".

By the mean result of eight azimuths and the amplitudes, the variation of the magnet was found to be 11° 14' NE.

Latitude by observation S 32° 31'.
Longitude by observation W 48° 23' 30".
Longitude by reckoning W 43° 43'.

20' more to the South than by reckoning.
Réaumur's thermometer +21½°, Fahrenheit's thermometer 80°.

From Saturday 26th to Sunday 27th February 1791

57¼

Until 5 o'clock PM, we had a calm or very light gusts of wind. The wind settled in a light gale at NW¼W with cloudy weather. All through the evening, we had lightning in the WNW. The weather was generally fine during the night and morning.

We saw fish much like whales and took a shark, which the people ate, we took another which was happy enough to escape. We saw sea swallows and colliers. We saw no more flying fish.

By the mean of thirteen azimuth, the variation of the magnet was found to be 11° 53' NE.

At 9h 56' 53" AM, from a set of eight distances of the moon and the sun, I found the longitude to be 48° 47' W.

Latitude by observation S 33° 18'.
Longitude by observation W 49° 10' 30".
Longitude by reckoning W 44° 30'.

7' more to the South than by reckoning.
Réaumur's thermometer +20°, Fahrenheit's thermometer 78°.

From Sunday 27th to Monday 28th February 1791

50¼

The whole of this day, the winds were very variable from East, round by the South, to W attended with squalls and a menace in the horizon.

At 5 o'clock PM, we saw a large turtle. We had but laid the sails aback and the yawl was ready to be hoisted out in order to take it, when it plunged under the surface of the sea.

We saw bonitos and took one.

A prodigious number of grey petrels which had white bellies, and others, which were of brown colour all over, fluttered about the ship. These latter birds are named by Mr de Buffon the Great Black Peteril and are very much like ravens.[53]

At 3 o'clock in the morning, the weather being of the worst appearance from North to South, we hauled up the top-sails, but we had nothing but heavy rain.

At 7 o'clock AM, we passed where a current stretched between WSW and ESE, which I had good reason to think set to ESE.

The variation of the compass by reckoning was 12° NE.

Latitude by observation S 33° 37'.
Longitude by observation W 49° 10' 30".
Longitude by reckoning W 44° 51'.

10' more to the North than by reckoning.
Réaumur's thermometer +18°, Fahrenheit's thermometer 73°.

From Monday 28th February to Tuesday 1st March 1791

75

At 1 o'clock PM, the wind having veered to the South and blowing a fresh gale in squalls, we took a reef in each top-sail, and as I supposed us to be near to the coast of America, we tacked and stood the East.

At 5 o'clock PM, there being a very great sea, we unrigged the main top-gallant yards.

During the whole of the night, the weather continued the same, but at day-light it become a little clearer, which permitted us to loose the reefs.

The grey and brown petrels still continued to flutter about the ship.

The variation of the compass was found to be NE 11° 15' by reckoning.

Latitude by observation S 33° 48'.
Longitude by observation W 48° 45'.
Longitude by reckoning W 44° 5'.

5' more to the North than by reckoning.
Réaumur's thermometer +18°, Fahrenheit's thermometer 73°.

---

53 Gannier (*journal*, op. cit., p. 183) cites Fleurieu who refers to Buffon's entry. In Buffon (Volume IX, p. 278), the description of the Brown Petrel-Puffin is as follows: *Edwards, though he gives this bird under the name of the Great Black Peteril, remarks, that the uniform colour of its plumage is rather blackish brown than jet black. He compares its size to that of a raven, and describes very well the conformation of its bill, which character places it among the Puffins.* Here then Marchand takes up Buffon's comparison to ravens.

From Tuesday 1ˢᵗ and from Wednesday 2ⁿᵈ March 1791

75

The whole of this day, the winds continued from S¼SW to SW¼W, blowing a light gale attended with squalls at intervals.

In the afternoon, we rigged the main top-gallant mast.

We continued to see a great number petrels.

By the mean result of six azimuths, the variation of the magnetic needle was found to be 12° 36' NE.

We saw bonitos and took two.

I had made a kind of fore stay-sail of sturdy canvas which would serve us in place of a true one in boisterous weather.

Latitude by observation S 34° 50'.
Longitude by observation W 47° 59'.
Longitude by reckoning W 43° 19'.

5' more to the North than by reckoning.
Réaumur's thermometer +17½°, Fahrenheit's thermometer 72°.

From Wednesday 2ⁿᵈ to Thursday 3ʳᵈ March 1791

40

Until midnight we had light variable winds from SSW and SE¼S and near calms, then the wind veered to the East board, continuing light but attended with clear weather. We continued to shape a course which would bring us nearest to our route. In the afternoon, we put in the hold the two canons we had had on the deck.

I saw from afar a bird of great extent. I was not able determine if it was an albatross or a great petrel named quebrantahuessos (breakers of bones) by the Spaniards.[54]

Besides the grey and brown petrels, we saw stormy petrels of which we had seen none since our departure from the region of the equator.

It was to my astonishment that we did not see pintados[55] in the latitude in which we found ourselves. If bound for the Cape of Good Hope, we may get sight of

---

54 *The Greatest petrel quebranthuesssos of the Spaniards. QUEBRANTHUESSOS signifies bone breaker and this denomination refers no doubt to the force of the bill of this great bird, which is said to approach the bulk of the albatross. We have not seen it; but Forster, a learned and accurate naturalist, describes its magnitude, and ranges it among the petrels* (Buffon, op. cit., Volume IX, p. 219).

55 *The White and Black petrel or the Checker. The plumage of this petrel, marked with white and black, regularly intersected and checkered, has procured it the name damier (chess-board) from our navigators. For the same reason the Spanish have termed it pardelas, and the Portuguese pintado, which the English have adopted . . .* Like Buffon, Marchand discusses the presence

them as early as in 29° or 30° latitude South, but I became convinced during the course of the voyage, that on the coast of America, they keep very much more to the South for we saw them only after having passed Staten's Land.[56]

By the mean result of ten azimuths and by the amplitudes, we found the variation of the compass to be 12° 48' NE.

At 5 o'clock AM, we rigged the fore top-gallant mast and the studding sails.

During the morning, the fine, clear weather gave me the opportunity to take down the hammocks. We cleaned and washed with vinegar the between decks which had been cleared.

Latitude by observation S 35° 6'.
Longitude by observation W 48° 12'.
Longitude by reckoning W 43° 32'.

4' more to the North than by reckoning.
Réaumur's thermometer +17½°, Fahrenheit's thermometer 72°.

From Thursday 3rd to Friday 4th March 1791

82½

There winds which had been very light and variable until 10 o'clock in the evening, settled at NNW and blew a strong gale attended by hazy weather. During the night, there was lightning and thunder at WNW, which did not however prevent us from carrying the studding sails.

At 9 o'clock AM, we had a violent squall from the NNW quarter, attended with thunder, which obliged us to loosen the top-sails. After this squall, the wind settled at NW, varying at N and blowing a strong gale with a menacing horizon all around. We took a reef in the top-sails and continued under the four main courses.

The variation of the compass determined from 9 azimuths and the amplitudes, was found to be 12° 53' NE.

We saw many petrels of the sort that I have previously mentioned.

Latitude by reckoning S 36° 3'.
Longitude by observation W 49° 19'.
Longitude by reckoning W 44° 39'.

Réaumur's thermometer +17°, Fahrenheit's thermometer 71°.

---

of this species of bird in the vicinity of the Cape of Good Hope, and around Cape Horn (Ibid. pp. 258–261).

56 Both Portlock and Dixon use Staten's Land, Cook (2nd voyage) on the other hand, writes Staten Land.

From Friday 4ᵗʰ to Saturday 5ᵗʰ March 1791

126

The wind continued at NW blowing a fresh gale in squalls. At 2 o'clock PM, the weather cleared and we set the main top-gallant sail and the studding sails. During the afternoon, we unrigged the fore top-gallant sail and struck the mast in order to ease the ship as she worked much while pitching.

At 1 o'clock AM, the sea became very heavy from WNW and the wind continued to blow hard at NW in hard squalls.

At 7 o'clock, we had a violent squall of wind and rain which obliged us to furl the top-sails.

At 9 o'clock, the colour of the sea became very dull, we sounded but found no bottom with 130 fathoms of line.

Much care is required in this space for the squalls, most particularly those at SW, for no sooner do we take notice of their forming than they are violently upon us.

We saw many albatrosses and petrels of the sort that we had before seen.

Latitude by reckoning S 37° 39'.
Longitude by observation W 50° 48'.
Longitude by reckoning W 46° 8'.

5' more to the North than by reckoning.

In this situation, Cape San Antonio in the South formed the entry to the River of Plate and bore W¼ NW of the globe, distant 100 leagues.

Réaumur's thermometer +15½°, Fahrenheit's thermometer 68°.

From Saturday 5ᵗʰ March to Sunday 6ᵗʰ March 1791

16¼

The wind varied between W and W¼NW, blowing a fresh gale in squalls, it continued thus until 6 o'clock. At this time we saw a squall of the most violent sort forming in the horizon from SSE, round by the W, to NW. We hauled up the top-sails and the fore sail but the squall made only the wind vary at SW with heavy rain.

In the afternoon we had unrigged the yard of the main top-gallant sail.

At 10 o'clock PM, the wind being contrary at E ½ SE, we led on the larboard tack; but at midnight we tacked on the starboard side.

My intention was to approach the coast of America in the latitude of 47 or 48° South, that is to say in the region of Cape Blanco. As the SE course was driving us away, at 10 o'clock in the morning we tacked and stood to the West. The wind which blows on this coast is generally in this quarter and this is good reason enough to keep the wind as much as possible. Mr de Bougainville says in 1767 in the journal of his voyage around the world, that bound for the Falkland islands, he had not taken the precaution early enough to approach the coast of America, and finding himself leeward, was thus obliged to come back and find the soundings off the Patagonian coast, before proceeding thither.

The variation of the compass by reckoning was 13° NE.

Latitude by reckoning S 38° 12'.
Longitude by observation W 50° 41'.
Longitude by reckoning W 46° 1'.

Réaumur's thermometer +13½°, Fahrenheit's thermometer 64°

From Sunday 6th to Monday 7th March 1791

54½

The wind continued at SW, blowing heavy gusts and squalls. At 4 o'clock AM, the weather became clear which allowed us to make sail under single reefed top-sails.

We saw albatrosses and many petrels.

I distinguished two kinds of brown petrel Puffins, one of which had a yellow bill and the other, a black one.

We had clear weather during the morning and a very light wind at SW, or scarce no wind at all. I made use of this time to make ready for any bad weather and I ordered four new courses bent.

The variation of the magnetic needle by 10 azimuths, was found to be 12° 19' NE.

Latitude by observation S 36° 35'.
Longitude by observation W 51° 18'.
Longitude by reckoning W 46° 38'.

This was 52' of difference more to the North than that which was had by reckoning in two days.

This great difference could only arise on account of the difficulty in reckoning the ship's way and in determining the extent of her driving during the critical weather we had just suffered. We had been obliged, upon every half hour at least, to haul up the main sail, and to often loose the top-sails, due to the squalls. I supposed also that we had been carried to the East of the reckoning.

Réaumur's thermometer +15°, Fahrenheit's thermometer 67°.

From Monday 7th to Tuesday 8th March 1791

We had light gusts with intervals of calm until 10 o'clock PM. The wind then shifted to NW and WNW, light. I directed our course to SW¼W.

It being the last day of Carnival, fresh meat and a double allowance of wine was served to the people. They gave themselves up to noisy diversion as they are much wont to do whenever the moment allows. During the day, we had a light wind from the NW¼N attended with very clear weather.

By the mean result of six azimuths, the variation of the needle was found to be 12° 52' NE.

We saw but few petrels or albatrosses. When the weather is fine, these birds rest themselves on the water and we see them flutter about only when the wind blows fresh.

Latitude by observation S 36° 47'.
Longitude by observation W 51° 52'.
Longitude by reckoning W 47° 12'

6° more to the North than by reckoning.
Réaumur's thermometer +17½°, Fahrenheit's thermometer 72°.

From Tuesday 8ᵗʰ to Wednesday 9ᵗʰ March 1791

During the afternoon, we observed six sets of five distances each between the moon and the sun at 3h 52' 25' apparent time, which gave the results as follows

The 1ˢᵗ by Mr Chanal	48° 59'.
The 2ⁿᵈ *ditto*	48° 35'.
The 3ʳᵈ by myself	48° 9'.
and the 4ᵗʰ *ditto*	48° 6'.
Mean result	48° 25'.

Our longitude computed from the last observations made on the 26ᵗʰ of previous month, was found to be at this same instant, 52° 10'. Consequently, we had been carried 3° 45' to the Eastward, which was considerable in so short a time.

I gave fearnought jackets to the people, which they call Magellan jackets, hoods and other slops to those most in need of them. I gave leaf tobacco to those who wished for it.

The wind blew a gentle gale at NNW and North during this day, attended with fine weather though a little hazy.

By the azimuths and amplitudes, the variation of the compass was found to be 14° 11 NE.

Latitude by observation S 38°.
Longitude by observation W 50° 40'.
Longitude by reckoning *ditto* 49° 46'.

26' more to the South than by reckoning.

Réaumur's thermometer +17°, Fahrenheit's thermometer 71°.

From Wednesday 9th to Thursday 10th March 1791

The wind varied at NW¼N and continued to blow a gentle gale until 6 o'clock PM. The weather became increasingly hazy. At this moment, we heard claps of thunder in the South. Very soon after, a squall sprung up in this quarter, which in ten minutes spread over the horizon. It was attended with heavy rain and a variable wind which then settled at SE, blowing a fresh gale. The sky was all in a flame with thunder and lightning from 6 to 8 o'clock.

At 7 o'clock, the weather was so very dark that we were able to see one another only in the glimmering of the lightning. It was at this moment that suddenly we witnessed a most singular phenomenon. I leave it to the natural philosophers to explain the cause of it. The utmost darkness was thus succeeded by a brightness so great that it was as if the sun was 10° above the horizon. The whole sky was indued with a superb yellow colour. This brilliant spectacle lasted 10 minutes and we were after once again plunged into the darkness. I observed that the moon was not yet set, but as it was only four days old it was hardly possible for it to have given such great brightness. The presence of this planet could not have been the cause of this sudden passage from dark to light and from light to dark. The storm had been very violent during this time.

The weather cleared at near 11 o'clock in the evening and permitted us to carry the four main courses. At day-light, we set all the sails. There was a great swell from the SW and the ship made little progress and laboured much.

The variation of the compass by observation was 14° 30' NE.

Latitude by observation S 38° 44'.

Longitude by observation W 53° 2'.

Longitude by reckoning *ditto* 52° 8'

4' more to the South than by reckoning.

Réaumur's thermometer +16°, Fahrenheit's thermometer 67°.

From Thursday 10th to Friday 11th March 1791

96¾

In the afternoon, we observed four sets of five distances each of the moon and the sun at 3ʰ 56' apparent time which gave the results as follows:

The 1st by Mr Chanal	53° 20' 45".
The 2nd by *ditto*	53° 58' 30"
The 3rd by myself	54° 15'
and the 4th by the aforesaid	53° 50' 30"
Mean result	53° 47' 30"

The longitude determined from the four observations made on the 8th and reduced to this time, was found to be 53° 26'. At 8 o'clock in the evening, by two sets of the distance between Pollux and the moon, the longitude reduced to the above, was 53° 33' 30".

At 6 o'clock PM, I directed the course SW.

During the day, we had in succession winds at SE¼S and ESE. They then veered to NNW, round by North blowing gentle gales with clear weather.

During the morning we saw much rock weed and some patches of sea weed.

The variation of the compass by several azimuths was found to be 15° 35' NE.

Latitude by observation S 40° 2'.
Longitude by observation W 55° 8'.
Longitude by reckoning W 53° 59'.

38' more to the South than by reckoning.
Réaumur's thermometer +14°, Fahrenheit's thermometer 65°.

From Friday 11th to Saturday 12th March 1791

77

During the afternoon, the wind was at NW and blew a hard gale which obliged us to take a reef in our top-sails. It moderated in the evening and shifted to W¼NW. We had calm weather a part of the night. At 4h 12' 11" apparent time, we took four sets of five distances each of the moon and the sun and determined the longitude. We obtained the results as follows

The 1st by Mr Chanal gave	56° 16' 30".
The 2nd by the aforesaid	56° 29' 15".
The 3rd by myself	56° 16' 30".
And the 4th by *ditto*	56° 38' 15".
Sum	225° 40' 30".

At 8h 10' 15' apparent time, by two sets of the distance of the moon and Pollux, the longitude reduced to the above was found to be 56° 26' 30"

Mean result 56° 25' 24"

The rock weed continued to pass by the ship in large quantities. We were surrounded by prodigious crowds of birds. I saw two species which we had not yet seen. One was perfectly white all over and the size of a pigeon, the description of which will be found in this journal. The body of the other was white underneath and of a fallow colour on top. This bird had much difficulty in raising itself up into the air and seemed even to walk upon the surface of the water than to fly. It perfectly resembled a duck. I believe Mr Cook to have named them race horses[57] but which the English[58], at the Falklands, named gray geese.

The variation of the compass computed from amplitudes was found to be 16° 32' NE. At 8 o'clock PM the sea seeming a whitish colour, I sounded but did not find any bottom with 200 fathoms of line. There fell a heavy dew during the night. At 6 o'clock AM, the wind veered to the West, attended with serene weather and a smooth sea. We started to complain of the cold which we felt no doubt because we had taken leave of a very warm climate for the thermometer had not yet gone below 11¼° at midnight.

Latitude by observation S 40° 48'.
Longitude by observation W 56° 52'.
Longitude by reckoning *ditto* 55°.

Réaumur's thermometer +15°, Fahrenheit's thermometer 67°.

From Saturday 12ᵗʰ to Sunday 13ᵗʰ March 1791

91¼

During the afternoon, we had calm weather, at 4 o'clock the wind settled at NW, smooth sea, hazy weather.

We saw many marine productions floating on the surface of the water, many birds, whales, tunny fish and we saw penguins for the first time.

At 4h 50' 18" I took one set of five distances of the moon and the sun which gave the longitude of 56° 34'. Mr Chanal observed 56° 14'.

By five distances of the moon and Regulus, I found the longitude to be 56° 34', reduced to 4h 50' 18". Mr Chanal found also 57° 4'. Mean result 56° 34' 30".

---

57 Cook (2ⁿᵈ voyage, op. cit., Volume 2, p. 186) here cites pages 213 and 244 of Pernety's journal in a note. Pernety himself describes the bird in question thus: *Upon the sea-coast is almost always seen a kind of duck, which flies in pairs and sometimes in flocks: the feathers of its wings are very short, and only serve to support it in running upon the water, for it never flies. Its plumage is grey, its bill and feet yellow. When it is not shot dead, it continues its flight upon the surface as long as the least breath of life remains. Its flesh is oily, and has a fenny taste: it was eaten however by our ships companies when no bustards were given them. These ducks usually weigh at least between nineteen and twenty pounds each. We called them grey geese, to distinguish them from the kind which affords that fine down of which muffs are made. The wild gander is of a dazzling white; its bill is short and black like a bustard's, and its feet are yellow. The bill and feet of the female resemble those of the male, but the feathers upon its back are grey. The border of the white feathers which cover the neck and bread is black, and forms a spot which takes the round shape of the feather. The wings of both resemble those of the bustard and have likewise a hard knob like a horn at the articulation of the pinion. After stripping the large feathers from the body of the female, there appeared a grey down extremely fine and very thick. The down of the male is at least as beautiful as that of a swan. They would both make beautiful muffs.*

58 Considering Cook's entry and reference to Pernety, which English navigators Marchand is here referring to is unclear.

This result put us 25' more to the East than the former had. We may consider that the agreement of the two observations must be near to the truth, the observations of Regulus and of the sun being set together.

There was lightning during the night and cloudy weather.

At day-light, we set the studding sails. At ½ past 7 o'clock AM, from my cabin, I heard called out *land a-head*. Though I very much believed that it could be nothing but haze, I came upon deck and, in effect, it was nothing other. This curtain of haze resembled land so much in appearance that the officer of the watch, himself mistaken, had altered the ship's course immediately. Upon my arrival on deck, I ordered the former course to be steered forthwith. I was loathe to destroy the illusion of the people who swore it was land.

At 8 o'clock AM, the wind blew a hard gale at NW, the horizon very hazy. We felt a damp coldness that was disagreeable in the extreme. The thermometer at 7 o'clock in the morning had fallen to +10°.

At ½ past 11 o'clock, the weather being hazy, the wind chopped violently to SW, which obliged us to reef the top-sails. As we had but just hauled up the main top-sail, the helmsman cried out that he could no longer steer the ship and that the tiller of the helm had got foul. We looked immediately for what could be the cause and found it to be a cleat, which had been fashioned for the middle piece of the rudder, under the first googing, in order to prevent it from jumping out of its place in case of the ship running aground. This cleat had worked loose and fixed itself between the stern post and the rudder. We removed it forthwith. If this accident had occurred a quarter of an hour before, that is to say during the change of the wind, we would have found ourselves in danger of losing at the least the top masts. This cleat had been nailed in with three small nails of iron which had been eaten by the acid of the copper.

The variation of the compass was found by several azimuths to be 17° NE.

Latitude by observation S 41° 39'.
Longitude by observation W 56° 37' I mean by reckoning
Longitude by observation 58° 5'.

Réaumur's thermometer +13°, Fahrenheit's thermometer 63°.

From Sunday 13th to Monday 14th March 1791

68

During the whole of this day, the wind blew a hard gale at SW, attended with a very heavy sea which broke with violence. The weather was clear and cold.

At 8 o'clock PM, we tacked and stood to the NW.

The variation of the compass by observation was 17° 30' NE.

At 8 o'clock AM, we put about ship.

We caught sight of the first white petrels.[59]

Latitude by observation S 41° 15'.
Longitude by observation W 57° 41'
Longitude by reckoning 56° 13'.

15' more to the North than by reckoning.
Réaumur's thermometer +12°, Fahrenheit's thermometer 61°.

From Monday 14th to Tuesday 15th March 1791

56¼

At 1 o'clock PM, the wind and sea having much increased, we struck the top-gallant mast and at 6 o'clock in the evening, we unrigged the mizen top mast.

At ½ past 4 o'clock, the sea broke across us and filled the two boats on deck with water,. We immediately took out one foot of the planks of the floor to make the water flow out more easy. We saw much sea weed, albatrosses, petrels, penguins, gulls and quebrantahueosses.

At 8 o'clock PM, we tacked and stood to the W under our two courses. At 9 o'clock AM, we tacked in the SE.

During the morning, we loosed all the reefs out of the top-sails and swayed up the top-gallant mast.

Longitude by observation W 57° 45'
Longitude by reckoning *ditto* 56° 17'.

9' more to the North than by reckoning.
Réaumur's thermometer +13°, Fahrenheit's thermometer 63°.

---

59 *The White petrel, or Snowy Petrel.This petrel is very justly denominated the Snowy Petrel not only on account of the whiteness of its plumage, but because it is always met with in the vicinity of the frozen regions, and announces to the navigator in the South Sea his approach to the ice-islands. Captain Cook, when he first saw them at a distance, termed them* white birds; *but afterwards he discovered from the structure of their bill that they belonged to the genus of petrels. They are as large as a pigeon; their bill is blueish black; their legs are blue, and their plumage seems to be intirely white.* "When we approached a broad ridge of solid ice," *says Forster, the learned and laborious companion of the illustrious Cook,* "we observed at the horizon, what the Greenlandmen call an* ice-twinkle; *insomuch that, from the appearance of this phaenomenon, we were sure of meeting ice at a few leagues distance."* Then it was that we commonly saw flights of white petrels of the size of pigeons, which we called Snowy Petrels, and which are the* "fore-runners of the ice." *These white petrels, intermingled with the antarctic petrels, seem to have constantly accompanied these adventurous navigators in all their traverses amidst the islands of ice, as far as the vicinity of the immense glaciere of the Southern pole* (Buffon, op. cit., Volume IX, pp. 266–267).

From Tuesday 15ᵗʰ to Wednesday 16ᵗʰ March 1791

30½

In the afternoon, the wind at SSW blew very light going off to a calm that we had at 7 o'clock PM. I made use of this moment to clean the between decks and sweeten them by fires. The sea was smooth with very serene weather.

At 8h 15' apparent time, we took two sets of five distances each of Regulus and Aldebaran and the moon, which gave the longitude 57° 32' W, mean result.

We had calm weather all night and at 6 o'clock AM, a light breeze sprang up at NNW with which we made sail SW, all sails set.

There had fallen a very heavy dew during the night.

The variation of the compass by ten sets of azimuths was 17° 55' NE.

We saw many whales. I shot and killed a penguin but as the sea was a little heavy and we were otherwise making good progress, I did not haul the yawl out to take it.

Latitude by observation S 41°.
Longitude by observation W 57° 52'
Longitude by reckoning 56° 23' W.

13' more to the North than by reckoning.

We discovered that we were suffering a violent current but we could not determine the direction. It would have been necessary for this to hoist out the yawl but I chose instead to make use of the favourable winds.

Réaumur's thermometer +13°, Fahrenheit's thermometer 63°.

From Wednesday 16ᵗʰ to Thursday 17ᵗʰ March 1791

142¼

We had seen hardly any birds during the day, at 4 o'clock PM though a prodigious flock of them rose up directly a-head, which consisted of all the species we had hitherto met with. I presumed that a shoal of fish had brought them thither. We saw *Mollusca* and seaweed which had in its roots pieces of rock, which was proof that it had come loose but a short while since.

During this day, the wind blew a constant hard gale at NNW, attended with a smooth sea, serene weather though a little hazy and a gentle breeze.

At day-light, I discovered that the sea had changed its colour and was of a dirty green. I did not sound however, in order not to stop our progress.

The variation of the compass was found to be 18° 30' NE by the mean result of 9 azimuths.

At ½ past 10 in the evening, the longitude by observation putting us no more than 30 leagues from the Bay Noyée, we steered SSW in order to pass along the coast.

Latitude by observation 42° 4' S.
Longitude by observation 60° 40' W.
Longitude by reckoning 59° 11' W.

2' more to the North than by reckoning.

Réaumur's thermometer +12°, Fahrenheit's thermometer 60½°.

From Thursday 17th to Friday 18th March 1791

77¼

Until 8 o'clock PM, the wind blew a steady gale at NNW and WNW, very hazy. During the night, the wind was variable attended with rain, lightning and thunder.

At ½ past 3 o'clock, we sounded and had 70 fathoms over a bottom of fine sand of a yellow greenish colour mixed with very small black and yellow gravel. At 8 o'clock, we had 75 fathoms, same bottom.

At ½ past 9 o'clock, in a gust of wind at SW, we suffered great heat which was nearly insupportable and which lasted three minutes. I had time enough to observe the thermometer which rose from 11° to 20° and afterwards fell almost immediately again to 10°. The very same thing had occurred in the Gulf of Valence in the Mediterranean Sea in the very midst of winter. I leave it to those who are more fit than myself to determine the causes of such physical phenomena.

At 7 o'clock AM, I saw two land birds. The first flew in exactly the same manner as our wagtails, the second was a sort of sparrow hawk which seized upon a stormy petrel and ate it. I saw also whales and a great number of gulls.

At ½ past 7 o'clock, the wind settled at SW and blew a hard gale which obliged us to close-reef the top-sails. The air was keen. To ease the upper end of the top mast, I ordered the yard to be unrigged and we struck the top-gallant mast. This disposition had also the advantage of keeping the ship from driving. Near 10 o'clock, the sea regained its natural colour and I believed this to show that that there were no more soundings to be had.

Latitude by observation 43° 5' S.
Longitude by observation 61° 6' W
Longitude by reckoning 59° 38' W.

8' more to the North than by reckoning.

Réaumur's thermometer +10°, Fahrenheit's thermometer 54°.

In the journal of his voyage around the world, M. De Bougainville says that in this part of the sea (from Rio del Plata to 45° South latitude), he had experienced currents which carried him South. I experienced the exact contrary for they carried me generally to the North. It is probable that the difference in seasons is the most likely cause of it. He was here in November and we were there in March.

From Friday 18th to Saturday 19th March 1791

47½

Until 6 o'clock PM, the wind blew a hard gale at SW. Soon after, it began to blow very hard which obliged us bring to under the stay-sails. The sea ran prodigious high and I did not recall it having ever been so, even in the midst of winter at the Cape of Good Hope, where everyone knows that the sea is very heavy. This I attributed to the shoals near which, or on which, we found ourselves.

At 8 o'clock in the morning, we tacked and stood to the West.

During this day, we lost six sheep which died of the cold which was extremely keen during the night, indeed at midnight the thermometer had fallen to +7°. This was a great loss and all the more trouble to us for there remained only five which were in great danger of suffering the same fate.

At this time, the people were in the best of health except two seamen who were suffering from the venereal disease, though not very seriously, as in spite of the cold and the rain as they were employed about their duties on deck though I said to them to remain below.

The variation of the magnetic needle by reckoning was 18° 30' NE.

Latitude by observation 43° 15' S.
Longitude by observation 60° 18' W.
Longitude by reckoning 58° 49' W.

2' more to the North than by reckoning.
Réaumur's thermometer +10°, Fahrenheit's thermometer 54°.

From Saturday 19th to Sunday 20th March 1791

48½

The wind having blown with violence until 7 o'clock PM began to abate and we were enabled to carry the top-sails close-reefed, which we loosed during the night.

At 6 o'clock in the morning, we tacked and stood to the East.

The weather was calm and we had a heavy sea from the SW during the morning. I made use of this moment to shoot and kill one brown petrel puffin and two albatrosses. We immediately hoisted out the yawl to take them up. The description of the petrel is given in the Natural History of Buffon and which is extremely exact. I will give only that of the albatross.[60]

Description of the albatross

This bird is generally known by French seamen as the Mouton du Cap.[61] I do not know for what reason this is so except they may appear to be nearly as big as the quadruped though its size is very inferior. Of the two I shot, one was 9 feet

---

60 Portlock gives similar (though shorter) descriptions of birds he sees at the Falkland Islands (op. cit., pp. 36–37).

61 *The very great corpulence of the albatross has procured it the appellation of* Cape Sheep (Buffon, op. cit., Volume IX, p. 290).

4 inches crossways, and the other 9 foot 6 inches and three feet from the tip of the beak to that of the tail. The wings, divided as those of other birds, were more thick and better feathered, possessing after the six quills, seventy-two of a smaller size which mixed together were arranged in three rows up to the body and were covered with very small white feathers at the origin, and others about a third of their size, the rest being black in colour. The feet, like those of a goose, have only three toes joined together by a brown membrane, the outward one has four joints, that in the middle three, and the third or inward one, two. Their legs are bare of feathers. The head is 8½ inches in length, five of which are occupied only by the beak. In one of the two birds, whose plumage was more variegated, the mandibles were of a beautiful ivory colour up to 1½ inches from their tip, which was formed of a white horny substance. In the other, these same parts were impressed very lightly with a pale pink colour. The upper jaw is formed of four principal parts. This upper part is formed, I mean to say cut away, in a sloping fashion, at about 1½ inches from its root, and the part which appears to be separate is formed of six lines, like a volvulus, on the right and on the left, and these are its nostrils. It is depressed in a very perceptible manner in the middle and rises up at the tip where the horny substance there planted forms a hook which goes beyond the lower mandible by three lines. The two lateral parts of the upper mandible possess a sort of moulding on their upper edges, which runs in the longest direction, and a deep furrow at the posterior end of the lower edge, destined to cover the same parts in the lower mandible which is itself made of three parts, very like those of the upper mandible, but which end in a blunt point made of the horny substance. The largest of the two, whose plumage was of the darkest colour, weighed near eighteen pounds, the other which was a female, weighed a little less. This bird was of a beautiful white colour on the upper and lower body, the wings were black on the upper side and white beneath. It had much less down than the other, which is explained by the moulting which was more advanced. They had both a prodigious number of insects of the type of lice found on chickens, but which were much longer in form. Their tongues were an inch in length and more than eight lines in breadth. The flesh of these birds has a very strong odour of fish but the liver makes very good eating.

Remainder of Saturday 19ᵗʰ and from Sunday 20ᵗʰ March

We discovered a strong current and I had reason to believe that it was carrying us NE.

Latitude by observation 42° 24' S.
Longitude by observation 60° 41' W
Longitude by reckoning 59° 12' W.

19' more to the North than by reckoning.
Réaumur's thermometer +11½°, Fahrenheit's thermometer 57°.

From Sunday 20th to Monday 21st March 1791

During the whole of this day, we had variable winds from NNE to South, round by W, attended with a great swell from the SSW and clear weather, though a little hazy. The air was keen and sharp.

At 2 o'clock PM, I had sounded and had not found any bottom with 130 fathoms of line.

During the night, there fell a very great dew.

We found a current which carried us very fast and most certainly to the NE, because these last few days we had found the ship to be constantly more to the North than by reckoning and then at noon, we found ourselves in the same situation, and even more to the West, than the place where we had found 70 fathoms, for we could not find any bottom with 120 fathoms of line.

By the mean result of ten azimuths, the variation of the compass was 18° 27' NE.

At 8 o'clock AM, we tacked and stood to the West.

We saw much seaweed which had worked loose from the rocks but a short time ago, many penguins, albatrosses, petrels, sheerwaters and whales.

Latitude by observation 42° 28' S.
Longitude by observation 61° 14' W
Longitude by reckoning 59° 45' W.

21' more to the North than by reckoning.
Réaumur's thermometer +10°, Fahrenheit's thermometer 54°.

From Monday the 21st to Tuesday 22nd March 1791

52

At 8 o'clock PM, we sounded and found 85 fathoms over a bottom of fine sand of a yellow greenish colour, mixed with yellow and black gravel, that is to stay the same we had found on the 17th at 2 o'clock AM. We found 65 fathoms; and at 8 o'clock, 55 fathoms, same bottom. We saw many sea plants but few birds.

The wind was variable from SSW and SSE until 8 o'clock AM. At this time, it fell calm.

During the night, there fell a very great dew.

The little progress that we had made to Southward since some little time, and the necessity that I believed we had of making the latitude of Cape Horn, in order to attempt to double it as early as could be was a matter of great concern for I could not deny that the season was well advanced and that I could only succeed if we departed in April, unless we were very much favoured (which indeed we were to be). Consequently, I would be able to make the coast of America only at the end of summer and would be able to spend very little time in commerce, with the risk I should run in missing the object of my expedition. I would advise all those who may undertake a voyage like mine, and who might wish to spare themselves great trouble, to depart from Europe at the very beginning of November, at the very latest.[62]

By the mean result of six azimuths and the amplitudes, the variation of the compass was found to be 18° 8' NE.

Latitude by observation 42° 5' S.
Longitude by observation 62° 27' W
Longitude by reckoning 60° 53'.

12' more to the North than by reckoning.
Réaumur's thermometer +11°, Fahrenheit's thermometer 56°.

From Tuesday 22nd to Wednesday 23rd March 1791

89½

During the whole of this day, the wind blew gales at NNW, more or less fresh, attended with clear weather though a little hazy and a smooth sea. We steered SSW and S¼SW to make Cape Blanc or the soundings of this cape.

We saw several bundles of sea plants, whales, seals but few birds.

At 8 o'clock, and at midnight, we sounded and found 55 and 60 fathoms, same bottom as yesterday.

By five sets of azimuths, the variation of the compass was 18° 41 NE.

At 2h 56' AM, by a set of five distances of Altair in Aquilae and the moon, the longitude (reduced to 7h 28' AM, at which moment we set the watch) was 61° 49' 45".

The longitude determined by our last observations was 63° 4'.
Difference to the East 1° 14' 15".

That which was deduced by reckoning from La Praya was 61° 35'. It is somewhat singular after the large differences to the East and to the West that we have had after taking our departure, that the longitude by reckoning was so near the true longitude that the difference was no longer more than 14'. If we had not be in a situation to make observations, we could have been led to suppose that the ship had not been carried by any current during the passage, and that we had very well reckoned the ship's course.

Latitude by observation 43° 26' S.
Longitude by observation 62° 15' W.
Longitude by reckoning 62° W.

---

62 Dixon and Portlock double Cape Horn in February and even then Dixon notes that *they are later in the season than could have been wished* (op. cit., p. 45).

12' more to the South than by reckoning.

It has been a few days that we have not had a difference to the Southward.

Réaumur's thermometer +14½°, Fahrenheit's thermometer 66°.

From Wednesday 23rd to Thursday 24th March 1791

83¾

The wind which had been blowing a hard gale since 8 o'clock in the morning, abated in the afternoon. At midnight, being in a near calm with very clear weather, the wind began immediately to blow a hard gale at SSE which reduced us to close-reefed top-sails and which obliged us to steer SW.

At 4 o'clock AM, the top-sails were handed due to the violent gusts which succeeded one another.

At 8 o'clock PM, we sounded and found 70 fathoms over a bottom of fine sand which was grey, yellow and of a dirty green colour.

At 9 o'clock AM, we stood to the East.

By six sets of observations of the azimuths, the variation of the compass was found to be 18° 48' NE.

Latitude by observation 44° S.
Longitude by observation 63° 16' W
Longitude by reckoning 63° 1' W.

4' more to the North than by reckoning.

Réaumur's thermometer +10 °, Fahrenheit's thermometer 54°.

We saw but few birds.

From Thursday 24th to Friday 25th March 1791

In the afternoon, the wind blowing very strong, gust after gust, we were reduced to the two courses and the close-reefed main top-sail.

A barrel which was as dark on both sides and which seemed to have been in the water but a short time, passed by the ship.

At 6 o'clock AM, after having lain under the stay-sails during the night on account of the violence of the wind, it fell almost calm. We saw a bird of a species we had not yet met with. It was perfectly white and the size of a pigeon which for this reason we named the White Antarctic Pigeon. An account of it may be had on page 107 of this journal.[63]

---

63 Gannier points out that this manuscript then was the fair copy for this reference is not an addition or an emmendation but rather an integral part of the text.

In the morning, we observed four sets of five distances each of the sun and the moon in order to determine our longitude. Having reduced them all to 8h 34' AM, we obtained the results as follows

The 1st by myself gave	63° 23' 45".
The 2nd by Mr Chanal	63° 25' 30".
The 3rd by myself	63° 17' 30".
The 4th by Mr Chanal	63° 25' 15".
Mean result	63° 23'.

The longitudes determined from the observations we had made of the stars put us 50' more to the East.

Latitude by observation 43° 55' S.
Longitude by observation 63° 23' W
Longitude by reckoning 62° 18' W.

6' more to the North than by reckoning.
Réaumur's thermometer +11°, Fahrenheit's thermometer 56°.

From Friday the 25th to Saturday 26th March 1791

123

At 1 o'clock PM, the wind set in at NNW and increased by degrees until 11 o'clock, attended with a very thick haze. At this time, we were reduced to the foresail and the two tops sails, two reefs in. There continued to be signs of a violent storm in the SW quarter. The sea ran very high and short, breaking as upon a beach.

At 5 o'clock AM, the wind varied light at NW, then at WNW, WSW and SW, attended with fine weather. We set all our sails and steered to the SE.

By 6 sets of azimuths observed with two compasses, the variation of the magnetic needle was found to be 19° 54' Northeasterly

We saw albatrosses, quebrantahuessoses, penguins, whales, seals, porpoises, sea plants but few petrels.

Latitude by observation 45° 37' S.
Longitude by observation 64° 49' W
Longitude by reckoning 63° 44' W.

3' more to the South than by reckoning.
From this point, Cape Blanc bore true SW½S, distant 38 leagues after Arrowsmith's chart, and was by the same compass, distant 45 leagues, following the

position given by the *Connaissance des Temps* of 1788[64] and which put it in 47° 20' latitude South and in longitude 67° 1', West of Paris. Mr Bellin's chart is false in all the points of the bearings assigned to this Cape and to the whole of the coast of Patagonia which he puts 20 leagues too far to the West. At noon we sounded and found 65 fathoms over a fine grey sand bottom.

Réaumur's thermometer +14°, Fahrenheit's thermometer 62°.

From Saturday 26th to Sunday 27th March 1791

100¾

During the afternoon, the light winds were variable from SSW to SW, attended with fine clear weather. After a calm from 7 to 9 o'clock, the wind started to blow at NW and NNW, becoming a hard gale. It then veered to W and WSW, with a very moist air.

By the observation of eight sets of azimuths and the amplitudes, with different azimuth compasses, the variation was found to be 20° 11' NE.

We saw whales and seals. Birds were scarce. The stormy petrels continued to accompany us whether foul or fair weather.

The observation of two sets of distances of the sun and the moon, reduced to 9h 1' 39" AM, gave the longitude of 64° 56' W, mean result.

We saw for the very first time Port Egmont Hens.[65] These are brown birds possessing some white feathers under the tips of the wings which are very wide. They very much resemble our crows and fly high up in the air.*

*This is Mr de Buffon's Brown Gull,[66] named by Mr Forster (the son), the Great Northern Gull.[67]

Latitude by observation 47° 2' S.
Longitude by observation 65° W
Longitude by reckoning 64° 29' W.

---

64 The full title was *Connoissance des temps à l'usage des astronomes et navigateurs*. See G. Boistel, "Les ouvrages et manuels d'astronomie nautique en France 1750–1850," *Le livre maritime au siècle des Lumières*, op. cit., pp. 155–130. See also G. Boistel http://dictionnaire-journaux.gazettes18e.fr/journal/0221-la-connaissance-des-temps.

65 *. . .saw one of the same sort of Birds as we saw last Saturday, these Birds are of a dark brown or chocolate colour with some white feathers under their wings and are as big as ravens; Mr Gore says that they are in great plenty at Port Egmont in about Faulklands Islds and for that reason calles them Port Egmont Hens* (Cook's *Endeavour* journal, 5th October, 1769). Cook, according to his journal, was in latitude South 38° 23' and longitude 176° 3' West of Greenwich, nearing New Zealand.

66 *The Brown Gull*, Buffon, op. cit., Volume XVIII, p. 368.

67 *To this account Mr. Forster adds, that he recognized it to be the great Northern gull, Larus Catanades, common in the high latitudes in both hemispheres; that a few days after they saw another of the same kind, which rose to a great height above their heads, which they regarded as a novelty, the birds of that climate keeping near the surface of the water* (Ibid., p. 271).

Cape Blanc bore West, some few degrees to the Southward, distance 25 leagues. Réaumur's thermometer +10°, Fahrenheit's thermometer 54°.

From Sunday 27ᵗʰ to Monday 28ᵗʰ March 1791

63¼

The wind blew a fresh gale until 5 o'clock PM, at which time it started to abate and vary.

From 9 o'clock it fell calm, succeeded at midnight by a light wind at WNW with clear, mild weather.

At 4 o'clock PM, we had sounded and found 75 fathoms over a bottom of greenish sand, black and white. At 8 o'clock, we found 75 fathoms, same bottom, somewhat oozy. At 10 o'clock, 80 fathoms, same bottom, and at 4 o'clock, 80 fathoms, *ditto*.

At 5 o'clock AM, we observed five distances of the moon and Antares, which when reduced to 8h 27' 34", gave us the longitude of 65° 12' 45" W.

During the morning, we observed 4 sets of five distances each of the moon and the sun, which reduced to the same time, gave the results as follows:

The 1ˢᵗ by Mr Chanal	65° 4' 45".
The 2ⁿᵈ by the aforesaid	64° 56' 45".
The 3ʳᵈ by myself	64° 55' 315".
The 4ᵗʰ by *ditto*	65° 15' 45".
Mean result	63° 5' 3".

It fell calm for a part of the morning then the wind set in at NW and we crowded sail S¼SW. The variation of the compass was found to be 20° 25' NE by two sets of six azimuths each.

Latitude by observation 47° 55' S.
Longitude by observation 65° 7' W
Longitude by reckoning 64° 53' W.

6' more to the North than by reckoning. We were distant about 25 leagues from the coast of Patagonia.
Réaumur's thermometer +10°, Fahrenheit's thermometer 54°.

From Monday 28ᵗʰ to Tuesday 29ᵗʰ March 1791

136

During the whole of this day, the wind blew fresh gales variable from NNW to W, with very hazy and unpleasant weather.

In the afternoon we saw a great number of birds and porpoises.

A 5 o'clock in the evening, we took in the studding sails which we had carried until this time, in spite of the violence of the wind.

Having the intention of rallying the coast of Patagonia, on account of the Westerly winds which generally blow in this part of the sea, we continued to shape our course S¼SW, sounding at every watch. At 8 o'clock, we had 82 fathoms, black and yellow sand bottom, rocks and small stones, broken shell and coral rocks. At midnight, 80 fathoms, soft bottom of black sand, and at 4 o'clock, 78 fathoms over a black and yellow, fine sand bottom.

At 10 o'clock in the evening, due to the heavy squalls of wind which succeeded one another, we had been obliged to close-reef the top-sails, which we loosed at day-light. The air was very mild.

In the morning, we took the precaution of clinching a cable to an anchor. The spritsail yard was unrigged.

We saw fluttering about the ship one of those birds which we have named the White Antarctic Pigeon, and of which I have already made mention. I shot and killed it and sent the yawl to take it up. I have not seen a description of this bird in any voyager's journal and thus it will be perhaps to useful to give it here.

Description of the White Antarctic Pigeon

Of all the navigators who have seen this bird and taken note of it, I know of none who has observed it and called it by a name other than the white bird. It is perhaps too much to presume to give it one which will endure but I will make use of the right of travellers who have always given names to unknown species. The whole plumage of this bird is perfectly white, and of the twelve I saw, there was with no other spot of colour, and it is the size of a large pigeon.

Remainder of 28th to 29th March 1791

It flies with a rapid beating of its wings which are wide throughout their length. This discriminating feature distinguishes them already from other aquatic birds. Either large flocks of these birds are pushed by violent winds into the offing, or they are travellers, but it is certain that many of them are to be met wth at some considerable distance, 40 or 50 leagues, from the land. More than two of them together are seen only seldomly. They seem to like very much to perch and sometimes do so on the ship, about which they like to flutter. If fear or tiredness weighs down upon them, they take rest on the surface of the water but never remain there for long. But I have never seen them play on the surface. One of those I saw had its legs dirtied by red earth.

Its entire length from the tip of the beak to the extremity of the tail, is fourteen inches. Each wing is one foot in length and the diameter of its body, from one wing to the other, is fourteen inches. The bill has the form of that of the gallinaceous tribe, but much bigger, and measures one inch in length and six lines in diameter at its base. The two mandibles exactly cover each other in length, excepting the superior mandible which projects by a small hook which measures about ½ of an inch and which is like that of a hen. The nostrils are in the middle and are covered with a sort of scale which finds its origin at the base of the bill which is itself surrounded by small, fleshy nipples of a white colour, in the centre of which shoot out small feathers. The gills are placed under the posterior angle of the eyes at a distance of six lines. The iris seems to be black and the cornea of a greyish colour. The tongue which is a little shorter than the bill takes up the whole width. The palate is spread with a quantity of nerves which must render its sense of taste more delicate than that of other birds. The inside part of the bill, opposite to the larynx, is traversed by yet another row of nerves, of a much bigger size, two of which, in the middle, form two small hooks towards the front. The feet, of a dark grey colour, as regards their proportion, are bigger and longer than those of seabirds but not enough so to resemble those birds which live on the shore. There are only three toes placed towards the front and there is no membrane. The nail at the very end is black and very hard. It also possesses a spur towards the back, very short in size. When we cut it open, we found the stomach empty and the interior of the gizzard, which is covered nearly all over with a membrane which is indented, full of small gravel and egg shells. At the extremity of the first articulation of the wing, there is a small horny callosity, which had the form of a wart, and which is natural to all the birds of this species for all those I had seen were possessed of it.

Mr de Bougainville and Mr Portlock[68] say they had seen such birds in this same sea and had assigned them the name of white bird. Mr Cook in his voyage to the South pole reports having seen a bird on the Island of Georgia which he named the new white bird but as he does not give a description, I cannot know if it is the same.

Latitude by observation 49° 50 'S.
Longitude by observation 67° W.
Longitude by reckoning 66° 45' W.

Réaumur's thermometer +11°, Fahrenheit's thermometer 56°.
At noon, we sounded and the lead found 80 fathoms over a bottom of fine black and yellow sand.

From Tuesday 29ᵗʰ to Wednesday 30ᵗʰ March 1791

65¾

During the afternoon, we saw numerous penguins whose cries were sharp and disagreeable and which deafened us, some few White Antarctic pigeons, porpoises

---

68 *We saw a large flock of white birds about the size of a tern, and which I am inclined to think are of the same species with those we met with in great abundance at Christmas Island during Captain Cook's last voyage* (Portlock, op. cit., p. 54).

and but few petrels. We got sight of a bird which we had not seen before. It had the form, size and flight of a tropic bird and its tail which was very long, opened into a fork and closed in a point. The body was white all over. I thought it to belong to the gull family.

At sun-set, we saw on the surface of the water some pink crawfish of which Dampier and other voyagers take note, but in a small quantity.[69] The variation of the compass was found to be 21° 41' NE by the mean result of five azimuths and the amplitudes.

Until 3 o'clock AM, we had a calm and at intervals a light wind which varied from S and W, attended with hazy weather and a smooth sea. At this time, the wind veered to NW blowing a gentle gale with very clear weather. At ½ past 3 o'clock, we sounded and had 90 fathoms over a bottom of fine yellow, black and white sand.

At 5 o'clock, by the observation of a set of distances of the moon and Antares, the longitude (reduced to 7h, 47' 15") was 67° 23' 15". During the morning, by 8 distances of the sun and the moon, reduced to the same hour, it was (observed by myself) 67° 27' 15", and by Mr Chanal, 67° 30'. Mean result 67° 17', which was in perfect agreement with the result of the longitudes which we had observed on the preceding evening, taking into account the course of the ship.

During the morning, we saw two whales which passed so near by the ship so as to touch us, their length with respect to the ship was, at the least, 60 feet. They had near flat heads and the body was speckled with black and white. We saw in addition, numerous porpoises, seals, albatrosses, penguins, petrels, quebrantahuessoses, little divers, seaweed and white Antarctic pigeons. I shot and killed several of the latter sort but our progress was too advantageous to send out for them.

Latitude by observation 51° 6' S.
Longitude by observation 67° 41' W.
Longitude by reckoning 67° 26' W.

22° more to the North than by reckoning in two days.

69 *From the time that we were in 10 degrees South till we came to these islands we had the wind between East-North-East and the North-North-East, fair weather and a brisk gale. The day that we made these islands we saw great shoals of small lobsters which coloured the sea in red spots for a mile in compass, and we drew some of them out of the sea in our water-buckets. They were no bigger than the top of a man's little finger, yet all their claws, both great and small, like a lobster. I never saw any of this sort of fish naturally red but here; for ours on the English coast, which are black naturally, are not red till they are boiled: neither did I ever anywhere else meet with any fish of the lobster shape so small as these; unless, it may be, shrimps or prawns: Captain Swan and Captain Eaton met also with shoals of this fish in much the same latitude and longitude. January 28th 1683.* William Dampier, *A New Voyage Around the World* (1697). Dampier's account was translated into French in 1698 and was reprinted in various corrected editions throughout the century. See Gannier (op. cit., p. 204) for other examples of the observation of this type of shell fish by other naviagtors.

Réaumur's thermometer +11°, Fahrenheit's thermometer 56°.

In this station, the islands of Sebald de Wert bore E, distant 30 to 35 leagues, following the charts of Arrowsmith, of Mr Cook and Mr de Bougainville.

Remainder of Tuesday 29th to Wednesday 30th March 1791

The prodigious quantities which I have seen in this part of the ocean has led me to reflect upon the advantages which may be had here. I do not presume to give any instruction; I desire rather to disburthen my memory and will do so by recording my reflections here.

Reflections on the advantages of whale, seal and sea-lion fishing in the Southern Atlantic ocean in the parts adjacent to the Falkland Islands, Staten's land and the Straits of Magellan[70]

It appears to me that the quantity of whales which may be seen in this part of the ocean and the ease with which these cetaceous animals would be taken in an open sea which is never frozen, should have opened the eyes of the government for this branch of commerce and the advantages it could procure for the nation.

Train oil is the object of a very considerable commerce for it is employed in diverse sorts of manufactures. Until present, whale fishing has been carried out mostly in the North only. It is very profitable and the Dutch have endeavoured to their utmost to keep it for themselves, in spite of the labour and danger with which it is attended, for the whale is difficult to prick on the surface of a sea which is scattered with masses of ice (see the voyage of Mr Pagès to the North Pole).[71]

---

70 Portlock considers the advantages of a fur trading settlement on the North West coast, as does Dixon. In the introduction to Cook's third voyage, King also makes its clear that in . . . *consequence of all these improvements, lessening apprehensions of engaging in long voyages, may we not reasonably indulge the pleasing hope, that fresh branches of commerce may, even in our time, be attempted and successfully carried on? Our hardy adventurers in the whale-fishery, have already found their way within these few years, into the South Atlantic; and who knows what fresh sources of commerce may still be opened, if the proposect of gain can be added, to keep alive the spirit of enterprize?* (op. cit., p. lix). Similarly, Gannier (*journal*, op. cit., p. 206) shows that Bougainville (and later La Pérouse) also discusses the advantages of commercial enterprise in the South Atlantic. Marchand is thus following in the textual footsteps of those having come and gone before him.

71 François de Pagès' *Voyages autour du monde et vers les deux pôles, par terre et par mer, pendant les années 1767, 1768, 1769, 1770, 1771, 1773, 1774 & 1776 par M. de Pagés,Capitaine des Vaisseaux du Roi, Chevalier de l'Ordre du Roi, Chevalier de l'Ordre Royal & Militaire de Saint Louis, Correspondant de l'Académie des Sciences de Paris* was published in 1782 and translated into English in 1792 — *Travels Round the World in the Years 1767, 1768, 1769, 1770, 1771, by Monsieur de Pagès, Captain in the French Navy, Knight of the Royal and Military Order of St Louis, and corresponding member of the Academy of Sciences. At Paris, Translated from the French.* Pagès in Chapter XXVII describes the whale fishing process in detail, highlighting as Marchand points out, the arduous and dangerous methods used in frozen seas.

The people of Biscay had heretofore been the masters of this sort of fishing of whales in the North. In the middle of the past century, the Dutch shared it with them, today they shut out nearly intirely our nation and do not send less than 200 ships every year for this fishery. It is quite possible no doubt, but not with ease, to take possession of it once more. Is it not more simple to seek elsewhere a commerce which is all the more profitable for us in that we are obliged to procure a part of this oil in foreign markets? The parts adjacent to the Falklands, Staten's Land and the straits of Magellan are in everything very favourable to this fishery, it would be more abundant, more easy and less dangerous to carry out.

All know that the whale is now seldom to be seen in the North, for we are today obliged to seek them in the midst of masses of ice instead of in the parts I have indicated, where hundreds are to be seen, and they are generally of a larger size. But without applying the mind absolutely to whale fishery, which consists in much trouble, we can replace it with two other sorts of fish with blubber which are very common in the Falklands, in Staten's Land and parts adjacent to the straits; these are the sea lion and the seal which are amphibious animals which give much oil and of which the hunting is less costly than that of the whale, and more easy for it is carried out on land on very heavy animals

Remainder of Tuesday 29th to Wednesday 30th March 1791

which are reached and struck down easily without trouble with blows from a bludgeon. Their skins make for an advantageous commerce. These two species are smaller in size than a whale and would give less oil, but their numbers would compensate for the want of volume.

The English, our rivals in everything, do not scorn this trade and have formed an establishment on Staten's Land (New Year Harbour) to favour this fishery. The ships *Prince of Wales* and *Princess Royal* were charged with this commission in the year 1786.[72] They proceeded to trade from this point on the North Western coast of America.

---

72 Dixon meets with the two ships on the 8th of August, 1787: . . . *we learned, to our great joy, that they were from London, and fitted out by our owners. The ship was called the Prince of Wales, Captain Collnett; and the sloop, the Princess Royal, Captain Duncan [. . .] These vessels left England in September, 1786, and had settled a factory at Statens Land, for the purpose of collecting seal skin and oil, from thence they had made the best of their way to King George's Sound, without touching at any other place. During so long a passage, the scurvy had got a great height among them, and and though providentially no lives had been lost, yet many of their people recovered very slowly* (op. cit., pp. 230–231). Dixon suggests at this point that all ships bound for the Northwest coast should in fact consider a stay at the Marquesas in order to avoid bad weather and scurvy (*Captain Dixon observed that it would be by far the best for all vessels bound to the North-West coast of America, after doubling Cape Horn, to steer directly for the Marquesas; there they might obtain refreshments, and at the same time would be well to the Westward, that in the further prosecution of their voyage, he had every reason to think, they would escape those climates which we had experimentally found to be so very unhealthy* (Ibid., p. 231). This is what Marchand decides to do.

Captain Portlock found a ship from Boston at the Falklands which was employed in hunting the sea-lion and the seal.[73] In addition to the advantages that this particular branch of trade would procure us every year, we would grow a stock of excellent sailors. The colony which Mr de Bougainville formed in Falkland's Island, following the orders of the government in 1764, and which we then ceded to the Spanish in 1764, was very suitable with regard to the extension of this fishery. Perhaps this was indeed his design?

I beg forgiveness for such considerations; I do not know if reason of state or covenants between our Court and that of Spain have until now prevented this fishery in this part of Atlantic Ocean, but I know very well that the Spanish have not at all taken it up.

From Wednesday 30ᵗʰ to Thursday 31ˢᵗ March 1791

144¾

My intention being to pass East of Staten's Land, and not within the Straits of Le Maire, at half past noon, we steered S¼SE, all sails set, the wind, variable, blowing a hard gale at WNW, attended with very fine weather.

At 8 o'clock PM, after having sounded and found 95 fathoms over a bottom of coarse grey sand, somewhat oozy, mixed with small yellow stones, we directed our course to SSE.

At this moment, Cape Virgin Mary bore W¼SW by the globe, distant 25 to 30 leagues.

The weather was so very fine during the night that we set the studding sails, which is not often the case in this part of sea. At 4 o'clock in the morning, we directed our course to the SE in order to make the Eastern part of Staten's Land.

During the night we had heard the cry of penguins.

The variation of the compass was 23° 19' NE, by the mean result of six azimuths and the amplitudes.

We saw seaweed and numerous birds amongst which was a sort of petrel we had not yet seen. The whole body was white excepting the top of the wings which were of a pale grey colour with a few black feathers. The exact account may be had in folio _____ of this journal.[74] We named it the Grey White petrel.

---

73 *At nine o'clock this evening a sloop arrived in the harbour, and anchored off the town. Early next morning, captain Coffin came on board the King George and informed me that his sloop is named the Speedwell, and is tender to a ship called the United States, commanded by captain Huffey, and now lying in a good harbour at Swan Island, in company with the Canton, captain Whippy: both these vessels were employed in the oil trade, and had nearly completed their cargoes; the United States having 300 tons of oil on board, and the Canton about half that quantity* (Portlock, op. cit., p. 34).

74 Gannier (*journal*, op. cit., p. 207) points out that Marchand had probably initially planned to insert the page number in question (6ᵗʰ April entry).

Latitude by observation 53° 26' S.
Longitude by observation 67° 34' W.
Longitude by reckoning 67° 19' W.

From this position following the chart to be found in the 4th volume of the second voyage of Mr Cook,[75] of which I have made use since Cape Blanc and which I consider to be very true like all this immortal navigator has left to us.

Cape St John, Staten's Land, bore true SSE 3° E, distant 28½ leagues.

Cape St Diego, Tierra de Feugo bore true South 4° W, distant 24 leagues. The chart of the South ocean of Mr Bellin was in very near agreement with it.

Réaumur's thermometer +9°, Fahrenheit's thermometer 52°.

From Thursday 31st March to Friday 1st April 1791

54

In the afternoon, we saw a vast number of birds and mostly blue petrels. We got also sight of whales, seals, many sea plants of different sorts, amongst which was to be found a bunch of very long seaweed named *fucus giganteus* by Mr Banks.[76] We see much of it says this learned naturalist in the parts near Staten's Land and Tierra del Fuego.

At 8 o'clock PM, we sounded and had 80 fathoms over a bottom of gravel, coral, broken shell and small, living shell fish. At this moment we were but 11 leagues NNW of the New Year Isles but I did not consider it prudent to stand in shore during the night. We brought to under close-reefed top-sails and steered East.

At midnight, having sounded again we could not find any ground with 135 fathoms of line. We tacked and stood to the West. This want of ground made me consider that the currents had carried us to the Eastward, for by reckoning, we had progressed but two leagues since 8 o'clock and should not have lost all ground.

The wind at NW, very clear, varied at W, WSW, SW, and then at South in the morning, attended with a very thick haze, a heavy sea and a violent current which

---

75 In Cook's published account (op. cit.,), in Book IV, Chapter IV is entitled *Observations, geographical and nautical, with an account of the islands near Staten Land, and the animals found in them.* Cook refers to an annexed chart which . . . *will, very accurately, shew the direction, extent and position, of the coast, along which I have sailed, either in this or my former voyage and no more is to be expected from it.* He goes on to specify how the latitudes and longitudes were calculated and gives precise bearings of the different capes and islands. In the translated version cited above (the Hotel de Thou edition) this passage is situated in the 4th volume (op. cit., p. 217) of the 1778 publication (which is the edition which Marchand most probably had with him on board).

76 *This evening many large bunches of sea weed came by the ship; we caught some of it with hooks, it was of an immense size every leaf 4 feet long and the stalk about twelve, the footstalk of each leaf was swelld into a long air vessel. Mr Gore tells me that he has seen this weed grow quite to the top of the water in 12 fathom, if so the swelld footstalks are probably the trumpet grass or weed of the Cape of Good Hope; we describd it however as it appeard and calld it Fucus Giganteus.* Joseph Banks (*Endeavour* journal), 3rd January, 1769 entry. The *Endeavour* was sailing along the Argentinian coast at this time.

made it impossible to steer the ship in spite of a relatively hard gale. I believed I saw it setting to the NE. The air was cold for the mercury in the thermometer fell to +6°;

We sounded several times during the morning and could not find any ground with 200 fathoms of line.

We perceived a small land bird which strongly resembled a skylark, and of the same size. Its flight was also the same. It took a Southerly direction. We continued to see the same birds and bundles of *fucus giganteus*.

At 10 o'clock AM, the weather became a little clearer, and at 11 o'clock, in the horizon extending before us, we had sight of Staten's Land, which stretched S¼SE to S¼SW. We were no more than 18 leagues distant by the latitude we had observed at noon. I will say nothing of this island which I saw only at little more than 10 leagues distance. It appeared very broken and from the distance at which we saw it, it must be very high. In the Eastern part, which we saw more clearly, we had sight of a round mountain which is to be seen first, the island comes to an end on this side at Cape St John, which is of middle height. A thick haze covered the Western part and it escaped our view.

Latitude by observation S 53° 56' S.
Longitude by observation W 66° 59' W.
Longitude by reckoning *ditto* 66° 44'.

11' more to the North than by reckoning.
Réaumur's thermometer + 17½°, Fahrenheit's thermometer 49°.

From Friday 1st to Saturday 2nd April 1792

137

At noon, we had a light wind at NW, which then increased and of which we made use to steer SSE, that is to say a little in the offing of the most Easterly land in sight. Finding that the currents were carrying us to the NW, we steered SE by SE¼E in order to pass at a reasonable distance from this land during the night, and not to suffer the effects of the very violent current which is to be met with near Cape St John and which sets NW. At 4 o'clock PM, we feared that we should lose sight of the land with the haze which was coming upon us, Cape St John bore SSE½S, distant 14 leagues.

The most Westerly land within sight bearing SSW 7°, and the round mountain of which I have made mention, S¼SE 4° E.

From this point, we took that of our departure in latitude 54° 6' S, and longitude 66° 27' West, following the chart of Mr Cook.

The longitude by observation since the 30th, reduced to this moment, was found to be 66° 58' and 66° 43' W by reckoning from La Praya.

Towards 5 o'clock the wind gradually increased at North, blowing a hard gale attended with haze. It then varied at NNE and NE. In spite of the want of prudence in carrying much sail during this darkest of nights, we did not take in the studding sails. At 11 o'clock in the evening, reckoning I was 8 leagues distant from the East of Cape St John, we bore away SE; at 1 o'clock AM, SSE½E, at 2 o'clock South, and at 3 o'clock S¼SW, which was the course I purposed to steer in order that we distance ourselves from the coast, that we avoid the currents which carry into the Strait of Le Maire, and that we make use of the favourable winds at SW and NW which generally blow in this part of the sea.

At day-light, we believed we saw land at NNW, but it was most certainly the haze, for the horizon was nothing more than a league distant from us as the haze was so thick. In the morning, we saw some seaweed and but few birds.

A species of bird which we had not yet seen presented itself to our sight. It was perfectly black, the neck was very long, the head small and the bill very sharp. Its flight was slow and encumbered. I served an allowance of brandy per day to the people.

Latitude by reckoning 55° 52' S.
Longitude by reckoning 66° 41' W.

Réaumur's thermometer + 6°, Fahrenheit's thermometer 46°.

From Saturday the 2nd to Sunday the 3rd April 1791

53¼

Until 4 o'clock PM, the wind continued to blew a gentle gale at ENE, attended with so thick a haze that it fell in a fine drizzle, which prevented us from seeing one another fore and aft of the ship.

At this moment, we had near a perfect calm, we took in the studding sails and handed the main top-gallant sail which we had continued to carry in spite of the uncertain weather. I was fully determined to crowd all the sail we could, thinking to double Cape Horn at the earliest.

At 7 o'clock, we had a sudden squall at SW which obliged us to haul up the close-reefed top-sails. At ½ past 7 o'clock however, the wind obliged us to hand them.

At 8 o'clock we unrigged the top-gallant yard and struck the mast along-side the top mast.

At ½ past 11 o'clock, the wind increased violently and we were compelled to lie under the stay-sails, head to the SE. Notwithstanding, the sea was not heavy in proportion to the wind we had. The squalls succeeded each other and the weather was cold.

At 6 o'clock AM, the wind having abated a little, we kept under the foresail. This permitted us soon after to carry the main sail and close-reefed top-sails, and to direct our course South.

During this day we saw White and Black Spotted Petrels for the first time, some albatrosses, a vast number of tropic birds and porpoises.

The variation of the compass by reckoning was found to be 24° NE.

Latitude by reckoning 56° 25' S.
Longitude by reckoning 66° 32' W.

Réaumur's thermometer + 5°, Fahrenheit's thermometer 43½°.

From Sunday 3rd to Monday 4th April 1791

78½

At half past noon, the wind at WSW blowing violently once more, attended with a large quantity of hail the size of peas, we lay once more under the stay-sails, head to the South. At 3 o'clock PM, we set the foresail, and at 7 o'clock, the main sail and close-reefed top-sails.

We had sight of a White Antarctic Pigeon fluttering about our yards, I shot it in such a fashion as to make it fall in the ship. It was excellent eating. It did not have any fishy taste.

We saw but few birds.

The weather was cold and the mercury in the thermometer kept at +3°.

During the whole of this day, the wind varied from WNW to WSW, blowing something more or less than fresh, still attended with falls of snow. At 10 o'clock AM, the wind blowing a hard gale at WNW with clear weather, suddenly veered to WSW and the sails were taken all aback. Fortunately, the squall was not so very violent and we had sufficient time to work the ship. In this part of the sea, we are subject to the wind shifting and the greatest care is required if the ship is not to suffer damage to the masts and yards.

It was not prudent to carry the top-gallant sails in such critical weather, we struck the mast close down.

Latitude by observation 57° 24' S.
Longitude by reckoning 66° 56' W.

13' more to the North than by reckoning.
We found the variation of the compass by four azimuths to be 25° 5' NE.
Réaumur's thermometer + 3¾°, Fahrenheit's thermometer 40°.

From Monday 4th to Tuesday 5th April 1791

42¼

During the afternoon and until midnight, when there fell a calm, we had a commanding breeze which varied from SSW to SW, attended with near continual snow. The sea was generally smooth. At 5 o'clock PM, we tacked and stood to the West under the four courses with a reef in each top-sail.

At 4 o'clock AM, the thermometer stood in the open air at +3°, by plunging it into the sea and leaving it there for half an hour, it fell to 2½ +. A quarter of an hour after, it rose again to +3°. It kept between 10° and 11° in my cabin.

We saw albatrosses, White and Black Spotted Petrels, sheerwaters, blue petrels and small white gulls.

At 3 o'clock, a wind at NNW succeeded the calm. It was attended with a very great swell from the SW and the snow continued to fall so thickly that we could not see one another on the deck. We directed our course to SW¼S to gain latitudinally and to the South.

The wind did not continue for long for towards 6 o'clock we had no more than a gentle breeze, but the snow did not abate. The air was cold and that which renders it even more disagreeable in this hemisphere is the constant wet state of it.

We perceived albatrosses which were of a slate grey colour all over.

We worked the ship with much difficulty for the cold froze our ropes and made them stiff. I would have much wished to bring relief to the people by putting the company to three watches but this could not be carried out if we were to continue to work the ship neatly by crowding as much sail as we could day and night, which now was of the utmost necessity. In order to surmount a little the difficulties of the cold and the fatigues of our people, I served a dram of brandy to each man in addition to the allowance.

The variation of the compass was by reckoning found to be 25° NE.

Latitude by reckoning 57° 27' S.
Longitude by reckoning 67° 18' W.

Réaumur's thermometer + 2½°, Fahrenheit's thermometer 37°.

From Tuesday 5th to Wednesday 6th April 1791

72

We had a calm until 11 o'clock, a great swell from the West and nearly continual showers of snow and hail. The wind then began to blow a hard gale at SE. The snow continued still to fall in great quantities.

During the afternoon, we amused ourselves by attempting to take the petrels with the hook and line. We took about twenty which I gave to the people. I tasted them and found them good eating. They were of the White and Black sort, or of the grey petrel species, of which I have before made mention. I will here describe the both sorts of petrel.

During the morning, the wind still blowing a hard gale, varied from SE to SSE, with snow. The mercury in the thermometer fell to the freezing point, that is to say nought, but towards 10 o'clock, the sun appearing a little, it rose to +1°. We saw albatrosses which seemed to us to be of a much larger size than those we had yet seen.

There remained but one sheep, seeing it every day become more sickly, we killed it.

We reckoned the variation of the compass to be 25° 30' NE.

Latitude by reckoning 57° 47' S.
Longitude by reckoning 69° 27' W.

Réaumur's thermometer +1¼°, Fahrenheit's thermometer 34°.

Description of a petrel we have called the Grey White Petrel

This bird measures three and half feet broadways including four inches for the diameter of the body, one and a half feet from the tip of the bill to the extremity of the tail. The legs are of a grey colour and measure two and half inches in length to the joint of the toes, which are also two and a half inches in length, including the nails. The toes are webbed together and it has three of them and a claw at the heel. The outer toe has four joints, the middle toe three, and the inner toe, two. Its neck is three inches in length, the head one inch in diameter. The forehead is well covered and the beak is two inches in length and six lines wide and is hooked at the extremity of the upper mandible, which is formed of three bones, of which the two lateral meet the middle one, forming on each side two grooves. The nostrils, separated by a thick skin covered by a membrane of a blue colour, open six lines from the forehead at the point where the upper mandible is lightly compressed. At four lines distance from the nostrils, the bend of the beak begins, the whole of the lower edges are cut sloping all the way. The ears are well covered and are two lines in diameter, they are to be found four lines from the outer angle of the eye, a little above the joint of the lower mandible. The lower mandible measures one inch and eight lines from the back part, which is covered by feathers, to the extremity which ends in a rounded point which fits exactly in the convex part of the upper mandible, of which the tongue occupies the whole of the inside. The palate ends in a fleshy part which hangs from the arch of the hook and which is lined with the organs of taste. The tip of the wing measures one foot in length and is formed of ten quill feathers which are black at the extremity. The upper surface of the wings are of a grey white colour and become perfectly white on the head, the belly is intirely white. The tail is formed of twenty quill feathers, in two rows, which the bird displays freely.

In several of the birds we had cut up, we found the stomach and the gizzard intirely filled with feathers. In one we found a bill that we supposed to belong to a stormy petrel. The inner membrane of the stomach is like the touch of the tongue of a cat. This bird has a social turn, like all petrels, and is to be found in large or small flocks. I have always seen two together which I supposed to be the male and the female. It does not use precaution, due either to stupidity or trust, and comes very near ships.

Nature has with great care lined the bird with a sort of prodigiously thick down, as with all those birds which live in these latitudes.

This bird seems to be the same bird which Mr Cook and Forster named the snowy petrel[77] and of which Mr de Buffon makes only mention and of which he does not give a description. The sole difference is that these gentlemen saw them only near the floating ice whereas we saw had sight of them from 53° latitude S, and in a part of the sea where they have never before been seen.

Description of the White and Black Petrel named by the Spanish Pardelas, by the Portuguese and the English, Pintado

Though this bird is of only two colours, black and white, the variegated nature of the plumage is most pleasing to the eye. The head is near round and, like the neck, is of the most beautiful black, the breast and belly of the brightest white. The upper surface formed of small feathers rounded at the end and speckled with black and white spots, offers the sight of a thousand small lozenges, all like one another. The rump appears more agreeable even to the eye, for it is covered in a greater number of these lozenges, but more distinct, and in all the individuals we had seen of this species, forms a square if viewed from one angle. It has a very gentle nature and is very familiar. I have said in another place that we took them with a hook and line which we baited with pieces of chicken gut. We attached a piece of cork 6 inches from the hook in order to keep it on the surface of the water. It is more often after a squall of wind that we take more of them and more easily. Its cry is raucous and sharp when it quarrels or when it is engaged in sport. The cry may be denoted like this sound *Crra Crra*. We were able to touch it and it did not seem to want to take flight or to defend itself. It generally crosses its wings in the form of a pair of scissors when it is quiet. It did not seem to want its liberty though at the beginning it made some effort to regain it. It is very lively indeed and its eye is black and bright. The bill is ebony black curved at the extremity and measures only fourteen lines in length, which gives it less stupid an expression than other aquatic birds. It is formed, like theirs, of three parts, of which the two lateral ones meet the middle one by means of ligaments and a membrane, which permits them to rub one against the other. The nostrils are separated by a thick skin and are round in shape and covered by the

Description continued

projection of the forehead bone which seems to form a fourth piece, feathers cover the root. The extremity of the upper mandible ends in a small hook which is very sharp, it is to be found three lines from the point in the most convex

77 See Buffon, op. cit., Volume IX, pp. 266–267.

part. The lower mandible is intirely occupied by the tongue and fits exactly in length the upper mandible, ending in a blunt tip which is a little shorter, ears placed like those of other birds. The feet are webbed, the leg is black and two inches in length. It has three toes on each foot and a moveable nail at the heel. Its tail is formed of eighteen quills in two rows and the white colour is most prominent in two thirds of the length. The first row of them ends in a small black stripe two inches in breadth. The second is formed of feathers only three or four lines in length. The covering of the tail, as I have before mentioned, is regularly spotted. The wings which have ten quills measure two and half feet in length, of which three inches form the diameter of the body. The largest of them have the outer edge, and one third of the inner, black, the remainder is white. The smaller birds have only the tip black which makes for a black edge all around the white ground. The whole length from the tip of the bill to the tail is one foot.

This bird is one the most beautiful we may see when it flies but is not so comely on close sight. It lives throughout the year in the Southern hemisphere for we have never seen it North of Tropic of Capricorn. It seems even to prefer the high latitudes, where indeed we have seen more of them.

From Wednesday 6th to Thursday 7th April 1791

71

During the whole day, the wind blew more or less a gentle gale and was variable from SE to SSE, attended with dark weather and falls of snow at intervals. Towards 5 o'clock PM, the snow fell in such a great quantity that the deck and the rigging were covered. It did not thaw during the night, the thermometer standing at nought. But at 7 o'clock in the morning, it rose to +2° and the snow began to melt.

During the morning, we had falls of snow at intervals. We saw A White Antarctic Pigeon and penguins, albatrosses and petrels.

The variation of the magnetic needle was 26° 1' by azimuths. At 8 o'clock AM, we set the studding sails which we were obliged to take in one hour after on account of the squalls of wind.

In the place of coffee, I served to the people tea in which we put a little brandy.

The weather continued hazy and we had been unable to make an observation of the latitude for three days, which by reckoning was 58° 15' S.

Longitude by reckoning 71° 28' W.

We had, by reckoning at least, passed the meridian of this famous Cape Horn of which the name alone frightens most navigators. In consequence, we had entered the Southern Pacific Ocean.

Mr Cook places the Cape Horn in latitude 55° 57' South and longitude 70° 6' West of the Meridian of Paris and the *Connaissance des Temps*, in latitude 55° 58' and longitude 69° 45'.

Thermometer +3° Réaumur, Fahrenheit's thermometer 38°.

From Thursday 7ᵗʰ to Friday 8ᵗʰ 1791

61

This day was the finest of all we had had some while since. The wind was variable and light from NNW round by East to SE. All sails were set.

The variation of the magnetic needle was determined to be 26° 22' NE by the mean result of ten sets of azimuths.

At midnight, we directed our course SW.

We saw but few birds except penguins.

The morning was much like the previous one and as agreeable a fine spring morning as in France, which is rarely to be had in these parts. I made use of it and ordered the hammocks to be taken down, the ship to cleaned and washed with vinegar, and the slops of the seamen to be aired.

Latitude by observation 58° 24' S.
Longitude by reckoning 73° 16' W.

14' more to the North than by reckoning in four days
Réaumur's thermometer +5¼°, Fahrenheit's thermometer 43°.

From Friday 8ᵗʰ to Saturday 9 April 1791

101¼

In the afternoon, the weather being very clear, we waited with a degree of impatience for the rising of the moon to observe the distances and determine the longitude. But no sooner had it passed the horizon, the winds varying at NW¼W, the whole of the atmosphere became loaded with a thick haze. Nothwithstanding, we had the time to take one distance which gave the result of longitude 72° 19' W. As I believed it to be uncertain, I continued to pursue the longitude by reckoning. The observation was sufficient however to prove that no considerable error in the reckoning had arisen.

During the day, the winds blew a hard gale and varied from NNW to NW, attended with an extremely thick haze which occasionally fell as rain. We worked to windward upon the starboard tack with all the sail we could crowd.

We saw little divers, albatrosses and petrels.

The variation of the compass by observation was 26° 30'.

Latitude by observation 59° 14' S.
Longitude by reckoning 76° 7' W.

2' more to the South than by reckoning.
Réaumur's thermometer +5°¼, Fahrenheit's thermometer 43¼°.

From Saturday 9ᵗʰ to Sunday 10ᵗʰ April 1791

93½

At noon, the wind veered to NNW and blew a hard gale. By our reckoning, as we were South enough, we directed our course W¼SW, inclining South. At 6 o'clock PM, the wind at NW and WNW became very hard, attended with squalls and an extremely high sea. We were brought under the foresail, the close-reefed main stay-sail and the main top-sail. We carried more sail than prudence would direct, but the desire to gain to the Westward, and not drive to the South, prevented us from looking too narrowly. The squalls continued with a prodigious rolling swell during the night and a part of the morning. At 10 o'clock AM, the weather became a little clearer and allowed us to set the main sail.

By seven azimuths, the variation of the compass was 26° 45' NE.
We saw but few birds.

Latitude by observation 59° 54' S.
Longitude by reckoning 78° 41' W.

2' more to the North than by reckoning.
Réaumur's thermometer +5°, Fahrenheit's thermometer 43½°.

To prevent the appearance of the scurvy, I ordered the company to use a gargle of the spirit of Cochlearia.[78] I served coffee twice in the week, or tea with brandy. Every single day, the officers had an eye upon their soup, in which we served sauerkraut. In the least inclement weather, they were given an allowance of brandy. I was most careful to have the between decks cleaned and washed with vinegar whenever the weather permitted us to do so. I did the same with the hammocks and slops, which all acquire a most rotten smell when they are closed up in moist weather of the sort we had during a little more than a month. Until this moment my labours had been well rewarded for not a single man aboard had the least symptom of a malady. The two men with the venerial distemper before

---

78 During the third voyage, Cook mentions *scurvy-grass* which in the French version (*Troisième voyage de Cook ou Voyage à l'Océan Pacifique* translated by Jean Nicolas Demeunier and published in 1785) is translated as *cochléaria*. Anderson, the Surgeon, refers specifically to *cochléaria*. In *Observations on the Scurvy. By Charles de Mertan, M.D. Dated Vienne, Jan. 14, 1778*, the use of cochléaria as a remedy for scurvy is largely recognised: *During the spring, those who had the scurvy took, in proportions, suitable to their ages, a drink of whey, in which were infused antiscorbutic plants, such as* cochlearia, nastutium, acquaticum, becca bunga, ascetosa. *This infusion was sweetened with plain syrup or syrup of sugar. Besides this, in the course of the day, they used a gargle, made of an infusion of herbs, rue, sage, agrimonia, in water, to which was added spirit of cochlearia and honey of roses. Philosophical Transactions*, Vol. LXVIII, 1778, Part II.

mentioned, were now intirely recovered. Our Surgeon made use of L'Affecteur's anti-syphillitic rob with great success.[79]

From Sunday 10th to Monday 11th April 1791

64

The wind, which had continued to blow until midnight from NW¼W to W, attended with squalls, varied to WSW. By our reckoning, we were in a high latitude and we thus tacked and stood to the North. At this moment, we were in latitude 60° 16' S and longitude 79° 19' W. This was the most Southward point we had yet found ourselves in.

Until 9 o'clock AM, the winds were changeable and varied from W¼SW to SW¼W, with the sea running high from the NW, the ship laboured much, which slowed her progress. The winds then veered violently at SSW, which brought us under the foresail and the close-reefed main stay-sail, we directed our course WNW, driving North. We caught sight of a great number of whales and but few birds.

At 4h 45' 56" o'clock PM, by seven distances of the moon and the sun, the longitude by observation was 76° 40' W.

The variation of the compass by observation of the azimuth was 27° NE.

The reckoning was found to be at this moment 78° 59'.

2° 19' more to the East.

This difference was occasioned most probably by the violent currents which are to be found when rounding Staten's Land and whose effects are felt even in the offing. Mr Cook determined that at 12 leagues from the coast the currents quite disappeared, but until a greater number of observations are to be had on this subject, we can hardly be sure. I am of the opinion that a current exists, even in the offing, which sets to Eastward for the winds blow almost constantly at West in this space, which obliges the waters of the ocean to run back to the Eastward. This is the case between the Tropics where the winds blow generally at East and the currents set always Westward. Lord Anson found this to be true by unfortunate experience when believing himself to be much Westward of land, he ran to the North and during the night he met most unexpectedly with Cape Noir at Tierra del Fuego, which caused him much distress and loss of a part of

---

79 See *Venereal Disease and the Lewis and Clark Expedition*, Thomas Power Lowry, University of Nebraska Press, 2004, p. 28: *Another enterprising charlatan was Denys Boyveau-L'Affecteur with his "anti syphilitic nectar" which he has termed "L'Affecteur's Anti-Syphillitic Rob", rob being an archaic word designating a vegetable juice thickened by heat. He would not reveal the secret ingredients, but it seemed to contain fruit juice, cumin, sarsaparilla, and mercury.* Gannier (*journal*, op. cit., p. 219) cites Roblet who, contrary to what Marchand affirms here, was extremely disappointed in the remedy.

the crew, for he was obliged once again to keep a high latitude towards the pole. Furthermore, he had thought he was lost with the other ships of his fleet.[80]

Latitude by observation 59° 46' S.
Longitude by reckoning 79° 27' W.
Longitude by observation 77° 10' W.

Réaumur's thermometer +3½°, Fahrenheit's thermometer 29°.

From Monday 11ᵗʰ to Tuesday 12ᵗʰ April 1791

70½

At 4h 41' 24" o'clock PM, by the mean result of two sets of eight distances each of the moon and the sun, the longitude was 77° 2' West. That of yesterday evening, reduced to this time, was found to be 77° 14'.

Mean result 77° 8'.

During the whole of this day, the winds varied from SW to NW¼W, attended with a very high sea from the WNW and squalls which brought hail and snow. The cold was much more intense than pointed out by the thermometer, which kept at +4°.

At 10 o'clock PM, the wind veering to North from West, we tacked and stood to the South.

---

80 Anson's account (*Voyage Round The World In The Years MDCCXL, I, II, III, IV by George Anson, Esq; Commander In Chief Of A Squadron Of His Majesty's Ships, Sent Upon An Expedition To The South-Seas. Compiled From Papers And Other Materials Of The Right Honourable George Lord Anson, And Published Under His Direction By Richard Walter, M.A. Chaplain Of His Majesty's Ship The Centurion, In That Expedition*), published in 1749, was translated into French that same year (*Voyage autour du monde, fait dans les années MDCCXL, I, II, III, IV par George Anson, Commandant en Chef d'une escadre envoyée par Sa Majesté Britannique dans la mer du Sud. Tiré des journaux & autres papiers de ce seigneur, & publié par Richard Walter*). Marchand obviously had this narrative with him and refers specifically to this episode: . . . *the next morning, between one and two, as we were standing to the northward, and the weather, which had till then been hazy, accidentally cleared up, the Pink made a signal for seeing land right a-head; and it being but two miles distant, we were all under the most dreadful apprehensions of running on shore; which, had either the wind blown from its usual quarter with its wonted vigour, or had not the moon suddenly shone out, not a ship amongst us could possibly have avoided: But the wind, which some few hours before blew in squalls from the SW, having fortunately shifted to WNW, we were enabled to stand to the southward, and to clear ourselves of this unexpected danger; so that by noon we had gained an offing of near twenty leagues. By the latitude of this land we fell in with, it was agreed to be a part of Terra del Fuego, near the southern outlet described in Frezier's Chart of the Streights of Magellan, and was supposed to be that point called by him Cape Noir. It was indeed most wonderful, that the currents should have driven us to the eastward with such strength; for the whole squadron esteemed themselves upwards of ten degrees more westerly than this land, so that in running down, by our account, about nineteen degrees of longitude, we had not really advanced above half that distance.*

We heard the disagreeable cries of the penguins during the night. We saw grey albatrosses of the species which Captain Cook had seen in the high Southern latitudes. We caught sight of some fish which resembled pilchards, but which we could not take, though we had good fishermen on board ship.

Latitude by observation 59° 24' S.
Longitude by reckoning 79° 27' W.
Longitude by observation 80° 26' W.

Réaumur's thermometer +4½°, Fahrenheit's thermometer 41°.

From Tuesday 12ᵗʰ to Wednesday 13ᵗʰ April 1791

82½

In the afternoon we took fifteen White and Black Spotted Petrels with a hook and line. We saw many birds of the grey albatross species, many sheerwaters and blue petrels.

Until 9 o'clock in the morning, the winds blew in fresh gales and varied from NW to W¼SW, with continual rain and a heavy sea from WNW. It then fell calm. At ½ past eleven o'clock, the wind settled at North, contiuning very hazy, we steered thus N¼NW.

During the morning, we saw penguins and little divers. We caught some more White and Black Spotted Petrels which were eaten dressed with an anchovy sauce, we found them tolerably good.

The variation of the compass by reckoning was 26° 30' NE.

Latitude by observation 59° 54' S.
Longitude by observation 80° 28' W.
Longitude by reckoning 82° 54' W.

Réaumur's thermometer +4½°, Fahrenheit's thermometer 41°.

From Wednesday 13ᵗʰ to Thursday 14ᵗʰ April 1791

104

The wind varied from NE¼N to NW, blowing a hard gale with a thick haze and a very hard sea from WNW.

Several of the people began to complain of colds and rheumatick pains. It must be observed that for more than a month we had daily suffered rain, snow, haze and hail, with variable winds which had blown hard and which had required the presence of all the people on deck, tiring them much. In addition to this, we had crowded sail, day as well as night until a want of prudence, in order to leave behind as soon as possible this sea, which is as much unwholesome as disagreeable, more especially in such an advanced season. Since Staten's Land, we had not had one single day when we had not taken or loosed the reefs three or four times. What was all the more pernicious was that we could dry nothing, for we never saw the sun, and the cloathes in our chests were as wet as those we had on our backs on the deck, for the haze penetrates to the utmost everywhere. Our books and charts were in the same situation and we could hardly unstick one leaf from another. To prevent such inconvenience, I did not let pass a single day without smoking the between decks. The cook rooms and the oven were placed in the between decks and this was indeed, I believe, a most favourable circumstance for both served greatly to purify the air in this part of the ship in which the crew is accommodated. I believe that without this, we would have been more hard put to it on board. I would advise those in this situation making the same voyage as this, to place the cook rooms under the lower deck where the people are generally accommodated.

Latitude by observation 59° 27' S.
Longitude by observation 83° 37' W.
Longitude by reckoning 86° 5' W.

The variation of the compass by reckoning was 25½° NE.
Réaumur's thermometer +5°, Fahrenheit's thermometer 42°.

From Thursday 14th to Friday 15th April 1791

96¾

The wind was light at NNW until 4 o'clock PM when a calm fell. The sea was very heavy from NW. At 9 o'clock, a hard gale began to blow at SW attended immediately with continual snow. The air seemed to us to be much colder than the thermometer, which kept at +3° above the freezing point, seemed to point out,. We steered NW¼W, but soon after, the wind veering closer to West, we hauled close upon the wind, keeping the sails full.

At 2 o'clock AM, the snow eased a little and fell only in showers. We took more than twenty White and Black Spotted Petrels with a hook and line during the morning.

The sea increased from the NW and ran as high as we had ever seen it. In this space, when the wind blows hard, the sea must, I believe, be most dreadful.

Latitude by observation 58° 45' S.
Longitude by observation 84° 22' W.
Longitude by reckoning 86° 50' W.

We found ourselves 43' more to the South than by reckoning. This difference in four days may be ascribed most probably to the heavy sea from the NW we had suffered now for several days.
Réaumur's thermometer +2°, Fahrenheit's thermometer 36°.

From Friday 15ᵗʰ to Saturday 16ᵗʰ April 1791

65¾

After a calm of short duration, the wind shifted at SE, blowing a light breeze It varied to the East and settled at South, round by W, still attended with a great swell from the NW.

The weather was more or less fine during the night but cold, for the mercury in the thermometer fell to +1½° at midnight.

We had very fine weather in the morning and I took the opportunity to order the between decks to be washed with vinegar and the hammocks and slops of the crew to be sweetened and aired. The variation of the compass by observation of the azimuths was 25° NE.

Latitude by observation 57° 46' S.
Longitude by observation 84° 40' W.
Longitude by reckoning 87° 8' W.

3' more to the South than by reckoning.

In this position, the land supposed to have been discovered by Drake, and which no navigator has ever found since, bore North, distant 4 leagues. Might this navigator have mistaken a haze or an ice island (though from my own knowledge, we have seen none in this space of the sea) for land? Or could this land have disappeared by some extraordinary revolution? Whatsoever may be the case, it is not be found where the charts lay it down. Some authors claim this land exists but that it is to be found closer to the polar circle and they ground what they say upon what Drake relates, that is, when he was on this land, there were only two hours of darkness and the sun was already 8° from the Tropic of Cancer, the inhabitants of the country had said to him that at a certain period of the year, there were no hours of darkness. This may be the truth for it seems hardly likely, and is even impossible, that Drake would have claimed to have seen land, if he had not. The crew moreover would have spoken against it.

We saw albatrosses, White and Black Spotted Petrels, the White-Gray Puffin Petrel,[81] blue petrels and some grey gulls. These last days, the stormy petrels had quite deserted us.

Réaumur's thermometer +4°, Fahrenheit's thermometer 40°.

From Saturday 16ᵗʰ to Sunday 17ᵗʰ April 1791

101

Until 8 o'clock PM, the wind varied from WNW to N very nearly resembling a calm. At 5 o'clock, we had tacked and stood to the SW, meeting with a calm. At

---

81 This might be a reference to the *Fulmar or White-Gray Puffin petrel of the Island of Kilda* (Scotland). This is the only white and grey petrel in Buffon (op. cit., Volume IX, p. 277). In the original, Buffon adds a note *Martin, dans Edwards*. Marchand refers to these birds as *petrels gris blancs*.

midnight the wind began to blow at SE¼S and veered, in hard gales, to SE and SSE. We steered NW¼W.

During the night, the wind blew in hard squalls, attended with snow and hail. In spite of such critical weather, we carried our studding-sails which the violence of the wind obliged us at last to take in at 5 o'clock in the morning. By the mean result of 16 azimuths, the variation of the compass was found to be 21° 29' NE.

I much wished to make observations of distances in order to determine our longitude yet so dense was the haze, within which we were constantly buried, that it was impossible. These two lines of Gustave would describe most properly this part of the Pacific Ocean:

> "I passed under a sky which was more of an enemy to me, Where the sun did but warm and shine in half measure." *Piron.*[82]

During the morning the wind blew with great strength attended with snow and hail.

Latitude by reckoning 56° 27' S.
Longitude by observation 86° 22' W.
Longitude by reckoning 88° 50' W.

Réaumur's thermometer +2½°, Fahrenheit's thermometer 37°.

---

82 Marchand is here quoting from *Gustave Wasa* (1733) by Alexis Piron. Alex Connon outlines the historical basis of the play: *The young Gustav Wasa was certainly an attractive character, heroic and swash-buckling, "with as many hairbreadth escapes and desperate adventures to his credit as Bonny Prince Charlie," as one noted historian puts it. Vertot gives an animated account of his colourful escapades, during which he sometimes dons disguises to escape detection; of the way his charm would lead strangers – sometimes female – to help him; and of his ability to win over the rebellious peasants of the region of Dalarna. Clearly Piron has been inspired by this figure, and has responded enthusiastically in his dramatic re-creation.*

Piron has also made a brave attempt to fill in the complex political background so carefully set out by Vertot. Gustav's campaign brought to an end the Union of Kalmar, officially consecrated in 1397 when Erik of Pomerania became King of Denmark, Norway, and Sweden. During the period of the Union, the Swedes had often had their own regent, with Sten Sture the younger taking this role from 1312 until 1320, when Kristian II bloodily asserted his right as King of Denmark to govern Sweden. The Bloodbath of Stockholm is the most famous of his atrocities but is far from being the only one, and it is undoubtedly the cruelty of his rule that allowed Gustav to gather such overwhelming popular support. Hence, the sanguinary character depicted by Piron in his Chris-tierne is true to historical fact (*Identity and Transformation in the Plays of Alexis Piron*, Modern Humanities Research Association and Maney Publishing, 2007, p. 48). See also Gannier (*journal*, op. cit., p. 224) who compares Marchand's taste in contemporary literature to Bougainville's more classical penchants.

From Sunday 17ᵗʰ to Monday 18ᵗʰ April 1791

178

The wind continued to blow with the same strength attended with snow and a hoar frost. It varied from SSW and SSE.

We saw some albatrosses, White and Black Spotted Petrels, blue petrels and numerous sheerwaters.

The variation of the compass by observation was found to be 20° 7' NE.

Latitude by observation 54° 45' S.
Longitude by observation 86° 9' W.
Longitude by reckoning 91° 37' W.

40' more to the South than by reckoning in two days. I was much surprised to find so great a difference for we took the greatest care in the reckoning.

Réaumur's thermometer +3°, Fahrenheit's thermometer 38°.

From Monday 18ᵗʰ to Tuesday 19ᵗʰ April 1791

153¾

The wind continued violent between SSW and SSE until 10 o'clock attended as before with snow and hail and a great sea from the South. It then varied at SW and WSW and continued to blow in hard gales.

At 3 o'clock in the afternoon, we had directed our course NW in order to hurry our progress Northward, for I believed to be enough West to shape this course.

It was very cold during the night for on the deck the snow did not melt. The mercury in the Réaumur's thermometer kept at +1°, and in that of Fahrenheit's thermometer, 34°.

Since the morning of the 17ᵗʰ, we had been sailing under the fore sail and the top-sails with the reefs in or loosed.

The weather was very pleasant during the morning though we had snow at intervals.

The variation of the compass determined from 7 azimuths was 16° 52' NE.

Latitude by observation 52° 32' S.
Longitude by observation 91° 10' W.
Longitude by reckoning 93° 38' W.

Réaumur's thermometer +3°, 38° Fahrenheit's thermometer.

In this situation, we had perfectly rounded Cape Horn for we were East and West with the Westerly entrance of the Strait of Magellan. I remarked by and by that we must have been been very fortunate in rounding this famous Cape, or that Mr Anson had been very unfortunate, or that the narrator of the voyage had overcharged somewhat the situation, for having rounded it in the same season as he had done, we met with none of the fearful storms or great high billows of the sea ready to swallow us up. We had suffered the winds and the heavy seas which are to be found in any place, and which I dare to say are much less great than at the Cape of Good Hope in May, June or July. What is most unpleasant in this passage is that the sun is almost never to be seen and we are constantly enveloped in haze, snow, hail and rain.

From Tuesday 19th to Wednesday 20th April 1791

62½

At 9h 20' 37" PM, by two sets of seven distances each of Spica Virginis and the moon, our longitude was found to be 93° 44' W. At this same moment, that reckoned from Staten's Land was found to be 94° 9' and 91° 36', deduced from our last observations. It appears that during the time we had taken to round Cape Horn the currents had balanced each other, for by the observations made on the 11th we had been carried a little more than 2° to the East, but by those of today, we found ourselves near the same, but more to the West.

By a set of six azimuths, the variation of the compass was 16° 10' NE.
In the afternoon we had billows of snow.

The wind which had blown rather a fresh gale at SW until 10 o'clock in the evening, veered South, SE, ENE and NE and blew a light air attended with intervals of calm.

During the morning, we rigged the main top-gallant mast and yard. The air was mild and pleasant, which offered me the opportunity to air the slops of the people and sweeten the ship by fires between decks.

I began to make use of the greens mixed with vinegar. I must here do justice to Mr Sapet of Marseilles who had prepared them for me. They are in the best condition and what was most remarkable was that they had not lost either their natural colour or their taste. It is to be recommended for the good state of health of the crew that all Captains making long voyages make use of sauerkraut and greens in vinegar. I gave orders to put them three times a week in the soup of the crew, and the remainder of the time to serve sauerkraut.

Latitude by observation 51° 38' S.
Longitude by observation 94° 5' W.
Longitude by reckoning 94° 25' W.

Réaumur's thermometer +6°, Fahrenheit's thermometer 45°.

From Wednesday 20th to Thursday 21st April 1791

115

During the afternoon, the weather was pleasant enough. We had a fine breeze at NE and ENE which blew fresh, but at 7 o'clock in the evening the weather became hazy all round, which was a most certain sign of a violent squall of wind to come. The wind was then blowing in heavy gusts and the horizon was no more than four leagues distant, the clouds appeared to be bearing down upon us. I unrigged the top-gallant yard.

At ½ past 10 o'clock, the wind had increased so much at NE that we were reduced to the fore-sail and the main stay-sail. At ¾ past 7 o'clock in the morning, the wind becoming furious at ENE, attended with squalls, the ship was no longer able to carry the fore-sail though we kept the ship four or five points from the wind. I gave orders to lie to under the stay-sail on the starboard tack, at the same time we got down the fore top-gallant mast. This much relieved the ship.

We suffered an extraordinary rolling on account of three large seas, from the South, the West and the third caused by the wind. Several of the people were thrown down as a result of the rolling and were very materially hurt, amongst them one of the volunteers, who I thought had been struck down dead. He recovered however a half hour after and was bled twice and seemed to grow easier, though he still complained of a pain in his head which was the place where he had received the blow, but three days afterwards he was perfectly recovered.

The wind which had continued to blow with the same strength until noon began to abate. This was the stiffest gale of wind, or it is better to say the only one which deserved to be called such, we had suffered since our departure from Marseilles.

The variation of the compass by reckoning was 14° 30' NE.

Latitude by reckoning 50° 19' S.
Longitude by observation 96° W.
Longitude by reckoning 96° 20' W.

Réaumur's thermometer +6°, Fahrenheit's thermometer 45°.[83]

From Thursday 21st to Friday 22nd April 1791

71

At ½ past 3 o'clock, the wind had a good deal abated and decreased even to a calm, we made sail under our four main courses and close-reefed top-sails. The sea still ran high.

During the gale, the birds in great quantities had kept close to the ship and appeared to have an inclination to rest themselves upon it.

The wind shifted to NW¼N, round by N, at 6 o'clock in the morning. At 8 o'clock, we tacked on the larboard side.

During the night, the weather was moderate attended with a very hard sea from the NNE.

Louis Coriol, sailor, who had fallen three days since and received a violent blow to the head, and who had not wished to be bled immediately saying that it

---

83 Omitted in Gannier's transcription (*journal*, op. cit., p. 227).

was a trifle, complained to the Surgeon that he was sickly. He was found to have a violent fever. He complained of a heaviness with excessive pain in the head and not only the back part where he had received the blow, but in the front part, whereby Mr Roblet judged there to have been a counter blow. After bleeding, he made a crucial incision and discovered a crack in the parietal bone on the right side, but with care and attention he was able to perform his duties at the end of twenty days.

Latitude by reckoning 50° 13' S.
Longitude by observation 97° 6' W.
Longitude by reckoning 97° 26' W.

Réaumur's thermometer +7½°, Fahrenheit's thermometer 48°.

From Friday 22ⁿᵈ to Saturday 23ʳᵈ 1791

83½

The winds varied all day from N¼NW to NW¼W, blowing a fresh gale attended with squalls and a great swell from the NNE. At 8 o'clock in the evening, we tacked and stood to the West and at 8 o'clock we put about and stood to the East.

At 9h 7' 34" AM, by two sets of four distances each of the sun and moon, our longitude was 96° 57'.

We saw the same birds and took White and Black Spotted Petrels with a hook and line.

The weather was very mild.

The variation of the compass was 14° NE by reckoning, the great rolling prevented us from taking the azimuths.

Latitude by reckoning 50° 39' S.
Longitude by observation 96° 58' W.
Longitude by reckoning 97° 18' W.

Réaumur's thermometer +7°, Fahrenheit's thermometer 47°.

From Saturday 23ʳᵈ April to Sunday 24ᵗʰ April 1791

123

During this day, the winds prevailed from NW to W¼SW, blowing hard gales attended with squalls and a hard sea from the NW. We made sail under our four courses and close-reefed top-sails, directing our course to Northward.

By two sets of five distances each of the moon and the sun, our longitude reduced to 8h 35' 38" AM was 95° 28' W.

As it was Easter this day, I served a feast of bread and fresh pork to the people and a double allowance of wine. As for ourselves, we drank with much cheerfulness to the health of our owners, to all our families and friends and to the success of the voyage.

The variation of the compass was 13° NE by reckoning.

Latitude by observation 48° 49' S.
Longitude by observation 95° 58' W.
Longitude by reckoning 95° 59' *ditto*.

Réaumur's thermometer +7°, Fahrenheit's thermometer 47°.

From Sunday 24ᵗʰ to Monday 25ᵗʰ April 1791

163½

The winds fixed at WSW and W¼SW and blew in hard gales with gusts attended with cloudy weather and squalls at intervals, the air was very mild. The sea was not as great as the preceding evening. We continued to see albatrosses, White and Black Spotted Petrels, grey white petrels and those of the blue kind. Since leaving the parts adjacent to Cape Horn, we had seen no more stormy petrels.

At 9h 22' 56" AM, by two sets of observations of the distance of the moon and the sun, we found the longitude to be 96° 9', mean result.

That which was deduced from the observations made the preceding evening, reduced to this moment, and taking account of the distance sailed, was found to be 95° 21'. Mean 95° 45'.

The variation of the compass by observation of the azimuths was 12° 1' NE.

Latitude by observation 46° 9' S.
Longitude by observation 95° 45' W.
Longitude by reckoning 96° 2' W.

Réaumur's thermometer +7½°, Fahrenheit's thermometer 48°.

From Monday 25ᵗʰ to Tuesday 26ᵗʰ April 1791

151½

The winds continued to blow fresh gales from WSW and SSW, though we met with squalls at intervals. The weather was in general pleasant because the sun appeared immediately afterwards. We directed the course to NW¼N when the wind permitted our doing so.

We were much pleased with having rounded Cape Horn with so much ease during a season which was much advanced, and having such favourable circumstances as these to work Northward.

In spite of the general system, I am almost led to believe that the finest of all seasons for rounding the Cape is March and April according to the several Captains I met with at Cadiz, who were making the voyage from Lima.*

*This is not the opinion of the English for we may read the following passage in the introduction of the 3rd Voyage of Mr Cook: "We shall, for the future, be less discouraged by the labours and distresses experienced by the squadrons of Lord Anson and Pizzaro, when we recollect, that they were obliged to attempt the navigation of those seas at an unfavourable season of the year (in March and April) and that there was nothing very formidable met with there, when they were traversed (in January) by Captain Cook."[84]

We read also in the relation by letters of the voyage by Mr Dixon that "our Captains determined to get to sea the first opportunity, as the season was already too far advanced for us to expect a good passage around Cape Horn." They were then at Falkland's Islands and the date was 20th January.[85]

The Spanish vessels which carry out this voyage depart, moreover, in any season. I saw one get ready for sea in the middle of the month of April to round the Cape in the very depth of winter. They generally depart notwithstanding in the months of November or December.

We saw some brown gulls or Port Egmont Hens.

The variation of the compass determined from azimuths was 11° 34' NE.

Latitude by reckoning 43° 46' S.
Longitude by observation 97° 2' W.
Longitude by reckoning 97° 19' W.

Réaumur's thermometer +8°, Fahrenheit's thermometer 49°.

From Tuesday 26th to Wednesday 27th April 1791

48½

At 4 o'clock in the morning, it fell calm, until that moment we had had a light wind at SW with grey weather.

We rigged the mizzen, main and fore top-gallant masts and yards. We saw albatrosses, blue petrels, sheerwaters, White and Black Spotted Petrels and brown gulls.

By the mean result of 9 azimuths, we found the variation of the compass to be 11° 14' NE.

Latitude by reckoning 43° 2' S.
Longitude by observation 97° 17' W.
Longitude by reckoning 97° 34' W.

Réaumur's thermometer +9½°, Fahrenheit's thermometer 52¼°.

---

84 In the translation of the third voyage, and in the original, there is no mention of *March and April* or *January*, which Marchand himself inserts into the quotation.
85 Dixon, op. cit., p. 38.

From Wednesday 27ᵗʰ to Thursday 28ᵗʰ April 1791

77½

We had a near calm until 3 o'clock PM, we got a light wind at NNE soon after which varied at NNE, attended with grey weather and a smooth sea.

We continued to make the tack to the Westward for it brought us close to our route.

We had some squalls during the night.

We saw many whales which all had a great white spot on each side of their backs.

The variation of the compass by reckoning was 1° 3'.

Latitude by reckoning 42° 31' S.
Longitude by observation 98° 49' W.
Longitude by reckoning 99° 6' W.

Réaumur's thermometer +11°, Fahrenheit's thermometer 55°.

From Thursday 28ᵗʰ to Friday 29ᵗʰ April 1791

97¾

At sun-set, we got sight of a vast quantity of birds of the sea swallow species from which I conjectured that we were near some islands, though none are laid down in this space on any chart.

Notwithstanding, Mr Pingre in a short treatise on the transit of Venus published in 1768 speaks of an isle which is said to have been discovered in 1714 by Juan Fernandes and which lies in latitude 38° S, distant 550 leagues from the coast of Chile, that is to say longitude 112°, West of Paris thereabouts.[86] As we could not

---

86 Marchand copies this specific reference from Cook's account, as it appears in the translation. In the original: *Mr Pengre in a little treatise concerning the transit of Venus published in 1768, gives some account of land having been discovered by the Spaniards in 1714, in the latitude of 38° and 550 leagues from the coast of Chili, which is in the longitude of 110° or 111° West, and within a degree or two of my track in the* Endeavour, *so this can hardly be its situation. In short, the only probable situation it can have must be about the meridian of 106° or 108° West, and then it can only be a small isle as I have already observed* (op. cit., p. 274). Pingré published a whole series of pamphlets in the 1760s and 1770s on the transit of Venus but the one being referred to here by Cook, and indirectly by Marchand, is *Mémoire sur le choix et l'état des lieux où le passage de Vénus du 3. Juin 1769 pourra être observé avec le plus d'avantage, et principalement sur la position géographique des isles de la mer du Sud* published in 1767. Pingré (op. cit., p. 70) recounts that *Depuis quelques années un marin de S. Malo, nommé Benard de la Harpe, a fait imprimer à Rennes chez Vatar un Mémoire pour la France, servant à la découverte des Terres Australes. 15 pag. In-4°. Il y rapporte qu'en 1714, le Capitaine d'un brigantin Espagnol, sortant du Callao pour aller à l'isle de Chiloé, se trouvant par 38 dégrés de latitude sud, & à 550 lieues à l'Ouest du Chili, découvrit une terre élevée, qu'il côtoya pendant un jour; qu'il jugea qu'elle*

exactly determine the longitude at sea then with as much ease as at present, and relying thus upon reckoning, it is possible that it lay more to the East. It is also the inclination of Mr Cook who believes it cannot but lie between longitude 108° or 110°. Whatever the case may be, this island has never been seen since its discovery. The swallows were flying Northward.

During this whole of this day, the winds were variable from NE to N¼ NE and blew in more or less fresh gales attended with a great swell from the NW and grey weather.

In the afternoon, there was so great a number of White and Black Spotted Petrels about the ship that we took more than 40 with a hook and line.

The variation of compass by the amplitudes and the azimuths was found to be 10° 20' NE.

The morning was rainy.

I gave orders to the gun-smith to begin to clean and make ready our fire-arms.

Latitude by reckoning 41° 30' S.
Longitude by observation 100° 28' W.
Longitude by reckoning 100° 45' W.

From Friday 29ᵗʰ to Saturday 30ᵗʰ April 1791

79

Until 2 o'clock AM, the winds were variable from NNE to E¼NE with near continual rain. They then shifted to WNW blowing in gusts, which obliged us to tack on the larboard side. We felt the effect of several, very great swells.

During the morning, the weather was generally pleasant though dark. The sea had become much less heavy.

We saw Port Egmont Hens or Brown gulls, albatrosses, White and Black Spotted Petrels, blue petrels and sheerwaters.

By the mean result of eleven azimuths, the variation of the compass was 9° S.

Latitude by observation 40° 19' S.
Longitude by observation 100° 49' W.
Longitude by reckoning 101° 6' W.

était habitée, par les feux qu'il apperçut durant la nuit; & que les vents contraires l'ayant obligé de relâcher à la Conception, il y trouva le vaisseau le François, de Saint-Malo, commandé par M. du Fresne-Marion, qui a assuré avoir eu communication du Journal du Capitaine Espagnol, & y avoir trouvé le fait que nous venons de rapporter. Ceux qui connoissent M. Marion savent que c'est un Officier sage, intelligent & véridique, aussi incapable d'être trompé que de tromper personne.

4' more to the North than by reckoning in five days.

Réaumur's Thermometer +11½°, Fahrenheit's thermometer 56°.

From Saturday 30ᵗʰ April to Sunday 1ˢᵗ May 1791

64¼

At half past midnight, the weather became clear and the evening was the finest we had had for more than a month. The winds were variable from NW¼W to N¼NE, fine clear weather and mild. We continued to make the tack to the Westward or to the Eastward, following the route most advantageous to us.

We saw Brown Puffin-Petrels.[87]

I observed two kinds of blue petrels, one was of a much smaller size than the other, but they have the same plumage exactly and the same blackish line which stretches from one end of the wing to the other.

By the mean result of 31 azimuths taken in the evening and in the morning, we found the variation of the compass to be 7° 35' Northeasterly.

During the night, there was lightning in the West. During the morning, we had squalls and fine weather at intervals. The squalls brought hail.

Latitude by observation 39° 59' S.

Longitude by observation 100° 6' W.

Longitude by reckoning 100° 23' W.

4' more to the North than by reckoning in five days.

Réaumur's Thermometer +12°, Fahrenheit's thermometer 57°.

From Sunday 1ˢᵗ to Monday 2ⁿᵈ May 1791

115

Until 4 o'clock PM, the wind was variable from North to NNE, and blew by squalls. It then began to shift to East and to South. At midnight, it veered to SSW and then to W, blowing a hard gale attended with heavy squalls and lightning in all quarters of the horizon.

The weather bearing a threatening appearance at sun-set, we unrigged the top-gallant yards.

---

87 *The Brown Puffin-Petrel. Edwards, though he gives this bird under the name of the Great Black Peteril, remarks, that the uniform colour of its plumage is rather blackish brown than jet black. He compares its size to that of a raven, and describes very well the conformation of its bill, which character places it among the Puffins. "The nostrils," says he, "seem to have been two tubes joined together, which rising from the fore part of the head, advance about a third of the length of the bill, of which both points bent downwards into a hook, look like two pieces added and soldered." Edwards reckons this species a native of the seas adjacent to the Cape of Good Hope; but this is merely conjecture* (Buffon, op. cit., Volume IX, p. 278).

The variation of the compass was 7° NE by observation.

Latitude by observation 38° 29' S.
Longitude by observation 100° 57' W.
Longitude by reckoning 101° 14' W.

8' more to the South than by reckoning in five days.
Réaumur's Thermometer +11½°, Fahrenheit's thermometer 56.

From Monday 2ⁿᵈ to Tuesday 3ʳᵈ May 1791

119¾

During this day, the winds were variable from WSW to NW¼W, generally fresh, attended with squalls at intervals. At noon, we rigged the main top-gallant yard. We set the studding sails which we were taken in at 5 o'clock PM on account of the frequent squalls.

We saw White and Black Spotted Petrels, sheerwaters and but few albatrosses. The variation of the compass by reckoning was found to 6° 30' NE.

Latitude by observation 36° 34' S.
Longitude by observation 100° 48' W.
Longitude by reckoning 101° 5' W.

Réaumur's Thermometer +14°, Fahrenheit's thermometer 63°.
*Note this page of the logbook belongs to the next page and should be placed 3ʳᵈ and 4ᵗʰ May.[88]

From Tuesday 3ʳᵈ to Wednesday 4ᵗʰ May 1791

108

We had a fresh gale at NW and WSW the whole of this day, blowing in gusts as if we had been under steep mountains. From time to time we had squalls but the weather was generally fine and mild.

The variation of the compass was found to be 7° NE by observation of the azimuths.

Latitude by reckoning 35° 4' S.
Longitude by observation 99° 34' W.
Longitude by reckoning 99° 51' W.

Réaumur's Thermometer +14°, Fahrenheit's thermometer 64°.

---

[88] These errors may be further evidence of the "fair copy" status of this particular manuscript.

*Note this page of the logbook belongs to the preceding page and shows the routes of 2nd and 3rd May.

Wednesday 4th to Thursday 5th May 1791

75

At noon, the winds varied at SSW, attended with a prodigiously thick haze which dissipated during the night. They shifted then to South and South East, continuing variable.

At 8 o'clock PM, I directed the course to NW¼W.

We saw but few albatrosses, some White and Black Spotted Petrels, many sheerwaters and a Port Egmont Hen.

The variation of the compass by reckoning was 6° 30' NE.

Latitude by observation 33° 56' S.
Longitude by observation 100° 14' W.
Longitude by reckoning 100° 31' W.

Réaumur's Thermometer +16°, Fahrenheit's thermometer 67°.

From Thursday 5th to Friday 6th May 1791

69

We had baffling winds varying from ESE to WSW, round by the North, attended with grey weather and a smooth sea.

At 8 o'clock in the morning, we tacked and stood to the NE.

I set the sailmakers to make sails for our longboats and boats, and the carpenters to make chests for aft of the boats in order to carry provisions and power in a dry condition. Lastly I made ready all that I could in order to make easy our trade on the coast of America.

We saw no more sheerwaters or albatrosses The White and Black Spotted Petrels had disappeared.

The variation of the compass was 6° 1' by observation of azimuths.

Latitude by reckoning 33° 14' S.
Longitude by observation 100° 45' W.
Longitude by reckoning 101° 2' W.

Réaumur's Thermometer +16½°, Fahrenheit's thermometer 68°.

From Friday 6th to Saturday 7th May 1791

99¼

The wind blew a steady gale at NW with fine weather though we had a great swell at SSW. The sea was smooth.

By 18 azimuths taken in the morning and in the evening, the variation of the compass was found to be 8° 14' NE, and by 16 others with another compass, it was 7° 40'. It having decreased until now, I was astonished to see it increase once again.

Except a white gull and some few sheerwaters, we did not see any birds at all during this day.

Latitude by observation 31° 40' S.
Longitude by observation 99° 37' W.
Longitude by reckoning 99° 54' W.

14' more to the North than by reckoning.
Réaumur's Thermometer +19°, Fahrenheit's thermometer 75°.

From Saturday 7ᵗʰ to Sunday 8ᵗʰ May 1791

96

The wind continued constantly at NW blowing a gentle gale attended with very fine weather and a hot air which we enjoyed with so much pleasure as we had passed two months in the most unpleasant of climates. The crew appeared to spring up again.

I continued all my efforts to prevent the scurvy. I feared the passage between the Tropics for it is in this hot climate that the fatal disease most frequently lays hold. Mr Roblet, who has the most watchful eye on every one, informed that there was not a single symptom of that disorder on board.

The variation of the compass determined from five azimuths was 9° NE.

At 10 o'clock AM, we tacked and stood to the W.

We saw but a white gull and a sheerwater during this day.

Latitude by observation 30° 26' S.
Longitude by observation 98° 49' W.
Longitude by reckoning 99° 6' W.

Réaumur's Thermometer +20°, Fahrenheit's thermometer 77°.

From Sunday 8ᵗʰ to Monday 9ᵗʰ May 1791

45

Our longitude determined from six sets of 5 distances each of the moon and the sun, and a set alike of 5 distances of Regulus and the moon, all reduced to 2h 48' 18" PM, gave 96° 33' W.

The longitude determined following the last observations made on the 24ᵗʰ of the preceding month, was found to be at this moment 98° 55'. By consequence, since that moment, we had been carried more than 2° to the East than was shown by the log.

It is worthy of note that these most recent observations differed by only 19'.

During this day, the winds were variable with intervals of calm. There was a great hollow swell from the WSW. The weather was fine and hot.

The variation of the compass, determined from amplitudes and eleven azimuths, was 9° 8' NE, mean result.

We saw gulls, sea swallows and whales.

Latitude by observation 30° 2' S.
Longitude by observation 96° 41' W.
Longitude by reckoning 99° 3' W.

5' more to the N than by reckoning.
Réaumur's Thermometer +21°, Fahrenheit's thermometer 79°.

From Monday 9th to Tuesday 10th may 1791

107⅓

By two sets of observations of the distance of the moon and the sun, reduced to 4h 7' 30" o'clock PM, the longitude was found to be 97° 8' 30" West. The difference was only 11' W of that determined from the observations of the preceding evening, allowing for the distance sailed. At the same moment, by thirteen azimuths, the variation of the magnetic needle was found to be 9° 10' Northeasterly.

The wind was variable from NNE to NNW attended with violent squalls at intervals and with a great swell from the South.

We had seen neither albatrosses nor White and Black Spotted Petrels these last few days. The people were sorry for they had a particular liking for the latter birds which were good eating, but they were hardly sorry, and left behind them with great joy, the climate in which the birds are to be found. They wondered that these birds did not prefer to fix themselves between the Tropics.

Latitude by observation 29° 33' S.
Longitude by observation 98° 17' W.
Longitude by reckoning 100° 28' W.

12' more to the South than by reckoning.
Réaumur's Thermometer +20°, Fahrenheit's thermometer 77°.

From Tuesday 10th to Wednesday 11th May 1791

77¾

Until 11 o'clock PM, the wind blew a fresh gale at NNW and N. At this time, the wind chopped at W and WNW blowing a hard gale, attended with violent squalls. We were brought under the fore sail and directed our course North, inclining to the East.

At midnight, we were able to set the close-reefed main top-sail. The sea was heavy and the wind blew in violent squalls.

At ½ past 7 o'clock in the evening, the top-gallant yards had been unrigged.

At 8 o'clock AM, following a squall which had obliged us to loose the top-sails, which we had previously set, the weather became fine and permitted us to steer North, all sails set.

The variation of the compass by observation of the azimuths, was 7° 7'NE.

Latitude by observation 29° 9' S.
Longitude by observation 98° 51' W.
Longitude by reckoning 101° 2' W.

Réaumur's Thermometer +20½°, Fahrenheit's thermometer 78°.

From Wednesday 11th to Thursday 12th May 1791

42½

This day we had very light winds at W, with intervals of calm, attended frequently with a light rain and a great swell from the NW.

To my great surprise we had not yet got the trade wind in spite of the latitude in which we found ourselves, while in the journals of diverse navigators they had been met with in the latitude of 32° and 33°. I attributed this to the sun, which was advanced towards the Tropic of Cancer, at least this is what is to be found, by my experience, in the Atlantic Ocean. When the sun is North of the equator, close to the Tropic of Cancer, the trade wind prevails but little to the South and much more to the North. The contrary is to be observed when it is close to the Tropic of Capricorn.

By eight azimuths observed with different compasses, the variation of the compass was 6° 33' NE.

We saw a bird of the kind named frigate and sea swallows.

Looking into the condition of our provisions which were subject to leakage, we found a barrel of common oil half empty of which the loss was irreparable to us.

Latitude by observation 28° 25' S.
Longitude by observation 98° 54' W.
Longitude by reckoning 101° 5' W.

Réaumur's Thermometer +18°, Fahrenheit's thermometer 73°.

From Thursday 12th to Friday 13th May 1791

95

At 3h 28' 38" o'clock PM, by the mean result of two sets of five distances each of the sun and the moon, our longitude was 98° 51' 30" West.

By also two sets of distances observed the preceding night, and reduced to this time, of Spica Virginis and the moon, it was 98° 56' 30".

Mean result 98° 54'.

There was very little difference between this result and the longitude determined from the observations of the preceding days.

By the mean result of 8 sets of observations of the azimuths, made with different compasses, the variation of the magnetic needle was 6° 31' NE.

During the afternoon, the wind was variable at SSW and then at SSE, attended with fine weather. We steered NW¼N to get within the reach of the trade wind.

Having opened the fore-hold during the morning to get up some water, I was vexed to find it spoilt and of the greenish colour which is to be seen in a pool of stagnant water. For the purification of it, we aired it and some few drops of oil of vitriol were poured into the barrels. I gave orders to examine the rest and found them to be in the same condition. Until this time, the water had been tolerable, though diffusing an unpleasant odour which disappeared with the simple ventilation of it.

Latitude by observation 26° 59' S.
Longitude by observation 99° 39' W.
Longitude by reckoning 101° 53' W.

Réaumur's Thermometer +19½°, Fahrenheit's thermometer 76°.

From Friday 13th to Saturday 14th May 1791

120½

At noon we directed our course to the NW.

In the afternoon, we spliced two cables so that we should be able to veer away two hundred and thirty fathoms on a single occasion. It is a precaution which I believe is necessary in voyages of any great length for a ship is obliged frequently to come to anchor before a bold shore, in deep water.

During the whole of this day, the winds continuing between SE and NE and blowing in fine breezes, we flattered ourselves that, founded in reason, we had at last met with the trade wind. In this we were very greatly mistaken, as will become clear in the course of this journal. We were destined to suffer numerous difficulties in these spaces where we should have expected to meet with but only a very few.

By three sets of azimuths, the variation of the compass was found to be 7° 49' NE.

For some days past, the caulkers had been employed in caulking the decks and the boats. I had the pleasure of seeing that the seams of the planks had not in any place become loose for the oakum was still very firm. This is rarely to be met with in a new ship on its very first voyage, which was a sure proof that the upper works had not yet worked enough, in spite of the bad weather, the high seas and stress of weather she had endured since our departure from Marseilles, and most particularly near the Cape Horn, where we had carried sail to the utmost limits.

Latitude by observation 25° 29' S.
Longitude by observation 101° 16' W.
Longitude by reckoning 103° 30' W.

12' more to the South than by reckoning.
Réaumur's +20° Thermometer, Fahrenheit's thermometer 77°.

From Saturday 14ᵗʰ to Sunday 15ᵗʰ May 1791

79½

The winds were light and variable from NE to NW, attended with squalls and calms at intervals.

The variation of the magnetic needle by six azimuths was found to be 8° 11' Northeasterly.

We saw some sea swallows or crossers,[89] and a small white gull.

Latitude by observation 25° 20' S.
Longitude by observation 102° 36' W.
Longitude by reckoning 104° 50' W.

14' more to the South than by reckoning.
Réaumur's Thermometer +20°, Fahrenheit's thermometer 77°.

From Sunday 15ᵗʰ to Monday 16ᵗʰ May 1791

59¼

The wind settled at N and N ½ NW and blew a light gale, with at times squalls. We continued to make a tack to the Westward which was the most advantageous to us.

We saw some few sheerwaters.

---

89 *They likewise glide and circle, sink and rise the air, crossing and entwining their various irregular track in a thousand directions;* * *their flight is impelled by starts of momentary caprice, and led by the sudden glimpse of their fugitive prey. They snatch the victim on wing, or alight only a moment on the surface; for they are averse to swim, though their half-webbed feet might contribute to that purpose. They reside commonly on the seashores, and frequent also lakes and great rivers.*

Sailors call those nimble birds found at sea, croiseurs (crossers) "when they are large; goelettes when they are small." Remarks made by the Viscount de Querhoënt (Buffon, op. cit., Volume VIII, p. 298).

The variation of the compass determined by three sets of azimuths was 6° 57' NE.

Latitude by observation 25° 29' S.
Longitude by observation 103° 41' W.
Longitude by reckoning 105° 55' W.

13' more to the South than by reckoning.
Réaumur's Thermometer +20½°, Fahrenheit's thermometer 78°.

From Monday 16ᵗʰ to Tuesday 17ᵗʰ May 1791

53¼

The winds continued at N and NNW and blew in light gales, with clear weather. In the afternoon, we took four bonitos which we found to be excellent eating and more especially as we had not eaten any fish these last two months and a half.

We saw two small grey gulls with a forked tail. Though navigators are of the general opinion that this species of bird is hardly to be found flying far from land, I cannot confirm it for the nearest land known to us was Easter Island, and we were no less than 160 leagues from it. It is true to say that some small low island not yet known may possibly have lain in this space.

We now met also with the first tropic birds or Arrow-tails.[90]

By the mean result of six azimuths taken with different compasses, the variation of the needle was 7° 39' NE.

Latitude by observation 25° 36' S.
Longitude by observation 104° 39' W.
Longitude by reckoning 106° 53' W.

4' more to the South than by reckoning.
Réaumur's Thermometer +21°, Fahrenheit's thermometer 79°.

From Tuesday 17ᵗʰ to Wednesday 18ᵗʰ May 1791

49½

We had light winds which continued at NNW and at N. The weather was fine and the sea was as a pond. I was much concerned that these winds were slowing our progress Northward.

We saw small grey gulls and tropic birds.

---

90 *The Tropic Bird or Oiseau du Tropique ou le Paille en Queue*. * In French paille-en-cul or fetu-en-cul (Straw-in-Arse) and Queu de Flêche (Arrow-tail)*, Buffon, op. cit., Volume VIII, p. 316. Buffon adds here that Linneaus gave this bird the poetic name of *Phaeton* or *Phaeton Aethereus*.

Having observed that the ship was not sailing as was usual, for she was too much by the stern, I ordered six barrels to be filled with water in the fore-hold of the ship, after which the ship sailed much better. The variation of the compass was determined to be 6° 26' NE by the mean result of six azimuths.

Longitude by observation 105° 29' W.
Longitude by reckoning 107° 43' W.
Latitude by observation 25° 44' S.

5' more to the South than by reckoning.
Réaumur's Thermometer +21°, Fahrenheit's thermometer 79°.

From Wednesday 18th to Thursday 19th May 1791

64¼

At sun-set, we were surrounded by frigate birds, gulls, grey gulls and tropic birds of both species, one with a white tail and the other with a red tail*, boobies and sheerwaters. I observed at this time all the birds to be on the wing towards the NE, notwithstanding that no neighbouring land was known in that direction.

At 9 o'clock PM, the wind veering to NW, we tacked and stood to the NE.

During the morning, the wind blew by light gusts from the SW quarter with cloudy weather.

By several azimuths, we found the variation of the needle Northeasterly 6° 8'.

Latitude by reckoning 25° 27' W.
Longitude by observation 105° 38' W.
Longitude by our observation 107° 52' S.

Réaumur's Thermometer +19°, Fahrenheit's thermometer 75°.
*Mr de Buffon names this last species of tropic bird, the Red Shafted Tropic bird[91] or Isle of France Tropic bird.

From Thursday 19th to Friday 20th May 1791

57¼

Until midnight, we had light winds varring from W to E, round by the South with squalls, the wind then settled at NNE and blew a light breeze with clear weather and a great swell at SW.

In the afternoon, we had seen bonitos but had not managed to take any one of them, notwithstanding the industry of our fishers.

91 *The Red-Shafted Tropic Bird. The two long shafts of the tail are of the same red with the bill; the rest of the plumage is white, except some black spots on the wing near the back, and a black horse-shoe which environs the eye* (Buffon, op. cit., Volume VIII, pp. 323–324).

The variation of magnetic needle determined from six sets of azimuths was 5° 48°.

I observed a petrel of a new species of which the description is nowhere to be found. It was twice the size thereabout of the stormy petrel and was like it in all particulars. The back was of a smoky colour and the belly, of a very dark grey. There was a very marked white line on both wings, two fingers in breadth, which made it very pretty. I believe this species to be uncommon for we caught sight of but two or three of them.

Latitude by observation 24° 47' S.
Longitude by observation 106° 23' W.
Longitude by reckoning 108° 37' W.

Réaumur's Thermometer +21½°, Fahrenheit's thermometer 80°.

From Friday 20ᵗʰ May to Saturday 21ˢᵗ May 1791

84¼

During the whole of this day, the wind varied from North to NE¼N blowing a gentle gale, attended with a smooth sea though we had a long swell from WSW.

We got sight of the first flying fish.

We saw but few birds save some few frigate birds and sheerwaters.

By the mean result of four azimuths and the morning amplitude, the variation of the magnetic needle was found to be 6° 41' Northeasterly.

Latitude by observation 24° 6' S.
Longitude by observation 107° 40' W.
Longitude by reckoning 109° 54' W.

6' more to the South than by reckoning.
Réaumur's Thermometer +22½°, Fahrenheit's thermometer 82°.

From Saturday 21ˢᵗ to Sunday 22ⁿᵈ May 1791

26

This day we had light airs which varied from NNE to NNW and calm.

During the morning, I took the opportunity of the calm to hoist out the yawl and scrub the sides of the ship clean of seaweed at the water line.

By 19 azimuths and the amplitudes, taken by different compasses, we found the variation of the compass to be 6° 26' NE.

Latitude by observation 23° 59' S.
Longitude by observation 108° 7' W.
Longitude by reckoning 110° 21' W.

Réaumur's Thermometer +23°, Fahrenheit's thermometer 83°.
We saw only a few sheerwaters.

From Sunday 22ⁿᵈ to Monday 23ʳᵈ May

68¾

We had near calm and variable winds until midnight. They then settled at East blowing gentle gales attended with clear weather and a smooth sea. With this wind in our favour, we steered NW¼N under all courses with the top-gallant mast studding sails set in order to gain ground to the Northward and get within reach of breezes which blow more fresh and are more settled.

We took two tunny fish and one bonito. In their stomachs we found flying fish and a species of fish which was long and thin and of a silver colour. I served tunny fish to the people. We saw sheerwaters, tropic birds and numerous flying fish.

Our longitude determined from six sets of observations of five distances each of the sun and the moon, taken in the morning and reduced to 8h 31' 22" AM, was 111° 45' 30". The longitude determined from our last observations, reduced to this time, was found to be only 108° 36', which was a proof that a current had carried us to Westward. Such a great difference in nine days cannot be accounted for by an error in the reckoning, which had been effected with the greatest attention. The longitude by reckoning from Staten's Land was 110° 50'.

At 7 o'clock in the morning, we crossed the Tropic of Capricorn, longitude 111° 37' W.

During the morning, we got up the spare sails and canvas to air them. We immediately set to repair some few sails found to be full of holes made by the rats.

The variation of the compass determined from amplitudes and azimuths was 5° 40' NE.

Latitude by observation 23° 5' S.
Longitude by observation 111° 56' W.
Longitude by reckoning 111° 1' W.

In this position, Easter Island bore South of the globe, distant 72 leagues.
Réaumur's Thermometer +24°, Fahrenheit's thermometer 85°.
The mercury in the thermometers stood so high that the air must have been very hot, however it was cool.

From Monday 23ʳᵈ to Tuesday 24ᵗʰ May 1791

108¾

Upon the most mature deliberation, and on the advice of my officers who were all of the same opinion, I resolved to gain a port, prior to our arrival on the coast of NW America. The reasons which decided us are as follows.

1. The sailing since La Praya had been long and hard.
2. All our water was found to be spoilt and very unpleasant to drink, in spite of the airing and the oils of which we had been making use in order to purify

it. I was under the fear of some diseases which it might cause and it was the opinion of the surgeons that it might prove fatal to the people.

3. Except 30 hens reserved for the sick, no more fresh provisions remained on board. It was impossible moreover to procure provisions on the coast of America and consequently, in order to supply ourselves with them, a delay five months at least would be necessary, that is upon our return to the Sandwich Isles after our departure from the coast.

We resolved for all these reasons to gain a port. There was no choice left to us but the Sandwich Isles or the Marquesas de Mendoça. We chose the last. The first, which were situated in longitude 158 or 159°, were quite out of our route. The Marquesas, lying in 141° thereabout, did not occasion the same inconvenience and fell in with the route we were taking. My intention was to cross the line in the longitude of 140° W in order to avoid the calms which diverse navigators have met with in crossing more to the East, and to avoid a current which carries to the East towards the Gulf of Panama. Though the people were at this moment in tolerable health on account of the care I have attended to it, I saw them to be weary of so long a voyage. The seamen shared a general joy on learning that we were to put in for water which we could no longer drink without extreme aversion.

I was convinced that on our arrival on the coast of America with our stock of water nearly complete, I would busy myself with nothing but trade, and would for the rest, regain the so short a time I would stay in the Marquesas.

It is known by all that the scurvy makes its appearance principally between the Tropics and following a long voyage. During the stay in the Marquesas, I hoped to prevent the effects of such cruel a disease with fresh water and all the refreshments which could be had there.

Remainder of 23rd to 24th May 1791

During this day, the breeze varied from East to North East and blew a gentle gale with cloudy weather.

During the morning, I observed ten sets of five distances each of the sun and the moon in order to determine our longitude. All these observations reduced to 10h 2' AM, gave the mean result of longitude 113° 34' W.

Messrs Masse observed two sets	112° 24' 30".
Chanal, eight sets	113° 30'.
Marchand the younger, by two *ditto*	112° 51'.
Infernet, one,	113°
Murat, *ditto*	112° 58'

The variation of the compass determined from amplitudes and azimuths was 5° 26' NE.

We saw tropic birds and numerous flying fish.

Latitude by observation 21° 54' S.
Longitude by observation 113° 41' W.
Longitude by reckoning 112° 58' W.

10' more to the South than by reckoning.
Réaumur's Thermometer +23½°, Fahrenheit's thermometer 84°.

From Tuesday 24ᵗʰ to Wednesday 25ᵗʰ May 1791

86½

The breeze was variable from NE¼E to SE, blowing more or less fresh, with squalls at intervals.

The variation of the compass deduced from azimuths and amplitudes was 24° 52' NE.

By the observation of three sets of distances of the moon and the sun, reduced to 8h 34' 6", our longitude was 114° 38' W. By two sets of Antares and the moon, reduced to the same time, it was 115°. Mean result 114° 49'.

The observations made two days before, reduced to this instance, put us in 114° 4', and those of the preceding day, in 114° 49.

It is clear to see that these observations put us daily more to the Westward and that the ship had been affected by a current and carried in this direction, that is to say more to the WSW, for in the last few days we had had differences to the Southward.

Messers Masse, by two distances of the moon and the ☉ had observed	114° 39'.
Chanal, Stars and the sun, *ditto*	114° 49'.
Marchand the younger, and the sun	114° 56'.
Murat, *ditto*	114° 52'
Infernet, *ditto*	115° 1'.

The sailmakers were employed in finishing the sails for the longboats and boats and in reducing the top-sails, for they were a little too large on account of the stretching of the canvas.

Latitude by observation 21° 3' S.
Longitude by observation 114° 57' W.
Longitude by reckoning 113° 6' W.

14' more to the South than by reckoning.
Réaumur's Thermometer +24°, Fahrenheit's thermometer 85°.

From Wednesday 25th to Thursday 26th May 1791

50

The breeze was light at SE during this day, attended with fine weather and a smooth sea.

We saw some few tropic birds and sea swallows which were exactly like our Martins.

By the mean result of 17 azimuths and some amplitudes, the variation of the magnetic needle was found to be 5° 41' NE.

At 8h 12' 44" AM, by two sets of observations of the distance of the moon and the sun, our longitude was 115° 32' 15" NE.

This differed from the longitude determined from the observations of the preceding day by only 8' West.

Latitude by observation 20° 22' S.
Longitude by observation 115° 38' W.
Longitude by reckoning 113° 40' W.

3' more to the South than by reckoning.
Réaumur's Thermometer +24½°, Fahrenheit's thermometer 86°.

From Thursday 26th to Friday 27th May 1791

70¾

The light breeze continued and varied from SE to East. So smooth was the surface of the water that we appeared to be sailing on a pond rather than on so vast a sea.

The tropic birds and the swallows followed us constantly. By the mean result of 17 azimuths, the variation of the magnetic needle was found to be 5° 11' Northeasterly. The observations had been made with three different compasses and differed very little between them.

At 4h 36' 8" AM, our longitude was 116° 20', determined from two sets of observations of five distances each of α in Aquilae and the moon, reduced to 7h 40' 50" AM. By two other sets of the moon and the sun, reduced to the same time, it was found to be 116° 26'. Mean result 116° 23'.

The observations of the preceding day, allowing for the ship's run, put us in 116° 15'. Hence I concluded that we had no more current for there was no difference neither to the West nor to the South.

I concluded that so great an agreement between 50 observations of the ☉-☾ made during this lunation, set together with those observations of the moon and the stars, was a proof that the longitude could hardly be determined better and that it must be very near true.

Latitude by observation 19° 34' S.
Longitude by observation 116° 34' W.
Longitude by reckoning 114° 28' W.

Réaumur's Thermometer +23°, Fahrenheit's thermometer 83°.

From Friday 27ᵗʰ to Saturday 28ᵗʰ May 1791

17

In the afternoon I shot a tropic bird and as the ship was making very little progress, I sent the boat out to take it. It was found to be of the species named by Mr de Buffon the Red Shafted Tropic Bird or Isle of France Tropic Bird. As this learned naturalist has not given us a minute description of this bird, it will here perhaps be of some use.[92]

This tropic bird was like a very large pigeon in size but it was of a more striking appearance. The plumage and the belly were white in colour with tints of a pale flesh colour in places. The quill feathers of the first articulation of the wings nearest the body, were black in colour throughout their length and white at the extremities of the webs. All the shafts of the remaining quills, of the tail or of the wings, were absolutely black, which made for a plumage which was agreeably variegated. The two shafts, whence its name, was one 13 inches in length, and the other 11. At the extremities, the webs were naked and narrow and of a deep red colour, attached to each side of a black shaft, which was three and half feet in length. From the tip of the bill to the tip of the tail, and not accounting for the two shafts just described, it was 15 inches long. The bill was of a beautiful coral red and two inches and eight lines long. It was very thick and very hard, indented on the edges and slightly convex throughout. The eyes are very black and jut out and are inclosed by small black feathers. The nostrils on each side of the upper mandible, two lines from the root, were formed of a membrane of a bluish tint. The feet intirely palmated had four toes of which the interior one was very small. The feet and legs were grey and the membrane which connected the toes was of a bright black colour.

We had calms and light gusts of wind with clear weather.

---

92 Buffon decribes the "generic" Tropic Bird and then devotes a few paragraphs to the three types he identifies, that is the Little Tropic Bird, the Great Tropic Bird and the Red-Shafted Tropic Bird. This latter is only briefly described, as Marchand points out: *The two long shafts of the tail are of the same red with the bill; the rest of the plumage is white, except fome black spots on the wing near the back, and a black horse-shoe which environs the eye. The Viscount de Querhoent was so obliging as to communicate the following note on this bird, which he observed at the Isle of France. 'The Red-Shafted Tropic Bird breeds in this island, as well as the common Tropic bird; the latter in the hollow trees of the principal island, the former in the cavities of the small neighbouring islets. The Red-Shafted Tropic Bird is scarce ever seen on land and, except in the season of courtship, the common Tropic bird seldom comes ashore. They live by fishing at large, and come to repose on the small isle of Coin de Mire, which is two leagues from the Isle of France, and is the haunt of many other sea birds. It was in September and October that I found the nests of the Tropic birds: each contained only two eggs of a yellowish white, marked with rusty spots. I was assured, that no more than one egg is found in the nest of the Great Tropic bird: and none of the species seem to be numerous.' None of these species or varieties, which we have just described, appears attached to any particular spot; often the two first or the two last are found together and the Viscount de Querhoent says, that he saw all the three collected at the island of Ascension* (op. cit., Volume VIII, pp. 323–325).

The variation of the magnetic needle determined from 9 azimuths and the amplitudes was 5° 40' NE.

There is reason to believe that the variation of the needle is not subject to great change in the part of the sea, for in 1774, being in this same position, Mr Cook found it to be 3° 4' NE.[93] He had departed from Easter Island and was bound for the Marquesas.

Latitude by observation 19° 21' S.
Longitude by observation 116° 46' W.
Longitude by reckoning 114° 40' W.

Réaumur's Thermometer +24°, Fahrenheit's thermometer 85°.

From Saturday 28th to Sunday 29th May 1791

71½

During this day, the breeze was light at first and then strengthened to a light gale at NE and N. We had a great swell during the night.

The variation of the compass by observation of the amplitudes was NE 5° 32'.

We took two bonitos. After having eaten of them, we were almost all taken ill. Some were attacked by a bilious disorder and others by vomiting. I was amongst the last. I could attribute this effect to nothing but the bad quality of the fish, for the quantity we had eaten could certainly not account for the disorder. I had seen such an accident with my own eyes in the island of St Helena, where a great quantity of this kind of fish is caught. All who had eaten of the fish were out of order. Several were subject to vomiting and others were covered with numerous small red spots on the skin.

Latitude by observation 18° 46' S.
Longitude by observation 117° 50' W.
Longitude by reckoning 115° 44' W.

Réaumur's Thermometer +22°, Fahrenheit's thermometer 81°.
We saw a frigate bird, tropic birds, sheerwaters and many flying fish.

---

93 *After leaving Easter Island, I steered N.W. by N and N.N.W., with a fine Easterly gale, intending to touch at the Marquesas, if I met with nothing before I got there* [. . .] *On the 22nd, being in the latitude of 19° 20' South, longitude 114° 44' West, steered N.W. Since leaving Easter Island, the variation had not been more than 3° 4', nor less than 2° 32' East; but on the 26th, in latitude 15° 17' South, longitude 119° 45' West, it was no more than 1° 1' East; after which it began to increase* (Voyage to the South Pole, op. cit., Volume 1, p. 297).

From Sunday 29ᵗʰ to Monday 30ᵗʰ May 1791

84¼

During the afternoon, the horizon became dark and fixed with thick clouds to the NE and W, round by N, with lightning which foretold of hard winds. At 7 o'clock PM indeed, a squall obliged us to loosen the top-sails, the wind at NW shifted suddenly to W¼NW and began to blow a hard gale.

We tacked and stood to the North under close-reefed top-sails and the four main courses.

During the remainder of the day, the winds varied continually from N¼NW to WNW. We kept the most advantageous boards.

I confess I did not expect to have winds so little settled as those we had met with for some little time in this latitude, where near but all navigators have got the fixed trade wind. I was vexed to see that these disagreements would greatly delay our arrival on the coast of America, and without good fortune we would have difficulty in opening an advantageous trade this year.

We took a bonito.

Latitude by observation 19° 7' S.
Longitude by observation 118° 47' W.
Longitude by reckoning 116° 41' W.

Thermometer +24° of Réaumur, Fahrenheit's thermometer 85°.

From Monday 30ᵗʰ to Tuesday 31ˢᵗ May 1791

51¾

During this day, the winds varied from NNW to WSW blowing in near continual squalls with intervals of calm.

At 7 o'clock in the morning, a squall in the West, round by North and then to the South, had the most violent appearance but it gave only little wind and pouring rain.

We had several great swells and the dashing of one against the other made a chopping sea.

We continued to see tropic birds and sheerwaters.

The variation of the compass by reckoning was 5° NE.

Latitude by observation 18° 36' S.
Longitude by observation 118° 34' W.
Longitude by reckoning 116° 28' W.

5' more to the North than by reckoning.
Thermometer +23° of Réaumur, Fahrenheit's thermometer 83°

From Tuesday 31ˢᵗ to Wednesday 1ˢᵗ June 1791

32½

During the whole of this day, we had variable lights gusts attended with rain and suffocating heat.

We had now nothing more than a very long swell from the SW.

We saw many porpoises whose bellies were all of a beautiful flesh colour.

The variation of the compass by reckoning was 5° NE.

Latitude by observation 18° 6' S.
Longitude by observation 118° 40' W.
Longitude by reckoning 116° 34' W.

5' more to the North than by reckoning.
Réamur's Thermometer +21°, Fahrenheit's thermometer 79°.

From Wednesday 1ˢᵗ to Thursday 2ⁿᵈ June 1791

29½

During the whole of the afternoon, we had very heavy rain. With the stock of water, I obliged the people to wash their clothes for I believed this to be better than washing them with seawater which never dries well and keeps the clothes humid, which is apt to make the people sick

We saw bonitos but as the ship was making so little progress we were unable to take any.

We had calms and light winds which were succeeded at 10 o'clock by a fresh breeze at SSW, we set all our sails forthwith and directed our course NW¼N in order to get the trade wind sooner.

By the mean result of seven azimuths, the variation of the compass was found to be 4° 50' NE.

Between each meal I served the people with the beer we had made on board with wort. Mr Cook has fully explained in the accounts of his different voyages the manner in which the beer is made and it is I believe needless to repeat the same here.[94] It is enough to observe that this skilful navigator has made it known

94 In the published account of Cook's voyage and in the Hotel de Thou French version (Tome IV), Cook's thoughts on how to ensure the good health of ship's crew were relayed by Sir John Pringle, President of the Royal Society from 1772–1778, in the form of a Discourse. Sir Pringle's account of Cook's method is taken from Cook's own paper, *The Method Taken for preserving the Health of the Crew of his Majety's Ship the Resolution during her late Voyage round the World. By Captain James Cook, F.R.S. Addressed to Sir John Pringle, Bart. F.R.S.* published in the *Philosophical Transactions*, 1ˢᵗ January 1776, pp. 402–406. In his presentation Cook discusses the effectiveness of certain remedies including wort: *We had on board a large quantity of malt, of which was made sweet-wort and given (not only to those men who had manifest symptoms of the scurvy, but to such also as were, from circulstances, judged to be most liable to that disorder) from one to two or three*

by way of experiments, which have been repeated, that it is one of the most highly antiscorbutic articles to be found.

Latitude by observation 17° 36' S.
Longitude by observation 118° 46' W.
Longitude by reckoning 116° 40' W.

3' more to the North than by reckoning.
Réaumur's thermometer +21°, Fahrenheit's thermometer 79°

From Thursday 2nd to Friday 3rd June 1791

135

The wind veered at SSE from SSW, blowing a fresh gale and then a steady breeze attended with grey weather making ready to rain. The sea running high from the SW until now, abated by little and little.

I hoped now we had got in with the trade wind at last and at 5 o'clock PM we directed our course North West to fall in with the Marqueses as early as possible. We saw tropic birds, sheerwaters and many flying fish. We also got sight of a dolphin, the first we had seen in these seas.

Latitude by observation 15° 48' S.
Longitude by observation 120° 13' W.
Longitude by reckoning 118° 7' W.

Réaumur's thermometer +21½°, Fahrenheit's thermometer 80°.

From Friday 3rd to Saturday 4th June 1791

163¼

At noon, we steered NW¼W. We had a steady breeze at SE¼S during the whole of this day with pleasant weather.

We set all our sails with the top-gallant mast studding sails.

By the mean result of 12 azimuths, the variation of the compass was determined to be 3° 10' NE.

Latitude by observation 14° 13' S.
Longitude by observation 122° 26' W.
Longitude by reckoning 120° 20' W.

4' more to the South than by reckoning.
Réaumur's thermometer +23°, Fahrenheit's thermometer 84°.

---

pints in the day to each man, or in such proportion as the surgon thought necessary [. . .] This is without doubt one of the best antiscorbutic sea-medecines yet found out . . .

From Saturday 4ᵗʰ to Sunday 5ᵗʰ June 1791

150¾

At noon we directed our course WNW.

The breeze continued fresh at SE and ESE attended with cloudy weather at intervals.

Several flying fish pursued by bonitos threw themselves upon the deck of the ship. We should have desired such accidents to occur more frequently for we had nothing more than salted beef left to eat. To render the fish more wholesome, we dressed it with sauerkraut, or greens in vinegar.

The variation of the compass by 17 azimuths was found to be 2° 43' NE.

Latitude by observation 13° 12' S.
Longitude by observation 124° 45' W.
Longitude by reckoning 122° 39' W.

Réaumur's thermometer +24½°, Fahrenheit's thermometer 86°.

Monday 6ᵗʰ to Tuesday 7ᵗʰ June 1791

138

The very fresh breeze of wind continued at ESE.

By five sets of five distances each of the moon and the sun, all reduced to 4h 22' 48' PM, I found our longitude to be W 127° 44'. By two more sets of Spica Virginis and the moon in the evening, reduced to the same moment, it was 127° 29'. Mean result 127° 36' 30".

The longitude, determined from our last observations, was found to be 127° 20'.

Messers Masse ☉-☾ observed	127° 43'.
Chanal ☉-☾ and ☾-*	127° 33'.
Marchand the younger ☉-☾	127° 19'.
Infernet ☉-☾	128° 15'.
Murat ☉-☾	127° 13' 30".

It would be an act of injustice not to give my officers their due. There was none amongst them who did not observe the distances very exactly in order to determine the longitude.

We saw tropic birds, grey gulls and sheerwaters.

By 17 azimuths, the variation of the compass was NE 4° 3'.

Latitude by observation 11° 12' S.
Longitude by observation 129° 24' W.
Longitude by reckoning 127° 2' W.

Réaumur's thermometer +24½°, Fahrenheit's thermometer 86°.

From Tuesday 7ᵗʰ to Wednesday 8ᵗʰ June 1791

123

During this day, the breeze continued light at ESE. A seamen named Paul Auguste fell sick. The Surgeon thought him to be attacked by an obstruction of the liver. It must be said that he was very pale when he came aboard at Marseilles and since then he had been attacked with some slight fevers. I had remarked also that he nearly never slept.

By the mean result of four sets of distances of the moon and the sun, reduced to 3h 20' 33" PM, I found the longitude to be W 129° 42' which is nearly the same as that determined by observations the day before, taking into account the distance sailed Westward.

Messers Masse found it to be	130° 5'.
Chanal to be	129° 40'.
Marchand the younger to be	129° 58'.
Infernet to be	128° 52'.
Murat to be	129° 29'.

The coopers were employed in setting up the casks, which we had put in frame, in order to have them ready upon our arrival in the Marquesas, where I wished to remain as short a time as possible.

By 7 azimuths and by the Easterly amplitude, we found the variation of the magnetic needle to be 4° 37' NE.

Latitude by observation 10° 18' S.
Longitude by observation 131° 17' W.
Longitude by reckoning 128° 52' W.

Réaumur's thermometer +25°, Fahrenheit's thermometer 87°

From Wednesday 8ᵗʰ to Thursday 9ᵗʰ June 1791

119

At noon, I gave orders to steer W¼NW.

We had a light breeze which varied from ESE to SSE attended with cloudy weather.

We saw tropic birds, sea swallows or gulls of several kinds. We saw petrels which have a white stripe on each wing and of which I have already spoken of in another place – I called them Great Stormy Petrels.

At 3h 2' 27" PM, by the mean result of four sets of observations of the distances of the ☉-☾, I found our longitude to be 131° 35'. By two others sets of observations, made in the evening, of Spica Virginis and the moon, reduced to the same moment, it was 131° 11'. Mean result 131° 23'.

The longitude deduced from the observations of the preceding day, was found to be 131° 31'.

Messers Chanal ☉-☾ and ☾-*ob[ed]	131° 21'.
Chanal ☉-☾	131° 21'.
Marchand the younger ☉-☾	131° 10'.
Infernet ☉-☾	130° 58'.
Murat ☉-☾	130° 38'.

By the mean result of 19 azimuths and the amplitudes, the variation of the needle was found to be 4° 52' NE. I believe I have said in another place that the variation does not seem to be subject to great change in this space of the sea for in 1774, being in this same position, Mr Cook had found it to be 4° 40'NE.

In the morning we bent the cables to the anchors.

Latitude by observation 9° 47' S.
Longitude by observation 133° 5' W.
Longitude by reckoning 130° 56' W.

Réaumur's thermometer +25°, Fahrenheit's thermometer 87°.

The latitude we kept to being that of the North point of St Christina (one of the isles of the Marquesas), I directed our course W½S.

From Thursday 9th to Friday 10th June 1791

112½

This day, we had a light breeze whch varied from E to SE, attended with fine and pleasant weather.

We got sight of the same birds as the day before. We also saw frigate birds notwithstanding what may be read in the *Nouveaux Voyages aux Iles d'Amérique* by Père Labat,[95] an author who abounds more in quantity than in truth, that this bird is to be found four hundred leagues from land, nothing is however more false. During the course of my navigations both to America and to India, I have observed it with the greatest attention and I have never met with it more than two hundred leagues in the offing, and most frequently at less than a hundred and fifty.

---

95 *Nouveau voyage aux isles de l'Amérique, contenant l'histoire naturelle de ces pays, l'origine, les moeurs, la religion et le gouvernement des habitans anciens et modernes, les guerres et les événemens singuliers qui y sont arrivez . . . le commerce et les manufactures qui y sont établies . . . ouvrage enrichi de plus de cent cartes, plans et figures en taille-douce,* Jean-Baptiste Labat, P. Husson, 1724 (Volume VI, p. 394): *Il n'y a pas d'oiseau au monde qui vole plus haut, plus longtems, plus aisément, & qui s'éloigne plus des terres que celui que je vais decrire [. . .] on trouve cet oiseau au milieu des mers, à trois ou quatre cens lieües de la terre . . .* Lebat goes on to provide a detailed description of the *fregate* in question.

Of all the equatorial birds, the bird whose flight is the most rapid and the most vigorous and which we see farthest in the offing, is the tropic bird for I have seen them fluttering about the ship frequently, four hundred leagues from land.

The variation of the compass determined by 10 azimuths was NE 5° 38'.

Latitude by observation 9° 47' S.
Longitude by observation 134° 59' W.
Longitude by reckoning 132° 50' W.

Réaumur's thermometer +23½°, 84 Fahrenheit's thermometer 84°.

From Friday 10ᵗʰ to Saturday 11ᵗʰ June 1781 (1791)

109

During the afternoon, Mr Chanal and myself observed eight sets of five distances each of the sun and the moon, and in the evening we observed also two sets of the moon and Regulus, and two of the moon and Antares, which were all set together. When all reduced to 4h 45' 34" PM, we obtained the results as follows:

Mr Chanal 1ˢᵗ Observation ☉-☾	136° 20'.
2 *ditto*	136° 21' 15".
3 *ditto*	136° 9' 15".
4 *ditto*	136° 9' 30".
5 of the moon and Regulus	136° 42' 45".
6 of the moon and Antares	136° 46' 45".
Myself 1ˢᵗ ☉-☾	136° 26' 45".
2 *ditto*	136° 34' 15".
3 *ditto*	135° 41' 45".
4 *ditto*	136° 20' 15".
5 of the moon and Regulus	136° 8'.
6 of the moon and Antares	135° 54' 30".
Mean result	136° 12' 55".

Our longitude, determined from observations made two days before, was found at this moment to be 135° 20'. As it is near impossible to doubt the truth of such numerous observations set together, made with the greatest attention and computed with utmost care, it may be concluded that there was a current which had carried us 52' West in two days, of which we became convinced upon touching at the Marquesas.

We saw during this day, frigate birds, tropic birds, swallows and gulls of several species, small white gulls and bonitos. I observed also a species of flying fish which to my knowledge no navigator has ever before seen.*

*When I wrote this passage, it was unknown to me that Mr de Bougainville had seen the same in his *Voyage around the world*, 2ⁿᵈ edition, Tome 2, p. 162.

Instead of possessing two wings, as is generally the case, this fish had four, two on the side of its head and two more very near to the tail. What induced me to notice it was that the body and the wings were of a fine red colour. I had at a later date an opportunity of seeing many of this kind, which I think are indigenous to this sea.

During the morning, we got four guns out of the hold and mounted them on the deck, we bent the cable to a third anchor and brought it to the cathead.

During this day we passed the uncertain position ascribed to the Marquesas in the chart of Mr Bellin. It is astonishing to see that we do not possess a chart of the Pacific Ocean after the new discoveries, though we pretend to have, and truly do have, the best of charts for all the other seas.

Latitude by observation 9° 59' S.
Longitude by observation 137° 41' 30" W.
Longitude by reckoning 134° 40' W.

10' more to the South than by reckoning.
Réaumur's thermometer +25°, Fahrenheit's thermometer 86°.

From Saturday 11ᵗʰ to Sunday 12ᵗʰ June 1791

99¾

At noon, I directed the course to W.

During this day, we had a light breeze variable from ESE to ENE, attended with grey and stormy weather which I believe was occasioned by the nearness of the land. We saw an infinite number of birds.

Though at 8 o'clock in the evening the longitude by observation put us at a distance of 59 leagues from the Marquesas, being careful of a difference West and the very dirty weather, precaution was taken to take in the studding sails. We had set them day and night until this moment, notwithstanding running over seas which the most famous navigators have seldom visited. At 4 o'clock AM, we once again set the studding sails. This day experienced excessive heat.

By three sets of five azimuths, each taken with different compasses, we found the variation of the magnetic needle to be 5° 42' NE.

At 10 o'clock in the morning, we caught sight of an extremely high island bearing SW, distant about 17 leagues, towards which immediately directed our course though I was very certain that it was La Magdalena,[96] which was confirmed at

---

96 Fatu Hiva today. Cook's first sight of the Marquesas was on the 6ᵗʰ April 1774: *I continued to steer to the West till the 6ᵗʰ, at four in the afternoon, at which time, being in the latitude of 90° 20' longitude 138° 14' West, we discovered an island, bearing West by South, distant about nine leagues. Two hours after we saw another, bearing S. W. by S., which appeared more extensive than the former. I hauled up for this island, and ran under an easy sail all night, having squally unsettled rainy weather, which is not very uncommon in this sea, when near high land. At six o'clock the next morning, the first island*

noon for the latitude by observation was 9° 59'. Our longitude deduced from the observations made the day before was found to be at this time 139° 19' 30", and the reckoning from Staten's Land to be 136° 18'. That which was given by the chart of Mr Cook, according to the bearings, put us in 140° 33' 30', which was a proof that the ship had been carried 1° 14' West by a current (as was noticed in the last observations we had made) in 42 hours. The longitude by reckoning was found to be E 4° 15' 30".

Réaumur's thermometer +26°, Fahrenheit's thermometer 88°.

From Sunday 12ᵗʰ to Monday 13ᵗʰ June 1791

At noon, La Magdalena bore SW distant 14 leagues, I steered WNW in order to observe the situation of the Isle of St Pedro which we caught sight of very distinctly half of an hour after. It stretched from NW¼W to WNW, distant 9 leagues thereabouts. At 1 o'clock, we saw the East point of La Dominica bearing NW.

We continued to steer WNW and W¼NW with a fine breeze from East until half past 5 in the evening, at which time the middle of Isle of San Pedro bore WNW, distant 3 leagues.

The middle of the Isle of La Magdalena South 3° W.
The East point of La Dominica NNW 3° W.
The channel which divides La Dominica and Santa Christina WNW 4° N.

The island which Mr Cook named Hood's Island[97], is I believe the one which Mendana named Mendoça Island, NNW.

We saw nothing but the highest mountains of Santa Christina, which lay in the same direction as San Pedro. I must do Mr Cook justice for his little chart of these isles which is as exact as can be, for I took fifty or more bearings in different positions and could find no error at all.

The weather becoming very dark at six o'clock in the evening I hauled our wind to SE under the top-sails. At 8 o'clock, the weather clearing and observing that it would prove difficult to come to anchor the next day in the bay of Madre de Dios (Isle of Santa Christina) if I remained abreast all through the night, I resolved to

---

bore N.W., the second S.W.W., and a third W. I gave orders to steer for the separation between the two last; and soon after, a fourth was seen, still more to the West. By this time, we were well assured that these were the Marquesas, discovered by Mendana in 1595. The first island was a new discovery, which I named Hood's Island after the young gentleman who first saw it. The second was that of Saint Pedro, the third La Dominica and the fourth, St Christina (Voyage to the South Pole, op. cit., Volume 1, p. 298). On Tuesday 12ᵗʰ April, Cook leaves the Marquesas and sees La Magdalena from a distance: *At five o'clock in the P.M. Resolution Bay bore E.N.E. ½ E. distant five leagues, and the island Magdalena S.E., about nine leagues distant. This was the only sight we had of this isle* (op. cit., p. 306). Cook uses both spellings, that is Magdalena and Magdelena.

97 See above.

sail onward under the top-sails and to sound continually. After about three leagues WSW, at ¼ past ten o'clock, we found suddenly only 12 fathoms over a rocky bottom, whereas one minute before we had no bottom with 30 fathoms of line. We immediately put the shore on the larboard hand, hauling our wind and sounding. We found 30 fathoms by little and little from 12 fathoms. After making two leagues SSE we had no bottom with 60 fathoms of line. On finding so unexpected a bottom, I took forthwith the bearings of the SE part of San Pedro and found it to be situated NNW distant about one and a ½ leagues, and in such a manner that this point, or I say bank, stretches about 3½ leagues SSW. I do not believe it to be dangerous but the bottom is very much unequal for we found 12, 12, 15, 18 and 30 fathoms successively. As no other navigator had passed South of Santa Christina and San Pedro, fearing to meet with the shoals, I set the anchors all clear in order to be ready to come to anchor if the water continued to decrease in its depth.

At ½ past 1 o'clock AM, we steered once again for the South point of Santa Christina which was very distinctly to be seen to the West of us, we sounded continually. At four o'clock we were but two leagues from it, we brought to once more. At day-light, we steered for it, all sails set, with a gentle breeze at ENE and at E.

At ¼ past 6 o'clock, the middle of La Magdalena bore SE 3° S. the middle of San Pedro NE and the South point of Santa Christina WNW, distant 2 leagues. When we were within the latter point (it was then 8 o'clock), we caught sight of several double canoes steering leeward, very close to the coast. I displayed the new French colours[98], and congratulated myself on being the first navigator to fly in this vast ocean these colours, an emblem of the liberty we had just but gained. I looked however at this same moment to my native country and was moved to pity for we had left it not intirely free from confusion.

I also had hoisted a small white flag at the top of the main mast as a sign of our friendly disposition.

Though we directed our course towards the canoes, making signs of friendship and showing to them nails, mirrors, etc., they never came near us. In all appearance, they remembered still Captain Cook who ordered musquet balls to be fired at them in 1774.[99] What followed convinced me of this for they repeated often

---

98 On the 21st and 24th October 1790, the Constituent Assembly voted in the new French flag. Fleurieu (Minister of the Navy – *Ministre de la Marine*) in December 1790, issues instructions which directs the Eastern sea ports to fly the new ensign which was made up of blue, white and red vertical bands on a white background.

99 Cook's first encounters with the islanders were fraught and ended in bloodshed. Cook anchors in Resoluton Bay (Port Madre de Dios), at St Christina, on the 7th April 1774: *This was no sooner done than about thirty or forty of the natives came off to us in ten or twelve canoes; but it required some address to get them along-side. At last a hatchet, and some spike-nails, induced the people in one canoe to come under the quarter-gallery: after which all the others put along-side, and having exchanged some bread-fruit, and fish, for small nails, &tc. retired ashore, the sun already being set. We observed a heap of stones in the bow of each canoe, and every man to have a sling tied around his head.*

Toute, Pouhi, Matté. The first signifies Cook, which they cannot pronounce better, the second is some allusion to the sound of our firearms, for they name them in no other way than this, and the third means killed, dead or hurt.

Monday 13th to Tuesday 14th June

During the afternoon we had sudden gusts of wind and calms which prevented our nearing the bay of Madre de Dios, which I had observed attentively after the descriptions of Mindina, Cook and Forster, and after the descriptions taken down by Mr Chanal, who had been sent in the longboat, armed, to look for it.

I was finally successful in convincing the natives to put along-side the quarter of the ship, where after giving them nails, they came on board, though shaking. In order to remove their fears, I touched my nose to theirs, according to the customs of the country, and we became the greatest of friends. To a few amongst them, I gave some trifles by way of present, looking glasses and nails gave them the greatest pleasure. They never tired of looking at themselves in the looking glass, turning this way and then that way, as monkeys would do. They gave us all the fish they had and a few cocoa-nuts and also bread-fruit.

Upon the boat making a signal to us, I ordered the English colours to be hoisted at the fore-mast in order to indicate that we had seen it. When the Indians who were aboard discovered it, they became fearful and timid. They pointed to it and saying amongst themselves Touti, Pouh, Matté. They remembered yet the colours of Mr Cook, for it is true to say that it is most difficult to forget any harm done us above all when we are convinced that it is not deserved.

At ½ past 4 o'clock in the evening, the boat returned. The calm and the currents had carried us into the offing and I lost all hope of coming to anchor that day. But near to 7 o'clock in the evening, the wind blowing a steady gentle gale

---

Very early next morning, the natives visted us again, in much greater numbers than before, bringing with them bread-fruit, plaintains, and one pig, all of which they exchanged for nails, &tc. But in this traffic, they would frequently keep our goods and make no return, till at last I was obliged to fire a musquet ball over one man who had several times served us in this manner; after which they dealt more fairly, and soon after several of them came on board. At this time we were preparing to warp farther into the bay, and I was going in a boat, to look for the most convenient place to moor the ship in. Observing too many of the natives on board, I said to the officers, "You must look well after these people, or they will certainly carry off something or other." I had hardly got into the boat, before I was told they had stolen one of the iron stanchions from the opposite gang-way, and were making off with it. I ordered them to fire over the canoe till I could get round in the boat, but not to kill anyone. But the natives made too much noise for me to be heard; and the unhappy thief was killed at the third shot. Two others in the same canoe leaped over-board, but got in again just as I came to them. The stanchion they had thrown over-board. One of them, a man grown, sat bailing the blood and water out of the canoe, in a kind of hysteric laugh. The other, a youth about fourteen or fifteen years of age, looked on the deceased with a serious and dejected countenance: we had afterwards reason to believe he was his son (Voyage to the South Pole, op. cit., Volume 1, pp. 299–300).

at ENE, I once again sent the boat with Mr Chanal in command and ordered him to come to anchor with two lanterns at the head of the mast; I stood in for the bay, but having had a calm and gusts of wind at a ¼ of league in the offing, and seeing the impossibility of anchoring, I signalled for the boat to return on board, and resolved to spend the night plying to windward between Santa Dominica and Santa Christina.

At sun-set, the canoes stood in for the shore as is generally the custom of the natives of the South Sea, for they never pass a night away from their huts. If the sight of a ship, which is so new and rare a sight to them, cannot engage their attention then we may suppose that nothing is capable of doing so.[100] In the afternoon, one of the natives came on board and pronounced something like a rather long harangue, which we did not understand, but as he was holding in his hand a piece of white cloth fastened to a small stick, I supposed it to be an olive branch, in which I was not mistaken for on having it fastened to the shrouds,[101] all the natives expressed the greatest joy.

I had further occasion to see on shore the speech maker for he was a juggler and made me a present of a pig during an entertainment. He was about fifty years of age and had a long grey beard.

When the natives addressed me or talked of me, they called me *Otohou* or *Othou*, which means in their language king or chief.

During the night, which we spent plying to windward under the top-sails between Santa Dominica and Santa Christina, the wind was light and varied from ESE to NE. We sounded continually with a line of 30 fathoms but found no bottom. At day-light, we steered for the Bay of Madre de Dios* in which we came to anchor at 8 o'clock in the morning, in 30 fathoms water over a fine, clear sandy bottom.

*Mr Cook, though I know not why changed the name of this bay and called it Resolution Bay[102] after the name of his ship. As the bay had a name given to it by Mendana, why not leave it thus? This eagerness which some navigators had for changing the names of islands or bays discovered previous to them, has caused not a little confusion in the geography of the Pacific Ocean.

---

100 Here Marchand reproduces Forster's remark (the French translation of the second voyage collates both Cook and Forster's observations as mentioned above): *As soon as it was dark, the canoes retired, according to the general custom of all the nations in the South Sea we had hitherto seen, on whom the novelty of an European ship cannot prevail to wake a single night* (Forster, *A Voyage Round the World*, op. cit., Volume 2, p. 9).

101 *. . .but at first they brought their canoes close along-side, and offered us some pepper roots, which were doubtless signs of peace, as at the Society islands and Friendly Islands. After we had fastened these roots to the shrouds, they sold us a few fish in exchange for nails . . .* (Ibid., p. 8).

102 *The port of Madre de Dios, which I named Resolution Bay, is situated near the middle of the West side of St Christina, and under the highest land in the island, in latitude 9° 55'30", longitude 139° 8'40" West; and N. 15° W. From the West end of La Dominica* (*Voyage to the South Pole*, Volume 1, op. cit., p. 307).

We immediately carried an anchor into the offing with which we moored in 40 fathoms over the same bottom.**

**Bearings at anchor. The South point forming the Bay lies S 18° W. The South point of the cove at South, S 34° E. The North point of this same cove, S 54° E. The South point of the cove at North, E 14° S. The North point of this same cove, E. The North point forming the bay lies with the West point of Dominica, N 19° W. The middle of the rock which separates the two coves S 69° E.

We had much difficulty in coming to an anchor for we were surrounded by more than fifty canoes, double and simple, which all had between 3 and 12 men in them. Besides the natives in the canoes, I counted more than 600 of them swimming along-side the ship. There were as many women within the canoes as in the sea, and all asking me to permit them to come on board. Their reasons were very clear, as they made use of signs so little equivocal to express them. The men pressed me, making me understand that I had but to choose the most pleasing to me. They showed me a girl, the prettiest of them all, she was 13 or 14 years of age with a modest air and the prettiest countenance of them all, which made her as bewitching as any our pretty French girls, powdered and with their cheeks painted red. If this young Indian girl had many charms, she did not owe them to any artificial means. She was very well made and, save a piece of cloth made of the paper-mulberry which was like a fig leaf, she was perfectly naked. I am obliged to say that I saw none other with this air of modesty.

I thought myself obliged to prevent them from coming on board, but it was impossible to succeed in such an undertaking, for while driving away one from one side, four would come on board on the other, for they are nimble in climbing. Moreover, believing it would please the natives, I had given them leave to come on board. There then came to pass between decks and in all the corners of the ship, such scenes over which I must draw a veil. To imagine it, we must fancy forty or fifty young Frenchmen after a navigation of six months, surrounded by pretty women. It was certainly not the easiest of matters to keep a command of oneself.

I did not wish to trade during that day for we were too busy in other things, and the care which I considered to be necessary in order not to increase the trouble on board the ship, and to procure the quiet of which we were in need, was like to prove fatal to the inhabitants. Those who had brought off bread-fruit, cocoa-nuts and other articles, seeing that no trade was to be had, gave themselves up to occasioning much disturbance and riot. After stealing everything that was within their reach, they pelted us with cocoa-nuts, bread-fruit and pieces of wood attaining several of us. They struck even the few seamen in the boats, who complaining of them to me, asked if I intended to leave them without protection and to be killed, for I had interdicted them to attack the natives, knowing well the degree of improper excess which sailors will indulge in without punishment. I replied that this was not my intention and that a little patience was yet necessary. Notwithstanding, we had fired the great gun over their heads twice, one after the other, once with a charge of powder and then loaded with ball, in order to stop their insolence by means of our guns. But I was far from successful and I was vexed to discover that they took my calmness of mind for fear, or, that having caused no harm to any person, they did not believe us to be very formidable. They grew so daring as to come under the bow-sprit and take away with them a piece of lead from the tube of the pump, aft of the ship, and two copper rudder bands. Until then, I had considered both the fear of killing some of them and our very own protection, but one of the natives being ready to attack me with a spear, I took aim with a musket but fortunately for him, the gun miscarried. I immediately gave orders to two of the officers to fire their pieces over his head. When he heard the balls whistle past him, he retreated forthwith and the others followed his example and left us in peace. I noticed in time that the most troublesome amongst them came from the neighbouring isles.

I did not see, as did Mr Cook, the canoes laden with stones and the men with slings.[103] It is likely that the honest manner in which we had received the natives on board the preceding day had removed their fears.

From Tuesday 14th to Wednesday 15th June 1791

Around 3 o'clock in the afternoon, I went ashore in the longboat accompanied by two of the officers and six armed men to take a view of the watering place. On our arrival in the North cove,*

*in the description of the bay which is given afterwards, we see that there are two coves, one at North, and the other at South.

we were very kindly received by the natives who proposed that we should fol-low them, which we did with the guards in a very orderly fashion. When I noticed them to much crowd around us, I made a sign and they retired forthwith. If we stopped to observe something, I would mark out a circle around us in the centre of which we would stand and no man would dare to cross the line.[104] They call this

---

103 In the published account, Cook writes of slings tied around the heads of the islanders. In the translation, the slings are described as being twisted around the hands of the Marquesans: *chaque homme avoit une fronde entortillée autour de sa main* (op. cit., p. 352). Forster does not mention how these particular slings were carried.

104 De Brosses (op. cit.,) in his article on Alvar di Mindaña (Volume 1, p. 253) mentions this recourse to virtual barriers in the Marquesas: *Les insulaires, au nombre d'environ 300 tournoient tout au tour de sa troupe. Il leur fit signe d'approcher, & de ne pas passer une raye que l'on traça sur la terre, ce qu'ils exécutèrent; appprtant de l'eau, des des noix de cocos et autres fruits.* Cook also adopts this very same strategy during his first voyage. At Tahiti, on April 15th, 1769, he notes *I went a Shore with a party of men accompanie'd by Mr Banks, Dr Solander, and Mr Green, We took along with us one of Mr Bank's Tents, and after we had fix'd upon a place fit for our pur-pose we set up the Tent and Mark'd out the ground we intended to occupy — by this time a great number of the Natives had got collected together about us, seemingly only to look on as not one of them had any Weapon either offensive or defensive — I would suffer none to come within the lines I had marked out excepting one who appear'd to be a Chief and old Owha,ª* In Hawkesworth (Marchand probably had access to the French version *Relation des voyages entrepris par ordre de sa majesté britannique, actuellement régnante; pour faire des découvertes dans l'hémisphère méridional*, published for the first time in 1774), the marking out of lines is recounted thus: . . .

ceremony *Tabou* in their language. They say a place is taboued when it is forbidden to go there. They conducted us through a grove, about one hundred and fifty paces from the shore, and proposed, still giving me the title of Otouhou, that my people and I should be seated under the large bread fruit trees in the most elevated place. They then sat down in a half circle around us. To reach this place, we had passed through several enclosures surrounded by stone walls two feet in height. I observed that the natives had stopped in the enclosure before the one we found ourselves in, which I supposed to be due to their inferior rank which prevented them from entering a place which was destined, it seemed, for great ceremonies. A quarter of an hour thereabout, a native was presented to us who said he was the Otohou. I believe it was a part they wished him to play in order to get some few presents for he was all a tremble and appeared much confused at the honour I did to him in touching my nose to his. Whatsoever the case, I gave him some few nails. Presently came a few natives, each with a pig under his arm. After haranguing us with much passion and violence, shouting rather than speaking, they set the pigs at my feet. I thanked them and made them presents of nails and beads, etc. We walked to the shore and were accompanied as before by more than four hundred natives. I tasted the water of the stream which I intended for the watering place, and found it to be excellent.

When I was about to get into the boat, my handkerchief and snuff box were stolen very neatly. Amongst the crowd, I caught sight of he who had taken the handkerchief and took up my musket, at which they all fled, but they returned when I called them back for I did not believe it was necessary to use force to recover an article of so little value. I made the pickpocket a present of it, who thanked me. I exchanged nails for spears which are made of a very hard wood, and for some of their articles of dress.

We observed that the naturals wore around their necks, several of the small implements which had been stolen from the ship and they appeared not to be apprehensive of those things being forced from them by us, which is almost enough to think that they do not believe they have committed a crime in thieving. This would have us believe that if they are not taken in the act, they fancy the stolen article to belong to them.

Before returning on board, I made a tour of the South Cove of the bay accompanied by several canoes. As birds were flying over our heads, I believed this to give us a fine opportunity to give the natives an advantageous idea of the superior power of our arms, I shot at and brought down two of the birds, which much surprised them.[105] The first bird was a kind of grey heron, and the second a sea swallow.

---

not being a single weapon of any kind among them. I intimated, however, that none of them were to come within the line I had drawn, except one who appeared to be a chief.

105 Marchand attempts here to intimidate the Marquesans, in spite of the frequent references to his peaceable intentions, as Banks ineffectually does at Tahiti on the 15ᵗʰ April: *While we with a*

The commanding officer on the ship informed me that the natives who had come aboard in the afternoon had behaved very well, which pleased me for I desired much to live peaceably with them in order not to be obliged to have recourse to some extreme measure of which they would undoubtedly be the victims. I found some women in the ship who wished to spend the night aboard but I obliged them to take leave of us, which they did by swimming back to the shore.

I had forgotten to say that the preceding evening at sun-set, being between Santa Christina and Santa Dominica, we thought to have caught sight of land at WNW. Today, we saw it again, lying in the same direction, and this convinced me that it was land indeed. I estimated it to be 20 to 25 leagues distant and resolved at the moment to take a view of it by making sail from this bay. We saw it no more the following days for the horizon was always hazy in this quarter. It was a new discovery for no land is to be found in the neighbourhood of the Marquesas on any chart.

There was a watch every night, as at sea, and I ordered out six guards under arms at different points of the ship.

In the morning I sent the longboat ashore with three officers and a party of nine men for water and to make trade. So as not to spoil the prices, Mr Roblet, who possessed all the necessary patience, was appointed alone to trade aboard the ship, if any was to be had,.

The officer commanding the longboat informed on his return that he had been very well received. On landing, the natives had with much eagerness rolled the barrels on the shore and made a sort of bank to facilitate the work of making water. An unhappy accident occurred at this moment which brought about a quarrel with them. A blunderbuss, charged with balls and left thus through inadvertency, was discharged and overturned a barrel, one of the balls made a hole in the arm of a young man sitting beneath a tree at more than fifty paces. Most of the natives fled forthwith, not knowing what had taken place. Some amongst them picked up stones but did not make use of them. The officer requested to see the wounded man, but he had been carried away. Once the officer had allayed the fears of those who had remained near the watering place, and made some presents, the others ventured near once more and repeated with a sorrowful air *Tayo eto, Matté eto* which signifies *you call us friends but kill us when we assist you* to which it was impossible to make a reply. They endeavoured to make them understand that they

---

nother party took a walk into the woods and with us most of the natives, we had but just cross'd the River when Mr Banks shott three Ducks at one shott which surprise'd ^ them so much that most of them fell down as tho they had been shott likewise. I was in hopes this would have had some good effect, but the event did not prove it, for we had not been gone long from the Tent before the natives again began to gather about ^ it and one of them more daring than the rest push'd one of the Centinals down, snatched the Musquet out of his hand and made a push at him and then made off and with him all the rest, emmidiatly upon this the officer order'd the party to fire and the Man who took the Musquet was shott dead before he had got far from the Tent but the Musquet was carried quite off . . . (Endeavour Journal).

had not done this wilfully, which appeared to comfort them. Some of the people thought themselves to be the victims of their very own heedlessness, for all the balls had passed very near them. I had heard the report from the ship, but as I had not observed with my glass that there was any disturbance on the shore, the officer had not made the signal for assistance in case of danger, I had come to understand within a small matter, what had taken place.

From Wednesday 15ᵗʰ to Thursday 16ᵗʰ June 1791

In the afternoon, I sent Mr Reynier the Surgeon in the longboat to the watering place with orders to endeavour to see the wounded man and to dress his wound, which he put in execution. He found a bone of the arm (the radius) to be broken. The natives had already very ingeniously dressed the wound. He was made a most considerable present which satisfied himself and his countrymen.

At 6 o'clock the longboat returned loaded with water.

During the morning of the 16ᵗʰ, I went ashore with Mr Roblet to once more make the wounded man a visit. Mr Roblet did not consider the wound to be dangerous. The longboat was employed in making water, and after having manned the watering place and leaving two officers to take charge of it, I advanced into the interior parts of the country with my servant. I was accompanied by more than thirty natives who took my hand and assisted me when I made a false step. At about one mile from the shore, I saw that the natives speaking very loudly amongst themselves, and that they were most likely forming some bad design, on which I resolved to return to the shore. I observed also that they took less notice of me for they no longer gave me their hand as they had been wont to do. They attempted several times to make me fall to the ground by pushing each other towards me, for which reason I was upon my guard against them. After three hundred paces thereabouts, I was unfortunate enough to fall to the ground by accident, and as I attempted to seize a root in order not to plunge into the precipice on one side of the path, one of the natives took the advantage and violently seized my musket very dexterously from behind and carried it off. Fortunately or unfortunately, the servant did not carry a musket, for I would have fired at the man. I stood however firm and drew my sword and pursued the thief through the woods, but when I was on the point of running him through, I heard my servant shout for help. I left the musket and ran to him. Seven natives had attacked him, who all fled when they caught sight of me. Their design was to carry off his sword and my bag which the servant carried around his neck, for they had seen that it was filled with nails, but they had only time enough to take his hat and a box he had and in which was to be found glass beads and hooks. One of them desiring to seize the sword by the blade found his fingers to be cut. During this walk into the woods, which was not of the most agreeable kind, they had requested me to shoot at a tree to see the consequence, but as I had begun to be upon my guard, I had refused them.

No sooner had the musket been carried off than I heard shouts in the woods. I made haste to the watering place where my officers learning of the circumstance which had occurred, proposed immediately to seek for redress, but I laid before them the danger in which Mr Roblet would find himself for he was at the same moment also taking a walk in the woods. It would be useful for the moment to proceed gently, and on his return we should consider what was to be done.

I called back the natives who had fled and made them comprehend that I did not desire to revenge the insult and punish a nation for the fault of one man.[106] Almost at the same instant, I caught sight of the Surgeon in the woods, returning in appearance most peaceably. When I had informed him of the proceedings, he said he had been much alarmed by the cries he had heard in the woods and could not account for them. One man, who seemed to have some authority over the others, and who had received many presents, had accompanied the Surgeon and had most likely prevented insults and theft being committed.

When we were all assembled on the shore and the water casks were all aboard, under the protection of the guard I addressed myself to the chief who had accompanied Mr Roblet. I made him comprehend that it was my firm purpose that the musket which had been stolen must absolutely be recovered. He took leave of us immediately and returned with it in one half of an hour. I observed that the gun stick was missing, he promised to bring it to me in the afternoon.

As we were awaiting the musket, one of the natives, who by his age appeared to have more importance than the others, stood up in the middle of them and spoke with firmness. I considered by his actions (for they make many gestures while they are talking) that it was a reproach, to those amongst them who had accompanied me, for their unworthy behaviour towards me. The others desired to be excused saying that it was not their fault and that they should not be held accountable for the behaviour of particular persons. He pointed thus to Mr Roblet and said that those men who had accompanied the doctor had prevented him from being robbed. He frequently pronounced the word *Othou* in his speech pointing to me and shouting very much. This was doubtless a reproach to his countrymen for the insult made to the chief of the ship. I had forgot to mention that one of the natives, who always called me *Tayo* (his friend), brought me a club which had but only just been broken, saying that he had *matte* (killed) the man who had stolen my musket. I doubted the veracity of his account, his intention being to receive some few nails for it. He was very much mistaken for I expressed my dissatisfaction with his action and made him comprehend that the man did not deserve death.

I confess myself very surprised at the ease with which I recovered the musket, for these people attach the greatest importance to the meanest pieces of iron, and the musket, a weapon much superior to any they have in their possession, should

106 Cook makes the same observation at Tahiti (Sunday 8th 1774): *This story of theirs, although it did not quite satisfy me, nevertheless carried with it the probability of truth; for which reason I thought it better to drop the affair altogether, rather than punish a nation for a crime I was not sure any of its members had committed* (*Voyage to the South Pole*, op. cit., Volume 1, p. 333).

in their eyes have been the greatest treasure in all the universe. I ascribed it to their fear that we would destroy their bay if they did not bring back the musket.

From Thursday 16ᵗʰ to Friday 17ᵗʰ June 1791

In the afternoon, we were employed in blacking the yards and the ship sides. The longboat was sent ashore for water where the officer was received very well, as before. The natives rolled themselves the casks and filled them. We rewarded them with glass beads.

The gunstick was found to be hanging from the ear of a native who made not the smallest protest at giving it up.

We continued to make exchanges in a peaceful and honest fashion on both parts, but save cocoa-nuts, bread-fruit and bananas, of which they brought down a great quantity, we got nothing more from them, for until this moment we had procured only six hogs and four fowl.

I regretted two great losses during the day. Due to the unskillfulness of the commander of the longboat, the grappling was lost. It had doubtless been badly bent to the ring, we swept the bottom for it to no purpose. Afterwards, the nets we had left in the water to take up fish were carried off, as well as I could understood it, by a company of porpoises which we observed to be in the bay. If the natives had stolen them, with the greatest of difficulties I should say, I would have discovered it, after all the enquiries I had made in order to inform myself, and after all the rewards I had promised to some few chiefs if the least intelligence could be had on this head.

The natives sold us a kind of nut of which the shell was very hard and which contained an oily white substance, the taste of which was like that of our nuts in Europe. All who partook of them were attacked, purged above and below. I had but tasted them and was not in anything affected by them. I gave orders to throw forthwith into the sea all those nuts aboard the ship, and I prohibited their purchase for the future.

One of the officers informed me that while we were employed in purchasing them, one of the women, finding herself alone aboard had made signs to him that he should not eat any of them but that a terrible look from he who was selling them had prevented her from doing more. This same officer took little heed of so sound advice, as he should have done, and was amongst the first to try them and suffered all the effects.

Following this incident, I advised the crew to take more care in the future and not to eat of all that was presented to them.

In the morning of the 17ᵗʰ, I did not send the longboat to the watering place. All the people were employed in removing from the hold of the ship, the wine, salted meat and spirits of which were in need, and to place within reach the articles which would serve for the trade on the NW coast of America.

We attempted to sweep for shells but to no purpose for the coast was bordered by coral rocks.

From Friday 17th to Saturday 18th June 1791

The weather was rainy during the afternoon and we suffered violent gusts of wind blowing from the valleys in the bottom of the bay, which however did not prevent the natives, both men and women, from coming off to the ship in their canoes and by swimming. We saw several who had come from Santa Dominica and the neighbouring bays. All of them brought us cocoa-nuts which we purchased twelve for the price of one nail, 4 or 5 inches in length. We also purchased two fowls, for they are not very plentiful in these islands. The natives possess many hogs but do not like to sell this article. They desired in exchange nails or looking glasses, but in a moment they would neglect them and wish for only glass beads, combs or whistles.

Only the women were permitted to come aboard (save our particular friends) and when the number became too great, we made signs that they should jump overboard, which they proceeded to do very cheerfully and very neatly.

An Indian who appeared to have some authority and who had come aboard several times and had once dined at my table, made me a visit and presented me with a fowl. I thanked him according to the custom, and made him a present of a nail, a looking glass and a folding knife with which he was extremely pleased. I requested him to attempt to procure some hogs and some fowls which he promised he should do. Before taking leave of us, he desired to know how much longer we should remain in the bay. I replied that I would remain five days more (though it was not my intention to do so), which appeared to give him great joy. He forthwith informed his countrymen who were about the ship, upon which they all shouted acclamations of joy.

At day-light on the 18th, we were surrounded as before by canoes and people swimming about the ship who brought us nothing but cocoa-nuts. As we had lain in a great stock and they observed that we no longer minded them, they gave us one for only one glass bead. I continued to desire them to bring fowls and hogs, but I saw none. We had procured but two fowls during the afternoon.

We found the log book, which was kept in one of the apartments of the binnacle, to be missing. I was not much sorry for its loss, for it happened fortunately that my journal was in good order.

From Saturday 18th to Sunday 19th June 1791

At one o'clock in the afternoon, I sent the longboat to the watering place under the command of an officer and the guard as usual.

At three o'clock I went ashore in the ship's boat accompanied by two officers to see if the natives would at last decide to sell hogs to us. But with much ado and patience, we procured but two hogs and three chickens. I showed them for the very first time some coopers' draw knives, bill-hooks, vine knives, files, etc., but they set no value on them and preferred the nails, the mirrors etc. to anything else.

At sun-set we returned on board.

During the night we had very violent squalls accompanied by rain.

At 8 o'clock in the morning of the 19th, we made an expedition in the boat, accompanied by three officers, to visit the coves situated Southward of the Bay which we were then in, in order to see what could be done there.[107] The first in our route, which we did not enter, was the smallest of them and is called by the natives *Napaho*, the second is called *A Natevaho* and the third, which is of a much larger size than the previous two, *A Potoni* which I named Friendly Cove[108] due to the honest manner with which we were received by the people.

We landed in the face of more than six hundred natives amongst which we caught sight of a chief who seemed to have some authority, for he seated us under a great tree and dispersed the people if they pushed themselves too much upon us. As the rain was pouring down upon us, he proposed entering a large house which I did not like to do. Though I placed the greatest confidence in them, I continued to think it prudent to take the greatest precaution. For the whole duration of the market, he kept the point of his spear upon our bag of articles and told us frequently to take heed for he knew the thieving disposition of his countrymen.

We procured in this cove twelve pigs in exchange for nails, looking glasses, combs etc., amongst the twelve, six were yet sucking pigs, the remainder weighed between 20 and 30 pounds.

We purchased likewise five fowls.

The sea broke in a surf with violence upon the shore and we landed and embarked with difficulty.

The natives appeared to be more shy of us than those of the two coves in our bay, for they never attempted to steal from us and carried us on their shoulders if they noticed our trouble in walking upon the rocks. On leaving the ship, I had taken with me the chief who had once dined with us and who had presented me with a hen. He was of great use to me.

The inhabitants of this cove appeared to be more at their ease than those of the bay in which we had come to anchor. The houses are of a larger size and more neatly made. There is a great quantity of coconut trees and bread-fruit trees and many more pigs and fowl. The trees on the shore, under which the houses are to be found, are planted with symmetry, those on the top of the neighbouring hills, in an agreeable disorder of nature, which all consists in a most picturesque prospect. We saw an infinite number of handsome women and several of the gentlemen suffered themselves to be seduced by their allurements.

When we saw that the natives would bring no more articles to market, we embarked and from there went to the cove which lies North of this one, and named as I have previously said *A Natevaho*. There we purchased but two pigs which I attributed solely to the bad weather. I resolved to return on board, where we

107 As does Cook on the 10th April, 1774.
108 *Anse des Amis.*

arrived thoroughly wet for the rain had never left off during the whole of our expedition.

We should have been obliged, in landing in this last cove and putting off, to walk more than two hundred paces upon great rocks which were prodigiously slippery, but the natives who were most honest and very obliging, carried us to the shore and back again upon their shoulders. We presented them with glass beads with which they seemed very satisfied.

Our watering completed, I resolved to leave this place the next evening. Before leaving the ship, I had given orders, put in execution, to hoist in the longboat and the boat.

From Sunday 19th to Monday 20th June 1791

In the afternoon I was accompanied by three of the officers to the cove Southward of our bay where we were able to procure but one pig. I desired from there to go with all the company to the one situated in the North by climbing up the rock which separated one from the other. We had completed no more than a quarter of the way when I saw the want of prudence in following such a very slippery path, which was so very narrow in some places as hardly to admit of our feet. We were obliged to take hold of a kind of fern in order not to plunge into the sea. I must here do justice to the natives for we, each one of us, went hand in hand with a native who gave us strength in the most difficult places. They proposed to carry me several times but I believed myself to be less in danger whilst walking and so I refused still. They never attempted to rob us during this time, which they could have done with impunity, for we could not have prevented them on account of the difficulty we had in keeping the way.

Fortunately, we reached at length the North cove where we were employed in filling two casks and the galley barrels with water. The night came fully upon us before we accomplished this operation. Through the negligence of the guard, the natives stole two barrels, and through that of the seamen in the boat, we lost one of the large barrels for it was not sufficiently made fast. When they caught sight of it, or so I was told, they were obliged to let it go, for the natives from the shore threw stones at them. So attacked, they fired a musquet in the direction of the shore which fortunately did not harm any one of them. During this scene in the cove, we had directed our way towards the rock caves of the North of the bay, which was the usual landing place. The night was so very dark that we could hardly see one another, and the sea broke with such great violence upon the slippery rocks that we were from time to time up to our waists in water. Several of the people hurt very much their legs. We at length embarked, while running the risk of death and of dashing the boat to pieces. I may say that this was the most disagreeable day's work I had ever made.

The breeze being most uncertain, and blowing in violent gusts sometimes from the sea and sometimes from the land, I resolved to remain at anchor until the wind became fixed.

After the scene of the previous evening, the natives came off to us once again as usual, but with the precaution of two chiefs who came before, and in whom they knew us to place confidence. By this means, one of the barrels was returned to us though they had not yet discovered where the other barrel and the water cask were to be found.

At 9 o'clock in the morning, the weather remaining variable, and not being able to get under sail, I sent the boat to *A Napaho* Cove under the command of Mr Masse, with orders to do the best he could to procure pigs and fowls, for I had not visited this place the preceding evening. Nothing was to be had however for the inhabitants are but a few.

We purchased two pigs and some few fowls on board the ship. One of the natives brought off a very large pig, for which he wanted a cat in return (called *pouhigo* by them). As we had but two on board, I could not give him satisfaction and he took away the pig, I proposed many other articles but he refused them all.

We had procured during our stay here but twelve or fifteen hundred cocoa-nuts, twenty-seven pigs, of which ten were yet sucking pigs, twenty seven fowls, bread-fruit and greens, etc. I believe we should have procured many more pigs and fowls if we had started the trade by refusing any other article, for at the beginning they would have given up all they possessed in order to procure nails.

From Monday 20th to Tuesday 21st June 1791

The breeze which had varied greatly until 4 o'clock PM, fixed at ENE and blew a hard gale. Though the flurries over the high land in the bay were of the utmost violence, I resolved to get under sail and I gave orders to heave the shore anchor. Notwithstanding all our efforts, we got under sail after having hoisted in the boats, an hour after midnight. The natives made a great fire on the shore for a reason I do not know, in either joy or pain at our departure.

At this moment,

The North point of Santa Christina bore	NE¼E.
The South Point idem	SE¼S.
And the West point of Dominica	N¼NW.

From hence, we took our departure in 9° 55' South latitude and 141° 33' longitude, W of Paris following the chart of Mr Cook, which is very accurate as I believe I have previously had occasion to notice elsewhere.

Before leaving the Marquesas, it might prove of some use to the reader to find here some observations on these islands and their inhabitants. These isles were discovered in 1595 by Mindina who gave them their name and they were then visited by Captain Cook who fixed their situation. They are five in number, La Magdelena, Santa Pedro, La Dominica, Santa Christina and Hood's Island which was named by Mr Cook as I have previously indicated and which I believe is the same island which Mendana named Ile Mendoça following the *Histoire des*

147

Navigations aux Terres Australes, 1ˢᵗ Volume, Book 2, page 251[109] in which the passage from the journal of Mindana or of Quiros, the Master of the ship, is to be found:

> *At a small distance of this island we discovered three others which the Captain named St. Pierre, Magdalena and Dominica. The first two of these are low and clothed with wood and about four leagues in circuit. I am not able to say if they are inhabited or not. La Dominica is the largest of them all and is more than thirteen leagues in circuit. The aspect is agreable and full of great trees and very good bays. It is separated from a fourth named Ile Christine by a channel, deep and clear, a league broad. The Captain named the whole of these together the Marquesas of Mendoça.*[110]

This passage shows in the most certain manner that Mindana, in addition to the four principal islands which are still called by the same names, had sighted a fifth at no great distance from them. And it is indicated in this same journal that it was called by him Mendoça Island,[111] which cannot be anything other than Mr Cook's Hood Island. Besides this, on all the ancient charts, we see that this group is composed of five islands.

Hood or Mendoça Island, the Northermost isle, which I saw but at a distance, lies in latitude 26' 9° S, longitude 141° 11'West.

St Pedro which the natives call *O niteyo*, latitude 9° 58' and longitude 141° 10'. It is I should suppose 3 leagues in circuit. Magdelena, latitude 10° 25' and longitude 141° 8' West, is five leagues in circuit. St Christina (bay of Madre de Dios) which the natives call *O Vaïtahou*,[112] latitude 9° 55' 30" and longitude 141° 27' 40', is 8 leagues. La Dominica, the largest of them all, called *O Hivahoua*, latitude 9° 40' South and longitude 141° 20' is about 15 or 16.

All these islands are inhabited, Mr Cook could not be sure if St. Pedro was equally so; but I was afforded the opportunity of being convinced of this fact as pirogues from this island came off to the ship. I was told that there was there an abundant supply of hogs. Excepting St. Pedro which is not a low island, they

---

109 Translated into English by John Callendar in 1766 *Terra Australis Incognita or Voyages to the Terra Australis, or Southern Hemisphere, during the Sixteenth, Seventeeth, and Eighteenth centuries* (3 volumes).

110 Callander does not translate this article on *Mindana* which appears in de Brosse's original text (Article XIX, p. 252).

111 The source of this particular detail is unclear as de Brosses does not make any mention of a Mendoça Island.

112 Forster op. cit., gives the Marquesan names for the Islands in his journal: *St Christina was called Waitahoo, La Dominica Heevaroa, and St Pedro Onateyo* (Volume 2, p. 19). and the circumferences are practically identical in both Cook and Forster. Marchand's estimates of the circumferences of these islands are very similar.

are all very high and divided by ridges of mountains which fall in gentle slopes towards the sea forming deep, fertile valleys, adorned with fruit trees, watered with streams of which the water was excellent.[113]

The bay of Madre de Dios is very easy to distinguish whether coming from the North or from the South of the island. It is situated towards the middle under the highest mountains of the island. When opposite to it, there are two sandy coves to be seen at the bottom, divided one from the other by a large round rock on which there is an appearance of verdure. The bay is bounded by a seacoast of black rock full of holes, which is the mark of a volcano, and very steep, for at landing on this coast we had 15 fathoms all round. When coming to anchor in this bay, proper care must be taken for the wind blows in violent squalls from the top of the mountains in the bottom of the bay, otherwise there is a risk of losing a top mast or of being dashed upon the rocks. Mr Cook thought the Resolution to be lost there.[114] The South point is high and steep topped with a peak impossible of access[115] but which can be noticed only on entering the bay for it cannot be distinguished from the interior mountains.[116] The North point is not as high and the slope is more moderate. The trees we had sight of are not the casuarinas as Mr Forster believed them to be, they are a sort of spruce of which the wood is very rosiny, for this naturalist depicts the casuarina, named *Toa* (war) by the Tahitians for it furnishes them with the instruments of death, to be a very hard wood of great weight and near black in colour, which appears red on occasion. This wood is however very soft, light and of a yellowish colour. In the bottom of the bay, there is a ridge of high and steep mountains with peaked summits. The houses of the inhabitants are to be found under the trees in the two coves.

113 This description is very similar to what Cook has to say about the topography of St Christina: *There are other ridges, which rising from the sea and with equal ascent join the main ridge. There are disjoined by deep narrow vallies, which are fertile, adorned with fruit and other trees, and watered by fine streams of excellent water* (Voyage to the South Pole, Volume 1, op. cit., p. 307).

114 *At length having come before the port we were in search of, we attempted to turn into it, the wind being right out; but as it blew in violent squalls from this high land, one of these took us just after we had put in stays, payed the ship off again, and before she wore round, she was within a few yards of being driven against the rocks to leeward* (Voyage to the South Pole, op. cit., Volume 1, p. 299). Forster in his account mentions the broken mast in question: *We found a harbour on the West side of the island, which looked so tempting, that we eagerly wished to come to an anchor; but just as we were turning about, in order to run into it, a heavy squall came over the high mountain with prodigious violence, and laid the ship on her side, so that we sprung our mizen-topmast, and narrowly escaped being driven againt the Southern point of the harbour* (A Voyage Round the World, op. cit., Volume 2, p. 7).

115 This does not quite correspond to what Cook appears to have seen: *The South point of the bay is a steep rock of considerable height, terminating at the top in a peaked hill, above which you will see a path-way leading up a narrow ridge to the summit of the hills* (Voyage to the South Pole, Volume 1, op. cit., p. 307).

116 The *Nouvelle Bibliothèque des Voyages* (cited in Gannier) occasionally mistranslates Cook's journals. The NBV is a compilation of Forster and Cook.

The North cove is the most convenient to make water, which is excellent. It is drawn up from a stream which runs into the sea in the middle of the shore. There is also a stream to be found in the South cove, but there would be many more difficuties to land and load the barrels due to the swell, which is greater than that which is found in the other cove.

Excepting the disposition of the natives of the Marquesas to claim as their own everything which belongs to us, we may say that they are perhaps the most gentle, most human and generous of all the peoples of the South Seas; they are most obliging and their friendly manner would honour the most polite societies of all Europe, and in their appearance we have seen that Mr Cook did not in any way exaggerate when he described them as one the finest races of people under the sun; they are rarely less than five feet four inches, and several are five feet eight inches; their countenances express feeling and their features are regular, though varying much. They seem to be of several species, some possessing hooked noses and others flat; some have hair which is straight and lank, others have it short and it is curled, but none of them had thick lips. Their skin is of a variety of colours, though their food, their dress and their occupations seem to be of the same kind. The darkest and the lightest were a red copper colour, a yellowish white and a clear black. Though we did not find much difference in their words for the same objects, we are lead to believe that the reasons for which the individuals of one race came to be here, were the same as those which brought the individuals of another race, which the former welcomed with their natural good nature and with whom they then united.[117]

It cannot be expected that we provide a complete account of their habits and customs, for we stayed so short a time amongst them, and the events occurred in such a manner as to allow us very little time for all the enquiries we would have wished to make, that is if we had better known their language, which we did not have occasion to learn for the men and women of the different islands with whom we had traffick though speaking in the main the same language, pronounced it differently.

They are very full of talk, and have a very strong and very loud voice. They talk all at once; their chests and shoulders wide, thighs strong and muscled, well-limbed, wide feet most probably due to their habit of going about barefoot. Their bodies are tattooed*,

*as are their faces which gives them a dark, fierce air.

---

117 Gannier points out that this sentence is to be read in the context of Roblet's remark (see Gannier, *journal*, op. cit., p. 278). What Roblet makes clear, and what Marchand attempts to put across, is that both men believe that, from a historical perspective, the differences in skin color are the remaining traces of demographical variations due to the arrival in the islands of different populations, at different moments in time. The fact that they all now speak the same language is proof, according to Marchand, of the benevolent attitudes of the orginal populations towards the newcomers.

some all over, and others less so, and some few hardly so and the children of ten or twelve years of age, not at all. Age or courage or birth or perhaps a mix of all three are the causes of so great a difference.

Tattooing[118] is a method which some of the men adopt, and which others do not. They possess for this, small pieces of shell of this shape,[119] which they fasten in the form of a hammer into a piece of wood of six or eight inches in length. After having covered the points with a black substance which seems to be nothing more than coal which they dilute with water, they strike small blows on the handle of the hammer with a stick made of the casuarina wood, driving the points in to the quick, which causes a slight inflammation, after which the part remains swollen for some time, though without much pain. The face, the shoulders, the breast, and lastly all the parts of the body, are marked with a diversity of figures of which are most perfect circles drawn as with a compass, quarter circles, straight lines, spirals and chequer work and squares crossed over in different directions; but there are never any figures of animals or of plants.[120] I observed that there reigned a perfect proportion of parts in their tattooing for the figures of one leg, of a thigh, of a shoulder were in exact correspondence with those of the other. It is principally, and even only, on the buttocks, that three or four concentric circles may be seen.

They all go about quite naked, most likely in order to preserve their glans from injury, they cover it with the prepuce which they tie up with a string after having brought it forward. They seem to have no idea of what we call decency, for their movements are of the utmost freedom and expressiveness. It is likely that they are not ignorant of the refinements of lewdness; in the water with the women, they adopt with no modesty all the attitudes necessary to the act of propagation. They watched with the greatest satisfaction one of our men, who cared little to do it in public, and in day-light, that which decency does not allow me to describe more clearly.

Some of them drank wine but seemed not to find it to their taste, whereas those to whom we offered spirits, drank with pleasure, which makes it likely that they have strong liquor amongst them which would be easy for them to procure for they dispose of ginger. To the strong liquor they give the name *ava*. They drink seawater with no expression of disgust, and most likely without indisposition. They eat fish and meat uncooked though they know the use of fire to dress the victuals.

A longer stay among them would be necessary to explain all the contradictory judgements in their conduct, for their incredible disposition for theft is joined to

---

118 Spelling used in the English translation of Fleurieu and which will be adopted here.
119 Page 107 of the manuscript (Livre 1).
120 Banks *Endeavor* Journal mentions crudely designed birds and animals at Tahiti: . . . *some have ill designed figures of men, birds or dogs* . . . Forster says much the same: *They never assumed the determinate form of an animal or plant, but consisted of a variety of blotches, spirals, bars, chequers, and lines, which had the most motley appearance* (*Voyage Round the World*, op. cit., Volume 2, p. 15). Forster also mentions the symmetry in the tattooing which Marchand also points to.

their uncommon mild and friendly disposition, and to their uncommon honesty in the trade we had with them. Not one of them to my knowledge took away the goods after having received the price for them, and several of them added articles which they may very well have kept for themselves. I know not if questions of property are respected by them, but I observed that not only did they give to the rightful owners, the glass beads and other trifles, but neither did they attempt to seize from their fellows those things they brought to us. They even made gifts to to one another of those items for which a moment before they would have paid with their most precious effects. When one of them succeeded in stealing from us, the object was passed from one to another, with little regard for the person to whom it was given.

The women, in general small, do not wait for the state of puberty to give themselves up to the men. Some few young girls, who seemed no more than eight years of age, were brought to us and seemed already used to the practice, though they were not instructed in the art as are the least of our Lais. For these young girls, all is bound by nature, and I would believe, even to that which is contrary to nature, if our gifts and presents had been powerless to convince them to accept of a thing of which they have no notion; but they are most ignorant of the art to make rise again the desire which they have but satisfied. This act renders within them some contradictory sentiment which I have not been able to explain the nature of. They are not voluptuous and must be led by profit alone, though this seems not always to be the case. They gave themselves freely, and the men, even those with whom we had no acquaintance, brought to us almost by force those women who desiring to raise the price, would not allow themselves to give up the commodity too early. So did the men satisfy their desires, or more, their brutishness, and it was I believe impossible to find by the experience, the pleasures so long wished for. I must observe however that I noticed within them a sort of modesty which consists of closing up their thighs diligently, which gives them a constrained appearance when sitting, standing or even swimming. They never came on board without a mat or some leaves about their person, particularly behind, for they are with ease able to substitute for the fig leaf, their hands.

We can say they are in general pretty though not beautiful; their features are not as regular as those of the men; though naked and continually in the water, they are whiter than the men, their eyes are lively and show intelligence; their teeth are good, the breasts of the young women are firm but soon lose their form*

*Their hands are small and well made, their plump fingers are extremely delicate.[121]

Some few of the women are marked with the *tattoo* on their arms, legs and hands, the others have no marks. Their limbs are rounded and supple. They have their hair long and I know not if they pluck it out in all parts of the body, but it is certain that few have their privey parts very full. Moreover, I know not whether

---

121 Mindana also mentions these *mains très jolis* (de Brosses, op. cit., Volume 1, p. 256).

they eat with the men, and consequently what rank they possess in society. However, it is probable that they are looked upon, as with all savage peoples, as nothing more than slaves.

They may remain for the whole day in the water with no inconvenience. They are, if not like monkeys, as children who desire all they see but who forget the following instant. They show no jealousy as regards each other, those who were refused would gaily seek out their more pleasing companions.

Notwithstanding the licence of their customs, it is certain that a union between kinsfolk is most strictly prohibited, but to what degree I am unable to determine.

We taught them to cry *Long Live the Nation*[122], and they said it often perceiving that it gave us pleasure. They pronounced each letter of the alphabet excepting b, c, e, l and t, with which they had difficulty. Their language is in general full of aspirations and I was never able to make them say the word France, and though they pronounce F and A separately, they were incapable of joining the r and always said rance.

As I have before made mention, we one day made a visit to the cove to the South of our bay which I had named Friendly Cove. It is with great difficulty that the great difference in the manners of the inhabitants of this neighbouring cove may be accounted for. These stole from us immediately, whereas the others had not attempted to commit such thefts, though they had come on board and had sorely tried our patience. Mr Forster in his description of these islands estimates the population to be near 50 000[123] persons. It appears though this number is much less, for though a great number of canoes which came off to us were from La Dominica, we never saw more than three hundred natives together, excepting the first day and when we were at Friendly Cove, where the those from other coves had come to that place.

In speaking of canoes within which they travel some distance, it is proper that I give an account of them. I am very far from thinking of them so advantageously and relating their construction from so favourable a point of view, as the observer I mention above.[124] They are made of three principal pieces which are sewn

---

122 Shouts of "Vive la Nation" were characteristic during the French Revolution. Marchand seems to have been a fervent supporter, at least in this fair copy, destined probably for publication, of the Revolution, as various remarks in his journal show. The slogan later became more commonly known as the French war cry at the Battle of Valmy in 1792.

123 See Forster, *Voyage Round the World*, op. cit., pp. 33–34.

124 Forster is not particularly enthusiastic concerning the Marquesan canoes: *Their canoes were likewise very similar to those of Taheitee, but of no great size. The heads commonly had some flat upright piece, on which the human face was coarsely carved; and their sails were made of mats, triangular, and very broad at the top. The paddles which they used, were made of a heavy hard wood, short, but sharp-pointed and with a knob at the upper end* (Ibid., p. 29). Cook is equally non-committal: *Their canoes are made of wood, and pieces of bark of a soft tree, which grows near the sea in great plenty, and is very tough and proper for the purpose. They are from sixteen to twenty feet long and about fifteen inches broad: the head and stern are made of two solid pieces of wood, the stern rises or curves a little, but in an irregular direction, and ends in a point;*

together in a rough manner and so badly wrought that the canoes make prodigious water. The first piece, which forms all of the bottom, is a tree hollowed out. The two other pieces are fitted on top and sewn to the first with ropes made of the fibres of cocoa-nuts which pass through holes bored to that purpose. They are 20 to 30 feet in length and one foot or 14 inches in breadth, the head curves a little under the piece of the bottom and projects out above the water about 1½ feet, the surface of which is convex in relation to the sea and 9 inches in breadth. The highest point ends in the form of a man's head or that of a monstrous fish.

The back part ends with the side which rises in the form of a circle; when this board comes loose by some accident, which I have often seen happen, the canoe fills immediately with water. Some of these canoes have a length of wood, which curves a little and rises from the stern, and which forms an angle of 45° with the keel. Sometimes (when the weather is dirty or they must travel a long distance), they join two together with two pieces of wood lashed strongly to the four ends of both canoes. On other occasions, they are content to fashion an out rigger,[125] which is nothing more than a log of very light wood of the *mapou* species, which is found in our American possessions. There are many to be seen which are formed of nothing but a hollowed out tree, not more than 12 feet in length and in breadth 10 inches. These canoes carry 2 to 12 men who manage them tolerably well, and when they over set or fill with water, all those on board throw themselves into the water to right them, or to empty them, and then come back on board and look upon it as of little consequence. The double canoes have in general a sail of a triangular shape made of matting, which is hoisted along the masts of the two canoes.

The most part of the natives wear their hair divided in two parts by a parting of two fingers' breadth,[126] which is perfectly free of hair and which extends from the forehead to the nape. Others have it long, but in general they wear it short and tied up on each side by a knot.

They wear their beards, which are most commonly long, in different modes: some divide them into two and tie them up in bunches and have the space

---

the head projects out horizontally, and is carved into some faint and very rude resemblance of a human face. They are rowed by paddles, and some have a sort of latteen sail made of matting (*Voyage to the South Pole*, op. cit., Volume 1, p. 311).

125 Joseph Banks describes the canoes at Tahiti and mentions the outrigger: *All these imbarkations which indeed are all that I saw us'd in any of the Islands are disproportionaly narrow in respect to their length, which causes them to be so very easily overset that not even the Indians dare venture in them till they are fitted with a contrivance to prevent this inconvenience; which is done either by fastening two together side by side as has been before describd, in which case one supports the other and they become the most steady vehicle that can be imagind, or if one of them is to go out single a log of wood fas[t]ned to two poles which are tied across the boat serves to balance it tolerably, tho not so securely but that I have seen the Indians overset them very often. This is upon the same principles as that usd in the flying Proa of the Ladrone Isles describd in Ld Ansons voyage, where it is calld an outrigger* (Banks' Descriptions of Places, Endeavour Journal).

126 Marchand uses the term *doigt* which was the equivalent of an inch.

between the two parts plucked clean, others plait them, some leave them loose, and some others ornament them with small shells which they bore with holes and through which parts of the beard pass. They wear around their neck a small ornament of white stone in the form of a cone and which is polished, a sort of string of red pods from a fruit in the form of a pineapple, which sometimes I saw them suck upon and which I found to be of a sweetish taste. Their head is sometimes ornamented with a half-circle of cock's feathers, plaited together. Some also wear a sort of head-piece, covered with cloth of a white colour on which they draw figures of black. There are others who wear a plaited crown on which they fix large circles of mother of pearl in the middle of which they put a piece of tortoise shell which is also wrought in a circular shape and very finely perforated.[127] There is sometimes above this last piece a third ornament of a smaller size and made of mother of pearl. They also wear around their neck a sort of gorget of a very light wood on which they glue with symmetry, or very even, a red seed. I saw some others who had upon their head a helmet of the black feathers of a frigate bird, I believe a foot in length, and on the sides they fix a plume from the tail feathers of tropic birds.

They have among their most precious ornaments those objects which we gave to them, or which they had stolen. They fastened these around their neck, and sometimes around the waist, taking no pains to conceal them from our view. We saw a shaving bowl, some pieces of wood and even a gun stick, of which I believe I have before made mention. They adorn also their heads, legs and a sort of spear, with bunches of hair belonging probably to the enemies they have overcome. They carry on their shoulders and around the waist, one two and sometimes three skulls of men, which they offered to truck with us. I must say that I saw only four or five natives who wore this last ornament, and they did not belong to the bay of Madre de Dios. Men, like the women, sometimes paint themselves yellow all over with ginger. They all had their ears pierced but wore few ornaments in them. The women anoint their heads with an oil made of coco-nut which is rancid.

It seems that they war amongst each other for they have long lances of wood, clubs very well wrought and swords shaped like a paddle, daggers and slings. I did not see amongst them either bows or arrows. Their fondness for iron is most extraordinary. Of all articles that Mr Cook left with them, there is no trace. What use have they made of them? No man amongst them is capable of changing the form we have given to the objects, and they seem to be very ignorant of their qualities and prefer nails and knives to the iron ware with cutting edges which we showed to them.

---

127 Here Marchand's descriptions of the various ornaments are similar to those of Cook and Forster (see Gannier, *journal*, op. cit., p. 283). The drawings (in the manuscript) of the Marquesan objects are also extremely similar to those in *Voyage towards the South Pole* (*Ornaments and weapons at the Marquesas*, Plate XVII, op. cit., p. 311).

I saw no chiefly authority amongst them. We observed that those who possessed the most influence amongst the crowd owed their authority, as I have before mentioned, to a pleasing countenance or to a vigorous character, or to the power of the family. But in any of these cases, their power is very restrained. This was our opinion in regard to he who assisted us in bringing back the musket, and he who accompanied us to Friendly Cove.

All the instruments that we have seen wholly consist of gourds of different sizes which close tightly enough to prevent the liquid within it from leaking; of stone axes lashed strongly to a handle of wood, like that of our pick axe, the stone is blackish and very hard, some I saw weighing about 25 pounds, of grinding stones, of mats upon which they sleep, of knives which they make from the shell of pearl oysters, of vessels of wood in a round or oval form of different sizes and which are well made, of fishing lines quite ingenious. Some are made of the fibres of cocoa-nuts and others of the bark of a kind of nettle. Their nets of the same materials are made in exactly the same manner as ours, their hooks are wrought from mother of pearl and very well worked. They make harpoons of bone which are very roughly made. They also have a polisher which they make with the skin of a fish which is much like that of shagreen.

The roof of their houses, of which the ridge rose up to a height of nine or ten feet, is supported by several posts formed of bamboo canes fixed aslant, covered with the leaves of the Latania or bread-fruit tree. The inside is paved with large stones neatly laid out next to each other and spread over with mats. On one side there is a door or a window, which distinguishes it from the other side which is open in general. I saw more than fifty of these houses which I found to be very clean, much like the kitchens, which usually touch the houses. I cannot say like Mr Cook that I saw the natives eating in the same vessel as hogs, but on the contrary, that I found them to be very delicate in their manners.[128] Beside fish, which the sea provides for their subsistence, though these waters seem not to abound in fish, which I saw them eat raw, even as they do hogs, though in general they dress them, they possess cocoa nut trees of which the advantages are already known and have no need to be described here. They have vegetables which have the same taste as scorzonera, and which grow upon a parasitical plant, bananas, ginger, the sugar cane and above all the bread fruit. This they dress upon a fire which is surrounded by hot stones, and from which they make a sourish paste to which they add ripe bananas, in order that it may keep for a longer period. The bread-fruit tree furnishes them with the matter for their cloth, even as does the paper mulberry tree. Without needs other than those which Nature most liberally satisfies, and untroubled by the future, they live in almost continual indolence and amuse

---

128 Cook though tempers this remark, goes on to say that his judgement cannot be applied to all: *The actions of a few individuals are not sufficient to fix a custom on a whole nation* (Ibid., Volume 1, p. 311).

themselves by dancing, singing and by putting themselves upon stilts.[129] For this, they work two lengths of wood into a pyramid form of about one foot and half in length upon which they carve roughly the figure of a man who wears on his head a sort of head-dress about two inches high and hollowed out behind in order that there be space enough for the foot to be inserted against the pole, which serves as a support. After having strongly lashed the foot to the pole to the desired height, they make use of them as we do ours. Before discovering the use to which they put these machines, and which they call *Etoui*, we took them to be rough daggers as they were somewhat like them in form.

The ground though mountainous, is covered with a rich black soil on which flourish various species of lichens, cow grass, purslain, cress and other bushes. The valleys are cloathed with trees of which I do not know all the names but which formed a very pleasing prospect. Amongst them I saw the cocoa-nut tree, the bread-fruit, the casuarinas of which they make their weapons, a species of fir tree which is predominant due to its height and the spread of the branches. But it is a soft wood and is little different from the fig tree of our American possessions. They use it to build their canoes. I saw the paper mulberry tree and another of which the blossom, the pods and the leaves are perfectly like those belonging to the Portia tree in India, but the trunk is not as straight. The banana tree is very common but we did not see any lemons or oranges. We tasted a sort of small cucumber which was the size of an apricot and which made excellent eating. There is also a kind of walnut tree, the fruit of which has a most agreeable taste but which poisoned some of the people; but on drinking tea and after four hours, the effects were no longer to be felt.

They have no recourse to the art of surgery in their wars, or in case of some accident. Nature has thus many resources amongst such sobre a people whose disposition is not disturbed by neither our passions nor our savoury dishes. I saw only natural cures of which the most ingenious of our Surgeons would have gained honour: a native who was wounded by a wooden knife which had entered under the shoulder blade and come out between the second and third rib on the right side, and which had pierced a hole right through, seemed to feel no indisposition from it, and only the mark on the back was prominent. We saw also three large depressions of both the coronal and parietal bones caused by the sling.

I saw only one deformed man, whose legs were exceedingly thin and the feet turned inwards. After having inquired into the reason, they made signs that he had fallen from the cocoa nut tree and had been in this state ever since.

---

129 Fleurieu published an engraving of these Marquesan stilts in his *Voyage autour du monde* in the 1809 edition (see Gannier, *journal*, op. cit., p. 286). But the English translation of Fleurieu published in 1801 already includes the engraving in question and the paratext is *J. Bye of St John's Squr*, Clerkenwell. The 1809 French engraving specifies that the original was done by a certain Gemillion from life. Marchand's manuscript does not contain any drawings of the Marquesan stilts at all.

The quality of the rock of a red or rusty colour is a mix of volcanic productions of a black and ferruginous nature which is spongious, hard and soon broken.
There is a sort of crust in the inland which seems to be clear of all verdure. The
tumbled rocks indicate the great changes. I caught sight of some shells fixed to the
rocks 600 feet above the sea. Of the animals on this island, I saw only a species
of hog which was very small and of which the meat is full of gravy. The fowls
were few and rats in great number. There are likewise lizards, some land birds, all
species of sea birds, herons.

The dance of the inhabitants of the islands is not worthy of notice. They form
a circle and all, excepting the women, make a loud noise by striking their elbows
at the joint while holding them against their sides, or by clapping their hands all
together while one of them moves his legs by crossing them alternately one over
the other, upon the same spot. This dance is invariably accompanied by a song of
which the chorus always ended with the word *Tayo* (friend) if we were present.
There is also sometimes a kind of drum which is perfectly like the *tamtam* belonging to the Indians, and which is covered with a skin on one side. The skin that is
made use of is that of hogs. They also have an instrument which is a nautilus to
which they fix a gourd in the form of a tube and into which they blow to make a
noise which is dull and disagreeable, varying but very little. They do much the
same with a cane of bamboo to which they join one of a smaller size at an acute
angle. We played before them the violin, the flute, the oboe and the flageolet,
which pleased them very much for they all set to dancing.

It is quite certain that there are no sharks to be found in these seas for the inhabitants take to the water with all confidence which is no doubt a result of their never
having known an accident of any sort.

Note: some part of these observations have been communicated to me by
Mr Roblet.[130]

During our stay in the Bay of Madre de Dios, the mercury in the thermometer
kept from +27° to +28 degrees, though another spirit thermometer rose to +28¼.
By means of 37 observations of the azimuths, and by the amplitudes, we found the
variation of the magnetic needle to be 3° 45' NE. The day before our arrival, we
had observed it to be 5° 41', and the day after our departure 4° 29'.

We had here variable winds from ESE to NNE, accompanied sometimes with
rain, if the wind veered from South to East. When the weather was fine, I observed
that in the afternoon the wind shifted to the West, but it was light and of short
duration. We were constantly employed during our stay at this place, which prevented us from observing the longitude in order to determine that of the bay. But
we may most certainly refer to the map of Mr Cook. After our departure, we made
several sets of observations of the stars and of the sun which reduced to this bay,

---

130 Gannier points out that many of Marchand's observations are in fact Roblet's. This correlation
is also identifiable in the *Endeavour* journals for example when both Cook and Banks recount
various episodes in almost exactly the same terms.

determined the longitude to be 141° 24' 40", which is but 3° different from the true situation, or that given by Mr Cook.

The natives no longer amusing themselves in fishing, I sent out the yawl with three or four men, morning and evening. But they rarely took more than 10 pounds each time for they fished only with the line and hook.

Vocabulary of words in the language of the Marquesas

A-tahi	One
-houah	Two
-tohou	Three
-fâh	Four
-hima	Five
-hono	Six
-fittou	Seven
-vahou	Eight
-hiva	Nine
-Onohouhou*	Ten
E-houma	Body or perhaps the waist
Haé	The forehead
Bouhouahina	Ears
Moutou	Mouth
Matta	The eyes
Toukiahi	Eyebrows
Niho	Teeth
Cohouh aï	Chin
Ecaqui	Neck
Tapouvahi	Feet
E-hou	Breasts
Houma	Throat or chest
Vaïvahi	Leg
Pouha	Thighs
Homo	Natural parts of the female
Houhouhou or Titohi or Titoï	Privy parts of a man
Coopu	Stomach
Ima	Arm
Manamana	Hand
Mayouhou	Nails
Houpoco	Head
Hou hoho	Hair
Behouhaï	Hat or ornament for the head
Cahou	Gummed cloth, Cloth, handkerchiefs, linen, etc
E poutetoutahi	Buttocks
Ouhakeho	Anus
Toukahima	Elbows
Pouhi	Guns or muskets
Cahahou	Bayonet, the same word is employed for spear
Cohé	Swords
Pahouha	Daggers
Epah	Hook

159

Hika	Fish
Moha	Hen or cockerel
O Maihi	Bread-fruit
Ahehi	Cocoa nut
Aheho	Tongue
Oukahouka	The venal act[131]
Ehah	The sun
Oumati	The moon
Ehani	Sky or perhaps the stars
Vaka	Canoe
Comaï	Testicle
Ouhi	Knife of shell
Pouhnah	Grinding stone
Toki	A very hard stone with which they make their axes
Pouhé	Shell
Epoh	Wait or later
Bohaka ou Pohaka sometimes Boah	Hog
Otohou or Othou	King or Chief
Haheho with great aspiration of the three Hs –	Come
Tahi	Go
Taihi	Sea
Evahi	Water
Ava	The name they give to Spirits
Taÿo, Taÿë	Friend and friends
Mahi	Follow me
Nohou	Sugar cane
Pappah	Nails
Pippi	Glass beads
Matté	Killed, dead or wounded
Pito	The naval
Mouhôh	The knee
Oukévahi	The heel
Ssssah while hissing the four Ss	Rain or rather cold
Hapÿ	Vessel or long boat
Tatou	The pricking of the skin. Tattooing
Tabou	To forbid something (to lay an embargo on)
Eh (very open sound)	Yes
Ouatta, Ouhatta	Looking glass
Pouiÿo	Word they used for cat
Moutou	Silence, quiet
Etouï	Parts upon which they rest their feet when they make use of stilts. They are in the form of small human figures.

* They count until 10 and from thence they begin again, marking each ten with their fingers or, to remember, by putting aside one of the things they are counting.
  It is necessary to mention that sometimes, in saying the number, they add an A to the beginning of each word, and sometimes they omit it, as they do in other words where they add an E. These two letters seem I believe to serve as articles.

131 Marchand truncates this word in the original: *L'acte Ven*. . . . . .

160

I have compiled a vocabulary[132] which is much longer but I have inserted here only those words of which the pronunciation and the signification I am perfectly certain.

Remainder of Monday 20th June to Tuesday 21st June 1791

57¼

I now return to my Journal which I put aside when, after having hoisted in the boats and having taken our bearings, we directed our course WNW in order to make the land of which I have already made mention, and which we had seen while at anchor bearing in this direction. No map shows this land in the situation I have indicated, I was in hopes this would prove to be a new discovery.[133]

During the night, we carried little sail. At day-light, we caught sight of an island directly a-head, bearing WNW to NW, at a distance of about 10 or 11 leagues. We were very certain that this island had not been seen by any navigators before us and my officers desired to do me the honour of calling it by my name. It was thus called Marchand Isle.

At a distance of about 9 leagues, we saw peaks which were very broken. We perceived at the Southermost point, a rock which rose perpendicular and was like an obelisk. It was separated by a small channel which was scattered with rocks and shelves level with the surface of the water. As we approached, we saw a small flat island (for which reason I called it Flat Island[134]) which was about ¾ of a league in circumference and lined with reefs, it was separated from the principal island by a channel which seemed to me to be a league in breadth. The land seems to have a barren aspect for we saw neither trees nor bushes. We saw only a few plants and mosses of a yellowish green colour. As we came nearer, the principal island afforded us a most pleasing prospect of numerous valleys and slopes covered in the most agreeable verdure, ornamented with great, strong trees, the aspect of the whole being so very different from that of the Marquesas Islands. There the tired voyager can find repose only upon the black rocks, burnt, but though of volcanic origin verdure and trees are to be seen, only at a very great and fearful height. The sides of the hills themselves are very steep. Here, on the contrary, the colour of the rocks and their layers in the horizontal position, the gentle slopes which rise by degrees to the summits which are commanded themselves by peaks standing alone and much like church steeples, the valleys, in the middle of one we saw a great stream falling with great speed more than 600 feet, the whole forms a most pleasant and majestic prospect. The mountains of which the highest tops are

---

132 Cook, Banks, Dixon and Portlock and many other navigators compiled vocabularies of this kind. The longer vocabulary was probably in the rough journal which has been lost.
133 Gannier (*journal*, op. cit., p. 291) points out that Joseph Ingraham had discovered these islands a month before Marchand. But Ingraham discovered the islands almost two months before Marchand (see *Introduction* to this translation).
134 *Île Plate*.

lost in the clouds, are cloathed in verdure and the rocks which line the shore are covered with the same where the waves of the sea come up against them.

At ¾ past 11 o'clock, being opposite the cove of the cascade of which I have just made mention, lying on the SW side of the island, being the third when coming from the South, we sounded and had 50 fathoms over fine white sand mixed with gravel. We were ½ or ¾ of a league distant from the shore. I am certain that were we to come along-side a little more, we would be able to anchor. It is true to say that no shelter is to be found there from the wind, but the sea is calm and as the breeze blows from the shore, we should at any moment be ready to weigh if we desired.

At noon, we were unable to observe the latitude for the land was at North, it was by reckoning found to be 9° 25' South and the longitude 142° 25' W.

At this moment, the Southermost part of the island bore ESE½S, and the West point NNW½ N, being distant from the shore about ¾ of a league. We discovered another point bearing in the same direction as the West point.

During the morning, we found with different compasses the variation of the magnetic needle to be 4° 29' Northeasterly.

From Tuesday 21ˢᵗ to Wednesday 22ⁿᵈ June 1791

37⅔

In ranging along the coast, one hour after noon, to the South of the NW point of the island, I caught sight of a large opening which appeared to be a fine bay. We immediately hoisted out the boat in order to examine it, to sound, to look for a watering place and to observe the disposition of the natives, under the command of Mr Masse, accompanied by an officer and the Surgeon. Soon after the boat sheered off, we saw a canoe with three men inside, paddling towards the ship. Perceiving that they could not overtake us, for we were sailing too swiftly, we brought to. At a cable's length from the ship, they stopped in order to admire the ship. We made signs to them to come to us with a small white flag, which they did after much hesitation. To invite them on board, I showed them nails and looking glasses which they seemed not to value. At last, the boldest of them came on board, very much afraid. I gave him a looking glass and his astonishment was so great in seeing himself in the glass that I cannot describe it. He did not tire of admiring all that he saw and it was with ease that we understood that he had never before seen a ship.[135]

At 4 o'clock, two more canoes approached the ship and in each were three men. Two came on board and were amazed as the first of them. I made them some

---

135 In China, Marchand discovers that Joseph Ingraham had been in these waters before him. In this fair copy, he chooses to overlook this. Extracts from Ingraham's journal were published in 1793 in the *Collections of the Massachusetts Historical Society for the Year 1793* (Boston), Volume 4, p. 298, by Jeremy Belknap. It appears that the journal itself was not published contemporaneously and there is little trace of a corresponding translation (see *Introduction* to this translation).

presents and they went away. They had between them only one lance, which they gave to me.

At ½ past 6, o'clock, the boat returned and was hoisted in. During the afternoon, we had lain to, or tacked on and off near the shore, in order to be within reach of the boat and put it under our protection if it became necessary.

Mr Masse reported to me on his return that the bay was good and that there was shelter for the ship but that it was narrow and there would be a difficulty in sailing into the bay due to the gusts of wind from the valleys in the bottom of it, he found 25 fathoms over a fine bottom of sand mixed with gravel. This bay contains two coves, one at North and the other at South, and it is formed by the NW point of the Island and by a rock, which wore a pyramidical form, situated SSE of it and which may be distinguished with much ease. Our people had met with a favourable reception and thus we named it Warm Welcome Bay.[136]

I will here report some details which Mr Roblet communicated to me. They landed in the South cove where the shore was stony and whereon the sea breaks with more noise than danger. The effect of the swell is not felt in this place; two streams, one of which forms a small pond 20 paces from the waterside, run on to the pebbles on the beach and flow into the sea. Two or three springs are to be found amongst the rocks in the shade of the cocoa-nut trees, of the bread-fruit trees, of the cresses and ferns, and a great variety of climbing plants, which rendered the place cool at all moments. Some few huts here and there in confusion on the sides of the hills formed an agreeable view to the eye, contrary to a tedious sameness.

The inhabitants are like those who we are told lived on this earth during the golden age, they enjoy the fruits of nature with no other desires, no fear and no troubles. Not knowing neither who we were, nor our intentions, they came however to meet our people with confidence, which is near sure proof that they had never before seen neither Europeans nor their terrible arms, and understood the troubles they have caused in this sea.

Most respectable old men introduced to us young girls whom they lead by the hand, which is a sure sign of the great hospitality with which they welcomed us. These innocent victims of so sacred a duty obeyed, trembling with their eyes lowered, the orders of their parents. We must indeed guard against the belief that profit guided them. They had knowledge neither of our pretty trifles nor our iron, which so turns the heads of the inhabitants of the islands which are already known to us. They accept our presents with no haste and no scorn. How shall I describe so considerable a difference between such a gentle and peaceable a people, not one of whom seemed to possess a weapon, and who expressed their surprise only by silence, and the noisy reception and the disposition to thieving of the inhabitants of the Marquesas, which had so tried us? As tall and as strong, their beauty is not of the same form, naked as all the peoples of this sea, they are true to the elegance

---

136 *Bon accueil.*

of form and are perfectly well-limbed. If something is wanting in their physiognomy, it is the way, due to their courage, which warriors have with them. They have tattoos also, but they saw hardly ten out a hundred who had undergone this operation. They distinguished only a few words which were like the language of the natives we had seen, even the word *Tayo* (friend) is not known to them, though common in such places. They easily repeated it but did not seem to apply the same idea to it. The women are very different from those of the Marquesas, and appear chub-cheeked and taller. They are covered all over with a cloth like that of the Marquesas made of the paper mulberry plant. They do not anoint themselves with oil of the cocoa-nut, but they have ornaments such as necklaces and garlands of flowers and sweet smelling plants, which were very agreeable. They did not torment our people as did the women of St Christina, with no degree of shame, by the most lascivious motions. These, on the contrary, kept a distance and even separated themselves from the men and seemed to submit with much trouble and as if by force, to the pressing demands of their relations.

Mr Forster[137] reflects on the Friendly Isles and Society Isles in I believe a judicious manner, but his observation cannot be applied to this island. This observer believes that only the common sort of women offer themselves to the strangers: this may be true as regards those islanders who, owing to their hospitality, and having learnt of the terrible and cruel consequences of their traffic with Europeans, have left it to the most common sort of people, and this is what Mr Forster saw. But how shall be justified the ease with which the supposed virtue of the better sort is sacrificed, if the price is paid? How shall the thieving disposition, which is common to all, be justified? Unless it is said that after the landing of the first navigators, the common sort have left a part of their lewdness and vice to the better sort, who came to know new desires. Whereas, the natives of this island who appear to have had no communication, do not yet fear us. It might be found desirable for them to keep this want of knowledge, which is their happiness.

All night, we plied to windward under the top-sails in the same space of sea over which we had sailed during the day. At ½ past 6 o'clock, the NW point of Marchand Island bore NE, the South point SE and the opening of Warm Welcome Bay, East.

I have forgot to mention that I named those peaks which rise above the middle of this Island the Murat Peaks for the officer who first caught sight of them from the bay of Madre de Dios. During this night, we had a fresh breeze varying from SE¼E to ENE, attended with squalls and rain.

At a quarter past six, the South point of Marchand Island in the form of an obelisk, which I named Obelisk Point, bore SE½E, Warm Welcome Bay bore NE¼N, distant 1 league from the land. At this time, we worked to windward upon the starboard tack in order to observe the North part of the island.

---

137 Forster, op. cit., Volume 2, p. 54.

At 7 o'clock, we caught sight of more land a-head, stretching from N¼NE to NNW, distant about 9 leagues. I thought I saw more land to the West through the haze. After half an hour, we tacked and stood to the South.

My intention was to take possession of Marchand Island (and of the others at the same moment, for we had seen another to the North) in the name of the King, though I never could imagine how a governed nation, and according to which law, may seize of an inhabited land without the consent of the natives.[138] But in complying with the custom, I affirm that my object was honest. I thought but to put them under our protection against injustice if some European nation was to make any future attempts to bring them under subjection.

Though we had a swell and a fresh gale, variable, being two leagues distant from the land, at 9 o'clock I took a boat with three of my officers and eight sailors along with me. We landed only at 12 o'clock in a cove, in which we saw some trees and to which I proposed to fix a copper sheet with the following inscription cut upon upon it

Captain Etienne Marchand of Marseilles, Commander of the ship Solide *took possession of this Island in the name of his Majesty Louis XVI, King of the French people 22nd June 1791*[139]

We were met by a crowd of natives who seemed to be of the same gentle disposition and of the same honesty as those we had seen the previous evening, only they seemed to make more noise. But the trifles we gave to them, and the things that they saw in our possession, like the looking glasses, the glass beads, nails, hooks, etc., had certainly produced this effect.

I remarked that the women were not as comely as had been described to me, though they were enough so to bring into subjection even a difficult man. Their behaviour though was the same as those of yesterday, and they were as decent.

The inhabitants gave us water, which they call *Evahi* like the natives of the Marquesas, and sugar cane which was thick as my arm but which was of not of the best sort for too watery.

The inscription of which I have just made mention was attached to a vigorous and strong tree of the Island Fig tree species at the bottom of the bay, on the left side. I gave the islanders three bottles with seals in which I had enclosed the same inscription. They had watched us in silence and had not attempted to commit the

---

138 The political, legal and philosophical legitimacy of taking possession of newly discovered lands was a complex issue and Cook in his instructions (*Endeavour* voyage) was to do so, officially at least, only with the consent of the natives. In the second half of the eighteenth-century, thinkers like William Blackstone and Emerich de Vattel had examined the issue. Gannier also points to Diderot's approach and Marchand here seems to be giving voice to the concerns of his time.

139 As Gannier specifies (see *journal*, op. cit., p. 297), Louis XVI was arrested that day and Marchand in his *Brochure* (*Découverte des Iles de la Revolution dans l'océan Pacifique méridional*, 1792), which was written later, amends this to *au nom de la Nation Françoise*.

least species of theft. We distributed pennies amongst them and other large coins of France, also knives, glass beads, nails, hooks, looking glasses, etc. We embarked very well pleased with our late conduct with the natives and shouted three times *Long Live the King*, to which the natives answered with more shouts of joy.

When I was on the point of embarking, I caught sight of a young girl who was wearing a pair of earrings wrought of shell, I told her by signs that she should give them to me, which she did expressing the greatest joy. The girl received a reward for her modesty.

There is no anchorage for a ship in this cove, which I called Possession Cove, but there is a fine stream of excellent water. It lies about 2 leagues NE of the North point of Warm Welcome Bay. It cannot be missed for it is the first cove covered with wood which is to be seen after this point. It is formed in the West by heaps of rocks leaning in all directions, some to the East and others West, while others are perpendicular, which is a sure sign of great changes, but the stone is of the original colour and shows no trace of volcanoes.

In the North part, which projects out into the sea but little, the layers of rocks are formed horizontally and make on the edge a sort of platform about eight feet wide and ending in a small ledge. We landed on this platform and the natives seeing that we could not descend from it, carried us on their shoulders. They were of service to us in the same way when we wished to embark again.

At 3 o'clock, we returned to the ship. I did not desire to fire the great guns as I took possession in order not to frighten the natives who most certainly do not know the effects of our firearms, I was glad to leave them perfectly unacquainted with them.

At noon, the latitude by observation had been 9° 21' South.
The longitude from the Marquesas by reckoning was 142° 30' W.

During the night, we observed four sets of distances between Altair of the Aquilae and the moon, and in the morning four sets of distances of the moon and the sun, which reduced to noon, gave the mean result of 142° 27'.

At the same time
Obelisk point bore SE½E
The North Point of the island NE¼E 3° N
And the North point of Warm Welcome Bay East ½ North, distant 1½ leagues from this last.

The variation of the magnetic needle determined from 19 observations of azimuths, was 4° 45' NE.
Réamur's thermometer +27°, Fahrenheit's thermometer 91°.
I have forgot to mention that in Warm Welcome Bay, our officers saw hogs and fowl which they proposed to buy, but the natives said that the owner was away fishing and they could not proceed to sell them without his consent.

From Wednesday 22ⁿᵈ to Thursday 23ʳᵈ June 1791

75½

The ship had plyed on and off with a very variable breeze during the time I was on shore. When we had hoisted in the boat, we stretched out close upon the wind on the starboard tack, crowding sail in order to make an attempt to examine the land we had caught sight of in the morning. We saw it very soon afterwards. It appeared to be a large island, quite high but not craggy.

At ¾ past 5 o'clock, Marchand Island bore SSE½E and SE¼E, and the most Westerly point of the land we saw a-head at N¼NW, distant about 5 leagues.

At 6 o'clock, the sea having changed colour, we sounded with 90 fathoms of line but had no bottom.

A quarter of an hour after, we tacked and stood to the South. We spent the night standing on and off in the space we had reconnoitred during the day, with a breeze varying from ESE to ENE attended with rain and violent gusts of wind.

At day-light, I noticed the currents had carried us to the Westward.

At 6 o'clock in the morning, the Westermost point of the land a-head bore NNE, with the Murat Peaks on Marchand Island bearing ESE½E, distant 6 leagues from the first. We thought we saw more land at W¼SW. We continued to haul close upon the wind.

At ½ past 9 o'clock, the weather clearing we saw distinctly the whole of the island stretching from NE to E½N. It afforded the most pleasing prospect. It is much larger than Marchand Island and though high, the top of the mountains is flat and not thick set with peaks like those of the last. We noticed the gentle slopes of the hills, well cloathed with wood and with a pleasant verdure, all had the appearance of fertility. If the beautiful prospect of a land, if its climate, if the nearness of peaceful and mild neighbours, can all be advantages in the forming of a judgement of these people, I dare say that never did any navigator possess such strong proofs so favourable to those he has discovered.

It is a most particular circumstance that all the peoples observed by Mr Cook were possessed of pride – or even a fierceness of which he at last proved to be the most unfortunate victim. Those we have just met with form a perfect contrast, owing to the many marks they shewed us of their sweetness of temper and of their obliging disposition.

This island I have named Baux island in honour of the merchants who have fitted out this ship, the Southermost point is called Marc Point and the North point Elisée Point.

My intention was to make a visit to this island but I saw with great regret that it was impossible unless we lost much time beating to windward, against the wind and with the currents running strong against us, which I could not do. I was already too long in these seas to assure the success of the commission with which I was entrusted, and I did not wish to receive the imputations of my owners that I had sacrificed their interest and proceeded to make discoveries with which I was not charged. I resolved thus, with regret I must say, to give up this design and stand for two small islands which we had seen at NW¼N, and which I named the Two Brothers.[140]

They lie together E½N and W½S, ¾ of a league distant one from the other. The Westerly isle is larger than the other and higher. They both appear to be white from the dung of birds who alone inhabit these isles. We passed to the Westward of them. They are but rocks on which moss can be seen. The largest is about half a league in circumference, and the other a mile. They lie W¼NW, distant 10½ leagues from Point Elisée on the Island of Baux. In the ESE part of the most Easterly island, I noticed a small shoal which stretched but little into the main.

At noon, our latitude by observation was 8° 50' South.

The longitude of St Christina by reckoning was 142° 52' 30" West, and 142° 49' determined from our last observations at Marchand Island.

We found ourselves 4' more to the South than by reckoning.

At the same time,

Point Marc on the Island of Baux	bore ESE 3° E
Point Elisée *ditto*	bore E¼E
The middle of the Island *ditto*	bore E¼SE
The Westermost of the Two Brothers	bore NW 3° N
and the most Easterly	bore NW½N, distant 3 or 4 leagues

We could not see Marchand Island on account of the hazy weather.

The variation of the compass determined from 17 azimuths was found to be 4° 57' NE.

Réamur's thermometer +27°, Fahrenheit's thermometer 91°.

From Thursday 23rd to Friday 24th June 1791

98¼

At ¾ to 1 o'clock, the Two Brothers, one by the other, bore E½N, ½ a league from the most Westerly of the them.

We steered NNW with a light breeze at East.

I thought that we had now left this group of islands behind us when towards a quarter past five o'clock, the lookout cried Land! We caught sight of it immediately, stretching from N¼NE to NNE½E. It appeared to be high and of a blackish colour. As night was approaching and we believed more land was a-head (in which we proved to be mistaken), I determined to make short boards in the sea over which we had sailed during the day, as it would have been a great want of prudence to continue our route. During the night it blew a hard gale from E to ESE, attended with clear weather.

---

140 Motu Iti.

At 6 o'clock in the morning, the Island which we had seen in the evening and which I had named Masse Island for my first officer, stretched from NNE½N to NNE 8° E, distant about 7 leagues. It afforded an indifferent prospect but it is true to say that we found it difficult to form a judgement on account of the distance and above all, due to the hazy weather. A great quantity of birds such as boobies, gulls, frigate birds and tropic birds, fluttered about the ship.

At ½ past 6 o'clock, in about the ENE part of Masse Island, we perceived another island which I named Chanal Island after my second Captain.[141] It bore NE 8° N, distant about 11 leagues. It appeared to be less mountainous and less broken than the first.

I would have desired to make a visit to these islands which were on our route, but the wind was unfavourable and I resolved upon crowding sail at NNW in order to attempt to leave this archipelago before night.

At ½ past 10 o'clock AM, Masse Island bore ENE ½ E, East ½ South, and the middle E 8° N, while Chanal Island stretched from ENE 3° N to ENE 6° E.

At noon, the latitude by observation was found to be 7° 54' South, and 7° 44' by reckoning, that is to 10' more to the North.

Our longitude by reckoning from the Marquesas was found to be 143° 13' and 143° 10', determined from the observations at Marchand Island and from those we made this morning.

By the observation of eleven sets of azimuths the variation of the compass was 5° 3'.

At this moment, at noon, Masse Island stretched from E½S to ESE 5° South and the middle bore ESE½E, distant 6 or 7 leagues. Chanal Island E¼NE 1° E, distant about 10 leagues.

These islands must absolutely be considered as a new discovery for we found them nowhere marked on any chart, as I have before mentioned. They are named in no navigator's journal, of old or of this time. I named all these islands the Revolution Islands in memory of the most remarkable occurrences of the century which have taken place in France. At noon, we drank several times to the health of this address.

Before leaving these islands, it appears to me necessary to give their position.

Marchand Island is greatest in length from North to South, four leagues. It is 3 leagues at the broadest and 10 to 12 leagues in circumference. The middle lies in the latitude of 9° 21' South and longitude 142° 19' W by observation. Obelisk point lies NW¼W 1° W of the globe, distant 20 leagues from the bay of Madre

---

141 Fleurieu is extremely elogious here as concerns Masse and Chanal (which is not the case in Marchand's journal): *Captain Marchand gave to the former the name of Ile Masse (Masse's Island), and to the latter that of Ile Chanal (Chanal's Island), the two officers employed on board the ship as second captains, who had, with equal intelligence and zeal, seconded the labours of the commander, in the discovery of a new archipelago, undoubtedly deserved that their names should be attached to two of the islands of which it is composed* (Volume 1 of the translation, op. cit., p. 244).

de Dios (Christina Island). The opening of Warm Welcome Bay is situated in the latitude of 9° 22' South.

Baux Island* was in circumference at least 17 leagues, the North point, which I named Elisée Point, lies in the latitude of 8° 48' South. It is very low. The Westermost point lies in the longitude of 41° 31' and bears N¼NW, distant 7½ leagues from the Western part of Marchand Island. I supposed by observation that the middle of the island was to be found in the latitude of 8° 54' and in the longitude of 142° 25' W. This island is the capital city of the Revolution Islands so much for its beauty as for its size.

*The navigators who will be better able to survey these islands will no doubt find that Baux Island is formed of two islands lying East and West and separated by a narrow channel, for seeing it from the NNE, I caught sight of two lands but I only presume this to be so for the wind and currents prevented us from gaining to the East.

The Eastermost of the two islets, which we called the Two Brothers, lies in the latitude of 142° 55' South and in the longitude of 142° 55' W. They bear W¼NW, distant 10 to 11 leagues of the Northern extremity of Baux Island.

As for Masse Island and Chanal Island, they were situated at too great a distance and I could not determine their size. The middle of the first one lies in the latitude of 8° 1' South and in the longitude of 142° 50' W, distant 16 leagues, and is situated NNW 2° W of Baux Island and North ½ E of Two Brothers. The second lies in the latitude of 7° 51' South and is situated in very near 142° 35' longitude. These two islands face each other ENE 9° N and WSW 9° S, distant 4 or 5 leagues.

During the time we remained between the two islands, we were very exact in observing the variation of the magnetic needle, which was 4° 29' to 5° 3' NE with different compasses.

During this day, Réamur's thermometer kept at +27°, and at night kept from 24 to 25.

In the channels which separate these islands, we found a current which set sometimes to the West and sometimes to NW, running near ½ a mile per hour.

After the marks which may be seen upon upon the rocks bordering the shore of Possession Cove (Marchand Island), the sea rises sometimes two feet. We observed the same in Warm Welcome Bay, where the sea is very smooth.

The bearings of these islands may be seen as being determined with near perfect exactness and I may assert that the longitudes which I have assigned to these islands do not vary more than a quarter of a degree. In Mr Cook's account of his second voyage in, Tome 4, page 120 of the French translation, and in the introduction to the third, it appears that the search for new lands in the Pacific Ocean South of the line by himself and by the those who followed leaves little to be discovered in this part of sea.[142] But I am pretty well convinced that there are easy proofs to the contrary in

142 Marchand had the Hotel de Thou version on board, on page 120 of Volume IV of the translation, Cook writes: *I had now made the circuit of the Southern Ocean in a high latitude, and traversed*

examining but the general map of this most famous navigator, on which all the different tracks may be seen. From the Marquesas, situated near longitude 141° 20', to the Dangerous Isles or St Bernard Isles, seen by Mr Biron,[143] lying in 169° 20' longitude, the 8th, 9th, 10th, 11th and 12th parallels have not yet been run over. Mr Cook did but cross them at 156° 10' in 1777, on the route from the Society Islands to the North Coast of America. No navigator, of whom I know at least, has ever crossed this vast ocean near the lines where more islands are yet most certainly to be found.

Mr Cook hardly suspected that so near the Marquesas, there lay such a considerable number of islands as this. We have discovered the four principal islands and I am convinced that West of these, there are others to be found, for I thought to have seen land there. It is with regret that I could not assure myself of this for the reasons I have above mentioned. The discovery of these islands is more valuable still for the inhabitants,* among all those that have been met with in the Pacific ocean, are the most gentle and are possessed of the most friendly disposition imaginable.

*I visited only Marchand Island but I believe we may presume, and even be well assured, that the inhabitants of the other islands possess the same manners. It would be most ridiculous to suppose the contrary: lambs cannot live near to wolves without being devoured by them

Articles which are to found in the Marquesas may be easily had here, and the weary voyager may, at the least, find refreshments and walk about in the magnificent groves which we caught sight of, without the least insult or fear of thieves. I am most certain that the space of sea before mentioned has never before been examined, which will permit to come to a resolution to more exactly reconnoitre the shores, and even the interior of New Holland, as well as the stretches of land situated to the North of Japan and North East of China.[144] I believe that despite the numerous discoveries made by the famous Cook, the King and Minister who determines to fit out new expeditions, will see themselves forever remembered amongst the most distinguished benefactors dedicated to the service of mankind and to the protection of the sciences.

---

it in such a manner so as not to leave the least room for the possibility of there being a continent, unless near the pole, and out of the reach of navigation By twice visiting the tropical sea, I had not only settled the situation of some old discoveries, but made there many new ones, and left, I conceive, very little more to be done even in that part. Thus I flatter myself that the intention of the voyage has, in every respect, been fully answered; the Southern hemisphere sufficiently explored (February 1775, Volume 2, p. 239). In the translation of the third voyage, the *General Introduction* is missing in the 1785 Hotel de Thou edition. It is probable then, that Marchand had the English copy of the third voyage with him and is here referring to King's *Introduction* which reproduces the above passage. (op. cit., p. xxviii).

143 Byron

144 This sentence is badly constructed in French and I have translated it so as to make it as meaningful as possible. It is of course open to other interpretations: *D'après la certitude que j'ai que les parages que je viens de citer n'ont jamais été parcourus et les motifs qui peuvent déterminer à reconnaitre plus parfaitement les côtes, meme l'intérieur de la Nouvelle Hollande et l'étendue qui se trouve au NE de la Chine et au Nord du Japon.*

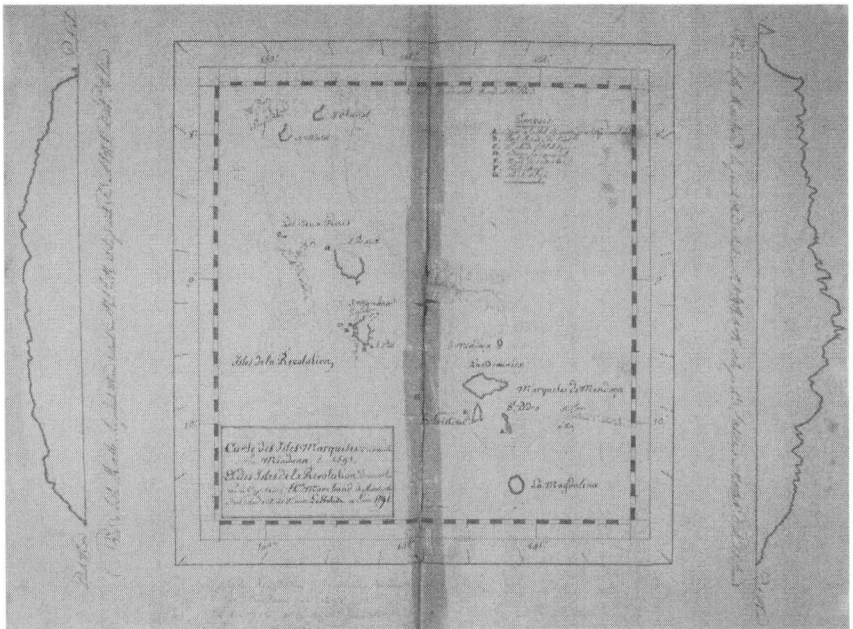

Figure 2 Map and profiles of the Marquesas (Volume 1 of the manuscript)
Courtesy of the Bibliothèque Alcazar, Marseilles, France.

Indeed, it is not be doubted that, in procuring to these savage peoples who are sometimes barbarous, the knowledge of only those of our arts which can augment their happiness, and that in bringing to their countries the means by which their chief sustenance may be increased, our national industry will improve, new routes for our trade and commerce will open, and navigators will find new means to recover their strength after their long voyage.

I will not here mention a motive which is more than sufficient to oblige the French Ministry to sacrifice all in hopes of meeting with Mr de la Peyrouse,[145] or the unfortunate remains of his companions, who are perhaps abandoned in some of these islands which are scattered all about the sea in these parts of the globe. Without the critical juncture in which France has found herself at this time, I am persuaded that the Ministry would never resolve cruelly to abandon our brave countrymen, and that it would be most unwilling not to relieve from their situation those who have faced the greatest of dangers for the dignity of their nation.[146]

---

145 Marchand's spelling.
146 Gannier (*journal*, op. cit., p. 308) underlines that Marchand is right to have faith in the government. A few months earlier, on 9th February 1791, the Assembly had decided to send out an expedition in search of La Pérouse. D'Entrecasteaux left Brest in September. A different interpretation

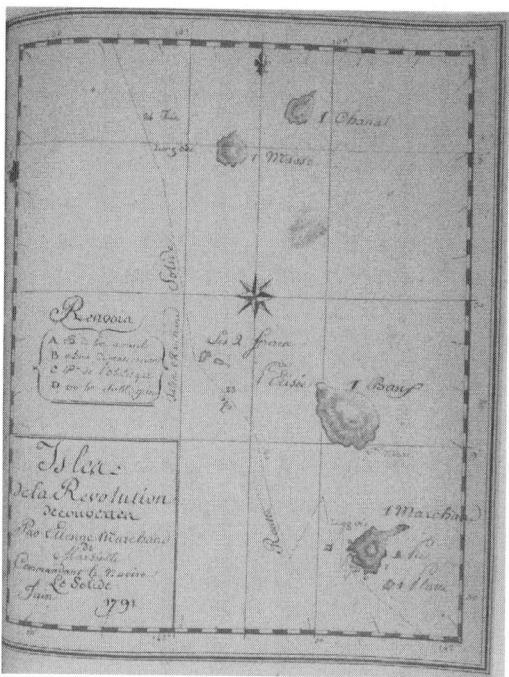

Figure 3 Track of the *Solide* through the Revolution Islands (Volume 1 of the manuscript)
Courtesy of the Bibliothèque Alcazar, Marseilles, France.

Such a blot on the honour of the Ministry in the eyes of all the nations of Europe, cannot be considered.

Other political reasons may perhaps determine even more France to keep one or two frigates in this sea where the ambition of England is to go further still. How may any Frenchman view with a composed mind, this nation, which is already master of the most profitable places in Asia*, secure itself, by open force or by a trick, some of the treasures of Spain in the New World by the establishment of new colonies, as Nootka Sound and others which will be formed forthwith on the North West coast of America, and which will most certainly be well managed and profitably situated?

*To be assured of the great extent of the English possessions in India and in other parts of the globe, it is enough to examine the catalogue of the countries of which they have mastery in Asia. They have in their possession the Mogul Empire of which the sovereign is but a shadow in their pay, the rich countries named

---

may be that Marchand is here attempting to plead his own cause and hoping, on his return, for a commision to command a voyage with this objective in mind.

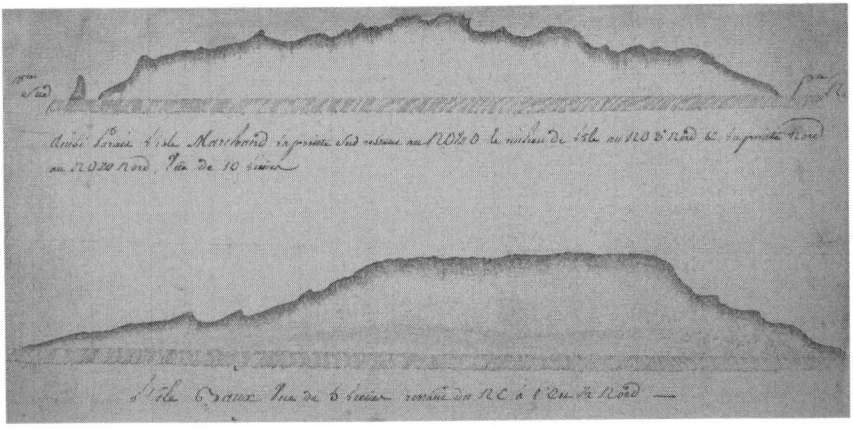

Figure 4 Profiles of Marchand Island and Baux Island (Volume 1 of the manuscript)
Courtesy of the Bibliothèque Alcazar, Marseilles, France.

Bengal, the four Circars, the Coromandel Coast where we have but a precarious power, the Kingdom of Arcot of which the sovereign is their prisoner, great establishments in the Tanjore, the Malabar Coast, Sumatra, Africa, New Holland, and even Gibraltar in Europe.

It is, I repeat, to the advantage of science and of the humanity of France and her friends, to not let slip any opportunity to acquire a certain knowledge of these regions within which our conduct must be of the most respectable kind. The expence which England has been at, and the formidable fitting out of ships, in order to make succeed their design, is sure proof of the soundness of the reasons I have given. Voyages of which the purpose is to observe, to examine the state of the colonies and the state of the industries, but of which the object is also to explore, must serve fully the interests of geography and natural history. This navigation, attended with dangers of all kinds, will bring up sailors of the most skilful sort from whom the Nation will find the greatest benefit.

From Friday 24th to Saturday 25th June 1791

124¾

During this day, we had a fine gentle gale, varying from NE¼E to NE. We directed our course as much to North as possible and set the studding sails. At 3 o'clock there was no land in sight.

The look-out at sun-set saw nothing a-head, and the weather being clear, we continued our route.

The variation of the compass, determined from 9 azimuths, was NE 5° 6'. We saw very few birds which is a near sure sign that we were near no more land.

We noticed many large flying fish with red wings.

Latitude by observation S 5° 42'
Longitude by reckoning W 143° 38'.

After 4 sets of observations of 5 distances each of the sun and the moon, reduced to noon, it was 143° 54'.
Réamur's thermometer +27½°, Fahrenheit's thermometer 92°.
12' difference more to the North than by reckoning.

From Saturday 25ᵗʰ to Sunday 26ᵗʰ June 1791

138¾
Until 8 o'clock PM, the breeze blew a gentle gale at East attended with clear weather. At this time, we had squalls and rain without intermission. We caught sight of some tropic birds but almost none others.

Latitude by observation S 3° 14'.
Longitude by reckoning W 143° 27'.
Longitude by observation 143° 43'.

10' difference more to the North than by reckoning.
Réamur's thermometer +24½°, Fahrenheit's thermometer 86°
I am told by Mr Roblet that one of the seamen has the symptoms of scurvy upon him. I recommended the greatest vigilance and care. During our stay at St Christina, a prodigious number of spots were found upon him, and upon on some of the others, but which went away by degrees. The company was in general in a very good state of health for there was no one man under the care of the Surgeon.

From Sunday 26ᵗʰ to Monday 27ᵗʰ June 1791

117¼
The wind blew a gentle gale from E¼NE to ESE, attended with fine weather. We saw tropic birds and some grey gulls.
By the mean result of 11 azimuths, the variation of the needle was 5° 6' NE.
During the evening, a flying with fish with red wings landed on the deck. It was 10 inches in length.

Latitude by observation S 1° 2'.
Longitude by observation 143° 44'.
Longitude by reckoning W 143° 28'.

15' difference more to the North than by reckoning.
Réamur's thermometer +24°, Fahrenheit's thermometer 85°.

From Monday 27ᵗʰ to Tuesday 28ᵗʰ June 1791

68½

During this day, we had but a light breeze variable from ESE to ENE and clear weather.

During the morning, we saw tropic birds, gulls, dolphins and very large flying fish with red wings and with white wings, and bonitos.

By 8 azimuths and by the amplitudes, the variation of the compass was observed in the evening to be 5° 15', and in the morning 5° 4' NE.

Latitude by observation N 19'.
Longitude by observation 143° 34'.
Longitude by reckoning W 143° 18'.

13' difference more to the North than by reckoning.

Crossing the line

We crossed the line at ½ past 6 o'clock in the morning for the second time, in longitude 143° 34' West.

Réamur's thermometer +25°, Fahrenheit's thermometer 87°.

From Tuesday 28ᵗʰ to Wednesday 29ᵗʰ June 1791

78¾

We saw in the afternoon considerable flocks of birds of the grey gull and white gull species, and birds like the booby, etc. which indicates that we are near to the land.

At a ¼ past 6 o'clock in the evening, the look-out shouted Land! at North and at West. Having myself ascended the cross trees of the top mast, I too believed I sighted land, like several of the officers. We were in this though all mistaken, the illusion being perfect.

At 7 o'clock in the evening, we steered W under the two top-sails in order to reconnoitre the land which lay in the West, for it was here that it seemed to be the largest. At 1 o'clock AM, we sounded with 90 fathoms of line and found no bottom. During the night, we lay to, with her head to the South until day-light. Having discovered our mistake, for there was nothing more to be seen, we stood again to the North. The great quantity of birds which we had seen and which were still to be seen, had occasioned the error. During the whole of the day we had a light breeze, attended with squalls at intervals.

The variation of the needle by the azimuths was found to be 5° 10' NE.

Latitude by observation N 1° 16'.
Longitude by observation W 144° 13'.
Longitude by reckoning 143° 57'.

10' difference more to the North than by reckoning.

Since our departure from the Revolution Islands, the currents had carried us one degree to the North of that given by the log.

Réamur's thermometer +24°, Fahrenheit's thermometer 85°.

From Wednesday 29ᵗʰ to Thursday 30 June 1791

116

We saw many sea swallows, seagulls, boobies, tropic birds of two species, and birds of the gull species of a black colour all over.

The breeze blew a gentle gale attended with squalls and much rain.

In the evening, the variation of the compass by observation was 5° 7', and in the morning 5° 2' NE.

Latitude by observation N 3° 12'.
Longitude by observation W 144° 23'.
Longitude by reckoning 144° 76'.

Réamur's thermometer +24½°, Fahrenheit's thermometer 86°.

Two of our people were much grieved to find that they had got the distemper, spread on occasion by the favours of the nymphs of the Marquesas.

From Thursday 30ᵗʰ to Friday 1ˢᵗ July 1791

104½

We caught sight of considerable flocks of sea swallows and grey gulls, etc.

The breeze continued to blow a gentle gale with squalls and much rain.

By the mean of seven azimuths, the variation of the needle was 5° 15' NE.

Latitude by observation N 4° 54'.
Longitude by observation W 144° 37'.
Longitude by reckoning W 144° 21'.

Réamur's thermometer +23°, Fahrenheit's thermometer 83°.

From Friday 1ˢᵗ to Saturday 2ⁿᵈ July 1791

77½

We had a variable breeze from NE to ESE, attended with lightning and rain without intermission.

We continued to see frigate birds, sea swallows, boobies and black gulls. We caught sight of dolphins and tunny fish.

Latitude by observation N 6° 18'.
Longitude by observation W 144° 52'.
Longitude by reckoning 144° 36'.

10' difference more to the North than by reckoning.
Réamur's thermometer +24½°, Fahrenheit's thermometer 86°.

From Saturday 2nd to Sunday 3rd July 1791

50½

During the whole of the day, the rain continued without intermission attended with lightning and thunder, the breeze varied much from SSE to NE½N.

The same birds of which I have made mention continued to flutter about the ship.

We took a bonito which I served to all the people.

Latitude by observation N 7° 10'.
Longitude by observation W 145°.
Longitude by reckoning 144° 44'.

5' difference more to the North than by reckoning.
Réamur's thermometer +22°, Fahrenheit's thermometer 81°.

From Sunday 3rd to Monday 4th July 1791

14

Excepting some few gusts of wind at West, between the North and the South, we had calm weather all this day and lightning at intervals.

We saw bonitos, dolphins, a shark and very few birds.

By a set of seven azimuths, the variation of the magnetic needle was 5° 27' NE.

Latitude by observation North 7° 23'.
Longitude by observation W 144° 53'.
Longitude by reckoning 144° 36'.

Réamur's thermometer +25½°, Fahrenheit's thermometer 88°.

From Monday 4th to Tuesday 5th July 1791

60

The heat was suffocating during the afternoon.

We had calm weather or light gusts of wind until 5' o clock. At this time, the wind veered at SSE and it grew cooler. We had rain at intervals, attended with lightning.

We saw very few birds this day but at night we heard their cries.

We had sight of porpoises once more.

By 9 azimuths, the variation of the compass was found to be 5° 48' NE.

Latitude by observation N 8° 34'.
Longitude by observation W 144° 45'.
Longitude by reckoning 144° 29'.

12' difference more to the North than by reckoning.
Réamur's thermometer +26°, Fahrenheit's thermometer 89°.

From Tuesday 5ᵗʰ July to Wednesday 6ᵗʰ July 1791

103

At 4 o'clock, we passed a trunk of a tree, 15 feet in length and 7 or 8 inches in diameter with barnacles upon it. It seemed to have been some time at sea.[147] We saw a great quantity of fish in the adjacent parts. At the same moment we took a bonito.

The breeze continued to blow variable from WNW to SSE round by South, attended with much rain.

We saw sea swallows, small white gulls, tropic birds and boobies. We caught sight of bird of a white colour, the size of a goose, its flight was very low never rising more than two or three feet above the surface of the sea.

Latitude by observation N 10° 21'.
Longitude by observation W 144° 32'.
Longitude by reckoning 144° 16'.

6' difference more to the North than by reckoning.
Réamur's thermometer +25°, Fahrenheit's thermometer 87°

From Wednesday 6ᵗʰ to Thursday 7ᵗʰ July 1791

The wind continued very variable attended with rain and a great swell from the NE.

We saw sharks, dolphins and many birds of the species of which I have already made mention.

During the night, we had much lightning.

---

147 Here Fleurieu in his account (in French and in the translation op. cit.,) suggests the exact opposite: *On the 5ᵗʰ of July, towards noon, in latitude 10° 20' North, and longitude 144° 30' West, there was seen passing a large trunk of a tree, which appeared to have been floating but a short time: from this sign, it might be supposed that the ship was in the vicinity of some land, but no other sign supported this conjecture* (op. cit., p. 261 of the translation).

By a set of 5 azimuths, the variation of the magnetic needle was 6° 15' NE.

Latitude by observation N 11° 42'.
Longitude by observation W 144° 33'.
Longitude by reckoning 144° 17'.

6' difference more to the North than by reckoning.
Réamur's thermometer +22°, Fahrenheit's thermometer 81°.

From Thursday 7ᵗʰ to Friday 8ᵗʰ July 1791

68¾

We lay almost becalmed until 9' o clock in the evening when the wind settled at NE blowing a gentle gale and attended with a great swell from this quarter. By two sets of 5 azimuths each, we found the variation of the compass to be 6° 26' NE.
We saw sharks.

Latitude by observation N 12° 32'.
Longitude by observation W 145° 12'.
Longitude by reckoning 144° 56'.

4' difference more to the North than by reckoning.
Réamur's thermometer +23½°, Fahrenheit's thermometer 84°.

From Friday 8ᵗʰ to Saturday 9ᵗʰ July 1791

92¾

The breeze was variable from N¼NE to NE blowing a gentle gale with squalls and a great swell from the NNE.
We saw dolphins, bonitos, tropic birds of both species, sea swallows and a frigate bird.
These last few days we have not caught sight of any flying fish with red wings.
By the mean result of four sets of azimuths, the variation of the magnetic needle was found to be 6° 41' NE.

Latitude by observation N 13° 31'.
Longitude by observation W 146° 27'.
Longitude by reckoning W 146° 11'.

3' difference more to the North than by reckoning.
Réamur's thermometer +24°, Fahrenheit's thermometer 85°.

From Saturday 9ᵗʰ July to Sunday 10ᵗʰ July 1791

74½

We had a gentle gale at NE and NNE until midnight. At this moment we lay becalmed until 6 o'clock AM. The wind fixed at SSE, SE and E still attended with squalls.

As soon as it was day-light, we were surrounded on every side by a great number of tropic birds, sea swallows, gulls and other kinds of birds which hardly ever quit the land. The nearest to us were the Sandwich Islands, which were more than 200 leagues distant, unless there is in this sea, which is very possible, some islands which have yet to be seen by navigators.

The variation of the compass by observation was 6° 58' NE.

Latitude by observation North 14° 29'.
Longitude by observation W 147° 6'.
Longitude by reckoning 146° 50'.

6' difference more to the North than by reckoning.
Réamur's thermometer +23½°, Fahrenheit's thermometer 84°.

From Sunday 10ᵗʰ July to Monday 11ᵗʰ July 1791

115½

In the afternoon, the great number of birds that we had seen in the morning left us, taking flight towards the NE.

We had a fresh breeze of wind at NE and ENE, attended with a very thick haze and drizzling rain.

During the night, we took a reef in each top-sail which we loosed at day-light.
The variation of the compass by reckoning NE 7° 30'.

Latitude by observation N 16° 17'.
Longitude by observation W 148° 4'.
Longitude by reckoning W 147° 48'.

9' difference more to the North than by reckoning.
Réamur's thermometer +23°, Fahrenheit's thermometer 83°.

From Monday 11ᵗʰ July to Tuesday 12ᵗʰ July 1791

114

The breeze continued variable from NE to ENE blowing a fresh gale attended frequently with hard squalls. We continued taking a reef in each top-sail.

We did not see any birds this day excepting a Frigate.

By seven azimuths we found the variation of the compass to be 8° 38' NE.

Latitude by observation N 18° 11'.
Longitude by observation W 148° 39'.
Longitude by reckoning 148° 23'.

6' difference more to the North than by reckoning.
Réamur's thermometer +21½°, Fahrenheit's thermometer 80°.

From Tuesday 12th July to 13 July 1791

116¾

The breeze continued at NE and NE¼E blowing a fresh gale attended at intervals with squalls.

We caught sight of tropic birds, some sea swallows, a turtle and dolphins or dolphin-fish.[148]

By the mean result of six azimuths, the variation of the compass was found to be 9° 2' NE.

Latitude by observation N 20° 3'.
Longitude by observation W 149° 34'.
Longitude by reckoning 149° 18'.

Réamur's thermometer +21⅓°, Fahrenheit's thermometer 80°.
In this position, the island of Ouhaihi[149] (one of the Sandwiches) bore W by the globe, distant 145 leagues.

From Wednesday 13th to Thursday 14th July 1791

127½

The breeze was variable from NE to ENE and blew a fresh gale with squalls.
We saw flying fish with red wings and few other birds during this day.

---

148 Gannier refers here to Cook's account (*Voyage to the South Pole*, op. cit., 3rd September 1772) and points to a confusion between dolphins and sea-breams or gilt-heads: *dorade-coryphène (coryphoena hyppurus)*, supposedly named dophin-fish in the account (op. cit., p. 318). On the 3rd September 1772, Cook makes no mention of a dolphin fish. Forster, on the contrary, the same day, refers to the *coryphena hippurus*: *We were lucky enough two days after to take a dolphin (coryphena hippurus,) whch is likewise dry meat; but the inimitable brightness of its colours, which continually change from one rich hue to another, whilst drying, is, in my opinion, one of the most admirable appearance which can occur to the voyager's view during a tropical navigation* (Volume 1, op. cit., pp. 47–48). In the Hotel de Thou translation (which was the edition which Marchand had on board with him), there is no mention of a dophin-fish either.

149 Hawai'i (present day spelling) was spelt in various ways by the European navigators. Cook calls the island *Owhyhee*, like both Dixon and Portlock.

By the azimuths, the variation of the compass was 9° 45' NE.

Latitude by observation N 22° 1'.
Longitude by observation W 150° 35'.
Longitude by reckoning *ditto* 150° 19'.

4' difference more to the North than by reckoning.
Réamur's thermometer +22°, Fahrenheit's thermometer 81°.
We kept today the Festival of the Federation[150] and served a double allowance
to the ship's company.

From Thursday 14ᵗʰ to Friday 15ᵗʰ July 1791

122

We crossed the Tropick of Cancer during the morning.

Latitude by observation N 24° 4'.
Longitude by observation W 151° 41'.
Longitude by reckoning W 151° 25'.

18' difference more to the North than by reckoning.
The mornings now grew cooler though the sun was directly over our heads.
Réamur's thermometer +22°, Fahrenheit's thermometer 81°.

From Friday 15ᵗʰ to Saturday 16ᵗʰ July 1791

133

During this day, the breeze blew a fresh gale at NE, attended with hard squalls
and very hazy weather in the horizon.

At ½ past 1 o'clock AM, we took a reef in each top-sail.

We caught sight of a considerable flock of large sea swallows and flying fish
with red wings.

The variation of the compass by observation 10° 27' NE.

During the morning, we unrigged the fore top-gallant masts. The ship worked
much forward under the top-gallant sail, and we seldom carried it if the sea was
great, in such case our progress was retarded, and not hastened.

Latitude by observation N 25° 58'.
Longitude by observation W 153°.
Longitude by reckoning 152° 44'.

Réamur's thermometer +20°, Fahrenheit's thermometer 78°.

---

150 For a discussion of this particular commemoration see "The Festival of the Federation: Model
and Reality," in Mona Ozouf, *Festivals and the French Revolution*, Harvard University Press,
1988, pp. 33–60.

From Saturday 16th to Sunday 17th July 1791

125½

Until 4 o'clock in the morning, the breeze was at NE, blowing a gentle gale with cloudy weather. At this time, it varied at NNE falling to a calm: I took the opportunity to examine the stays and haul taught the top shrouds, which we had not had the time to do in the Marquesas.

At ½ past 6 o'clock, we tacked and stood to the East, and at 10 o'clock, to the West. By the Easterly amplitude, the variation of the compass was found to be 11° 48' NE.

We saw porpoises and some few sea swallows.

Latitude by observation N 28° 36'.
Longitude by observation W 154° 47'.
Longitude by reckoning " 155° 3'.

Réamur's thermometer +20°, Fahrenheit's thermometer 77°.

From Monday 18th to Tuesday 19th July 1791

54½

During this day, we had by turns very variable light winds, calm and rain.

We saw gulls, stormy petrels, a prodigious quantity of small blubbers (a species of *Mollusca*) on the surface of the sea.

The variation of the compass by observation was 12° 15' NE.

Latitude by observation N 28° 40'.
Longitude by observation W 154° 8'.
Longitude by reckoning W 153° 52'.

Réamur's thermometer +20°, Fahrenheit's thermometer 77°.

From Tuesday 19th to Wednesday 20th July 1791

28

We had light gusts of wind, calm and rain.

It may be imagined that I could not see this calm and light winds with nothing but the greatest impatience, for I could not convince myself that the season was not too greatly advanced, and that there would be time enough to assure a profitable trade on the NW coast of America. It is above very certain that the Spanish and the English have come before me. The variation of the compass by observation of 15 azimuths was 12° 31' NE. We took a shark upon which we found a sucking fish.

We saw this day only stormy petrels and some sea swallows.

I served beer every day to the ship's company which was made on board. They received coffee twice a week. We boiled greens in vinegar or sauerkraut among the soup. It is I believe unnecessary to say that during our time in warm climates, we lashed up the hammocks every day and the between decks were swept clean or scrubbed. The good health of the company may, I believe, be accounted for by these precautions. At this time, one of the sailors was down with the scurvy as I have before mentioned, but due to the care of the Surgeon, all the symptoms were soon checked. However two of the seamen were afflicted with the vene-real[151] distemper which they had contracted in the Marquesas.

By two sets of 5 distances each of the moon and the sun, reduced to 7h 34' 26", our longitude by observation was 156° 5' 52". The longitude computed from the observations made near the Revolution Islands was found to be 154° 20', that is 1° 42' 52" more East. Since our departure from this group, the currents seem to have carried us about NW, for our differences were N and W.

Latitude by observation N 28° 42'.
Longitude by observation W 156° 2'.
Longitude by reckoning 154°.

11' difference more to the South than by reckoning.
Réamur's thermometer +19½°, Fahrenheit's thermometer 76°.

From Wednesday 20ᵗʰ to Thursday 21ˢᵗ July 1791

60¼

The wind being light and the sea smooth during the afternoon, we took the opportunity to paint all the outside of the ship and the masts, which we had not had time enough to do in the Marquesas. We saw a quebrantahuessos, stormy petrels and porpoises.

By the mean result of five azimuths, the variation of the compass was found to NE 13° 32', and by the amplitude, 13° 33'.

During the remainder of the day, we had light winds at South and South East, attended with squalls and a very smooth sea. We directed our course to N¼NE.

We saw flying fish with red wings and with white wings. We had not seen tropic birds for some days.

We took two bonitos.

Latitude by observation N 29° 36'.
Longitude by observation W 155° 37'.
Longitude by reckoning 153° 35'.

Réamur's thermometer +21°, Fahrenheit's thermometer 79°.

---

151 This term is again truncated in the manuscript to *maladie ven . . .* (Gannier, *journal*, op. cit., p. 321).

From Thursday 21ˢᵗ to Friday 22ⁿᵈ July 1791

78

In the afternoon we passed a small quantity of rock weed.

We saw quebrantahuessoses, crossers, stormy petrels and porpoises.

During this day we had light winds varying from SSE to W, attended with squalls and a smooth sea.

By the observation of eight sets of azimuths, the variation of the magnetic needle was 13° 46' NE, mean result.

Latitude by observation N 30° 52'.
Latitude, I mean longitude by observation W 155° 1'.
Longitude by reckoning 152° 49'.

5' difference more to the North than by reckoning.
Réamur's thermometer + 22°, 81 Fahrenheit's thermometer.

From Friday 22ⁿᵈ July to Saturday 23ʳᵈ July 1791

79½

We had a light breeze varying from SSW to SE attended with fine weather. The mean result of six azimuths gave 14° 23' NE variation.

By the mean result of 4 sets of 5 distances each of the moon and the sun, reduced to 7h 4' in the morning, our longitude was found to be 154° 34' 35". That determined from the observations three days before was at this same moment, 154° 32'.

In the morning, we saw quebrantahuessoses, a Red-Shafted Tropic Bird, porpoises and patches of sea weed.

Latitude by observation N 32° 10'.
Longitude by observation W 154° 25'.
Longitude by reckoning " 152° 21'.

6' difference more to the North than by reckoning.
Réamur's thermometer + 21½°, Fahrenheit's thermometer 80°.

From Saturday 23ʳᵈ to Sunday 24ᵗʰ July 1791

104¼

During this day, we had a gentle gale varying from South to SE with cloudy weather, clear at intervals and a smooth sea.

The variation of the compass by observation of the azimuths was 15° 1' NE.

We saw a Red-Shafted Tropic Bird, some quebrantahuessoses and stormy petrels.

No more flying fish were to be seen.

By the observation of two sets of the distances of the moon and the sun, reduced to 8h 3' 58' in the morning, our longitude was W 153° 42' 15". That determined from the observations made the evening before, accounting for the course we had steered, was found to be at this same moment, 153° 40'.

Latitude by observation N 34° 5'.
Longitude by observation W 153° 32'.
Longitude by reckoning 151° 26'.

21' difference more to the North than by reckoning.
Réamur's thermometer + 20½°, Fahrenheit's thermometer 78°.

From Sunday 24ᵗʰ to Monday 25ᵗʰ July 1791

110¼

We had a gentle gale at ESE attended at intervals with squalls. We saw porpoises and tropic birds. I was much surprised to see these birds in such high latitudes for they but seldom remove from the Tropics.

The variation of the compass determined from the azimuths was 15° 30' NE.

At 9 o'clock in the morning, in order not to gain to the East and to get the NW winds, which blow in 45° or 50° latitude, we directed our course to North.

Latitude by observation N 35° 51'.
Longitude by observation W 152° 32'.
Longitude by reckoning 150° 26'.

7' difference more to the North than by reckoning.
Réamur's thermometer + 19°, Fahrenheit's thermometer 75°.

From Monday 25ᵗʰ to Tuesday 26ᵗʰ July 1791

115¼

All this day, we had a breeze at ESE and East attended with showers at intervals. The sea continued smooth. We caught sight of a large turtle asleep on the surface of the water. I did not desire to hoist out the yawl to take it as the weather was favourable to our route. The mean result of two sets of 5 distances each of the moon and the sun, reduced to 8h 21' 20" in the morning, gave longitude 152° 19'. That determined from the last observations (reduced to this moment) was 152° 2'.

Latitude by observation N 37° 49'.
Longitude by observation W 152° 17'.
Longitude by reckoning 149° 54'.

8' difference more to the North than by reckoning.
Réamur's thermometer + 17½°, Fahrenheit's thermometer 72°.

From Tuesday 26th to Wednesday 27 July 1791

109½

We caught sight of crossers, stormy petrels, quebrantahuessoses and porpoises.

The surface of the sea was covered with different species of *Mollusca*. By 11 azimuths, the variation of the compass was found to NE 16° 34'. During the morning, we passed a great quantity of sea fruit[152] which were all of a circular form. They were perfectly like chestnuts which still possess their first outer coats, excepting their colour, which was dirty-white and not brown.

The breeze continued at East and blew a gentle gale with cloudy weather. The surface of the sea was as calm as in a pond.

Latitude by observation N 39° 48'.
Longitude by observation W 151° 42'.
Longitude by reckoning 149° 19'.

13' difference more to the North than by reckoning.
Réamur's thermometer + 17°, Fahrenheit's thermometer 71°.

From Wednesday 27th to Thursday 28th July 1791

102½

In the afternoon, the sea fruits continued to pass by the ship with *Mollusca* of several species. During the night we were made deaf by the cries of the birds. At day-light we caught sight of great flocks of birds among which we distinguished several species: brown gulls, another much resembling the frigate, which like these, was possessed of a long forked tail. Only the flight was different, for it was much more rapid. And finally another species which was the size of a pigeon and whose cries and whose flight resembled that of our sea larks, and thus I believe it to be a bird of the sea shore. We saw flocks of ten to thirty of these. These were signs that we were near to some island not yet known to navigators. Captain Portlock in 1786, in steering for the North West coast of America, had caught sight of a shag in this same sea, and these birds are known almost never to travel far from the land. Mr Cook during his third voyage (in 1778) had also caught sight of a pieces of wood in this position which seemed to have been in the water but a short time.

It seems however that the galleons of Spain which go from Manilla to Acapulco in these same parallels, to get the wind at West, would have discovered such lands if they do indeed exist.

By three sets of observations of azimuths, the variation of the needle was 16° 54' NE.

---

152 *Sea fruit* is the term used in the translation of Fleurieu's account (op. cit., p. 263).

We had this day a gentle gale which varied from SE to East.

Latitude by observation N 41° 35'.
Longitude by observation W 151° 4'.
Longitude by reckoning 148° 41'.

9' difference more to the North than by reckoning.
Réamur's thermometer + 16°, Fahrenheit's thermometer 69°.

From Thursday 28ᵗʰ to Friday 29ᵗʰ July 1791

48¾

We saw a great flock of a species of duck, flying to the Westward. We saw the birds we had seen the evening before taking the same direction, from which I presume that if any such islands exist about this sea, they must be situated Westward of the meridian in which we found ourselves.

Having a near calm, we hoisted out the yawl in the morning to scrub the sides clean of the moss which had grown very long at the water-line.

We unbent the four main-sails and bent new ones. We got up the spare sails in order to dry them, and found they had been damaged by the rats, but we set immediately to work to repair them.

The sea was covered with several species of *Mollusca* and the feathers of the birds. It was most likely the season of moulting.

The variation of the compass by observation was NE 17° 14'.

This day we had very light winds varying from South to East falling to a calm. We have not seen such smooth and quiet a sea that I remember since our departure from Marseilles.

Latitude by observation N 42° 37'.
Longitude by observation W 150° 14'.
Longitude by observation[153] " 147° 51'.

15' difference more to the North than by reckoning.

The considerable differences to the North we have run into since our departure from the Revolution Isalnds can only be accounted for by the setting of the currents.

Réamur's thermometer + 18°, Fahrenheit's thermometer 73°.

---

153 This entry should read *Longitude by reckoning* (see Gannier, *journal*, op. cit., p. 326).

From Friday 29ᵗʰ to Thursday, I mean, from Saturday 30ᵗʰ July 1791

26

At ½ past 6 o'clock in the evening, having seen on the surface of the water, at a short distance from the ship, what appeared to me to be a turtle, by the movements of the fish about it, we hoisted out a yawl in order to take it. It was though found to be a sea plant about 14 feet in length, and in breadth four inches at its widest extremity, and which very gradually decreased to no more than the size of a finger at the other end. It was in the form of a bamboo and likewise hollow but there were no joints to be seen. It had barnacles almost all over fixed by pedicles of a white colour, four, five or six inches in length of a thick, elastic consistence much like a glass tube filled with water. It is the same seen by Captain Cook and named the sea-leek.[154]

We lay becalmed and had light gusts at all points of the compass during this day.

We saw sheerwaters and stormy petrels.

The variation of the compass had been found in the evening by observation to be 17° 33' NE, in the morning it was 17° 51'.

We saw whales.

Latitude by observation N 43° 3'.
Longitude by observation W 150° 37'.
Longitude by reckoning 148° 14'.

8' difference more to the North than by reckoning.
Réamur's thermometer + 15½°, Fahrenheit's thermometer 68°.

From Saturday 30ᵗʰ to Sunday 31ˢᵗ July 1791

59

During this day we had winds varying from NW to W, more or less light, attended with mild weather and a smooth sea.

We saw quebrantahuessoses, sheerwaters, stormy petrels, whales and a sea plant which was like the one we had taken the day before.

The variation of the compass by observation of the amplitudes and of the azimuths was 18° 33' NE.

Latitude by observation N 44° 1'.
Longitude by observation W 150°.
Longitude by reckoning W 147° 37'.

---

154 Cook, *Voyage to the Pacific Ocean*, op. cit., Volume 2, p. 255. Fleurieu points out that neither Cook (nor Anson) had given a detailed description of this species of seaweed. Both Portlock (op. cit.,) and Dixon (op. cit.,) also mention the presence of the *sea-leek* (op. cit., p. 95 and p. 57 respectively) in this area.

8' difference more to the North than by reckoning.

Réamur's thermometer + 15°, Fahrenheit's thermometer 67°.

One of the sows we had brought with us from the Marquesas died while giving birth.

From Sunday 31ˢᵗ July to Monday 1ˢᵗ August 1791

152

We had a fresh gale at W and W¼SW this day attended with hazy weather.

We directed our course to N¼NW for fear that the winds which blew almost constantly from this quarter on this coast, and above all from NW, should oblige us to attack more to the South than we wished.

The season was too far advanced to attempt to meet with the entrance of Prince William or with Cook's River. I resolved to rally the coast around Cape Edge-combe, situated in latitude 57° 4' N, in order to spend time in the Queen Char-lotte's Islands, where abundant skins are to be found.

We saw a piece of wood in the water and whales.

During the morning, we saw several species of petrel, among which was the quebrantahuessos, the stormy petrel, the blue petrel and a fourth which perfectly resembled the White and Black Spotted Petrel, excepting the plumage which did not consist, on the back, of longitudinal lines of black and white.

During the night, we double reefed the fore top-sail and took one reef in the top-sail. There was a great swell from the SW and another from the NW, which obliged us to unrig the main top-gallant mast.

The variation of the compass by azimuths was found to be 18° 43' NE.

Latitude by observation N 46° 29'.
Longitude by observation W 149° 14'.
Longitude by reckoning *ditto* 146° 51'.

Réamur's thermometer + 12°, Fahrenheit's thermometer 61°.

From Monday 1ˢᵗ August to Tuesday 2ⁿᵈ August 1791

139

The wind continued to blew a fresh gale, attended again with a very thick haze varying from WNW and becoming very suddenly cold, Réamur's thermometer at 11° fell to +8°. We found it very cold, for only three or four days since, we had been complaining of the heat.

We saw the trunk of a tree with its roots, covered with its bark and sea plants of several species. A great quantity of petrels, of which I have before made mention, fluttered about the ship.

We also saw a small white gull with a forked tail.

The variation of the compass by reckoning was 20° NE.

At noon, the haze dispersing, the latitude by observation was found to be 48° 44'
N. Our longitude by observation was 148° 21' W, and by reckoning, 145° 58' *ditto*.
4' more to the North than by reckoning.

Réamur's thermometer + 10½°, Fahrenheit's thermometer 58°.

From Tuesday 2nd to Wednesday 3rd August 1791

134½

Until 10 o'clock PM, the wind blew a hard gale at WSW attended with a thick
haze and a prodigious swell from the West. At this time, due to the squalls which
succeeded one other, we were reduced to the foresail and the double-reefed
top-sail. At day-light, the wind moderating, we set the four main courses.

In the afternoon, I perceived that the sea had altered its colour to a whitish
shade which seemed to indicate our approach to soundings, but I did not sound for
our progress was very favourable to our route.

We saw the same birds as in the last two days and some sea plants.

The variation of the compass was 21° 30' NE.

Latitude by reckoning N 50° 56'.
Longitude by observation W 147° 41'.
Longitude by reckoning " 145° 18'.

Réamur's thermometer + 9½°, Fahrenheit's thermometer 56°.

From Wednesday 3rd to Thursday 4th August 1791

131½

The hard gale continuing to blow at WSW, the wind began to veer at SE, attended
with a thick haze and so much rain that the horizon stretched no more than ½ a
mile. The swell from the West these last few days now affected us but very little. The sea was still discoloured and at 5 o'clock in the evening we sounded but
found no bottom with 150 fathoms of line.

At 9 o'clock PM we loosed all the reefs out of the top-sails and set the studding
sails, which I was obliged to take in at 7 o'clock in the morning on account of the
violent gusts of wind.

In the morning, we caught sight of large piece of wood in the water and several
kinds of petrels, of which I have already made mention, and puffins and brown gulls.

The variation of the compass by reckoning was 22° 30' NE.

Latitude by reckoning N 53° 6'.
Longitude by observation W 147° 4'.
Longitude by reckoning " 144° 41'.

Réamur's thermometer + 9°, Fahrenheit's thermometer 55°.

From Thursday 4th to Friday 5th August 1791

141¼

At noon, we directed our course North, and at 3 o'clock PM, N¼NE in order to come up with the coast of America. The wind blew a hard gale at SE and South, attended with squalls and a great swell from the West. During the night we continued under the foresail and close-reefed top-sails.

We saw petrels, sheerwaters, a flock of small birds like sea larks and sea plants.

In the morning, we clinched a cable to the two anchors and brought them to the cathead.

By four sets of azimuths, the variation of the magnetic needle was found to be 23° 36' NE.

Latitude by observation N 55° 12'.
Longitude by observation W 144° 50'.
Longitude by reckoning 142° 27'.

8' more to the North than by reckoning in three days.
Réamur's thermometer + 10°, Fahrenheit's thermometer 57°.

From Friday 5th to Saturday 6th August 1791

138

At noon, we steered NNE with the wind at South and SE blowing a hard gale with clear weather.

At 2h 10' 12" PM, the observation of four sets of five distances each of the moon and the sun, made by Mr Chanal and myself, gave the following results

The 1st by Mr Chanal gave	143° 31' 45".
The 2nd *ditto*	143° 42' 30".
The 3rd by myself	143° 14' 15".
The 2nd by *ditto*	143° 30' 15".
Mean result	413° 29' 40".

That determined from our last observations, reduced to the same moment, was 144° 34', that is 1° 4' 20" more to the West, or 12½ leagues.

All the officers had also made observations and obtained about the same results.

In the afternoon we brought another anchor to the cathead to which we clinched a cable.

Many birds were to be seen of which I have already made mention, as well as sea plants.

The colour of the sea grew suddenly a very whitish colour, but knowing with great accuracy the distance at which the coast lay, by the observations we had just made, and the weather being favourable, I did not sound.

At 7 o'clock in the morning, in latitude 56° 33' and longitude 141° 20' 40", we directed our course to NE¼E. Cape Edgecombe bore then NE, some degrees to the E, distant 35 leagues. The wind continued to blow a hard gale at SE, attended with hazy weather.

We saw on the surface of the water a fish of a red colour which had been dead for a short time for it was still whole. It was about 18 inches in length. Several of the company informed me that they had seen another, but very much larger.

At noon the latitude by reckoning (we had been unable to take the altitude) was found to be 56° 38'.

Longitude by observation was 140° 40'.
By reckoning from the Marquesas it was 139° 21'.

The variation of the compass by observation was 25° 1' NE.
Réamur's thermometer + 10°, Fahrenheit's thermometer 57°.

From Saturday 6ᵗʰ to Sunday 7ᵗʰ August 1791

64

This day the wind was very variable blowing from almost all quarters and attended with rain without intermission, excepting in the morning when the weather grew clear and fine.

We had continued to lead on the starboard side until 11 o'clock in the evening, at which time we had tacked.

At 8 o'clock in the morning, being in the latitude of 57° 1' N by reckoning, and in longitude 140° 23' W, the wind fixing at South and SSE, we directed our course to E¼NE all sails set, in order to fall in with the land before night. Cape Edgecombe was distant but about 24 leagues, following our observations.

We continued to see petrels, puffins, brown gulls, sea plant, drift wood and a great number of whales.

At 9 o'clock, the wind veered at SSW, which permitted us to set our studding sails.

The variation of the compass by observation was NE 26° 30'.

Latitude by observation N 57° 20'.
Longitude by observation W 139° 56'.
Ditto by reckoning 138° 37'.

We were carried 23' North of the reckoning in two days. As my intention was to anchor in the entrance of Norfolk, we found ourselves too much to the North of its latitude, we worked to windward, the wind being at SE¼S.
Réamur's thermometer +12°, Fahrenheit's thermometer 61°.

From Sunday 7ᵗʰ to Monday 8ᵗʰ August 1791

55½

Many very large whales, gulls, several species of petrels, sea plants, the trunks of trees and small pieces of wood, which seemed to have been wrought, were to be seen.

At 6 o'clock PM, we had, at last, sight of the long-looked for coast of America. The land extended from E to E¼NE, distant by estimation about 14 leagues. In the Southermost land appeared a very high mountain of a pyramidical form, which we recognized as Mount Edgecombe. The summit was covered in snow. To the North of it we perceived two others, which were of a more moderate height, and which at such a distance appeared to stand alone.

We were distant 11⅓ leagues following the longitude computed from our last observations, and 15 leagues more to the East of the reckoning from the Marquesas.

During the night we continued to make for the land with a light wind varying from SSW to SSE, but at day-light I saw that we had made little progress and that the current had carried us to the Northward.

At 7 o'clock in the morning, we had sight of land to the North and to the South of that which we had seen the day before. We discovered to the North very high mountains which were very broken and which were separated from Mount Edgecombe by what appeared to be low land. To the South we saw land of a moderate height. The land extended from NE¼E to ESE. After a quarter of an hour, the clouds, which had gathered above it, hid it from our view. But at 9 o'clock, we saw it once more and we distinguished very clearly Cape Edgecombe bearing ESE, and the neighbouring mountains of the Bay of Salisbury bearing NE½N. We were distant about 7 leagues from the shore which appeared to form several bays.

Note that the view of Mount Edgecombe[155] drawn by Mr Cook in his atlas is very well done and it is impossible to mistake it.

At ¼ past 10 o'clock, we had a light wind at ESE. As I desired to double Cape Edgecombe in order to make the entrance to Norfolk, we tacked and stood to the South.

When Cape Edgecombe bears E¼SE at a distance of 7 leagues, the extremity of it appears to terminate in a very low point beyond which no more land is to be seen. A little to the NE of this cape, the land increases in height and joins the foot of the mountain of the same name.

At noon our latitude by observation was 57° 12' N.
The longitude determined from our last observations was 138° 29' 30", and that taken from Dixon's chart, from the following bearings, was 138° 55' 30".

Mount Edgecombe bore E½NE 2° E, the Cape of the same name and the Northermost land in sight, bearing NNW, the Cape was distant about 8 leagues by estimation.

---

155 Cook, *Voyage to the Pacific Ocean*, op. cit., Volume 2, p. 258.

During this day, we found a difference of 15' N, and I perceived that we had been carried W 4 or 5 leagues since the first bearing we had taken of the land, which proves to a demonstration that we had been carried by the current about 6 leagues NW.

Réamur's thermometer +11°, Fahrenheit's thermometer 59°.

The variation of the compass determined from the azimuths and the amplitudes was NE 28° 13'.

From Monday 8ᵗʰ to Tuesday 9ᵗʰ August 1791

55½

At ½ past 1 o'clock PM, we tacked and stood to the East in order to fall in with the coast and to have the advantage of a favourable wind for the doubling of Cape Edgecombe.

We continued on this tack with a light wind varying from SSE to S¼SW until ½ past 6 o'clock. Near becalmed and perceiving that the swell and the currents were carrying us quickly on the shore, leeward to us, we sheered off in order to get an offing.

When we tacked, Cape Edgecombe bore ESE½E, distant 5 leagues. The inlet which Mr Cook named Bay of Islands, bore NE½E, and Pitt's Island point, which Mr Portlock named Cape Georgiana, N¼NE.

It is unnecessary to say that Mr Portlock was the first to discover that Cape Edgecombe is situated on an island and that he named it Pitt's Island.[156] It is separated from the continent by a strait which he named Hayward Strait but which did permit the passage of a boat. It forms a channel between the Bay of Salisbury and the entrance to Norfolk. Mr Cook so well understood such things that on examination of this coast, not having come to anchor, he presumed that such a passage must exist.

Near where we tacked, we sounded and had no bottom with 80 fathoms of line.

We were near enough to the land to permit us to observe that between Cape Edgecombe till Cape Georgiana, three remarkable openings were to be seen. The land there is very high and much broken, the shore rises perpendicularly. I believe it would be possible to find there an anchoring place, which I however could not discover for I had so little time at my disposal. My intention was to fall in with the entrance of Norfolk as early as I could for I was in hopes of finding skins there. Inland, the mountains and the gullies were covered all over with snow.

We continued to stand to the West until midnight, at which time we stood in for the shore. During the night we had winds varying from SE¼S to S, more or less light, attended with hazy weather threatening at West.

156 Portlock, op. cit., p. 275.

At ½ past 4 o'clock in the morning, Cape Edgecombe bore E¼SE, distant 8 leagues, and the Northermost land in sight bore North. We had sight of Mount Edgecombe at intervals, for it was otherwise covered in clouds.

At 9 o'clock, the wind abating and perceiving that we were to be becalmed a quarter of a league to the leeward, the swell and the current carrying us towards the shore, we tacked and sheered off in order to get an offing. At this time, Cape Edgecombe bore East, distant 4 leagues, and the low land and the islands which form the South East shore of the entrance to Norfolk, E¼SE.

During the morning we had rain without intermission attended with a very light wind at South.

This day, we caught sight of a very large number of whales, porpoises, seals, puffins or sea parrots,[157] stormy petrels, gulls, and a kind of crested bird which resembled the blackbird in form but not in colour, for its mantle, though of a black and white colour, was with rufous speckles. The belly was white and the bill and feet of a reddish colour.

At noon, Cape Edgecombe bore East 9° N, distant 7 leagues.

At noon, our latitude by observation was N 57° 5', and our longitude determined from the above bearing, was 138° 50' 30".

The currents had carried us 16° more to the North this day, for the latitude by reckoning since noon yesterday was found to be only 56° 49'.

Réamur's thermometer +10°, Fahrenheit's thermometer 57°.

From Tuesday 9th to Wednesday 10 August 1791

20

During the afternoon, we had sudden gusts of wind and calms with variable light airs from SE¼S to SSW, attended with rain.

At 5 o'clock we sounded and had 80 fathoms over a bottom of rocks mixed with a few grains of grey sand.

Cape Edgecombe bore at this time ENE½E, distant about 3½ leagues.

At ½ past 7 o'clock, we had the following bearings:

Cape Edgecombe:	ENE½E
Mount *ditto:*	NE½E
the islets forming the the SE shore of the entrance of Norfolk:	East
Entrance of the Bay of Islands:	NNE
Cape Georgiana:	bore N½W

---

157 *This imperfect analogy to the bill of the parrot, which is also edged with a membrane at its base, and the no less distant analogy to the short neck and the round shape, have procured the Puffin the name of* sea parrot, *a denomination as improper as that of* sea dove *for the little guillemot* (Buffon, op. cit., Volume IX, p. 308).

At this time, we were no more than 2 leagues distant from Cape Edgecombe. The currents, or I think the tide, had brought us very near.

The weather growing a little clearer at 6 o'clock, I had caught sight of very high mountains covered in snow in the bottom and North of the entrance of Norfolk.

At 8 o'clock, some few gusts of wind permitted us to stand off to sea in order to get a little clear of the coast. We lay in a perfect calm all night, attended with rain without intermission. At 8 o'clock in the morning, we had a light wind at NW and stood in for the entrance. At 4 o'clock in the morning, Cape Edgecombe bore ENE, distant 4 leagues. At noon, it bore NE and Southermost land adjacent to it, NE½E 3°, distant 2½ leagues. We discovered at the South extremity, a small island which lies East of this Cape, at ENE½N.

Our latitude by observation was found to be N 57° 0' 20" and our longitude, determined from the above bearings, was 138° 27' W.

According to our latitude, observed with the best of sextants and with the greatest exactness, Cape Edgecombe, or that part of it which is situated most West, and which bears NE, lies in the latitude of 57° 3' as determined by Captain Cook.[158] But the land contiguous to the Cape which stretches ESE of the globe, lies in the latitude of only 57° 1'. It may happen frequently that one may be mistaken for the other, according to the position from which it is seen.

Réamur's thermometer +13°, Fahrenheit's thermometer 63°.

From Wednesday 10th to Thursday 11th August 1791

32¾

At 10 minutes past 2 o'clock PM, having made 7½ miles E¼NE since noon, Cape Edgecombe bore NNW 3° W, distant ½ a league. Several small islets formed the SE shore of the entrance, bearing E¼NE to East ½ S. The islet which lies East of the entrance of Cape Edgecombe bore NE, and White's Point bore NE 8° N.

From this position, we commanded all of the entrance. At 3 o'clock we hoisted out the boat and under the command of Mr Chanal, I ordered that they sound a-head, and then go near the ledge of rocks, which is very steep and which extends near 1½ miles SE¼E true of White's Point

After having passed the island which lies to the East of Cape Edgecombe, we had in turn 30, 25, 20 and 17 fathoms over a rocky bottom. We steered to NE in order to avoid the ledge of which I have just made mention, and near the extremity of which the boat had come to anchor. When we had doubled it, we made signs for the boat to leave its station and sound a-head. The wind which had fixed at WNW until this time, veered to NNW. Perceiving that to double a chain of small

---

158 *This mountain I called Mount Edgecumbe; and the point of land that shoots out from it, Cape Edgecumbe. The latter lies in latitude 57° 3'* [. . .], Voyage to the Pacific Ocean, op. cit., Volume 2, p. 345. Here Marchand confirms Cook's bearings, but also attempts to consolidate the nautical data already available.

islands, lying at ENE of the ledge of rock, would prove to be impossible now that we had the tide against us and a contrary wind, and that the passage besides being far too narrow to ply to windward during the night, I made the signal for the boat to come on board and we sheered off in order to get an offing, which I would not have resolved to do if we had been able to come to anchor. The bottom though was everywhere formed of very sharp rocks and we should have run the risk of losing the anchor and a part of the cable, without any degree of safety for ship. We tacked, White's Point at this time bore W 17° South, the middle of the small chain of islands lying ESE of the ledge bore NE 17° N, and the highest point of the ledge of rocks, SW 28° S. All corrected of the variation.

At 8 o'clock in the evening, we fired a great gun to raise the curiosity of the natives,[159] if any were to be found here. In the afternoon, we hoisted out the second boat to tow the ship in case of a calm.

At 10 o'clock in the evening, the middle of the small island East of Cape Edgecombe, bore NW¼W, Cape Edgecombe W½S and the land forming the SE shore of the entrance bore SE½E.

We had calms and light airs at intervals during the night.

At day-light, I sent the second boat under the command of Mr Chanal to visit the harbour in which Mr Dixon had come to anchor in 1787, and to see if the entrance was inhabited at this time, for it is very well known by all that the inhabitants of this coast (like all savages) leave their dwellings to take up their abode in a better place when the fishing and hunting are no longer profitable.

At 4 o'clock, we had a light wind varying from NNW to NNE which permitted us to make several boards in order to approach the anchoring the place. At 7 o'clock, we had a perfect calm. The weather was clear and hot for the thermometer kept at 15½°.

At 4 o'clock AM, the middle of the small island situated E of Cape Edgecombe bore 7° E, Cape Edgecombe W 3° S, and the SE point of the entrance, which is formed of nothing but a chain of small islands of which I have before made mention, bore ESE½E, distant 1½ miles.

At ½ past 7 o'clock, to our great satisfaction, we had sight of a canoe with two men inside it who were singing and making towards the ship, they would have no doubt come along-side the ship very soon after. At a very short distance, one of the two stood up in the aft of the canoe, stretched out his arms and continued to sing. On finishing his song,[160] he approached the quarter of the ship without the least

---

159 Marchand here adopts the same strategy as Dixon at Edgecombe: *Though this appeared a most eligible spot for the natives to take up their abode in, yet no people were to be seen. On this, a four pounder was fired in the evening, in order to excite the curiosity of the inhabitants, if there should be any within hearing* (op. cit., p. 193).

160 Marchand often borrows from the Cook, Dixon and Portlock accounts in this part of his journal, choosing to recount similar episodes in similar terms. For example, Cook in Nootka Sound in March 1778 (*A Voyage to the Pacific Ocean*, op. cit., pp. 273–274) writes: *A considerable number of natives visited us daily; and, every now and then, we saw new faces. On their first coming, they*

fear, for we had shown them marks of friendship. One wore a sort of coat made of the skin of a bear exactly like a carter's.[161] The other had a waistcoat of English wool which was almost new, being a sure proof that others had come before us and that we were to glean after those happier voyagers.[162] It is true that we could not expect better at this time for we had arrived on this coast at a moment when we should have been considering our departure from it.

After having purchased three bear skins in exchange for three tin basins, they made signs for us to come to anchor[163] for we would find many good skins. They also sold us a small sea otter, which had been dead for a very short time, which I had skinned in order to preserve the skin. I ate the flesh which I found to be sweet meat. This canoe had come from the Eastern side of the bay, and at 9 o'clock, it left us and returned the same way. At noon, Cape Edgecombe bore WNW½W, and the small islands which lie ENE of the ledge of rocks, NNE½E.

Our latitude by observation was 57° 2' 46" N
and our longitude 138° 8'.

By the mean result, determined from 12 sets of azimuths taken with different compasses, the variation of the magnetic needle was found to be 28° 46' NE. Captain Dixon in 1787 had found only 24° variation.

Réamur's thermometer +15½°, Fahrenheit's thermometer 68°.

From Thursday 11th to Friday 12th August 1791

At noon, we had the advantage of a little wind at SSW which permitted us to make for the entrance, after having sent another boat to keep near the ledge. At 5 o'clock, a perfect calm succeeded these light airs and prevented us yet again from coming to anchor.

---

generally went through a singular mode of introducing themselves. They would paddle, with all their strength, quite round both ships, a Chief, or other principal person, in the canoe, standing up with a spear, or some other weapon, in his hand, and speaking, or rather hollowing all the time. Sometimes the orator of the canoe would have his face covered with a mask, representing either a human visage, or that of some animal; and instead of a weapon, would hold a rattle in his hand, as before described. After making this circuit around the ships, they would come along-side, and begin to trade without further ceremony. Very often, indeed, they would give us a song in which all in the canoe joined, in a very pleasing harmony. Similarly, Dixon (op. cit., p. 188) also mentions the singing of the inhabitants of Norfolk Sound, before any trading initiatives would begin.

161 Dixon also compares the jacket to a *waggoner's frock* (Ibid., p. 189).

162 Dixon uses the same terms to describe his trading encounter with the people of Port Mulgrave Sound: *They shewed us plenty of beads, and the same kind of knives and spears we had seen in Prince William's Sound; and as a melancholy proof that we only gleaned after more fortunate traders* (Ibid., p. 168).

163 *The cove in which the anchor had been dropped is situated on the Southern coast of Pitt's Island,* * *which forms, on the North-West side, Dixon's Norfolk Sound, to which the natives give the name of Tchinkitânay.* *See in the Introduction Portlock's *Voyage in 1786–7* (Fleurieu, op. cit., p. 283).

At ½ past 5 o'clock, the boat which I had sent to find an anchoring place, returned. The commanding officer informed me that he had examined the harbour in which Mr Dixon had come to anchor, but that more to the North he had found a cove which afforded much more shelter and was a place of safety for the bottom appeared to him to be better and smoother. The cove was very commodious for a river was to be found at the bottom of it and water could be made there, but also it was full of fish which was yet another advantage. Excepting some marks of huts, which seemed to have been abandoned some time since, they saw not the least signs that this place was inhabited.

At 5 o'clock, we had a perfect calm, of which I have already made mention, and which obliged us sheer off to get an offing in order to avoid during the night the dangers of the rocks and banks.

At ½ past 6 o'clock, we had sight of a canoe carrying two men and soon after two others wherein were 15 natives. They came again from the Eastern coast of the entrance. After performing the usual ceremony, that is singing the song, they came along-side the ship. We purchased in all five sea otter skins and twelve strips of the same, two bear skins and three sea calf skins in exchange for tin, daggers, files, nails, etc.

Before leaving us, they gave us to understand by the most expressive gestures, that were we to anchor in the entrance, they should sell to us many skins and that we would find there many inhabitants from the Eastern shore of the entrance, which was at this time their usual place of abode. I did not doubt them and had no cause to be sorry for my faith in them, as we shall have occasion to see.

At 9 o'clock in the evening, the weather became hazy and the wind fixed at SE. We made the tack to the Eastward until half past midnight, when we put about. At ½ past 2 o'clock in the morning, we were very near to the shore, we sheered off in order to get an offing and upon day-light, we immediately steered for the entrance, after having hoisted out a boat and sent it to keep at the high rock of which I have already made mention. At ½ past 6 o'clock, they made the signal for anchorage in the place assigned.

The islands lie ENE of the bank, which bore at this time from NE to N¼NE, the boat having come to anchor WNW 3° N at the rocky ledge, Cape Edgecombe and the Northern extremity of the island, which is Eastward of the Cape, bore WSW½W, White's Point bore WNW½W, and the most Northward point of the Western shore of the entrance, South of which we came to anchor, bore NNW 4° N.

Towards 7 o'clock, we had a perfect calm and I sent a boat a-head in order to tow the vessel, we also shipped the oars. At ½ past 7 o'clock, upon passing the bank, I perceived that the currents were setting the ship very fast near the small islands at ENE of the bank, from which we were but two cables length distant. I called in the boat, which I had sent to the ledge, in order to assist in towing the ship. Since our arrival within the banks and small islands, we had soundings from 15 to 25 fathoms over sometimes a rocky bottom, and at other times small stones.

At 9 o'clock, we had passed the small islands altogether and steered towards the Northermost point of the Western shore of the entrance. We had then 15 to 18 fathoms over a sandy bottom, successively rocky and then of small stones.

A 10 o'clock, we came to anchor opposite the river in 12 fathom water over a sandy bottom with small pebble stones. I think worthy of remark that I found the bottom to be foul for it was extremely uneven. The sounding shows that there is but a very thin bed of sand upon the rocks. I had perceived the first of the flood to have begun towards 7 o'clock in the morning, that is to say when we were between the bank and the islets at ENE of it.

Upon coming to anchor, a wind sprung up at South blowing a fresh gale attended with a thick haze. We attempted to moor across, after having hoisted out the boat. At noon, we finished mooring the ship, and when we had secured it the North point of the cove in which we found ourselves, bore N¼NW, White's Point bore S¼SW 3° W, and the river's mouth W¼SW. We were distant about ¾ of a mile from the shore. While we had been engaged in towing the ship to the anchoring place, we had been attended constantly by four canoes which had left us undisturbed, not daring to come along-side the ship until we had come to anchor. Several of the natives within the canoes asked leave to go on board the boats to assist in the paddling, which I gave them and which seemed to please them very much. When we had finished mooring the ship, we made signs to them to draw near, which they did. We had but time enough to purchase one bear skin for the wind increasing constantly obliged them to withdraw into the cove in which we had come to anchor.

From Friday 12th to Saturday 13th August 1791

In the afternoon, several canoes came off to the ship from the Eastern side of the entrance. Some of them came on board but were soon obliged to fall back into the cove in which we had come to anchor on account of the wind and the rain. We purchased some sea otter skins and other furs of an inferior kind. For the remainder of the evening, we continued to see canoes from the same side which could not reach the ship and which repaired all to the cove. In the evening, they numbered sixteen, having on board 150 persons, whereas the preceding day not one inhabitant was to be found there.

At 7 o'clock in the evening, the wind blowing a fresh gale at South, we struck the main top-gallant mast and the main yard and the fore yard. During the night, we had a wind which blew more or less fresh from South to SSE attended with rain. At 6 o'clock in the morning, the weather moderating, the canoes began to come along-side. At 8 o 'clock, there were sixteen about the ship, having 135 persons on board including the women and the children. It would be so very difficult to describe the great satisfaction we had on seeing that each of these canoes contained some item for purchase.

We traded with the natives all through the morning. At noon they all retired to the shore, most likely to eat their dinner. They did not return this day.

We gave them in exchange boilers, pans and tin basins, large daggers, brass pots and other trifles. They scorned in general glass beads and all other such toys which were not necessaries. They made hardly nothing of our axes, adzes, saws, etc. although we showed them what use could be made of them. To obtain some few of their most beautiful sea otter skins, I was obliged to give them waistcoats and breeches of wool which I had on board to issue to the company if I thought necessary. One of them, who had one of the finest sea otter skins we had yet seen, insisted in exchange upon a cloak of wool after the Spanish fashion, which I wore, and to please him and in order to acquire the skin, I gave it, and one of my hats, to him.[164] Here I must observe that he had a kind of influence over his countrymen and I desired to make a friend of him.

From Saturday 13th to Sunday 14th August 1791

At 5 o'clock in the evening, I visited the cove accompanied by two of the officers. The inhabitants received us in the most friendly manner. They offered to carry the casks in order to fill them at the river and bring them back again to the boat. As a reward, I made them presents of rings with which they seemed very satisfied for they had asked for nothing.[165] After having having finished our work, we proceeded to cut some hazel twigs, which they permitted us to do in a most peaceable manner.[166] We also took leaves of the pea, which we found to grow about the shore, in order to be boiled with the soup for the people. I had no sooner indicated to several of them that I would be glad of the opportunity to see their huts, than they offered to lead me to them. We found there the women busy boiling fish in a pot which we had sold to them. These huts are formed of four poles fixed in the ground across which they put some few boards and which they cover with the bark of trees or the skin of sea calves. The back of the roof which slopes very much, or at the lowest point, is always to the windward. They keep very close to the fire due to which their eyes appear always sickly and bleary.

We returned on board at ½ past 6 o'clock in the evening. During the night the wind blew a fresh gale at South and the rain continued without intermission.

In the morning, the canoes came along-side the ship and we commenced a brisk trade in a good quantity of sundry furs. For a fine sea otter skin, the natives required a coat, breeches or a tin basin. For the others, more or less of these.

---

164 Here Fleurieu notes that clothes had not been envisaged of as exchange articles (op. cit., p. 284).

165 Fleurieu presents another interpretation: . . . *they even showed themselves officious, and assisted the sailors in filling a few casks with water: it was not, it is true, without having previously stipulated for the remuneration which should be made to them; but the price of their labour was only a few metal rings* (op. cit., p. 286).

166 Gannier (*journal*, op. cit., pp. 342–343) points out that Cook, on the contrary, met with quite strong resistance when he attempted to cut grass, make water or cut wood (see Cook, *Voyage to the Pacific Ocean*, op. cit., Volume 2, p. 284).

We found the cables very much rubbed. We served them. I remarked that the ship had dragged the anchor at South while the boat had been under the cable.[167] Distrusting the bottom which I knew to be foul, we swayed up the main yard and the fore yard in order to be ready to get under sail if it became necessary. I resolved also to put to sea as soon as the weather became favourable, for almost no more furs were to be had, and we had little reason to expect that they would fulfil their promise of bringing more.

From Sunday 14ᵗʰ to Monday 15ᵗʰ August 1791

At 4 o'clock PM, the canoes left us, the largest part directing their course to the East side of the entrance, making signs to us that they would soon return. The others fell back into the cove. During the night the rained continued almost without intermission attended with a light wind at South.

At 3 o'clock in the morning, we cast off the mooring at East in order to bring it into the offing, where we moored in 15 fathoms over a sandy bottom, which seemed good and better even than that in which we had let go the anchor at South.

Upon anchoring once again, we took the bearings as follows:

The North point of the cove bore N¼NW.
White's Point bore S½W.
The rocky ledge of the entrance bore S¼SE.
Mount Edgecombe bore SW¼W
The river bore WSW bore 8° S.

The canoes which had remained in the cove came along-side the ship at 7 o'clock in the morning. After having purchased from the natives some furs of a very inferior kind, they left us for the East side. There remained however two canoes in the cove though they had nothing more to sell.

At 11 o'clock, I sent the boat to the watering place and the two carpenters were set to work to cut down a tree to make boards.[168]

From Monday 15ᵗʰ to Tuesday 16ᵗʰ

In the afternoon, we had a light wind which continued at South attended with cloudy weather. At 4 o'clock, I went ashore to hasten the work. I found the carpenters squaring a great piece of wood which they had found pulled down along-side the river. I cannot be better satisfied with the manner in which the natives received me at every visit. It is true to say that I did not enter into any of their huts before

---

167 Cook had experienced similar problems with the cables (*Voyage to the Pacific Ocean*, op. cit., Volume 2, p. 272).
168 See Cook, Ibid., p. 289.

asking of them their sentiment. At ½ past 7 o'clock, we returned on board and found there some few natives who, having nothing more to sell, had more the intention of amusing themselves than of trading.

Towards evening, two canoes which came from the bottom of the entrance, passed along-side the ship and went away to the cove. These were the same Indians whom we had previously traded with. I believe that in showing themselves to us, they wished to indicate that they had returned.

We had a calm during the night and some light winds at North towards the morning, attended with clear weather. This proved to be the first fine day since we had come into the entrance. We took the opportunity to dry somewhat our furs, which were in great need of it for we had traded for them in rainy weather. They were spread out and the skinners were employed in beating them with flails.

At ½ past 10 o'clock, the wind veered to South.

I had sent the boat to the watering place in the morning and it returned at noon with the tree which had been cut into pieces, measuring six feet in length, as I had ordered. The officer in command reported that, desiring to approach a hut within which there were some women, one of the natives inside had threatened him with a spear and made signs for him to withdraw, which he did with much caution.

In the morning we purchased two canoes of which I have just made mention, three sea otter skins and some other furs of an inferior kind. At noon, we took with the greatest accuracy and with very good instruments, the sun's Meridian altitude, we found our anchoring place to be in latitude 57° 3' 45" North. I believe I have before mentioned that we had excellent fishermen and there was no want of fish. In the river, they took as many as they wished of different kinds, particularly salmon. Then, during the night on board ship, they took soles and some fish of a red colour which ate deliciously. The rocks on the shore furnished us with very good shell fish and the ship's company would choose what they desired to eat and dined on good cheer. If our employments or the foul weather prevented us from taking fish, the Indians brought us as many as we could wish, in exchange for some few nails.

From Tuesday 16th to Wednesday 17th August 1791

In the afternoon, I sent the yawl a shore with the carpenter to cut sticks for the skinners.

Towards the evening, we had calm weather and a breeze from the shore in our favour which I was in hopes of in order to put to sea the next day. We tripped the anchor at South, which we found to be no more damaged than when he had examined it last. We rode a peek the other anchor in order to be ready to put to sea, but the wind was against us for at 10 o'clock it started again to blow at South attended all day with rain without intermission.

The canoes remained along-side until 8 o'clock in the evening. We purchased some sea otter skins for which we were obliged to pay more every day, the otters had been killed but a short time ago for the skins were still stretched upon sticks.

As I was free with the natives, I came on board one of their canoes which contained ten men and I sat down with them. I spoke to the most intelligent of them all, or whom I believed to be so, and by signs, as plainly as I could, I made him understand that he should tell us the number of vessels which had come to this entrance. He answered very clearly that he had seen but three, a two-master, this was Captain Dixon, whose name he said most distinctly, a three-master which was very large and carried many guns, and our ship. Another native to whom I had not spoken and who had understood our conversation, made signs that beyond these three he had seen a long boat (pointing to ours) which had come from the North of the entrance and which had burnt and destroyed several of their canoes. This was I understood the vessel of Captain Portlock who had indeed come here and the commanding officer had burnt two or three of their canoes for the natives had cut the cable of the longboat.[169]

This account was confirmed by several of them. I proposed to the native with whom I had the previous conversation without speech, to come on board and that I would bring him back, to which he replied that he would come readily but that I was in return to leave as hostage one of our people.[170]

Towards 11 o'clock in the evening, in spite of the rain which was very heavy, a canoe came off to the ship, paddling very slowly and coming aft where we had our boats. I cannot be positive as to the intentions of those within the canoe who had come along-side, against common practice, at such an undue hour and with such bad weather. I believe notwithstanding that we may presume it was but to attempt to steal from us. When they caught sight of us, they came near the ship to sell a sea otter skin of an inferior kind.

During the morning, no canoes came off due to the bad weather.

From Wednesday 17ᵗʰ to Thursday 18ᵗʰ August 1791

During this day and until 10 o'clock in the morning, the wind was at South, attended with drizzly rain without intermission. It veered to WNW at this time

---

169 *A short time before they intended sailing to return to the ship, and while the people were busy in putting the boat to rights on deck, the Indians went in two boats, and took an opportunity of cutting their cable. The anchor lay in twenty-eight fathoms water, without a buoy, so that there was no chance of recovering it. After doing this piece of mischief, the Indians made for the shore with all the haste imaginable, and landed at a little distance from the long-boat. Our people pursued them, and being a good deal exasperated at their daring and insolent behaviour, they landed with the boat, and intirely destroyed both the Indian boats. The natives fled with precipitation into the woods, which put a stop to our people's pursuit; and I believe they did them no further injury. I was sorry that the boat's crew should have been under the necessity of taking this step; but undoubtedly this crime committed by the Indians was of so very mischievous a nature, that it became necessary to punish them in some measure for it; and it is very probable that destroying their boats (which it must cost them much time and trouble to rebuild) would make a greater impression than even taking away numbers of their lives* (Portlock, op. cit., p. 277).

170 Similarly, hostages were left, and taken, by Portlock.

and was soon succeeded by a calm. We hoisted up the long boat notwithstanding, in order to get under sail in case of fine weather.

The natives came along-side and we purchased two or three good sea otter skins and sundry furs of various kinds, but all of a very inferior sort.

From Thursday 18ᵗʰ to Friday 19ᵗʰ August 1791

In the afternoon, we amused ourselves in hunting along the coast. We landed half a mile from the river and marched Northward where we had a view of rocks which were fearfully steep though covered with pine trees which had not grown up very well. Half an hour after, we returned on board. The natives retired all at once within 20 cables length of the ship. This was worked with the same diligence as if all had been decided together. I must own that I was most surprised for I knew not why they had made such a retreat. But the natives soon removed our fears for they made us understand that they had caught sight of a whale very near the surface of the water and feared that this cetaceous creature of an enormous size would over-set their canoe. Indeed we saw it at 30 cables length aft of the ship. The natives set upon it notwithstanding, even in one canoe with three men within it, they proceed to strike it with a harpoon.

Towards 6 o'clock in the evening, the wind veered to WNW. But soon after at 8 o'clock it veered again to South and SSE attended as usual with a very thick haze on account of which the land could hardly to be seen. This weather continued thus all the morning. At 10 o'clock, I had sent the boat out under the command of Mr Infernet, with orders to sound the East part of the entrance in order to beat to windward in safety if I resolved to put to sea with the wind against us. He reported to me upon his return that East of the cove in which had come to anchor, he had found a good depth of water until the shore, but that he had not been able to examine the islets of the entrance for he had had the wind and the tide against him. I was assured afterwards that these islets, those which form the passage and which lie to the NE of the ledge, are safe in the West part and that we may approach them within half a cables length without danger. But vigilance is required in case of a calm due to the flood in the different passages which the islets form between themselves.

From Friday 19ᵗʰ to Saturday 20ᵗʰ August

As I suspected and do so still, according to what the natives told me very clearly and according to the turnings which the mountains form between themselves, the entrance to Norfolk and Port Banks[171] to the Southward of it, communicate with

---

171 *This harbour is situated in 56 deg. 35 min. North latitude and 135 deg. West longitude: it obtained the name of Port Banks, in honour of Sir Joseph Banks* (Dixon, op. cit., p. 195). Portlock (op. cit., p. 75) also honours Joseph Banks on the island of Woahoo (Sandwich Islands): *The Southern extreme forms itself into a flattish point, which I distinguished by the name of Point Banks, in honour*

one another by a narrow strait. I sent a boat under the command of Mr Masse with orders to examine all the entrances he should find in the NE part of Norfolk entrance. But the foul weather obliged him to return to the ship and he arrived at 10 o'clock in the evening. He had nonetheless examined a channel which runs SE where he found no bottom.

In the afternoon, I visited the cove to have some conversation with the natives to whom I made a promise that we would return, for they told me that many superior furs should be prepared for trade. I should fire our guns three times in order that they should know us again, and they would all come to take up with me the business of trading. I was desired to bring upon my return daggers of a particular design, coats, red breeches with great shining buttons of white or yellow, pots with rings of iron in order to put them upon the fire and remove them from it conveniently, and large copper basins, for those of tin proved to be too thin and unsoldered upon the fire.

One of them told me that Captain Dixon had given him two muskets in exchange but that he had destroyed them in great fury for they made only a slight noise, a *crick* sound. He used this word to say that they miscarried always. It is likely, as it was fit, that the Captain had not given him powder.

Being alone in the hut among fifty natives, both men and women, I asked them if they could in the very depth of winter continue in such miserable huts. They answered by showing me the bottom of the bay where they possessed huts of a much larger size and better made which afforded them shelter in bad weather.

Several among them proposed to go with me if I left with them one of the company as hostage, which I refused to do. It is perhaps of some surprise that we were able to understand each other so very well for the language spoken by the one was not known to the other, but if the reader could know the clearness and expressiveness with which these savages make signs, he would certainly not be surprised.

At ½ past 6 in the evening, I left the natives and returned to the ship well satisfied with their understanding and the presents they had made me at every visit.

The next day in the morning, we purchased five good otter skins and other furs of an inferior kind.

I sent the boat to the watering place and gave orders to the carpenters to cut spars for the ship.

During this day, the winds blew from South to SSE attended with a very thick haze and rain without intermission.

The season was already far advanced and I was in the greatest expectation of a wind which would permit us to leave the entrance and visit Queen Charlotte's

---

of Sir Joseph Banks. Joseph Banks had christened the *Queen Charlotte* and as Portlock recounts: *The novelty of this enterprise attracted the notice of several persons, who were eminent either for talents or station, and who promoted this voyage by their countenance, or strengthened the company by their approbation. When Sir Joseph Banks and Lord Mulgrave, Mr. Rose and Sir John Dick, came on board, the Secretary of the Treasury named the largest vessel The King George and the President of the Royal Society called the smallest The Queen Charlotte. Exclusive of the profits of traffic, or the advantages of discovery, this voyage was destined to other national objects* (op. cit., p. 6).

Islands where I hoped to procure a quantity of furs of a good quality. But he that reckons without his host, must reckon over again, as shall be seen in the following.

From Saturday 20ᵗʰ to Sunday 21ˢᵗ August 1791

In the afternoon, the weather clearing, we took the opportunity to air the skins and beat those which we had stretched for they were found to have grown damp on account of the rainy weather during which we had purchased them. A great part of the otter skins besides had yet fixed upon them the blubber of the animal.

Several canoes came along-side the ship but the natives had nothing more to sell. I distributed amongst them many coins of France, and I gave to one of the girls of fourteen or fifteen years of age, who had a most remarkable face, a medal struck in Lyons, of which the subject was the Federation of May 1790.

The same canoe which had made us a visit one day at 11 o'clock in the evening, attempted at 10 o'clock to come off warily once again. It was no longer doubted that those within it certainly had no other intention but to steal from us. When they saw themselves discovered, they came along-side the ship very quietly, speaking with us. I did not wish any harm to come to these men for we would not be long amongst them.

During the night, the weather was clear. At 3 o'clock in the morning, with a very light wind at North and the boats towing, we put to sea with no great regret for the stock of furs which the natives possessed had been disposed of and we left them all near stripped. At ½ past 7 o'clock, Cape Edgecombe and the Southern extremity of the island which lies to the East of this Cape, bore WSW½W, the Western extremity of the islets which lie ENE of the ledge of rock, bore NNE½E. At this moment, we had a calm but at ½ past 9 o'clock, we got a trade wind at W and W¼SW blowing a gentle gale. We hoisted in the boats and steered SSE having passed the islands situated close to the SE shore of the entrance.

At noon the latitude by observation was found to be N 56° 54'. Cape Edgecombe at the same time bore W 9° N, and the island most offward SE of the entrance bore SE 4° E which put us in longitude 137° 56' W of Paris, from whence we took our departure.

As the season was very far advanced and that we might lose as little time as possible, I gathered the officers and on their advice, we determined to repair directly to Queen Charlotte's Islands in place of examining the intermedial coast where we were not likely to find furs if the navigators who had preceded us were to be believed. However we were hardly to do better elsewhere than here, as experience was to teach us.[172]

---

172 Marchand does not provide a list of his purchases (though Chanal and Fleurieu do – see Gannier, journal, op. cit., p. 349). Remarks such as these also show the narrative strategy Marchand had decided to employ in this fair copy.

During our stay in Norfolk entrance, which the natives name Tchinkitanay, the thermometer kept between + 10 to 15½°. The weather was in general hazy with rain. We moored in latitude 57° 3' 45" by very exact observation. We were prevented by the weather from taking distances in order to determine the longitude which was 137° 59'. The variation of the compass computed from at least twenty sets of azimuths, taken with different compasses, was found to be 28° 46'. We found the tide to rise 10 feet upon a perpendicular, but it is not certain. The winds at SE and SW bring much haze and mist, and rain, though the weather is very clear when winds are at N or at NW.

From Sunday 21ˢᵗ to Monday 22ⁿᵈ August 1791

147¾

A 2 o'clock PM, Cape Edgecombe bore N 50° W, the mountain of the same name N 37° W, and Southermost land in sight bore East 14° South. A chain of islands which borders the coast and from which we were distant about 2 leagues, extended from N 4° E to E 7° N.

The wind continued to blew a gentle gale at WNW and NW, attended with very clear weather.

At 20 minutes past 7 o'clock in the evening, Mount Edgecombe bore NNW 8° W, an opening in the coast, which I understood to be Port Banks, ENE½N, and the Southmost land ENE½E. We were distant about 9 or 10 leagues from the shore by our estimation.

Ranging along the coast, the land appeared to be very high. All the mountains were covered in snow and seemed quite bare, very much like those in Norfolk Entrance.

By the mean result of five sets of azimuths and amplitudes, the variation of the magnetic needle was found to be 28° 49' NE.

At midnight we directed our course to SE¼S, at 3 o'clock AM to SE, and at 8' clock to East ½ S in order to examine the Northerly island of the Queen Charlotte chain, near Cloak Bay.[173]

---

173 Dixon is here able to trade very successfully and Beresford explains why Cloak Bay was the name chosen for this particular entrance: *A scene now commenced, which absolutely beggars all description, and with which we were so overjoyed, that we could scarcely believe the evidence of our senses. There were ten canoes about the ship, which contained, as nearly as I could estimate, 120 people; many of these brought most beautiful beaver cloaks; others excellent skins, and, in short, none came empty handed, and the rapidity with which they sold them, was a circumstance additionally pleasing; they fairly quarrelled with each other about which should sell his cloak first; and some actually threw their furs on board, if nobody was at hand to receive them; but we took particular care to let none go from the vessel unpaid. Toes were almost the only article we bartered with on this occasion, and indeed they were taken so very eagerly, that there was not the least occasion to offer any thing else. In less than half an hour we purchased near 300 beaver skins, of an excellent quality; a circumstance which greatly raised our spirits, and the more, as both the plenty of fine furs, and the avidity of the natives in parting with them, were convincing*

210

The wind blew a gentle gale at NW all this day.

Latitude by observation N 54° 35'.
Longitude by reckoning W 137° 16'.

The mean result of four sets of lunar observations, reduced to noon, made by Mr Chanal and myself, gave 137° 9' 30" longitude – that is to say 6' 30' more to the East than by reckoning.

Réamur's thermometer +11½°, Fahrenheit's thermometer 60°.

Before departing from Norfolk entrance, I believe I must give an account of this entrance, of the inhabitants and of their manners and their customs which is to be found on p. 348, and within the following pages of this book.[174]

From Monday 22nd August to Tuesday 23rd August 1791

86¾

Soon after noon, the coast presented itself to our view. It extended from ENE½N to NE½N. It appeared to be very high and distant 18 to 20 leagues by our estimation.

At ¾ past 6 o'clock, we caught sight of Queen Charlotte's Islands which stretched from E¼NE to SE, the coast of the continent extending from NE¼N to NW¼N. We were 9 leagues distant by our estimation.

At 8 o'clock, we brought to under the top-sails after having sounded and finding no bottom with 115 fathoms of line.

At ½ past 3 o'clock AM, we filled the top-sails and soon after we caught sight of land a-head.

At ½ past 4 o'clock, the Northern extremity of the Northern island bore E¼NE, the Southern extremity bore ESE and the entrance of Cloak Strait bore ESE½S, distant 3 leagues. The Southermost land in view bore SSE.

We steered in direction of the strait in hopes that the natives would come off to the ship in their canoes to begin a trade in furs, as they had done with Captain Dixon.

We saw some few small islets situated near the Northern extremity of the Northern island.

---

proofs, that no traffic whatever had recently been carried on near this place, and consequently we might expect a continuation of this plentiful commerce. That thou mayest form some idea of the cloaks we purchased here, I shall just observe, that they generally contain three good sea otter skins, one of which is cut in two pieces, afterwards they are neartly sewed together, so as to form a square, and are loosely tied about the shoulders with small leather strings fastened on each side [. . .] At noon the head of the bay we had made, and which I shall distinguish by the name of Cloak Bay, bore nearly East, about four leagues distant (op. cit., pp. 201–202).

174 Gannier notes (journal, op. cit., p. 350) that this sentence is in different handwriting and may have been added later by someone other than Marchand. On close examination of the manuscript this may not necessariy be the case.

At ½ past 6 o'clock, we came to the entrance of Cloak Strait. We fired a great gun to excite the curiosity of the natives but none appeared. We then tacked and stood out to sea for half an hour. Believing that they had not yet seen the ship, we stood directly into the strait but as I knew not whether an anchoring place was to be found there, I resolved to go out again and to send a boat to attempt to procure furs.

At ½ past 8 o'clock, the boat departed under the command of Mr Chanal with orders to go to the strait and to look for an anchoring place and to purchase as many furs as could be had, in exchange for the articles I gave to him.

Until 10 o'clock, we were obliged to make the tack to the Southward, keeping very close to the reefs which run along the shore for we could not have doubled them on the other board. At this time I attempted to tack and stand to the North but perceiving that we were nearing the reefs more and more and that we were no more than half a mile distant from them, we tacked once more. The great swell from the West and a strong current had occasioned this hard situation.

Due to these circumstances we had found ourselves distant 5 leagues from Cloak Bay, but fortunately at 1 o'clock in the afternoon, a gentle gale sprung up which carried us away from the coast and permitted us to draw near the strait. The

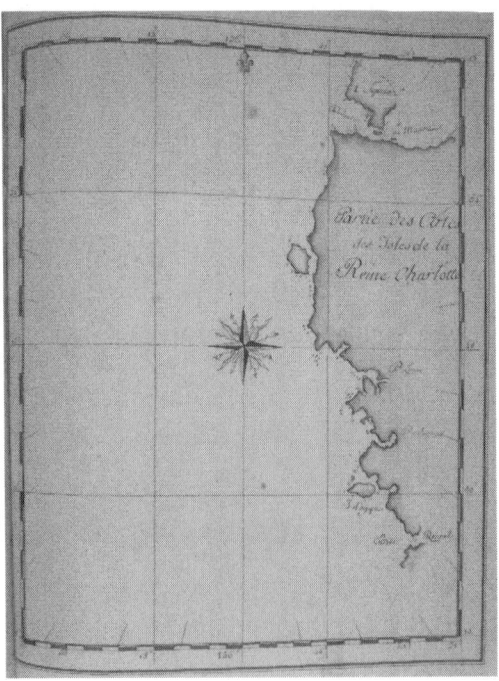

Figure 5 Part of the coast of Queen Charlotte's Islands (sewn into Volume 1 of the manuscript)

Courtesy of the Bibliothèque Alcazar, Marseilles, France.

currents then altered their direction carrying us NW. Though we had run along the coast very near the shore, we had seen neither inhabitant nor even any smoke.

The North point of the island at North bore N, the entrance to the strait bore NNE½E, the Southermost point in view bore SE about 5 leagues, South South West of the globe. We perceived from the strait an island whose Northermost point bore SE½E. From the strait to this island, reefs and islets run along the coast and extend into the offing, as I have before made mention, and these are very dangerous. At noon, our latitude by observation was 54° 4' N, and our longitude determined from the bearings, following Dixon's chart, was 135° 53' W, and that which was computed from our last observations put us in 135° 57' 30".

The variation of the compass determined from azimuths was 28° 3' NE.

Réamur's thermometer +12°, Fahrenheit's thermometer 61°.

The weather was fine and mild.

We saw a very great number of whales, gulls, ducks, herons, mackerel, etc., and much sea-leek and other marine productions.

From Tuesday 23rd to Wednesday 24th August 1791

55½

We continued to make the Northward board until 9 o'clock in the evening. At 7 o'clock, we had caught sight of the boat in the entrance of the strait which was returning to the ship, but as we had just about doubled the West coast of the Northern island from which were but ½ a mile distant, and finding it impossible to tack without falling in on the reefs situated South of the entrance, I preferred to leave the boat aft of the ship. At 8 o'clock, the islets which lie at the Northern extremity of the North island, bore E 8° N.

The middle of the entrance of Cloak Strait bore SE¼S 3° S. We were at a distance of about 2 miles from the islands.

We spent the night with no small uneasiness about the boat, and continued to make short boards between the North island and the continent, that is to say in Dixon's strait. We fired from time to time our guns and displayed the rockets so that the boat would be able to keep the ship in view in case it was to keep to sea during the night.

At 5 o'clock AM, Cape Pitt bore W¼NE, the Northern point of North island bore E¼SE, the entrance of Cloak Strait ESE½S, the Southermost land in view bore SSE½ South. Soon after, we steered towards the strait to regain the boat which came on board but at 10 o'clock, which we hoisted in immediately.

The commanding officer[175] informed me that no good anchorage for the ship was to be had, but that natives were to be found there and he had purchased five otter skins, a beaver cloak and some beaver tails and sundry furs of an inferior

---

175 According to Fleurieu, Chanal was accompanied by Lieutenant Murat, Roblet, and Volunteer Décany (op. cit., p. 391).

quality and worn. The Indians were of a very gentle disposition and had promised to him that should we remain amongst them, they would bring furs. They showed to Mr Chanal a small cove where some European longboats had come to anchor. The great coats, the blankets, and new instruments which they were possessed of was sure proof that these had come but a short time since. It was impossible to bring the ship into the strait for there was no safe anchorage to be found, but in the hope however of procuring furs there, I resolved to send the longboat under the command of Mr Chanal. I gave him provisions enough for twelve days and arms with which to assure their own protection if they found it necessary. I gave them all kinds of articles for exchange. This is what we agreed upon: after three days, if the weather permitted us to do so, the ship would come to the bay, and on catching sight of the ship, Mr Chanal would come off to us in the longboat, or with his fowling piece, fire two shots if he did not yet wish to return, which would then be a proof that furs were still to be had. If the contrary, or if he were now missing articles of traffic, he would return to the ship.

At noon, the islands situated at the Northern point of North island bore E½N, distant 3 leagues, Cape Pitt bore NNE and the entrance of the Cloak Strait bore ESE 8° S.

Our latitude by observation was 54° 26' N, and our longitude determined from our bearings was 137° 57'.

We were carried this day 6' more to the North than by reckoning, and 18' to the West. The variation of the compass determined from five sets of azimuths (mean result) was 27° 59' NE.

Réamur's thermometer +11½°, Fahrenheit's thermometer 60°.

During this day, the wind varied from WNW to WSW, more or less light, attended with very clear weather. We availed ourselves of these fine days to dry and beat the furs we had purchased in Norfolk entrance in order to prepare them for packing.

From Wednesday 24th to Thursday 25th August 1791

47½

We were employed in equipping the longboat which left us at ½ past 5 o'clock, armed with 13 men and accompanied by the Surgeon, at his request. I recommended to Mr Chanal to be particularly careful as was consistent with prudence, and always exact caution amongst the natives, in spite of their demonstrations of friendship. I requested that he would draw a sketch of the strait.

At 7 o'clock in the evening, Forster Island bore NW¼N, distant about 9 leagues, Cape Pitt bore NNE 3° N, the Northern extremity of North Island bore E½N, the entrance to Cloak Strait bore E 8° S.

Forster Island is high and wooded. In fine weather, it can be seen with ease 15 leagues distant. The part of the coast of the continent in view was very high, but no snow could be seen on the summits. The North island is of moderate height and very even. To the South of this island, high mountains are to be seen, wooded to the very tops.

I did not intend to quit the entrance of Cloak Strait and we spent the night making short trips to the Northward and to the Southward. At 7 o'clock, we caught sight of a great piece of pine on the surface of the water which was covered with mussels.

At 8 o'clock, the Northern point of North island bore E 8° S, the entrance of the Strait bore ESE 3° S, Forster Island bore NW¼N, distant 5 leagues. The part of the continent in view extended from NNW¼N to NE½E. We perceived some islets to the NNW of Forster Island.

During this day, we had a wind which varied from WNW to WSW, attended with magnificent weather.

At noon, the middle of Forster island bore NW½N, the Northern point of North island bore E½N, Cape Pitt bore NNE½E, Cloak Strait bore E 8° S, and the Southermost land in view bore SE½S.

We were at a distance of about 6 leagues from the strait.

Our latitude by observation was 54° 25', and our longitude determined from the bearings was 135° 57'.

We found this day 2' difference more to the North and 22' difference more to the East.

The variation of the compass by observations made of great exactness, made with different compasses, was 28° 7' NE.

Réamur's thermometer +12½°, Fahrenheit's thermometer 62°.

From Thursday 25ᵗʰ to Friday 26ᵗʰ August 1791

38½

We continued to make boards in order to remain near North Island of which the Northern point bore North NE¼E at ¾ past 6 o'clock in the evening, distant 9 leagues.

During the afternoon, we perceived that the ship had been carried to the SW by a strong current.

There fell a very large dew during the night.

At ¼ past 5 o'clock in the morning, Forster Island bore NNW½W, distant 5 leagues, the coast of the continent in view stretched from NNE 3° E to N¼NW. The weather was hazy about the horizon which prevented us from seeing Queen Charlotte's Islands, but at ½ past 7 o'clock, the weather becoming clear, we saw the point of North island at ESE½E, distant 7 leagues.

During this day, we had light winds variable and calm at intervals.

At noon, the Northern point of North island bore E¼SE, the entrance of Cloak Strait bore ESE½S, and Forster Island bore NW¼N, distant 6 leagues from the point.

Our latitude by observation at noon was N 54° 29', and our longitude computed from the bearings was 136° 5'.

We had 4' of difference more to the South and 4' of difference more to the W this day.

Réamur's thermometer + 13°, Fahrenheit's thermometer 63°.

From Friday 26ᵗʰ to Saturday 27ᵗʰ August 1791

26¼

At noon, I ordered that we avail ourselves of all the gusts of wind to get close to Cloak Strait in order that the next day we draw near the entrance as we had agreed upon with the commanding officer of the long boat.

At 7 o'clock in the evening, the Northern point of North island bore E¼SE, the entrance to the strait bore SE¼E, Forster Island bore NW½W, Cape Pitt bore NNE 3° N. We were 5 leagues distant from North island by our estimation.

At day-light, a small air of wind sprang up at NE, we steered for the entrance of the strait which bore ESE½S, 4 leagues distant. At 9 o'clock we caught sight of the longboat which came along-side at half past eleven o'clock.

Mr Chanal had procured these last three days 9 good otter skins, 2 others in the form of a mat, which was worn, and other furs of a very inferior kind. When they had sold all they had, they made signs to Mr Chanal to return in six days, at which time they would be in possession of some skins to sell. He told them that he would return but only in ten days. The natives made him understand that at this time, the furs would be disposed of in favour of an English vessel which was now at the East shore but which was soon to arrive. Indeed the people caught sight of it the next day at the East entrance of Cloak Strait. She was an English brig of 150 tons burthen. As I had advised Mr Chanal not to speak with any ship he might meet, he withdrew into a cove and returned to the ship, having nothing more to do on shore. He also discovered from the natives that a three-master had come to the entrance but a short time since and had purchased from them some furs. This circumstance was an undoubted proof that a profitable trade could not be carried on about these islands, as we had proposed to do. As I did not wish to lose the least opportunity, nor to have anything laid against my charge, and though in spite of all our endeavours we had not here found a brisk trade, I resolved to send the long-boat out the next day to run to the South till Rennell's Strait.

At noon, the Northern point of North island bore ENE½E, distant 2 miles.

Our latitude by observation was 54° 15' N, and our longitude, computed from the bearings, was 135° 50'. We had 1' of difference more to the South, and 7' difference more to the East this day. The wind was variable, with calm at intervals and clear weather.

Réamur's thermometer +12°, Fahrenheit's thermometer 61°.

From Saturday 27ᵗʰ to Sunday 28ᵗʰ August 1791

At noon, we steered so as to double an island which bore South, distant about 4 leagues. I had reason to believe that this part of the coast, situated between Cloak

Strait and the island, was not inhabited, or very little, for on our arrival at the entrance of Cloak on the first day, the currents and the heavy sea had obliged us stand along this shore no more than a mile distant, and we saw neither huts nor inhabitants.

At ½ past 7 o'clock, the island of which I have just made mention, bore ESE½E, the Northern point of North island bore NNE. We were distant 2 leagues from the nearest land.

We spent the whole night making short trips, keeping close to the land, but the currents carried us in to the offing. At 6 o'clock in the morning, the two extremes of the land extended from N½E to ESE. We were distant about 2 leagues from the nearest land.

At ¼ past 7 o'clock, the longboat departed, armed with 12 men with provisions enough for 15 days and with commodities and implements for trade. The longboat was under the command of Mr Chanal to whom I gave the following instructions.

Copy of the instructions given to Mr Chanal

You are to run along the coast until Rennell's Channel, which lies in the latitude of 53° 25', according to Mr Dixon's chart. You will not lose the least opportunity to obtain all the furs to be found on the way, and to discover a good anchoring place in which to secure the ship. On your way, you will take the bearings of the coast in order to determine its situation. If you find harbours or ports, you will not forget to draw a view of them. We will keep close to the shore as long as the weather and the circumstances will allow, and we will come to Rennell's Channel only on the fourth day after your departure, that is to say on the 31st August, in order that we may come to anchor in case you have found such a place to the North of the Channel. I will however not be uneasy if you are not to be found at this moment in this place, for it will be a proof that you have found a brisk trade, which is to be wished for.

When the ship is near the entrance of Rennell Channel, two guns will be fired in order that you may know us.

If the weather should be bad, obliging us to draw away from the shore, you need be under no apprehension or any fear, for we will return after the bad weather.

Knowing you to be most prudent, I believe it to be unnecessary to advise you to be extremely circumspect and to use caution in your behaviour with the natives in order to avoid as much as possible all surprise.

Given on the Solide, 28th August 1791

Soon after the departure of the longboat, we stood out to sea, at ½ past 11 o'clock we stood in for the shore. My intention was to rally the shore as close as we could in order to begin a trade with the natives if any were to be found there, as Mr Dixon had done in 1787 in this same place.[176]

At noon, our latitude by observation was North 53° 55'.

And our longitude determined from the bearing was 135° 47'.

At this time, the Southermost point in view bore ESE½E, and the Northermost land bore N. We were about 2 leagues distant from the land.

The variation of the compass determined from several sets of azimuths was 28° NE.

During this day, we had a light wind varying from WNW to N attended with fine clear weather.

Since our arrival within these islands, we were affected by violent currents which carried us sometimes to the North, and at other times to the South, always along the coast.

Réamur's thermometer +12°, Fahrenheit's thermometer 61°.

From Sunday 28ᵗʰ to Monday 29ᵗʰ August 1791

At 1 o'clock PM, we were but a mile from the shore, the coast there forming a great opening in the bottom of which I thought there to be be a bay situated amongst the few islets bound by reefs. We immediately steered towards them while sounding, but in coming close and observing that the place appeared to afford little shelter, we tacked and stood out to sea.

Though we had coasted very close along the shore for about 3 leagues, we saw neither inhabitants nor huts. It appears however to be a very good place of abode, and for Captain Dixon it cannot be doubted that it is inhabited for beautiful beaches, with sand of a greyish white colour, are to be seen.

At ½ past 7 o'clock, the coast extended from SE½S to NNW½N. We were about 1½ miles distant from the shore.

We spent the night making trips. At 5 o'clock in the morning, the Southermost land bore ESE½E, and the Northermost land N¼NW. We were about 2 leagues distant from the land. At 8 o'clock, we were but a mile from the land. We had extremely fine weather but nonetheless we saw no canoes, which is a sure proof that the natives had nothing to dispose of and the vessels which had come before us had purchased all the furs.

During this day, we had a light wind varying from NNW to WNW, attended with a smooth sea and very fine weather.

In this part of Queen Charlotte's Islands, the land is very broken and the mountains are somewhat high. On the summits of some amongst them, small patches of snow are to be seen.

---

176 See Dixon op. cit., pp. 203–204.

At noon, the Northermost land bore NNW½N, and the the Southermost land ESE½E. We were distant about 4 miles from the land.

Our latitude by observation was found to be 53° 40' N, and our longitude from the bearings above, was 135° 30'.

The variation of the compass by observation of the amplitudes and the azimuths was 28° 10' NE.

Réamur's thermometer +13½°, Fahrenheit's thermometer 64°.

From Monday 29ᵗʰ to Sunday, I mean, from Tuesday 30ᵗʰ August

48

We continued to keep as close in with the coast as was consistent with prudence. At ½ past 5 o'clock PM, being but half a league from it, we caught sight of the longboat standing towards the ship. I thought for an instant that she was coming along-side and made ready to wait for her, but seeing that this was not her intention and that she was ranging along the shore, we stood out to sea under the top-sails.

At ¼ to 7 o'clock, the Northermost point in view bore NW¼N, the Southermost land bore SE¼E, distant ⅔ of a league from the land. We had fine weather during the night though somewhat hazy.

At 5 o'clock AM, the extremes of the land stretched from N¼NW to ENE. We were 2 leagues distant from the land by our estimation.

Until 8 o'clock in the morning, we could not rally the land as I desired to do on account of the haze which covered it. But at this time, the weather cleared somewhat and we stood straight in for it.

At 9 o'clock, the entrance of Rennell was in view and we directed our course towards the mouth of it.

At 11 o'clock, finding ourselves between the two points which form the strait, and perceiving no sign of the inhabitants, we tacked and stood out to sea. The part of the strait we had seen stretches from East to West.

At ¼ past 11 o'clock, Hippah Island bore NNE½E, a point at South forming the opening bore E¼SE, another point more to the South formed the entrance of Rennell Strait and bore E 8° N, the entrance of the strait bore E 3° N. We were distant about 1 mile from Hippah Island.[177]

The mountains in the interior part of the country around this strait are high much like those which form a border on the coast. To the Southward, peaks of a moderate height or even, it may be said, of a low height, can be seen.

At noon, the Northermost land bore NNW 8° N, the Southermost land bore ESE 3° S, the entrance of Rennell Channel bore NE¼E 3°, and Hippah Island bore NNE, distant 4 miles. The channel between this island and the shore appeared to be narrow and encumbered with shoals and islets.

---

177 *View of Hippah Island* in Dixon, Ibid., p. 205.

Our latitude by observation was 53° 28' North, and our longitude determined from the bearings above, was 135° 24'. We had 1' of difference more to the South, and 3' of difference more to the East.

The variation of the compass was found to be 27° 47' NE. During this day, we had light winds varying from WNW to NNW attended with hazy weather clear at intervals.

Réamur's thermometer +12½°, Fahrenheit's thermometer 62°.

From Tuesday 30th to Wednesday 31st August 1791

69¼

During the afternoon, we kept plying to windward making the trips which circumstance would admit, and keeping as near the shore as possible.

At 8 o'clock in the evening, the Southermost land bore SE½E, and the Northermost bore NNW ½W and the middle of Hippa Island bore North, distant 1½ miles.

I must mention that to the West and to the South, Hippa Island is surrounded by shoals which stretch half a mile into the offing and upon which sea-leek is to be seen.

At ¼ past 8 o'clock, we tacked and stood out to sea under the four main courses in order not to set to leeward, for in general we made sail only under our top-sails.

At 5 o'clock, Hippa Island bore N¼NW, distant 1½ leagues. The variation of the compass by observation of several azimuth and by the amplitudes, was 28° 11' NE.

At noon, the extremes of the land extended from SE¼E to NNW. Hippah Island bore N¼NE, distant 3 miles, and the entrance of Rennell Strait bore ENE½N.

In Mr Dixon's chart, this strait is laid down as a simple entrance, and in the chart of Arrowsmith, as a strait which runs from East to West.

At noon, our latitude by observation was 53° 25' N
and our longitude 135° 25' W.

During this day the wind constantly blew a gentle gale at NW, attended with hazy weather. We perceived nowhere any inhabitants though we kept in very close to the shore.

Réamur's thermometer +11°, Fahrenheit's thermometer 59°.

From Wednesday 31st to Thursday 1st September 1791

57

At ½ past 3 o'clock, we caught sight of the longboat which was standing for the ship and which came along-side at ½ past 4 o'clock.

After having run along the shore and inspected every cove to be seen, Mr Chanal was able to procure only 4 good otter skins, one of an inferior sort and but a few beaver tails. We have been unsuccessful and this was owing certainly in great measure to the English and the Spanish who had come before us and who had procured for themselves all the furs that were to be had. Besides, the European clothes which the natives wore and the various implements of which they were possessed, were sure proofs of this.

Mr Chanal told me that he had not found it necessary to examine Rennell Strait and that he had preferred to return to the ship to make his report to me.

The weather becoming hazy towards 6 o'clock in the evening, we hoisted in the longboat. During the night, we stood out to sea and at 4 o'clock, we stood in for the shore which could not be seen on account of the haze.

At ½ past 7 o'clock in the morning, the officers and myself came together in a consultation in order to determine the manner in which to proceed for the success of the expedition, that is to procure furs, for we had no other object. After a run along the shore of Queen Charlotte's islands of 18 to 20 leagues, and having obtained only 18 otter skins, it could no longer be doubted, unless we bear little respect for the plain truth, that all over the others had come before us and no more furs were to be had. We resolved unanimously that it was not necessary to remain any longer, unless we desired to lose yet more time, which we could not do for the season was already far advanced. In consequence, and without further delay, we must abandon these islands and as soon as it would be possible and repair to the entrance of Berekley's Sound where we might find a better trade. This was though as uncertain as in Queen Charlotte's islands and we had in truth hardly any hopes of success. But we resolved to take our departure for it was very certain that no more furs were to be had in these islands. At 8 o'clock we directed our course to the SSE. At noon, the latitude by observation was 52° 56'. The haze had cleared a little and we caught sight of a part of the coast bearing ENE½N, distant 5 leagues, finding ourselves in 135° 18' W, following Dixon's chart from which we took our departure.

Description of Cloak Strait

Before leaving these islands, I believe it is necessary here to give Mr Chanal's account of the performance of the tasks of which he had the charge. The reader recalls that on the 23rd of August in the morning I had sent Mr Chanal to Cloak Strait to examine it, but also to commence a trade in furs. He speaks here.

1ST TASK

We set sail from the ship at ½ past 8 o'clock in the morning. We arrived at the Westerly mouth of the strait which appears like a great bay. We directed our course towards the small island to the East of this bay and lying within the strait, we sounded and had 30 to 18 fathom water over a bottom of rock and shells, sometimes white sand and at other times small stones. The strait extends to the East at the bottom of the bay, where it becomes considerably narrow before the small island above. To the Southward, some reefs are to be found, one of which extends to the North and which leaves but a narrow entrance of about 3 cables length in breadth at most, between itself and a cape stretching out from the North coast of the strait. We found 32 to 40 fathom water over a bottom of coarse sand and broken shell. The North coast of the reef is steep and clear.

While we were in the bay formed by the entrance of the Strait, three canoes having 30 persons on board, including women and children, came towards us from the South shore of the bay. The Indians had no arms amongst them and made signs of peace. They had but fish to sell and a few old furs. They had coats and blankets from Europe and gave us to understand that an English vessel had this year come to this place. Having passed the narrow entrance situated near to the island which is to be found in the strait, we sounded and got 25 fathom water over a bottom of rocks. The channel to the North of this island is very narrow. There appearing to be no anchoring place, we stood to the South where beaches and huts were to be seen. If we had found a good anchoring place, we would have accomplished our first task for a vessel is afforded shelter from all winds in this place. But all along the shore we had 20 to 30 fathom over a bottom of coral of a bright red and white colour. In standing more to the East, South of the island, we had 30 fathom water over a bottom of rock, and we caught sight of the Easterly mouth of the strait which we had not yet quit. But the South coast of the strait extends 3 or 4 leagues Eastwards and is open to the wind. I did not find it necessary to continue and as the day was drawing to a close, I resolved to return to the ship. Upon departing, more canoes came off, and in order to give the natives the time to gather, in hopes of procuring some furs, we stopped at the West point of the island, which is situated within the strait. We went on shore in order to satisfy our curiosity and examine the fences we thought to be the work of Europeans. We found these fences to form an enclosure around a platform of a moderate height, supported by the rock on one side, and supported in other places by stakes and cross pieces, etc. We reached the top of this sort of gallery by means of a kind of stair case made of the trunk of a tree. This was the work of the natives and appeared very old. We observed several barrels with no cover, of which the Indians showed us the use by striking the sides with their fists making a noise like a drum. The most curious of all were the two large pictures 8 or 9 feet in length and 5 in breadth, though formed of only two boards. In one of the pictures, in bright colours (red, black and green), the different parts of the human body, painted separately, were to be seen. The second was doubtless a copy of the first for the colours were all near faded. The natives named the pictures Caniac in their language. We had no reason to believe that this place served as a stronghold, or a place of security for the Indians should there be an attack, though it appeared to be such and could be well defended. But I rather think, following what we have seen and after what the Indians have told us, that it was a place of religious worship or of public entertainments.

Towards 3 o'clock we put to sea in order to quit the entrance. But having the wind and the tide against us, our progress was slow. The natives left us after having, in the short time that they were with us, disposed of 4 good otter skins, one the same but inferior, some old skins of otters and pieces of otter skins. We had seen in all seven or 8 canoes and 60 natives of various ages and of both sexes. But we judged the inhabitants of this strait to be much more numerous on account of the number of huts we had seen. The Indians pointing to the East, I mean the East part of the South coast, gave us to understand that if we remained a few days amongst them, they would go for furs which they would then bring to us. Some of those who visited us did not wish to sell us good skins for we did not have the articles of traffic they required, that is to say coats and blankets. We remained here for too short a time to determine if this place could furnish a quantity of furs at this instant. But it seemed that a stay of two or three days would procure a small quantity. At 6 o'clock in the evening, we left the strait and caught sight of the ship which was standing to the North. We followed her until 8 o'clock but could not reach her, and night coming on, the ship escaped our sight for she could neither tack nor shorten sail being less than half a mile from the rocks which were situated directly to the leeward. At 9 o'clock, we resolved to enter the strait once more for the night. We withdrew behind an islet situated at the bottom of the bay on the North shore, where a good beach of small stones was to be found and where we landed very easily. We spent the night quietly in this place. This place is opposite to those where the Indians live as well as being at some distance from them, for they are to be found on the South shore of the strait.

2ND TASK

The next day 24th. We returned early to the mouth of the strait. We immediately caught sight of the ship which directed her course towards us as soon as she saw us. At noon we came along-side. I made a report to Mr Marchand of our voyage and of the impossibility of mooring the ship for there was no safe anchorage to be found in Cloak Strait. He resolved to send the longboat out once again under my command, in hopes of procuring some few furs following what I had told him. The longboat was furnished with various articles of trade and provisions for eight or ten days and armed with a swivel, two blunderbuss, besides muskets and other arms. I was ordered by Mr Marchand to return in three days if, after this time, there were no more furs to be had, or if we had not been able to obtain any. Mr Roblet, Mr Murat and a midshipman, with a crew of nine, came on board for this expedition, which made in all 13 men. We were armed well enough not to fear any insult the natives could offer us. We left the ship at half past five o' clock in the evening and spent the night in the same place, as we had previously, in the boat.

25th August. In the morning, we passed to the East of the channel after having tacked several times and firing our guns in order to be seen by the inhabitants. But during the morning, we saw only one canoe within which were two women who came off to us in a cove to the South of the place where we had landed. They gave us to understand that Indians were engaged in hunting and would soon return with furs. We took the opportunity to examine the huts of which I have made mention.

In the afternoon, we were joined by nine or ten canoes, having on board around 60 persons, who had to sell but one sea otter skin and two cloaks of the same, which were worn.

Towards the evening, we saw some large canoes coming off from the East which landed on the beach North of the island situated in the strait. We went to the place immediately, where there were two fine residences and a considerable number of inhabitants who were no doubt of the same tribe. The chief of the canoes which had just come to the place, desired to come on board our long boat, which I permitted him to do. He sold us 4 otter skins and it was with the chief that I carried on this traffic, though the skins were not his own. He asked in exchange, muskets and powder, and when he saw that we did not want to comply with this request, he resolved to take coats, breeches, boilers, small basins and large knives. The Indians thought it advisable to put an end to their traffic that evening, after the purchase of the four furs. They told us to spend the night in this place and the next day they would bring many furs for sale. We had seen some Indians bringing canoes to the residence. The avidity with which the Indians pressed us to stay, and the certainty that they possessed yet more furs, put us in hopes of a profitable traffic. We judged it prudent however to spend the night at the usual place, promising to return the next day, early in the morning. Their conduct had been very polite and we parted good friends.

On the 26th, we came early in the morning to the market place where we found the Indians waiting for us. The chief we had seen the previous day came along-side, but seemed to have forgotten the reasons for our visit for he hardly looked at the articles which we laid before him in order that he determine which he would like to have. He contented himself with occasionally promising us many furs and telling us that we must wait for them. During this interval, we surprised him immersing into the sea a small bell, which he had taken away, and which no doubt he thought to get out of the water after our departure. We pretended to pass over this trick but we resolved that we would observe his neat-handedness and put it out of our way if he were to attempt something again. This was the only theft of which we had fallen victim during the time we were amongst these Indians. Their conduct was honest and even polite. Even if they had not told us that an English vessel had remained a long while in this place, and even if the slops, the iron stakes and a great quantity of articles which had been obtained from her had not been convincing proofs that the English had stayed here, their behaviour, their manners and the friendly intercourse we had with them were undoubted proofs that they were accustomed to the Europeans. They told us the Englishmen had frequently slept in their huts and that they had provided them with women, they made us the same offer but we contented ourselves with visiting their residences in order to become acquainted with their manner of life, etc. The chief of the district in which we found ourselves took us into his own hut and entertained us with much consideration and in the most civil manner, for which praise is due.

At 11 o'clock, we had had no traffic though we were most certain that furs were yet to be had from the Indians. We became thus angry against the chief, who was still on board and who was not eager to speak of the traffic, in spite of the small presents we had made him. I had given him to understand in the morning that at noon, we would make our departure and return no more. We made as if to depart and this device proved advantageous. The Indians, seeing us getting under sail, were earnest that we should come back and that they would sell us their furs with procurement of the chief. It is to be agreed upon that no other was as firmly attached to their interest as the chief. He resolved to traffic only after a minute inspection of the articles we offered, and his choice was always the best one. He never forgot to come to an agreement with us with regard to the present we were to make him upon each purchase, and which consisted of a knife, a bell, or some other trifle. The bargains he concluded were always approved of by those who were the owners. During the morning, we purchased seven otter skins, some otters and two cloaks, one made of old otter skins and another of marmot. They asked without intermission for muskets and powder, but upon refusing constantly to give them any, they took boilers, pewter basins, large spears, some few implements and few pots.

Until this moment, they had insisted upon our remaining one more day amongst them, but as soon as they had disposed of their furs, they declared that we should depart whenever we wished for they had nothing more for sale. I gave them to understand that we were to visit the West part of the strait but they answered that no more furs were to be had there for they had sold all that they were possessed of before our arrival. It seems that the English three-master had left the strait very recently and the skins we had purchased were from animals killed after their departure for they were still very new.

The Indians desired us to come back again in six days for they said they would then have killed some otters whose furs they would sell to us. I promised to return, but only in ten days, on which they said on account of such a considerable delay, an English ship would have the precedency and that if we desired to avail ourselves of these furs, it would be necessary to return in six days as they had directed us to do. It today being high water in the strait at 11 o'clock, at ebb at one o'clock, occasioned my observing that the currents which set to the West towards the channel were very strong. They formed between the passage and the island a violent eddy. We waited for the current to cease in order to visit a cove which lies on the North coast of the strait between the channel and the island.

While we were eating our dinner, several Indians of all ages and of both sexes came to the cove. They behaved in a very friendly manner. Having no more skins to sell to us, they brought with them instead young girls to dispose of.

In the afternoon, the wind which had been at West since our arrival in the strait, shifted to East, attended anew with fine weather.

Between ½ past 4 o'clock and 5 o'clock, the tide began to flow. The flood sets to Eastwards and the currents were found not to be as strong as those of the ebb.

As the Indians had indicated that the English ship, of which I have made mention, had anchored at East, outside the mouth of the strait, I desired to spend the remainder of the day examining the South coast stretching to the Eastward in order to assure myself that an anchoring place was not to be found there. In pursuing my route through the canal to the South of the island, we caught sight of a brig of 150 to 200 tons burthen, standing for the South coast which it had been my intention to examine. The ship was but a league distant, and a small Dutch boat of 12 tons burthen was following her. They did not hoist their colours. I judged them to come from the continent, and having orders to avoid speaking with any ship, we abandoned our survey and stood for the entrance through the canal at North, where we sounded and had 4 or 5 fathoms over a bottom of small stones. This channel is so narrow and bounded by rocks that it would prove dangerous for a ship to run through it. The channel to the South of the island is broad and deep, but only a bottom of rocks is to be found.

We saw a canoe and the Indians on board were those we had traded with, they were standing off for the brig, pointing to it and shouting English, which was proof that they knew her to be an English vessel.

We spent the night in the usual place with an intention to go on board the next day.

The account of the two runs in Cloak Strait shew that no safe anchoring place for a ship is to be found there. The least troublesome place is situated in the middle of the Westward entrance, but the bottom is uneven and the place appears to afford little shelter from the violence of the winds at West. If however a ship were compelled to come to anchor in this place, there is means to cross the strait in case of an unfavourable event. Any wind which blows at sea may be felt in this place. But as the bottom to the East is full of rocks and coral, and as it would be dangerous to be compelled to moor the ship there, it is advisable to compute the hour of the tide, either with regards to the beginning of the flood, or of the ebb, for the currents are too strong then. As far as possible, one can do no better than to avoid this channel, and in the other place of which I have made mention*, that is the Westward entrance of the strait, only in the last extremity should one resolve upon anchoring there.

*The chart of the strait made by Mr Chanal which I add here and in which all the soundings are marked, will better assist in making known the direction and bearings of the coasts and the course to be directed, than discourses can do.

After the small number of observations I was able to make on the tides, they flow every six hours each way, and the time of high water is 12 o'clock in the Westerly mouth of the strait on the full of the moon and the new moon. In the strait, the sea rises about 10 feet and the currents follow its direction: the flood comes from Westwards, and the ebb from the Eastwards.

The land in the strait is low and covered with pine trees which are not as numerous as in Norfolk entrance. At a certain distance from the shore, the woods are very much like fine glades, planted in uniformity.

The shores of the coasts are formed of heaps of steep rocks and most of the beaches are scattered with rocks which renders landing difficult.

The soil is drier than we had found it in Norfolk entrance, and the climate no doubt is not as rainy. In the short time that we stayed there, we had enjoyed very fine weather with light airs. There fell heavy dew during the last two nights.

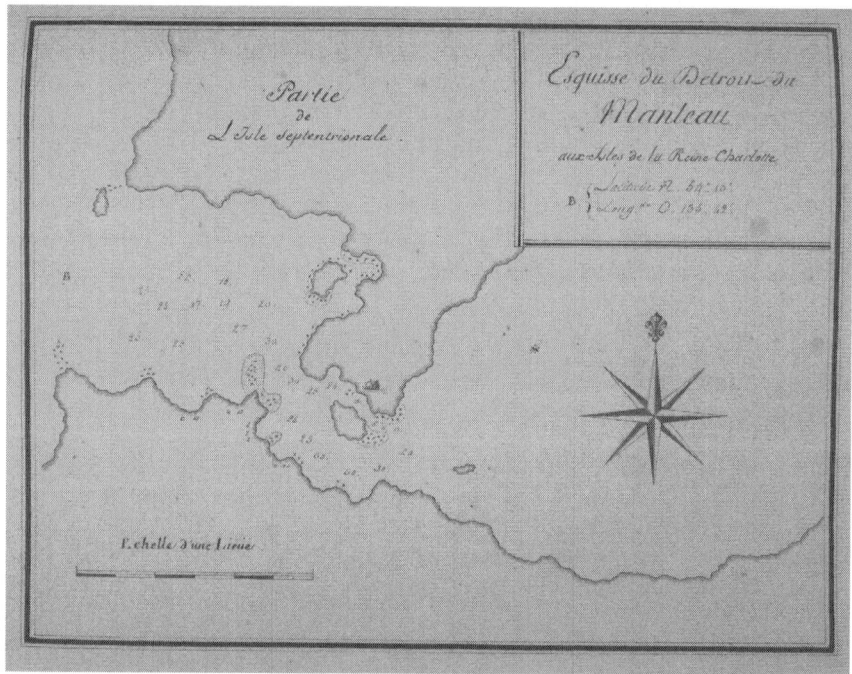

Figure 6 Sketch of Cloak Strait (sewn into Volume 1 of the manuscript)[178]
Courtesy of the Bibliothèque Alcazar, Marseilles, France.

The productions are as those which are to be found at Norfolk. The sea is full of fish and the cove in which we had retired had furnished us with a great abundance of fine mussels and good rock fish.

The rocks under the surface of the sea produce sea-leek, as at Norfolk, and several species of fucus. Many whales and sea calves are to to be seen.

There are numerous species of birds but I cannot account for all of them here. Amongst the sea birds or wild fowl, I observed many gulls, divers, puffins, geese, wild ducks and a heavy bird with a long neck and webbed feet much like the Cormorant, of which it has the habits, for they were gathered together in great numbers upon the rocks. On our approach, they went away from their retreat with great trouble, but came back immediately upon our going away. This bird would be thought a true Cormorant if the flesh did not have the taste of a duck. The flesh of the Cormorant we knew from another place to be very badly tasted.

We saw amongst the land birds, eagles, vultures, sparrow hawks, crows, grey herons of the largest kind, sparrows and other small birds.

---

178 There are in fact two almost identical drawings of Cloak Strait in the manuscript at this point, these are very similar to those published in Fleurieu's *Voyage* op. cit., They are both unsigned.

We saw about the residences, many tame dogs of the same species as our sheep dogs.

The inhabitants scattered about the various parts of the strait, seem to belong to the same tribe, formed of several families of which each has a chief. The greatest number of persons that we saw gathered together at one time in the place where we had traded, was about 200 men, women or children, but I observed that most of those we had seen on the 23rd were not to be found here. It is to be supposed that, not having furs to dispose of, some had not gone to the place, others may have been engaged in hunting, fishing, etc. On this account as nearly as we can estimate 350 people are the whole of the natives to be found here of all ages and both sexes.[179]

These natives are in general as tall as Europeans and better proportioned than those at Norfolk entrance. They do not possess the grim and fierce air we had observed at Norfolk entrance. Their features are regular and their looks are much like those of Europeans. They are of a brown colour, but had they been cleaner in person and lived less in the open air etc., the whiteness of their skin should be equal to ours. I observed amongst them some who were fairer than our common farm labourers. Their hair is black and in general pleasing, some wear it short, that is to say cut all around. Their eyes are not small and do not run like those at Norfolk, they are rather large and lively. They differ from them in other points. They do not daub their hair with ochre and other filth, and their faces are not besmeared with red and black, I saw only two like this. They are not free from lice, for the old cloaks we purchased from them were covered in them.[180]

I have mentioned that they were civil and cheerful, and I will further add that they had nothing of the savage in their looks. But this may be accounted for by their keeping company with Europeans. Indeed they acted towards us with great propriety and with circumspection. Excepting the theft of which I have made mention, they neither stole anything from us nor attempted to do so. It is not they have no propensity to thieving. But it is not their interest to set us at variance with them and that which they would have undertaken previously with less prudence, they will not attempt to do unless they are without fear of detection. The commerce which has been carried on has made them civilized to this point, and if we continue to bring to them with our articles of traffic, the knowledge of the polite arts and of our manners and customs, they will soon equal certain European nations.

---

179 Chanal's figure of 350 differs somewhat from the estimation of the size of the population in Dixon, though the method of calculation seems to have been the same: *I endeavoured to make a calculation of the number of inhabitants who reside in the sound, and its environs; the greatest number I ever saw about the ship at one time, was 175, including women and children. Were I to estimate these at half the number who live here, it would perhaps not be far from the truth; but supposing an allowance to be made for the aged and infirm, and for those who were absent, engaged in hunting, fishing, etc. I think 450 people will be the whole of the natives found here, taking the computation in its utmost extent, and including men, women, and children* (Dixon, op. cit., p. 186).

180 These decriptions, and later Marchand's, are similar to those in Cook, Dixon and Portlock.

I find them to be very intelligent and they seem to understand us in the smallest degree. Although we could converse but with signs, they never left us in any doubt as regards their meaning, and they also understood us very well. I was much surprised at this manner of conversation between us.

The women are less ugly here than at Norfolk entrance though much like them, they wear in an opening made in the under lip, a piece of wood,[181] which gives them a disgusting aspect. This ornament is larger here than at Norfolk entrance, and enlarges the form of the opening. Their manner of wearing it is the same, and the size is in proportion to age, much like at Norfolk.[182] I saw old women wearing

181 Chanal, Dixon and Portlock (and Vancouver) all describe this form of ornament as though it had never before been observed. But Cook (both Dixon and Portlock had made the voyage to the Northwest coast with Cook, and Chanal had access to Cook's accounts) decribes it in detail: *But the most uncommon and unsightly ornamental fashion, adopted by some of both sexes, is their having the under-lip slit; or cut, quite through, in the direction of the mouth, a little below the swelling part. This incision, which is made even in the sucking children, is often above two inches long; and either by its natural retraction, when the wound is fresh, or by the repetition of some artificial management, assumes the true shape of lips, and becomes so large as to admit the tongue through. This happened to be the case, when the first person having this incision was seen by one of the seamen, who called out, that the man had two mouths and, indeed, it does not look unlike it. In this artificial mouth, they stick a flat, narrow ornament, made chiefly out of a solid shell or bone . . .* (*Voyage to the South Pole,* op. cit., Volume 2, p. 369).

182 *This curious operation of cutting the under lip of the females, never takes place during their infancy, but from every observation I was able to make, seems confined to a peculiar period of life. When the girls arrive to the age of fourteen or fifteen, the center of the under lip, in the thick part near the mouth, is simply perforated, and a piece of copper wire introduced to prevent the aperture from closing, the aperture afterwards is lengthened, from time to time, in a line parallel with the mouth, and the wooden ornaments are enlarged in proportion, till they are frequently increased to three, or even four inches in length, and nearly as wide, but this generally happens, when the matron is advanced in years, and consequently the muscles are relaxed; so that possibly old age may obtain greater respect than this very singular ornament* (Dixon, op. cit., p. 187). Portlock also describes this ornament: *. . . but the women disfigure themselves in a most extraordinary manner, by making an incision in the under-lip; in which part they wear a piece of wood made in an oval form a little hollow on each side, and about the thickness of a quarter of an inch; the outer part of the rim is hollowed all round: this curious piece of wood is thrust into the hole, and is secured there by the rim of the lip going round it, fixed in the hollow which is made round the wood. They appear to be worn large or small in proportion to the age of the women, or perhaps to the number of the children they have bore; those that I took to be between thirty and forty years of age wore them about the size of a small saucer, and the older larger in proportion; one old woman, I remarked particularly, having one as large as a large saucer. The weight of this trencher or ornament weighs the lip down so as to cover the whole of the chin, leaving all the lower teeth and gum quite naked and exposed, which gives them a very disagreeable appearance. When they eat, it is customary for them to take more in the mouth at a time than they can possibly swallow; when they have chewed it, the lip-piece serves them as a trencher to put it out of their mouths on, and then they take it occasionally. It seems a general pratice among the females to wear the wooden ornament in their underlip; the children have them bored at about two years of age, when a piece of copper-wire is put through the hole; this they wear till the age of about thirteen or fourteen years, when it is taken out, and the wooden ornament introduced; its first size is about the width of a button* (op. cit., p. 289).

Figure 7 A young woman of Queen Charlotte's Islands[183]

Courtesy of the National Library of Australia

this ornament which was three inches in length and one and a half in breadth. The young girls who are not required to wear this troublesome ornament, without the dirt attending them, are agreeable enough.

Like the men, the women were of a friendly disposition, without suspicion and virtuous enough, that is those of them who were married. The young girls, without appearing to be put in a fright, were offered to us by the natives. The men were not jealous of their women[184] and I did not observe amongst these last, the shyness and constraint of those at Norfolk Sound. I believe the women here to be true to their husbands, and these were under no great uneasiness in this respect. I could not say if they had been once again influenced by the intercourse with Europeans in this regard, or if this difference had existed before they came to know them. It is for the English and the Spanish to determine, for they were the first to sojourn amongst them.

183 See Dixon, op. cit., p. 226.
184 See Dixon Ibid., p. 223.

The men possess clothes of many kinds which they have received from the English and the Spanish, and which make a substitute for the fur cloaks which they wore in times past, they have waistcoats, long breeches, cloaks or great coats, habits, etc. Our clothes pleased them very much. They preferred above all our great coats and our suits and trowsers. Some few of them had hats, stockings, shoes and those who were intirely dressed in this manner would have had nothing of the savage about them in our towns. The dress of the women consists of a cloak of fur which rests upon the shoulders and which is tied in front with a string, and of a large apron made of skins which are tanned and which they tie around their waist at the back and which covers their thighs much like a petticoat. Both men and women, as well as the children, have holes in their ears and wear earrings and necklaces or glass beads. They in general wear upon their head, a small hat which they weave themselves.

Their canoes, their weapons for hunting and their implements for fishing are about the same as those belonging to the inhabitants of Norfolk. They work their canoes with paddles but have come to understand the benefit of sails, for we saw a canoe bearing away which carried a blanket in place of a sail.

Their houses are well-built and one of the finest we measured to forty five feet in length and 35 in breadth, in the form of a parallelogram. The timberwork was very firm and formed of strong posts which are squared and joined together with mortises. On the outsides, the sides and the roof are built of planks which are two feet in breadth. The sides are about 7 feet in height and the middle of the roof 12 feet. At the very top in the middle, there is a square opening to carry out the smoke and let in the light of day. There are small windows in the sides. The door is a large hole oval in shape and three feet in height and two feet in breadth, which from its shape is like the mouth of I know not what animal. The hole is one and a half feet from the ground and made from a large piece of wood lifted up on its edge perpendicularly in the middle of one of the sides. This same side is ornamented with carved work with images of various animals such as lizards, frogs, etc., and with the busts of men, arms, thighs and other parts of the human body. The top is the figure of a man standing and wearing a hat in the shape of a sugar loaf. These figures may be nothing more than emblems of their religion. But the chief who accompanied us informed us that the statue at the summit was a chief. This may perhaps be how these people perpetuate the memory of those persons for whom they entertain veneration. These various carved figures, however imperfect, and the construction of their buildings, give us to much better understand the resource which these people possess, as well as their genius and patience.

On the inside, many chests are to be seen piled upon each other on the sides or in the corners. They told us that their provisions for winter and their bows and arrows were to found inside. Their rods, their javelins, nets and hook and lines were hung up in different places of the house. In the midst of all, there was a picture with various figures and very much like the one of which I made mention on our first run, which we saw on the island situated in the middle of the strait. Their furniture, in the form of cooking utensils consists of wooden vessels, spoons wrought of horn or of the beard of whales, iron pots, pewter basins and other things which they have received from Europeans and which they know how to put to very good use. They make a fire in the middle of the house and the women appear to take charge of the domestic occupations and some are employed in weaving the mats or in needlework, and others, by means of smoke, drying the fish for their winter provision.

They have no fixed place for sleeping and in all likelihood they lie down confusedly on the ground and do not mind the filth of the place, which is to be found everywhere. They care more for their children. In this regard, the chief of the residence which I am describing showed me a cradle hung up for one of his own children. Mothers and fathers have the greatest affection for their children. The residence which I have described was situated in the place where we had trafficked with them. Another of the same kind and of the same size was being built along-side this one. Only the timber work had been completed and a cellar reached along the inside six feet distant from the sides. Three steps constructed all round led down into it. The beams upon which the floor of the residence above was to be built were already put up. Our guide told us that this subterranean was their place of abode during the winter. It seems that all their houses possess such a cellar reserved for this use.

There were in this place, some small huts. They were but dwellings of a moment for the use of those who had come to the place to traffick with us. They do not deserve any mention. Those we saw on the South shore of the strait were neither as fine nor as large as these and did not have the front of the door carved in the manner in which I have just made mention. But in other aspects, they were built in the same manner and contained about the same things. I have forgot to mention that they bring their canoes into their residences for we saw them within almost all of them.

At about a hundred paces from the residence, we observed several tombs or graves. These were chests supported by two posts, 8 or 9 feet in height, covered in a plank loaded with stones. We had reason to believe what the chief, our guide, told us about this place, that these tombs were those of their dead relations.

The shortness of our stay amongst these Indians did not permit us to understand their religion. I have but imperfectly described their character, but I have made a report of what I saw. I will say over again that I found them to be fair and good men. They never came to us armed and were never troubled even when they saw our muskets, satisfied no doubt that they had nothing to fear from us if they did not provoke us. Credit must be given for this circumstance to the conduct of the first navigators who landed amongst them.

Over and above the articles which were given to them by the English, and of which I have before made mention, the natives had in their possession copper plates, large iron bars, axes, adzes, chisels, daggers, spears etc. The chief alone had four muskets which he showed to us, and half a pound of powder. We left them in a state of ignorance concerning the necessity of shot and bullets. He never thought to request any from us, though he had none, but he asked constantly for powder and musquets. I will not enquire whether it was well or ill to furnish them with these sorts of arms. We know it to be true that the English, who deserve our good opinion in many other respects, take a great latitude if they find it beneficial to themselves. But even in this case, it appears that in addition to the other numerous articles which they had received, they could very well have dispensed with the distribution amongst the Indians of muskets, for they will soon learn of their destructive powers which may one day they may be turned upon the givers.[185] A proof of this assertion is that upon our refusal to give them muskets, we obtained from them all the furs they possessed, though our articles of traffic did not please them over much.

On the 27th early in the morning, we sailed out of the strait having a breeze at SE, and as we progressed the wind shifted to NE. We arrived on board at 11 o' clock in the morning.*

*Some other remarks upon this Strait and its inhabitants communicated to me by Mr Roblet are to be found in the second book of this journal.

3RD TASK

On the 28th August we set sail from the ship at ¼ past 1 o'clock in the morning and landed on the shore at 11 o'clock. Seeing no indications that this part was inhabited, we steered South, standing along the shore which was a quarter of a mile distant. Fine weather and clear. At noon, the latitude by observation was 53° 47' North. At this time, the first island to be found on the South shore of Cloak Strait extended NW to NNW, at a distance of about 5 miles. Hippah Island bore SE 9° South, and the nearest point Southward bore SE 3°, distant 1 league.

185 Portlock is extremely critical of this practice (and implicitly of Cook) in the Sandwich Islands: *As they are very dangerous and destructive weapons, I did not suffer any to be made in either ship, though strongly importuned to it by many of the natives: indeed I always thought it [during ?] the last voyage, a very imprudent action to furnish the Indians with weapons which, at one time or other, might be turned against ourselves; and my suspicions were but too well founded; for with one of the daggers given by us to the natives of Owhyhee, my much lamented commander captain Cook was killed; and but for them, that ornament to the British nation might have lived to have enjoyed the fruits of his labour – in ease and affluence, after a series of years spent in the service of his country, and for the benefit of mankind in general: he, however, unfortunately set the example, by ordering some daggers to be made after the model of the Indian Pahooas; and this practice was afterwards followed by every person who could raise iron enough to make one; so that during our stay at these islands, the armourer was employed to little other purpose than in working these destructive weapons; and so liberally were they disposed of, that the morning we were running into Karakakooa bay, after the Resolution had sprung her foremast, I saw Maiha Maiha get eight or nine daggers from captain Clarke, in exchange for a feathered cloak; though since our arrival at Woahoo, I have purchased some cloaks considerably better than that of captain Clarke's, for a small piece of iron worked into the form of a carpenter's plane-bit: these the Sandwich islanders make use of as adzes, and call them towees; and to them they answer every purpose wherever an edge-tool is required* (op. cit., p. 78).

The part of the coast we were navigating is of moderate height and guarded by reefs through which there is no passage. Beyond the first point of land, which is also surrounded by islets and reefs, the shore forms a large gulf within which we were in hopes of finding some bays. In navigating the North shore of this gulf, we saw first a fine beach of easy access. There were two huts to be seen which appeared to be vestiges. We fired our gun at a distance of one mile from the shore, but no inhabitants appeared. We had between 12 and 20 fathoms over a bottom sometimes of sand and at other times, of rocks. Two miles to the Eastward of the Northern extremity of the gulf, we found a bay about half a league deep, extending N¼NE by compass. It is 3 or 4 cables in length and we had between 20 and 12 fathoms and everywhere a bottom of fine sand. The bay is bounded by two sandy beaches and supplied by a stream on the East shore upon which we landed. We saw neither inhabitants nor any sign that this place had ever before been examined by Europeans, but we saw trees cut down and others stripped of their bark, and heard the sound of dogs barking. We did not see however any canoes or Indians, in spite of having fired our guns. I named this place Otard Bay, after my friend. The two points which bound this bay stretch by the compass NE and SE. At 3 cables length South of the East point, there is a shoal which guards the entrance, and it is requisite upon approaching it, to keep a little more to the West point. Though the bay is open to the winds at South, it affords good anchoring and it appears to me that a ship may moor in this place in safety for we did not observe the sea to have destroyed it in any way. The land round about is of moderate height, but the hills inland are much higher. In sailing out of this bay, we steered towards an opening which bore SE½S, at a distance of ¾ of a league. On drawing near, we observed it to be very deep, stretching ENE. On our starboard side, we passed an island which had a low point upon which the sea breaks. We stood along the North coast at a proper distance and had constantly 15 to 25 fathoms over a rocky bottom. We caught sight of a canoe a-head with two Indians on board and which ran away upon seeing us. We saw them land on the North shore and carry their canoe away into the woods. One mile at least from Otard Bay, we entered through a channel of middling width into an entrance, which appeared to be of a considerable size. We continued to have 25 to 30 fathoms over a bottom of rocks, but we found the sea to be smooth and calm. As night was approaching and we could no longer see around us, we were obliged to stop and land upon a small beach which afforded good shelter on the North coast, and there we spent the night.

29th. It was high water at midnight and ebb tide at ½ past 6 o'clock in the morning. It rises about 10 feet. We saw in the woods no other signs of the Indians but the vestiges of a hut and the remnants of fires which had been made in various places. We left this place and steered to the ENE in order to conclude our examination of the entrance. We fired our fowling piece once again to persuade the inhabitants to shew themselves. After proceeding one mile to the ENE in the direction of the entrance, we turned to the SE and found ourselves guarded intirely by the land in a place which formed a spacious and commodious harbour. We had everywhere soundings from 16 to 20 fathoms over a muddy bottom. We named this place Port Louis after Mr Louis Marchand, the brother of the Captain who had accompanied me in the longboat. It is closed at West by an island, which is to be found at the mouth of the entrance. We had the day before, followed the canal situated to the North of this island which we had believed to be the main, but we saw today that there is to the South a canal which is equally deep but very narrow. In the midst of sounding, we saw a canoe with five persons on board which had come from the side by which we had entered. We suspected them at first to be those who had run away at our approach the day before, which afterwards was to be confirmed by the Indians themselves. No sooner had we seen them than we waved a white flag and we made every sign of friendship that could be thought of to persuade them to come off to the boat. They drew near, somewhat wary, and the chief before coming along-side made himself known asking who was the chief amongst our people. He next came on board and after I had embraced him, he asked me to exchange names, which we proceeded to do. From this moment he addressed me as *Nousk*, this was his name, and he answered to nothing but the name of Chanal. He made me a present of an old cloak, which he wore himself, and I gave him some few trifles. This was a great sign for the conduct of the Indians differed greatly from the generality of the natives we had hitherto seen. We concluded that though they had previously seen Europeans, the intercourse they had had with them had been it seems of short duration. We expected thus to engage in a profitable traffic with them if the entrance was inhabited, which the situation seemed to promise. We could do no better than to give ourselves up to these Indians who offered to take us to their habitation, which they pointed to as lying in the SE. We believed they meant to bring us furs and we attended them thither. The channel to which they led us extended to the Eastward and was deep and narrow. A short distance from its mouth, we stopped before a cove at South, which was their place of abode and which was hid amongst them woods. Some Indians appeared upon their hallowing to them, and those who had brought us here landed forthwith, promising to return very soon. They indeed came back very soon. But we were much surprised to see them in European dress with waistcoats, breeches and English hats and having nothing to sell but fish. We thus were well persuaded the English ships, which had come to this shore before us, had penetrated into this place likewise. After having purchased but one very fine cloak of otter skin, which we were obliged to much haggle for, we departed. They had no arms and seem to be of a very gentle disposition. They had with them in their canoes large skins very tanned, or rather well buffed. I desired to bring one off to the ship but they did not wish to part with any. I know not if they were the skins of deer but they very much resemble them. We did not come to the entrance until noon, which prevented us from observing the latitude. We made our way out of the channel situated to the South of the island which is to be found in the middle of the mouth of the entrance. In the afternoon, we stood along the South shore of the gulf and on our starboard side, we passed two small islands of a moderate height near which we had 15 fathoms over a bottom of sand and rock. Off the second of these two islands, we entered a channel stretching to the SE but were soon stopped by the rocks which guarded it. Beyond these rocks, a lake of salt water extending to the SW was to be seen, but we could not see at what distance it continued. The Indians we had seen in the morning, joining us in this place, gave us to understand that the channel communicated with the sea beyond the South point of the gulf, but I believe that this was a trick, or rather that we had not understood them well enough. We were now without hopes of finding a greater number of inhabitants and furs in this place. We continued our route in order to double the South point of the gulf. The two points of the gulf, at the bottom of which the entrance we have named Port Louis is to be found, lay by compass SE¼E and NW¼W, at a distance of 2 leagues. By reckoning, Port Louis lies in 53° 41' North latitude, and in order to reach this place, it is adviseable rather to run along the North shore of the gulf, passing all the small islands of which I have made mention on the starboard side. At the bottom, ranges of high mountains are to be seen. The shores are bounded by steep rocks and the main rises rather abruptly. From the channel which leads to Port Louis, there is by compass to the E¼NE, a remarkable round mountain of considerable height.

At 6 o'clock in the evening, we rounded the South point of the gulf, offward there are two shoals to be found which are distant about 1 mile. We caught sight of our ship standing to the North under the top-sails. She tacked and stood to the South at this moment, and we continued to coast along the shore. The Western extremity of Hippah Island bore SE½S, about 3 leagues distant. At the SE, a point of the land, distant 2 leagues, was to be seen. Between this point and the coast, there appeared to be a deep opening bearing ESE, towards which we directed our course. The night falling, we stopped on the coast amongst rocks which afforded some shelter, after having doubled the point of which I have made mention. But as the shore was also guarded by rocks and it was impossible to land. We spent the night at anchor over a sandy bottom.

30th August. At day-light, we put to sea and as we approached the channel which we had the intention of entering, a canoe with three natives on board came off to us. We purchased two cub, a fine cloak of otter skins and the skin of an animal recently killed. The islanders had no arms and shewed no knowledge of our articles. The bargain was concluded in a very short time, which was not their usual practice. They left us soon after and we continued to steer towards the channel. We sounded at this moment and found 30 fathoms over a fine bottom of sand, distant at least one mile from the North shore. We next passed on the larboard side a small island upon which several dogs were to be seen. Immediately afterwards, we entered the channel which is a little less than a mile in breadth, situated between high, steep land. We continued E¼NE for one mile, at which point the channel turns back to ENE for quite a considerable distance. The land was here very high and steep on both sides, with a line of 50 fathoms we had no bottom. We saw a canoe following and waited for it. These were the same Indians from whom we had purchased a cloak of otter skins, somewhat worn. They brought with them this time a young girl of 14 or 15 years for their own profit for they offered her to me several times. The filthiness of this girl rendered her very loathsome. The

Indians gave us to understand that furs were to be had at the bottom of the chan-nel. We went to the place favoured with a sea breeze which had been blowing since 10 o'clock. The weather had been calm until this time. They followed us with their canoes. After a mile, we found 25 to 30 fathoms over a bottom of rock and broken shells. The canal was here narrower and we were inclosed by the land. The canal stretched NE. We had now a bottom of 50 fathoms over coarse sand. We sounded and had 42 fathoms, same bottom. In coming near the place, the anchor-ing became by degrees better. We sounded and had successively 32 fathoms over shells and sand, 30 fathoms over sand and mud, 30 fathoms over black sand and 28 fathoms over black sand and shells. We were at this moment but ¾ of a cables length from each side of the channel, and some two cables length from a beach at the bottom, cloathed in verdure, and which bore NE½N. We had thought the channel to terminate at this beach but we soon found it to extend further to the North where it came to form a wetdock, or an excellent port in which we had 15 fathoms over a bottom of mud. Very near the shore of rocks, we found 10 fathoms over a muddy bottom. We stopped there to eat our dinner. The channel continued into a small branch to the NNW and we made the Indians who had followed us here understand that they should give the inhabitants notice, in hopes that they would bring furs. But they soon returned bringing nothing, and we supposed that no inhabitants had been found there. In order to assure myself that no inhabitants were to be found, I followed the shore attended by two of the gentlemen, and after half a a mile we reached the bottom of the channel. Two streams fell from the mountains and flowed into the channel. We saw neither huts nor any signs of inhabitants and so we returned to the longboat. Though I am very certain that this place is not inhabited, it is necessary to say that the barking of dogs was to be heard and we saw in the woods paths, but which had been in truth little used. The port in which we had come to anchor was a fine place and had a very agree-able aspect. Though it is surrounded on all sides by high mountains, the sides are moderately elevated. We discovered in the woods many of our European plants of which I will presently make mention. We made our water at the stream nearest to us. It was of the sweetest sort and did not possess the remarkable reddish colour of all those we had seen in the other places.

This port was named Port Chanal by Mr Marchand upon our return. There is here room enough for several ships, no better shelter nor bottom could be desired. The sea is very smooth here and it is impossible herein to suffer the effects of any sort of inclement weather. It was high water in this port this day at 1 o'clock in the afternoon, and as this day was the second of the moon, the time of high water is at about 12 o'clock on the days of the new and full moon. After our observations the following night, having departed from the canal, the sea rises but 7 or 8 feet. The whole length of the canal is intirely free from danger and there is a consider-able depth of water near the shore for the banks are steep. The sea breeze blows to the bottom of the channel and a ship may reach this port with no great difficulty if she waits for the sea breeze to settle before coming to the mouth. A difficulty may arise on the way out of the channel, and though we did not have land breezes during our stay there, it is very possible and most likely that sometimes they blow here when the haze does not oppose them. In case of a calm, the ship could otherwise be towed out of this place by the boats with the tide of the ebb. On the outside of the channel, the ship may be warped over a bottom of sand in order to get under sail with the breeze at WNW, which is usual here as it blew from this point of compass during the whole of our stay on this coast. Making the SW board will soon bring a ship into the offing. Following the observation I made the next day, the mouth of the channel, at the bottom of which Port Louis is to be found, lies in latitude 53° 34' North. During the afternoon we sailed out of the channel and at 8 o'clock, we secured a sandy beach on the North shore near to the place we had seen the Indians in the morning. In this place, where we spent the night, there were to be found the remains of a house, which had been deserted, and a coffin which had been left to decay and which was of the kind we had seen in Cloak Bay. There were about the place rose-bushes perfectly like those of our gardens.

31ˢᵗ August. We had a thick fog until 8 o'clock in the morning which prevented our leaving the cove until this time. It was low water in this place at 7 'clock. At 9 o'clock, the fog clearing away intirely, we saw at the point of the cove from which we had just departed, a canoe with five men on board, soon after we saw another to the Westward. As we rowed towards the place, they seemed to run away from us, which obliged us to stop and wave a white flag, making all the signs we could in order to engage their attention. But they seemed to mind us little and we saw them land amongst the rocks which bordered the shore. Upon following them to the landing place, we saw neither the Indians nor their canoes, which they no doubt had carried away into the woods. Two hours had passed since the moment we had perceived the first canoe. We could not land with the longboat in this place and lose yet more time waiting for them, for this day we were to regain the ship. The breeze had settled at West attended with fine weather, we took the opportunity to stand to the South. At noon, the latitude by observation was 53° 36' North. At this time, the entrance of Port Chanal bore E¼SE, one league distant. The extremities of the opening in which we found ourselves, stretched from NNW, distant 1 league, to SSE½E, distant 1 league. Some few coves or bays are to be found on both the North and the South coasts, but no safe anchoring place is to be had there. The West point of Hippah island, for which we were steering, bore SSE½S, distant 2 leagues between the South point of the gulf and Hippah Island. The shore is guarded from the sea by shoals and small islets of rocks. An opening bends to the SE and forms a passage between Hippah Island and the mainland. At ½ past 1 o'clock, having made a run of 6 miles since noon, we doubled the West point of Hippah Island near to which shoals and a ledge of rocks, covered in sea-leek, stretch 1 mile into the offing. We passed over them and found 10 fathoms of water. We followed the island very close to the mouth of the channel which forms the separation between it and the shore. The South West part is formed of beaches bordered by rocks and there is no convenient landing place to be had, we saw neither huts nor inhabitants. The East part is a high round mountain and though steep, well wooded notwithstanding. It is bordered by steep rocks and is not easy of access. We perceived two small huts on this shore, but no inhabitants appeared. We saw on this island no fortification or hippah of which Captain Dixon makes mention, though we had kept close enough to the shore in order to be well assured that no such thing exists. Towards the South opening of the strait, which separates the island from the mainland, there is a shelf and a ledge of rocks covered in sea-leek. The tide flowing full, attended with the wind, carried us violently to the Southward. From here, we steered towards Rennell entrance, waiting to fall in with ship. The East coast of Hippah Island is very high and steep. There is to be found there a deep bay at the bottom of which there is a fine beach of white sand. At ½ past 3 o'clock, we caught sight of the *Solide* standing in for the land, bearing SSW½W, distant 2 leagues. We bore up to the ship and came on board at ½ past 5 o'clock in the evening. The whole part of this coast is wooded and only the summits of the highest mountains are bare and appear barren. Amongst the pine trees and fir trees composing this great forest, we observed some very fine hazelnut trees, some birch trees and a kind of willow. In the various places we had landed, I had discovered many of the plants which grow at home in France such as the rasberry bush, the wild goose-berry tree, the rose bush of which I have already made mention, celery, purslain, water cresses, the lily of the valley, the dock plant, the greater centaury, a species of mallow, nettles, starwort like that which is to be found in our gardens, a species of fern whose root tastes like liquorish, etc. We saw everywhere peas and vetch scattered about in tufts, and which I believe to be native to the country for there was hardly a possibility of those navigators who had come here before us, having sowed the seeds of these plants in such great quantities in the places in which we had discovered them. These peas are tender and as pleasant to the taste as any kind found in Europe. They take root at the top of beaches in open country like those we saw in Norfolk. In Port Chanal, we saw a crab apple tree bearing fruit, which though very small is proof that the ground of these islands were it cultivated would produce plentifully all that the fields of France produce, in the Southerly provinces I mean to say. We cannot speak of the climate on account of our very short stay in these places. Suffice it to say that we had fine and very agreeable weather. On land, we bore a considerable degree of heat during the day, most particularly in a calm. The dew fell heavy during the night. The sea and the land birds are of the same kind as those we had observed in Cloak Bay. There is so much fish to be had on this coast that in no more than half an hour, we took with two lines as much fish as could be eaten in a day by twelve men. The rock fish proved excellent eating, better than any I had ever tasted. The little chart I have drawn will better illustrate the route of the longboat from Cloak Bay to Hippah Island.

From Thursday 1st to Friday 2nd September 1791

126½

I now resume my narrative which I had put aside on the 1st September at noon, after having resolved to steer for Berkley Entrance.

During the whole of this day, we had a steady wind at NNW and WNW, more or less fresh, attended with hazy weather.

At ½ past 6 o'clock in the morning, we directed our course ESE, and at noon E¼SE in order to fall in with coast.

The variation determined from azimuths and the amplitude was 26° 3' NE.

At noon, having been prevented from determining the latitude by observation on account of the haze which was very thick, it was 50° 58' North by reckoning, longitude 134° 54'.

Réamur's thermometer +12½°, Fahrenheit's thermometer 62°.

From Friday 2ⁿᵈ to Saturday 3ʳᵈ September 1791

The wind blew more or less fresh at NNE and WNW variable, attended still with a thick haze and a smooth sea. We saw whales, stormy petrels and other sea plants.

The variation of the compass was NE 24° 30' by observation.

Latitude by observation 49° 49'.
Longitude by reckoning W 132° 52'.

11' more to the South than by reckoning.
Réamur's thermometer +14°, Fahrenheit's thermometer 65°.
The weather was mild and pleasant.

From Saturday 3ʳᵈ to Sunday 4ᵗʰ September 1791

99

During this day, we had a wind at NW and NWN with hazy weather.

The variation of the compass 23° 37' NE by observation.

At 8 o'clock in the morning, we directed our course Eastward and at noon, after having found the latitude by observation to be 49° 1' N, in which lies the North point of Berkley Entrance, whence I had determined to come to anchor, we steered ENE. The longitude by reckoning was 130° 44'.

We were carried 4' to the North of the reckoning this day.

Réamur's thermometer +14°, Fahrenheit's thermometer 65°.

We saw few birds but many sea plants of the *Fucus* kind, and sea-leek.

From Sunday 4ᵗʰ to Monday 5ᵗʰ September 1791

95¼

By the mean result of four sets of lunar observations made by Mr Chanal and by myself, reduced to 4h 24' 51" PM, our longitude (mean result) was 129° 58' 30" W. By reckoning, the longitude was at this moment found to be 130° 2' 30", that is 4' more to the Westwards.

At ½ past 4 o'clock, the weather clearing, we caught sight of the coast extending N to NE½N, distant 13 or 14 leagues. It seemed to be very high. Towards evening, the weather became very hazy.

The variation of the compass by observation was 22° 45' NE.

At 8 o'clock in the evening, distant only 7 leagues from the West point of Breakers Island by estimation, and 11 leagues from the North point of Berkley Sound, we brought to under the top-sails with her head to the SW, and I gave orders to put about ship every two hours. The wind blowing a fresh gale we reefed the top-sails.

In the afternoon, having a very light wind at NW, we took the opportunity to stand in for the land which we could not see on account of the thick haze which covered it.

At 10 o'clock, the haze clearing a little, we caught sight of very high mountains the summits of which were covered in snow. They stretched from NNW to NE¼E. Soon after, the sea becoming so to say muddy, we sounded and found no bottom with a line of 80 fathoms. This change in the colour of sea gave me reason to suppose that the current from the River Pinack, called the Strait of Juan de Fuca in former times, and situated but a few leagues to the Southwards of us, was the cause. At noon, the North point of Nootka Sound bore NW¼N, the middle of Breakers Island, N¼NW, the middle of Nootka Sound bore NNW and the North point of Berkley Sound bore NE¼E, distant 6 or 7 leagues.

Latitude by observation N 48° 51'.
Longitude by observation W 128° 56'.

8' more to the South than by reckoning.
Réamur's thermometer +14°, Fahrenheit's thermometer 65°.

From Monday 5th to Tuesday 6th August 1791

43

During the afternoon, the weather was pretty clear. We saw what appeared to be several openings North of Berkley Sound, which seemed to form bays.

At ¼ past 5 o'clock PM, the weather becoming hazy, the entrance to Nootka Sound bore NW½W, the middle of the entrance bore NW, the Southermost land in view bore ENE½E and the North point of Berkley entrance bore NE¼ E, distant 4 leagues.

We spent the night making trips, making ready to stand in for the shore at day-light.

At 2 o'clock in the morning, after a calm of three hours, we had a light wind at SE and ESE attended with a haze prodigiously thick which prevented us from seeing the shore though we were very close to it. By means of some few mountains, which I caught sight off above the haze, I found our position to be the same as yesterday at the time that the bearings were taken.

At 8 o'clock, the weather clearing a little, the North point of Berkley Sound was found to be bearing NE¼E, distant 5 leagues, and the middle of the entrance of Nootka, NW½W.

The wind continued at ESE and E and prevented us from standing in for the entrance. On account of the curtain of haze with which the coast is almost constantly covered and which moves from one place to another, examining the coast in this sea proves very tedious and does not leave time enough to determine the situation. At noon the North point of Berkley Sound bore ENE½E, distant 4 or 5 leagues, and the South point of this very same sound bore E.

Latitude by observation 48° 59',
Longitude by observation 128° 43½'.

On Mr Dixon's chart it was found to be 128° 50', following the bearings above. The variation of the compass determined from 13 sets of azimuths was found to be NE 22° 39'.

Réamur's thermometer +14°, Fahrenheit's thermometer 65°.

From Tuesday 6ᵗʰ to Wednesday 7ᵗʰ September 1791

4

During the afternoon we had light gusts of wind at SSE, or rather a calm attended with a pretty large swell from the West.

At 6 o'clock, observing that the currents were carrying us quickly to the NW shore of Berkley Sound, we sounded and found 50 fathom water over a fine bottom of grey sand, a little muddy and mixed with very small, broken shells. We came to anchor, clinching a hawser on the kedge anchor.

In this situation, the North point of Berkley Sound bore ENE 4° E, distant 4 leagues. We were about 2 leagues distant from the NW shore of the Sound. Our latitude was 48° 58', the longitude computed from our observations, was 128° 49½', and by Mr Dixon's chart, it was 128° 50' in comparison to our observation of it.

At the anchoring place, the variation of the compass by observation with different compasses, was found to be 23° 1' NE.

After coming to anchor, the head of the ship was to WSW and the currents were setting to ESE, it being now the flood, running at the rate of 1 mile per hour. At 9h 40' PM, it was high water and at 9h 55' the ebb began to make and continued until ¾ past 4h AM, which is proof that the tides are regular. At 6 o'clock, we perceived five canoes paddling towards the ship. They had come out of a sort of opening situated to the North of us. Our joy at such a sight can hardly be imagined for we believed them to be loaded with furs, but in this we were cruelly disappointed. Half a mile from the ship, they advanced in only slow degrees. Finally, after shewing them every mark of friendship and following the song with which the natives of this coast entertain most often their visitors, they came along-side. There were six persons in each canoe and we counted thirty all together. There were no women or children to be seen. We saw in a very short time that they did not have a single fur amongst them, excepting one who wore an old piece of bear skin, which he did not desire to sell. In the beginning, we supposed they had concealed them from us, as they had done often at Norfolk, but after we showed them all that we possessed in order to tempt them, they left us very quietly to engage in fishing in the offing. A canoe with only two men on board came off to us soon after, but they likewise brought nothing to dispose of and left us in like manner.

On our enquiry for furs, they made signs which could not be easily understood. I perceived nonetheless that they wanted to make us understand that several ships had come to this place and they had trafficked all that they were possessed of, which I believed to be true for they showed us woollen blankets of Spanish manufacture, shirts after the English fashion, hooks, glass beads, etc. Very soon we were unfortunately to become convinced of the truth of the information given by the natives, but this is to take up the account before time.

Their canoes are the best wrought of all those we have seen on this coast and are most proper for keeping the sea. They were 35 to 40 feet in length and about 3½ feet broad. In some, the forepart is fixed very neatly to the canoe about two feet from the stern or from the prow. The head rises a little. They contained the same instruments for fishing as in Norfolk, and large skins for wine or whale oil very well made of what I believe to be sea calf skin. I presume they are intended to serve as buoys when a whale is struck in order to keep them in sight and to tire them. In such a case, I saw them fill them with air. On these skins, they paint figures, in a large part fish, which are rudely executed.

In addition to these implements of fishing, each canoe is furnished with a harpoon which was not like any we saw neither at Norfolk nor at Queen Charlotte's Islands. It was about ten feet in length and eight inches in circumference and made of a very hard wood. The point was sharpened and appeared to have been made hard with fire. From near one end to the other at intervals, there was a kind of gammoning intended to prevent the harpoon from slipping from their hands. They gave us to understand that they used it for whale fishery.

Like the natives of Norfolk, they paint their faces and sometimes their bodies, like their hair, a red and a black colour. In the short time I saw them, they seemed to live in the same manner as those at Norfolk. They expressed either surprise or joy at the sight of the ship and of all the articles of traffic we showed to them.

I believe them to be very bold in venturing to sea on board their canoes for we saw them more than 4 leagues distant from the shore. When I saw them so far distant, I could not but reflect upon the power which Providence has given to the most ignorant of men over the strongest of animals in the sea or on the land. That those numerous men of the civilized world have tamed the elephant, that they have subdued it and managed the horse in order assure its labour in their favour, that they have made the King of all beasts, the lion, a slave, and made the tiger flee, is no surprise to me for I have an esteem for the arts and sciences which have increased a hundred times their strength, and have made them understand how to put it to the most advantageous use. But these men, quite independent, having but very imperfect learning and possessing no other resource which society otherwise affords to other men, that they put to sea in their frail canoes made of nothing but the trunk of tree hollowed, and at a considerable distance from the shore, and they set upon the largest fish ever (the whale) which may so easily swallow them up or drown them, is most astonishing to me. If as I am persuaded, men of nature, as in the most civilized states, seek to engage in hunting for their own sustenance, it is to be believed with the utmost ease that these navigations have resulted in the most ordinary manner, in the population of the islands scattered in the South seas. Should a canoe with men, women and children on board be pushed out of its way and be carried away to sea by a strong wind or by some other accident, they not being able to return home, would be obliged to proceed in direction of the winds and be scattered amongst the vast archipelagos which navigators have so frequently visited since. It is true that we did not find amongst these islanders the same language or customs as those belonging to the peoples of the continent we had seen. Would it be too great a presumption to say that I have sufficient knowledge all these peoples to be a good judge of these matters? Yes. May all those who have ever visited these people say they have never been mistaken? Did they always understand those who spoke to them? I can hardly believe it. Let us hold for a certainty only that which we know and not seek through fruitless supposition, to penetrate the secrets of the past with nothing more than our opinions to guide us.[186] I return to my account. In spite of the faint hopes of finding furs in Berkley Sound, we resolved to come to anchor. As we all liked to entertain ideas of success, we said to ourselves that the Indians were engaged in nothing but fishing for they had with them no women or children, and that in consequence they had left their furs at home, having no idea of meeting with a ship with which they might traffic.

During the night we had successively a calm, light gusts of wind at SE with hazy weather and a great swell from the West. In the morning, the weather became unsettled and dark in the horizon at West, the swell increasing from that quarter at each instant. Our situation at anchor proving most dangerous, I resolved to get under sail as soon as the wind would permit. As early as ½ past 11 o'clock, a very thick haze prevented our seeing the land, from which we were distant but 2 leagues, as I have before made mention. Our situation would become more dangerous still in case of strong wind at West for it was impossible to come to anchor in Berkley Sound which we had not examined and knew only as it is laid down in chart of Mr Dixon.

I was surprised to see several sharks about the ship of which there are few in such cold a climate.[187]

Réamur's thermometer +14°, Fahrenheit's thermometer 65°.

---

186 Gannier identifies the textual source of Marchand's philosophising here as being Roblet's journal (*journal*, op. cit., p. 390).

187 Dixon makes the same remark: *In the afternoon we had a large shark along-side. I mention this as it is a fish rarely seen in such Northerly latitudes* (op. cit., p. 77).

From Wednesday 7th to Thursday 8th September 1791

22

At ½ past 1 o'clock, a breeze springing up at SE, we put to sea and stood to the Southward.

At ½ past 2 o'clock, the haze cleared a little and we observed the North point of Berkley Sound bearing E¼NE, distant 5 leagues.

Soon after the weather became so very dark and rainy we could hardly see from fore to aft of the ship.

At 5 o'clock in the evening, the wind varied from W to WSW. We continued to stand to the Southward and only at half past four in the morning did we tack and stand to the Northward. During the night, we had a calm and light gusts of wind at West. The swell had gone down a little. The weather cleared at 6 o'clock in the morning, though a very thick bank of haze remained all round the horizon. We had sounded every hour during the night with a line of 80 fathoms and had found no bottom.

Until 10 o'clock AM, we had a calm, a great swell from the West and very hazy weather at intervals. At this moment, a light breeze springing up at WSW, we stood once again for the entrance of Berkley Sound.

At noon, our latitude by observation was found to be 48° 40' North and our longitude 129° W.

The currents had carried us 4' to the Southward since we had got under sail.

The variation of the magnetic needle was found to be 22° 31' NE by a great number of observations of the azimuths.

Réamur's thermometer +14°, Fahrenheit's thermometer 65°.

From Thursday 8th to Friday 9th September 1791

73¼

As our latitude by observation at noon had put us 20' more to the South of the N point of Berkley Sound, we steered NE and NE¼N.

At 3 o'clock o'clock PM, we saw the land through the haze. It extended NNW and E¼SE.

At ½ past 5 o'clock, being but 5 leagues distant from Berkley Sound, which bore NE¼N, we perceived a three-master coming out of the Sound and coasting South. Not intending to speak to her, we directed our course SE in order not to draw near.

After what the natives had told us and after having seen the ship, it was now of no use to come to anchor in a place where there was certainly no traffic to be had. I assembled a council of officers in order to determine the manner in which to proceed. We considered the time that would be lost in seeking out an anchoring place more to the South, as no place was laid out between Berkley Sound and Cape Mendocino on the charts we had in our possession, though all quite new, excepting Point Trinidad, which is adjacent to this Cape and in consequence, to the Spanish possessions. Having considered, as I have made mention, if furs were to be had here or not, the season being besides too advanced to continue with researches of this sort in a space of sea in which the land is frequently covered in haze which prevents our seeing it, we resolved by mutual consent that for the greater success of the expedition, there was nothing more to do but to direct our course to the Sandwich Islands, where after providing ourselves with refreshments, we would make all possible haste to Canton in order to outrun the other ships which we knew to be about this coast. There we would sell at the most advantageous price the skins we had obtained here. After compiling the minutes of this resolve, signed by all the officers at 7 o'clock in the evening, we steered S¼SW.

Thus all the hopes we had entertained since our departure from Marseilles, of procuring a great quantity of fine furs on the North West coast of America, vanished. What prices are to be had at China I know not and only then, when I discover the price of furs in China, will I give my opinion concerning so uncertain a commerce.

At 6 o'clock in the evening, the North point of Berkley Sound bearing NNE½E, distant 5 leagues, we took our departure, following Mr Dixon's chart, in latitude 48° 46' North and longitude 128° 48' West. At this moment, we had observed a current which had set to the North until noon.

At day-light, we perceived the coast stretching E½N to NE, distant about 14 leagues. It seemed to be very high. During this day we had light winds varying from W to ENE round by North. The weather was clear enough though hazy in the horizon. There was great swell from the WSW.

Latitude by observation N 47° 45'.
Longitude by reckoning W* 129° 26'.

*As the longitude will be constantly West of Paris, I will not make mention of the denomination in the remainder of the journal in order to avoid a tiresome repetition.

16' more to the South than by reckoning.
The variation of the compass was NE 21° 15'.

From Friday 9th to Saturday 10th September 1791

84

We had during this day light winds at North which shifted to ESE round by North East, attended with a thick haze. We saw sea plants of various kinds and very few birds. The variation of the compass determined from the amplitudes and the azimuths, was 20° 5' NE.

Latitude by observation N 46° 16'.
Longitude by reckoning 130° 30' 30".

17' more to the South than by reckoning.
Réamur's thermometer +15°, Fahrenheit's thermometer 67°.

From Saturday 10ᵗʰ to Sunday 11ᵗʰ September 1791

79

Variable winds from W to SE round by South, blowing more or less fresh, with calms at intervals, hazy weather and a great swell from the SW. We caught sight of whales, sea plants, stormy petrels and considerable flocks of a kind of sea lark.

Latitude by observation N 45° 8'.
Longitude by reckoning 131° 28'.

Réamur's thermometer +14½°, Fahrenheit's thermometer 66°.

From Sunday 11ᵗʰ to Monday 12ᵗʰ September 1791

Until 5 o'clock PM, the wind blew a gentle gale at West. At this moment it began to fall calm. The weather was fine and pleasant.
We continued to see many whales, sea plants, stormy petrels and sea larks.
The variation of the magnetic needle determined from 9 sets of azimuths and amplitudes was NE 18° 7'.

Latitude by observation N 44°.
Longitude by reckoning 132° 10'.

14' more to the South than by reckoning.
Réamur's thermometer +18°, Fahrenheit's thermometer 73°.

From Monday 12ᵗʰ to 13ᵗʰ September 1791

62¼

Until 5 o'clock in the morning, we had light winds varying from WSW to W, attended with a very thick haze. At this moment, they shifted to WNW and blew gentle gales, it continued hazy. We had a large hollow swell from SW which greatly retarded our progress.
We saw this day only stormy petrels, crossers and one albatross.
The variation of the compass by observation was 17° 30' NE.

Latitude by observation N 42° 56'.
Longitude by reckoning 132° 48'.

9' more to the South than by reckoning.
Réamur's thermometer +16°, Fahrenheit's thermometer 69°.

From Tuesday 13th to Wednesday 14th September 1791

137½

Wind at NW blowing a fresh gale, cloudy weather and hazy.
The variation of the compass determined from azimuths was 16° 31' NE.

Latitude by observation N 40° 39'.
Longitude by reckoning 134° 13'.

15' more to the South than by reckoning.
Réamur's thermometer +15°, Fahrenheit's thermometer 68°.

From Wednesday 14th to Thursday 15th September 1791

117

At 10 o'clock in the evening we caught a small land bird which resembled a linnet and which had settled upon a yard. We were now distant 150 leagues from coast of America, which was the nearest land to us. It is difficult to imagine how such small an animal could cross so large a distance, particularly with the winds which blow constantly from the West quarter in this space. The winds varied from NW to W¼SW, blowing fresh in a greater or less degree, attended with cloudy weather and a great swell from the WSW.

By 7 sets of azimuths, the variation of the magnetic needle was found to be 15° 30' Northeasterly.

Latitude by observation N 38° 45'.
Longitude by reckoning 135° 20'.

9' more to the South than by reckoning.
Réamur's thermometer +17°, Fahrenheit's thermometer 71°.

From Thursday 15th to Friday 16th September 1791

107¾

At noon, we steered SSW when the wind permitted. The wind was still at W, blowing fresh in a greater or less degree attended with squalls at intervals.
The variation of the compass by observation was 14° 43' NE.
We continued to see stormy petrels and some few quebrantahuessosses.

Latitude by observation N 36° 58'.
Longitude by reckoning 136° 7'.

8' more to the South than by reckoning.
Réamur's thermometer +16½°, Fahrenheit's thermometer 70°.

From Friday 16ᵗʰ to Saturday 17ᵗʰ September 1791

123½

During this day, the wind varied from NW to NNE blowing a gentle gale with hazy weather.

I had forgot to mention in its proper place, that the man named Muller, one of the skinners, had been on the 30ᵗʰ of the month, attacked by the pleurisy. On the 9ᵗʰ day of the disease, he was dangerously sick but he is now in a fair way of recovering from his late illness by the great care of our Surgeons.

One of the officers had also lain ill of the consequences of a gonorrhoea which had been suppressed, he was now well recovered.

All the people at this time were in the finest health, and no man had the least symptoms of scurvy upon him, which was very surprising following so long a journey. It is true that I continued to keep a strict course of diet of which I have made mention several times in the course of this journal. That is to say, we continued to add to the soup, sauerkraut or greens in vinegar. We served coffee twice a week and the company had a plentiful supply of beer which we brewed on board ship. The ship was kept very clean, which is of the greatest importance against the fatal consequence of this disease which on some vessels has carried away more men than any engagement of the most violent kind. Every fine day was dedicated to upping all the hammocks and airing and sweeping the ship, and washing the between decks with vinegar.

The variation of the compass by observation was NE 14° 3'.

Latitude by observation N 35° 3'.
Longitude by reckoning 137° 39'.

16' more to the South than by reckoning.

We continued to see stormy petrels, crossers and quebrantahuessosses but only a small number.

Réamur's thermometer +18°, Fahrenheit's thermometer 73°.

From Saturday 17ᵗʰ to Sunday 18ᵗʰ September 1791

154

The wind continued to blow a fresh gale at NNE attended with a heavy sea and cloudy weather.

The variation of the compass by observation was 13° NE.

Latitude by observation N 32° 43'.
Longitude by reckoning 139° 27'.

15' more to the South than by reckoning.

We continued to see stormy petrels, crossers and quebrantahuessosses but only a small number.

Réamur's thermometer +17°, Fahrenheit's thermometer 72°.

From Sunday 18ᵗʰ to Monday 19ᵗʰ September 1791

123½

During the afternoon we caught a small bird of the finch species which settled upon the rigging.

Bird Island, which is placed upon Mr Roberts (Cook's atlas) in 30° latitude North and in 136° longitude West of Paris, bore at this moment SSE 5° E, 60½ leagues distant, following our observation of the longitude made the next day. This bird I thus presumed to have come hither from this island, but upon Arrowsmith's chart, which is the newest of them, this island is laid down in 27° 10' latitude and in 137° 10' longitude, under the Spanish name of Passaros Island (Sparrow). Such a great difference in the situation of this island can be accounted for in only two ways. Either the first navigator who discovered it was in ignorance of its true situation, or those who had made the charts had received information which could not be depended on.[188]

I observe by and by that in this sea the navigators of late have searched to no purpose for Los Majos, Roca Partida and Maria la Gorta[189] in the situations laid down in the Spanish charts and those of Mr Roberts.

The wind blew a hard gale at NE attended with hard squalls which obliged us to take in the studding sails until midnight, at which time it began to abate.

At 6 o'clock we thought we saw land at SW¼W but it was but imaginary and only clouds.

At 8h 34' 44" AM, by two sets of observations of five distances each of the moon and the sun, taken by Mr Chanal and myself, the longitude (mean result) was 138° 53' 30". The longitude from Berkley Sound by reckoning, reduced to this moment, was found to be 140° 41' 30". Difference to East 1° 48'.

The variation of the compass by observation was NE 11° 56' NE.

During the morning, we saw the first flying fish and whales, quebrantahuessosses, crossers and stormy petrels.

Latitude by observation N 30° 58'.
Longitude by observation 139° 3'.
Longitude by reckoning 140° 51'.

4' more to the South than by reckoning.
Réamur's thermometer +20°, Fahrenheit's thermometer 77°.

---

188 Portlock questions the position of this "small island" as well (op. cit., p. 297).
189 Both Dixon and Portlock remark on these errors (Dixon p. 86 and Portlock p. 143).

From Monday 19ᵗʰ to Tuesday 20ᵗʰ September 1791

81½

All this day we had variable winds from E to SE¼S blowing fresh to a greater or less degree, attended with dark weather, rain at intervals and a great swell from the North.

Several observations with different compasses in order to determine the variation of the magnetic needle, gave the following results.

By the Easterly amplitude 11° 53', by the passage of the sun upon the prime vertical, 10° 30' and by the azimuths, 11° 4'. Mean result 11° 9' NE.

Latitude by observation N 29° 50'.
Longitude by reckoning 139° 27'.

15' more to the South than by reckoning.
Réamur's thermometer +17°, Fahrenheit's thermometer 72°.

An account of Norfolk Sound,[190] of the inhabitants, their manners, their customs, etc[191]

The mountains which surround the bay, and which are all along the coast, are very high and covered in snow very probably the whole year round for at this time it was not melted after suffering the heat of the summer. However they appear to be covered with trees almost to the summits. The face of the country presents a very picturesque and agreeable aspect as we look upon the plains covered in snow right up to the clouds, and then cast an eye over land where the commencement of the ancient forests of pines, of fir trees and others, are to be found, and which grow upon the remains of those trees having fallen long since.

On the shore of the cove in which we had come to anchor, there was a small part which was sown with peas which appeared to have been planted two months, or two months and a half since. I was of the opinion that the weeds with which it was over-run had given the peas a slight degree of bitterness. A great quantity of the plants were still in blossom and others had grown to maturity. The raspberries, having the taste of weeds and being full of water, were large and full. I found strawberries and a species of *lillium convallium*, or lily of the valley, whose flowers were of a blue colour and which was of a larger size than our ordinary lily. Another plant, whose stem was two or three feet in height, also bears flowers which are blue. I saw also birch trees. We could hardly penetrate into the interior part of the woods on account of the old trees, which are so well twisted and covered in moss that it renders the ground very broken.

---

190 Named after the Duke of Norfolk (Dixon, op. cit., p. 184).

191 Gannier here points out that Chanal, Roblet and Marchand all write very similar accounts of Norfolk Sound (*journal*, op. cit., p. 397).

Figure 8 Sketch of Norfolk Entrance (sewn into Volume 1 of the manuscript)
Courtesy of the Bibliothèque Alcazar, Marseilles, France.

The inhabitants of this Sound are of a middle size and in general none was as tall as five feet four inches but they are well made. They are of a light red colour but appear to be blacker on account of the dirt which gathers upon their skins and of the various substances of red and black with which in general they cover themselves. Their features are not unpleasant though some appear fierce. They are not strangers to cheerfulness. They possess at intervals a degree of boisterous liveliness which is a proof of the confidence that we may place in them.

They are almost all of them marked with the small-pox[192] and when I enquired the reason of such pitted faces, they gave us to understand very plainly that it

---

192 In Portlock's Harbour, Portlock also notices smallpox scars: *I observed the oldest of the men to be very much marked with the small-pox, as was a girl who appeared to be about fourteen years old. The old man endeavoured to describe the excessive torments he endured whilst he was afflicted with the disorder that had marked his face, and gave me to understand that it happened some years ago. This convinced me that they had had the small-pox among them at some distant period. He told me that the distemper carried off great numbers of the inhabitants, and that he himself had lost ten children by it; he had ten strokes tatooed on one of his arms, which*

was on account of a disease which made their skin swell and which covered their bodies with sores filled with pus, causing itching. They observed that we must suffer from the same disease for some amongst us had the same marks upon the skin. My account of their disposition must no longer be understood as that of a description of savages. Their intelligence, assisted by the circumstances, their progress towards civilization had been exceedingly rapid. Though they be brutes and savages and nothing but wandering tribes, they have laid themselves open to the knowledge of some particular morals. The cunning with which they engage in traffic with us is proof that they are capable of making great progress.

The women, whiter or rather less black than the men, are however ugly in the extreme. Though their faces are intirely round and their nose is flattened in the middle, and though their eyes are small and they are exceedingly dirty, it is not this which incurs the greatest disgust. It is common practice for the women to make a hole about six lines below the under-lip, and to wear there a skewer of iron or of wood, which is frequently made larger in order to then introduce another piece of wood, very well wrought, about two and a half inches in length, and amongst the largest, one and a half inches in width. This piece weighs the lip down and uncovers intirely the teeth and the lower jaw giving the mouth the most disagreeable appearance we can imagine.[193] The lip continues to hang down in front once this piece of wood is removed making it impossible to perceive the opening and I cannot understand how the first navigators who came to this coast believed at first these people to have two mouths.

They are thick and short and much the same size as the men. They are maternal and regard their children with feeling. Those who were nursing their children have much milk, and those whom we saw beating the most grown up and troublesome of their children, struck them very lightly on their arms or on their hands which in general brought their cries and importunities to an end.

The boys at three years of age have already pieces of wood in the form of arrows or of spears with which they amuse themselves. Mr Dixon affirms that it is only at fourteen years of age[194] that the operation of the lip takes place. He could not have seen any girls younger than this having their lips slit. We ourselves saw some who were no more than four months for they had as yet no teeth, but a needle of iron was already worn in the under-lip. No men that I saw had such ridiculous a slit.

I understood were marks for the number of children he had lost. I did not observe any of the children under ten or twelve years of age that were marked; therefore I have great reason to suppose that the disorder raged a little more than that number of years ago; and as the Spaniards were on this part of the coast in 1775, it is very probable that from them these poor wretches caught this fatal infection. They, it should seem, are a nation designed by Providence to be a scourge to every tribe of Indians they come near, by one means or other (op. cit., p. 71).

193 See above Cook, Portlock and Dixon.
194 See Dixon, op. cit., p. 287.

They did not appear, as all the voyagers agree to say of the female savages, to be over burthened with employments of the rudest kind, and to be regarded by the men as being unlike themselves in their disposition. They take their meals with the men and their children, and the men seem to take advice of them in regard to the traffic. They do not appear to have the charge of the cooking, and I saw several times the men cutting up and cleaning the fish and putting it into the pot for as soon they purchase one they put it to use immediately in order to dress their articles of food. They then pour the mess into vessels of tin or of wood, and eat it with spoons of the beard of whales or of a sort of horn, which are very well wrought. I showed them ours while they were being made, but they made signs that they did not want them for they were too easily broke. The children and always males, engage in fishing in the river, in getting up fresh water in order to boil the fish they catch, and in bringing wood to make a fire, which they light hitherto with European tinderboxes. The employment of the women, at least of those I saw with own eyes, consists in cleaning the skins of animals which their husbands or other men have killed during the hunt. They then sew them together to make clothes. They carry and take care of their children when they have any. Some few conduct the canoes, but when no men are on board. They walk in an awkward fashion and their constrained manner of going is uncertain, which is proof that they little exercise their bodies and are sedentary. However I cannot affirm it with certainty for I did not see their habitations and I perceived only their temporary huts, which did not require any great skill to build and which afforded little shelter against the bad weather. All places suit their purpose for they generally carry all that they possess with them. They place their war spears and their fishing harpoons against a tree and cover them with green or dry branches, without any distinction, upon which they then lay large pieces of bark taken from the pine trees and the skins of sea calves. This then forms their shelter of which the highest part is intirely open but which is in general turned in the direction opposite to that of the wind. This is where they have their fire outside rather than inside the hut.

I have mentioned that the women are principally employed in the care of their children[195] and it might be believed that these unfortunate infants have at least the free use of their limbs and like their parents, they must suffer the cruelty of a sharp winter. Not at all. In a hot climate, nature has taught the inhabitants not to inclose their children in swaddling clothes for they could not then take the advantage of

---

195 *It might be imagined, that the children of these savages would enjoy the free and unrestrained use of their limbs from their earliest infancy; this, however, is not altogether the case: three pieces of bark are fastened together, so as to form a kind of chair, the infant, after being wrapped in furs, is put into this chair, and lashed so close, that it cannot alter its posture even with struggling; and the chair is so contrived, that when a mother wants to feed her child, or give it the breast, there is no occasion to release it from its shackles. Soft moss is used by the Indian nurse to keep her child clean, but little regard is paid to this article, and the poor infants are often terribly excoriated, nay, I have frequently seen boys of six or seven years old, whose posterieurs have born evident marks of this neglect in their infancy* (Dixon, op. cit., p. 239).

the coolness. Here, on the contrary, they know very well that warmth is better preserved in a confined space. In consequence, they make small cradles, which are much like one of our chairs of which the top part has been cut off very near to the seat, excepting that the back is a rounded shape and there are sides. These cradles, made of small twigs of wood which are easily bent, are covered outside with a dry leather and lined inside with otter skins. The place where the buttocks rest, to keep the child from its excrements, they place some dry moss which they put between the thighs. The child thus sits with its legs stretched out in front covered with an otter skin up to chin which is fixed by straps and lashed up so tightly so as to cause great pain, for all those I saw without their swaddling clothes, had deep furrows which the skins, the straps, the moss and sometimes the cradle itself, had impressed upon their bodies. Thus here as at home, ignorant mothers have confined innocent creatures in order to dispense with the care and constant vigilance which would be required of them if the children had the free use of their limbs. These peoples are perhaps under the necessity of making frequent journeys and of carrying their children in very light canoes, which are consequently liable to accident and to overturn, which has made them shut their eyes to such a barbarous transaction. For all that, in this I am not mistaken and am well assured, the leaness and the weakness of all the infants in swaddling clothes is due to nothing else but this restraint, for all those who are free from these shackles are plump and in good health.[196]

Almost all of the women and some men, have some few tattoos on their hands, legs and above the knees.

The modesty for which we gave credit to the women, was owing no doubt to the jealousy of the men. We saw no indecency in the few days of our stay. They were very scrupulously covered, and only those as at home sometimes suckled their child before us. After having asked by signs one of the women accompanied by her husband, if they were married and if the man was the father of the child she was nursing, she immediately took up a dagger very much in a passion. She seemed to present a danger for I was very near enough to touch her. At this same instant her husband being less agitated, or better understanding what I had desired to say, took hold of the dagger and pointing it to the child gave me to understand plainly that were he not the father, he would stab the child to death. This made us conjecture as regards to this scene which had surprised us all and which had caused fear amongst the officers for the safety of myself. Our conjecture was that the woman who had not well understood the signs that I should like to know if the savage was the father of the child, believed that I had said that the man was not the father of the child, and had subsequently become furious for her husband was a spectator. This last made us believe that these women were not as full of scruples and not as nice if they could go unpunished, for in exchange for a few trifles, several of the gentlemen made some of them who were without the men,

196 From Roblet's journal (see Gannier, *journal*, op. cit., p. 400).

and very distant from them on board a canoe, uncover their bosoms and almost all else. I observed furthermore when I was ashore, the little trouble they took to avoid me; on the contrary they desired to come close but the islanders prevented them from doing so. I have made a report of the preceding incident which is of no great interest by itself, in order to make known the jealousy of the men, of which they are justified if what I have said afterwards is heeded.

They have large heads and their cheekbones are very prominent, their shoulders wide and their bosom is high and well rounded in the girls who are less than sixteen years of age, but it hangs downwards very much and is very soft in those who have suckled their children. Their knees and their feet face inwards to such a degree that they rub together frequently, as can be perceived in their manner of walking. Their hair, which is very thick and bushy, and long very nearly like a mane, is worn tied up with leather straps in the form of a knot. The men though have theirs in great disorder and full of paint, which gives it a dismal aspect. They cover it also with the down of birds. I am satisfied that, as I have already mentioned, the piece of wood which they place in the underlip disfigures them, for the young girls who wear but very small ones are pretty enough. The young men have engaging faces, but their features, with time, become hard, coarse and even ferocious in some, on account most probably of the passion into which they fall frequently. A face which is flat and round with the eyes sunk into the head, cheeks which are large and swollen, flat noses but which are not broad, are common to almost all. They do not wear a beard before attaining a certain age. The lines of colour which they paint upon their faces are not all of the same form but they contribute to rendering them hideous. One and the other sex are covered in vermin which they eat when they come upon them.[197] We had no reason to complain of any ill treatment, though some of the gentlemen had gone alone into the woods as far as the thick of the forest would let them, and had met with some few men here and there who had appeared very suddenly, as if from the ground or from under the roots. It is true to say that all those we had met with in this manner were not armed and found themselves there with a particular design, as I shall have occasion to explain more plainly.

During our traffic with them along-side the ship, we perceived that only once did one of them attempt to keep those articles belonging to himself and the ones we had given to him in exchange, though they seem to desire greedily some of the objects we exhibited to them. The manner in which they traffic shows great judgement and cunning. They preferred most often that which was most useful

---

197 Cook and Portlock both comment on this habit of eating lice: . . . *what is still worse, their heads and their garments swarm with vermin, which, so depraved is their taste for cleanliness, we used to see them pick off with composure, and eat* (*Voyage to the Pacific Ocean*, op. cit., Volume 2, p. 305). *But with all this fancied finery, they are remarkably filthy in their persons, and not frequently shifting their garments, they are generally very lousy; and in times of scarcity those vermin probably serve them as an article of food; for I have seen them pick and eat to the number of a dozen or more; and they are not very small* (Portlock, op. cit., p. 249).

to that which was beautiful, and this last only rarely in order to please the women.[198] They do not make noise, and on the contrary they wait with the greatest patience till the bargains have been made and only then do they offer their own things. Indeed, they trust to those they believe to be more skilful in the market. The first who came off to us sang on his arrival and upon concluding a bargain to his advantage, the seller would shout out the word *Ouhoh* to which all the others would answer together.[199] But this was not in general the case. Their custom or method is to ask for the *stock* when a bargain is almost concluded. It consists in general of one or two nails, or some other articles of little value of which we make them presents. If the present is not made, they sometimes change their mind.

Though their gestures were neither as expressive nor as easily understood as when the first navigators had met with them, they had made great progress in commerce and we cannot but give them credit for their skill, for they were able to make us understood very easily each object they desired, either shirts, coats, breeches, kettles, pots, iron vessels, pans, boilers, axes, spears, etc. I succeeded over and above to make them understand some abstract moral points of view, for example that it was not just or possible to break a bargain one hour after it had been concluded unless fixed on by both parties. Mistaken in their first experiments with the tinwork, or the vessels of pewter which had been given to them, they no longer put them on the fire. They gave us to understand that some of them had become unsoldered, and others had melted.

I know nothing of their idea of religion, or if they adore a Supreme being, but there was no indication of it. I observed only that sometimes while singing, they pointed to the sky. The population is not very large and women seem to be much less in number than then the men, from which springs perhaps their extreme jealousy of them and their inclination for pederasty. Several of our people were convinced of it, in a most certain manner. What was still worse, for very little in exchange, they give themselves over to the passions the most immoderate licentiousness has been able to contrive for its shameful enjoyment. I would have drawn the curtain over such a matter if I had not intended to give the most exact account of what I had observed amongst these peoples whom we call savages.

---

198 Dixon makes a similar observation in the Sandwich Islands: *Besides nails, we found buttons very useful in our traffic with these people. To the credit of the men be it spoken, they looked on them as things of no value; but the females saw them in a very different point of view, and were exceedingly fond of wearing them round their wrists and ankles as bracelets, calling them Booboo, and sometimes Poreema. As gallantry is perhaps equally prevalent here, as in more civilized nations, the men frequently preferred buttons to nails (contrary to their better judgment) in their traffic. This is an incontestible proof, that the power of beauty is not confined within the narrow limits of our polite European circles, but has equal influence all over the world* (op. cit., p. 97).

199 Marchand here notices the same custom as Dixon: *One peculiar custom I took notice of here, which as yet we had been strangers to. The moment a Chief has concluded a bargain, he repeats the word* Coocoo *thrice, with quickness, and is immediately answered by all the people in his canoe, with the word* Wheeh, *pronounced in a tone of exclamation, but with greater or less energy, in proportion as the bargain he has made is approved of* (op. cit., p. 189).

Though we had seen no proof of it and had no indication that these people appeared to be cannibals, I could not be persuaded that they were not.[200] I desired to clear up my doubts. Several times, I asked them if they ate the flesh of the men they had killed in battle, and after assuring me that they had understood me, they would look at each other without answering neither yes nor no. And so I asked them if they would eat me if I remained amongst them. At this, they drew back as if in a kind of horror and said that they would give me food and provide me with furs to wear. I concluded hitherto that they ate their enemies, for if they did not, they would have expressed the same horror in regard to their enemies as for me. Perhaps the various European nations which have previously come to this place have made them blush at such barbarous a custom, and they dare no longer to own it. If I am right in this conjecture, there is but one short step to be taken in order to call them man eaters no more. We had found them to be a more civilized than those who had come before us had described them to be.

After the account I have given of the decency of the women, which is required of them by the men, perhaps these last should also put it a little into practice. But everywhere man has made laws such as to oppress the weaker sex. Here the inhabitants take off their clothes and go naked before the women and strangers. On shore they go about naked if the weather is not overly rude, otherwise they squat down, which position they frequently keep, and if they stand in need of making water, they do so without the least disturbance to themselves, not believing they are committing any indecency.

---

200 Cook in Nootka Sound is convinced of the North Americans' cannibalism: *But the most extraordinary of all the articles which they brought to the ships for sale, were human skulls, and hands not yet quite stripped of their flesh, which they made our people understand they had eaten; and, indeed, some of them had evident marks that they had been upon the fire. We had but too much reason to suspect, from this circumstance, that the horrid practice of feeding on their ememies is prevalent here, as we had found it to be at New Zealand, and other South Sea Islands* (op. cit., p. 271, see also Volume 2, pp. 209–214 when Cook questions the Hawaiians as to their cannibalism). Dixon suspects cannibalism but without any direct evidence: *A number of circumstances occurred, since our first trade in Cloak Bay which convinced us that the natives at this place were of a more savage disposition and had less intercourse with each other, than any Indians we had met with on the coast, and we began to suspect that they were cannibals in some degree. Captain Dixon no sooner saw the hut just mentioned than this suspicion was strengthened, as it was, he said, built exactly on the plan of the* Hippah *of the savages of New Zealand* (op. cit., p. 206). Captain King (*Voyage to the Pacific Ocean*, op. cit., Volume 3, p. 69), also questions the Hawaiians (just after the death of Captain Cook and their presentation of a part of his body) in much the same way as Marchand does the North Americans: *This afforded an opportunity of informing ourselves whether they were cannibals; and we did not neglect it. We first tried, by many indirect questions, put to each of them apart, to learn in what manner the rest of the bodies had been disposed of; and finding they were constant in one story, that after the flesh had been cut off, it was all burnt; we at last put a direct question, Whether they had not eat some of it? They immediately showed as much horror at the idea, as any European would have done; and asked, very naturally, if that was the custom amongst ourselves.* King later comes to the conclusion that the Hawiians are not in fact cannibals (Volume 3, op. cit., pp. 132–134).

Since their possession of iron, their arms have undergone a material alteration, as has perhaps the manner in which they make use of them. However, they still have the bow and arrow, much like their ancestors made them in time past. Their knives, which in former times were of bone or of wood, are now wrought of metal, which the men would better put to use in order to satisfy their needs and for their own convenience, and not to cut one another's throat. Their lances are made of two pieces and the handle is 15 to 18 feet in length, the lance itself is in nothing inferior to the spears of our ancients. But they have not yet found it convenient to change the materials of their harpoons for fishing. They are still wrought of a bearded bone fixed to a long pole. Furnished with this arm, no more than three men will most readily go to meet a whale. When they are near to the place where the enormous creature dived down the very last time, they slow their progress and play, so to say, with their paddles upon the surface of the water, and when it appears they throw their harpoons at the head. I did not myself see them striking it but bore witness only to the working of the canoe which I have indicated here. They assured us that they seldom missed putting out both the eyes and killing it. The fat of the whale gives an oil which they like very well. They keep it in bladders of a very large capacity, and they make various household utensils of the beards and of the bone of the whale. Their food in general consists of fish from the sea and from the river, fresh or smoked, of the flesh of animals they kill, and of a sort of cake which they prepare with roe and a kind of root which is floury. In the interval between their meals, or during their journeys, when they feel hungry they eat the cake of which I have spoken above, or blackberries or other berries which are to be found in great abundance in the woods. They continually chew upon a kind of grass. Some tasted of our tobacco and found it to their liking. Their journeys are at present much more encumbered than before their commerce with the Europeans, from which we may conjecture that if the trifles we give to them continue to please, and that if a person or a ship remains long enough amongst them to give them an idea of fixing themselves and of cultivating the land, they may very well give up the wandering life they lead. They are industrious, neat-handed, quick and laborious. Their canoes, which they make intirely by themselves, their wickerwork, their well-woven cloaks with strips of otter skin knotted across very agreeably, others are spun very well with the hair of animals, and their wooden dishes very handsomely done, are all proofs of these accomplishments, even though their eyes and gestures may not foretell of them. I will have occasion to dwell a little more upon this subject.

All the open places we have seen produce a gramineous plant of which the stem and ears are like European rye, but the grain was not yet ripe and I was not able to examine it. It is certain though that this plant was not carried here neither from Europe nor from any other place, for it is to be found in all the places above the high water mark and consequently it is indigenous to the country and very likely to greatly improve with culture.

Amongst the other plants which the natives eat are berries. One bush which bears a small black berry is very like the gooseberry and has a sourish taste which is quite agreeable. Another bush, which is quite different from the first, produces a small red fruit filled with a mucilaginous substance and seeds 10 to 14 in number. I know not why the English navigators determined to call it by the name of gooseberry, for the leaf, the fruit, which is always alone, and the taste resemble in nothing those of what we know to be the gooseberry. It is not to be confounded with a fruit of an oblong shape, which grows upon a plant and not upon a bush, and which is very much like a cornel in form but has no stone, and it is not fit to eat. All the other plants which we saw during a walk, are like those in Europe forasmuch as we can call to mind.

It is not to be doubted but that the climate has an influence upon the customs of the inhabitants as well as upon the productions of the earth. It should from this principle follow that the inhabitants of the Marquesas, whom we had found to be of so friendly a disposition and so free concerning their women, and to be such thieves though without any ill-usage of us, be jealous and their passions allowed to take full swing in the most dangerous and violent manner. The blood of the Americans, on the contrary, should partake of the cold climate which reigns in this country, without the heat of the passions. The things for which they stand most in need should alone excite them, but it is precisely the contrary. I will not take it upon myself to assign the causes of such effects but will be well contented by describing only what I saw.

I believe I have observed that these peoples are extremely slow in their tiresome manner of conducting their traffic, which they do with circumspection.[201] We did not observe in general that they attempted to keep our articles as well as their own, but some few did indeed do so. They know very well the advantages of trade and have as a result put a stop to their inclination to steal. It is not to be doubted that they were possessed of such an inclination, for two canoes came off very slowly to the ship at 11 o'clock in the evening, and making no noise, in order to steal from us. It is true to say that if the natives did not steal from us as they desired to do, it is I believe intirely on account of our proceeding very warily with them and never letting them come on board.[202] The traffic was carried on in the boats along-side the ship. For all that, we found them in general to be of mild disposition, honest, skilled and obliging enough. We did not entertain any great suspicion of them for two of the Officers told me that they would fain spend the winter amongst them if I would allow it, in order to persuade them to engage in hunting and to sell us the skins the next season. As hostages, two of the natives offered to accompany me to China. I thought myself obliged to refuse this scheme for reasons which are quite evident. I cannot believe that a European nation would engage in such a settlement in this place, for it would soon be ruined. In a very short time, the manners and customs, the implements and even the moral

201 Dixon notes *the slow and deliberate manner in which these people conduct their traffic* (op. cit., pp. 169–170).
202 Marchand probably decided on this as a result of reading the Dixon account (Ibid., pp. 160–161).

thought of natural man, would no longer be found. The great change which has been wrought in their ideas on account of the new things we have brought them, is hardly to be believed. Stones of axe which the first navigators spoke of, are no longer to be found amongst them. Their lances and daggers, wrought of wood and of bone in times past, are now armed with iron. Having furnished them with murderous weapons turned against their equals, they are now ready to oppose with more ease the oppression of the strongest men and the fierceness of beasts. A pure intention during an intelligent distribution of such murderous weapons, humanity would no doubt approve such philosophical views. But as we are not yet in readiness to thus travel the world only to bring the savage peoples to the state of civilization, and to teach them agriculture, while exposing ourselves to all the dangers therewith, like the heroes of ancient times, we must at least encourage them to traffic. By bringing them thus little by little to a better state and to a knowledge of new articles, putting in repute those nations who are therein employed, they will free themselves from barbarousness and draw any advantage to be had from this last. A happy circumstance for the inhabitants, and ourselves alike, if some few navigators more greedy of riches than others, do not furnish them with the most fatal of weapons. Mr Dixon, whose name they pronounced most distinctly, himself or one of his men, gave to one of them two muskets, it is true without powder. He broke them in vexation for they would not *pouh* like those of the Europeans, but only *cric* as he said so himself. Should he have waited, with some little understanding, another vessel (ignoring that he was in possession of muskets) would not have refused him had he demanded powder and shot in exchange for fine furs, and this knowledge, of which they should have the least intelligence, would have fallen into their hands.

I know that in all places there are men who have invented the means of killing one another. I know further that some affirm indeed, in paradoxical fashion, that the invention of gun powder has not rendered battles more murderous than in times past, and that instead the advantages of it are certain. With gun powder the most formidable of animals, which ordinary arms cannot destroy, may be killed, the strength of men has been increased a hundred times and the polite arts could have no existence without it, etc. Despite all these reasons which overburthen me, for I am not learned enough to answer them all, I ask only if the savage, to whom nature and instruction have given strength to fight hand to hand, and to stab the bear which inhabits the same forest as himself and with which he must sometimes contend for his sustenance, cannot make better shift without the musket, which can miscarry and leave him without the least defence and at the mercy of his enemy. Suffice it to say that others will hear these thoughts upon which I have insisted for a moment. I now return to the industry of my savages which is most stimulated in the manner of building their canoes. With the advantage of fire, they cut down the largest trees which they hollow out and shape into the most convenient form. Nonetheless they posses axes but fire has the advantage of hardening the wood and I have reason to believe that they have knowledge of this, for when they desire to drive a stake into the ground, they harden the end in the fire. They are in general 15 feet in length inside, and two feet and a half broad. They have cross pieces or floor timbers upon which they sit in order to paddle. The two extremities are identical in all points to one another and are but an inch thick and in the form of a sheerwater, 12 to 15 inches in length. Their paddles are of the usual shape and they do not yet make use of the sail to navigate, as do the Marquesans who dispose of both. In making mention of the dimensions, I speak of the common sort which carry a family in general of 7 or 8 persons including the children. But I saw a larger one within which I counted fifteen people and which could have contained more. All I can say of them is that they are very finely executed and very well wrought. On the sides of some them and on the paddles are to be seen figures rudely painted.

I know not if they have a permanent chief or what authority he has over them. Families came to strike their camp near to us but we saw neither authority nor sub-ordination within any of them, excepting the power of a chief over the members of the family. Notwithstanding, the very first day, a savage came along-side with attendants who appeared more numerous and who seemed to be in esteem with them. I did not treat him in any different manner from the others for I perceived that he wanted to prevent the canoes which had come before him from draw-ing near to us. He returned the following days with the crowd and was of very small consequence amongst them. He appeared to have put aside the part he had wished to play. We also saw marks of authority in another person but they were too ambiguous and too particular to be of any consequence.

It is more certain that they have superstitions and a kind of mountebank in whom they have some confidence. I will content myself with giving here the details of the particular garments which they wear during some few ceremonies of which I know not the signification. It did not appear that a particular age was necessary in order to cloathe themselves in these, for he who thus dressed him-self before us was no more than twenty five years of age. The first article is a sort of cap which consists of two parts which are fixed together by a band of leather which is wrapped about the head and tied behind. These two parts, about ten inches in length, cover only the temples. They are bordered with very long hair and fur. They are ornamented with various rude figures upon the surface of which they fix long plaits of hair or of the threads of a bush very much like the hemp, which hangs behind in the form of a tail. The breast is covered in a kind of armour made from cloth and the hair of animals woven and bordered with straps of skin of which the inner edge is ornamented with a prodigious number of shells or dried hoofs[203] of some animals. The middle part is painted with various figures of irregular form. They wear on each thigh a small piece of cloth which is varie-gated in colour and bordered with skins. Above the knee they fix yet more pieces of cloth nearly in all respects similar excepting that they resemble very rudely a human face whose nose is wrought of a piece of wood which was moveable and

---

203 See Cook, *A Voyage to the Pacific*, op. cit., Volume 2, p. 308.

about four inches in length, very much like a hook. These last two are like those which are worn on the breast and ornamented with shells, which make in a very imperfect manner the noise of small bells. In one of their hands they hold a hoop of wickerwork within which, from the middle to the circumference, stretch various lines ornamented with shells. In the other they hold a small stick eight inches in length at the top of which is a human figure of bark which is painted and which terminates in a point. It is filled with small stones and makes a noise much like that of a rattle which is given to children for their amusement.[204] I believe these garments serve on various occasions for they have several sorts, mostly of caps.

Desiring to procure such a dress, I proposed to give them in exchange a suit of clothes of my own and other utensils. But the owner refused to part with it at any price.

During our stay of eight days within this bay, we went ashore frequently though it rained almost continuously. We did not find the plant which Mr Dixon called the wild celery. If that which they once showed to us was the same as the one to which he gave this name, we recognized neither the leaf, nor the root nor the taste. In consequence, Mr Roblet dared not to serve it to the people, or another somewhat resembling parsley but of which the stem was much thicker. If our people had been down with the scurvy, or if they had been in the most pressing need of greens, he would have without a moment's hesitation procured some article for them at random. But all our people enjoying good health, he was more circumspect in his behaviour than he otherwise would have been.

We had proposed planting cucumbers, peas, beans, some gourds and Danish cresses, etc. But considering that the season was too far advanced for these plants to flourish, and that they would grow rotten and be intirely lost, we left nothing.

The only animals we have seen alive are dogs of one species alone and which are like our sheep dogs excepting that the hair is longer and softer. They bark and are very fearful with regard to strangers. Their paws are very large, the tail is thick and the muzzle pointed, the ears are pointed, their eyes lively and their body is thick and about 18 inches in height to the withers. They show the greatest affection for their masters, who commend them enough for their intelligence and their courage in hunting in the woods and in the water. Notwithstanding, a puppy which I had purchased and which I gave back again afterwards, upon seeing its master did not dare to jump into the sea to go to him. I also saw a small otter cub of which I tasted the flesh and found it to be very good eating.

I have little to say of the birds for the species which I saw were not very numerous. Amongst the sea birds, two seagulls and a diver are the only birds I saw within the bay, for outside of it there are albatrosses, puffins, etc. The swimmers or water birds, are a sort of goose which is black all over and which is different from ours for the head is smaller, the neck thinner and a little longer. It makes very good eating. There is a duck the size of a teal but which has wings spotted with a

---

204 Cook describes similar garments and accessories in Prince William Sound (op. cit., p. 383).

brighter white and a beak which is a little longer. We saw a heron which was black all over and so shy that we could never get within a musket shot of a single one. We saw a great number of sea swallows. The land birds are less numerous, for in the account I can give of our stay in the place, I saw but two vultures, a dozen crows, a few small Sky larks and three wrens. I had reason to think that the sharpness of the winter with the addition of very little food for the granivorous species, for impenetrable woods cover the face of the country, were the reasons for which there are so few to be found. The language of the American Indians is very harsh, all the sounds are first made in the throat with a strong nasal aspiration. Of all our consonants, only two or three prove difficult for them and two are impossible for them to pronounce, b and d, n for the first, and the last are f and v.[205]

I will here give a few words of their language which will make known the harsh nature of it. If we reflect upon the difficulty with which a European makes himself understood, and with which he apprehends what these peoples wish to say to him (though they are very intelligent), the very few words which I have obtained will not be matter of surprise to anyone. It is a wonder that I was able to question them at all, and then to understand if they had answered me. I give here only those of whose pronunciation and meaning I am certain. I have attempted to spell them after the French pronunciation. But I am obliged to indicate where Ci must be pronounced like the Italians for I cannot render this sound in our language.[206]

Norfolk American	English
clerrk	One
terrg	Two
nelšk	Three
tācoŭnn	Four
Kēciň (pronouncing the ci like the Italians)	Five
clēloňchoŭ	Six
tărrāloŭchoŭ	Seven
nētscāloŭchoŭ	Eight
coŭchāckoŭ	Nine
Tcinnkat (pronouncing the ci like the Italians)	Ten
clerrkătt	Twenty
terrgkăt	Forty

After having counted to ten, they begin again with one, and when they have counted their fingers and their toes, they remember scores, but I believe them to count to forty only for they never have need for more.

205 Cook (quoting from Anderson) comments on the phonetic make-up of the Indian languages (see for example *Voyage to the Pacific Ocean*, op. cit., Volume 2, p. 334).

206 Dixon (op. cit., p. 241) compares the languages from different areas on the coast, Portlock (op. cit., p. 293), Cook (op. cit., p. 336 and p. 375) all give vocabulary lists Gannier (*journal*, op. cit., p. 410) also points out that Marchand seems here to collate Chanal and Roblet's lists.

*Names for parts of the human body
and others*

Norfolk American	English
kăhoŭhăc	The eyes
kătsī	The eyebrows
kākăc	The brow
kāchīloŭ	The nose
kāoŭrg	The teeth
kăkăkăt chăăgŭi	The moustache
kāhāi kŭtechoŭcoŭ	The throat
kărĭqŭe	The arm
kălīssēijou	The forearm
klăthergue	The hand and the fingers
kăgoŭgā	The stomach
kājoŭ	The belly
kăgătz	The thighs
kătsēijou	The legs
kăgoŭsătzgli	The feet
kătglīgz	The privy parts of the male
kăgrĭehăÿ	The hind parts
Koŭgzā	The hairs
Koŭgz	The privy parts of the female
kēintăkă	The piece of wood which the women insert into the under-lip
kătvaĭgz	The lips
kăkoŭqŭe	The ears
kāchă kăou	The hair
kătchītā	The breasts
kăkoŭoŭ	The skins with which they cover themselves
krăgoŭn	A tree which has been cut or wood
kăsānī	The male children
jăquĕsānī	The females
tchăsse	The fish
kăseīstănĕ	An ant
kēitlĕ	A dog
kărākoŭ	The nails
kătchŭtinā	The top of the hand
kătchĭkoŭttĭa	The wrist
kăoŭcoŭ	The shoulder
kăstoŭtchī	The septum of the nose
kati . . .	The chin
kaouttaki	The eyelids
katkaska	The mouth
ketsloug	The tongue
katslata	The neck
katoucotchi	The buttocks
kakissakanoukou	The knees
kakoustou	The soles of the feet
katchoutouk	The shins
kahiny	The arm-pits

katslougou	The ribs
yacou	A canoe
téhée	Stones
ass	Standing trees or a forest

The remainder of the vocabulary

Norfolk American	English
tchkaa	A pole or a fishing line
kahouk	A chest after their fashion
youkatskou	A particular flower or in general flower
takha	Mosquitoes or midges
krota	A chisel foxed to a handle of wood in the shape of an axe
koutesk	A waistcoat
kaïkouts	Buttons of a suit of clothes
thausou	A hat
hill	Water
ketchle	Tatou or marks on the skin
klettaqui	A ring
kané	Fire
heïte	Their huts or thatched houses
stock	Present they request after concluding a bargain
ouoh	Word they shout when they have concluded a good bargain

The syllables of the words of which I have not indicated the quantity, are those of which I am uncertain or which are sometimes pronounced long by various individuals, and short by others. They pronounce the g at the end of words by a rolling which cannot be expressed in our language. It is clearly to be perceived by the very few words which I have gathered together, and by the various significations of each, that their language is very rich. This abundance is most worthy of remark in regards to the human body, of which all the outward parts, however small they may be, have a particular name. I know not if the names of new articles which they Europeans have given to them are distinguished by names taken from some other language or if they have made over to them the names of objects which previously were employed for the same purpose.

I had forgot to mention their music which is of a very melodious kind.[207] They sing in parts and like ourselves, they make use of semi-tones and B-flats. It was most pleasing, and when we invited them to sing to us, which we did frequently, they never refused to do so. Our instruments such as the violin, the clarinet, the flageolet, etc. did not occasion any degree of emotion amongst them. They make more

207 Cook, Portlock and Dixon all describe the Indian music and instruments. As in Dixon (op. cit., pp. 242–243), Marchand includes a score in his journal, written by Louis Marchand (his brother).

Figure 9 Score sewn into Volume 1 of the manuscript
Courtesy of the Bibliothèque Alcazar, Marseilles, France.

account of our singing, most particularly that in a slower time. They have a sort of instrument which is made of a long bone in the shape of a flute and which has only three holes. They make sharp sounds with it much like those of our whistles but they never accompany their songs with it. When they sing, the beat time on the sides of their canoes,[208] they have such a good ear that we never hear more than one stroke.

I have said nothing I believe of their common dress. The men have a coat or a sort of jacket made of furs which are like those of our waggoners in France. In addition to the jacket and a sort of apron or a skirt of skin tanned, the women wear over these a cloak of fur. They wear on their heads a small hat made of the bark of trees, which is very well woven. But most frequently, they are bare-headed. The hair of the furs they make use of rarely form the inside part.

In order to moor in Norfolk Sound, after meeting with Cape Edgecombe, which is very easy to distinguish for it is formed of low land terminating in a round mountain of the same name and the highest on this shore, it is necessary to direct the route half a league to the South of it. Upon reaching this point or just before it, a small island is to be seen lying East of this point which must be left to the larboard side and to which it is possible to come quite close for there is no danger. When this island bears North, one must direct the course ENE in direction of a chain of small islands which are to be seen directly a-head. When half a mile distant, it is necessary to steer North ½ W in order to pass them on the starboard side and avoid, by this means, the ledge of rocks which extends about SE¼E. The mooring place is almost directly a-head, opposite the place where the river is to be found. It is near the best place or, rather the least unsafe, for the bottom is neither good nor even, for we found our cables rubbed there. My advice to those who wish to anchor in this entrance would be to send a boat to the edge of the ledge of rocks and as soon as the ship has doubled it, the boat should thence proceed

208 See Cook, *A Voyage to the Pacific Ocean*, op. cit., Volume 2, p. 283

to examine the bay which is very easily to be found in relation to the river. When the ship reaches the bay and the river lies to the West, she may come to anchor in 12 fathom water. By this means, much trouble will be avoided. If there is a calm upon entering, as we had, it would be convenient to have the boats hauled out in order to tow the ship on account of the currents which might carry her too near the small islands or the ledge of rocks. These small islands are safe on their West side. The chart of the entrance here annexed will illustrate the course, better than any discourse can ever do, which must be taken in order to enter.[209] I must say beforehand to the reader that the shaded parts of the chart are most accurate, as is the position of the small islands situated ENE of the ledge. The remainder is but a sketch which I drew however from a very short distance. It is to be observed that there is no good anchoring ground to be had until one has sailed beyond the ledge and raised the West shore at a distance of one mile, or of one and half miles. The bottom is there uneven with large gravel and sand. Otherwise, it is everywhere a rocky bottom. The dangers which lie on the West shore, further along or North of the ledge, are close to the land and visible enough. The depth of the water gradually decreasing indicates where they are to be found but they are not dangerous. Captain Dixon's[210] sketch of this entrance I found to be wanting in several points.

All the points of the compass which I have indicated are corrected by the variation which was found to be 28° 46'.

Bureau des classes of the Navy
According to the Law of 13ᵗʰ August 1791
Given under our hand on the Twenty-Eighth of August 1792 at Toulon,
Year 4 of Liberty.
Dauniez[211]

---

209 Marchand here is almost imitating Cook, textually and materially speaking: *But the chart or sketch of the Sound* (Nootka), *here annexed, though it has no pretensions to accuracy, will with all its imperfections, convey a better idea of these islands, and of the figure, and the extent of the Sound, than any written description* (*Voyage to the Pacific Ocean*, op. cit., Volume 2, p. 289).

210 Dixon, op. cit., p. 184

211 Dauniez's signature.

VOYAGE ROUND THE WORLD PERFORMED UNDER THE DIRECTION OF CAPTAIN ETIENNE MARCHAND IN THE *SOLIDE* OF MARSEILLES

Second volume

From Tuesday 20ᵗʰ to Wednesday 21ˢᵗ September 1791

66

During the afternoon, we saw the first tropic birds with white shafts, quebran-tahuessoses, cut-waters, stormy petrels and flying fish with red wings and with white wings.

At 9 o'clock in the morning, having seen a turtle, we hoisted out the yawl in order to take it but it dived down upon our approach.

The variation of the compass by observation of the azimuths was 10° 39' NE.

During this day we had light winds which varied from SE to S¼SW with rain at intervals.

At 8 o'clock AM, by the mean result of two sets of distances of the moon and the sun, our longitude was 141° 38'. The longitude by observations made on the 19ᵗʰ, reduced to this moment, was 141° 11', that is 27' more to the East.

Latitude by observation N 29° 46'.
Longitude by observation W 141° 46'.
Longitude by reckoning from Berkley entrance 143° 7'.

21' difference more to the North than by reckoning.
Réamur's thermometer + 21°, Fahrenheit's thermometer 79°.

From Wednesday 21ˢᵗ to Thursday 22ⁿᵈ September 1791

During this day, we had light winds which varied from SSW to SE, attended with cloudy weather and a long swell from NNW.

We saw quebrantahuessoses, tropic birds, crossers, stormy petrels, whales, por-poises and bonitos.

The variation of the magnetic needle determined from the azimuths was NE 10° 35'.

Latitude by observation N 29° 32'.
Longitude by observation 142° 42'.
Longitude by reckoning 144° 9'.

Réamur's thermometer +21½°, Fahrenheit's thermometer 80°.

From Thursday 22ⁿᵈ to Friday 23ʳᵈ September 1791

88

During this day, we had winds from the SE quarter, attended with dark cloudy weather.

We saw quebrantahuesosses, tropic birds, tunny fish and porpoises.

The variation of the compass by observation of the azimuths was 10° 25' NE.

At 9h 37' 4" in the morning, by the observation of two sets of five distances each of the moon and the sun, our longitude was 143° 38'. The longitude computed from the last two observations had been 143° 45'.

Latitude by observation N 28° 29'.
Longitude by observation 143° 47'.
Longitude by reckoning 145° 21'.

3' more to the South than by reckoning.
Réamur's thermometer +21½°, Fahrenheit's thermometer 80°.

From Friday 23rd to Saturday 24th September 1791

80

Lights winds from SSE to East, with cloudy weather and gusts of wind all round the horizon.

We took note of three species of flying fish, the first with white wings, the second with red wings and the third with four red wings. As I have before mentioned in another place, I believe the last two kinds to be natives of the Pacific Ocean for I have never seen them in America, in the Caribbean Sea or in India. By the mean result of several sets of azimuths, and by the amplitude, the variation of the magnetic needle was 10° 15' Northeasterly.

Latitude by observation N 27° 36'.
Longitude by observation 142° 50'.
Longitude by reckoning 146° 24'.

Réamur's thermometer +20°, Fahrenheit's thermometer 77°.
I gave orders to direct our course S¼SW if the wind permitted us to do so, considering that if we reached 24 or 25° latitude rapidly, we would meet with the steady trade winds as quick as possible.

From Saturday 24th to Sunday 25th September 1791

66

We had winds which blew more or less light varying from ENE to SE and attended with cloudy weather clear at intervals. The variation of the magnetic needle by observation was NE 9° 51'.

Latitude by observation N 26° 30'.
Longitude by observation 145° 22'.
Longitude by reckoning 146° 56'.

5' more to the South than by reckoning.
Réamur's thermometer +21°, Fahrenheit's thermometer 79°.

From Sunday 25th to Monday 26th September 1791

35½

The whole of this day, we had a very light wind from the SE quarter.

We saw tropic birds, sheerwaters and some few sea larks, as well as tunny fish and dolphins. The cunning of our fishermen could not overcome them and we did not take a single one.

The variation of the compass by observation, by several methods and with different azimuth compasses, was 9° 42' NE.

The weather being fine, we got up the spare sails to air them. They were found to be full of holes made by the rats, the sailmakers set immediately to work to repair them. At the same moment, we paid the deadwork with tar.

Latitude by observation N 26° 7'.
Longitude by observation 145° 45' 30".
Longitude by reckoning 147° 19' 30".

5' more to the North than by reckoning.
Réamur's thermometer +23°, Fahrenheit's thermometer 83°.

From Monday 26th to Tuesday 27th September 1791

20

We had only light airs and a calm the whole of this day. During the calms, we felt a suffocating heat.

The variation of the compass by observation was 9° 36' NE.

We saw considerable flocks of sea larks and some few tropic birds. The tunny fish and the dolphins continued to follow the ship.

Latitude by observation N 25° 49'.
Longitude by observation 145° 55' 30".
Longitude by reckoning 147° 29' 30".

Réamur's thermometer +23°, Fahrenheit's thermometer 83°.

From Tuesday 27th to Wednesday 28th September 1791

102½

A 1 o'clock PM, with a light wind springing up at ENE, we got in with the trade winds.

The variation of the compass determined from the amplitudes and the azimuths, was 9° 33'.

We continued to see flocks of sea larks, tropic birds, tunny fish and dolphins.

The breeze varied from ENE to ESE and blew a gentle gale with cloudy weather clear at intervals.

Latitude by observation N 24° 16'.
Longitude by observation 146° 40'.
Longitude by reckoning 148° 14'.

4' more to the South than by reckoning.
Réamur's thermometer +21½°, Fahrenheit's thermometer 80°.

From Wednesday 28ᵗʰ to Thursday 29ᵗʰ September 1791

131¼

At 2 o'clock PM, we steered SW¼S with the help of breeze at East, blowing a gentle gale.

The variation of the needle by observation was 9° 7' NE.

Some of the seamen perceiving that Jacques Teissier, the baker, had been sickly for a few days and lamenting not, informed Mr Roblet, who after having looked at him, found him to be attacked with the scurvy of the second stage. After reprimanding him in very strong terms for his carelessness, he ordered the necessary medicine.

During the night we crossed the Tropic of Cancer for the third time in 147° 20' longitude.

Latitude by observation North 22° 37'.
Longitude by observation 148° 15'.
Longitude by reckoning 149° 49'.

Réamur's thermometer +23°, Fahrenheit's thermometer 83°.

From Thursday 29ᵗʰ to Friday 30ᵗʰ 1791

128

Breeze at East blowing a gentle gale, fine weather.

By the mean result of several observations, the variation of the magnetic needle was found to be NE 8° 34'.

During the morning, we took a tunny fish weighing sixty pounds, half of which I served to the people.

We continued to see sea larks, tropic birds, stormy petrels and crossers.

Latitude by observation North 21° 2'.
Longitude by observation 149° 47'.
Longitude by reckoning 151° 21'.

Réamur's thermometer +22½°, Fahrenheit's thermometer 82°.

From Friday 30th September to Saturday 1st October 1791

123½

The breeze at NE blowing a gentle gale, clear weather and a smooth sea.

By four sets of observations of five distances each of the moon and the sun made by Mr Chanal and myself, reduced to 4h 1' 10" o'clock PM, we obtained the following results:

The 1st by Mr Chanal gave	149° 34' 30".
The 2nd *ditto*	149° 15' 15".
The 3rd by me	149° 48' 35".
And the 4th by *ditto*	149° 34' 15".
The mean result of them gave	149° 33' 9".

The longitude, determined from our last observations, reduced to this moment, was 150° 5', that is 31' 51" more to the West.

The variation of the compass by observation of several sets of of azimuths was found to be 8° 14' NE.

At 8 o'clock PM, we directed our course to the SW.

We continued to see sheerwaters, tropic birds, flying fish and tunny fish.

Latitude by observation North 19° 46'.
Longitude by observation 150° 49'.
Longitude by reckoning 152° 55'.

5' more to the South than by reckoning.
Réamur's thermometer +24°, Fahrenheit's thermometer 85°.

From Saturday 1st to Sunday 2nd October 1791

106¼

At noon, we steered WSW.

During this day we had squalls which made the breeze vary.

By four sets of observations of five distances each of the moon and the sun made by Mr Chanal and myself, reduced to 3h 28' 32" PM, we obtained the following results:

The 1st by Chanal gave	151° 9' 45".
The 2nd by *ditto*	151° 15' 30".
The 3rd by me	151° 16' 30".
And the 4th by *ditto*	151° 22' 15".
Mean result	151° 16'.

The longitude computed from the observations made the day before, and allowing for the distance sailed to the Westward, was found at this moment to be 15° 6'.

Latitude by observation North 19° 15'.
Longitude by observation 152° 49'.
Longitude by reckoning 154° 55'.

Réamur's thermometer +24°, Fahrenheit's thermometer 85°.

From Sunday 2ⁿᵈ to Monday 3ʳᵈ October 1791

122

At noon, we directed our course W¼SW and W.

During this day, the breeze was variable from NE¼E to South attended succes-sively with clear weather and rain.

The variation of the compass determined from the azimuths and the amplitudes was 8° 17' NE.

We continued to see tropic birds, sheerwaters and stormy petrels.

During the morning, we took a bonito, there was a great quantity of them fol-lowing the ship.

Latitude by observation North 19° 14'.
Longitude by observation 154° 59'.
Longitude by reckoning 156° 55'.

31' more to the South than by reckoning.
Réamur's thermometer +24°, Fahrenheit's thermometer 85°.

From Monday 3ʳᵈ to Tuesday 4ᵗʰ October 1791

91½

We continued to steer W¼SW, all sails set, with the breeze blowing a light gale at East and cloudy weather, clear at intervals.

At 2h 15' 33', by the observation of two sets of distances of the moon and the sun, made by Mr Chanal and myself, the longitude was found to be 155° 16' 30", mean result. The longitude carried on since the last four observations was found to at this moment 155° 9' 3".

In the afternoon, we took three bonitos.

At 8 o'clock in the evening, we were but 35 or 36 leagues distant from the point of the island of Ouhahi. We took in the studding sails which were set again at 5 o'clock in the morning.

By several sets of azimuths and by the Easterly amplitude, the variation of the magnetic needle was found to be 7° 55' Northeasterly.

At 10 o'clock in the morning, the island of Ouhahi presented itself to our view, extending from W¼SW to WNW½N. I estimated it to be at a distance of about 10 leagues. We saw only low land or of a moderate height, the summits of the mountains being hidden by clouds. At noon, the Eastermost point of the land bore W 30° North, distant 9 leagues, and the Southermost land in view bore W ½ South. Our latitude by observation at the same moment, was found to be 19° 12' North; our longitude computed from the observations made the day before was 156° 43'. The longitude carried on from Berkley Sound was found to be 158° 47' by account.

We had 4' difference to the North.

We observed that since our departure from Berkley Sound, we had been carried much to the Southward of the reckoning, and to the Eastward, and if this difference was on account of a current, of which I make no doubt, the ship was carried more or less SE.

Réamur's thermometer +24°, Fahrenheit's thermometer 85°.

From Tuesday 4ᵗʰ to Wednesday 5ᵗʰ October 1791

92¾

During the afternoon, we steered towards the South point of the Island. At 4h 35', the Eastermost point which is low, and which appeared not unlike islands, bore North of the globe, which put us in longitude 157° 11' following the chart of the Sandwich Islands which is to be found in Mr Cook's atlas, whereas the observations made yesterday gave 157° 0' 30", that is 10' 30" more to the East. The longitude carried on from Berkley Sound, was found to be 159° 5', or 1° 54' to the Westward.

At 2 o'clock PM, we passed by a great piece of wood which appeared to have belonged to the mast of a large vessel for I believed I saw the place where it had broken.

At 6 o'clock, the East point of the island of Ouhahi bore N 3° E, distant 8 leagues. We spent the night beating to windward under our top-sails. At ½ past 5 o'clock AM, I gave orders to bear away W¼SW with an intention to double the South point of the Island. At 6 o'clock, the East point bore N¼NE, and the South point W ½ South. The East point was at a distance of 9 leagues by estimation. I perceived that a current had carried us 2 leagues to the East during the night. At ½ past 6 o'clock, we caught sight of Mouna Roa, a high mountain of Ouhahi, which bore NW and of which I shall have occasion speak, and of *Kaah* which is to be seen on this same island. *Mouna* signifies mountain in the language of this country.

At 11 o'clock, having doubled the South point of Ouhahi, we steered WNW, coasting along the shore, distant no more than two leagues. At noon the East point bore ENE 8° E, and the Westermost point of the land in view bore NW. We were about 1½ leagues distant from the shore.

Our latitude by observation was 18° 54', and our longitude determined from the bearings above-mentioned, was 158° 13'. The current had carried the ship 3° to the South in 20 hours.

The variation of the compass, determined from a great quantity of observations of azimuths, made with different compasses, was 8° 4' NE. During this day, we had a breeze which blew a gentle gale from E to NE.

Réamur's thermometer +24½°, Fahrenheit's thermometer 86°.

From Wednesday 5th to Thursday 6th October 1791

It was not my intention to come to anchor at the Sandwich Islands but only to get a supply of provisions while standing along the shore, as near as was consistent with prudence. At half past noon, having caught sight of a canoe, we shortened sail in order to wait for it. There were four men on board and it came along-side the ship without the least hesitation. But they were only fishermen, from whom we purchased some fish. I attempted to make them understand that we desired to procure some provisions such as hogs, vegetables, etc. and that we wished them to acquaint their countrymen of our arrival in order that they might come along-side the ship to bring some off to us, which they promised to do. I made them a present of a few nails in order to effect my purpose. They fulfilled their promise for immediately upon arriving ashore, we saw several canoes come off, we brought to in order to wait for them and to trade with them more easily. During the afternoon, eight of them came along-side with thirty persons on board including the women. I permitted some of them to come on board. We got three small hogs, a few sweet potatoes, very few yams and bananas, but the natives promised to return the next day with many provisions.

Having seen a very pretty canoe with one man on board, I took a fancy to purchasing it. No sooner had I informed the owner than he immediately began to perform all manner of exercises with great agility which was amazing to see, and most likely to show to me how well it was built. When the price was settled after some difficulty on his part, we hoisted it up.

At nightfall, the canoes left us.

At 6 o'clock, the Westermost point of the island of Ouhahi bore North and the Southermost point E ½ S. We were about 5 miles distant from the shore. We perceived at NNW½N, the island of Moouhi, though it was 35 or 27 leagues distant.

Yet again, we spent the night making boards. The fear of falling to leeward determined me to carry the four main courses, but notwithstanding this precaution, I perceived that we had drove to the West though we had had a fresh breeze during the night. We had much difficulty in regaining the land on account of the baffling winds and calms.

At 6 o'clock in the morning, the West point of Ouhahi bore W½W, the South point NE¼E, distant 5 leagues, and Mouna Roa bore NNE.

At 11 o'clock in the morning, being two leagues distant from the shore, several canoes came along-side the ship. But I saw with concern that they had come out of mere curiosity for we procured but a few potatoes and some bananas.

The variation of the compass determined from 15 sets of azimuths was 8° 5' NE. At noon, the South point of the island bore E¼SE½S. We were distant about 1½ leagues from the shore. The West point bore N, and Mouna Roa NE½E.

Latitude by observation N 18° 58'.
Longitude computed from the bearings 158° 23'.

Réamur's thermometer +24°, Fahrenheit's thermometer 85°.

From Thursday 6th to Friday 7th October 1791

During the afternoon, we had about fifty canoes along-side ship but they did not all bring provisions, for we purchased but 19 hogs and some vegetables. A great number of them came to offer us women, but I did not wish them to come on board for fear of the misfortune which might follow should the seamen keep company with these dangerous creatures. There were about 210 people on board the canoes.

We traded very peaceably with the natives and had no reason to complain of them. Several of them said they had come from Keraguegoa Bay and made signs to us to proceed to that place and that we should find many provisions there. I informed them that it was not my intention to come to anchor and that I desired to procure provisions whilst under sail. They then told me that I should keep in close with the land the next day and that I would not be short of provisions.

I spoke of Orono (which was the name they had given to Captain Cook whose misfortune it was to have been killed in Keraguegoa Bay after an unhappy dispute with the natives) to some of the natives. They told me that they had killed him and that one part of his body had been returned to the ship and that they had eaten the other. Prompted by curiosity, I then asked them if they would eat me in a similar case to which they all answered in the affirmative without the least hesitation, which astonished me. The natives of Norfolk answered neither yes nor no to this question. My report here may destroy the opinion of *Mr King* who believes that these people are not[212] to be supposed cannibals, though Mr Cook did not appear to have any doubt but that they were.[213]

At 6 o'clock in the evening, the canoes left us, as was the custom.

At this moment, the West point of the island bore N½E, the South point E¼SE, distant 2 leagues from the shore.

We spent the night beating to windward, close in shore. We found a current setting to the SW.

At 6 o'clock in the morning, the South point of the island bore E ½ South, the West point N½W. We were about 2½ leagues distant from the shore.

At 10 o'clock, finding ourselves but a league from the shore, the canoes began to come along-side. At noon, we took the following bearings: the South point bore

212 See *Voyage to the Pacific Ocean*, op. cit., Volume 3, p. 132.
213 See *Voyage to the Pacific Ocean*, op. cit., Volume 2, pp. 209–214.

ESE½S, the North point bore N½W, and Mouna Roa NE½E, distant 3 miles from the shore.

Our latitude by observation was at that time 19° 6' N, our longitude deduced from the bearings, was 158° 26'. The variation of the compass by the observation of the azimuths and the amplitudes was 8° 11' NE, mean result.

During this day, the winds varied much with intervals of calm and rain.

Réamur's thermometer +25°, Fahrenheit's thermometer 87.

From Friday 7th to Saturday 8th October 1791

We lay to all afternoon, about three miles from the shore. We continued to have about a dozen canoes along-side ship, all with something to sell.

At ½ past 5 o'clock in the evening, they withdrew, as was the custom. The refreshments we had got, now consisting in number of 41 hogs of 15 to 100 pounds each, 3 fowls and a great quantity of vegetables, I resolved to continue our route.

We gave in exchange nails, Dutch knives, clasp-knives and other articles of hard-wares. For one pig, we gave three or four nails. The natives preferred in general nails and knives. For one pig, according its size, we gave two or three nails. They demanded almost as many for a hen, which very near convinced us that there were very few of them or that they made much of them. At 6 o'clock, the South point of the island of Ouhahi bore East 12° South, the West point bore N½W, distant 4 miles from the land. From this point, we took our departure in latitude 19° 4' North and 158° 29' longitude. The Mouna Roa peaks bore NE 8° E.

My intention being to go to China by the shortest of routes in the 20th and 21st parallels of latitude, we went a little out of our way and then directed our route WNW½W.

During this day, the winds varied much and we had some squalls. At day-break, we caught sight of Mouna Roa at ENE, distant about 17 leagues, and Mouna Kaah at NE. The island of Moohui was in sight at NNE.

The variation of the compass by observation was 8° 29' NE.

Latitude by observation N 19° 19'.
Longitude by reckoning 159° 42'.

9' more to the South than by reckoning.

Fahrenheit's thermometer 84°, Réamur's thermometer +23½°.

Before taking our departure from the Sandwich Islands, the reader may find it convenient to find here the observations I was able to make respecting the country as well as its inhabitants during the short time we kept abreast of Ouhahi.

The Sandwich Islands were discovered as we know by Captain Cook* during his third voyage to the Pacific Ocean.

They are 11 in number, that is to say: Ouhahi, Moouhi, Morokine, Tahouroua, Ranai, Morotay, Ouhahou, Atoui, Onihiou, Ohiroua and Tahoura.[214] Captain Collnet and Captain Duncan discovered a twelfth island which they named Mountain Island, the latitude of which is 23° 10' N and the longitude 163° 50' W. It is most probably the island which the natives spoke of several times to Mr King, and which they named *Modoupapapa*, excepting that they said that it was to be found WSW of Tahoura, whereas it lies – of this very same island. The eleven of which I have spoken stretch from latitude 18° 54' to 22° 15' and from longitude 157° 11' to 162° 43' West. These islands are very fertile and very plentiful in all kinds of provisions.

The island of Ouhahi and Moouhi, the only ones I saw, are very high and may be seen from 40 to 50 leagues distant,[215] more particularly the first which has two mountains named by the natives *Mouna Kaah* or Kaah Mountain and *Mouna Roa*. The first is situated in the NE quarter of the island, and the second, in the South. Mr King, the continuator of the journal of Mr Cook, supposes these two mountains to be as high as the Peak of Teneriffe.[216] One of the proofs, the sole proof of this (though he did not measure the height of it by the barometer or geometrically), is the line of snow which is says he, permanent. I do not seek to speak against Mr King in regard to the height of these mountains, but at the moment we saw them, no signs of snow were to be seen on the highest of the summits, thus it is not constant. We perceive then what becomes of his computation.

Mount Kaah rises in three peaks and is broken by deep ravines. The other is even and terminates in a gentle slope towards the shore as well as inland and which appeared neither wooded nor cultivated in the South quarter, for the verdure I saw there was nothing more than under-wood.

---

214 *They are situated from 18 deg. 54 mins. to 22 deg. 15 min. North latitude; and from 154 deg. 56 mins. to 160 deg. 24 min. West longitude, and are eleven in number; viz. Owhyhee, Mowee, Ranai, Morokinne, Tahoaroa, Moretoi, Whahoo, Atoui, Oneehoura, Nehow, or Oneehow, and Tahouroa* (Dixon, op. cit., p. 262).

215 In accordance with King's remarks: *The districts of Amakooa and Aheedoa are seperated by a mountain called Mouna Kaah (or the mountain Kaah), which rises in three peaks, perpetually covered with snow, and may be clearly seen at 40 leagues distance* (*Voyage to the Pacific Ocean*, op. cit., Volume 3, p. 103).

216 *On doubling the East point of the island, we came in sight of another snowy mountain, called Mouna Roa (or extensive mountain), which continued to be a very conspicuous object all the while we were sailing along the South East side. It is flat at the top, making what is called by mariners table-land. The summit was constantly buried in snow, and we saw once its sides also slightly covered for a considerable way down; but the greatest part of this disappeared again in a few days.*

According to the tropical line of snow, as determined by Mr Condamine, from the observations taken on the Cordilleras, this mountain must be at least 16,020 feet, which exceeds the height of Pico de Teyde, or Peak of Teneriffe, according to Dr. Heberdeen's computation, or 3680, according to that of the Chevalier de Borda (*Ibid.*). Marchand follows Dixon (op. cit., p. 263) in commenting on the height of Mouna Roa.

It appears however that following Mr Robert de Vaugondy's chart published in 1766 and which is to be found at the end of the second volume of Histoire des navigations aux Terres Australes[217] Mendana saw them in 1568. For there is a large extent of land laid down in latitude 22° North and longitude 154° 30', West of Paris, and lying like these islands, SE and NW. About 2° 30' to the Southward, on the same chart, an island named San Francisco is to be found, which discovered by I know not which navigator, is most likely to be one of the group. We know but little of the means by which during this earlier period the navigators succeeded in determining the true position of the lands they discovered, and thus we cannot make objections to the difference in the longitude. Besides, from California and 700 leagues West of these islands, no other land has been found in this latitude, which destroys beyond doubt all the reasons which can be given in order to prove that Mendana was not the first to have seen them. It is much the same for so many of the islands which the moderns believe they have discovered, but which most probably had previously been examined by those of former times.

I certainly do not speak of this in order to remove the honour of this discovery which belongs to Mr Cook, for his abilities were numerous enough to render him forever famous without the honour procured by chance alone.

The whole presents a prospect which confirms to the very utmost the opinion of Mr Cook, who believed that a volcano, now extinct for there was neither smoke nor fire, had formed the whole by its eruptions. The ground, dry and yellowish, broken by ravines which the melting snow and the water of storms had formed, terminated at the sea by a steep cliff. At this point, a reef is to be found stretching out to sea for about a third of mile. The West shore presents a more pleasing prospect and more variegated.

Some of the inhabitants who came off to the ship to sell us refreshments appeared to be darker than the those of the Marquesas. Like these, they are of an intermixed race for I saw some with curly and frizzling hair, and others with it straight. I believe these individuals intermix without concern, for we perceived easily a face with a flattened nose and thickish lips and with long hair, or a head of curly hear with a straight nose. In general, their looks are neither pleasant nor intelligent, and I did not see the least degree of ferocity in their countenance. I met with only a few who were suspicious during the traffic, most likely because they had been cheated in exchanges. But most of them gave us their articles even before the market had been concluded. They make much noise and made no attempt to steal anything from us. They are of an ordinary size and quite well-formed.

They women they brought off to us do not have the least claim to the praise of their beauty. In general, they are tall and quite well made, but their features are forbidding and hard. The women are very much like the men in their looks, which they distort even further by, like the men, pulling out their fore-teeth on

217 See Gannier, p. 429.

certain occasions as upon the death of their relations.[218] I must here observe that we saw individuals of the lowest class. I know not if they were accustomed to all the results of their excessive licentiousness before the infection brought by the English[219], but at present they are better at it than any of our most impudent Messallinas. They are of a gentle disposition, but much less lively than the Marquesan ladies. Like these, their fore-arms are tattooed very slightly, as are the lower parts of their legs, whereas those of the men do not resemble in anything those of the inhabitants of the Marquesas whose tattoos are variegated in a very agreeable manner. These consist of lines in great confusion and very close together, which make it impossible to perceive anything but a block of colour a little in opposition to the colour of the skin.

The clothes of the men and the women, or of those whom we met, consist of a belt of cloth of the mulberry plant which they name *Maro* and which scarce hides their privy parts. They wear around their necks a small ornament of ivory in the shape thereabouts of one of our hooks and near two inches in length and half an inch in breadth. It hangs about their necks by a plait of hair prettily wrought. In addition to this ornament, they wear also around the neck the head, a kind of necklace which is three quarters of an inch thick and which consists of small red, yellow and black feathers[220] so closely woven together and so very finely worked, that it seemed like velvet. The ground is red with alternate small circles of yellow and black.

They also make use of fans and fly flaps.[221] The first is in general made of the fibres of cocoa-nuts, and the second of feathers of an indifferent sort. The finest of them are made with the tail-feathers of the tropic bird. Their industry and taste most excel in the manufacture of the paper mulberry tree cloth which they paint with all sorts of patterns which are all very fine.[222]

---

218 King here argues the opposite: *To this class of their customs, may also be referred that of knocking out their foreteeth. Scarce any of the lower people, and very few of the chiefs, were seen, who had not lost one or more of them; and we always understood, that this voluntary punishment, like the cutting off of the joints of the finger at the Friendly Idlands, was not inflicted on themselves from the violence of grief; on the death of their friends, but was designed as a propitiatory sacrifice to the* Eatooa, *to avert any danger or mischief to which they might be exposed* (Voyage to the Pacific Ocean, op. cit., Volume 3, p. 162).

219 Marchand here takes up Cook's acknowledgement of British responsibility for the introduction of sexually transmitted disease in the South Pacific islands: *The order not to permit the crews of the boats to go on shore was issued, that I might do everything in my power to prevent the importation of a fatal disease into this island, which I knew some of our men laboured under, and which, unfortunately, had been communicated by us to other islands in these seas. With the same view, I ordered all female vistors to be excluded from the ships* (Voyage to the Pacific Ocean, op. cit., Volume 2, p. 196).

220 Marchand's descriptions here correspond closely to those given by Cook (Voyage to the Pacific Ocean, op. cit., pp. 206–207). Both King (Voyage to the Pacific Ocean, op. cit., Volume 3, p. 139) and Dixon (op. cit., p. 271) note the velvety texture of the ruffs.

221 Both King (Voyage to the Pacific Ocean, op. cit., Volume 3, p. 135) and Dixon (op. cit., p. 272) describe this particular device.

222 Like King and Dixon.

They put upon their heads a kind of paste which makes the colour of their hair change, which some wear long and which others cut short. The beards of the men are left to grow.

Their mats are the most beautiful I have ever seen, and most beautifully manufactured. They are of a very large size and some of these are painted in diverse colours.

The natives have two sorts of spears of a hard wood much like that of the cedar tree. The first are about 7 feet in length and very well polished. One extremity is very sharp and the other terminates suddenly with a barb. The others, of which I saw only two, are about fourteen feet in length and terminate at both ends in sharp points.[223]

Their *pahoua*, or daggers, are one and half feet in length and they are made of a very hard wood of a black colour and very heavy. I saw some of which the handles were ornamented for six to eight inches with the skin of a dog with the hair outermost.

I saw neither slings nor clubs.

Their canoes are made much like those belonging to the Marquesans, but are better wrought. They have single ones, which have outriggers, and double ones. Their paddles are of the largest size that I have ever seen. The double canoes carry a sail which consists of a mat of a triangular shape with the point at the bottom.

Their hooks, which serve usually as bait, and of which they have many sorts, like those of the Marquesas, are made of the pearl oyster shell in the form a small fish.

Their fishing lines, with which they also make their nets, are very well wrought. They make use of the same tree which furnishes the material for their cloth.

Like the inhabitants of the Marquesas, they are very dextrous in swimming and diving; after having shown them some very small hooks, I sometimes let them fall overboard upon which they immediately dived down under the surface of the water, always bringing them back again. Mr Portlock and Mr Dixon make mention of the natives swimming in the greatest confusion amongst the sharks who durst not attack them.[224]

The honesty of the natives is not to be doubted. We purchased of them potatoes, yams, tarrou, which is the same root as the yam found in the West Indies, cocoa-nuts, water-melons, pumpkins, sugar cane, salted fish, fresh fish, fowls and hogs. These last appeared to be of two kinds, the greater part of them more numerous and of a small size, and the other kind of a larger size. We did not, like Mr Cook or his continuator, find them to remain alive but for a short time on board ship. Amongst the forty we took on board, all of them continued to eat,

---

223 See *Voyage to the Pacific Ocean*, op. cit., Volume 3, p. 152.
224 Cook also mentions the Hawaiians' swimming skills (*Voyage to the Pacific Ocean*, op. cit., Volume 2, p. 229), as does King (*Voyage to the Pacific Ocean*, op. cit., Volume 3, p. 145). Portlock describes how at ease they were with sharks (op. cit., p. 180).

and even several days after we had taken our departure, those we killed were in as good health as when they were first brought to us. As the English navigators do not make mention of having procured water-melons or pumpkins as we had done, I presumed that they had been sown here by the English. The fowls appeared to be scarce for they brought off very few and they bore a high price.

In addition to the articles of which I have spoken, the natives brought to market[225] a great quantity of white salt which is of great use and which is in general scarce in all of the islands of the Pacific Ocean.

We took the precaution of conducting all our traffic along-side ship and did not permit them to come on board in order to remove any opportunity for them to commit a theft. This also prevented any disputes which should have occurred after such attempts. In consequence, we took leave them the best of friends.

I hope I may be allowed to say again in regard to these people what I have said of the inhabitants of the Marquesas, that their desire for iron cannot be comprehended. We can hardly imagine from whence comes their knowledge of it, which is besides of the most useful that Mankind has ever procured. We know not what use they make of it for we saw neither arms nor utensils made of it. I do not believe them to possess the least capacity in the working of it,[226] though they make all kinds of vigorous efforts in order to procure it for themselves.

The usual practice of the islanders, above and below the line, which consists of offering their girls and women to strangers, can be comprehended no less, especially after the fatal experience of infections their custom has given rise to, which derives always it appears from the hospitality of their behaviour. But I know of no peoples who live upon the continents who practice this. In truth, some few individuals, in order to yield to constant requests, and by lewdness, give up their women, which at Queen Charlotte's Islands some of the gentlemen had occasion to experience. Their aversion, whether true or false, is proof enough that they have not yet contracted a familiarity with such a custom. Whereas the inhabitants of Norfolk showed always extreme jealousy, the same has been observed by the voyagers of the Indians, whether they be Chinese, Malays, people of Peking, true Hindous or Arabs. For if amongst several of these peoples there are to be found temple dancers, nowhere are the men to be seen offering them to strangers. In the Marquesas Islands, the Friendly Isles, from the Society to the Sandwich Islands as well as in the Revolution Islands, it the usual custom to which the women yield too willingly for their perfect submission not to be an essential article of their early instruction.

I perceived upon some of them corrupted sores. The navigators who had some intercourse with this people and who had a tolerable knowledge of them, affirm with certainty that this infection may be attributed to their immoderate use of

---

225 Like Cook and King, Marchand notes the usefulness of salt and the fact that it is to be found in the Hawaiian islands.
226 See King, *Voyage to the Pacific Ocean*, op. cit., Volume 3, p. 131.

ava or *kava* which is a sort of liquor which is made of the root of the intoxicating pepper root.[227] The men do not tie up the prepuce as do the inhabitants of the Marquesas, however several of the Officers told me that they had seen several of them who practised this custom.[228]

I shall conclude my observations of the inhabitants of the Sandwich Islands, or rather those of the Island of Ouhahi, with a vocabulary of some words of their language which I collected during the short time of our stay near this island.

Tahi	One
Roa	Two
Toroa	Three
Fah	Four
Kemi	Five
Ohaine	Six
Hitou	Seven
Oualloa	Eight
Hiva	Nine
Houloua	Ten
Epou	The Head
Païpaïhi eho	The Ear
Erehi	The fore-head
Mettai	The eye
Pohivai	The arm
Pitou	The navel
Houhah	The thigh
Ouaouaï	The leg
Inihou	Cocoa nut
Ouharrai	Potatoes
Ouhaï	Yams
Boa or Boaka	Hog
Moa	Fowls or birds
Maro	Cloth
Ourou	Bread fruit
Matté	Dead or wounded
Vaha or Evaha	Canoe
Vahi or Evahi	Fresh water
A barbed point	Haïhaï
Héahou	A fishing line
Tabou or tapou	Prohibited, forbidden
Maï Taï	This is good, it is beautiful or I am pleased
Poé	A mixture of bread fruit and other roots of which they make into a paste
Ouahiné	A woman

227 Marchand here in referring to navigators in general, reproduces Cook, King and Dixon's remarks almost verbatim.

228 See Cook, *Voyage to the Pacific Ocean*, op. cit., Volume 2, p. 233.

Aïi	Yes
Ténété	A man
Eïnou	To drink
Maiténo	Present
Touhourrai	A rope
Taihi	The sea
Haïraï	The sun
Mahinai	The moon
Maihié	Bananas
Ouraï	Red feathers
Eréyé	A necklace of red feathers
Maitou	Hooks
Pahoua	Daggers
Mohinai	Mats
Toa ou Tou	Sugar cane
Tomamaï	Come here or simply here
Aiboubou	Tomorrow
Toaï	Paddles
Hoou	A nail
Houbou	Button on a suit of clothes
Petaihi	Salt
Enoou	Bad
Tibou	Gourd

I observed that in front of each word, they often add an *a* or an *e* which I believe serves as the article.

If we take pains to compare this short vocabulary with that which I have given for the language of the Marquesans, there is to be found not only the greatest affinity between the two languages but also that the same words are assigned to the same things, most particularly with regard to the numerals.[229]

From Saturday 8th to Sunday 9th October

38

During the evening, we took a sea swallow which had settled upon the rigging. It was the size of a common pigeon. It was of a black brown colour all over, excepting the head which was of a light grey colour.

At 6 o'clock in the morning we perceived very distinctly the island of Ouhahi and of Moouhi. The first bore ENE½E, distant 41 leagues, and the second NE½N, distant 37 leagues by estimation of the distance sailed since our departure.

---

229 Cook also comments on the similarity between the Tahitian, New Zealand and Hawaiian languages (*Voyage to the Pacific Ocean*, op. cit., Volume 2, p. 250). Anderson constructs a vocabulary which Cook refers his readers to (*Voyage to the Pacific Ocean*, op. cit., Volume 3, Appendix V, p. 549). Anderson's list numbers 229 words (Marchand's vocabulary is 67 words long), Dixon also presents a sample of the Hawaiian language (op. cit., pp. 268–270).

These islands could have been seen from a distance of 12 or 15 leagues more, for they appeared at this moment still very high.

By several sets of azimuths, the variation of the compass was found to be NE 8° 50'.

During this day, we had very light winds and calms.

Latitude by observation N 19° 45'.
Longitude by reckoning 160° 18'.

10' more to the North than by reckoning.
Réaumur's Thermometer +25°, Fahrenheit's thermometer's 87°.

From Sunday 9th to Monday 10th October 1791

27

At ½ past 5 o'clock, the island of Ouhahi was still in sight bearing E¼NE, distant 48 leagues.

We saw tropic birds, frigate birds and sheerwaters. The variation of the compass determined from eight sets of azimuths, was 8° 37' NE.

During this day, we had light winds and calms.

At noon, we caught sight of the island of Atoui bearing NNW½W, 34 leagues distant. This island must be of a great height in order for it to be seen at so a great distance.

Latitude by observation N 20° 26'.
Longitude by reckoning 160° 47'.

We were carried by the current 29' more to the North than by reckoning these last 24 hours, which was more WNW½W, which was our course.
Réaumur's Thermometer +25°, Fahrenheit's thermometer 87°.

From Monday 10th to Tuesday 11th October 1791

70½

Since taking our departure from Ouhahi, we had got but light breezes and calms on account I believed of our being in the vicinity of the Sandwich Islands, I directed the course to WSW in order to go away from them.

Until 10 o'clock AM, we had baffling winds and calms, but at this moment there sprung up a light breeze, variable from NNE to ENE, attended with clear weather.

We saw sea larks, boobies, tropic birds and frigate birds.

A large quantity of mackerel was following the ship, and we took three with the harpoon.

The variation of the compass was 8° 38' NE by the amplitudes and by 12 sets of observations of azimuths.

Latitude by observation N 20° 10'.
Longitude by reckoning 162°.

Réaumur's Thermometer +26°, Fahrenheit's thermometer 89°.

From Tuesday 11ᵗʰ to Wednesday 12ᵗʰ October 1791

89

I have spoken before of my intention to go to China under the 20 and 21° parallels of latitude (which is a route which has been little used in order to cross the Pacific Ocean). But having observed that we would most likely meet with but light winds so near the Tropic, and at a period when the sun was to be found in the Southern hemisphere, I became of another mind and resolved to draw nearer the equator until the 13 or 14ᵗʰ parallel of latitude, and then direct our course West until we reached the Ladrones or Marianne Islands.[230] This is the track of the Manilla ships[231] which depart from Acapulco to come there. In consequence, I directed our course to SW¼S.

During this day, we had a light breeze from NE to East, attended with pleasant weather.

The variation of the magnetic needle determined from 9 sets of observations of the azimuths was 9° 1' NE, mean result.

Latitude by observation N 18° 53'.
Longitude by reckoning 163° 6'.

15' more to the South than by reckoning.
Réaumur's Thermometer +25½°, Fahrenheit's thermometer's 88°.

As all that which is in relation to the everyday life of the citizen is of great importance, we cannot reflect upon these points without the strictest attention. I find myself bound to set forth the smallest detail of a trial which may prove to

---

230 Marchand is not being particularly innovative here as Dixon makes exactly the same observations (himself following Cook's recommendations) concerning the route to China from the Sandwich Islands: *China was the place of our next destination, and we were already in the same latitude, and consequently had only the longitude to run down; but our Captain judged it most prudent to steer to the Southward, 'till we were in about 13 deg. 30 min. North latitude, and then bear away to the Westward; as that track was the most likely for a true trade, and it had been found in Captain Cook's last voyage, that in the latitude 20 and 21 deg. to leeward of these islands, the winds are at best but light, and often variable* (op. cit., p. 281).

231 See King, *Voyage to the Pacific Ocean*, op. cit., Volume 3, p. 408.

be of the greatest assistance to the sea. I will thus here draw very exactly from the original of my Surgeon Mr Roblet's reflections upon a means to cure the disease which he tried on board with regards to the baker of whom I have spoken, and who was affected in the second stage of that disorder (after Mr Roblet).

On the 11th October, ten months after our departure, we had no serious malady on board, excepting one man who was affected with the scurvy, and this though we had put into no harbour in which the crew had been sent ashore only in order to refresh themselves. For the three and half days at St Jago, the seamen had been employed in making the water which we were in need of. From St Jago to the Marquesas, we had passed from the extremes of heat and of cold. Thanks to the antiscorbutic medecines, to the cleanliness of the ship and to the kindness of the Captain, who without limitation did all that he could to relieve the seamen, we had no serious malady on board. During the four days we were at anchor in the bay of Madre de Dios, we stood in need of water and of refreshments, and on account of the diverse events which happened due to the character of the inhabitants, we did not secure the full benefit of our stay in this country, which had appeared to us to have so promising an aspect. On the North coast of America, we were not fortunate enough to stay in a port from which any benefit could be received for the good health of the ship's crew. We had however only two persons affected with the scurvy, whom we cared for and cured at sea, without making a stay on land. After having examined for about one month, the coast of America and that of the islands adjacent to it, and after the run to the Sandwich Islands, we had but two more sick, one of whom, the baker, was attacked with scurvy with great violence. As the circumstance would not permit us to come to anchor, we purchased everything which the canoes of the natives brought off to us, and though we had vegetables and fresh meat, I durst not flatter myself that this man would recover, for we had two months at sea before our arrival in China. The breeze from the shore alone had so affected him that he lost three of his teeth on the day we saw land.[232] I desired to give him relief, and thus on board ship I employed with success, sand, hot and dry, in which I buried him, the salutary effects of which method I had seen on land.[233]

To this effect, the sand was dried and heated in a great kettle, I then mixed it with a sufficient quantity of more sand to allay the heat to a proper temperature. After which the sick man was buried in it up to the hams. The weather was dry and pleasant, at noon Réamur's thermometer was at 25½ degrees in the shade. We took him out after a little more than half an hour. His legs were then benumbed,

---

232 This sentence is unclear in French: . . . *je n'osais pas cependant me flatter de conserver ce malade, car nous avions encore deux mois à rester à la mer avant d'arriver en Chine, et que l'air de terre seulement l'avait déjà affecté au point que trois dents lui tombèrent le jour que nous la vimes* (op. cit., p. 27 of the manuscript, Livre 2).

233 This recourse to hot sand is described in James Lind's *Treatise on the Scurvy* (1753) which was translated into French (*Traité du Scorbut*) in 1756. Later editions were also translated into French and Roblet must have been familiar with them.

most particularly the tendons of the extensors, which I ascribed to the troublesome position in which he had found himself. I made him lie down for half an hour and recommended to him that he keep warm in order not to suffer the effects of the open air. Two hours afterwards, his state of health appeared to be a wondrous thing, there was no longer any swelling or stiffness even in the joints, the eruptions upon the skin, almost dissipated, were now of a yellowish colour, in the soles of the feet, very painful previously, he no longer felt the least sensation. To conclude, it was a satisfaction to see that my trial had gone beyond my hopes of meeting with success.

It is I believe not improper to give the reasons which induced me to make this trial.

Very much concerned with the different diseases with which seamen are affected, I constantly reflected with melancholy upon the scurvy, the most dangerous of many others together. Upon reading the accounts of authors who have been acquainted with it, and being informed of the most probable causes and the effects, there remains in my mind much uncertainty with regards to the cures, though all of the authors end in saying that land was the specific. In an infinite number of situations, and particularly that in which we found ourselves, this was too long a time for what I was in hopes of, and what I desired. The remarkable observations, full of humanity, of Mr Cook, were proofs of how much his genius in this respect had been ready to consider all the means as might contribute to the success of the endeavour. This put me in mind of my desire for new remedies which could be put to use, for despite all his care, I saw in his journals that those seamen attacked by the malady were restored to good health only on land, in spite of their putting into ports many times, some of them dying even of the scurvy, whereas other diseases had touched them not. I employed as preventatives, over above the greens pickled in vinegar, wort, etc., I employed I say carbonic acid or fixed air in tisans for the sick. I mixed a certain quantity of spirit of vitriol with water, and I ascribed to these remedies our good fortune in passing the line, without any dangerous infections, through the hot weather to the severe cold which reigned in sixty one degrees of South latitude, and alternately from the cold to the heat, and then once more to the cold climate of North America, followed by a navigation of more than two months between the Tropics, and altogether without example, not putting into any sort of harbour which can be considered as worthy of that name.

I have been accustomed since my tender years to consider the government of my country as being one which has constantly at the largest expence, pursued the designs dictated only by humanity, proving it to the whole of Europe, which followed their example, by the hospitals for soldiers. But I cannot but give credit to England, which justly deserves commendation for the care given to such useful a class of men as seamen. France and England, already rivals on many other points, have continued without intermission and in emulation of one another, to make humanity thrive with knowledge of the most useful nature, in order that the advancement of a scourge so terrible as the scurvy, be retarded, the result of which is that it is now spoken of as any other disease which attacks all of mankind.

The most frequent diseases on board ships, in prisons and in hospitals where a great quantity of poor wretches are confined together in a small space, proceed from the air which they breathe, which is impure and which is corrupted immediately, as in damp or marshy places. The sea-air to which the seamen are exposed, most particularly in long navigations during which they suffer from fatal calms, as well as the salted foods of which they eat in general, their sorrow and their melancholy, are not the only causes to which may be assigned this scourge, but they contribute greatly to it. Badly salted meat liable to putrefaction, water which in casks is not purified thanks to communication with the open air during a long period, excepting the moment when it is drawn to drink, and above all the frequent want of this essential element, have appeared to be of such importance that the government has resolved in order to purify this last, to adopt all the measures which have been proposed to them by the doctors, physicians and other learned observers, such as the application of a hot iron, or even of sulphur, which however cannot dissolve in water, and finally of lime. There is in addition the caution that only the best quality of salted meat should be procured, with a prodigious quantity of greens, which form most efficacious remedy for this disease. It is in order to contribute to such noble designs that I will here make mention of my ideas on this important object.

I have given an account of the immediate causes of this disease. I will now describe the effects. The principal effect, from which all the others follow, is the dissolution of the blood. In this state, the watery part is in such a great quantity that the fibres are weakened and relaxed and it gets into the cellular membrane. The arterial system is still able to push the blood, but the veins are in want of the necessary strength to promote the circulation from which proceeds the stagnation of the blood. The nutritious humours, not being sufficiently formed, pass with increased difficulty in the small vessels whence they are bound, and if they are to be found there, the relaxation of the fibres makes them stagnate and they cause a choaking up. The patches and effusions of a livid colour under the skin follow the collection of the putrid blood, which is corrupted and which is the cause of the terrible ulcers and rottenness of the bones and the teeth. It is due to these effects that the doctors and Surgeons all agree that bleeding in this condition would prove fatal, for in decreasing in no very exact manner, the concreted mass of the blood, the bleeding will greatly increase accidents. But as the remedy is thought to be the evacuation of this excessive watery part, and that sweating is much reduced or stopped, and that gangrene is brought on if there is a recourse to scarification for the fibres are much weakened, a more gentle physic must be found in order to reach so important an object. It is very surprising indeed that the application of baths of sand on board ships has not been considered. It is true to say that those who have had recourse to this remedy, never having given an account of their designs, the use of them has not become the custom. In reflecting upon the causes and the effects of the scurvy, which have been ascertained, and also upon the qualities of absorption of sand, which is tonical when intermixed with saline particles, I determined to make a trial. The experiment will make known the advantages of this practice. The great success which the experiment will meet with is already evident if all answers my expectations. It is the least expensive and the easiest means to employ. The most essential instrument is a bathing tub of iron-plate with a double bottom, within which one or two chafing dishes may without danger be inserted, containing a quantity of sand sufficient to cover the thighs, the legs and even a part of the back. Three or four barrels of fine sand which is well-dried is the last necessary. The sand should I believe be washed with sea-water and not with fresh water on account of the saline particles which the former contains and which are tonical. I am satisfied even that this practice may be extended with great advantage to the proper treatment of the swelling of the legs which follows from chronic distempers as the dropsy, etc., etc.

Note: I continued to serve fresh food, pickled vegetables and other internal helps of which I disposed, though their effects were very slow and the relief procured by the bath proved to be immediate. Nonetheless, I believe the union of both to be more efficacious and even necessary.[234]

From Wednesday 12th to Thursday 13th October 1791

143

At noon I directed the course to SW. The ship was not making the usual progress for it was pooped. We filled four casks with water forward, which answered my expectations.

During this day, we had a very fresh wind which varied from NE¼E to East, attended with squalls at intervals.

We saw a great quantity of bonetta and took five, which were in great part served to the the the ship's company.

The variation of the compass by observation was 8° 59' NE.

Latitude by observation N 17° 22'.
Longitude by reckoning 165° 10'.

4' more to the South than by reckoning.
Réaumur's Thermometer +25°, Fahrenheit's thermometer 87°.

From Thursday 13th to Friday 14th October 1791

155

The breeze at ENE blowing a fresh gale, attended with clear weather and cloudy at intervals.

We continued to see frigate birds, tropic birds, boobies and sheerwaters.

---

234 Most of Roblet's theory and experiments (causes, effects, remedies) are based on Lind's observations and methods.

By 15 sets of azimuths, the variation of the magnetic needle was 9° Northeasterly.

Latitude by observation N 15° 48'.
Longitude by reckoning 167° 21'.

4' more to the South than by reckoning.
Réaumur's Thermometer +25½°, Fahrenheit's thermometer 88°.

From Friday 14th to Saturday 15th October 1791

145½
At noon, we steered SW¼W with the assistance of fresh gale blowing at ENE attended with clear weather, rainy at intervals.
We had the same weather during the whole this day.
The variation of the compass by observation of the azimuths was 9° 25' NE.
We continued to see the same birds as the previous days and great quantities of flying fish with red and with white wings.

Latitude by observation N 14° 45'.
Longitude by reckoning 169° 38'.

2' more to the North than by reckoning.
Réaumur's Thermometer +25°, Fahrenheit's thermometer 87°.

From Saturday 15th to Sunday 16th October 1791

114½
During this day we had a gentle gale at ENE. At 3 o'clock in the morning the wind shifted to SSW for one hour and then varied to ENE once again.
The weather was clear and dark at intervals and we had a great swell from the NE.
At noon, we had directed our course to WSW.
The variation of the compass determined from 9 azimuths was 10° 14' NE.

Latitude by observation N 14° 16'.
Longitude by reckoning 171° 33'.

3' more to the South than by reckoning.
Réaumur's Thermometer +26½°, Fahrenheit's thermometer 90°.

From Sunday 16th to Monday 17th October 1791

122½
Fresh wind at E¼NE, cloudy weather, lightning in the South quarter and rain during the night.

By 7 azimuths, we found the variation of the magnetic needle to be 100° 26' Northeasterly.

Latitude by observation N 13° 39'.
Longitude by reckoning 173° 37'.

11' more to the South than by reckoning.
Réaumur's Thermometer +25½°, Fahrenheit's thermometer 88°.

From Monday 17ᵗʰ to Tuesday 18ᵗʰ October 1791

121½
At noon, we steered W¼SW.
Wind blowing fresh more or less from ENE to E, cloudy weather and rain during the night, clear and fine during the day.
We saw sheerwaters, gulls, boobies and bonetta.
Variation of the compass by reckoning 10° 30'.

Latitude by observation N 13° 34'.
Longitude by reckoning 175° 42'.

3' more to the South than by reckoning.
Réaumur's Thermometer +25°, Fahrenheit's thermometer 87°.

From Tuesday 18ᵗʰ to Wednesday 19ᵗʰ October 1791

97½
Light breeze at East, attended frequently with squalls and rain, most particularly during the night.
We saw a great many tropic birds, sheerwaters, Grey gulls and boobies.
By two sets of observations of five distances each of the moon and the sun, reduced to 9h 41' 58" in the morning, our longitude was found to be 178° 39', and that deduced by reckoning since our departure from Ouhahi, was 177° 14'. Thus a difference of 1° 25' more to the West.
By the mean result of 9 azimuths, the variation of the compass was 10° 56' NE.

Latitude by observation N 13° 33'.
Longitude by observation 178° 48'.
Longitude by reckoning 177° 23'.

11' more to the South than by reckoning.
Réaumur's Thermometer +23½°, Fahrenheit's thermometer 84°.

From Wednesday 19ᵗʰ to Thursday 20ᵗʰ October 1791

79¾.

During this day we had a light breeze which varied from E to ENE with rain at intervals.

In addition to all the sea birds we saw daily, we caught sight of several land birds of the plover species.

At 8 o'clock 26' 39" AM, and by two sets of observations of the distance of the moon and the sun, our longitude was 180° 30' 45", and that deduced from the observations made the day before, and taking into account the distance sailed to the Westward, was 179° 57'.

Mean result 180° 14'.

The variation of the compass determined from the amplitudes and the azimuths was 11° 27' NE.

Latitude by observation N 13° 32'.
Longitude by observation 180° 27'.
Longitude by reckoning 178° 45'.

Réaumur's Thermometer +26°, Fahrenheit's thermometer 89°.

From Thursday 20ᵗʰ to Friday 21ˢᵗ October 1791

105½

Fresh breeze varying from East to ENE, attended with pleasant weather.
The variation of the compass determined from eight azimuths, was NE 12° 18'.

Latitude by observation N 13° 32'.
Longitude by observation 182° 16'.
Longitude by reckoning 180° 34'.

2' more to the South than by reckoning.
Réaumur's Thermometer +25½°, Fahrenheit's thermometer 88°.
We saw a number of land birds. Following the chart of Arrowsmith, St Peter's Island bore S¼SE of the globe, distant 62 leagues.

From Friday 21ˢᵗ to Saturday 22ⁿᵈ October 1791

121¼

Fresh breeze from ENE to East, cloudy weather and rain, great swell from the NW.

During the night, we heard the cries of a great many birds. During the morning, we saw tropic birds and a gull.

The variation of the compass determined from the amplitudes and the azimuths was NE 21° 30'.

At 8h 41' 11" AM, by two sets of observations of the distance of the moon and the sun, our longitude was 185° 4', mean result. According to these two observations, we found the ship 1° more to the West of the mean result of the last four.

Latitude by observation N 13° 36'.
Longitude by observation 185° 22'.
Longitude by reckoning 182° 40'.

2' more to the North than by reckoning.
Réaumur's Thermometer +25½°, Fahrenheit's thermometer 88°.

From Saturday 22ⁿᵈ to Sunday 23ʳᵈ October 1791

114½

Breeze at East and at E¼NE blowing a gentle gale, attended with squalls and rain. Great swell from the North.

We saw tropic birds, frigate birds and sheerwaters.

Variation of the compass by observation NE 12° 48'.

At 8h 42' 58" AM, by two sets of observations of the distance of the moon and the sun, our longitude was 187° 15' 15". That computed from the two sets of observations made the day before, and taking into account the distance sailed Westward, was 187° 2'. Mean result 187° 8' 373".

Latitude by observation N 13° 40'.
Longitude by observation 187° 26'.
Longitude by reckoning 184° 38'.

2' more to the North than by reckoning.
Réaumur's Thermometer +25½°, Fahrenheit's thermometer 88°.

From Sunday 23ʳᵈ to Monday 24ᵗʰ October 1791

124¾

Breeze at ENE blowing a gentle gale with cloudy weather and squalls at intervals.

We saw land birds of the plover species of which I have before spoke, and white gulls.

The variation of the compass by observation was 13° 27' NE.

Latitude by observation N 13° 44'.
Longitude by observation 189° 36'.
Longitude by reckoning 186° 48'.

2' more to the South than by reckoning.
Réaumur's Thermometer +25°, Fahrenheit's thermometer 87°.

From Monday 24th to Tuesday 25th October 1791

151½
A fresh gale at ENE, attended with squalls at intervals and a great swell from the NE.
Saw tropic birds, frigate birds, gulls and sea swallows.
Variation of the compass determined from the amplitudes and the azimuths 13° 15' NE.

Present latitude by observation N 13° 45'.
Longitude by observation 192° 12'.
Longitude by reckoning 189° 24'.

2' more to the South than by reckoning.
Réaumur's Thermometer +25°, Fahrenheit's thermometer 87°.

From Tuesday 25th to Wednesday 26th October 1791

152½
Breeze at ENE blowing a fresh gale, attended with gusts of wind and rain.
Variation of the compass by observation NE 11° 31'.

Latitude by observation N 13° 51'.
Longitude by observation 197° 37'.
Longitude by reckoning 194° 49'.

Réaumur's Thermometer +25½°, Fahrenheit's thermometer 88°.

From Thursday 27th to Friday 28th October 1791

117
During this day, we steered WSW and W¼SW with the help of gentle gale varying from ENE to East attended with squalls and a great swell from the NE.
We caught a bonetta.
Variation of the compass by observation NE 10° 32'.

Latitude by observation N 13° 42'.
Longitude by observation 199° 37'.
Longitude by reckoning 196° 49'.

Réaumur's Thermometer +26°, Fahrenheit's thermometer 89°.
6' more to the North than by reckoning.

From Friday 28ᵗʰ to Saturday 29ᵗʰ October 1791

138¾

Breeze varying from ENE to ESE blowing a gentle gale attended with violent squalls of wind and rain at intervals.

We saw during this day several birds as large as the albatross, and as broad. All the upper side of the body was of a black colour and the under-side was white speckled with black.

Variation of the compass by observation NE 9° 50'.

Whenever the weather permitted, the skinners were employed in drying the skins.

Latitude by observation N 13° 43'.
Longitude by observation 201° 59'.
Longitude by reckoning 199° 11'.

Réaumur's Thermometer +27°, Fahrenheit's thermometer 91°.
We felt a great heat despite the cool of the breeze.

From Saturday 29ᵗʰ to Sunday 30ᵗʰ October 1791

127½

Breeze varying from ENE to ESE blowing a gentle gale, violent gusts of wind, rain and a great swell from the NE.

Variation of the compass by observation NE 9° 20'.

We saw boobies, tropic birds, etc. and bonettas.

Latitude by observation N 13° 24'.
Longitude by observation 204° 8'.
Longitude by reckoning 201° 20'.

Réaumur's Thermometer +26°, Fahrenheit's thermometer 89°.

From Sunday 30ᵗʰ to Monday 31ˢᵗ October 1791

122¾

We had during this day a breeze which varied much from ENE to ESE attended with violent squalls and rain almost without intermission. We had squalls all from the Southeast quarter.

At noon we had directed our course W½S.

The variation of the compass by observation of several sets of azimuths was 8° 4' NE.

Latitude by observation North 13° 29'.
Longitude by observation 206° 16'.
Longitude by reckoning 203° 28'.

Réaumur's Thermometer +26°, Fahrenheit's thermometer 89°.

From Monday 31ˢᵗ October to 1ˢᵗ November 1791

105

At noon we directed our course to West. We had a variable breeze from SE to ENE with heavy squalls, constant rain and a great swell from the NE.

The variation of the compass by observation in the evening of the azimuths and the amplitude was 8° 10', and in the morning 8° 44'.

Present latitude by observation North 13° 42'.
Longitude by observation 208° 3'.
Longitude by reckoning 205° 15'.

Réaumur's Thermometer +24°, Fahrenheit's thermometer 85°.

From Tuesday 1ˢᵗ to Wednesday 2ⁿᵈ November 1791

116¼

At noon we directed our course W¼NW in order to fall in with the latitude of Tinian.

By two sets of observations of five distances each of the moon and the sun, reduced to 2h 10' 57" o'clock PM, our longitude was found to be 209° 24', mean result.

That which was determined from last observations made on the 23ʳᵈ of the preceding month, was at this moment 208° 13', that is to say 1° 11' more to the East.

Whilst making our observations this day, I must make mention of the weather which was a little hazy.

The variation of the compass by observation was 70 30' NE.

During the whole of this day, we had a breeze which varied from SE to ENE attended with violent squalls, rain and a great swell from the NE.

Latitude by observation North 14° 24'.
Longitude by observation 211° 18'.
Longitude by reckoning 207° 19'.

Réaumur's Thermometer +25½°, Fahrenheit's thermometer 88°.

I observed through a good telescope two spots upon the East part of the disk of the sun, which then disappeared on the 8ᵗʰ of this same month, in the Western quarter.

From Wednesday 2ⁿᵈ to Thursday 3ʳᵈ November 1791

126¼

At 2h 27' 30" o'clock PM, by four sets of five distances each of the moon and the sun, our longitude was 212° 28' 30".

Our situation determined by the observations of the preceding evening, reduced to this moment, was 211° 28'.

We steered W¼NW until 7 o'clock AM. Being by reckoning in latitude 14° 57' North, which is that of the island of Tinian, we steered Westward.

During this day, we had winds which varied much from SSW to East, round by South. At intervals, we suffered very violent squalls of wind which obliged us to haul up the top-sails. There was a great swell from this quarter.

We had lightning without intermission at SW during the night, the horizon being very dark all round the compass, which appeared to foretell the coming of a hard gale.

The variation of the magnetic needle was found to be NE 6° 47'.

Latitude by observation North 15° 6'.
Longitude by observation 214° 23' 30".
Longitude by reckoning 209° 23' 30".

8' more to the North than by reckoning.
Réaumur's Thermometer +25°, Fahrenheit's thermometer 87°.

From Thursday 3rd to Friday 4th November 1791

132½

During this day, and most particularly during the night, very dirty weather, that is to say hard squalls from the Southern quarter, attended with thunder and lightning and rain.

At 6 o'clock AM, the carpenter having refused to do what was his duty when ordered by the First Officer, was put in irons by this last. He seized forthwith an axe saying that he who came near him would have reason to repent of it. The officer sent word that I should come. After having listened to the reasons of his doing this, I gently told him to submit. Having heard me come upon deck, he had put away his axe.

We continued to see a great number of birds of several species, sparrow hawks, white boobies with the tips of their wing of a black colour, tropic birds, sheerwaters and stormy petrels.

Latitude by observation North 14° 50'.
Longitude by observation 216° 40'.
Longitude by reckoning 201° 40'.

8' more to the North than by reckoning.
Réaumur's Thermometer +25°, Fahrenheit's thermometer 87°.

From Friday 4th to Saturday 5th November 1791

93

At 3 o'clock PM, we caught sight of the Ladrone Islands trending from NNW to SW, they seem to form a single island. At ½ past 3 o'clock, the middle of Tinian bore W½N, and the Peak of Saypan NW¼N. We were 5 or 6 leagues distant from the first.

We steered thus WNW in order to examine the channel between these two islands, which I proposed to push through.

By four sets of observations of five distances each of the moon and the sun made by Mr Chanal and myself, reduced to 5h 1' 21", our longitude was 215° 54', mean result. The observation made on the 1st, reduced to this moment, was found to be 216° 10', and that of the 2nd, 217° 10'.

Mean result of ten sets 216° 25'.

At this time, Tinian bore West, distant 3 leagues, which put the East extremity of this island in longitude 216° 34' West of Paris, or longitude 143° 26' East.

These observations agreed to a point with those which Mr Wallis, Commander of the *Dolphin*, made near this island in 1767, for he determined the longitude of the middle of the island to be 214° West of Greenwich, or 216° 20' West of Paris. Following the chart of Mr Arrowsmith, which has been newly published in England, these islands are laid down in two different situations, one of after the observations of Mr Wallis, and the other about 40 leagues more to the Westward. I know not the reason for such an alteration.

At ¾ past 5 o'clock, the South point of Tinian bore SW¼W, the North point WNW½N, the middle of Aguigan bore SW, the Peak of Saypan NNW½N, its South point NW, its N point N½W, and the middle of the channel between this island and Tinian, bore NW¼W, distant 2 leagues from Tinian.

The channel between Tinian and Saypan was no more than 2½ leagues broad, and besides this, the weather having a threatening appearance, I resolved not to run in during the night. In consequence of this, we sheered off to get an offing with a breeze at SSE blowing a gentle gale. We spent the night making different boards. At day-light, observing that the currents had carried us Northward, making it impossible, with the wind at South and SSE, to push through the channel between Tinian and Saypan, we bore away to the NW that we might pass Northward of Saypan. We ran along the East shore, at a distance of less than 1½ leagues. This part of the coast is bordered by reefs and breakers but which do not extend out to sea.

Saypan presented a most pleasing aspect on account of the verdure. Cocoa-nut trees are to be seen even on the mountains. The peak, which is to be found in the middle of the island, is of moderate height and in clear weather may be seen at sea when 15 leagues distant. Tinian and Aguigan are low, the first, which I saw near at hand, was well-wooded.

These islands were discovered by Magellan in 1521 and were named the Ladrone islands on account of the thievish disposition of the inhabitants. The Spanish have since there settled in Guam, with a governor and a garrison. They were in times past very populous. I will not here make mention of the reasons of the destruction of the inhabitants, I will say only that today, inhabitants can be found only on the island of Guam and these engage in hunting expeditions at various times in the course of the year. If the reader is curious to find out more I shall leave him to refer to the voyages of Admiral Anson, Byron and Wallis.[235]

At ¾ past 8 o'clock, the Northermost point of Saypan bore W 8° S, distant about 2 leagues.

At 10 o'clock, we caught sight of a small island situated NW of the shore of Saypan, and flat in form. It lay about 1½ leagues from the land and was situated W¼SW, distant 4 leagues.

At noon, our latitude by observation was North 15° 30'. Our longitude, following the mean result of our previous observations, was 216° 41', the difference being 19' more to the North during this day. At this same moment, the Northermost point of Saypan bore SE½S, distant 4½ leagues, and the small island of which I have spoken, S¼SE.

After the latitude by observation at noon, and the bearing aforesaid, the North East point of Saypan lies very close to latitude 15° 20' North, and longitude 216° 30' West, or 143° 30' East. The peak lies in latitude 15° 13' and longitude 216° 34' West, or 143° 26' East.

Its greatest length, which lies in a direction nearly North to South, is 3 or 4 leagues.

Following our longitude by reckoning from the Sandwich Islands, we found that the currents had carried us 4° 15' to the West.

The wind was steady at SSE.

Réaumur's Thermometer +26°, Fahrenheit's thermometer 89°.

From Saturday 5th to Sunday 6th November 1791

65½

At sun-set, we saw still very distinctly the peak of Saypan, which bore SE, about 14 leagues distant.

At 8 o'clock PM, we directed our course W¼NW.

During this day, we had light winds from the South quarter, attended with rain and a very hollow swell from NW.

The variation of the compass determined from the observations of the azimuths was 5° 34' NE.

Latitude by observation North 16° 2'.
Longitude by reckoning 217° 41'.

Difference more to the North 4' than by reckoning.
Réaumur's Thermometer +26°, Fahrenheit's thermometer 89°.

---

235 Marchand may here be referring to the Hawkesworth edition (1773) of these voyages which includes the Byron and Wallis accounts, and which was translated into French in 1774.

From Sunday 6ᵗʰ to Monday 7ᵗʰ November 1791

26½

During this day we had in turn calms, light gusts from all round the compass, rain and still a very great swell from North West.

By the mean result of 16 azimuths, we found the variation of the magnetic needle to be 5° 9' North Westerly.

We continued to see a great number of birds and of flying insects of the butterfly species, and of dun flies.

Latitude by observation North 16° 12'.
Longitude by reckoning 218° 30'.

5' more to the North than by reckoning.
Réaumur's Thermometer +25¾°, Fahrenheit's thermometer 88½°.

From Monday 7ᵗʰ to Tuesday 8ᵗʰ November 1791

108

At noon the breeze settled at ENE and East, blowing light at first and then increasing to a fresh gale, attended with fine weather and a great swell from the North.

We continued to see a great number of birds of various species.

At 8 o'clock AM, we directed our course WNW.

The variation of compass by observation of several sets of azimuths was 4° 39' NE.

Latitude by observation North 17° 3'.
Longitude by reckoning 219° 52½ '.

16' more to the North than by reckoning.
Réaumur's Thermometer +25°, Fahrenheit's thermometer 87°.

From Tuesday 8ᵗʰ to Wednesday 9ᵗʰ November 1791

147¾

We had a fresh wind at ENE, attended with squalls at intervals and a great swell from the North.

We continued to see a great number of birds.

The variation by observation of the azimuths and the amplitudes was 3° 49' NE.

Latitude by observation North 17°.
Longitude by reckoning 222° 10 '.

9' more to the South than by reckoning.
Réaumur's Thermometer +25°, Fahrenheit's thermometer 87°.

From Wednesday 9th to Thursday 10th November 1791

125

During this day we had a variable breeze from ESE to ENE attended with rain. The swell from the North had now intirely ceased.

We continued to see a great number of boobies, tropic birds, sheerwaters and a species of bird which was black all over.

We took a fish which was very long and whose head was in the shape of a sword. I had seen several of this species in the Atlantic Ocean. The variation of the compass by observation was NE 2° 58'.

Latitude by observation North 18° 48'.
Longitude by reckoning 224° 9'.

5' more to the South than by reckoning.
Réaumur's Thermometer +25°, Fahrenheit's thermometer 87°.

From Thursday 10th to Friday 11th 1791

116½

During the afternoon, we had constant rain and an infinite quantity of birds of all species about the ship.

The wind was variable during the whole of this day from NNE to East, blowing a gentle gale. The variation of the compass by the observation of ten azimuths was 2° 38' NE.

Latitude by observation North 19° 41'.
Longitude by reckoning 226° 1'.

7' more to the South than by reckoning.
Réaumur's Thermometer +24°, Fahrenheit's thermometer 85°.

From Friday 11th to Saturday 12th November 1791

104½

Wind more or less fresh and variable from NE¼E to E, attended with cloudy weather.

Many tropic birds and gulls fluttering about the ship.

The variation was 2° 12' NE by the observation of 8 azimuths.

Latitude by observation North 20° 27'.
Longitude by reckoning 227° 41'.

3' more to the South than by reckoning.
Réaumur's Thermometer +25°, Fahrenheit's thermometer 87°.

From Saturday 12th to Sunday 13th November 1791

93½

During this day we had a gentle breeze from East to ESE with clear weather, cloudy at intervals.

By the amplitudes and azimuths, the variation of the needle was found to be 2° 11' Northeasterly.

Latitude by observation North 21° 5'.
Longitude by reckoning 229° 11'.

Réaumur's Thermometer +25°, Fahrenheit's thermometer 87.

From Sunday 13th to Monday 14th November 1791

115

At 4 o'clock PM, the wind shifted to NE and blew a hard gale with hard squalls attended with rain. We took in two reefs in the top-sails which we loosed at 7 o'clock in the evening.

We directed our course W¼NW.

The whole of this day we had violent gusts of wind.

We continued to see a very great number of birds.

The variation of the compass by observation was 1° 29' Northeasterly.

Latitude by observation North 21° 19'.
Longitude by reckoning 231° 11'.

8' more to the South than by reckoning.
Réaumur's Thermometer +23½°, Fahrenheit's thermometer 84°.

From Monday 14th to Tuesday 15th November 1791

96

Until 8 o'clock AM, we had a variable breeze from NE to SSW, round by East, with cloudy weather. At this moment, the wind veered to North with great fury and though we had hauled up all our sails, we found ourselves in the greatest danger. The fore top-sail being split while we were getting it off, we unbent it for repair and brought another to the yard.

A quarter of an hour before the squall, we had caught sight of a land bird of the falcon species.

At 10 o'clock, the wind shifted to NW, moderate, attended with fine weather.

The variation of the compass by observation was NE 47'.

Latitude by observation North 21° 46'.
Longitude by reckoning 232° 52'.

8' more to the South than by reckoning.

Réaumur's Thermometer +22½°, Fahrenheit's thermometer 82°.

From Tuesday 15ᵗʰ to Wednesday 16ᵗʰ November 1791

166½

During this day, the breeze varied from NNW to NE blowing a hard gale attended with cloudy weather and a great swell at NE.

At 4 o c'clock PM, I directed our course to the Westward.

We passed constantly a great quantity of pumice stone which most likely comes from Japan or Sulphur Island.[236]

At 9h 29' 10" AM, by 10 distances of the moon and the sun, our longitude was found to be 237° 34" 30", mean result. At this same moment, that by reckoning from the Ladrone Islands, was only 235° 31' 30", that is to say 2° 3' more to the East.

By several sets of observations of the azimuths and the amplitudes, we found the magnetic needle to have no dip neither East nor West, giving near the true meridian.

Latitude by observation North 21° 34'.
Longitude by observation 237° 54'.
Longitude by reckoning 235° 51'.

16' more to the South than by reckoning.

Réaumur's Thermometer +22¼, Fahrenheit's thermometer 81½°.

From Wednesday 16ᵗʰ to Thursday 17ᵗʰ November 1791

109¾

During this day, we had a breeze which blew more or less a fresh from NNE to NE, attended with clear weather and fine.

The variation of the compass was not perceivable.

At ½ past seven o'clock in the morning, we caught sight of land a-head and found it to be the Great Botel Tobago Xima. Soon after, we perceived the smaller Botel.

---

236 King's remarks are most probably the source of Marchand's thoughts on the presence of pumice stone in these waters: *On both days, we passed great quantities of pumice stone, several pieces of which we took up and found to weigh from one ounce to three pounds. We conjectured that these stones had been thrown into the sea by eruptions of various dates, as many of them were covered in barnacles, and others quite bare [. . .] We still continued to pass much pumice stone: indeed, the prodigious quantities of this substance which floats in the sea between Japan and the Bashee Islands, seems to indicate that some great volcanic convulsion must have happened in this part of the Pacific Ocean . . . (Voyage to the Pacific Ocean*, op. cit., Volume 3, p. 407 and p. 408).

At ½ past 9 o'clock, the North point of the larger Botel island bore W¼NW, the South point W¼N, and the middle of the smaller W½S. We were distant about 8 leagues from Great Botel. We thus steered WSW and SW¼W in order to pass to the Southward of both of the islands.

Latitude by observation North 21° 58'.
Longitude by observation the preceding day 239° 49'.
Longitude by reckoning from the Ladrone Islands 237° 46'.

10' more to the North than by reckoning. At the same moment, the North point of Great Botel bore W 21° N, the South point of this same island W 10° N, the middle of the smaller of the Botel islands bore W 3° S, and the middle of the channel between the both islands, West 6° 30' North, distant 6 leagues from Great Botel.

Following these bearings and our observations, the middle of Great Botel lies in latitude 22° 3 or 4' North, and in longitude 240° 15' West. The latitude of the smaller island is 21° 57' North and the longitude is same as that of the larger. The channel between these two islands may be 4 to 5 miles broad, and appeared to be free of rocks.

The large Botel island is about four leagues in circumference. It is high and may be easily perceived in fine weather from 15 leagues at sea. On the North point are to be seen rocks, which stand by themselves and appear quite like ships under sail, and to the SW, at a short distance there is a round islet. This island does not seem to be of the best sort. It is wooded in several places but the trees are low and stunted. Some few fields which are cultivated are to be seen. I know not which nation inhabits this island, but on account of its nearness to the island of Formosa, it may be supposed that it is the Chinese people.

The small Botel is nothing but a rock which is no more than half a mile in circumference. It is stripped of trees and the only verdure to be seen appears to be moss. At the South point, there is a reef which extends half a mile in this direction.

Réaumur's Thermometer +22°, Fahrenheit's thermometer 81°.

From Thursday 17ᵗʰ to Friday 18ᵗʰ 1791

99½

During the afternoon, having a light breeze at NE and at ENE, we made our way so as to pass the South point of the smaller of the Botel islands.

At 5 o'clock, the middle of both Botel islands, keeping in one with each other, bore NW¼N, which gives their respective situations.

At this moment, we directed our course to the Westward in order to examine the South point of the Island of Formosa before night came on, which indeed we saw soon after.

At 6 o'clock, the middle of Great Botel bore N½E, the smaller island NE, and the Southermost point of Formosa was in sight at West. We were about 3 leagues distant from Great Botel.

At ½ past 8 o'clock in the evening, having by estimation made 3½ leagues since we had taken the bearings, we found ourselves 6 leagues distant from Great Botel. We brought to upon the larboard tack under double reefed top-sails, her head to ESE.

Having come on deck at midnight, I was much surprised to find that the currents had carried us with great violence to the NNE and to the NE, and that we now found ourselves no more than a mile from Great Botel for we could perceive the breakers though the night was dark. We immediately bore away under only the top-sails, her head to the WSW. During the night, we saw many fires on shore. At 5 o'clock in the morning, with all the sail that we could crowd, we directed our course WSW, and at day-light, we caught sight of the island of Formosa extending from West to NW¼W, distant by my estimation 6 leagues. The middle of Great Botel bore ENE. We continued to steer WSW with a fresh wind at ENE in order to pass 2 leagues from the South point of Formosa.

At ½ past 9 o'clock, we caught sight of Villa-Rette at SW¼W, 1½ leagues distant. It is a ledge of rocks, lying very low above the surface of the water and upon which the sea breaks with terrible violence. It lies South ½ West and North ½ East, with the South point of Formosa at a distance of 2½ or 3 leagues following the bearings we took, and not 5 leagues distant, as laid down on all the charts. The latitude is 21° 44' or 45' North.

At ½ past 10 o'clock, the South point of Formosa bore North, distant 2 leagues, and Villa-Rete S¼SW, about ¾ of a league distant. At noon our latitude by observation was 21° 48' North. Our longitude computed from our last observations was found to be 241° 30', from which point we took our departure.

At the same moment, the South point of Formosa bore ENE½ North, the Westermost point in sight of the same island bore N¼NW, distant 4 or 5 leagues from the nearest land.

The South point of Formosa lies exactly in latitude 24° 52' North, and in longitude very near 241° 18' West, which agrees intirely with that which is ascribed to it by Mr d'Après in his general chart of India. I will say that it is falsely laid down in all of the charts I had before me.

This point is very low, and at the extremity a reef appeared to extend near half a mile out to sea.

During all the time that we had found ourselves East of this point, the currents had carried us NE. After doubling the point, the currents ran very strong to the Westward.

At 11 o'clock in the morning, we steered W¼NW.

The island of Formosa is in general high and there are mountains to be seen very much like the Peak of Teneriffe in height, but upon which I saw no snow. In the West part, there are great openings which appeared perhaps to be bays. I know not who distinguished this island with its name, I observed only that the mountains and the hills were very little wooded and the prospect was not in any way pleasing with regard to the verdure which a great part of the high islands of the South Seas possess.

Réamur's thermometer +22°, Fahreheit's thermometer 81°.

From Friday 18ᵗʰ to Saturday 19ᵗʰ November 1791

103

At 4 o'clock PM, I directed our course to WNW.

We saw a great quantity of birds, a large fish of the ray species, butterflies and dun-flies.

During the morning, we frequently passed the bones of cuttlefish.

During this day, we had a wind, more or less fresh, which varied from NE to SSE, attended frequently with rain.

At 11 o'clock, we met with a squall at NNE of which the violence obliged us to furl all the sails excepting the staysail. It was attended with thunder and hard rain. At noon, we were prevented from observing the latitude, it was by reckoning 22° 17'.

Our longitude was 243° 11'.

Réamur's thermometer +22°, Fahrenheit's thermometer 81°.

In sight of China

From Saturday 19ᵗʰ to Sunday 20ᵗʰ November 1791

134¾

During the afternoon, the wind settled at NNE blowing a fresh gale with overcast weather.

We saw large birds of the crane species.

At ½ past 4 o'clock, the wind beginning to blow high with squalls, we took two reefs in the top-sails.

At midnight we sounded and had 22 fathoms over a sandy bottom of very fine grey sand. At 4 o'clock, we had 25 fathoms over the same bottom.

At 10 o'clock in the evening, being by reckoning in the latitude of Pedro Blanco, I had directed our course to the Westward.

At 7 o'clock, we saw the coast of China at NW, at a distance of about 7 leagues. Soon after, we saw two Chinese junks or fishing boats towards which we steered in order to get a pilot for Macao. When we were at a small distance from them, we fired a gun, but seeing that they did not mind us, I sent the yawl along-side. The officer in command of the yawl brought back a man and I was never able to make him understand that our intention was to go to Macao and that would he carry the ship there, I dismissed him. While we were lying to, we sounded and had 30 fathoms over a fine grey sand.

During the morning, we passed a great quantity of boats. I no more sent to them, for after passing Pedro Blanco I imagined that I would not be in want of pilots.

At noon, having been prevented from observing the latitude, it was 22° 33' North by reckoning, and the longitude, 245° 33'.

Réamur's thermometer +22½°, Fahrenheit's thermometer 80°.

From Sunday 20ᵗʰ to Monday 21ˢᵗ November 1791

89½

During the afternoon, several boats made the signal as if to bring off a pilot, I sent the yawl but once again to no purpose.

At ¼ past 5 o'clock PM, the coast extended from W¼NW to NNW½N. We were at a distance of 8 leagues from the nearest land.

At 2 and at 6 o'clock, we sounded and had 25 fathoms over a grey sandy bottom. As soon as night came on, we plyed to Southward.

At midnight, we sounded and had 45 fathoms over a muddy bottom, we put about at NW. At 4 o'clock, we had 35 fathoms over a bottom of very fine muddy sand, and at 7 o'clock, 26 fathoms, same bottom.

During the night, the wind was variable from ENE to NNE, attended with violent gusts of wind and rain. We passed several boats.

At day-light, the coast stretched from N¼NE to West. We were at a distance of about 8 leagues. At 7 o'clock, we steered West ½ South. A quarter of an hour after, we caught sight of Pedro Blanco, which bore WSW 8° W, distant 5 leagues. We steered thus WSW to double it by the South. This rock has a form very much like sugar-loaf, it appears to be whitened in many places I believe by the dung of birds.

On account of the overcast and cloudy weather which is found to prevail in these parallels, ships which come to China from the West, I mean the East, are frequently not able to observe the latitude. In order not to lose time and be prevented from taking the bearing of Pedro Blanco, they must examine the coast of China, at a distance of 5 or 6 leagues, and they will seldom fail of seeing it, for it may be caught sight of easily at a distance of 5 leagues. At ½ past 9 o'clock, it bore North, distant two miles. Our latitude by reckoning was at this moment 22° 33' North, and our longitude 246° 25' West, or 113° 35' East. That laid down in the chart of Mr D'Après was 113°, which is proof that we had been carried 35' to the Westwards since our departure from Formosa.

At 10 o'clock, we brought to in order to make a visit to several of the junks and attempt to bring on board a pilot, but to no purpose. We purchased fish, which the Chinese in general salt after having taken them.

At ½ past 11 o'clock, having caught sight of a boat a-head, we steered towards it. When we were at a short distance, we brought to and the boat performed the same movement. I sent a boat and he who seemed to be the Commander told the officer to return to the ship and that he would follow with his vessel, which he hauled out immediately. When they came on board, I saw with much concern that the two men who had given us to understand that they could take the ship to Macao, would speak only Chinese. But after putting several questions by signs to them in regard of the course, to which they replied with the greatest exactness, I resolved to keep on with them and there was nothing more but the question of the price. They began by demanding 100 pieces of eight. At length they consented to 70, after having five or six times returned on board their boat. This was indeed a most immoderate expence, but we had fine weather which was favourable to sailing onward, and so I believed it unnecessary to look too narrowly into it. I asked if they would decrease the price if I took on board only one of them, having replied no, they both remained on board. They had a mind to be paid beforehand. When they received the pieces of eight, they tried them all with a nail in order to see if they were not false. I am convinced that had there been two or three boats of pilots and had they been in competition, we should have been carried to Macao for less than thirty pieces of eight.

From Monday 21st to Tuesday 22nd November

51

At half past noon, we filled the sails. The pilots made us ply to windward to the Westward. The weather was hazy and the wind at NNE. At ½ past 1 o'clock, Pedro Blanco bore ENE½N, distant about 4 leagues. At 4 o'clock, we caught sight of the coast of China, Single Island bearing North ½ East, a rock which resembles a ship named Pick Rock by Mr Dalrymple,[237] bearing North 8° East, and the Grand Lema WSW½W.

At a quarter past 5 o'clock, the pilots made us come to anchor opposite the bay, the depth of water 18 fathoms over a muddy bottom.

The island of Single bore NE½E, another island to the North of this last is not named on the chart of Mr Dalrymple, and was called by the pilots Teccosouhou, it bore NE¼N, the West point of the deep bay bore NW½N, the East point, NNW½W, the Grand Lema (named Tamcome by the Chinese) bore SW. Our distance from this last was about 7 leagues, and 3 leagues from the island of Single, we were 2 leagues from the land nearest to us.

This part of the coast is quite high and possesses no other sort of vegetation but an indifferent kind of moss.

During the night, we had very violent gusts of wind at NNW, attended with rain. Towards midnight, a most extraordinary change of the temperature took place. The thermometer which had kept at 18° until this moment, fell upon a sudden to +11°, which occasioned sudden cold. We were in consequence almost all laid up with colds. Our pilots who were dressed in nothing but linen, asked us for cloaks. At ¾ past 6 o'clock, we got under sail by the direction of the pilot with a fresh wind from North and NNE. We steered WSW and SW¼W, ranging along near the South part of the island of Poo Toy. At ¾ past 9 o'clock, it bore NNW and NNE, at a distance of half a mile. The Grand Lema and the other islands which lie to the West, extended from SE¼S to SW, the island of Lintin from W¼WS, Chi-Chow W½ S, the Peak of Lantao bearing WNW 3° N at the same moment.

---

237 Fleurieu (op. cit., Volume 2, p. 89) indicates that Marchand was using Alexander Dalrymple's *Chart of a part of the Coast of China*, which had been published in D'Après's *Neptune Oriental*.

We steered hauling our wind, it being the pilot's intention to sail along the coast of the South part of the island of Lantao. But as we were abreast of the Island of Lamina, the wind having varied to NNW and NW, permitting us neither to range along the coast nor to pass to windward of Lintin, we bore away to the leeward of this island in order to pass between it and the Sa-Moan Islands. To the North of Lintin, two small shoals are to be seen close to the surface of the water which are not laid down upon the chart of Mr Dalrymple. The first is about three cables length from the land and the other, half a mile. I do not believe them to be dangerous, and the pilots said the same. At the South point of this same island, there is small islet to which we can approach but at a distance of half a cable's length on account of some rocks under the water.

To the North of the Sa-Moan Islands, several large islets are to be found which are not laid down on the chart of which I have made mention.

The wind blowing a hard gale with hard gusts of wind made our navigation dangerous among so many islands.

The whole of the coast, from the deep bay to the Island of Poo Toy, is scattered all over with small islands which can be approached very near for we ranged along them at no more than a distance of a mile.

From Tuesday 22ⁿᵈ to Wednesday 23ʳᵈ November 1971

After having passed Lintin Island, we hauled our wind in order to pass leeward of the Chi Chow Islands. Mr Dalrymple has laid down only one Chi-Chow island, there are however three. We continued to stand to the West, with the wind at NNW, by the direction of the pilot. But perceiving two shoals a-head which were only a cable length's distant, I gave orders to veer, the strength of the wind not permitting us to tack. I then asked the pilots why they had not informed me and what their intention was in making so near an approach to the rocks. They answered that when I gave orders to veer away, at this same moment they were preparing to do the same. After changing the tack, they directed us to make for the Chi Chow Islands, South of which we came to anchor at ¼ past 3 o'clock in 13 fathoms over a moderate soft, muddy bottom.

The middle of the Chi Chow Islands bore NNE½E, Chook-Chow Island SSW½S, Tsou Island SE½S, the middle of the channel between these two islands bore S¼SE, the Peak of Lan Tao bore N¼NE, the island of Laf-sam-mee bore NW, the Westermost of the Sa-moan Islands bore SSE½E, and island of Potoe, West. We were at distance of one mile from the Chi Chow Islands. It is to be observed that I have kept the names which are to be found on the chart of Mr Dalrymple though my pilots frequently gave them others.

During the night we had a hard gale which blew NNE with rain. At day-light, the pilots did not think it proper to get under sail and told us that we should wait in this situation while the weather continued thus. All the islands along which we had coasted were barren in the extreme, and there was scarce any grass to be seen there.

During the morning, the boat from the sampane[238] of the pilots came along-side to inform us that they had lost a fluke of their anchor, which was made of wood, as was the custom on these vessels, and that would we give them a piece of wood in order to repair it, which we did.

It was very cold for the mercury in Réamur's thermometer kept at +9°. It may be judged from the circumstances that we were very sensible of it, for we had suffered great heat scarce two days before. I never would have conceived of such great cold in latitude 22°.

From Wednesday 23rd to Thursday 24th November 1791

The wind continued to blow a hard gale from NNE and NNW and we kept at anchor. At eleven o'clock in the morning, it was high water. At noon, the latitude by observations made very exactly was found to be 22° 3' 30", following the chart of Mr Dalrymple. After the bearings of our anchoring place, we were in 22° 11'. We observed that all the city of Macao, and all the islands of this chain, are laid down in the chart between 7 and 8' too much to the North.

From Thursday 24th to Friday 25th

During the afternoon and the night, we kept at anchor. At day-light, the wind blowing a gentle gale at North and the ebb just beginning, we got under sail by direction of the pilots. We stretched to the Eastwards towards the Island of Lintin. At ½ past 7 o'clock, we tacked and stood to the West. We coasted along the islands of Chi Chow and Laf-Sam-mee on the South side, at a distance of about half a mile. The wind now blowing a hard gale, we handed the top-gallant sails. The pilots directed us to work to windward as much as it was possible to do, in order to pass very near to the South of the Island of Chuctaan, which we doubled soon after. We next sailed onward to pass between the two small islands of Tai-lock and Sy-lock. In the middle of the passage between these two islands, there is a small rock which we passed on the larboard side. We coasted very near along the island of Sy-lock, that is to say within a musket shot, for the strait between it and the small rock is no more than two cables length broad. To the Eastward of Sy-lock, there is small islet to which one must not draw near for about ¾ of a cables length

---

238 King gives a detailed description of a Chinese sampane in Volume 3 (*Voyage to the Pacific Ocean*, op. cit., pp. 427–428): *These boats are the neatest and most convenient for passengers I ever saw. They are of various sizes, almost flat at the bottom, very broad upon the beam, and narrow at the head and the stern, which are raised and ornamented; the middle where we sat, was arched over with a roof of bamboo, which may be raised or lowered at pleasure; in the sides were small windows with shutters, and the apartment was furnished with handsome mats, chairs, and tables. In the stern was placed a small waxen idol, in case of gilt leather, before which stood a pot containing lighted tapers made of dry chips, or matches, and gum.*

from it, upon sounding, we found but five fathoms, soon after we had 7 or 8, over a muddy bottom still.

A ship may pass very close Northward of the rock of which I have made mention, and which lies in the middle of the channel between Tai-lock and Sy-lock. But the channel between the rock and Tai-lock is very dangerous. The pilots gave us to understand that it was necessary to be well acquainted with the channel between Tai-lock and Potoe, for this last is bordered by rocks.

At 10 o'clock, we entered the great Road of Macao. At 11 o'clock, we tacked and stood to the Eastward, and at ½ past eleven o'clock, we came to anchor in 5 fathoms over a an oozy bottom of mud, which was not a very good anchoring place. The city of Macao bore WNW½W, distant 2 leagues, Lintin island NNE½E, and the Peak of Lantao bore ENE½N.

From Friday 25th to Saturday 26th November

No sooner had we anchored than we hauled out the longboat with an intention of going the next day to Macao. At day-light, I left the ship accompanied by three of my officers. On landing, I was conducted to the Governor's house by a soldier. The reception which I met was not unkind, but quite cold, in consequence most likely of his circumspection in regard to the Chinese governor. After receiving the compliments as was the custom, I requested to learn the method of procuring fresh provisions. I was directed to Mr Bourgogne, a Frenchman who was resident in Macao, and who in past times had been the supercargo of the Anver's Company's. It must be observed, in justice to his conduct, that he was of great service to us in everything which lay in his power.

Upon taking leave of Mr Bourgogne, we made a visit to a French priest who was procurator of the missions of China, Cochin China and of others. His reception of us was one of great kindness and which I will never forget, for I was received into his house with every mark of attention, as were my officers, during the whole of our stay in this city. All that can be expected of a most civil and honest man was to be found in him, that is, manners plain and unaffected, great hospitality and lofty conversation without pedantry, a good table with no excess, the greatest marks of attention with no importunity. These were the means by which this agreeable clergyman made his hearty welcome of us. But I was most struck by the quietness of his life within his household, which was of an exemplary character. His servants, subjected to no strict discharge of religious duties, heard the prayers and mass on Sundays and on Holy-days. I conclude by observing that this would be a most happy retreat if the cares and the dangers of a worldly kind did not come to trouble the quietness of the place. On the one hand, and which draws the greatest attention, there is the jealousy of the Portuguese missionaries and the vexation of the Chinese, who see the priests as forming a seminary from within which the teaching of a religion forbidden in their country, will be occasioned. On the other hand, the confusion which has been occasioned in France, has caused great fear within the seminary, of an entire forsaking of it by the religious order.

Though these reasons have troubled the most cheerful countenances, I never did perceive anything of their trouble and, only on account of the confidence which they placed in us, did we learn of it. In addition to this, Mr L'Etondas, who is the procurator of the establishment, is much esteemed by all the honest and respectable citizens in this place, which is a great sign of the favour which he and the establishment inspire.

Soon after landing on shore, I learned that the Emperor of China (Tienlong) had prohibited since six months, the introduction of all furs of any kind in his country. This was most unfavourable to my designs, and my situation at this time was very critical, for I knew not where to go in order to be rid of those skins that I had. I learned that the Spanish had been obliged to carry back with them more than three thousand otter skins which they had brought to Macao, and which they had proposed to sell in Canton. The cargo of Mr Meares, taken by the Spanish on the North West coast of America, was to be found in the ware-houses of Macao, where the seals of the Mandarins had been affixed. This was also the case of the furs of another English vessel. The price of these articles had been so lowered that the otter skins of the finest sort, which in January 1791 had been purchased for 40 to 60 pieces of eight, the following year their price was 13 or 14.

Each gave a different reason for the prohibition. Some supposed it to be on account of the dispute between the Emperor and the Empress of Russia, which had occasioned the proclamation of the prohibition, with an intention to remove the branch of commerce which is most profitable to her subjects. Others say that the Mandarins in times past, having purchased a great quantity of furs at high prices, and which they had not yet disposed of, seeing the lowered price of this article and the competition of furs which were yet to come in the course of this year, feared very great losses. This had directed the Emperor to this prohibition, for since several years the Europeans had taken away a great quantity of tea and other merchandize by the sale of skins alone, and that the want of ready money was now being felt in Canton. However, upon mature consideration of the determination to take in so dangerous a situation, I resolved to remain in Macao and to dispatch a letter to Mr Blondi at Canton, to whom I had been recommended. I informed him of our present situation and begged that he should tell me of any measures to be taken for the sale of my furs, and what was his opinion of our situation. Knowing that Mr Pignatel, supercargo of the ship *Liberty* of Marseilles, Captain Guérin, who frequently had been a particular friend to us, I wrote to them about this same subject.

I myself was of the opinion that on account of the prohibition, the existence of which I have no doubt, it was intirely against the interests of my owners to go to Wampu. The very small quantity of furs I had, once sold by smuggling, which is a very dangerous practice and difficult to do, the sum collected would scarce amount to the excessive duties which the Chinese levy in the Tygris, and of which everyone has knowledge. I resolved nonetheless to await the answers from Canton before making any determination. The custom is that the European vessels, immediately upon their arrival in Macao Road, which is a little unsafe, take on board a pilot to direct them to Wampu. The Mandarins, observing my stay in the Road without asking for one, enquired of the Portuguese governor the reasons thereof, who then sent a sepoy with whom I went to his house. He asked if my intention was to go up to Wampu or to continue on my way. I answered that this was a private concern, and that meanwhile my masts had received some damage and I desired to repair them. He told me then of the Mandarins demand and recommended that I should proceed in such a manner so as not to occasion any disagreements to them, which I promised to do. As I had foreseen all these difficulties, I had got down the top-gallant masts and the lower yards.

It is to be observed that the Mandarins would perhaps have had no objection to our stay at Macao, had they not been informed by the sampanes which came along-side the ship, and by the pilots, of my return from the North West coast of America with furs of which they hoped to prevent the sale. As we had come to China from the West, and we had lost a day, I changed the date and instead of Saturday 26th, I counted Sunday 27th November.

From Sunday 27th to Monday 28th November 1791

After having got on board some fresh provisions, I departed and arrived along-side at ½ past 7 o'clock PM. I had not been able to procure neither meat nor bread. We could purchase nothing without the assistance of the *comprador* or broker, who being obliged to share his profits with the Mandarins, cheats with impunity. I had learnt that two vessels leaving the Tygris and bound for Europe, would come to this place the next day. I prepared in consequence letters for my employers which were put into their hands forthwith.[239]

---

239 Gannier (*journal*, op. cit., p. 471) here suggests that it was by this method that news of the discovery of the Revolution Islands reached France. Fleurieu (op. cit., Voume 2, p. 102) specifies that the House of Baux, having received a chart of these newly discovered islands, informed the National Assembly four and a half months before Marchand reached Toulon: *During the Solide's stay in Macao road, three English-East-Indiamen passed by without stopping, and continued their route in order to proceed to Europe. Captain Marchand availed himself of this opportunity of writing to his owners, and of addressing to them the particular chart of the Iles de La Revolution which he had discovered, on the 22d of June 1791, to the North-West of the group of Las Marquesas de Mendoça. We are certain that this chart reached France, and that the House of Baux laid it at the feet of the National Assembly upwards of four months and a half before the* Solide's *return; for on the 17th of April 1792, the chart was presented to that assembly, which decreed that honourable mention should be made of it in the verbal-process of that day.* *

**Captain Chanal has procured, from the Archives of the Republic, an extract from this verbal process, which is transcribed from the original that he put into my hands.*

Archives of the French Republic.

"*Extract from the verbal-process of the National Assembly of the 17th of April 1792, 4th year of Liberty;*

A Member presents to the Assembly a chart of several islands, newly discovered in the Indian seas by the Sieur

From Monday 28ᵗʰ to Tuesday 29ᵗʰ November 1791

During this day, we had a heavy wind at NNE attended with a very strong rippling. During the night we perceived that the ship had dragged the anchors although we had 65 fathoms of cable out. I gave orders to bear away 50 fathoms more. Seeing that the ship kept driving, we moored with an other anchor and she held fast. The ship had driven more than ¾ of a league.

From Tuesday 29ᵗʰ to Wednesday 30ᵗʰ

Towards ½ past 10 o'clock, the weather moderating, we got under sail with the flood in order to come to anchor more to the North, near the place we had left. After making two boards, we anchored in 5 fathoms over a soft muddy bottom.

The city of Macao bore W 8° S, the Eastern extremity of Mountain Island bore SW¼S, Potoe Island bore SSE ½ E, the Western extremity of Grand Ladrone bore S¼SE and the Peak of Lantao bore ENE½E. We were at a distance of about 1 league from the nine islands.

In the morning, I went ashore with the intention of remaining there until the answer to the express I had sent to Canton was received, and in order to attempt to sell if possible some few furs by smuggling. I spoke to more than twenty Chinese merchants who in past times were engaged in this commerce. They all told me that the prohibition was of too severe a kind, the Mandarins desiring to keep a strict hand over the whole, they would be hung if the fraud was discovered. Every day, visits were made to their houses, which prevented them from making such purchases. I was now without hope from this moment of doing our business in Macao. During this day, an American brig from the North West coast of America, like ourselves, came to anchor in the bay. The Captain informed us that a great vessel had lost her boat near Berkley Sound, and that the crew, amongst which was the second Lieutenant, had been murdered by the natives, which is a strong proof of the precaution which it is necessary to take with these savages.

He told us that on his return from the coast he had put in at one of the Sandwich Islands, and that two seamen who had deserted from an English ship, and who had lived for the whole period amongst the natives, had made their escape to the ship. I had occasion to see these two seamen and I learned from them that the Sandwich Islanders eat their enemies, whom they take as prisoners during their battles. They had had occasion to be present several times during such a horrible feast. Thus the dispute into which Mr King has entered, contrary to Mr Cook who

---

Marchand, of Marseilles, commander of the ship Solide dispatched to the South Sea, by Messers. J. and D. Baux, ship-owners; he moves that honourable mention should be made of this offer. The proposition is decreed. Collated and found conformable to the original deposited in the Archives of the French Republic, by me. Keeper of the Archives; in witness whereof I have signed and caused to be affixed the seal of the said Archives. Paris, fifth Ventose, year five of the French Republic one and indivisible. Signed to the original, Camus.

was of the opinion that the Sandwich Islanders were indeed cannibals, is now at a certain end if the accounts of eye-witnesses in favour of the arguments of Captain Cook, are to be referred to. This is indeed a proof of how fine an observer this great man was.

Immediately after these two men had deserted from their ship, and had made known to the natives their desire to remain amongst them, they were each given a wife and some land to cultivate food for their sustenance. They told me that in the Sandwich Islands a great quantity of pearls could be procured if the natives are encouraged to fish for them. During their stay there, they had collected twelve hundred pearls which were of rather a good quality, though they had not taken any particular care, for they affirmed that they had meant to spend the remainder of their lives on the island for want of an opportunity to leave it.

The American captain had on board two young Sandwich islanders who of their own accord had embarked with him. He had departed from Boston to engage in the fur trade, which he had previously done three times. He had like us put in at the Marquesas.[240] Though there was no Surgeon on board, and though he had in his possession few medicines, he had lost but his second Lieutenant some few days after his departure. Since then, he had had very few men lying ill. It is true to say that he had but twenty two men altogether, all of a robust constitution of body and less than 36 years of age thereabouts. However, his arrival here was fortunate indeed for the Captain was attacked by a violent fever and his recovery was despaired of. The officer who came on board gave a most terrible description of the malady and the effects of his being out of his senses. As the Surgeon was on shore, the officer in command sent the second Lieutenant in order to supply the remedy, which worked wondrously well and with great effect in a very short time. I had occasion to meet with him on shore three or four days afterwards.

He was not surprised to learn of the prohibition of furs. He said he had a quite a good quantity of them.

From Wednesday 30th November to Thursday 1st December 1791

We had a light breeze during this day. The ships of English Company left the Tygris and took on board our packets.

From Thursday 1st to Friday 2nd

In the morning of the 2nd, when the longboat was about to depart in order to come on shore, the watch, perceiving that a seaman had thrown on board a bag, which seemed to contain some object, asked to see it. Two large pieces of otter skin were found inside. One of the men had thrown the bag on board, and an other had received it. The officer in command obliged all the men to come on board the ship

---

240 Fleurieu identifies the ship in question as the *Hope*, captained by Ingraham (see Gannier, *journal*, op. cit., p. 473).

once again and gave orders for a search. Two pieces were found in the chest of another man, who said that he had them from someone on board ship. This person denied the thing and we could not convict him of it. As it was of the first importance to punish such misdemeanours, the three men who had been found out and convicted, were put in irons. I have forgot to say that upon our arrival at Norfolk Sound, I had expressly prohibited by a call, all members of the crew to engage in the fur trade for themselves. My owners had given me such orders and I had taken it upon myself to put them in execution.

During the morning, I received an answer from Mr Blondu who informed me that the prohibition of furs was indeed in existence, as I had learnt upon my arrival at Macao, and that it would be impossible to sell them at Canton without the running of the greatest risk, and that the sum from the sale of the furs, of which I had sent him the particulars, would not be fully sufficient for the very high taxes that we would be obliged to pay in the Tygris. In consequence, I had better continue our route in accordance with the orders of Messers. Jn and Dd Baux. He ended by saying that he had received no letter from the owners that year, neither for himself nor for myself, which surprised me greatly for I could not conceive that the owners (most particularly mine, whom I know to be very particular), who perfectly know their ship to be in in China at this moment, should not write not only to myself but also to the person of whom I would likely expect some assistance. After reflection, I concluded that the letters had been lost. I could not believe that it was for want of opportunity for the *La Royale Elisabeth* who was at Canton, had departed from Lorient in April, bound directly for China.

I received also a letter from Mr Pignatel who laid down the same as Mr Blondi.

Upon much consideration, I made a determination very willingly on the advice of Mr Pignatel, with whom I was in accordance. I did not however neglect any opportunity to attempt to sell all, or a part of the furs in my possession at Macao, but in vain.

From Friday 2ⁿᵈ to Saturday 3ʳᵈ November (sic) 1791

During this day we had a very light wind at NNE. After having taken the resolution to depart for Isle of France as soon as it was possible, I immediately set the men to make water. But as the watering place was to be found in the Typa, a distant part of the country, I requested of the French Captain, who was in the service of the Portuguese, that he come along-side and assist us in coming to anchor in a more commodious place, which he promised most willingly to do the next day.

The information I had collected at Macao, as well as my own remarks, have furnished me with several observations concerning this city which will perhaps be welcomed here.

Macao is quite a pretty city, built upon a small peninsula of land which is joined to another larger peninsula by a narrow piece of sand which is very low. It is commanded to the North and to the South by hills which are of a moderate height, the city itself is situated on the top of a small hill which rises with a gentle slope. It is perhaps five miles in circuit. The houses there are fine enough though they are not of very noble design. To the Northward and to the Southward, it is enclosed within a wall which is seven feet in thickness and it is flanked with some few bastions incapable of affording any great resistance. Four forts and some batteries protect it. The streets, narrow and badly paved, are not ornamented with any building deserving of that name. The churches, as in any of the Spanish or Portuguese colonies, are well situated and are of a fine appearance. I perceived the church of St Paul built by the Jesuits. The front is very high and quite finely built. A staircase of about 130 steps leads to the entrance, which is about 300 feet in diameter and which ornaments it. The interior is covered in pictures which are very much in want of taste or fancy. The seminary is as large, spacious and convenient. Several Chinese who are converts, and some of the Holy orders, are in residence there. What is the most striking inside the church are two pulpits which I believed to be designed for controversy. There is but one single public place, which is of a triangular form and not very spacious. It is to be found in front of the palace, which is a fine building and in which the Senate assembles. There is no promenade, excepting on the quay along the shore to the East of the city, and which ends at the North in a green plot ornamented with turf but no shade. The market-place is the most convenient of places for the accommodation of the inhabitants. It is at least 720 feet square. Well-kept cart-houses afford the tradesmen and the buyers shelter in the case of bad weather. They are at all periods furnished with vegetables, fresh and dried fish, meat, in general pork (for mutton and beef are very scarce) and fruit. However, as I have already made mention, the price of the provisions we saw we found to be exorbitant. Strangers are obliged to engage a *Comprador*, who being plundered himself by the Mandarins, lays the fault of all his troubles, upon the strangers themselves. Their shops are variegated in appearance although they are not furnished with all the commodities which are to be found in Canton. Their work houses, in particular those of the carpenters, are proof everywhere of the activity of this nation. I saw there a company of jugglers, whose tricks I did not find surprising in the least, excepting that of swallowing the blade of a sword without an edge and which was about 15 to 16 inches in length and one and a half inches in breadth. I was not much surprised nonetheless, for I had seen the same being done on the Coromandel coast.

The government of Macao is under the immediate subordination of the Viceroy of Goa and is composed of a Senate, which is noble and most powerful, the President of which is a Governor who has at his disposal two votes. He possesses no other authority here than the utmost discipline of his soldiers, who are either black men, mulattos or white men, and who are no more than one hundred and fifty in number. The Bishop equally disposes of two votes, but the other clergymen, who may possess some influence within the Senate, have only an indirect authority which is in consequence of the power they exercise in the private houses. The Senators are elected every two years.

Nothing I can say will make better known the[241] abjection in which the Portuguese languish at Macao than the account of what had occurred two days before our arrival and during the whole of our stay there. The day before we came to anchor, a man from Manilla had been put to death for he had killed with his knife three amongst several Chinese who had insulted and abused him. As the Europeans have become accustomed to giving up to the Mandarins any man guilty of whatever crime, there was no further application on this subject. In this particular case of three murders, the Mandarin of Macao affirmed that four men must be brought to him, this number he had then reduced to three saying, despite proofs of the contrary, that three men at least were necessary in order to kill three Chinese. The Senate held a council to consider the question and resolved, at the first sitting, that such a request was clearly unjust and could not be complied with. They informed the Mandarin of their refusal. This last persisted in his demands and threatened to leave the city unprovided, and to cut off all means of communication (method which the Chinese always have recourse to in case of disputes with the Portuguese). The Governor, who is nothing more than the President of the Senate, showed the resolution which redounded to the honour of his nation. Although I have to say with regret, that another Senator proclaimed that, in order not to provoke expressions of anger on the part of the Chinese, they should give up the number of men which the Mandarins had demanded of them. Some others appeared to be nearly of the same opinion. But the greatest part of them, amongst whom was the Governor, stood up very strongly against this opinion and declared that they would rather bury themselves in solitude within the ruins of their city, than consent to such a cowardly act. They finally gave up only the guilty man. It is with much trouble that we may moderate our indignation at seeing the base action of such an officer, who must work for the publick good and that of his country and that of its inhabitants. I desired very willingly that he would be given up to the Chinese himself, for he had approved of the sacrifice of innocents. Does not a government which trusts a part of it authority to those who are unworthy, deserve the reproach with which it is covered daily?

The insulting and criminal manner in which the meaner sort of Chinese conducted themselves with regard to the Portuguese Senate on the day of the execution of the man from Manilla, is yet another proof of the scorn with which they

---

241 Marchand takes up King's analysis of the situation: *On my arrival at the citadel, the fort-major informed. me, that the Governor was sick, and not able to see company; but that we might be assured of receiving every assistance in their power. This, however, I understood would be very inconsiderable, as they were intirely dependent on the Chinese, even for their daily subsistence. Indeed, the answer returned to the first request I made, gave me a sufficient proof of the fallen state of the Portugueze power; for, on my acquainting the Major with my desire of proceeding immediately to Canton, he told me, that they could not venture to furnish me with a boat, till leave was obtained from the Hoppo, or officer of the customs; and that the application for this purpose must be made to the Chinese government at Canton* (Voyage to the Pacific Ocean, op. cit., Volume 3, p. 421).

regard the former conquerors of the Indies. These officers of the nation were received with stones, and one amongst them, hurt very badly, came to us nonetheless, in danger of his life, upon the day of our departure. If he had then lost his life, it is very certain that no search for those guilty of the crime would have been undertaken.

Other such instances have happened several times, although this insult is directed at the Portuguese nation only by means of the representatives. The Governor, the garrison and the Senators are in the pay of the city itself, and in such a manner, the mother nation is saved all expence. It has happened sometimes that the Viceroy of Goa, drawing bills of exchange, has obliged the colony to pay forthwith, although the sum was certainly never to be reimbursed.

The language which is spoken here is Portuguese which is corrupted with the French, English, etc. of the worst kind.

The Portugeuse women are sequestered within lodgings and their fate may be compared with that of the sultaness. When they leave their houses, they are carried about in a kind of palanquin of a square shape and within which penetrates all the air which is necessary in order to prevent any suffocation. Those who are not rich enough to be carried are obliged to go about on foot, and are never without a veil.

They so little exercise their judgement, and are so ignorant of common practice, that they all of them, women or girls, yield quite willingly to demands made of them perchance by any over-bold man who is a fortune-hunter. They know not what it is to withstand the undertakings of a sex of whom they have no knowledge.

They being admitted to the table during the meals occasioned by weddings or other feasts (from what I have seen), they sit all together on one side, with the men on the other. They do not in any way contribute to increasing the agreeableness of the society. They seem rather to put a constraint upon it, and thus they leave it very promptly in order to withdraw into their apartments where they take tea and dance amongst themselves, while the men dance on their part with each other, which is an entertainment wanting in interest. The Portuguese do not engage in any retail commerce and do not possess any trade or art. They are too proud and lazy. They prefer to live wretchedly and with what is given to them by the government, or by begging charity than by any useful trade. Excepting the sail-makers, the caulkers and the carpenters, who are very small in number, no Portuguese has the wherewithal to maintain himself, save the sailors.

They depend altogether on the Chinese for their necessaries. Their weakened state with regard to the Chinese, the loss of their commerce which they had engaged in with great advantage on the coasts of Coromandel, of Malabar and of Bengal, are the necessary consequences of their indolence and of their dishonesty which is occasioned by their poverty. All the commerce of the merchants at Macao, the greatest part for the interest of the Chinese, is limited only to that carried out in Cochin China, to which place they import iron, nails and some weapons, and from which they export betel, rice, elephants' teeth, sapan wood for dyes. This commerce is not profitable and demands great management. When the stock of rice in China is reduced, they undertake sometimes expeditions to Manilla in order to procure some, which is profitable.

It is worth mentioning that every year the Senate fits out a ship of 3 or 400 tons bound for Timor. I have been informed, and even assured, that the profits to be had extend from 150 to 200 per cent. Iron, arms, lead, copper is carried thence.

Rice, elephants teeth, wood for dyes is brought back. The privilege of undertaking this commerce is limited to the Senate alone, but this last is careful to engage therewith the poor families and the merchants of the city, more or less. That is the greater the want of ability, the larger the interest, which is very well understood.

I asked of the Governor why, this expedition being so very profitable, he should not undertake more. He answered that this kind of commerce could not be extended further, for if more than one ship were sent to the place, they would feel a loss. Macao Road is very dangerous and the anchor will always drag if it blows a hard gale, unless two anchors are put to use, though this will frequently be not enough. We saw in the Typa itself, which affords very good shelter, ships with all their anchors in the sea driving onto the shore. But these may be set afloat again for the ships run aground upon mud. The Typa is an anchoring place situated three miles to the South of Macao, between four or five islands which afford it shelter from the wind and from the sea. Only the Spanish, the Portuguese and the King's ships may enter. Other ships may be received if they resolve to pay a considerable sum.

To the West of the city, there is a harbour named the Harbour of Macao, of which the entrance is situated to the South. It affords shelter from all the winds but there is so little depth of water that the large ships lay upon the mud and they are obliged to go to Typa when they wish to load. Those vessels of two hundred tons charge there their entire cargo. Excepting the Spanish, the other nations pay very large sums of money in order to enter this harbour. This advantage for the Spanish is a consequence of a particular agreement between these last and the Portuguese, who accord the Spanish the same advantages in all their colonies.

I have neglected my journal, to which I now return.

In the morning of the 3rd, before coming on board ship in order to change our place, I made a visit to the Governor in order to inform him of what was about to do. At his door, I found a negro who told me that he would enquire if his master would see me. Upon his return, he asked on his part what I wanted with him. I signified to him that he should tell his Master that I would not account for myself to a negro, and that it was with him in person that I wished to speak. I know not what effect this remark had but I was taken to him. I told him that my ship was not in a very commodious place for making water and I proposed to bring the ship to anchor near to the Typa. At this word, he jumped up once more and said that this was not possible to do for the Mandarins were already uneasy with regards to myself, and that we should give them no further object for concern. I observed to him that I did not intend to enter the Typa and had knowledge of the taxes which it was necessary to pay, and that I desired only come to anchor near the Easterly entrance in order take in fresh water. I gave him to understand that if Macao Road were free, and that I could come to anchor anywhere I pleased, he would nonetheless refuse me leave. I signified to him that I would do without, and that the step that I had taken was but a civility. He then told me that he was much troubled for the Mandarins had come to his house at every turn with regards to my ship and the reason for its presence in the Road. What is this vessel taking to Wampu? What business had I here in China? It is a smuggler who, attempting to delay, desires indeed to sell his furs. And other such talk. To all this, I replied nothing more than that it was necessary for me to take in water as I was in need of it. He finally concluded by saying that I should take my ship where I would, but that I should not make too near an approach to the Typa. During the morning I went on board with Mr Jocquet and Mr Brun. This last desired to go to the Isle of France and I agreed to his passage. He had come from Cochin China and had served the King for two years as Engineer. He had taken his departure for the King refused to pay.

From Saturday 3rd to Sunday 4th December 1791

At 3 o'clock PM, we got under sail with a gentle gale at North, at ½ past 5 o'clock we brought the ship to anchor abreast of the Eastern entrance of the Typa, in 5 fathom water over a muddy bottom, somewhat hard.

The city of Macao bore WNW½N, the extremity of the two islands forming the entrance to the Typa bore SWS 3° S and SW½W, the West point of the Grand Ladrone bore S¼SE 3° E. We were at a distance of about half a league from the land.

We immediately struck the masts and the main top-gallant yards.

At ½ past 11 o'clock in the evening, the wind blowing a hard gale at North, we perceived that we were driving, but upon mooring with a second anchor, she held tight.

From Sunday 4th to Monday 5th

During the afternoon we were employed in taking in water with the longboat.

I received that day a second letter from Mr Blondi, and another from Mr Pignatel, which confirmed me in the resolution which I had taken to go to the Isle of France.

At 6 o'clock, we saw a ship sailing out of the Tygris and recognizing it as being that of Mr Pignatel, I hurried to go along-side. Immediately upon seeing us hoist out my boat, he brought to in order to wait for me. I not know how to express the pleasure I had in embracing my countrymen and my friends after a voyage such as I just had made.

Mr Pignatel told me that had I arrived ten or twelve days before, he would have taken the ship to freight for Europe and would have given me himself 100 tons. He had delayed one day in taking his departure from Canton with regards to me, but that he had been able to do nothing more for all the supercargoes and the private persons who had engaged their capital. He concluded by advising that I continue on my way and that I remain in Macao for but a very short time, for the ships were not in a great degree of safety and the expence was excessive. Concerning the small quantity of iron and lead which I had, I should dispose of it with as much advantage at the Isle of France than in China where such commodities abounded. I had been sensible of all these reasons but was immediately much provoked on account of the freight of which I have just made mention, and for which profitable occasion I had arrived too late. However, after consideration, there was no reason to regret this delay for I could have taken on board, with such a large crew on board, only 200 to 500 tons to the value of £100 M. I was very certain that my entrance into the Tygris would have occasioned my employer the expence of at least 10 M pieces of eight for the taxes, the measurement of our vessel,[242] for the anchoring place and the victualling of the ship. This would have proved even less advantageous for it would have been impossible for me to dispose of the great quantity of tools and instruments of iron which I had on board.

From Monday 5ᵗʰ to Tuesday 6ᵗʰ December 1791

During this day, we continued to take in water and to make ready for sailing.

I had forgot to say that at the request of Mr Jocquet and Mr Le Brun, I released from irons the three men of whom I have before spoken.

From Tuesday 6ᵗʰ to Wednesday 7ᵗʰ December 1791

78¼

Completing our water at 3 o'clock PM, we hoisted in the longboat and determining to get under sail in the evening or during the night, we took up one of the anchors in the sea.

At 6 o'clock in the evening, Mr Le Brun who had secured a passage with us to Isle of France, and of whom I have already made mention, came on board. He reported that the Mandarins had taken note of our visits sometimes, once we were ashore, to Mr Jonquet. They had come to believe that we were there leaving our furs and that in consequence they had made a visit to his house with the Customs officers who made a most diligent search, which made me very angry for I had caused much trouble to a very honest man from whom I had had nothing but respect.

At 9 o'clock, the boat which I had sent ashore under the command of an officer in order to procure the last provisions, returned. All the vessels were hoisted in immediately and we hove in the cable. At ½ past 10 o'clock in the evening we

---

242 Dixon actually has to undergo this measurement process though . . . *this visit seems to be a mere matter of form, as they only measure from the foremast to the tassrel, and then athwart near the gangway, which certainly can give them but a very imperfect idea of a vessel's burthen: however they demand (I am informed) no less than a thousand pounds sterling, as a port charge, for this piece of mummery* (Dixon, op. cit., p. 296).

were under sail with the ebb and a gentle gale at N¼NE. At the same moment, the East point of Mountain Island bore SW, Cabaret Point bore WNW and Potoe Island bore E½S.

Until ¾ past midnight, we steered S¼SW and South. At this moment the South point of Grand Ladrone bore East, distant about 2 leagues. We took here our departure in latitude 21° 55' North and longitude 248° 38' West. After having taken this bearing, we directed our course S¼SE with the intention of striking soundings on Macclesfield or English Bank.[243]

During the morning, we had a fresh wind at NNE attended with a hard and short sea.

Latitude by observation North 20° 49'.
Longitude by reckoning 248° 25'.

Réamur's thermometer +18°, Fahrenheit's thermometer 73°.

From Wednesday 7th to Thursday 8th December 1791

160½

During this day, we had a breeze blowing a hard gale at NE attended with violent gusts and a very hard sea.

At 8 o'clock in the morning, we steered South under our four main sails and double reefed top-sails.

The variation of the compass by observation was 17' NE.

We saw tropic birds and sea swallows.

Latitude by observation North 17° 54'.
Longitude by reckoning 247° 56'.

18' more to the South than by reckoning.
Réamur's thermometer +22°, Fahrenheit's thermometer 81°.

From Thursday 8th to Friday 9th December 1791

168

A breeze blowing a hard gale at NE, violent gusts, hard sea running high.

---

243 Marchand decides to verify the soundings, as King does: . . . *being in latitude 18° 57', and longitude 114° 13', the wind veering to the North, we directed our course half a point more to Eastward, in order to strike soundings over the Macclesfield Bank. This we effected at eight in the evening of the 16th, and found the depth of water to be fifty fathoms, over a bottom of white sand and shells. This part of Macclesfield Shoals we placed in latitude 15° 51', and longitude 114° 20'; which agrees very exactly with the position given in Mr Dalrymple's map* (Voyage to the Pacific Ocean, op. cit., Volume 3, p. 449).

At ½ past 3 o'clock in the morning, reckoning that I was near the Macclesfield shoals, we sounded and found no bottom with a line of 80 fathoms. We steered S¼SW in order to gain the middle of the Bank. At 5 o'clock having sounded once again, we found 65 fathoms over a bottom of broken shells mixed with black and white gravel. I directed our course to the SW in order to gain Pulo Sapata.

Latitude by observation North 15° 18'.
Longitude by reckoning 248° 34'.

3' more to the North than by reckoning.
Réamur's thermometer +22°, Fahrenheit's thermometer 81°.

From Friday 9ᵗʰ to Saturday 10ᵗʰ December 1791

165
A breeze blowing a hard gale at NE, rainy weather and at intervals clear, a great swell from the NE.
We found one of the jars of oil belonging to the crew half-empty, and three supplies of biscuit and a barrel of rice, intirely spoiled.
We saw a great quantity of birds of diverse species and much floating wood.
The variation of the compass by observation of the azimuths 31' NW.

Latitude by observation North 13° 22'.
Longitude by reckoning 250° 35'.

Réamur's thermometer +22°, Fahrenheit's thermometer 81°.

From Saturday 10ᵗʰ to Sunday 11ᵗʰ December 1791

172¾
During this day, we had a breeze blowing a hard gale at NNE and at NE, attended with squalls at intervals. The sea remained very hard.
Many birds and much floating wood.

Latitude by observation North 11° 14'.
Longitude by reckoning 252° 40'.

4' more to the South than by reckoning.
Réamur's thermometer +22°, Fahrenheit's thermometer 81°.

From Sunday 11ᵗʰ to Monday 12ᵗʰ December 1791

127¾
At ¾ past 4 o'clock PM, reckoning that I was yet 25 leagues distant from the Three Brothers, following the chart of Mr Dalrymple (*Neptune*

Oriental),[244] we perceived them at WSW, distant 5 leagues. We immediately steered SW¼S in order to avoid them.

At 6 o'clock, they bore W 40° N at a distance of three leagues. We worked to windward on the larboard tack under the two top-sails close-reefed. But perceiving that we had fallen very much to the Southward, and fearing to meet with Pulo Sapata, we took in the courses. The Three Brothers are small, low islands. On the Northermost is a small hill which rises above the shore. On the North point and on the South point of these three islands, which seem to form together but two, according to the situation in which we found ourselves, we observed two small rocks separated from each other.

At the moment when I hauled close to the wind, we had a sounding of 80 fathoms over a bottom of red and black sand.

At midnight we saw Pulo Sapata bearing SW¼W, at about 2½ leagues.

At ¾ past midnight, it bore West, at one and a half leagues, from which we took our departure in latitude 10° 4' North and longitude 253° 1' West, following the situation assigned to this island by the *Connaissance des Temps* of 1788. After having taken this bearing, we steered in succession SSE, S½W, SSW½W in order to double the island and to avoid coming too near to it.

At 3 o'clock AM, I directed the course to SW. Having seen Pulo Sapata, I did not think it to much purpose to stand for Pulo Condor, but rather to proceed directly to Pulo Timon. We had been carried 26' to the Southward since noon the preceding day to three quarters past midnight.

Note. Following the chart of Mr Dalrymple (*Neptune Oriental*), Pulo Sapata lies in latitude in 105° 57' East of Paris. It is laid down in the *Connaissance des Temps* of 1788 in 106° 54', thus it is to be found 57' more to the Westward upon this chart. In consequence, I would by all means recommend to the navigators returning from China to take into account this difference without which, in making their way from Macclesfield Bank to Pulo Sapata, they will run the risk of finding themselves during the night at Three Brothers. This circumstance is one in which we should have found ourselves if we had not caught sight of them during day-light. Upon this chart, the same error is to be ascribed also to the situation of these three islands, for it was determined following that of Pulo Sapata. We had during this day a breeze which blew a hard gale at NNE and NE with violent gusts.

Latitude by observation North 9° 12'.
Longitude by reckoning 253° 44'.

4' more to the South than by reckoning.
Réamur's thermometer +22°, Fahrenheit's thermometer 81°.

---

244 The chart in *Neptune Oriental* (d'Apres de Mannevillette, 1775) is specifically Alexander Dalrymple's *A chart of the China Sea inscribed to Monfr. D'Apres de Mannevillette the ingenious author of the Neptune Oriental as a tribute to his labours for the benefit of Navigation and in acknowledgement of his many signal favours to Dalrymple.*

From Monday 12th to Tuesday 13th December 1791

136

A variable breeze from NNE to East blowing more or less hard, attended with continual rain and a smooth sea.

We saw many birds.

There was no variation of the compass.

Latitude by observation North 6° 53'.
Longitude by reckoning 255° 20'.

43' more to the South than by reckoning in two days.
Réamur's thermometer +23½°, Fahrenheit's thermometer 84°.

From Tuesday 13th to Wednesday 14th 1791

137¾

At noon, I directed the course to SSW½W. At ¾ past 11 o'clock in the evening, we sounded and found 49 fathoms, and at 6 o'clock in the morning, 50, oozy bottom.

During the whole of this day, we had a breeze blowing more or less a hard gale and varying from NE to SE¼E with overcast weather and rain at intervals.

We felt a suffocating heat.

We could perceive no variation of the compass.

Latitude by observation North 4° 40'.
Longitude by reckoning 256° 25'.

12' more to the South than by reckoning in two days.

As can be here seen, we had every day great differences to the South on account of the currents.

Réamur's thermometer +24½°, Fahrenheit's thermometer 86°.

From Wednesday 14th to Thursday 15th December 1791

97

At ½ past 1 o'clock PM, we caught sight of a ship at NW, going our way.

At ¾ past 5 o'clock in the evening, we sounded and found 45 fathoms over a soft bottom, at ½ past 3 o'clock in the morning, 36 fathoms, hard muddy bottom mixed with broken shells, and at 6 o'clock, 36 fathoms, same bottom.

At the same moment we caught sight of Pulo Timon stretching from SW¼S to South. The wind being at East and ESE, we worked to Southward in order not to fall in West of Pulo Pissang and of Pulo Aor, which we saw soon after, the first bearing South ½ W and the other SSE.

At 9 o'clock, the wind veered to South East, and perceiving that the currents had carried us very fast towards the passage between Pulo Timon and Pulo Pissang, we tacked and stood off NE.

The ship we had seen the preceding day was now 1½ leagues leeward of us. I believed she was the *Liberté*, Captain Guérin. At 10 o'clock, we had a violent squall from SSW which obliged us take in the top-sails. I took this opportunity to steer East and SE in order to avoid Pulo Timon and to be able to double Pulo Aor if the wind should shift again to East or to ESE.

After the squall, the wind settled at NW though the weather remained so dark and so rainy that we could no longer see the land.

At noon, not being able to determine the latitude by observation, it was 3° 23' N by reckoning. Our longitude by reckoning from Pulo Sapata was 256° 48'.

Réamur's thermometer +25°, Fahrenheit's thermometer 87°.

From Thursday 15ᵗʰ to Friday 16ᵗʰ December 1791

91½

At ¾ past 2 o'clock PM, the weather clearing a little, we took the bearings of the South point of Pulo Aor, distant 3 or 4 leagues.

From this point, we took our departure in latitude 2° 56' North and longitude 257° 34', following the *Connaissance des Temps*. By reckoning, our latitude was found to be at this moment 3° 17', and our longitude from Pulo Sapata, 256° 40' 30". We had thus had 21' of difference to the Southward in two days, and 53½' to the West since Pulo Sapata.*

> *Such a great difference in so short a time cannot be only on account of the defects in the charts which have falsely laid down Pulo Sapata with regard to Pulo Timon, for I directed my course towards this last following only its situation as determined in the same Connaissance des Temps, like that of Pulo Aor. I myself of course determined the situation of Pulo Timon, which is not to be found in the Connaissance des Temps, following that of Pulo Aor. Furthermore, I took several bearings at the same time of Pulo Timon, of Pulo Pissang and of Pulo Aor, and not one of these was in agreement with the charts of Neptune Oriental.*

At 10 o'clock in the evening, I directed the course to SSE in order to pass East of the Doogers Banks. During the whole of this day, we had a breeze varying from WNW to N, attended with rain. We saw a great quantity of snakes pass by the ship. They were yellow with black bands across. We also saw floating wood and plants which were still of a green colour.

Not being able to determine the latitude by observation, it was by reckoning 1° 46' North.

Longitude by reckoning 256° 55'.

Réamur's thermometer +22°, Fahrenheit's thermometer 81°.

From Friday 16ᵗʰ to Saturday 17ᵗʰ December 1791

109¾

Towards ½ past two o'clock PM, we caught sight of something on the surface of the water directly a head of us, and which appeared to be the wreck of a ship. We hoisted out the yawl. I was informed that it was a piece of bamboo near which there was a prodigious quantity of fish of all species. After hoisting in the yawl, we continued upon our way. While laying to, we had sounded and found 40 fathoms over muddy bottom.

At eleven o'clock in the evening we steered S¼SE, and at 2 o'clock SSW in order to fall in with Pulo Lingen.

At ¼ past 9 o'clock in the morning, we caught sight of a flat island bearing SSW, at a distance of about 7 leagues. At 10 o'clock, we lost sight of it on account of violent squalls all round the compass within one hour, and which obliged us to take in all our sails. At ½ past 10 o'clock, we sounded and found 20 fathoms over a bottom of muddy sand. I knew not what to make of this island in the hazy weather we had. By reckoning, it was very likely a part of Pulo Lingen, but we could see no other land to the West and thus I had some doubt of our true situation. I feared most of all, not having made any observations in order to determine our latitude since Pulo Aor, that we had been carried to the South by the currents.

At noon, we were yet again unable to observe the altitude on account of a thick haze, the latitude by reckoning was 0° 4', and our longitude, 256° 48'.

Réamur's thermometer +23°, Fahrenheit's thermometer 83°.

From Saturday 17ᵗʰ to Sunday 18ᵗʰ December 1791

33¾

The weather was hazy until 3 o'clock PM. At this moment, we caught sight of another small island bearing West ½ South, at a distance of about 6 leagues.

We steered thus S¼SW and SSW. At 5 o'clock, we directed our course to SW. Half an hour after, the watch shouted that land was in sight at SSE. I could not believe it to be a new land, our true position, of which I have already made mention, being very uncertain. We moored in 18 fathoms over a bottom of muddy sand mixed with broken shells.

The first island which we had discovered bore NW½W, and the second WNW. The last island we had seen extended from SSE to S¼SE.

Upon coming to anchor, we immediately perceived that the currents were setting to East about one mile per hour.

During the night, the winds varied from North West, attended with overcast weather and rainy with a swell from the NNW. At day-break, I immediately perceived that the islands we had seen the preceding day were Rigaudière Island and St Peter, and that the coast we had seen bearing SSE was that of Banca Island. We had thus been carried considerably farther to the Southward and to the East since seeing Pulo Aor.

At ½ past 7 o'clock in the morning, we got under sail with the help of a moderate breeze at NW¼N and NW. Immediately upon getting under sail, we worked to NE. Half an hour after, we tacked and stood to the West in order to attempt to gain the entrance of the Strait of Banca.

During the morning we sounded and found 18 to 19 fathoms over a bottom of sand and mud.

At noon, the coast of Banca stretched from SE½S and SW½S. We had a view of the Westermost of the two islands we had seen the preceding day and this morning, extending NNW½W.

Our latitude by observation was 1° 15' South.
The reckoning from Pulo Aor was found to be 20' South.

0° 55' difference South in 2½ days.

Longitude by reckoning from Pulo Aor 257° 3'.

Longitude determined from the bearing above, following the chart N° 49 of Mr D'Après, was found to be 256° 42'.
Difference East 0° 21'.

It can be seen that we were carried to the Eastward and to the Southward since Pulo Aor, whereas following the instructions of Mr D'Après, we had been upon our guard against a difference to the SW.

The part of the Island of Banca bearing SE½S was Point Pesant, and in consequence, the two small islands which we had seen to the NW could only be St Peter and Rigaudière. In this case Tolé Island is falsely laid down in the charts and must thus be found much nearer to these last two islands. However it be, these two islands, following the bearing which we have taken very exactly at different moments, lie N¼NW and NNW½N, about 13 leagues from Point Pesant on the Island of Banca.

From Sunday 18th to Monday 19th December 1791

13½

We had been directing our course along the shore of Banca Island since morning, it is very low near the sea but there are high mountains in the interior part of the country.

Towards ½ past three o'clock PM, having perceived that the currents were carrying us to the shore incredibly fast, and from which we were but no more than two leagues, we came to anchor in 16 fathoms over a red clay bottom which was exactly like the gum of which the glaziers make use. On sounding, we found a little sand and broken shells.

During the afternoon we had regular soundings from 17 to 19 fathoms over a bottom of sand, mud, shell and clay. Immediately upon coming to anchor, Point

Pesant bore E¼SE, an islet opposite the part of the shore where we had anchored bore SSE½E, distant 2 leagues. To the West of the islet, the shore formed a large opening. We also saw a hill which appeared to be the Westermost point of the island of Banca, it was perhaps Mount Monopin[245] bearing SW¼W, there was an islet in view bearing WSW½S.

We kept at anchor the whole day, the winds having settled at NW and blowing a hard gale attended with squalls and a great swell, though we did not think it to be the safest of anchoring places for the wind, as the sea and the currents, were setting straight towards the shore. But as I much depended upon the strength of our cables, I was quiet enough, though I meant to get under sail as soon as the wind permitted us to get clear of this coast.

While we were at anchor in this place, all the currents set to ESE at a rate of 1 or 1½ miles per hour.

Latitude by reckoning from the anchoring place South 1° 23'.
Longitude by reckoning W 256° 53'.

Réamur's thermometer +23°, Fahrenheit's thermometer 83°.

From Monday 19th to Tuesday 20th December 1791

11½

At 1 o'clock PM, the wind having shifted to NW¼W, we weighed. At ¾ past 1 o'clock, being under sail, we worked to windward, standing to the NE in order to coast along the shore while waiting for a wind in our favour to reach the Strait of Banca.

At ¾ past 4 o'clock, we caught sight of two small islands which we thought to be Rigaudière and St Peter.

At 6 o'clock, it falling calm and the currents setting to ESE, we came to anchor in 18 fathoms over a bottom of fine grey sand mixed with broken shells.

The island of Banca stretched from SSE to SW. The island of Rigaudière bore NNW and St Peter bore NW.

During the afternoon, we had soundings varying from 16 to 19 fathoms, same bottom, that is sometimes clay, sometimes ooze, sand and shells.

During the night, we had a hard gale at NW attended with squalls. The sea was running high and the ship pitched most violently. The current continued to set to East and ESE at a rate of 1½ miles per hour. At 7 o'clock in the morning, the cable was broke. We immediately let go another anchor and got on board the other, which we found broke near the clinch, which we attributed to the great pitching we had suffered during the night. We lost the anchor which had no buoy, but

---

245 This was called Hill by King and Dixon, and Mount by Portlock.

even this would not have saved it for it would have been impossible for the yawl to loosen the anchor on account of the high sea. We cut 60 fathoms of the cable which had broke in order to make rope yarn, gaskets and other articles which were become necessary to us.

As I desired to stow three anchors upon the bow to be ready always to come to anchor, we got another out of the hold, which was a work of great labour and time, for they were stowed at the very bottom. During the morning, we had a light wind at NNW attended with fine weather, the currents setting to ESE at a rate of two miles per hour.

From Tuesday 20th to Wednesday 21st December 1791

21¼

During the afternoon and the night, the wind blew a hard gale at NW and at NNW, attended with squalls and currents setting ESE at a rate of 1½ miles per hour.

Seeing that it was impossible for us to gain the Strait of Banca with the winds and current so unfavourable, and troubled by the loss of time, following the advice of my officers, I resolved to sail out by the channel or strait of Gaspar situated between Banca and Billiton.[246] In consequence, at ¾ past 7 o'clock in the morning, we got under sail and directed our course with a strong breeze at NW¼N.

This strait being very little, or not at all, visited by navigators, though a small chart of it is to be found in *Neptune Oriental*, and wishing to draw up one following our own observations, I desired Mr Le Brun, of whom I have already made mention, and Mr Chanal, the second Lieutenant, to take all the bearings answering to this object, examining thus the Banca coast as well as the strait itself during our passage through it, which was done most exactly.

In hoving up the anchor, we found one of the strands of the cable broke near the clinch. The sea had been hard and the pitching very violent during the night. Fortunately we were getting under sail at this time, one hour after wards we would perhaps have lost yet another anchor. We lost a lead of 80 pounds which had been kept in the sea in order to take notice should we drive nearer the shore.

At 9 o'clock, we steered SE to gain the coast of Banca.

During the whole of morning, we had soundings of 19 to 20 fathoms over a bottom of rocks and gravel.

At noon, Point Pesant, or the North of Banca, bore West 30° South and West 5° South and the Eastermost land SE¼S.

Latitude by reckoning S1° 29'.
Latitude by observation 1° 30'.

---

246 King, Portlock and Dixon all manage to sail through the straits of Banca.

1° difference South.

Longitude by reckoning W° 256° 28' or 103° 32' East.
Longitiude or bearing of the point of departure 256° 18' or 103° 42'.

10' difference East.
Réamur's thermometer +25°, Fahrenheit's thermometer 87°.

From Wednesday 21ˢᵗ to Thursday 22ⁿᵈ December 1791

46⁶/₁₀

At noon, we steered SSE, and then S½W and S¼SW to gain the coast of Banca, perceiving that the currents setting to the East were driving us away from it. We sounded and had 15 to 17 fathoms over sand and gravel.

At ¾ past 4 o'clock, Broken Point on the island of Banca bore South 30° W, the first island of this coast, to the East of this point extended from South 17° W to South 20° W, and the second island South 10° W to South 12° W.

At this moment, we plyed to windward on the larboard side in order to avoid some breakers which we saw to the Southward.

At 4 minutes past 5 o'clock, they were South 18° W, distant 2 or 3 miles. At 12' past 5 o'clock, we caught sight of more at North 15° E, distant 1½ to 2 miles.

We saw yet more at the same moment to the South 3° W, at a distance of 3 or 4 miles.

We bore away to the SE to avoid a fourth breaker directly a-head.

At 50 minutes past 5 o'clock, the first island to the East of Broken Point extended from South 43° to South 49° West, the second from South 38° to South 40° W.

At 6 o'clock, the breakers we had just seen bore South 67° E, at a distant of about 4 or 5 miles. Since ¾ past 4 o'clock, we had had soundings of 12 to 14 fathoms over a bottom of sand, gravel and broken shells. We had the same bottom until ¾ past 6 o'clock, at which moment we came to anchor in 14 fathoms, same bottom, in order to wait for day-light. In the afternoon, we saw a great quantity of frigate birds. We also saw much floating wood and seagrass.

At sun-set, the variation of the magnetic needle by observation was nought.

During the night, the wind was moderate at NW, clear weather. We had small currents setting to the SE and ESE. At day-break, from the anchoring place the bearings were: Broken Point South 72° W, the third island to the East of this point from South 35½° to South 38° W, and the fourth *ditto*, from South 2° to South 4½° W.

At 50 minutes past 7 o'clock, we got under sail and steered SSE½E.

We sounded and had 14 fathoms still over a bottom of sand and gravel mixed with broken shells.

At 50 minutes past 8 o'clock, Broken Point bore W 1½° S, the third island from S 66° to South 67½°, and the 4ᵗʰ from South 34½° to 35½° W.

At 40 minutes past 9 o'clock, the 3rd island bore South 83½° W and the fourth or last, from South 67° to South 70° W. This last is surrounded by breakers.

From this moment, we steered SE¼S. We sounded and had 13 or 14 fathoms over the same bottom as above.

At 4 minutes past 11 o'clock, Gaspar Island was seen from the mast-heads bearing East 6° South. We steered thus SE¼E. At 16' past 11 o'clock, the extremity of a most remarkable mountain on the island of Banca, which we named Sea-Mark Mountain for it may serve to gain the strait, extended from South 13° W to South 42° W. It is in the interior part of the country and can be seen only at a great distance.

At noon, the extremities of Sea-Mark Mountain bore South 22° West and South 49° West. The East point of Banca bore South 43° East, and Gaspar island to the East. We sounded and had 14 fathoms still over the same bottom.

Latitude by reckoning S 2° 10'.
Latitude by observation *ditto* 2° 21'.

11' difference South.

Longitude by reckoning W° 256° 4'.

We concluded from our observations of the currents and by the comparison of our own bearings, that we had been carried 19 miles SE¼E, which gives 0° 16' to East. Thus our longitude, which I corrected, was West 255° 48', or 104° 12' East.

From Thursday 22nd to Friday 23rd December 1791

52⁷/₁₀

At noon, we steered ESE½E in order to stand off a little from the East point of Banca. We sounded and had 12, 14 and 16 fathoms, and at 1 o'clock, 20 fathoms still over sand and gravel.

At ½ past 1 o'clock, the extremities of Sea-Mark Mountain stretched from South 48° to South 65° W. The East point of Banca bore South 22° East, and an islet situated in about the middle of the channel between Gaspar Island and the East point Banca, East 6° South.

A chain of breakers joined these two islets. A little to the South of the East point of Banca, there is a small islet very close to the shore.

From 42 minutes past 2 o'clock to 3 o'clock, we steered SE½S. We sounded and from ½ past 1 o'clock, we had 20 to 21 fathoms over the same bottom.

At 3 o'clock, the East point of Banca bore South 53° W and Gaspar Island N 53° E.

We could now see the entrance to the strait and steered S¼SE to gain the Salt Island,[247] which marks the strait to the Westward. We had 22, 23 and 24 fathoms until

---

247 *Several charts or plans have designated as an island the land which, on Gaspar's Plan, bears the denomination of the Ile de Sel: it is at this day admitted that it is only a peninsula, connected*

4 o'clock. The bottom was still of sand and gravel. At this moment, the East point of Banca bore North 71° West and the extreme NW point of Salt Island bore 32° W.

At 8 minutes past 4 o'clock, the Eastern extremity of one or several of the islands marking the strait, bore South 15° East. We observed that the currents were carrying us very fast to the Eastward, I steered thus S¼SW to coast along close to Salt Island, in direction of the strait. At ¼ past 4 o'clock, we sounded and had but 17 or 18 fathoms over a bottom of gravel and shells, we continued to have the same bottom as before.

At 5 o'clock, the East of Banca bore N 35° W and Gaspar Island N 22° E, the Eastern extremity of Salt Island bore South 9½° W, a small island to the Northward extended from South 40° to South 48° W, and quite a large island, which marks the strait to the Eastwards, which we named Solide Island after the ship, extended from South 28° to South 52° East.

Observing that the currents were carrying us to the SSE in the direction of the strait, we steered SSW½S. We sounded and had still 17 fathoms, same bottom.

At 6 o'clock, the East point of Banca bore N 23½° W, Gaspar Island bore North 17° E, the first island North of Salt Island bore South 79° and South 81° W, a second island North of Salt Island bore South 62° and South 75° W, the West point of Salt Island bore South 77° W, and the South East point of it South 15° W.

We steered South ½ E until 40' past 6 o'clock, at which moment we came to anchor in 17 fathoms over a bottom of sand and fine gravel mixed with broken shells. We had moored near the middle of the channel between the island which we had named Solide, and Salt Island.

During the night the wind varied from NW to WNW, overcast weather. The currents set to SSE until 2 o'clock in the morning, and then to the South. Their rate was one and a half miles per hour.

At day-light, still at anchor, we took the following bearings:

A hill on the East point of Banca bore N 21° W, Gaspar island bore N 13° 30' E, the second island to the North of Salt Island from North 68° to N 77° W, Salt Island from South 22° W to West 1° South, the South extremity of Solide Island bore South 64° E. To the South of this last island, four islets could be seen bearing South 76° E-South 70° E-South 65° E and South 56° E.

We weighed and got under sail at ¾ past 6 o'clock. We steered S½E, and soon after we directed our course SE¼S, and then SSE½S, for we saw on the East coast of Salt island, a line of breakers projecting out into the sea at a distance of about 1 mile. We had soundings which increased from 17 to 20 fathoms, sand and gravel.

At 22 minutes past 7 o'clock, the hill standing on the East point of Banca bore North 23½° W, the first island to the North of Salt Island bore N 55° W, the second *ditto* North 47½° to North 51½° W, the NE point of Salt Island bore North 65° W,

---

with the Island of Banca by a slip of land so low as not to be always perceived from the distance at which the reef, that terminates this land to the Eastward, requires that ships should keep from it (Fleurieu, op. cit., p. 140).

the South extremity of the same island South 54° W, Solide Island from N 19½° to North 55° E, a small island situated next to it bore N 17° E. We could see at North 71½° E and at N 75° E, two other islets between the four of which we had taken the bearings from the anchoring place, and Solide Island.

After having taken these bearings, we directed our course to the South. The soundings we had increased from 20 to 24 fathoms, same bottom. The SE part of Banca was to be seen more, insomuch that we had near left the strait. We saw a small islet very near the South point of Salt Island. We passed through the streams, which from a distance could have been taken for breakers.

At 20' past 8 o'clock, Solide Island bore from North 11½° to North 32° E, and the small island adjacent to it, N 9° E, the middle of the second island, which lies to the North of Salt Island, bore, from the East point of this last, North 34½° W.

From this point, we steered South ½ W, the soundings decreasing by degrees from 24 to 20 fathoms, same bottom.

At 7 minutes past 9 o'clock, the islets, which were seven in number and which lie SE of Solide Island, were in one with each other, bearing North 43° E. Solide Island bore from North 8° E to North 21° East, the South point of Salt Island bore N 53½° W, the island situated South of this point, N 55° W.

Until ¾ past 9 o'clock, we steered SSW½W and had regular soundings from 20 to 17 fathoms.

At this moment, the extremities of Salt Island bore from North 13½° to North 44½° W. Having now sailed out of the strait, we worked to windward upon the starboard tack to gain the coast of Sumatra, North of Two Sisters.[248]

At ½ past 10 o'clock, the soundings decreased from 17 to 9 fathoms. Fearing that we had come too close along-side shallow water which, following the chart of this strait in *Neptune Oriental*, lies South of Salt Island, we bore away to the Southward, but perceiving afterwards that the depth of water varied only from 9 to 12 fathoms, we once again worked to windward.

We could see no other land at noon, excepting the SE part of Banca, of which the extremes stretched from NW½W to NNW½N.

Latitude by observation South 3° 30'.
Latitude by reckoning 3° 5'.

25' difference South.

Longitude by reckoning W° 255° 43'.

---

248 Fleurieu (Ibid., p. 151) notes that on the English charts, these islands are called the Two Brothers. In effect, Dalrymple in his *Memoir of the Chart of the Straits of Sunda and Banka* (1787) indicates that: *They are generally named* The Brothers *by English navigators but Mr d'Après calls them* The Sisters, *which is sometimes used in English journals: I adopt the former because* Three Islands, *adjacent to North Island, are called* The Sisters (op. cit., p. 4).

But following our observations of the currents, and the comparison of the bearings, and after the difference to the South, I concluded that we had made 27½ miles more to SSE 1° E than by reckoning, the longitude is thus to be reduced by 11.

Longitude corrected W 255° 32'or 104° 28' East.

Réamur's themometer +25°, Fahrenheit's thermometer 87°.

The strait of Gaspar appears to deserve the preference over the strait of Banca for vessels proceeding from China to the Strait of Sunda. At first because it is so short a channel that it may be passed in 6 hours, and then because there is everywhere at least 17 fathoms over a fine bottom. I am all the more surprised that it should be so little frequented by shipping until the present time, and that Mr d'Après himself gives advice to the navigators not to enter it. A chart is to be found in *Neptune Oriental,*[249] and though very imperfect, it did not cause us to run into any error. When I was induced to give up the passage through the straits of Banca, the fear that I should not be able to stand in for the Two Sisters with the prevailing winds, and that we should find ourselves to the leeward if we passed the Straits of Billiton, induced me to give the preference those of Gasper. We proceeded with the greatest prudence and took all the bearings most exactly as possible, which I have inserted into this journal. By this means, we have been able to draw a chart of this strait and of a part of the coast of Banca from Broken Point to the East point.[250] We considered the currents, to which we paid the greatest attention, which we then compared by means of the differences, determined by the latitudes by observation and by the bearings which we took most regularly, of the principal points. We believe the chart to be correct. Concerning Billiton and the islets and banks with which it is surrounded, we have laid them down following the chart in *Neptune Oriental*. We did the same for the Eastern coast of Banca and the islets W of Salt Island. All these places, which we could not see on account of the distance or of other land which interrupted our view of them, did not in any way affect the strait, and are of very little importance as to the safety of the navigators who have no other intention but to sail through it.

We have, following our bearings and our course, laid down the four breakers which we saw at different distances to the North of the islands situated Eastwards of Broken Point. Mr d'Après in chart N°49 of *Neptune Oriental* lays down the breakers a little more to the North, after the observations and bearings of Mr Crozet, who was Captain of the *Mascarin*, bound for the Strait of Billiton, but the difference is but of a few minutes. A 5th breaker is laid down in the same chart between the others and Gaspar Island, which we did not see due very probably to

---

249 *Carte de la partie comprise entre la sortie du Detroit de Malac, le Detroit de Banca et l'Isle Borneo* (*Neptune Oriental*).
250 This chart is not in the Marchand manuscript.

the distance, but which we have placed on our chart. We have done the same for the breaker which is to be found North of Gaspar Island, following the chart of which I have made mention. The chart of the strait which is to be found in *Neptune Oriental* lays down several islets on the Eastern coast of Salt Island, but none was seen by us, though we passed very close to this island. Only a few breakers are to be found along this island.

The latitude of Gaspar Island was 2° 21' South and it was determined by the bearings taken at noon, at the moment of the observation, it bore East of us. The longitude, which we computed by reckoning and which we corrected on account of the currents of which I have made mention, is 104° 40' West and depends upon the longitude of the NE point of the Banca, following the chart N° 49 in *Neptune Oriental*, and from which we had taken our departure the previous day. The latitude of East point of Banca was found to be 2° 33' South, following our course and bearings which place it 13' more to the South than on the same chart. We place this point in longitude 104° 23' East, which is 11' more to the Westward than laid down in the chart of which I have just spoke. To conclude, the middle of the strait is laid down 5½ leagues more to the East upon this chart than following our bearings and our course.

From Friday 23rd to Saturday 24th December 1791

30

During the afternoon, we continued to steer to windward with the help of a gentle breeze at NW and at NNW.

At ¾ past 6 o'clock, the wind having fallen and the currents setting to the South, we came to anchor in 12 fathoms of water over a bottom of ooze and sand.

From noon to this moment, we had soundings from 9½ to 12 fathoms, same bottom.

Immediately upon coming to anchor, we observed that the currents were setting to SE¼S at a rate of a mile per hour. They continued thus all the time we were at anchor.

At ½ past 3 o'clock AM, the wind now blowing a hard gale, the ship began to drive, but after bearing away 10 fathoms, she held tight. While mooring, we had veered away 50 fathoms.

The breeze being very light until 11 o'clock in the morning, we remained at anchor, but veering to NW¼W at this moment, we got under sail and continued to work to windward in order to gain the coast of Sumatra.

During the night, we had had thunder and lightning.

Latitude by observation South 3° 51'.
Longitude by reckoning 255° 54'.

1' more to the South than by reckoning.
Réamur's thermometer +26°, Fahrenheit's thermometer 89°.

From Saturday 24th to Sunday 25th December 1791

26½

The wind blowing a gentle gale we continued our course until ¾ past 2 o'clock PM, when having a calm, we came to anchor in 10 fathoms of water over a bottom of light ooze and foul ground.

About an hour after coming to anchor, the breeze began to blow fresh at NNW upon which I resolved to get under sail. But at 5 o'clock, a squall at NNW, all round the compas in 10 minutes, obliged us to come to anchor once again in 11 fathoms over the same bottom as before.

During the night, the wind blowing a hard gale at NW¼W, attended with rain, thunder and lightning, we were drove about 4 cables length.

At day-light, we caught sight of two small vessels steering SE, and of a brig at anchor NW of us, at about a distance of three leagues. I supposed that she had sailed out of the strait of Banca. At eight o'clock in the morning, we got under sail with the help of a gentle gale at NW. The brig had weighed at the same moment and had directed her course SSW, whilst we steered SW in order to fall in with the coast of Sumatra.

During the time we were at anchor, the currents had continued to set to ESE at a rate of a mile and a half per hour, and we had had regular soundings from 10 to 13 fathoms over an oozy bottom.

Latitude by observation South 4° 25'.
Longitude by reckoning 256° 14'.

17' more to the South than by reckoning.
Réamur's thermometer +25°, Fahrenheit's thermometer 87°.

From Sunday 25th to Monday 26th December 1791

36¼

At noon, we were in sight of the coast of Sumatra extending from SW to WNW at a distance of about 5 leagues. It is very low in this place and there are no hills to be seen even in the interior parts of the country.

We steered thus S¼SW and then South, whilst attempting to keep a depth of 9 to 13 fathoms in order to fall in with the Two Sisters, following the instructions of Mr D'Après.

At 6 o'o clock in the evening, the coast of West Sumatra bore NW, distant 6 leagues. We sounded and had 10 to 11 fathoms at this moment over a bottom of mud and sand.

We had kept company with the brig of which I have spoke.

At ½ past 9 o'clock in the evening, the wind slackening, we came to anchor in 12½ fathoms over a bottom of soft mud and broken shell.

During the night, we had a light wind at SW, attended with thunder, lightning and rain. We had currents setting to ENE at a rate of a mile per hour.

At day-light, we saw a brig anchored at a very short distance from us.

At ½ past 6 o'clock AM, we weighed together with a light breeze at WNW. Desiring to know to which nation she belonged, we hoisted the ship's enseign and she hoisted Dutch colours.

Soon after getting under sail, we saw a three-master at anchor in the SW, at a distance of about 3 leagues which hoisted American colours.

At 7 o'clock, we saw the Two Sisters to the SW¼W at a distance of 6 leagues. We could also see Nordwack Island, or Nord Water,[251] to the SE½S.

A 8 o'clock, the coast of Sumatra extended from SW to WNW. The Two Sisters bore SW¼S and Nord Water island SE.

Immediately upon perceiving this island, the brig steered towards it. It was likely that she was bound for Batavia.

At ½ past 9 o'clock, having near a calm and fearing to be carried to the Eastward by the currents, we came to anchor in 13 fathoms of water over a muddy sand bottom with shells. The Northermost of the Two Sisters bore SW½S, and the Southermost SW¼S, at a distance of 1½ leagues from Nord Water Island bearing ESE½S. From this position, a very high mountain standing on the coast of Sumatra could be seen to the SW. It is to be found in the Strait of Sunda, above Hog's Point, a little inland. In departing from the Two Sisters, and steering directly towards it, we cannot but fall in with North Island, which is to be found in the same direction.

At ¼ past 10 o'clock, the American vessel got under sail and directed her course SW. At ¼ past 11 o'clock, the wind having shifted to NW and blowing a light gale, we weighed and steered towards the Two Sisters. At noon, the Northermost of the two bore SW½W, and the Southermost SW, distant 1 league.

Latitude by observation South 5° 4'.
Longitude by reckoning 256° 24'.

5' more to the South than by reckoning.

Réamur's thermometer +26°, Fahrenheit's thermometer 89°.

This was in agreement with the longitude determined from the bearings of the Two Sisters. The currents, which had always set to the East since our departure from the Straits of Gaspar, had made me expect a difference in this direction. But I believe that the Two Sisters and the coast of Sumatra are laid down too much to the Westwards upon the charts of Mr D'Après. Besides, the Two Sisters appeared not to lie as far from the coast of Sumatra as upon the charts.

Following the observation which I had made at noon with the greatest accuracy, the latitude of these two islands was 5° 6' South, and not 5° or 5° 1' as laid down in *Neptune Oriental*.

---

251 Northwatcher in *A Chart of the South Parts of Sumatra and of the The Straits of Sunda and Banca with Gaspar Straits corrected and improved from the observations of Josh.* Huddart (1794).

During this day, we had regular soundings from 9 to 13 fathoms over a bottom of mud, sand and broken shell.

From Monday 26ᵗʰ to Tuesday 27ᵗʰ December 1791

At ½ past 1 o'clock PM, we got sight of the high mountains of Java at South. Until 3 o'clock, we had a gentle breeze at WNW which then shifted to South with squalls, we thus tacked and stood to the West, at ½ past 4 o'clock, as we had a near calm, we came to anchor in 10 fathoms over a bottom of mud, sand and shell.

The Southermost of the Two Sisters bore NE¼N, and the Northermost NNE½E, distant 1 league. These two islands are surrounded by reefs and breakers which are not dangerous for they do not project into the sea more than half a mile. The coast of Sumatra could be seen from NW to SW¼W. In this place, the shore is very low, but in the interior parts of country, hills and mountains of quite a considerable height can be seen.

The American vessel came to anchor at about three quarters of a league SW of us.

The tide had set to the South until ¼ past 7 o'clock in the evening. At this moment, it began to flow NE and continued in this direction at a rate of a mile and a quarter per hour.

During the night, we had fresh winds at SSW attended with rain, thunder and lightning, all the squalls coming from Sumatra.

At day-light, we perceived that we had drove about three quarters of a league to the NE, and that in consequence we were very close to the Two Sisters. I resolved to get under sail immediately, in spite of the breeze which was blowing very light at W and W¼NW, and of the currents which were against us. In tripping the anchor, we perceived that the cable had become entangled with one of the flukes, which had made us drive. We found the cable to be cut where it had touched the anchor. We cut away three or four fathoms.

Immediately upon getting under sail, we worked to windward on the starboard side. The American vessel had weighed at the same moment. We saw another astern, belonging to the same nation.

During the morning, the breeze was very light and varied at W¼NW and NW, attended with fine and clear weather.

At noon, the Two Sisters bore NNE at a distance of about 5 leagues. The coast of Sumatra stretched from NW¼N to SSW½W, and that of Java, from South to SSW.

Our latitude by observation was found to be at the same moment 5° 22' South. Our longitude by reckoning was 256° 34'. We had a difference of 5 minutes to the South.

During this day, we had soundings of 10 to 14 fathoms over a bottom of sand, mud and shell.

Réamur's thermometer +26°, Fahrenheit's thermometer 89°.

From Tuesday 27ᵗʰ to Wednesday 28ᵗʰ December 1791

At 1 o'clock PM, we had sight of the small North Island at SW½S, at a distance of 6 leagues.

At 4 o'clock, having a calm, we came to anchor in 17 fathoms over a bottom of sand and gravel. North Island bore SW½S, distant 4 leagues. The coast of Sumatra extended from NNW½N to SSW, and that of Java from SSE to South.

From noon to two o'clock, we had regular soundings from 13 to 14 fathoms over a bottom of muddy sand. From 2 to 4, from 16 to 17 fathoms over a bottom of sand and gravel. At 5 o'clock, we had sight of two large vessels and a brig making boards at SSE.

During the night, the wind was variable from SW to West, attended with rain, thunder and lightning. We had currents setting to the South until 8 o'clock in the evening, and during the remainder of the night to NNE, at a rate of one mile per hour.

At ¾ past 6 o'clock in the morning, having no current and the wind blowing a gentle gale at SW, we got under sail in order to attempt to gain North Island by beating to windward.

During the morning, the winds settled at SW and SSW, attended with rain at intervals. We spent the morning beating to windward, keeping in as close as it was possible to the coast of Sumatra, which appeared to be very safe in this place for we frequently came within less than half a league of it and never had soundings less than 11 fathoms. We had 20 fathoms at two leagues from the shore.

At noon, Cape St Nicholas, or Bantam Point, bore SSE½E. The highest part of the coast of Java was to be seen from SE to S½W. North Island bore SW¼S. The coast of Sumatra extended from SSW to NNW.

Latitude by observation South 5° 34'.
Longitude by reckoning 256° 41' 30".

2' more to the South than by reckoning.
Réamur's thermometer +26°, Fahrenheit's thermometer 88°.

From Wednesday 28ᵗʰ to Thursday 29ᵗʰ December 1791

At ¾ past 1 o'clock PM, we stood in shore but the soundings suddenly varying from 11 to 15 fathoms, we stood off shore. When we tacked, North Island bore SW¼S at a distance of two leagues.

At ½ past 4 o'clock, having a calm, we came to anchor in 20 fathoms over a bottom of sand and large gravel.

North Island bore WSW½W, at distance of no more than a league. The Grand Toque bore South and the centre of Mid-channel Island,[252] SSW 7° S. The islands

---

252 This name used is by King (*Voyage to the Pacific Ocean*, op. cit., Volume 3, p. 471). Fleurieu calls it Middle Island (op. cit., p. 152)

which lie at the South point of Sumatra bore from SW¼S to SW 3° S. The coast of Sumatra from SW to NNW, and that of Java in sight, from SE to S½W.

Until 7 o'clock in the evening, we had currents setting to SSW, and then to NE. During the night, the wind settled at SW¼W, attended with rain and lightning.

At ½ past 10 o'clock in the morning we got under sail, which proved to be a work of great labour and time for we were obliged, in order to trip the anchor, to make use of the blocks and three tackles. Upon getting up the anchor at the cat-head, we perceived that the shank was broke near a third of its length, close to the arms, the two pieces holding together but by a very thin strip of iron.
It was rendered useless.

At anchor, latitude by observation South 5° 37'.
Longitude by reckoning 256° 42'.

3' more to the South than by reckoning.
Réamur's thermometer +26°, Fahrenheit's thermometer 89°.

From Thursday 29ᵗʰ to Friday 30ᵗʰ December 1791

We spent the whole of the afternoon plying to windward by boards, with a gentle gale at WSW and SW, we had soundings of 25 to 30 fathoms over a bottom of gravel, mud and broken shells. At 7 o'clock in the evening, we came to anchor in 22 fathoms over a bottom of mud and sand, the Grand Toque bearing SSE½S, the island in the middle S 13° W, the Southern extremity of the islands which lie on the Southerly point of Sumatra, named by Mr d'Après Pulo Relow, Pulo High, Pulo Woody, Pulo Kandang, etc., bore SSW½, and North Island NW¼W, distant ¾ of a league.
The three sail of which I have made mention passed close by us having hoisted Dutch colours. They came to anchor to the South of North Island where the two American ships were to be found. I supposed them to be compleating their wood and water and getting on board other provisions which may be purchased of the Malays.
During the night and the morning, we had violent currents setting to NE. Their rate was frequently two and a half miles per hour, which obliged us to remain at anchor.

Latitude by observation at anchor South 5° 45'.
Longitude by reckoning 256° 44'.

3' more to the South than by reckoning.
Réamur's thermometer +26½°, Fahrenheit's thermometer 90°.

From Friday 30ᵗʰ to Saturday 31ˢᵗ December 1791

The wind blowing light and the currents setting in the same direction, still NE, we kept at anchor during the afternoon and the night. But at ¾ past 7 o'clock in the morning, we got a trade wind at SW¼S blowing a gentle gale, and with scarce a current we got under sail and plied to windward by boards all through the morning.

The two American vessels at anchor near North Island got under sail at the same time.
The variation of the compass by observations of the azimuths was 49' NE.

At noon, the centre of the island in the middle bore SSW½W, Grand Toque bore South ½ East, the Peak of Cracatoa bore SW 8° W, North Island bore NNW½W, and the the Southern extremity of the islands lying on the Southerly point of Sumatra, WSW 3° South. We were at a distance of about 1 league from Grand Toque.

Latitude by observation South 5° 48'.
Longitude by reckoning 256° 45'.

2' more to the South than by reckoning.
Réamur's thermometer +26°, Fahrenheit's thermometer 89°.

From Saturday 31ˢᵗ December to Sunday 1ˢᵗ January 1792

At ¼ past 3 o'clock, we caught sight of the rock which lies near the middle of the channel between the islands on the South point of Sumatra and Mid-channel Island.[253]

We continued to ply to windward by boards with fine weather and the wind at SW¼S blowing a gentle gale. We were not able to double the rock, of which I have made mention, in order to enter the Strait of Sunda before night, I did not think it prudent to remain in so narrow a channel and at ¼ past 6 o'clock PM, we came to anchor near Remow Island, at a distance of half a mile from the shore and in 30 fathoms of water over a bottom of sand mixed with gravel and broken shells.

At anchor, Mid-channel Island bore from SE to SSE 4° S, the Peak of Cracatoa SW½W, Grand Toque ESE, and the rock in the the middle of the channel bore South ½ W.

I observed that in this place, if one stands off but a little from the shore, the depth of the water increases to 60 or 70 fathoms.

---

253 King keeps close to the shore in order to avoid the rock in question (*Voyage to the Pacific Ocean*, op. cit., Volume 3, p. 471).

During the night we had a light breeze varying from WSW to SSW attended frequently with rain, and we had currents setting either from NE or from SW, very irregular.

At ½ past 7 o'clock AM, we got under sail and with the help of a light breeze varying from NW to SSW, we doubled the rock in the middle of the channel.

This rock is very low and is of no great extent, all around it the depth of the water appeared to be considerable.

My intention being to sail out between the island of Cracatoa and that of Sambouricou, we continued our progress so as to keep close in with Sumatra.

At noon, Point Toca, or Hog's Point, bore ENE½E, the Peak of Sambouricou bore W¼SW, that on Cracatoa bore SW½W and the centre of Mid-channel Island, East ½ South. Our distance from Hog's Point was about 1½ leagues. Some small islets, level with the surface of the water, are to be seen at a short distance from this point.

At this moment we sounded and found 25 fathoms over a fine bottom of sand and large broken shells.

Latitude by observation South 5° 53'.
Longitude by reckoning 256° 59'.

2' more to the South than by reckoning.
Réamur's thermometer +24½°, Fahrenheit's thermometer 86°.

From Sunday 1ˢᵗ to Monday 2ⁿᵈ January 1792

With a light breeze at SW and at WSW, we continued to ply to windward by boards all the afternoon in order to fall in with the channel between Cracatoa and Sambouricou. We sounded and had 24 to 25 fathoms of water near Sumatra, and 30 to 35 fathoms close to Cracatoa, over a bottom of sand, mud and broken shells. At ¾ past 6 o'clock, the current being against us and making nothing to the Westward, we came to anchor in 30 fathoms over a bottom of muddy sand and broken shells.

The island of Cracatoa and the adjacent islands stretched from SW to WSW, Sambouricou from W¼NW to WNW½N, distant 2½ leagues from Cracatoa.

During the night, the currents set to NE with more or less strength, but their rate never exceeded ½ a mile per hour. The weather was fine and clear with a light breeze at SW.

At ½ past 8 o'clock AM, we got under sail with a very light breeze nearing a calm, which we would not have resolved to do had the currents been running against us.

During the morning, we had very little wind. We had regular soundings from 23 to 28 fathoms, still the same bottom.

A boat which was sailing through the strait passed by the ship and made no shew of stopping.

At 10 o'clock, while under sail we had seen the three Dutch vessels which we had left at anchor at North Island, between Mid-channel Island and Java.

At noon, the centre of Mid-channel Island bore ENE½E, the Peak of Sambouricou bore NW¼W, that of Cracatoa SW½S and the middle of the Island of Sabessi bore NNW½N.

Latitude by observation South, in agreement with the reckoning, 6° 3'.
Longitude by reckoning 257° 4'.

Réamur's thermometer +25°, Fahrenheit's thermometer 87°.

From Monday 2ⁿᵈ to Tuesday 3ʳᵈ January

At ½ past 2 o'clock, it falling quite calm, we came to anchor in 21 fathoms over a bottom of mud, the Peak of Cracatoa bore SW½S, that of Sambouricou NW and the middle of the Island of Sabessi, NNW½N. We were at a distance of about 2 miles from the shore.

An hour after having dropped anchor, the wind now blowing a little more fresh at SW, we got under sail once more, and after having made several trips between Sambouricou and Cracatoa, we again came to anchor at ¼ past 6 o'clock in 22½ fathoms, muddy sand bottom. The island of Sambouricou extended from NW¼N to North, Cracatoa and the adjacent islands from SW¼W to S¼SW, and the West-ermost extreme of Sumatra that was in sight, West. We were at a distance of about a mile from Sambouricou, on the SW point of which are to be seen some few rocks level with the surface of the water and very close to the shore. At about 5 miles to the West of this same point, we had sight of three or four large rocks very near to each other and amongst which there is one which resembles a ship under sail.

We could not discover any dangers in the South and SE part of island of Sambouricou, though we had frequently tacked less than half a mile from the shore. It seems that there are a few breakers to be found on the SW point, but they are within reach of the shore.

At 7 o'clock, a small canoe with an outrigger and two men on board came along-side the ship, we purchased three turtles for two pieces of eight, for this was all they had with them. They said they had come from the Island of Sabessi and that if we remained at anchor until tomorrow noon, they would bring off other provisions. They spoke a kind of corrupted Portuguese.

During the night, we had very light airs at SW attended sometimes with rain and lightning. We saw great fires on the Island of Sambouricou and Cracatoa. We scarce had a current in any direction.

At 6 o'clock in the morning, a light breeze springing up at West, and the currents setting to SW at a rate of half a mile per hour, we got under sail. We spent the morning plying to windward by boards in order to double the island of Cracatoa. The variation of the compass determined from the amplitudes and the azimuths was found to be 57' NE, mean result.

At noon, the island of Cracatoa extended from SSW to SSE. The rocks lying West of Sambouricou bore WNW½N and the middle of Sambouricou bore NE½N, distant 1 mile from the shore.

Latitude by reckoning South 5° 58'.
Longitude by reckoning 257° 8' 30".

2' more to the South than by reckoning.
Réamur's thermometer +26°, Fahrenheit's thermometer 89°.

From Tuesday 3rd to Wednesday 4th January 1792

During the afternoon, we continued to ply to windward by boards with a light breeze, which gave us an opportunity to gain to the Westward owing to the variableness of the wind. Upon tacking and standing to the WNW, steering away from Sambouricou, the depth of the water increased from 28 to 46 fathoms. But as night was falling, it was impossible for us to get clear of Cracatoa on the other tack, I resolved thus to come to anchor. We approached the island in order to decrease our depth of water. At ½ past 6 o'clock, we sounded and had only 39 fathoms and having very little wind, we dropped the anchor in a bottom of sand, mud and broken shells. The Peak of Sambouricou bore ENE 2° N, that of Cracatoa bore SE¼S, two islets lying to the West of the said island bore S¼SE, and the rocks to the West of Sambouricou, NE¼N 2° N. During the night we had a storm and light variable winds. The currents alternately set to SW and WNW. The weather being very variable and having squalls from SE to SW, we remained at anchor until ½ past 10 o'clock AM. At this moment, the wind shifting to North with a squall, we took the opportunity of getting under sail and steering WSW, but at 11 o'clock, the wind falling and having varied at WNW, we worked to windward and stood for the SW. At noon, the island of Cracatoa and the adjacent islands extended from E to ESE 8° S. The peak of Sambouricou bore ENE 7° N, and the middle of Prince Island, South. We here took our departure in latitude South 6° 4', which was in perfect agreement with the reckoning, and longitude 257° 5' West, following the bearings of Prince Island, after the situation which is assigned to it in *Connaissance des Temps*. The longitude by reckoning was found to be at this moment 257° 15'. We had thus a difference of 10' more to the East. However, as the currents had continually set to the West of South since our departure from the Two Sisters, we cannot have been carried to the Eastward whilst under sail, which is a proof as I have before mentioned, that the Two Sisters and the coast of Sumatra are laid down a little too much to the Westward in the charts of Mr d'Après.
Réamur's thermometer +25°, Fahrenheit's thermometer 87°.

From Wednesday 4th to Thursday 5th January 1792

59¼

During the afternoon, we had light winds and very variable, attended with squalls. We made the boards most advantageous to us in order to sail quite out of the strait. During one of the squalls, we caught sight of a water spout at two cables length of the ship, which disappeared in but a few minutes.

At 9 o'clock in the evening, Jean-Joseph Barri, our Steward, departed of this life. As the length of the voyage was not the cause of his malady, I will here give an account as communicated to me by the Surgeon.

On the 1st of January, he was slightly indisposed and we found him with a fever. After the symptoms, Mr Roblet believed him to be ill of a putrid fever. He was kept on a strict course of diet, and on the 2nd he was given a purgative. On the 3rd, he had recovered and the emetic had had the desired effect. He found himself better, but he was kept to diet drinks, broth, etc. He remained well and did not complain of any fever until this day, 1 o'clock PM. At ½ past 1 o'clock, he was taken ill with a violent fever and a burning heat, he began to be light-headed and became intirely delirious. At three o'clock, blisters were applied to his legs. At four o'clock, he recovered a little and the fever appeared to have left off. He had a mind to make his will but he did not have the time to do so for he soon after became delirious once more. His pulse was hard and he suffered a spasmodic affection of the nerves. At 7 o'clock, the convulsions began. The disease seemed now to be a fever of the acute and inflammatory sort. He was in so bad a state that five men could not keep him to his bed. He lived for one and a half hours, he ceased to drink and fell into a deep swoon, which was followed by death ten minutes after.

This unfortunate event was no small surprise to Mr Roblet for he knew not from what real cause it proceeded, and it was but two hours after that he perceived a bleeding at the nose and saw that the whole of the body was covered in black and livid spots. Perhaps, said he to me afterwards, bleeding would have had a fortunate effect if it had been performed at the beginning of the delirium, but having been continually at sea for thirteen months, and nothing indicating such a course to be necessary, he had not thought himself bound to do it.

He was the first man we had lost in the course of our voyage. We lamented him for he had always been most careful and untiring in his professional duties.

At 8 o'clock in the morning, after the usual ceremonies, we committed him to the the sea. In the morning, we set down in an inventory the list of all his effects, and the chief and warrant officers added their signature to it, the crew all being present.

During the night, the wind was very variable but then settled at NE. We steered SW¼W and then SW.

At 6 o'clock in the morning, the coast of Sumatra bore from NNW to NNE. We could neither distinguish that of Java nor the islands in the strait on account of the haze. We had now sailed quite out of the Straits of Sunda and we continued our route with fine weather.

Present latitude by observation South 6° 39'.
Longitude by reckoning 257° 49' 30".

9' more to the South than by reckoning.
Réamur's thermometer +26°, Fahrenheit's thermometer 89°.

At day-light we had sight of a vessel a-head which hoisted Dutch colours. She was standing the same way.

During the morning, I ordered all the hammocks to be lashed up, which we had not had time enough to do this great while. We cleaned and smoked the between decks, washing with vinegar. We daily found casks of biscuit intirely spoiled, and near three quarters of the wine was now wanting for it had grown sour. This was no small surprise after so long a voyage and during which we had experienced so great a number of different climates.

From Thursday 5ᵗʰ to Friday 6ᵗʰ January 1792

74

The breeze was variable from SSE and East attended at intervals with squalls and a hollow swell from the SW.

During the night we had lightning in the West.

At day-light, we had sight of the Dutch vessel at a distance of a league aft, and at 10 o'clock we lost sight of her in this same direction.

The variation of the magnetic needle determined from the azimuths was NE 36'. We saw boobies.

Latitude by observation South 7° 57'.
Longitude by reckoning 258° 35' 30".

20' more to the South than by reckoning.
Réamur's thermometer +26½°, Fahrenheit's thermometer 90°.

From Friday 7ᵗʰ to Saturday 7ᵗʰ January 1792

89½

During this day, the breeze, more or less fresh, was variable from SE¼E to SSE attended frequently with squalls.

We continued to have a large swell from the SE.

The variation of the compass by observation NE 29'.

Latitude by observation South 8° 54'.
Longitude by reckoning 259° 39'.

4' more to the North than by reckoning.
Réamur's thermometer +26½°, Fahrenheit's thermometer 90°.

From Saturday 7ᵗʰ to Sunday 8ᵗʰ January 1792

98¼

Variable breeze at SSE to SE¼S with clear weather and fine.

Many tropic birds and boobies.
The variation of the compass by observation NE 39'.

Latitude by observation South 9° 35'.
Longitude by reckoning 261° 7'.

4' 30" more to the North than by reckoning.
Réamur's thermometer +25½°, Fahrenheit's thermometer 88°.

Several of the people were ill of the flux, of which I myself had been indisposed for these last few days, and which had made me very weakly. This disease, which is in general to be met with in the Straits of Sunda, can scarce be attributed only to the unwholesome water which is taken on board in China, in Batavia or in the Strait itself. In this opinion I am confirmed, for in China and in Batavia, this disease is most common. The stock of water made at Typa being intirely spoiled, I gave our principal people the water from Marseilles, which was yet excellent for it had kept very well. I also gave orders to make a beverage for the people for their daily allowance. It was made of $^4/_5$ water and $^1/_5$ wine.[254]

From Sunday 8th to Monday 9th January 1792

74

During this day, the breeze was more or less light and variable from S¼SE to SE¼S, fine weather and clear, great swell from the SSE.
Few birds.
The variation of the compass by observation NE 29'.

Latitude by observation South 10° 22'.
Longitude by reckoning 262° 13'.

15' more to the South than by reckoning.
Réamur's thermometer +27½°, Fahrenheit's thermometer 92°.
We felt a suffocating heat which was almost intolerable.

---

254 King also recounts the fragile health of the crew in the same waters, but unlike Marchand, without loss of life: *From the time of our entering the Straits of Banca, we began to experience the powerful effects of this perstilential climate. Two of our people fell dangerously ill of malignant putrid fevers; which however we prevented from spreading by putting the patients apart from the rest, in most airy births* [. . .] *One of the two who had been ill of fevers, one after being seized with convulsions, on the 12th February, which made us despair of his life, was relieved by the application of blisters, and was soon out of danger. The other recovered, but more slowly. On board the Resolution, besides the obstinate coughs and fevers under which they very generally laboured, a great many were afflicted with fluxes . . . (A Voyage to the Pacific Ocean,* op. cit., Volume 3, pp. 478–479). In Dixon, the effect of the climate on the crews of both ships is also described as being particulary nefarious (op. cit., p. 336).

From Monday 9th to Tuesday 10th January 1792

70¾

The breeze was variable more or less light from SE¼S to S¼SW attended with small squalls at intervals.

We saw a large quantity of birds of the boobie species, tropic birds and frigate birds.

We took one tunny fish and two bonetta.

The variation of the compass by observation of the azimuths was 29' NE.

Latitude by observation South 10° 53'.
Longitude by reckoning 263° 18'.

4' more to the South than by reckoning.
Réamur's thermometer +25½°, Fahrenheit's thermometer 88°.

From Tuesday 10th to Wednesday 11th January 1792

83

During this day we had a light breeze varying from SE¼S to S¼SE, fine weather and a smooth sea.

We saw floating wood, bamboo and seagrass passing by the ship.

Many birds.

We took two tunny fish, weighing each eight pounds, which I served to the people.

No variation of the compass by observation.

Latitude by observation South 11° 28'.
Longitude by reckoning 264° 36'.

8' more to the South than by reckoning.
Réamur's thermometer +25½°, Fahrenheit's thermometer 88°.

From Wednesday 11th to Thursday 12th January 1792

69½

Variable breeze from South to SE¼S, fine weather a very smooth sea.

At ¼ past 4 o'clock, we saw the Island of Cocos from the mast-head, bearing SSE at a distance of 6 or 7 leagues.

It appeared low and regular.

Mr Malespina, Officer of the Spanish Navy, has laid down the situation of the largest of these islands in latitude 12° 11' South and in longitude 94° 3', East of Paris.

We saw a great quantity of birds and we took two tunny fish.
The variation of the compass by observation NW 48'.

Latitude by observation South 11° 53'.
Longitude by reckoning 265° 37'.

4' more to the North than by reckoning.
Réamur's thermometer +25¼°, Fahrenheit's thermometer 88°.

From Friday 13th to Saturday 14th January 1792

144

At ½ past 5 o'clock PM, we saw in the West a large vessel abreast of us, displaying Dutch colours. Seeing that she desired to speak to us, we bore down towards her. She had left the Cape of Good Hope and was bound for Batavia, with many troops on board.
We gave her our longitude and we then each continued on our way.
During this day, we had a fine breeze at SE and fine weather.
A great multitude of birds fluttered continually about the ship.
We again took two tunny fish.

Latitude by observation South 13° 30'.
Longitude by reckoning 268° 52'.

4' more to the North than by reckoning.
Réamur's thermometer +26½°, Fahrenheit's thermometer 90°.

From Saturday 14th to Sunday 15th January 1792

150

The breeze blew fresh attended with heavy squalls.
The variation of the compass determined from 6 azimuths was 1° 2' NW.
Few birds.
By two sets of observations of five distances each of the sun and the moon, reduced to 7h 8' 46" AM, we found the longitude to be 272° 20'. The reckoning was 270° 41'.
A difference of 1° 39' Westward.

Latitude by observation South 14° 42'.
Longitude by reckoning 272° 47'.

Réamur's thermometer +25½°, Fahrenheit's thermometer 88°.

From Sunday 15ᵗʰ to Monday 16ᵗʰ January 1792

149½

During this day, the breeze continued to blow a gentle gale from SE¼S to ESE. Variation of the compass by observation 1° 19'NW.

At 8h 53' 48" AM, by two sets of observations of five distances each of the ☉ and the ☾, our longitude was 274° 37'. That determined from the observations of yesterday, reduced to this moment, was 274° 53' 30". Mean result of the 4 observations, 274° 45' 15".

Latitude by observation South 15° 53'.
Longitude by reckoning 273° 43'.
Longitude by observation 275°

Réamur's thermometer +25½°, Fahrenheit's thermometer 88°.

From Monday 16ᵗʰ to Tuesday 17ᵗʰ January 1792

148

We had during this day a gentle gale from SE to East attended with squalls at intervals and a great swell from the SW.

We were steering WSW.

Variation of the compass by observation NW 1° 39'.

We caught sight of the first Red-Shafted Tropic Birds. Navigators of former times believed these birds to foretell of the proximity of Isles of France and Rodrigue, though we were yet very far removed from them.

Latitude by observation South 16° 52'.
Longitude by reckoning 273° 51'.
Longitude by observation 277° 21'.

Réamur's thermometer +25°, Fahrenheit's thermometer 87°.

From Tuesday 17ᵗʰ to Wednesday 18ᵗʰ January 1792

138

We continued to have a fresh breeze of wind at SE attended with strong gusts. The variation by observation NW 2° 32'.

Latitude by observation South 17° 48'.
Present longitude by observation 279° 33'.
Longitude by reckoning 278° 3'.

Réamur's thermometer +25°, Fahrenheit's thermometer 88°.

From Wednesday 18ᵗʰ to Thursday 19ᵗʰ January 1792

156¾

At noon, we steered WSW½W.

During this day, we had a fine breeze which varied from ESE to SE attended frequently with squalls.

The variation of the compass by observation of 10 azimuths was NW 3° 34'.

By four sets of five distances each of the ☉ and the ☾, reduced to 8h 1' 47" AM, we found the longitude to be 282° 1'. That computed from our last observations was found to be 281° 43', that is 18' more to the East.

We saw tropic birds and gulls.

    Latitude by observation South 18° 50'.
    Longitude by observation 282° 27'.
    Longitude by reckoning 280° 39'.

    Réamur's thermometer +25°, Fahrenheit's thermometer 87°.

From Thursday 19ᵗʰ to Friday 20ᵗʰ January 1792

131½

Fresh breeze of wind at ESE and fine weather.

We directed our course to W¼SW.

We saw a great quantity of White and Red-Shafted Tropic Birds.

By 10 azimuths, the variation of the magnetic needle was found to be 4° 53' North Westerly.

    Latitude by observation South 19° 38'.
    Longitude by observation 284° 41'.
    Longitude by reckoning 282° 53'.

12' more to the South than by reckoning.
Réamur's thermometer +24°, Fahrenheit's thermometer 85°.

From Friday 20ᵗʰ to Saturday 21ˢᵗ January 1792

106½

Moderate breeze and fine weather.

Variation of the compass by observation NW 6° 12'.

Few birds.

The people were employed painting the ship inside and out, and the caulkers and carpenters likewise employed in repairing the boats.

    Latitude by observation South 20° 10'.
    Longitude by observation 286° 32'.
    Longitude by reckoning 284° 44'.

11' more to the South than by reckoning.
Réamur's thermometer +25°, Fahrenheit's thermometer 87°.

From Saturday 21st to Sunday 22nd January 1792

119½

Breeze at E¼SE blowing more or less fresh, attended with fine weather. Course W¼NW.
We saw a few tropic birds.
The variation of the compass by observation was 6° 40' NW.

Latitude by observation South 20° 3'.
Longitude by observation 288° 39'.
Longitude by reckoning 286° 51'.

3' more to the South than by reckoning.
Réamur's thermometer +25°, Fahrenheit's thermometer 87°.

From Sunday 22nd to Monday 23rd January 1792

101¼

Light breeze at East, overcast weather.
The variation of the compass by observation 6° 47' NW.
We saw White and Red-Shafted Tropic Birds.

Latitude by observation South 19° 48'.
Longitude by observation 290° 25'.
Longitude by reckoning 288° 37'.

3' more to the South than by reckoning.
Réamur's thermometer +24°, Fahrenheit's thermometer 85°.

From Monday 23rd to Tuesday 24th January 1792

85

Light breeze from NNE to East. During the afternoon, we had a little rain followed by fine weather.
The variation of the compass by observation of the amplitudes and several sets of azimuths was 7° 35' NW.

Latitude by observation South 19° 46'.
Longitude by observation 291° 55'.
Longitude by reckoning 290° 7'.

5' more to the South than by reckoning.

Réamur's thermometer +25°, Fahrenheit's thermometer 87°.

From Tuesday 24ᵗʰ to Wednesday 25ᵗʰ January 1792

92½

Light breeze moderate at E and ESE. Clear weather and fine, great swell from the South.

We saw many tropic birds.

By the Westerly amplitude, and by several sets of azimuths observed with different compasses, the variation of the magnetic needle was found to 8° 13' North Westerly.

Latitude by observation South 19° 52'.
Longitude by observation 293° 34'.
Longitude by reckoning 291° 46'.

7' more to the South than by reckoning.
Réamur's thermometer +25½°, Fahrenheit's thermometer 87½°.

From Wednesday 25ᵗʰ to Thursday 26ᵗʰ January 1792

85

Light breeze moderate from East to ESE, clear weather and fine. A swell at SSW.

Variation of the compass by observation of the amplitudes and by 15 sets of azimuths, 9° 12' NW.

Many tropic birds fluttering about the ship.

Latitude by observation South 19° 46'.
Longitude by observation 295° 7'.
Longitude by reckoning 293° 19'.

4' more to the South than by reckoning.
Réamur's thermometer +25°, Fahrenheit's thermometer 87°.

From Thursday 26ᵗʰ to Friday 27ᵗʰ January 1792

91¾

Variable breeze from SE and ESE, light.

During the afternoon, we caught sight of Grey gulls.

Variation of the compass by observation of the amplitudes and by several sets of observations of azimuths, was 9° 36' NW.

By four sets of observations of five distances each of the moon and the sun, taken by Mr Chanal and by myself, reduced to 11h 2' 13' AM, our longitude was 297° 30', mean result.

That computed from our last observations was found to be at the same moment 296° 38', that is 52' more to the East.

Latitude by observation South 19° 37'.
Longitude by observation 297° 36'.
Longitude by reckoning from the Straits of Sunda 294° 56'.

4' more to the South than by reckoning.
Réamur's thermometer +25°, Fahrenheit's thermometer 87°.

From Friday 27th to Saturday 28th January 1792

122½

At 4 o'clock 34' 44" PM, we took two more sets of distances of the moon and the sun, Mr Chanal and myself, which gave 298° longitude. This result was in perfect agreement with that of the observations made in the morning and reduced to this moment.

At 6 o'clock PM, we perceived Rodrigue Island, bearing West ½ S.

At ½ past 6 o'clock, it extended from West 3° N to West 4° South, at a distance of about 13 leagues.

The variation of the magnetic needle, determined from the Westerly amplitude and from several sets of azimuths taken with different compasses, was at this moment 10° 18' NW, mean result.

Immediately upon perceiving Rodrigue Island, we had directed our course WSW in order to pass South of it.

From 8 o'clock PM to ¾ past 4 o'clock AM, we steered successively SW¼W, W¼SW and W 4° N in order to sheer off a little more during the night on account of the reefs which surround Rodrigue.

At this moment, we directed our course WNW½W.

At ¼ past 5 o'clock AM, it bore from N 54° E to North 59° E, distant 8 leagues. We took our departure from this situation in longitude 299° 32' West.

At this moment, the longitude, determined from our observations of the preceding day, was found to be 299° 6'. 26' more to the West.

It is to be supposed that the currents had carried us a little to the Westward during the night, in which direction they usually set here.

The longitude by reckoning since our departure from the Straits of Sunda was 3° 6'. In consequence, we had been carried to the Westward this far during our passage.

Rodrigue Island is in general regular and very little broken, it is high enough to be seen in fine weather at a distance of 12 or 13 leagues.

Latitude by observation South 20° 4'.
Longitude by reckoning 300° 6'.

3' more to the South than by reckoning.

Réamur's thermometer +25½°, Fahrenheit's thermometer 88°.

From Saturday 28th to Sunday 29th January 1792

119

We continued to steer WSW½W with the help of a gentle gale at ESE until 7 o'clock in the morning, at which moment we directed our course to W¼NW.

At ½ past 6 o'clock, we perceived a ship in the SE standing the same way.

We saw tropic birds and sea swallows.

The variation of the compass determined from several observations was 11° 20' NW.

Latitude by observation South 19° 47'.
Longitude 302° 12'.

8' more to the South than by reckoning.

Réamur's thermometer +25½°, Fahrenheit's thermometer 88°.

From Sunday 29th to Monday 30th January 1792

118⅓

During the afternoon, we had a gentle breeze at SE attended with a hollow swell from the South and clear weather.

At 8 o'clock in the evening, we handed the top-gallant sails and took in the studding sails. We carried this quantity of sail all night. At day-light we crowded sail and stood to the West.

At ½ past 6 o'clock AM, we had sight of Round Island in the WNW, at a distance of 8 to 9 leagues.

The ship we had seen the preceding day was ½ a league a-head.

At 8 o'clock, Round Island bore NW¼W, distant 6 leagues, and Isle of Serpents, NW 3° W.

A thick haze prevented us from seeing Isle of France, which we perceived one hour after.

At 11 o'clock, Round Isle bore North of the globe, which gave the longitude of 304° 35' West, following the chart of Mr D'Après. However, that computed from the moment we perceived Rodrigue Island, was 304° 15', that is 20' more to the East.

At noon, we took the following bearings.

Round Isle by Isle of Serpents NNW½W, Coin de Mire WNW½W and Le Pouce on the Isle of France, SW½W.

Réamur's thermometer +24°, Fahrenheit's thermometer 85°

From Tuesday [sic] *30th to Tuesday 31st January 1792*

We doubled Coin de Mire at ¼ past 1 o'clock, and at two o'clock we passed at a distance of half a league from Point of Cannoniers. We then worked to windward, ranging along the coast at a distance of ⅓ or ½ a league. At ½ past 3 o'clock, we bore away somewhat in order to avoid the reefs surrounding the Island of Tonnelier, having 5 fathoms over a coral bottom.

At ¾ past 3 o'clock, the pilot came on board ship, at 4 o'clock we came to anchor within musquet shot of the flag-staff opposite the entrance of the harbour. The Surgeon came on board in a boat at 5 o'clock, after which I went immediately ashore, having given orders to the commanding officer on board to tow the ship as soon as possible into Trou Fanfaron, which affords shelter from the hard gales which, in general, blow every year in this place at this moment. This was done the next day. The ship was unrigged immediately and the standing and running ropes were overhauled.

A few days after our arrival, I succeeded in selling the remainder of our cargo and all the stores of the ship for which we no longer had any use.

During our stay in this colony, I had built a poop in order to take more passengers. We gave the ship a parliament heel in order to repair the sheathing of copper which had been lost at the water line aft, and at the place where the flukes of the anchors had rubbed when getting under sail. The caulkers were employed caulking all the sides of the ship inside and out, and the coopers went to work to repair the casks. We set up the forge in one of the tents and the armourer was employed making the sundry iron work of which we were in need. I discharged from the ship, of his own accord, Mr Roblet, the Surgeon, who desired to settle in this place, with the carpenter, the armourer and some few seamen. These were replaced by three men and the crew in consequence was 42 in number. It was with the greatest satisfaction that, on account of the confidence that we placed in the ship, we reached the object of our wishes in taking her intirely to freight and procuring twelve passengers bound for Toulon, which conduced somewhat to making the cost of the expedition less exorbitant.[255]

From Wednesday 18th to Thursday 19th April 1792

76

After seventy-seven days at Port Louis, on the 18th April, at 5 o'clock in the evening, we got under sail with the help of a light breeze at SE. The pilot, and likewise our friends, accompanied us and left the ship once we had sailed passed the flag-staff.

---

255 Gannier suggests that Marchand may have engaged in slave trading while at Mauritius in order to make up for his failure in fur trading (*journal*, op. cit., p. 524). Marchand spends almost two and half months on the island (from the 31st January to 18th April 1792).

At 6 o'clock, Sandy Point bore SW¼W, Coin de Mire bore NE½E and the point of the island of Tonnelier SE 8° E.

At this moment, the breeze settled at East and varied afterwards at SE and SSE blowing a gentle gale.

As I was to take on board about three hundred bags of coffee at St Denis, on the Isle of Bourbon, I directed the course for this island after standing off a little from the Isle of France in order to avoid the calms.

At day-light, we perceived the Isle of Bourbon extending from SW¼W to West.

At noon, the Northern extremity of this island, called Latanier Point, bore W½N, and the South point, SW 2° South.

At this moment, our latitude by observation was found to be 20° 59' South.

Réamur's thermometer +23°, Fahrenheit's thermometer 83°.

From Thursday 19th to Friday 20th April 1792

62½

During the afternoon, we continued to stand in for the land with the help of a gentle gale at SE. But at ½ past 5 o'clock, I judged it to be impossible to gain St Denis before night, I resolved thus to make trips until day-light. In consequence, we worked to windward.

At this moment, the Northermost point of the Island bore WNW½N, and Piton Point, South.

During the night we had a hard gale varying from SE¼S to South attended with squalls.

Immediately upon day-light, we steered for the road of St Denis in which we came to anchor at ¼ past 9 o'clock, in 10 fathoms over a bottom of fine gravel mixed with broken shells.

Latanier Cape bore W¼N, Bois Rouge Point ESE¼S, and a warehouse which is situated very close to the shore, bore South aft of us.

The pilot had come on board ship at the moment of our coming to anchor.

The road of St Denis, laid down in the chart of Mr D'Après in latitude 20° 51' 40" South and longitude 53° 10' East, is very easy to make. On coming from the South East, it is necessary to range along the coast at a distance of about a mile, steering for a large point which is very steep and which is called Cape Latanier. The anchoring place is to be found directly West of this Cape, and once at anchor, it is no more than a quarter of a league distant. It cannot be mistaken, for it is the only point which is so steep, and it is the first to be met with if coming from the South. Besides, the mast of the pavilion, belonging to the fort, can be perceived from more than two leagues distant. Mount Signaux can also be seen, for it is to be found WNW and NW of the town, upon the slopes of a hill, which lies SW of the town. There is also a man who, for his own pleasure, makes signals to the ships with flags. On the point forming the anchoring place at East, there is a reef which stretches about ¾ of a cables length into the sea, but it does not present any danger from the breakers there. If making for the road with a hard gale, it would be better to enter with as little sail as is possible, and only with the fore stay-sail

Remainder of Thursday 19th to Friday 20th 1792

if the ship steers well, for it can swing but little in this place and must be moored NW and SE. As we were to remain here but a very short time, I anchored with one anchor.

This anchoring place is dangerous during the strong winds and a ship may drive from her anchor even in strong gales. It is the pilot who, in hard weather, will make the signal to unmoor from ashore. Upon coming to anchor, you are informed of the agreed signals.

Upon coming to anchor, I immediately went ashore in order to proceed with the taking in of the coffee.

From Friday 20th to Saturday 21st April 1792

During the afternoon, thanks to Mr Berthelot who had been charged with the purchase of the coffee, we loaded 240 bags. During the night we had a hard wind at SE attended with heavy squalls and rain.

During the morning, we took in the remainder of the coffee and some provisions which I had not been able to procure at the Isle of France.

From Saturday 21st to Sunday 22nd April 1792

85½

At 5 o'clock PM, I came on board and found all ready for sailing.

At 6 o'clock, we hove up the anchor, and at 7 o'clock we got under sail with the help of a breeze blowing a fresh gale at SE¼E.

At ½ past 7 o'clock, the Northermost point of the island bore W 8° S, and the road of St Denis SE¼S. We here took our departure in latitude 20° 42' South, and in longitude 306° 50' West of Paris.

After having taken the bearing above-mentioned, we directed our course first to NW and W in order to avoid the calms which are to be met with to the leeward of this island, and then to SW and SW¼W.

We left a brig from the Isle of France in the road of St Denis which had come to anchor the same day as ourselves.

During the night, the breeze blew a gentle gale at ESE and then varied at ENE.

At day-light, the Isle of Bourbon could yet be seen extending from E¼NE to ESE, distant by estimation about 11 leagues.

We saw many tropic birds and gulls.

Present latitude by observation South 21° 33'.
Longitude by reckoning 307° 52'.

9' more to the South than by reckoning.

Réamur's thermometer +21°, Fahrenheit's thermometer 79°.

From Sunday 22ⁿᵈ to Monday 23ʳᵈ April 1792

99

During this day, the breeze was at SE and SE¼E, blowing a gentle gale attended with grey weather and a swelling sea at NE.

The variation of the compass determined from several observations was NW 18° 20'.

We saw many tropic birds.

Present latitude by observation South 23° 6'.
Longitude by reckoning 308° 43'.

7' more to the South than by reckoning.
Réamur's thermometer +21°, Fahrenheit's thermometer 79°.

Monday 23ʳᵈ to Tuesday 24ᵗʰ April 1792

94

The breeze varied from ESE to NE and blew a light gale attended with overcast weather.

During the night, we had lightning in the North.

The variation of the compass by observation was NW 19° 50'.

Latitude by observation South 24° 23'.
Longitude by reckoning 309° 47'.

2' more to the South than by reckoning.
Réamur's thermometer +20°, Fahrenheit's thermometer 77°.

From Tuesday 24ᵗʰ to Wednesday 25ᵗʰ April 1792

64¾

At noon we steered WSW.

Until 8 o'clock in the evening, we had light breezes varying from NE to ENE. At this time, we had a squall from the West attended with rain, thunder and lightning, which made the wind vary from NE to West round by the South.

During the remainder, the wind was light from the NE quarter varying at ESE with rain at intervals.

The variation of the compass, determined from several sets of observations of the azimuths, was 20° 30' NW.

Latitude by observation South 25° 38'.
Longitude by reckoning 310° 40'.

32' more to the South than by reckoning.
Réamur's thermometer +20°, Fahrenheit's thermometer 77°.

From Wednesday 25th to Thursday 26th April 1792

32½
At noon, I directed our course to W¼SW.
During this day, we had baffling winds, calms, rain and frequently lightning all round the compass.
The variation of the compass by observation of the azimuths was 21° 30' NW.

Latitude by observation South 25° 56'.
Longitude by reckoning 311° 11'.

Réamur's thermometer +20°, Fahrenheit's thermometer 77°.

From Thursday 26th to Friday 27th April 1792

91
We had very light airs until 7 o'clock PM, at this time there began to blow a fresh wind which settled at ENE, blowing a gentle gale attended with squalls at intervals.
We saw albatrosses, brown gulls, sea swallows of several different kinds, Port Egmont Hens and tropic birds.
Variation of the compass by reckoning NW 22° 30'.

Latitude by observation South 26° 39'.
Longitude by reckoning 312° 34'.

9' more to the North than by reckoning.
Réamur's thermometer +20°, Fahrenheit's thermometer 77°.

From Friday 27th to Saturday 28th 1792

145
At noon, we steered W½N. During this day, we had a heavy wind at East, attended with fine weather.
We saw albatrosses, sea swallows and porpoises.
The variation of the compass determined from the amplitudes was 23° 11' NW.

Latitude by observation South 27° 11'.
Longitude by reckoning 315° 9'.

Réamur's thermometer +19½°, Fahrenheit's thermometer 76°.

From Saturday 28ᵗʰ to Sunday 29ᵗʰ April 1792

150½

At 2 o'clock, 45' and 6", apparent time, by four sets of five distances each of the moon and the sun, observed by Mr Chanal and myself in order to determine the longitude, the result of each was as follows:

The 1ˢᵗ by Mr Chanal gave	317° 23' 30"
The 2ⁿᵈ by the above-mentioned	317° 34' 45"
The 1ˢᵗ by myself	317° 34' 45"
and the 2ⁿᵈ *ditto*	317° 30' 45"
Mean result	317° 32'

The longitude by reckoning from St Denis, Isle of Bourbon, was found to be 315° 25'. Difference to the West 2° 7'.

During this day, the wind continued to blew a fresh gale from ESE to SE, fine weather.

Latitude by observation South 27° 50'.
Longitude by reckoning 318° 7'.
Longitude by observation 320° 14'.

7' more to the North than by reckoning.
Réamur's thermometer +19°, Fahrenheit's thermometer 75°.

From Sunday 29ᵗʰ to Monday 30ᵗʰ April 1792

138½

At 3h 16' PM, apparent time, our longitude determined from three sets of observations of five distances each of the sun and the moon, was 320° 58'. That by the observation of the preceding day, reduced to this moment, was 320° 33', that is 25' more to the East.

During this day, the wind settled at ESE blowing a gentle gale, clear weather and fine.

The variation of the compass by observation of five sets of azimuths was 23° 30' NW.

Latitude by observation South 28° 18'.
Longitude by reckoning 320° 37'.
Longitude by observation 323° 9'.

13' more to the North than by reckoning.
Réamur's thermometer +19½°, Fahrenheit's thermometer 76°.

Monday 30th April to Tuesday 1st May 1792

111
At 4 o'clock PM, we steered West.
Wind at ESE blowing a gentle gale, clear weather and cloudy at intervals.
We saw albatrosses.
The variation of the compass by observation was 26° 3' NW.

Latitude by observation South 29°.
Longitude by reckoning 312° 32' 30".
Longitude by observation 325° 4' 30".

3' more to the North than by reckoning.
Réamur's thermometer +20½°, Fahrenheit's thermometer 78°.

From Tuesday 1st to Wednesday 2nd May 1792

80½
During this day, we had light breezes at East and at ESE with overcast weather
at intervals.
The variation of the magnetic needle, determined from 24 observations of the
azimuths, was 26° 47' NW.
We saw a great quantity of sea swallows and some few albatrosses.

Latitude by observation South 29° 25'.
Longitude by reckoning 323° 55'.
Longitude by observation 326° 27'.

7' more to the North than by reckoning.
Réamur's thermometer +20½°, Fahrenheit's thermometer 78°.

From Wednesday 2nd to Thursday 3rd May 1792

66½
Light winds varying from ESE and ENE, clear weather and fine, smooth sea.
By 9 sets of observations of the azimuths, and by the amplitudes, we found the
variation of the magnetic needle to be 26° 54' NW.
We took three bonetta of which there were many around the ship.

Latitude by observation South 30° 28'.
Longitude by reckoning 325° 4'.
Longitude by observation 327° 36'.

33' more to the South than by reckoning.
Réamur's thermometer +19°, Fahrenheit's thermometer 75°.

From Thursday 3rd to Friday 4th May 1792

71¾

Until 5 o'clock in the morning, we had a light wind at NNE and at North, which was succeeded by light airs and calms.

We saw stormy petrels, albatrosses and sea swallows of several kinds.

The variation of the compass was 27° 3' by observation.

Latitude by observation South 31° 8'.
Longitude by reckoning 326° 12'.
Longitude by observation 328° 44'.

4' more to the South than by reckoning.
Réamur's thermometer +20½°, Fahrenheit's thermometer 78°.

From Friday 4th to Saturday 5th May 1792

84

We had a calm until 4 o'clock PM. At this time, the wind having settled at ENE, varying at North, we steered West, all sails set. Fine weather and smooth sea.

At 4 o'clock AM, the wind shifted to NE appearing to vary at NW.

Gusty winds and cloudy, took two reefs in the top-sails.

During the morning, the wind having shifted to W and blowing a hard gale, with the appearance of bad weather, we unrigged the fore top-gallant mast and the mizzen top mast.

At 10 o'clock, heavy squalls reduced us to the foresail and the close-reefed main top-sail, we tacked and stood to the Southward.

We saw many albatrosses, black petrels and stormy petrels.

Latitude by observation South 32° 11'.
Longitude by observation 327° 18'.
Longitude by reckoning 329° 50'.

16' more to the South than by reckoning.
Réamur's thermometer +17°, Fahrenheit's thermometer 71°.

From Saturday 5th to Sunday 6th May 1792

40

At noon, we led on the larboard tack. The wind continued to blow a hard gale at WSW until 10 o'clock in the evening, at which time, moderating, it shifted to SW and South.

We had squalls at intervals.

At 10 o'clock AM, we had a calm with a great swell from the SW.

We caught sight of White and Black Spotted Petrels and albatrosses. We took several with the line.

Latitude by observation South 31° 53'.
Longitude by observation 330° 18'.
Longitude by reckoning 327° 46'.

3' more to the South than by reckoning.
Réamur's thermometer +20°, Fahrenheit's thermometer 77°.

From Sunday 6th to Monday 7th May 1792

127½

Until 2 o'clock PM we had much difficulty in steering the ship on account of the swell from the SW. Soon after, a light breeze sprang up at ENE and began to blow fresh. During the remainder of this day, the wind blew a hard gale, varying to NNW round by North.

During the night, we steered W¼S and W in order not to meet with any land unexpectedly should we have a difference to the West, which is usual here. At day-light, I directed our course to W¼NW.

By several sets of observations of the azimuths, the variation of the compass was found to be 24° 34' NW.

Latitude by observation South 32° 51'.
Longitude by observation 332° 31'.
Longitude by reckoning 329° 59'.

Réamur's thermometer +19°, Fahrenheit's thermometer 75°.

From Monday 7th to Tuesday 8th May 1792

43½

Clear weather, swelling sea, difficulty in steering. During the calm, we took two female sharks. We found in their bellies more than two hundred young, still alive and ready to be born. After killing them we threw them into the sea.

At ½ past 1 o'clock AM, the wind began to blow suddenly at NNW in violent gusts, which brought us under close-reefed top-sails. At 4 o'clock, it shifted to W¼NW and blew with such strength that we were obliged to bring to under the mizen, after having got down the top-gallant mast until the back-stays.

During the whole of the morning the wind continued to blow a hard gale attended with violent gusts of wind and a very hard sea.

Greatest height at noon.

Latitude by observation South 32° 57'.
Longitude by observation 332° 49'.
Longitude by reckoning 330° 17'.

Réamur's thermometer +16°, Fahrenheit's thermometer 69°.

From Tuesday 8ᵗʰ to Wednesday 9 May 1792

61

The wind having fallen during the afternoon, we set the four main courses under close-reefed top-sails. The sea was still very hard and we laboured much.

At 3 o'clock PM we perceived the coast of Africa in the vicinity of Natal, I mean Point Natal, extending from N¼NW to NNE, at a distance by estimation of 9 leagues, in this situation we were about 10 leagues more to the West of the longitude determined from the observations made on the 29ᵗʰ of the preceding month.

During the night, we had moderate breezes and variable, attended with a great swell from the SW. We lost a hog on account of the great sea.

Until 7 o'clock in the morning we had stood off in order to get an offing from 6 o'clock in the evening, at which time we tacked and stood in for the land.

At noon, the South coast of Point Natal bore NW¼N at NNE, at 7 leagues.

Latitude by observation South 33° 33'.
Present longitude determined from the observations of the 29ᵗʰ: 333° 3'.

That computed from the bearing taken at noon 334° 3'.
Difference to the West which had most likely happened these last two days: 1°
We were carried 40' more to the South in two days.
Since our departure from Bourbon we had been driven 3° 32' more to the West than by the reckoning.
Réamur's thermometer +18°, Fahrenheit's thermometer 73°.

From Wednesday 9 to Thursday 10ᵗʰ May 1792

59¼

Clear weather, standing to the North under the four main courses, two reefs in the top-sails.

At 2 o'clock, the change in the colour of the sea announced that we were near Cape Aiguillas.

At ¼ past 3 o'clock, we sounded and had 75 fathoms over a bottom of gravel and broken shells. The coast extended at this time from NE¼E to WNW½N, distant 5 leagues. At ½ past 3 o'clock, we tacked and stood to the Southward.

The wind was variable and moderate until midnight, attended with drizzling rain, close overcast weather and a boisterous sea from the West. From midnight to 4 o'clock, the wind increased in such a manner that it obliged us bring to under the mizen and the fore stay-sail. The atmosphere promised a stiff gale, we unrigged the top-gallant mast and got it down until the back-stays.

During the whole of the morning, the wind blew with such strange fury, it was attended with the most violent gusts of wind and the sea ran prodigiously high. We lay to however, and I resolved not to bear away, though some amongst us were of this opinion. At 10 o'clock, the wind carried away the fore stay-sail, but which was immediately replaced by another for I had taken the precaution to bend it to the yard some few days ago. The sea carried away all that it could, even that which was lashed. Fearing that the two boats on the deck, in filling, would break through the gratings upon which they were placed, we removed a stopper from each in order to make easier the draining of the water.

Latitude by reckoning 33° 46'.
Longitude by reckoning determined from the bearing of yesterday 334° 8'.

Réamur's thermometer +14°, Fahrenheit's thermometer 65°.

From Thursday 10ᵗʰ to Friday 11ᵗʰ May 1792

52½

At noon, we stood close upon a wind to the Southward, continuing to try under the mizen and the mizen stay-sail. While tacking, and when the ship was almost wind right aft, a terrible wave struck us and broke through the windows of the poop which then filled almost completely with water, spoiling all the articles I had in my cabin.

The stiff gale continued to blow with the same violence until 4 o'clock in the afternoon, at which time it began to abate. The sea was a fearful sight. Several waves struck the deck and washed away several articles and broke the water barrel. The cabins were all afloat under the poop and between decks. But excepting this, the ship behaved well and did not make the least water in her hold. During the storm, we made two inches of water per hour which came from the upper works.

Towards the evening, we heard the storm, the wind began to abate and the sky to clear, but the sea continued to run very high, and it was only during the morning of the 11ᵗʰ that the wind moderating, permitted us to set the two courses. This gale was one of the hardest which it is possible to have, and while navigating I have never before seen any such winds, though I have experienced parts of hurricanes. We had not sustained all the damage which was to be expected of such violet weather and of the raging of the sea. This was owing most likely to the ship being a very good one, and she behaved exceeding well. It is not be doubted but that an old vessel, or one that was not well-built, would have been attended with the greatest dangers, for despite the strength of ours and the good repair in which she had been kept previously, the storm did not prevent all the seams of the planks of the deck, extending from the main mast to her bow, from splitting, and the water from getting in the between decks and in the steward's room which is situated before the fore mast. If we consider the dangers with which a ship is attended when wind is right aft, in such weather and in such a boisterous sea as we had experienced, and when we compare them to the advantages which may be had from lying to, and when a ship unites strength and other fine qualities, it is a matter of great surprise that many navigators have preferred to bear away in such cases as these, save when the ship is deep-waisted and may thus be brought into danger by being water-logged. Lying to appears to me to be the most preferable situation to keep in order to better bear the effects of stiff gales upon low vessels, or those with three decks, if they are made ready for the bad weather. The fore yard of the ship went a great way into the sea, to a third part of its length, on each rolling of the ship, as I had never seen and which I would scarce have imagined before.

During the bad weather we lost a hog, three goats and more than three hundred fowl owing to the waves and the hardness of the weather. We saved the remainder of the fowls and our animals by putting them in the great cabin. At 6 o'clock in the morning, we tacked and stood to the North under the four main courses wind permitting, two reefs in the top-sails. During the storm, we constantly saw spotted petrels, albatrosses, sea swallows and blue petrels.

Latitude by observation 34° 42'.
Longitude by reckoning 333° 40'.

During these two days, we were carried 1° 11' to the South of the reckoning, from which I imagined that we must have also a difference to the West, for the currents in general set to the SE in this place, following the direction of the coast.
Réamur's thermometer +14°, Fahrenheit's thermometer 65°.

From Friday 11ᵗʰ to Saturday 12ᵗʰ May 1792

80

The weather being fine, sailing under the four main courses, leading on the larboard tack and much difficulty in steering. The sea turbulent and short, which we judged to be in consequence of the currents. From 6 to 10 o'clock PM, we had a calm, and then a breeze sprang up at ENE which blew a gentle gale all night and with the help of which we directed our course NW¼W, all sails set, except the studding sails, the sea intirely smooth.

At day-light, we saw land to the Northward. It was high and we judged it to be the adjacent parts of Round Mountain, which seemed to indicate a great difference to the West, which was confirmed by our observations.

At 9h 18' 44', apparent time, by two sets of five distances each of the ☉ and the ☾, taken by Mr Chanal and myself, our longitude was found to be 337° 58' 30".

That computed by reckoning following the bearing of the coast of Natal, was found to be at this time 335°. Difference to the West in three days 2° 58' 30".

The variation of the compass determined from the azimuths was found to be 25° 29' NW. At noon, the part of the coast in sight, which as I have before mentioned was the adjacent part of Mountain Cape, extended from NE¼N to NNW½N, at a distance of 10 or 12 leagues.

Latitude by observation South 35°
Longitude by reckoning determined from the observations above-mentioned 338° 10' 30".

32' more to the South than by reckoning.
Réamur's thermometer +14°, Fahrenheit's thermometer 65°.

From Saturday 12 to Sunday 13ᵗʰ May 1792

61½

Clear weather and a smooth sea. We steered WNW, all our sails set, and under the studding sails.

We saw many spotted petrels, albatrosses, sea swallows and blue petrels.

By ten sets of observations of the azimuths, we found the variation of the magnetic needle to be 25° 30' North Westerly, and by the amplitude 24° 53'.

At 5 o'clock PM, the extremes of the land in sight stretched from N¼NW to NE¼E, and Round Mountain bore NE¼N. This part of the coast is high and very broken.

At 7 o'clock in the morning, the wind having shifted to WSW, we tacked and stood to the North, and at 10 o'clock AM, as it varied to NW, we stood once more to the South.

As we tacked, we caught sight of coast from which we were no more than four leagues distant, but the haze prevented us from distinguishing anything.

Latitude by observation South 34° 38'.

Our longitude determined from the observations made the preceding day, was found at noon to be 338° 56', and that computed from two other sets of distances taken at 10h 50' in the morning, was 338° 59'. Little sensible difference.

This day, we were carried 17' to the Northward of the reckoning.
Réamur's thermometer +17°, Fahrenheit's thermometer 71°.

From Sunday 13ᵗʰ to Monday 14ᵗʰ May 1792

70¼

The sea was somewhat hollow, standing to windward on the starboard side under the four main courses.

At 3 o'clock, the wind blowing a gentle gale, we took two reefs in the top-sails.
We saw Velvet Sleeves,[256] and more of the same birds of which I have before made mention.

At ½ past 2 o'clock AM, while we were hauling up the top-sails in the brails on account of a squall, the main yard broke near one third of its length. It had most likely been sprung during the storm, for the squall was not in the least heavy. We were soon employed in getting up another, which work was completed at 8 o'clock in the morning, and which would have been done very much earlier had I not taken the precaution of fishing the yard, for it had many knots in the middle of it.

Latitude by reckoning South 35° 13'.
Longitude determined from the observations 339° 0' 30".

The variation of the compass by observation was NW 25° 1'.
Réamur's thermometer +15°, Fahrenheit's thermometer 67°.

From Monday 14ᵗʰ to Tuesday 15ᵗʰ May 1792

65¼

During this day, the wind was variable from S¼SW to ESE, round by the South. Steering W¼NW and WNW.

We caught sight of seals, Velvet Sleeves, etc.

At 8h 43' AM, by two sets of observations of five distances each of the ☉-☾, taken by Mr Chanal and myself, our longitude was found to be 339° 48', whereas that determined from the preceding observations put us in longitude 340° 5', that is 17' more to the West.

The variation of the compass determined from several azimuths was 24° 7' NW, mean result.

Latitude by observation South 35° 19'.
Longitude determined from the observations made in the morning 340° 3'.

---

256 *The* velvet sleeves, mangas de velados, *of the Portugueze which, according to the dimensions and the characters that some give, seem to be pelicans, and, according to other notices, present more analogy to the cormorant. It is in the creek, at the Cape of Good Hope, that these birds are to be found. They owe their name to the resemblance of their plumage to velvet* (Hist. Gen. des Voy. tom, i, p. 248), *or to their tips being velvet black* (Tachard, p. 58) *said that in flying their wings appear to fold like the arm* (Hist. Gen. des Voy, ibid.). *According to some, they are all white, except the end of the wing, which is black; they are as large as the swan, or, more exactly, as the goose (*Merolla in the Hist. Gen. des Voyages, tom. i, p. 534) *according to others, they are black above and white below, (Tachard), Monsieur de Querhoënt says that they fly heavily and scarcely ever leave the deep water, he believes them to be of the same genus with the* margaux d'Ouessan *(*Remarks Made on Board His Majesty's Ship the Victory, by the Viscount de Querhoënt*) but the margaux, as we have said, must be cormorants* (Buffon, op. cit., Volume IX, p. 37). Gannier *(journal,* op. cit., p. 539) cites Fleurieu who refers to this quotation from Buffon.

3' more to the North than by reckoning.

Réamur's thermometer +15°, Fahrenheit's thermometer 67°.

From Tuesday 15ᵗʰ to Wednesday 16ᵗʰ May 1792

111¼

During this day, we had a light breeze from ESE to SE.

We steered Westward during the night in order to avoid Cape Aiguillas in case we should have a difference Northward. We steered during the day WNW and NW¼W.

At 5 o'clock in the evening, there was land in sight in the NNE.

At day-light, we saw two vessels in the North standing the same way as ourselves. We saw Velvet Sleeves and other birds.

At 8h 51' AM, apparent time, by two sets of observations of the distance of the ☉ and the ☾, our longitude was found to be 341° 57' 30". Mean result 341° 56' 34".

The variation of the compass by observation of the azimuths was 23° 28' NW.

Latitude by observation South 35° 44'.

Longitude by observation 342° 14'.

9' more the South than by reckoning.

At noon, we sounded and found 95 fathoms over a bottom of muddy sand, which agreed well with our observations putting us South of Cape Aiguillas.

Réamur's thermometer +16°, Fahrenheit's thermometer 69°.

From Wednesday 16ᵗʰ to Thursday 17ᵗʰ May 1792

109

During this day we had a light breeze at SE attended with clear weather and fog at intervals. We steered NW and NW¼N, carrying even the top mast studding sails in order to double as early as possible the Cape of Good Hope.

At midnight, we sounded but had no bottom with a line of 150 fathoms, from which I concluded that we were to the West of the bank of Aiguillas.

At 7 o'clock AM, we perceived a sail behind us making the same way.

We continued to see Velvet Sleeves.

Latitude by observation South 34° 46'.

Longitude by reckoning 344° 15'.

12' more to the North than by reckoning.

From this position, the Cape of Good Hope bore NE¼N, at a distance of 9 leagues. I had reason to think however that we were a little more to the West for having had a difference of 12' North, we should have had as much to the West the currents setting frequently to the NW in this place, following the coast. A thick fog prevented us from seeing the land which we would most certainly have perceived otherwise. But on account of the exactness of our last observations, the sight of land was of little consequence.

Réamur's thermometer +15½°, Fahrenheit's thermometer 68°.

From Thursday 17ᵗʰ to Friday 18ᵗʰ May 1792

101

During this day, we had a smooth sea and a light breeze varying from ESE to SSW attended at times with haze. The vessel which we had perceived in the morning was very near before night. At midnight, as she passed very near us, we hailed her. She proved to belong to the English Company and was from Bengal bound for London.

At day-light, she was 1½ leagues a-head.

The variation of the compass determined from several sets of azimuths, was 23° 19' NW.

Latitude by observation South 33° 45'.
Longitude by reckoning 345° 54'.

From this situation the Cape of Good Hope bore ESE, 35 leagues distant. We had therefore doubled the Cape intirely.

Réamur's thermometer +15½°, Fahrenheit's thermometer 68°.

From Friday 8ᵗʰ to Saturday 19ᵗʰ May 1792

56½

We had this day-light variable winds and calms. We saw Velvet Sleeves, spotted petrels, albatrosses, sea swallows, blue petrels and black ones.

At 5 o'clock PM, the English ship could still be seen a-head of us from the mast-head.

The caulkers were employed in caulking the seams of deck which had received some damage during the storm.

The variation of the compass by observation was 23° 1' North Westerly.

Latitude by observation South 33° 29'.
Longitude by reckoning 346° 54'.

Réamur's thermometer +15°, Fahrenheit's thermometer 67°.

From Saturday 19ᵗʰ to Sunday 20ᵗʰ June 1792

112

At 3 o'clock PM, we tacked and stood to the North.

The wind was variable from NNW to WSW until midnight, at which time it shifted to SW and blew a hard gale during a squall. The sea ran very high and the wind blew in violent gusts which obliged us to take two reefs in the top-sails.

The variation of the compass by observation was 22° 37' NW.

Latitude by observation South 31° 59'.
Longitude by reckoning 348° 6'.

15' more to the North than by reckoning.
Réamur's thermometer +13°, Fahrenheit's thermometer 63°.

From Sunday 20ᵗʰ to Monday 21ˢᵗ May 1792

144¼
During this day, we had a hard gale varying from SW to SE attended frequently with squalls.
We directed our course to NNW all sails set.
At day-light, we perceived a sail on the larboard side, steering NW¼N.
Variation of the compass by observation of the amplitude 22° 7' NW.

Latitude by observation South 30° 6'.
Longitude by reckoning 350° 4'.

10' more to the North than by reckoning.
Réamur's thermometer +13°, Fahrenheit's thermometer 63°.

From Monday 21ˢᵗ to Tuesday 22ⁿᵈ May 1792

133
Light breeze from SSE and SE. Clear weather and cloudy at intervals. At day-light we could no longer see the ship we had perceived yesterday.
The variation of the magnetic needle, determined from the azimuths, was 21° 34', and from the Easterly amplitude, it was 20° 34' North Westerly.
We saw spotted petrels, albatrosses and several kinds of sea swallows.

Latitude by observation South 28° 29'.
Longitude by reckoning 351° 50'.

2' more to the North than by reckoning.
Réamur's thermometer +14°, Fahrenheit's thermometer 65°.

From Tuesday 22ⁿᵈ to Wednesday 23ʳᵈ 1792

102½
Breeze blowing a light gale from S¼SE and ESE, smooth sea.

We saw spotted petrels, albatrosses, etc.

By the mean result of three sets of observations of azimuths, the variation of the magnetic needle was 20° 34' North Westerly.

Latitude by observation South 27° 13'.
Longitude by reckoning 353° 9'.

9' more to the South than by reckoning.
Réamur's thermometer +15°, Fahrenheit's thermometer 67°.

From Wednesday 23rd to Thursday 24th May 1792

69½

Light breeze varying from SE to SW, round by the South, grey weather and smooth sea.

We saw spotted petrels, albatrosses and whales.

Variation of the compass by observation 20° 39' NW.

Latitude by observation South 26° 11'.
Longitude by reckoning 354° 2'.

11' more to the South than by reckoning.
Réamur's thermometer +16°, Fahrenheit's thermometer 69°.

From Thursday 24th to Friday 25th May 1792

54½

We had light gusts variable and calms until 3 o'clock AM at which time the wind settled at NW and WNW and blew a gentle gale. Grey weather, swell from the West.

The variation of the compass by observation of the azimuths was 20° 48', and of the Easterly amplitude 20° 6'.

We saw neither spotted petrels nor albatrosses.

As we had taken a great quantity of petrels with the line, I had put 6 of them in a cage in order to attempt to bring them back to Europe, but they died one after the other, though the most proper care was taken of them.

Latitude by observation South 25° 28'.
Longitude by reckoning 354° 13'.

Réamur's thermometer +17°, Fahrenheit's thermometer 71°.

From Friday 25ᵗʰ to Saturday 26ᵗʰ May 1792

113¾

During the whole of this day, we had a light breeze varying from W¼NW to South round by W. Fine weather, swell from the SW.

At 3h 7' 12" PM, apparent time, by two sets of distances of the ☉-☾, our longitude was found to be 355° 0' 30".

That computed from our last observations made on the 16ᵗʰ, reduced to this moment, was 354° 17', that is 43' 30" more to the East.

Variation of the needle determined from ten azimuths 20° 24' NW.

Latitude by observation South 23° 48'.
Longitude by reckoning 355° 28' 30".
Longitude by observation 356° 12'.

12' more to the North than by reckoning.
Réamur's thermometer +16°, Fahrenheit's thermometer 69°.

From Saturday 26ᵗʰ to Sunday 27ᵗʰ May 1792

72½

Light breeze varying from South to ESE, attended with grey weather and a smooth sea.

This day we crossed the Tropic of Capricorn for the fourth time during this voyage.

We saw some few black petrels, stormy petrels and sea swallows.

Latitude by observation South 22° 49'.
Longitude by reckoning 355° 28' 30".
Longitude by observation 356° 12'.

Our longitude by observation, determined from the observations of the preceding day, was found to be 357° 5' West, or 2° 55' East, having departed from Marseilles, of which the longitude is 3° 12' East.

We had thus circumnavigated the globe, or made 360° of longitude in 17 months and 13 days, including the time we had put in ports and our stay at the Isle of France.

5' more to the North of the reckoning.
Réamur's thermometer +17°, Fahrenheit's thermometer 71°.

From Sunday 27ᵗʰ to Monday 28ᵗʰ May 1792

35

This day we had only baffling winds. Grey weather and smooth sea.

We saw upon the surface of the water many *Mollusca* of the species which is commonly called the Portuguese Man of War by the seamen.

The variation of the compass determined from azimuths and amplitudes was found to be 20° 28' NW, mean result.

Latitude by observation South 22° 6'.
Longitude by observation 357° 31'.
Longitude by reckoning 357° 31'.

18' more to the North than by reckoning.
Réamur's thermometer +17½°, Fahrenheit's thermometer 72°.

From Monday 28ᵗʰ to Tuesday 29ᵗʰ May 1792

98½

At 2h 27' 23" PM, apparent time, by four sets of observations of five distance each taken by Mr Chanal and myself, we found the longitude to be 359° 5', mean result. That determined from our last observations, made on the 25ᵗʰ PM, was found to be 357° 35', reduced to this moment. We had thus been carried from this moment 1° 30' to the West. This great difference in three days I attributed to the light winds which we had had, and during which we had observed most violent currents. Besides, it is very certain that differences to the North and West are very common in this place, and following this rule, those who go from the Cape of Good Hope to St Helena, and who do not observe the longitude, must keep at least 60 leagues to the windward of this island in order not to miss seeing it.

Until 5 o'clock in the evening, we had light gusts at West, but the wind shifting to SW, it began to blow fresh, varying from East, round by the South.

We caught sight of dolphins, black petrels and stormy petrels.

The variation determined from the amplitudes and the azimuths was 20° 4' NW.

We saw sea-leek, or bamboo, like that we had seen on the NW coast of America.

Latitude by observation South 20° 51'.
Longitude computed from the observations made this day 7' West.

That determined from the observations made South of Cape Aiguillas was 357° 54', that is 13' more to the East.
Réamur's thermometer +18°, Fahrenheit's thermometer 73°.

From Tuesday 29ᵗʰ to Wednesday 30ᵗʰ May 1792

125

During the whole of this day, we had a light breeze at East and ESE attended with cloudy weather and squalls at intervals.

381

At 2h 41' 10" PM, apparent time, by 10 distances of the ☉-☾, the longitude was found to be 23' 30" West, mean result. That determined from the observations of the preceding day, reduced to this moment, was 17'.

The variation of the compass by observation was 19° 47' NW.

Latitude by observation South 19° 13'.
Longitude by observation 1° 44'.
Longitude by reckoning 359° 25'.

6' more to the North than by reckoning.
Réamur's thermometer +18°, Fahrenheit's thermometer 73°.

From Wednesday 30ᵗʰ to Thursday 31ˢᵗ May 1792

126

During this day, we had a light breeze from ESE to SE, attended with squalls at intervals.

At 3h 46' 49" PM, apparent time, by two sets of observations of five distances each of the ☉-☾, our longitude was 1° 57', whereas that which was computed from the observations made the preceding day, reduced to this moment, was found to be 1° 58', which was in perfect agreement, with only a difference of 1'.

The variation of the compass by observation of 10 azimuths was 19° 17' North Westerly.

During the morning, we rigged the mizen top mast and yards.

I ordered the coopers to get up the casks which had been put in frame in order to clear the decks. My intention was to put into St Helena in order make water and replace that which had been used up by us, for we did not dispose of enough to return to Europe if we were meet with some difficulty. I intended also to procure provisions to make up for the fowls we had lost when doubling the Cape of Good Hope during the storm of which I have before spoken.

Latitude by observation South 17 26'.
Longitude by observation 3° 10'.
Longitude by reckoning 0° 52'.

13' more to the North than by reckoning.
Réamur's thermometer +18°, Fahrenheit's thermometer 73°.

From Thursday 31ˢᵗ May to Friday 1ˢᵗ June 1792

109½

At noon, we directed our course to NW¼N.
Light breeze varying from SE¼S to ESE, cloudy weather and smooth sea.
Variation of the compass by observation NW 18° 31'.

During the morning, we very distinctly saw a spotted petrel astern which fluttered for a long time about the ship. I was greatly surprised to see a bird of this species in these low latitudes.

Latitude by observation South 16° 13'.
Longitude by observation 4° 40'.
Longitude by reckoning 2° 22'.

6' more to the North than by reckoning.
Réamur's thermometer +19°, Fahrenheit's thermometer 75°.

From Friday 1ˢᵗ to Saturday 2ⁿᵈ June 1792

95½

At noon, we steered NW¼W, at midnight WNW and at 7 o'clock AM WNW½W, being by the reckoning in the latitude of St Helena, that is 15° 55'. The wind was blowing at SSE, varying at SSW, fine weather, cloudy at intervals.

By several sets of observations of the azimuths and the amplitudes, the variation of the compass was found to be 17° 46' NW.

Latitude by observation South 15° 47'.
Longitude by observation 6° 18'.
Longitude by reckoning 4°.

11' more to the North than by reckoning.
Réamur's thermometer +20°, Fahrenheit's thermometer 77°.

From Saturday 2ⁿᵈ to Sunday 3ʳᵈ June 1792

68¼

During this day, we had a light breeze varying from ESE to SSW.

Clear weather and smooth sea. Steered W¼NW.

By the amplitudes, the variation of the magnetic needle was determined to be 16° 18' NW.

At 6 o'clock AM, we perceived astern at a short distance, a three-master steering NW. We displayed our colours, and she hoisted French colours. At ½ past 7 o'clock, she was standing the same way as ourselves.

We saw many white gulls.

At ½ past 11 o'clock, we had sight of St Helena bearing W, at a distance by estimation of about 12 leagues.

We had no sooner seen the land than I hoisted the colours which we had struck in order to inform the ship which was astern. Either she must have understood the signal, or she must have seen the land, for upon making an answer to us, she altered her course and steered NW¼N. It is most likely that she did wish to make the land.

Latitude by observation South 15° 49'.
Longitude by observation 7° 28' 30".
Longitude by reckoning 5° 10' 30".

3' more to the North than by reckoning.
Réamur's thermometer +19°, Fahrenheit's thermometer 75°.

From Sunday 3ʳᵈ to Monday 4ᵗʰ June 1792

38¾

We caught sight of many gulls of several species, some amongst them were white all over.

The variation of the compass, determined from a great number of observations, was 16° 16' NW.

At ½ past 5 o'clock, we perceived a ship in the W¼SW, that is to say directly a-head and making the same way as ourselves. At 6 o'clock, St Helena extended from W to W 7° N, at a distance of about 10 leagues.

With the help of a very light breeze at South, we steered for the land during the whole of the night.

At day-light, the ship we had seen a-head was astern, at a distance of about 1 league. She hoisted English colours.

At 8 o'clock AM, the South East point of the island bore SW½S, Sugar Loaf Point (the North part of the Island) W½S, and Round Hill Point, WSW½W, distant about 1 league from this last.

At 9 o'clock, the Eastermost part of St Helena bore SSW½S, and Sugar Loaf Point W½S, which put us in longitude 8° 4' 30" West, following the situation given to it in *Connaissance du Temps*.[257] That computed from our last observations was found to be 8° 3' 30", that is only one minute more to the East. From the meridian of Cape Aiguillas, the current had carried us 2° 18' to the West, and as we had constantly had differences North on this route, we can be very certain that the currents set to NW in this place. Besides, all the navigators experience this difference. Our latitude by reckoning at this time, that is 9 o'clock AM, was 15° 56' South.

---

257 Marchand is particularly specific here as regards the bearings and the position of St Helena. Fleurieu explains why such detail may be considered important: *As the road of St. Helena is little frequented by the French, to whom however, it may be important to be acquainted with it, and as it is so well known to the English, that in the accounts of their voyages, they dispense with entering into any detail respecting the anchorage, I have thought that it would be useful to preserve the remarks which Captain Chanal was enabled to make, as well in regard to the precautions to be taken, as to the course to be held, by a ship that intends to anchor in this road stead* (op. cit., p. 177).

At 10 o'clock, being abreast of Sugar Loaf, we hoisted out the boats and at ½ past 10 o'clock we came to anchor in 13 fathoms over a bottom of fine sand. Fort Munden bore South ½ E, Sugar Loaf ENE½E, the Governor's House S½W, the Westermost point WNW½W and the Eastermost, E¼NE.

We were about two cables length distant from the land.

In this road, we found the *Lord Campbell* and the *Northumberland*, which were English Company vessels. One and a half hours after, the ship which had been astern of us, also came to anchor. She was the *Hawkesbury* belonging to the same Company. The Captains of these ships informed me that they had received much damage in the storm on the 10th May, above all the *Hawkesbury* which had remained for a great time water-logged for the pepper on board had moved out of its place under the wind. The *Northumberland* had lost her jib boom and the *Campbell* also suffered some averages.

Upon coming to anchor, I sent an officer ashore, following the custom of this Road, to apply to the Governor Mr Brooke in order to obtain leave to make water and purchase some few provisions, which was done. As soon as the ship had been moored across with a small anchor and a small cable extending in the NW (in this place a ship is moored across from NW to SE), I went myself to the Governor's House. After paying our compliments and receiving the same, he asked me several questions concerning the voyage, which I answered in the necessary manner, he informed with regret that he could not furnish me with the provisions I was in need of, for the colony was greatly in want of fowls and animals which I required, owing to the drought which had been continuing for eighteen months, and the animals had died as a result of it. He promised me six sheep, some few bags of potatoes and greens. I applied to Mr Masson in order to procure these articles.

It is to be remembered that while doubling the Cape, we had lost 300 fowls, goats and hogs and that I had twelve passengers on board ship, and this quantity of provisions was very small. We found ourselves in great difficulty for there remained a passage of three months to Toulon.

At noon, all the forts and the ships saluted us. It was St George's Day, in honour of the King of England.

By the observations made with the greatest exactness, our latitude at the anchoring place was 15° 36' South.

From Monday 4th to Tuesday 5th June 1791

During the afternoon, I ordered our empty casks to be filled with the greatest haste, intending to remain in this road as short a time as we could for we could not procure any fresh refreshments here excepting fish, which we caught in prodigious quantities. Before night, we had twenty eight casks filled with water. We were employed during the night, at 6 o'clock in the morning we completed our water. I wished to get under sail immediately, but it proved impossible to do so for the small amount of provisions we had procured were to be got on board in the evening. I employed the people setting up the shrouds and in taking fish which we salted.

By a great number of observations of the azimuths and the amplitudes, the variation of the compass was found to be 16° 11' NW, mean result.

Réamur's thermometer +21°, Fahrenheit's thermometer 79°.

From Tuesday 5ᵗʰ to Wednesday 6ᵗʰ June 1792

At 7 o'clock in the evening, having returned to the ship with 6 sheep, potatoes and greens, of which I have before made mention, we made ready to weigh. We got up the anchor at SE in order to get under sail under the small anchor at NW. At ½ past 10 o'clock, we weighed with a very light wind at ENE after hoisting in the boats and clearing the decks. At ½ past 11 o'clock, the town bore SSE at a distance of one league, the island extending from SW½S to ESE½S.

My intention was to cross the line in 28° or 30° longitude in hopes of meeting with more wind, and in order to avoid the calms which are to be found in this place in latitudes 17 and 19° on account of it being too near to the coast of Africa. We steered NW¼N.

The island of St Helena is known very well and several navigators have written very much about the population, which is no more than two thousand persons black and white together, including the Garrison, and about the productions which are so very few. I shall thus forbear to say anything more. Mr Forster, the son, in the fourth folio volume of the second voyage of Cook has pretty well exhausted the subject.[258] It is however to the credit of the English that they have made the most of this island which is thick-set with rocks and peaks which have suffered the effects of the volcano in all parts.

I acquaint my fellow navigators that in case of necessity they will find amongst the warehouses of the Company of this colony, main top masts, cordage etc. which is sold at a price which is 50% that of London and which can prove to be of great use.

When coming from the East, and on resolving to anchor in St Helena, the North point, which is round and high, must be steered for. When reaching this point, another will be seen in the West which terminates in a sugarloaf, at the summit an ensign staff is to be found, at the very foot of which is a battery. At a distance

---

258 Forster gives a detailed description of St Helena (Chapter VII, pp. 557–571) and comments on the size of the population: *The number of inhabitants on St Helena does not exceed two thousand persons, inlcuding near five hundred soldiers and six hundred slaves (Voyage round the World,* op. cit., Voume 2, p. 570). In the translated version, this figure two thousand had been mistranslated: *Il n'y a pas à Sainte-Hélène, plus de vingt mille habitans, y compris cinq cents soldats & six cents esclaves.* Marchand seems to have had access to both accounts in English and French. Gannier (*journal,* op. cit., p. 550) attributes this remark to Cook (in the *Nouvelle Bibliothèque des Voyages* version) and suggests that Marchand here is mistaken in his estimation of the size of the population (whereas Marchand is in fact correctly « copying » from Forster).

of 3000 feet to the Westward of this battery (Fort Munden), there is another to be seen on a point which projects out to sea and abreast of which it is possible to come to anchor. But the best anchoring place is about two cables length more to the Westward, when the Governor's House, which is very near the shore and which is situated to the East of the town, bears SSW. In coming to the anchoring place, proper care is required, the coast must be followed very near to the shore for there is no danger there from the violent gusts of wind from the mountains.

During the remainder of the day, we had but light winds and calms, clear weather and smooth sea.

At noon, the island of St Helena extended from S¼SE to SE½S, at a distance of about 4 leagues. From this point, we took our departure in latitude 15° 48' South, and in longitude 8° 14' West.

Réamur's thermometer +20°, Fahrenheit's thermometer 77°.

From Wednesday 6th to Thursday 7th June 1792

51¼

Light wind varying from North to W¼NW, clear weather. At 2 o'clock PM we were leading on the starboard tack.

By five sets of observations of the azimuths, the variation of the compass was found to be 15° 44' NW.

At 4 o'clock PM, the island of St Helena extended from SSE½E to SE¼E, at a distance of 5 leagues.

At day-light, it could be seen very distinctly still in the SSE. At 10 o'clock we lost sight of it. By observation of the sun's meridian at noon, we were at this time distant 20 leagues.

Latitude by observation South 14° 53'.
Longitude by reckoning 8° 8'.

8' more to the North than by reckoning.
Réamur's thermometer +21°, Fahrenheit's thermometer 79°.

From Thursday 7th to Friday 8th June 1792

68

Until 11 o'clock in the evening, we had a light breeze at WNW and West, at which time it started to blow a gentle gale varying from SW to SSE, smooth sea, overcast weather.

Variation of the compass by observation NW 16° 17'.
We took two bonettas.

Latitude by observation South 13° 55'.
Longitude by reckoning 8° 8'.

8' more to the North than by reckoning.

Réamur's thermometer +20½°, Fahrenheit's thermometer 78°.

From Friday 8ᵗʰ to Saturday 9ᵗʰ June 1792

49½

Light breeze variable from SW¼S to SE¼E, clear weather and fine.

We took a bonetta.

By the amplitudes and azimuths, the variation of the compass was found to be 15° 29' NW.

In the morning, the people employed in inspecting the skins which were found to be in the best condition.

Latitude by observation South 13° 20'.

Longitude by reckoning 9° 26'.

3' more to the North than by reckoning.

Réamur's thermometer +19½°, Fahrenheit's thermometer 76°.

From Saturday 9ᵗʰ to Sunday 10ᵗʰ June 1792

82½

Light breeze from SSE to ESE. Fine weather, clear and a smooth sea.

We took a very large tunny fish.

Variation of the compass by observation NW 14° 57'.

Latitude by observation South 12° 21'.

Longitude by reckoning 10° 29'.

4' more to the North than by reckoning.

Réamur's thermometer +20°, Fahrenheit's thermometer 77°.

From Sunday 10ᵗʰ to Monday 11ᵗʰ June 1792

108

Fresh breeze of wind from SE to ESE, cloudy weather and smooth sea.

We saw porpoises and we took some tunny fish.

Variation of the compass by observation of the azimuths, 14° 7' NW.

Latitude by observation South 11° 10'.

Longitude by reckoning 11° 51'.

Réamur's thermometer +19°, Fahrenheit's thermometer 75°.

From Monday 11th to Tuesday 12th June 1792

118¾

During this day we had a fresh breeze of wind from SE to ESE, attended with rain at intervals.

We took a very large porpoise which I served to the people, who found it very good eating.

The brains of this fish are a delicacy which make for very good eating.

The variation of the compass, determined from the azimuths and the amplitudes, was found to be 13° 53' NW, mean result.

Latitude by observation South 9° 56'.
Longitude by reckoning 13° 19'.

6' more to the South than by reckoning.
Réamur's thermometer +20°, Fahrenheit's thermometer 77°.

From Tuesday 12th to Wednesday 13th June 1792

121½

Breeze blowing a gentle gale, variable from East to SE, with squalls and rain.

At 6 o'clock in the morning, we steered N¼NW in order to cross the latitude of Ascension in day-light.

The variation of the compass determined by several azimuths was 13° 42' NW.

We saw many birds of a species very much resembling the Velvet Sleeve. The body is white all over and the tips of the wings are black. But their flight differs, for the Velvet Sleeve flaps its wings very often, whereas these have frequently a heavy flight.

Latitude by observation South 8° 29'.
Longitude by reckoning 14° 40'.

Réamur's thermometer +19°, Fahrenheit's thermometer 75°.

From Wednesday 13th to Friday 14th June 1792

126

At 8 o'clock PM, finding ourselves in latitude 7° 52' South, and having crossed the line of Ascension, which lies in 7° 57', we directed our course once again NW¼N.

We saw tropic birds and a Port Egmont Hen and a great quantity of birds of the species of which I have before made mention.

A fresh breeze of wind at ESE and SE, cloudy weather.

The variation of the compass by observation of the azimuths was NW 12° 57'.

Latitude by observation South 6° 56'.
Longitude by reckoning 16° 2'.

Réamur's thermometer +21°, Fahrenheit's thermometer 79°.

From Thursday 14th to Friday 15th June 1792

126

At noon, we directed our course to the NW in order to stretch further to the West and thus attempt to avoid, as I have before made mention, the calms which are in general to be met with when so near to the coast of Africa.

During this day, we had a fresh breeze of wind at SE attended with cloudy weather. The variation of the compass by observation was 12° 19' NW.

Latitude by observation South 5° 39'.
Longitude by reckoning 17° 49'.

9' more to the North than by reckoning.
Réamur's thermometer +21½°, Fahrenheit's thermometer 80°.

From Friday 15th to Saturday 16th June 1792

130

Breeze at ESE blowing a gentle gale, clear weather and cloudy at intervals.
We saw frigate birds, tropic birds, stormy petrels and boobies.
Variation of the compass by observation NW 12°.

Latitude by observation South 4° 20'.
Longitude by reckoning 19° 37'.

7' more to the North than by reckoning.
Réamur's thermometer +22°, Fahrenheit's thermometer 81°.

From Saturday 16th to Sunday 17th June 1792

124

Fresh breeze of wind from SE¼E to ENE, clear weather.
Saw frigate birds and boobies.
The variation of the compass determined from several sets of azimuths was NW 11° 22'.

Latitude by observation South 3° 8'.
Longitude by reckoning 21° 19'.

3' more to the North than by reckoning.

Réamur's thermometer +22½°, Fahrenheit's thermometer 82°.

From Sunday 17th to Monday 18th June 1792

124

At noon, we steered NW¼N with the help of a fine breeze varying from East to SE¼E. Clear weather and cloudy at intervals. Variation of the compass by observation of the amplitudes NW 10° 58'.

We saw boobies and a prodigious quantity of flying fish.

Latitude by observation South 1° 57'.

Longitude by reckoning 22° 46'.

16' more to the South than by reckoning.

Réamur's thermometer +22°, Fahrenheit's thermometer 81°.

From Monday 18th to Tuesday 19th June 1792

108½

Breeze at SE¼E blowing a gentle gale. Fine weather.

Saw tunny fish and boobies.

Variation of the compass NW, by observation of the azimuths and the amplitudes, 10° 46'.

Latitude by observation South 0° 57'.

Longitude by reckoning 24° 2'.

16' more to the South than by reckoning.

In this position, the breakers that we had sight of South of the line, as laid down in the chart of Mr Verdun, Mr Borda and Mr Pingré, bore North, at a distance of 10 leagues.

Réamur's thermometer +22°, Fahrenheit's thermometer 81°.

From Tuesday 19th to Wednesday 20th June 1792

111

During the afternoon the green colour of the sea appeared to be paler than common.

We saw many *Mollusca*.

During this day, the breeze at SE¼S blowing a gentle gale. Cloudy weather and clear at intervals, the sea rough.

Variation of the compass, determined from the azimuths and the amplitudes, 10° 10' NW.

During the night we crossed the line for the fourth time in the longitude of 24° 41' West by reckoning.

Latitude by observation North 0° 38'.
Longitude by reckoning 25° 19'.

16' more to the North than by reckoning.
Réamur's thermometer +21½°, Fahrenheit's thermometer 80°.

From Wednesday 20ᵗʰ to Thursday 21ˢᵗ June 1792

120

At 4 o'clock PM, the Island of Pénédo de Saint Pierre bore West of the globe, at a distance of 85 leagues.

During the afternoon, we caught sight of considerable flocks of sea swallows, tropic birds, boobies and a turtle, and by this I did suppose that we were more to the Westward than I imagined, and in consequence much nearer to the Island of Pénédo, or some other island yet unknown for this place has been very little examined by navigators. Since taking our departure from St Helena, we had not had the least opportunity to take distances in order to determine the longitude for we were hindered constantly by the clouds. During this day, we had a gentle breeze at SE¼S, attended at intervals with squalls and rain.

Variation of the compass by observation of the azimuths 8° 47' NW.

Latitude by observation North 2° 34'.
Longitude by reckoning 26° 30'.

28' more to the North than by reckoning.
Réamur's thermometer +22½°, Fahrenheit's thermometer 82°.

From Thursday 21 to Friday 22ⁿᵈ June 1792

118½

At noon, we steered NNW, at 7 o'clock in the morning, N¼NW. Fresh breeze of wind at SE, clear weather, cloudy and rainy by turns.

We had a swell from the North East.

The variation of the compass by observation was NW 8° 2'.

I perceived some few flying fish with red wings which I had never before seen in the Atlantic ocean.

Latitude by observation North 4° 34'.
Longitude by reckoning 27° 25'.

15' more to the North than by reckoning.
Réamur's thermometer +23½°, Fahrenheit's thermometer 84°.

From Friday 22ⁿᵈ to Saturday 23ʳᵈ June 1792

113

A breeze blowing more or less fresh, varying from SSE to SSW, with rain at intervals. Hot weather and sultry.

We saw sea swallows of several kinds. We took a very large porpoise. We caught sight also of tunny fish, but caught none of them.

The variation of the compass determined from the azimuths was NW 8° 17'. No observations.

Latitude by reckoning North 6° 20'.
Longitude by reckoning 28° 3'.

Réamur's thermometer +24°, Fahrenheit's thermometer 85°.

From Saturday 23ʳᵈ to Sunday 24ᵗʰ June 1792

61½

Until 4 o'clock AM, we had a moderate breeze at SSE attended with cloudy weather. At this time it abated and shifted to South and WSW. During the night we had lightning in the West and North West.

We heard the cries of several birds.

The variation of the compass determined from the azimuths was NW 8° 14'. No observations.

Latitude by reckoning North 7° 18'.
Longitude by reckoning 28° 24'.

Réamur's thermometer +23°, Fahrenheit's thermometer 83°.

From Sunday 24ᵗʰ to Monday 25ᵗʰ June 1792

46¼

Until 4 o'clock in the morning, we had a light breeze varying from NNE to N¼NW attended frequently with rain.

At 8 o'clock, after having it quite calm, the wind settling at NE¼E and NE¼NW and blowing a gentle gale, we congratulated ourselves on having got the trade winds.

I was very much surprised at finding them in such a low latitude as this, and in this season. I attributed the little variety of climate and the calms which we had met with in this place to the crossing of the line more to the Westward than the common. I am of the opinion that in order to avoid the calms, the line should be crossed, in coming from and going to India, in 25° thereabouts, notwithstanding all that Mr D'Après writes to the contrary in *Neptune Oriental* saying that the course must be shaped in order to cross the line in 16° or 18°. It cannot be ignored that the proximity of such a continent as Africa must stop the wind. It is the same on the North coast of America in the Pacific Ocean. All those navigators who have ranged too close along the shore say they met with almost constant calms, whereas having crossed the line to the Northward, we had continually fresh winds. We made good use of the experience of others for we had kept very far from the land. To this will object those who have but followed the ordinary course to India, in crossing the line in 25° or 30°, and running the risk of not being able to double the coast of Brazil, several vessels, they say, were obliged to put in at Rio de Janeiro. I give in answer to this that those who have embarked in such an undertaking were obliged to take this method, or did so for reasons unknown to us, and not on account of the winds. On departing from Rio de Janeiro, bound for India, why can we not continue even if the coast of Brazil is in sight? But this happens only to he who is so inclined. It is to be found by experience that before reaching this situation, the winds at SE shift to East and then to NE.

For a home-bound vessel, I can see no reason why the line should not be crossed in 25°, and even more to the Westward, for it is indisputable that more wind is to be found there than nearer to the coast of Africa. Mr d'Après, in advising ships to cross the line in 16° or 18°, relies on the direct course and if the passage should be lengthened in consequence, I must alter the course for the run to the Westward will be soon gained on account of the wind.

Everything I have said on the crossing of the line is founded on the information I had very exactly from the vessels bound for America from Mozambique,[259] and from those which come from the coast of Guinea bound for the same place. The first, in order to shape a direct course, cross the line far to the Westward and never lay becalmed, whereas the last remain sometimes several months in Gabon and cannot leave for want of wind. The English East-Indiamen have now begun to cross the line in 28 or 30° and find themselves well satisfied.

Variation of the compass by observation 8° 23' NW.

43' more to the North than by reckoning in three days.

Latitude by observation North 8° 15'.
Longitude by reckoning 28° 49'.

Réamur's thermometer +23½°, Fahrenheit's thermometer 84°.
We took a small shark.

From Monday 25th to Tuesday 26th June 1792

114

A breeze blowing a gentle gale varying from NE¼N to ENE, cloudy weather, great swell on account of the wind.

---

259 This may indicate that Marchand did indeed go to Mozambique from the Isle of France during his two-month stay there.

Our fore top-sail being very worn and of no further use to us, we bent another.

The variation of the compass, determined from a great number of observations, was 8° 2' NW.

No birds.

Latitude by observation North 9° 21'.
Longitude by reckoning 30° 21'.

Réamur's thermometer +23°, Fahrenheit's thermometer 83°.

From Tuesday 26ᵗʰ to Wednesday 27 June 1792

121¼

Fresh breeze of wind at NE¼N and ENE, cloudy weather and hazy, we hauled close upon a wind, sails ready filled.

No birds of any kind.

Latitude by observation North 11° 15'.
Longitude by reckoning 31° 51'.

22' more to the North than by reckoning.
Réamur's thermometer +23°, Fahrenheit's thermometer 83°.

From Wednesday 27ᵗʰ to Thursday 28ᵗʰ June 1792

130¾

We had during this day a fresh breeze of a wind varying from NE¼N to NE¼E attended with a hazy weather and a heavy swell on account of the wind.

No birds.

The variation of the compass by observation was 70 47' NW.

Latitude by observation North 12° 20'.
Longitude by reckoning 33° 43' 30".

6' more to the North than by reckoning.
Réamur's thermometer +23°, Fahrenheit's thermometer 83°.

From Thursday 28ᵗʰ to Friday 29ᵗʰ June 1792

112

At 2 o'clock PM we caught sight of a three-master in the NNE, steering W¼NW. I had great reason to believe her to be an African trader bound for the colonies of America. Neither the one nor the other hoisted colours.

During this day we had a fresh breeze of wind from NE to NNE, attended frequently with squalls and rain.

Latitude by observation North 13° 33'.
Longitude by reckoning 35° 19'.

9' more to the North than by reckoning.
Réamur's thermometer +22°, Fahrenheit's thermometer 81°.

From Friday 29ᵗʰ to Saturday 30ᵗʰ June 1792

101¾

A breeze blowing a gentle gale varying frm ENE to NNE attended with cloudy weather and rain at intervals.

The variation of the compass by the amplitude was found to be NW 5° 28', and by the azimuths 5° 46'.

Latitude by observation North 14° 58'.
Longitude by reckoning 36° 21'.

7' more to the North than by reckoning.
Réamur's thermometer +22°, Fahrenheit's thermometer 81°.

From Saturday 30ᵗʰ June to Sunday 1ˢᵗ July 1792

114¾

Fresh breeze of wind varying from NE to E¼NE in violent gusts, cloudy weather.
Variation of the compass determined by azimuths and amplitudes 5° 34' NW.
No birds.

Latitude by observation North 16° 37'.
Longitude by reckoning 37° 25'.

5' more to the North than by reckoning.
Réamur's thermometer +22½°, Fahrenheit's thermometer 82°.

From Sunday 1ˢᵗ July to Monday 2ⁿᵈ July 1792

125

Breeze at NE and ENE blowing a fresh gale, with squalls, overcast weather.
The variation of the compass determined by the azimuths was NW 5° 43'.

No observations.

Latitude by reckoning North 18° 10'.
Longitude *ditto* 38° 52'.

Réamur's thermometer +22°, Fahrenheit's thermometer 81°.

Monday 2nd to Tuesday 3rd July 1792

During this day we had a fresh breeze of wind at NE, varying at East, attended with violent gusts, squalls and dark weather.

We caught sight of bundles of the sea weed species which is commonly called sea grape or Sargoso.

By the mean result of five azimuths, we found the variation of the compass to be 5° 23' NW.

At 7 o'clock in the morning, we discovered at a distance of 2 leagues in the NW, a schooner steering WSW.

Latitude by observation North 19° 49'.
Longitude by reckoning 40° 8'.

4' more to the North than by reckoning in two days.
Réamur's thermometer +22°, Fahrenheit's thermometer 81°.

From Tuesday 3rd to Wednesday 4th July 1792

117

Fresh breeze of wind varying from NE to ENE, clear weather and smooth sea.

We saw tropic birds and several bundles of sea grape which we took, we found it to be small crabs.

By the mean result of ten azimuths, taken with different compasses, we found the magnetic needle 5° 23' North Westerly.

Latitude by observation North 21° 25'.
Longitude by reckoning 40° 58'.

4' more to the North than by reckoning in two days.
Réamur's thermometer +22½°, Fahrenheit's thermometer 82°.

From Wednesday 4th to Thursday 5th July 1792

114¼

During the whole of this day, the breeze blew more or less fresh, variable from NE to East. We had sometimes squalls attended with rain

We found in the large bundle of sea grape we had taken, two fish about two inches in length. They resembled a needle in shape but their noses did not open fully the whole length and they terminated in a kind of trunk. The body was spotted all over with small stripes which were black in colour across a grey ground.

The variation of the compass by observation of the azimuths was 6° 25' NW.

By the mean result of five azimuths, we found the variation of the compass to be 5° 23' NW.

Latitude by observation North 23° 3'.
Longitude by reckoning 41° 40'.

3' more to the South than by reckoning.
Réamur's thermometer +22°, Fahrenheit's thermometer 81°.

From Thursday 5ᵗʰ to Friday 6ᵗʰ July 1792

92

Breeze variable from ENE to East blowing a gentle gale attended with cloudy weather and sometimes rain.

The variation of the compass deduced from 10 sets of observations was NW 7° 13'.

At ¾ past 11 o'clock AM, during a squall, two whirlwinds passed by the ship with little ill effect though the water was raised in a column of more than six feet in height. I had taken the precaution of hauling up all the sails which were set again very soon after.

During this day, we crossed for the fourth time during the course of this voyage, the Tropick of Cancer.

No observations

Latitude by observation North 24° 30'.
Longitude by reckoning 42° 8'.

Réamur's thermometer +21°, Fahrenheit's thermometer 79°.

From Friday 6ᵗʰ to Saturday 7ᵗʰ July 1792

82½

Light breeze from NE to ESE attended frequently with squalls and rain. By the mean result of ten azimuths the variation of the compass was found to be NW 7° 35'.

Latitude by observation North 26°.
Longitude by reckoning 42° 19'.

9' more to the North than by reckoning.

Réamur's thermometer +22°, Fahrenheit's thermometer 81°.

From Saturday 7ᵗʰ to Sunday 8ᵗʰ July 1792

91¼

During this day, we had alternately fine weather and rain with a breeze varying from ENE to East.

The variation of the compass by observation was 8° NW.

Latitude by observation North 27° 50'.

Longitude by reckoning 42° 37'.

21' more to the North than by reckoning.

Réamur's thermometer +22°, Fahrenheit's thermometer 81°.

From Sunday 8ᵗʰ to Monday 9ᵗʰ July 1792

134¾

A fresh breeze of wind varying from E¼NE to E¼SE attended with cloudy weather and some few squalls.

We continued to see much sargoso.

We caught sight of a bird of a smoky black colour of the gull species, and some stormy petrels.

The variation of the compass deduced from a large number of observations was found to be 9° 11', mean result.

Latitude by observation North 30° 5'.

Longitude by reckoning 43° 0' 30".

2' more to the North than by reckoning.

Réamur's thermometer +22½°, Fahrenheit's thermometer 82°.

From Monday 9ᵗʰ to Tuesday 10ᵗʰ July 1792

128¼

Fresh breeze of wind varying from ENE to ESE attended with fine weather. At 2 o'clock, we had heavy rain but which lasted only half an hour.

The variation of the magnetic needle by the mean result of several observations of the azimuths, was determined to be 10° 44' NW.

A very large dew fell during the night.

By four sets of five distances each of the ☉-☾, reduced to 8h 22' 5" AM, we found the longitude to be 46° 22' 45". That deduced by reckoning since our departure from St Helena, reduced to this same time, was 43° 25' 15". Difference to West 2° 57' 30".

We had not been able even once to observe the distances in order to determine the longitude on account of the cloudy weather and the haze which we had had constantly since our departure from this island.

Latitude by observation North 32° 23'.
Longitude deduced from the observations 43° 29' 30", I mean 46° 27'.
Longitude by reckoning 43° 29' 30".

13' more to the North than by reckoning.
Réamur's thermometer +21°, Fahrenheit's thermometer 79°.

From Tuesday 10ᵗʰ to Wednesday 11ᵗʰ July 1792

116½

During this day, we had a light breeze at ENE and E¼NE attended with squalls at intervals.

By several azimuths and by the amplitudes, we found the variation of the compass to be 12° 22' NW.

Latitude by observation North 34° 15'.
Longitude by observation 47° 32' 30".
Longitude by reckoning 44° 35'.

10' more to the North than by reckoning.
Réamur's thermometer +21°, Fahrenheit's thermometer 79°.

From Wednesday 11ᵗʰ to Thursday 12ᵗʰ July 1792

101¾

A breeze of wind more or less fresh, varying from ENE to ESE, fine weather and a smooth sea.

By the Easterly amplitude the variation of the compass was determined to be 14° 31" NW.

We saw much sargoso.

Latitude by observation North 35° 59'.
Longitude by observation 47° 56'.
Longitude by reckoning 44° 58' 30".

10' more to the North than by reckoning.
Réamur's thermometer +21½°, Fahrenheit's thermometer 80°.

From Thursday 12ᵗʰ to Friday 13ᵗʰ July 1792

42

During this day, we had alternately light winds varying from North to ESE, and calms. Fine weather, small swell from the SE.

We took a small sea bream.

By several azimuths, we found the variation of the compass to be 14° 35' NW. No observations.

Latitude by reckoning North 36° 24'.
Longitude by reckoning 44° 45'.
Longitude by observation 47° 42' 30".

10' more to the North than by reckoning.
Réamur's thermometer +20½°, Fahrenheit's thermometer 78°.

From Friday 13ᵗʰ to Saturday 14ᵗʰ July 1792

74¾

Breeze more or less fresh, varying from NE to N¼NE, fine weather, swell from the NE.

We close hauled alternately upon starboard and larboard, choosing the best tack in order to gain to Northward.

By several observations, we determined the variation of the compass to be 14° 35' NW.

During the 14ᵗʰ, we kept the birthday of the Federation and fired our guns several times. I served a double allowance to the ship's crew.

At 9 o'clock AM, we saw a brig in the West, steering SW.

Latitude by observation North 36° 7'.
Longitude by observation 47° 12'.
Longitude by reckoning 44° 15'.

12' more to the North than by reckoning.
Réamur's thermometer +21°, Fahrenheit's thermometer 79°.

Saturday 14ᵗʰ to Sunday 15ᵗʰ July 1792

37

Until 2 o'clock after midnight, the breeze was light and variable from NNE to NE. Then, excepting some few light airs from the West quarter, we had a calm.

The variation of the compass by observation was 15° 1' NW.

W caught sight of a turtle. We saw many flying fish, much sargoso and *Mollusca*.

Latitude by observation North 36° 3'.
Longitude by observation 46° 30'.
Longitude by recxkoning 43° 33'.

5' more to the North than by reckoning.
Réamur's thermometer +21°, Fahrenheit's thermometer 79°.

Sunday 15ᵗʰ to Monday 16ᵗʰ July 1792

29½
Durng this day, we had very light winds varying from North to East, and calms.
Clear weather and fine, smooth sea.
    Variation of the compass by observation North 36° 16'.

Latitude by observation North 36° 16'.
Longitude by observation 46° 18'.
Longitude by reckoning 43° 21'.

10' more to the North than by reckoning.
Réamur's thermometer +21½°, Fahrenheit's thermometer 80°.

Monday 16ᵗʰ to Tuesday 17ᵗʰ July 1792

27½
    Some light airs at South which prevent me from saying that we had absolute calm until 8 o'clock AM. At this moment, a wind springing up at West, we steered NE¼N.
    The variation of the compass by observation of the amplitudes and the azimuths was NW 15° 45'.
    During the morning, we caught sights of sea-breams. We took one.
    We passed several pieces of wood covered all over with barnacles.
    At half past eleven o'clock, we perceived a three-master in the NEE, steering E¼NE. There was a kind of netting at the stern which I took to be bales of cotton. Though we passed very near each other, we did not display our respective colours.

Latitude by observation North 36° 52'.
Longitude by observation 46° 12'.
Longitude by reckoning 43° 15'.

Réamur's thermometer +21°, Fahrenheit's thermometer 79°.

From Tuesday 17ᵗʰ to Wednesday 18ᵗʰ July 1792

115½

We steered NE and NE¼E until 4 o'clock in the morning, at which time I directed our course ENE. In steering this course so much to the Northward, my intention was to pass North of the Açores and to leave these calms as soon as possible, which we know are to be met with between the trade winds and the variable winds,.

At sun-set, we could no longer perceive the ship which we had seen in the morning, but at day-light, we saw another directly a-head but of which we lost sight soon after the weather being a little hazy.

During this day, the wind continued at WNW and W, blowing a gentle gale attended with fine weather.

We caught sight of brown gulls and many flying fish.

The variation of the compass by observation was NW 16° 17'.

Latitude by observation North 38° 18'.
Longitude by observation 44° 30'.
Longitude by reckoning 41° 33'.

5' more to the North than by reckoning.
Réamur's thermometer +20°, Fahrenheit's thermometer 77°.

From Wednesday 18ᵗʰ to Thursday 19ᵗʰ July 1792

96¼

Breeze of wind more or less fresh at WNW. Weather a little hazy, hollow swell from NNW.

At 9 o'clock PM, we saw an *aurora borealis* which ended at ½ past 10 'clock.
The variation of the compass by observation was 17° 40' NW.

This day, we saw on the surface of the water several pieces of wood with barnacles upon them, which I supposed to be the remains of the masts of a ship. At 9 o'clock in the morning, we perceived a large ship in the SE, steering NE¼E. As we were steering ENE, she reached us at 6 o'clock in the evening and hoisted Dutch colours, upon which we displayed ours. We did not endeavour to speak with each other though we were almost within hearing.

Latitude by observation North 39° 20'.
Longitude by observation 42° 53'.
Longitude by reckoning 39° 56'.

2' more to the North than by reckoning.
Réamur's thermometer +19½°, Fahrenheit's thermometer 76°.

From Thursday 19ᵗʰ to Friday 20ᵗʰ July 1792

113½

During this day, we had gentle gale at West attended with a thick haze.

We continued to see at intervals pieces of wood on the surface of the water. We caught sight of brown gulls, grey gulls, stormy petrels, flying fish and a large quantity of *Mollusca* of several species.

By several observations, we determined the variation of the magnetic needle to be 18° 47' North Westerly.

At midnight, we directed our course to NW.

Latitude by observation North 40° 25'.
Longitude by observation 40° 25'.
Longitude by reckoning 37° 53'.

1' more to the North than by reckoning.
Réamur's thermometer +19°, Fahrenheit's thermometer 75°.

From Friday 20ᵗʰ to Saturday 21ˢᵗ July 1792

89

This day, the wind from WNW to W¼SW, blowing a gentle gale attended with a smooth sea and very hazy weather.

At noon, we had directed our course East.

The variation of the compass determined from azimuths and amplitudes was 20° 53' NW.

Latitude by observation North 41° 3'.
Longitude by observation 39°.
Longitude by reckoning 36° 3'.

7' more to the North than by reckoning.
Réamur's thermometer +19°, Fahrenheit's thermometer 75°.

From Saturday 21ˢᵗ to Sunday 22ⁿᵈ July 1792

97

Wind variable from W¼SW to W¼NW blowing a gentle gale, smooth sea and thick haze.

We took two bonettas.

We perceived many flying fish and much *Mollusca*.

The variation of the compass by observation was NW 22° 10'.

At midnight, we directed our course E¼SE.

Sargoso was no longer to be seen but we now caught sight of a kind of sea grass of a yellowish colour.

Latitude by observation North 41° 24'.
Longitude by observation 36° 56'.
Longitude by reckoning 33° 59'.

8' more to the South than by reckoning.
Réamur's thermometer +18°, Fahrenheit's thermometer 73°.

Sunday 22nd to Monday 23rd July 1792

88½

Light wind variable from NW¼N to W¼S, smooth sea and thick haze.
We caught sight of whales, brown gulls, stormy petrels and sea grass.
Variation of the compass by observation NW 22° 40'.

Latitude by observation North 41° 42'.
Longitude by observation 35°.
Longitude by reckoning 32° 3'.

8' more to the South than by reckoning.
Réamur's thermometer +18°, Fahrenheit's thermometer 73°.

From Monday 23rd to Tuesday 24th July 1792

94

Light wind variable from NW to W¼NW, smooth sea and very thick haze.
At midnight we directed our course ESE.

By two sets of six distances each of the moon and the sun, reduced to 2h 15' 43", we found the longitude to be 34° 13'. That deduced from the last observations, reduced to this moment, was 34° 41', that is 28' more to the West.

We saw stormy petrels and sea grass.

Latitude by observation North 41° 42'.
Longitude by observation 32° 25'.
Longitude by reckoning 29° 57'.

8' more to the South than by reckoning.
Réamur's thermometer +17°, Fahrenheit's thermometer 70°.

From Tuesday 24ᵗʰ to Wednesday 25ᵗʰ July 1792

90½

By two sets of observations of five distances each of the ☉-☾, reduced to 2h 55' 21" PM, I found our longitude to be 32° 5'. That deduced from yesterday's observations, reduced to this moment, was 32° 12'.

The variation of the compass by observation was NW 22° 37'.

During this day, we had a breeze varying from W¼SW to NW. The weather was very hazy until the wind veered to NW, at which time it cleared up.

We saw sea swallows.

Latitude by observation North 41° 46'.
Longitude by observation 30° 15'.
Longitude by reckoning 27° 54'.

2' more to the North than by reckoning.
Réamur's thermometer +17½°, Fahrenheit's thermometer 72°.

From Wednesday 25ᵗʰ to Thursday 26ᵗʰ July 1792

110½

Variable wind from WNW to North with violent gusts and attended with weather alternately clear and cloudy. Smooth sea.

We saw Black Headed Grey Gulls and a turtle.

The sea was covered with *Mollusca*.

By the mean result of several observations of the azimuths and the amplitudes, the variation of the compass was determined to be 22° 35' NW.

Latitude by observation North 41° 45'.
Longitude by observation 27° 39'.
Longitude by reckoning 25° 18'.

Réamur's thermometer +17½°, Fahrenheit's thermometer 72°.

From Thursday 26ᵗʰ to Friday 27ᵗʰ July 1792

123

At noon, we directed our course SE¼E.

At 4 o'clock PM, we had sight of a ship to the windward, steering WSW.

By several observations, the variation of the magnetic needle was found to be 22° 17' NW.

406

During this day, the wind was variable blowing a gentle gale from NW to N, clear weather and a smooth sea.

Latitude by observation North 41° 13'.
Longitude by observation 24° 58'.
Longitude by reckoning 22° 37'.

8' more to the South than by reckoning.
Réamur's thermometer +17°, Fahrenheit's thermometer 71°.

From Friday 27ᵗʰ to Saturday 28ᵗʰ July 1792

99½

Wind variable from NW to W¼NW, clear weather and hazy at intervals. Smooth sea. The variation of the compass by observation NW 22° 27'.

At 4h 26' 33" PM, by twelve distances of the ☉-☾, our longitude reduced to noon, was found to be 23° 22'. That deduced from the observations made on the 24ᵗʰ was found to be 22° 48'. Mean result 23° 5'.

Latitude by observation North 40° 55'.

Réamur's thermometer +17°, Fahrenheit's thermometer 71°.

From Saturday 28ᵗʰ to Sunday 29ᵗʰ July 1792

100

At noon, we steered SE with the help of a light gale at W¼NW and NW, attended with very hazy weather.

At 8 o'clock AM, we caught sight of a ship in the NNW, steering SW.
The variation of the compass determined from several observations was 22° 31 NW.
No observations.

Latitude by observation, I mean by reckoning, North 40° 61'.
Longitude by observation 21° 3'.
Longitude by reckoning 18° 53'.

Réamur's thermometer +16°, Fahrenheit's thermometer 69°.

From Sunday 29ᵗʰ to Monday 30ᵗʰ July 1792

95¼

At 6 o'clock, we spoke to Captain Barbier, Commander of the brig *La Société* from Dunkerque, bound for Virginia. As well as we could understand, he told us that we were at war with the Emperor.[260]

---

260 See Gannier, *journal*, op. cit., p. 569.

During this day, we had a breeze varying from NNE to NE¼E blowing a gentle gale. Cloudy weather.

Variation of the compass by observation NW 22° 19'.

No observations.

Latitude by reckoning North 39° 37'.
Longitude by observation 19° 17'.
Longitude by reckoning 17° 17'.

Réamur's thermometer +16°, Fahrenheit's thermometer 69°.

From Monday 30ᵗʰ to 31ˢᵗ July 1792

125

A very fresh breeze of wind at NE with the help of which we kept to the wind in order to attempt to make Cape St Vincent. At 4 o'clock PM, we caught sight of a ship, and the next morning we had in sight four others, steering NW.

Clear weather and cloudy at intervals.

Latitude by observation North 38° 28'.
Longitude by observation 16° 49'.
Longitude by reckoning 14° 39'.

20' more to the South than by reckoning in three days.
Réamur's thermometer +17°, Fahrenheit's thermometer 71°.

From Tuesday 31ˢᵗ to Wednesday 1ˢᵗ August 1792

112¾

At 6 o'clock PM, we had sight of a cutter directing her course South, and at four o'clock in the morning, a Dutch hoy steering NW. During the morning, we got two guns, two cannons and four guns out of the hold, which we had struck down upon our departure from the Isle of France.

At the same time, we bit the cables to the anchors.

During this day, we had a fresh breeze of wind from NE to NE¼N attended with hazy weather.

We perceived upon the surface of the water several bundles of sea weed of a reddish colour, with a somewhat yellow cast, and which the navigators commonly called *lacets* or *macaronis* or *marine creepers*.[261] It is thought that they come from

---

261 *Lianes marines* in Marchand.

the Tagus, for they are to be met with in general at a distance of 60 or 70 leagues from the coast of Portugal.

Latitude by observation North 38° 9'.
Longitude by observation 14° 19'.
Longitude by reckoning 12° 9'.

Réamur's thermometer +71°, Fahrenheit's thermometer 17.[262]

From Wednesday 1ˢᵗ to Thursday 2ⁿᵈ August 1792

120¼

At 8 o'clock in the evening, we steered SE with a very fresh breeze of wind at N¼NE.

At ½ past 3 o'clock in the morning, there appearing to be land a-head, we steered S¼SW along shore. At ½ past 4 o'clock in the morning, being day-light, we perceived it very distinctly extending from NE½N to SW¼S. We were at a distance of about 3 leagues from the nearest land.

We saw upon the surface of the water dead sea weed and other sea productions. At this time we lay becalmed, but soon after a breeze sprung up at NE, with the help of which we stood a little out to sea. We then steered in order to double Cape St Vincent which bore SW¼S.

At the time we had taken the first bearing, our longitude determined from the observations made on the 24ᵗʰ and 27ᵗʰ July, was 12° 28', and that laid down in the chart, 11° 35', consequently in the longitude by observation there was an error of 53' Westward, or 14 leagues in 6 days, and in that by reckoning from St Helena, an error of 1° 17', or 20 leagues East.

At noon, Cape Vincent bore ESE½S, at a distance of one and a half leagues. At this time, the latitude by observation was 37° 3' North, which is 1' different from that laid down in the chart of Mr Verdun, Pingre and Borda, which is 37° 2'. During this day, the currents carried us 12' to the South of the reckoning.

We had six ships in sight.

We saw some large gulls and many small ones.

Réamur's thermometer +18°, Fahrenheit's thermometer 73°.

From Thursday 2ⁿᵈ to Friday 3ʳᵈ August 1792

80½

After having doubled Cape St Vincent, we steered SE¼S until 9 o'clock, and then SE.

The wind which had settled at NNW, varied at midnight to NNE and ENE, which obliged us to haul our wind to the Southward. Hazy weather and smooth sea.

---

262 As in the original.

We perceived at day-light, 7 ships standing in different directions.
During the morning, we had a calm and light gusts from the East quarter.

Latitude by observation North 36° 8'.
Longitude by reckoning 10° 14'.

Réamur's thermometer +17°, Fahrenheit's thermometer 71°.

From Friday 3ʳᵈ to Saturday 4ᵗʰ August 1792

111½

We lay becalmed until 2 o'clock PM when a fresh breeze of wind at West
sprung up, and with the help of which we steered ESE and SE in order to examine
Cape Spartel, which at 5 o'clock in the morning, bore South, 3 leagues distant.
From Cape St Vincent, the currents had carried us 10 leagues ESE.

At ½ past 7 o'clock, we entered the Strait of Gibraltar with a strong breeze of
wind at West, in company with 7 sail.

By the mean result of several sets of azimuths, the variation of the magnetic
needle was found to be 21° 56' North Westerly.

At ten o'clock, Europa Point (the South point of Gibraltar) bore N½W, distant
2 leagues. At noon, it bore WNW½N, 7 leagues distant.

Réamur's thermometer +18°, Fahrenheit's thermometer 73°.

From Saturday 4ᵗʰ to Sunday 5ᵗʰ August 1792

87

At ½ past 3 o'clock, Windmill Hill bore NNE, at a distance of 9 or 10 leagues.
The variation of the compass by observation NW 22° 6'.
During this day, the winds were constantly at West, blowing more or less fresh.
We had in sight many ships standing in different directions.
At noon, the Point of Las Roquettas bore NE½E, 5 leagues distant.

Latitude by observation North 36° 32'.
Distance sailed by reckoning 29 leagues.

Following the bearing taken at noon, we had run 35 leagues in 24 hours, which
is 6 leagues more to the East on account of the currents.
Réamur's thermometer +18°, Fahrenheit's thermometer 73°.

From Sunday 5ᵗʰ to Monday 6ᵗʰ August 1792

89¾

At 2 o'clock PM, we had sight of Cape de Gata, which at 4 o'clock bore NE
3° N, distant 2 leagues. From this point, we steered E¼NE in order to make Cape

Palos. At 6 o'clock in the evening, we had sight of a brig directly a-head. I thought her to be a vessel from Marseilles and consequently, in order to have news, we worked the ship in order to speak with her. She perceived my intention immediately, and with a mark of civility, brought to. I was not mistaken for she was the *Le Vigilant*, commanded by Mr Cazeneuve, having departed from Marseilles 14 days since, bound for the Cape.

We were informed that we were at war with the Empire, Prussia, Sweden, Russia and Savoy. He also informed me that no pirates would be met with in the Mediterranean.

In taking leave of us, he requested me to give his employers, Mr Cailhol and Mr Barthélemi of Marseilles, some news of him, which I did upon my arrival in Toulon.

During the night, we had thunder, rain and a light breeze at West.

Latitude by observation North 37° 21'.
Course by reckoning NE¼E 1° E.

Distance sailed by reckoning 26½ leagues.

From Monday 6ᵗʰ to Tuesday 7ᵗʰ August 1792

81½

At 1 o'clock PM, we had sight of Cape Palos, which at 4 o'clock in the evening bore WNW½W, at a distance of 5 leagues.

Since the last bearing of Cape de Gata, the currents had carried us 12 leagues ENE.

At sun-set we had sight of 32 ships.

During the night, we steered NE and NE¼E with the help of a light gale at WNW which fell at day-light.

At 5 o'clock in the morning, Benidorme bore NNW½N, distant 1 league, Mount Karpi NE¼N, and Cape St Antonio (following the chart of Olivier), NE¼E.

By several observations, the variation of the compass was found to be 20° 23' North Westerly.

Latitude by observation North 38° 40'.
Course by reckoning NNE 3° E.
Distance sailed by reckoning 27 leagues.

6' more to the North than by reckoning.

At noon, Cape St Antonio bore NNE½N distant 1½ leagues, and Benidorme W½N.

Réamur's thermometer +18°, Fahrenheit's thermometer 73°.

From Tuesday 7th to Wednesday 8th August 1792

61¾

At sun-set, Cape St Antonio bore SW¼W, distant 8 leagues.

Until 10 o'clock in the evening, we had a gentle breeze from SSE varying to SW attended with clear weather. At this time, the wind veering suddenly to NW and then to NE, we tacked and stood to the NW.

At ½ past 7 o'clock in the morning, we tacked and stood East.

We continued to see many ships.

During this day we painted the sides of the ship and the boats. After laying one hour becalmed at 11 o'clock, a light breeze sprung up at South which permitted us steer NE¼E once again.

Latitude by observation North 39° 32'.
Course N½E.
Distance sailed by reckoning 16½ leagues.

12' more to the North than by reckoning.
Réamur's thermometer +21°, Fahrenheit's thermometer 79°.

From Wednesday 8th to Thursday 9th August 1792

47

At 1 o'clock PM, we had sight of the Monte Colibre Isles at NE¼E, 5 leagues distant. I immediately determined to pass to the Eastward and keep the wind, but finding it impossible to double them, we bore away along the shore to leeward.

At 4 o'clock PM, they extended from E½S to ENE, and at ¾ past 4 o'clock, the largest of these islands bore ESE, distant ¾ of a league, we steered ENE.

If sailing in close to these islands during the night, greatest care is required.

1   For several of them lie no higher than a boat upon the water and they are to be seen only when the ship is upon them.
2   On account of the currents which will often put the ship out of her way
3   For I do not believe that they have been laid down very well in the charts, which all differ from one another in the position. In the chart of Mr Olivier, they are to be found in latitude 39° 43', and in 39° 55' in that of the Navy.

Following the latitude by observation which was made very exactly at noon, and the reckoning of the distance sailed until ¾ past 4 o'clock, at which time the Northermost isle bore ESE, the true position may be considered as 9° 44' N.

During this day, we had light winds varying almost all round the compass.

Latitude by observation 40° 17'.
Course by reckoning NE¼N 1° N.
Distance sailed by reckoning 13½ leagues.

12' more to the North than by reckoning.

At noon Cape Oropesa bore W, at a distance of 10 leagues.

Réamur's thermometer +21°, Fahrenheit's thermometer 79°.

Thursday 9th to Friday 10th August 1792

29

At ¾ past 6 o'clock in the evening, the coast stretched from NNE to W¼NW. We were at a distance of 8 leagues from the nearest shore.

The variation of the compass, by observation of several sets of azimuths and of the amplitudes, was 20° 114 NW.

During this day, we had light winds variable, and calms. During the night there fell a heavy dew.

We saw a great number of ships steering different ways.

Latitude by observation North 40° 45'.

Course by reckoning NE 4° E.

Distance sailed by reckoning 9¼ leagues.

We were this day 3½ leagues more to the NE than by reckoning.

At noon, we had sight of the coast of Spain at a distance of 10 leagues, extending from NE to West.

Réamur's thermometer +20½°, Fahrenheit's thermometer 78°.

From Friday 10th to Saturday 11th August 1792

33

Light winds variable, fine weather and smooth sea.

At 2 o'clock PM, a ship passed very close and hoisted Dutch colours. While preparing to display ours, she struck hers, I followed the example, that is we did not shew our colours which she perhaps had perceived while we were rigging the ensign halyard. This was the second vessel belonging to this nation which had committed such an action.

At 6 o'clock in the morning, we perceived Mount Jui bearing NE½E, at a distance of 8 or 9 leagues.

We had at this time sight of 18 ships and 15 fishing vessels.

Latitude by observation North 41° 11.

Course by reckoning NE½E.

Distance sailed by reckoning 10 leagues.

7' more to the North than by reckoning.

At noon, Mount Jui bore NNE distant 3 leagues.

Réamur's thermometer +21°, Fahrenheit's thermometer 79°.

From Saturday 11th to Sunday 12th August 1792

71½

At 2 o'clock PM, Mount Jui bore NW¼N, distant 3 leagues, we steered East.

During this day, we had a light breeze at WSW attended with fine weather and a smooth sea.

We had sight of three ships.

By several sets of observations, we found the variation of the compass to be 20° 6' NW.

At 5 o'clock AM, Cape Begur bore N½W, and Cape de Creux N¼NE, distant about 9 leagues from the first.

Latitude by observation North 41° 40.
Distance sailed by reckoning 23⅓ leagues.
Course by reckoning E 34° N.

Réamur's thermometer +22°, Fahrenheit's thermometer 81°.

From Sunday 12th to Monday 13th August 1792

43½

During this day, we steered E¼NE with the help of a light wind varying from WSW to SSE, attended with fine weather and a smooth sea.

We saw four ships steering ENE. They were most likely bound for Marseilles.

Latitude by observation North 42° 9.
Course by reckoning ENE 9° N.
Distance sailed by reckoning 14½ leagues.

4' more to the North than by reckoning.
Réamur's thermometer +22°, Fahrenheit's thermometer 81°.

From Monday 13th to Tuesday 14th August

64½

During this day, we had a light breeze varying from SW to West. Fine weather.

At 5 o'clock in the morning, we made the coast of Provence, extending from NNE to NE½E, at 8 clock, Cape Sicié bore N 8° E at a distance of 8 leagues. We had sight of the Isles of Hières at NE¼E.

At noon, we took the following bearings.

Cape Sépet bore NE½N and Cape Sicié NNE, distant 3 leagues.

We saw a Man of War and two frigates leaving Toulon and bound Eastwards. We also saw two Navy brigs and a Dutch ship, steering for Toulon like ourselves.

At ½ past 3 o'clock, after having doubled Cape Sépet, and circumnavigated the globe, we came to anchor in Toulon Road, after a voyage of twenty months during which we had made a run of 14,833 leagues given by the log. During the twenty three months of the voyage, we had put into ports for only three months and twenty one days. All the remainder was employed in navigation. Of the fifty men I had on board, I lost but one in the Strait of Sunda on account of the apoplexy. Very few were attacked by the scurvy and those who had the symptoms of it upon them went about their work nothwithstanding.

Bureau des classes of the Navy within this Port
According to the Law of 13th of August 1791
Given under our hand on the twenty-eighth of August 1792, Toulon,
Year 4 of Liberty.
Daniez